# *an invitation to* health

## Second Canadian Edition

**Dianne Hales**

**Lara Lauzon**
University of Victoria

NELSON / EDUCATION

**NELSON** / EDUCATION

An Invitation to Health, Second Canadian Edition

by Dianne Hales and Lara Lauzon

**Associate Vice President, Editorial Director:**
Evelyn Veitch

**Editor-in-Chief, Higher Education:**
Anne Williams

**Executive Editor:**
Paul Fam

**Senior Marketing Manager:**
Sean Chamberland

**Developmental Editor:**
My Editor Inc.

**Photo Researcher/Permissions Coordinator:**
Nicola Winstanley

**Senior Content Production Manager:**
Imoinda Romain

**Production Service:**
S4Carlisle Publishing Services

**Copy Editor:**
Wendy Yano

**Proofreader:**
S4Carlisle Editing Services

**Indexer:**
S4Carlisle Editing Services

**Production Coordinator:**
Ferial Suleman

**Design Director:**
Ken Phipps

**Managing Designer:**
Franca Amore

**Interior Design:**
Carianne Bauldry

**Cover Design:**
Dianna Little

**Cover Image:**
Jan Greune/Getty Images

**Compositor:**
S4Carlisle Publishing Services

**Printer:**
Courier

**Library and Archives Canada Cataloging in Publication**

Hales, Dianne R., 1950–
    An invitation to health/Dianne Hales, Lara Lauzon.—2nd Canadian ed.

Includes bibliographical references and index.
ISBN 978-0-17-650009-2

1. Health—Textbooks. 2. Self-care, Health—Textbooks. I. Lauzon, Lara, 1955– II. Title.

RA776. H216 2009 613
C2008-908117-X

ISBN-13: 978-0-17-650009-2
ISBN-10: 0-17-650009-X

To my husband, Bob, and my daughter, Julia,
who make every day an invitation to joy.

**Dianne Hales**


To my husband, Ron, and my son, Lindon, whose love and
support allow me to climb every mountain and whose love of life
keeps me committed to living well.

**Lara Lauzon**

# Brief Contents

# Contents

# Preface

## To the Student

This textbook is an invitation to you—an invitation to embrace a healthy and well way of living. Every day, you make choices that can affect both how long and how well you live. The knowledge you acquire in this textbook will help you make better choices, ones that will have a direct impact on how you feel and function, now and for decades to come.

As you read through this textbook, ask yourself the following questions:

✔ How healthy or well are you?
✔ How well do you understand yourself? Are you able to cope with emotional upsets and crises?
✔ Do you participate in regular physical activity?
✔ Do you understand how nutrition plays a role in healthy living?
✔ Are your relationships with others solid and supportive? Are you conscientious about birth control and safe-sex practices?
✔ Do you use alcohol responsibly? Do you use medications wisely and say no to illegal drugs? Do you smoke?
✔ How much do you know about the Canadian health-care system and complementary and alternative health-care options?
✔ What do you know about your risk for infectious diseases, heart problems, cancer, or other serious illnesses?
✔ What steps have you taken to ensure your personal safety at home, on campus, and on the streets?
✔ What can you do to live a long and healthy life?
✔ What are you doing today to assist with global wellness?
✔ Are you spiritually connected? Are you living a meaningful and purposeful life?

Self-care, self-responsibility, and social responsibility are important concepts when it comes to personal and professional health and wellness. Over time, your priorities and needs will inevitably change, but the important connections between your mind, body, and spirit will remain the same. The values that guide you through today can keep you mentally, emotionally, physically, and spiritually well throughout your lifetime.

*An Invitation to Health,* Second Canadian Edition, provides you with information, advice, recommendations, and research, so that you can take charge of your own health. However, knowledge alone can't assure you a lifetime of well-being. The skills you acquire, the habits you form, the choices you make, and the way you live day by day will all shape your health and your future. We hope you will embrace health and wellness so that you have the opportunity to live a fulfilling life.

This is our invitation to you.

—Dianne Hales

—Lara Lauzon

## To the Instructor

Health and wellness is a subject that must be both learned and lived. Often for the first time in their lives, students in a college or university health class become aware of the importance of personal responsibility for their health and acquire the knowledge and skills they need to support their well-being and prevent serious health problems.

By its very nature, learning about health and wellness encourages interaction with the learning material. *An Invitation to Health,* Second Canadian Edition, offers many features designed to inspire and involve your students. Every chapter incorporates research on Canadian college and university students. We have also included numerous tables and graphs to report recent data on the health, habits, and concerns of Canadians.

We describe health and wellness as a process of discovering, using, and protecting all possible resources within the individual, family, community, and environment. The most recent health and wellness research is presented, along with practical information students can use to apply these findings.

As we tell students, *An Invitation to Health,* Second Canadian Edition, can serve as an owner's manual to their bodies, minds, and spirits. By using this book and taking your course, they can acquire the power to make good decisions, to assume responsibility, and to create and follow a healthy lifestyle. This textbook is our invitation to them to live what they learn and make the most of their health and of their lives.

# Your Quick Tour of This Outstanding Book Starts Here!

*An Invitation to Health*, Second Canadian Edition, includes everything your students need in a streamlined text. Dianne Hales and Lara Lauzon are known for the way they speak with students—not at them. Throughout this text, health is not just a subject to memorize and master, but one to be both learned and lived.

## A Text for the Canadian Student!

**The Spirit of Health and Wellness.** The Second Canadian Edition includes an entire chapter dedicated to the spiritual dimension of health and wellness, with current research on the link between spirituality and health. Included is a section describing the religions of the world, information on the connection of nature and spirituality, and a special section on First Nations' spirituality.

### Thea Maguire—A Message of Hope

Thea Maguire, a graduate in a recreation and health education program, is now living in Dubai, United Arab Emirates, with her fiancé. She is excited about her current career in real estate and hopeful about what the future holds for her. However, the story she would like to share is one that began in high school.

Thea was very active in sports and dance. There was also musical theatre, the leadership club, and community youth groups. She is convinced that the pressure to "do everything" came from within. "My achievements and success began to form my identity."

One year she also grew nine inches. There comes from a family that is genetically tall and thin; however, she did not think of family genes when she heard comments such as "Do you have a hollow leg?" and "You are a human coat hanger!" said in joking ways by people of all ages. As Thea says, when you grow that fast no amount of healthy eating is going to prevent you from being "skinny." Then there were the mixed messages. While attending a professional ballet school, she was told she had the perfect body type to be a ballerina but was asked to withdraw for growing too tall as there was no partner available for someone her height. That is when she began drinking coca-cola to stunt her growth.

Quitting dancing, entering into an outdoor education school, and physically maturing during her grade 11 and 12 years resulted in major changes in her outward body appearance. With the changes came comments such as "You are finally filling out" and "You look so different—not a skinny Thea anymore." "It was a loss of identity. It had a huge impact on me. If I wasn't skinny Thea, then who was I?"

She remembers the day when she read about a diet in a magazine—a diet that would soon go wrong. Thea is convinced that the media played a role in her eating disorder. The models were people she looked up to. She began restricting food and overexercising. New comments started right away—"You're so thin again." "Skinny Thea is back."

Thea's parents were concerned and sent her to a nutritionist. She went to "get them off my back." She

was thin but managed to convince them she was recovering. She also graduated the top of her class. After graduation she took a summer job away from home. She clung to her eating disorder losing thirteen more kilograms (30 lbs). At her lowest weight, she was 45 kilograms (100 lbs), still 183 centimetres (6 ft) tall. She lost control of her emotions and began crying all of the time. "Lying was my survival. Much of the deceit is meant for you. You don't even realize that you are lying. Anorexia became my life, all consuming. I did not care about anything except how much I ate and how much I exercised."

It was a visit from her brother—his shock at seeing her, his care and compassion, that helped Thea realize, for the first time, that something was very wrong. She returned home and started on the road of recovery. Initially, the recovery began for her family. Then it shifted to her. Thea says that "ultimately the recovery has to be for yourself." It was a two steps forward, one step back process. She feels that for some individuals, this is the way it will be, no matter what interventions are used. "You must reprogram your brain to think outside the disorder's reality. It can be a very long and painful process."

**Human Potential stories.** These special box features, found in every chapter, relate stories about Canadians who have faced challenges and made a difference in the lives of others. These stories help to illustrate the link between health and wellness and human potential.

### Self Responsibility

*The Law of Giving—*
*Every relationship is one of give and take, if you stop the flow of either, you interfere with nature's intelligence.*

**Deepak Chopra**

Building relationships takes time, energy, and commitment. In Prochaska's Stages of Change model, maintenance also demands care and attention to avoid a relapse. If you are in a relationship that is lacking in enthusiasm and energy, commitment and caring, it may

### Social Responsibility

*Go out into the world today and love the people you meet. Let your presence light new light in the hearts of people.*

**Mother Teresa**

be time to re-evaluate why this is so. What can you do to rejuvenate this relationship—Spend more time together? Seek out new adventures? Make a change in lifestyle habits that encourage healthy lifelong living? Take time to give and take.

**New to the second edition: Self-Responsibility/Social Responsibilities boxes.** To enhance behaviour change, this new element has been designed to help Canadian students reflect on the Stages of Change model throughout every chapter.

**Canadian-related research.** The most up-to-date health research and research on Canadian students and students around the world appear in every chapter.

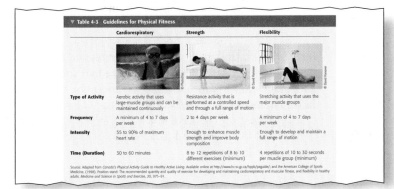

▼ Table 4-3  Guidelines for Physical Fitness

| | Cardiorespiratory | Strength | Flexibility |
|---|---|---|---|
| **Type of Activity** | Aerobic activity that uses large-muscle groups and can be maintained continuously | Resistance activity that is performed at a controlled speed and through a full range of motion | Stretching activity that uses the major muscle groups |
| **Frequency** | A minimum of 4 to 7 days per week | 2 to 4 days per week | A minimum of 4 to 7 days per week |
| **Intensity** | 55 to 90% of maximum heart rate | Enough to enhance muscle strength and improve body composition | Enough to develop and maintain a full range of motion |
| **Time (Duration)** | 30 to 60 minutes | 8 to 12 repetitions of 8 to 10 different exercises (minimum) | 4 repetitions of 10 to 30 seconds per muscle group (minimum) |

Source: Adapted from *Canada's Physical Activity Guide to Healthy Active Living*. Available online at http://www.hc-sc.gc.ca/hppb/paguide/; and the American College of Sports Medicine. (1998). Position stand: The recommended quantity and quality of exercise for developing and maintaining cardiorespiratory and muscular fitness, and flexibility in healthy adults. *Medicine and Science in Sports and Exercise, 30*, 975–91.

# Other Outstanding Features and In-Text Tools!

With outstanding, interesting features and in-text tools designed to help students take charge of their own well-being, *An Invitation to Health*, Second Canadian Edition, truly stands above the rest! The authors are unmatched in their ability to inspire and convey how attainable learning and living a healthy lifestyle can be.

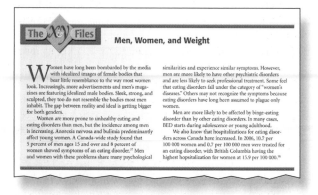

**The X & Y Files.** Topics related to gender differences in health are highlighted in this special feature, including "Men, Women, and Stress" and "Alcohol, Tobacco, and Gender."

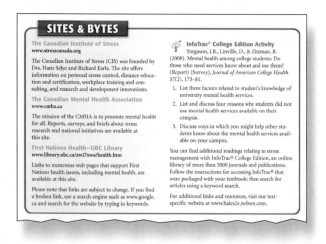

**FAQs.** Frequently Asked Questions appear at the beginning of each chapter and engage students with answers to the most commonly asked questions. Page references are included after each question, and each corresponding heading is marked with an icon, signalling where the answer can be found.

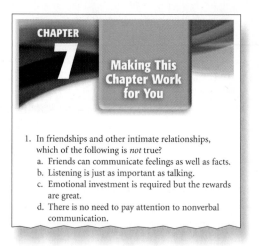

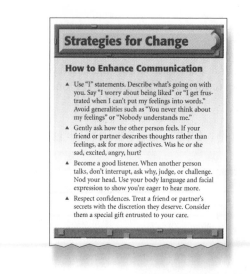

**Strategies for Change and Prevention.** Appearing throughout the book, the Strategies for Change boxes provide practical checklist-style behavioural change strategies for achieving better health. The Strategies for Prevention boxes provide effective, practical checklists for preventing health problems and reducing health risks.

**Making This Chapter Work for You.** To test their knowledge, students are invited to review important chapter material through a format of multiple-choice questions.

**Sites & Bytes.** Updated interactive websites and InfoTrac® College Edition activities include Canadian sources and encourage students to use these resources for additional information and learning.

**Critical Thinking questions.** At the end of each chapter, students are asked to consider some applications of the chapter's coverage or weigh in on a health-related controversy.

## The Latest Internet Resources Add Value for Instructors and Students!

**CENGAGENOW™** **CengageNOW™ for *An Invitation to Health*, Second Canadian Edition.** Designed by instructors and students for instructors and students, CengageNOW™ is an integrated, online suite of services and resources with proven **ease of use** and **efficient** paths to success, delivering the **results** you want—NOW! The most popular section for students consists of a pre-test, a study plan, and a post-test. Students gain a thorough understanding and excel in their studies with CengageNOW™ for *An Invitation to Health*.

**InfoTrac® College Edition.** *An Invitation to Health* is packaged with four months of FREE access to this extensive online library, giving instructors and students access to the latest news and research articles online—updated daily and spanning more than 20 years! Conveniently accessible from students' own computers or the campus library, InfoTrac® opens the door to the full text of articles from thousands of scholarly and popular journals and publications.

Each chapter includes an InfoTrac® College Edition activity to encourage use of this dynamic resource.

**Book Companion website.** For students, the *An Invitation to Health* website contains learning objectives, quizzes, crossword puzzles, flashcards, and web links. Instructors may download supplements from a password-protected section of the website. We invite you to explore the website at www.health.nelson.com.

## Overview of the Second Canadian Edition

The Second Canadian Edition of *An Invitation to Health* presents a wealth of new research, references, and features. The basic themes are personal responsibility, a commitment to prevention, practical applications of knowledge, and a focus on behavioural change and social responsibility. All chapters have been updated to keep the textbook as current as possible and to honour requests by students and reviewers. Two chapters have been expanded: Chapter 16, "Working Toward a Healthy Environment," and Chapter 17, "The Spirit of Health and Wellness." The environmental chapter includes current information on climate change and an introduction to Al Gore and Andrew Weaver, who shared the honour of receiving the Nobel Peace Prize in 2007. The spirituality chapter includes much more information on the link between spirituality and health, as well as references to new studies about college and university student spirituality.

The features in this edition include a special Self-Responsibility/Social Responsibility textbox and Making This Chapter Work for You at the end of each chapter. These elements give students the opportunity to reflect on how they might embrace lifestyle change and test their understanding of the key concepts in the chapter. Other features include the chapter FAQs, Strategies for Change, Strategies for Prevention, and The X & Y Files. We have also included a Human Potential story in every chapter. These moving stories are about individuals who have faced great challenges or who have made a difference to the lives of others. They show the connection between healthy lifestyle choices, the ability to leave legacies, and social responsibility.

The health and wellness field is advancing rapidly. We have attempted to provide you with the most current research, including the latest available statistics and hundreds of citations to support the text material. The majority come from primary sources, including professional books; medical, health, physical activity, and mental health journals; health educational periodicals; scientific meetings, federal and provincial agencies, and consensus panels; publications from research laboratories and universities; and personal interviews with specialists in a number of fields. In addition, Sites & Bytes presents reliable Internet addresses where students can turn for additional information and a suggested reading from InfoTrac® College Edition, an online library of thousands of academic journals and popular periodicals.

Following is a chapter-by-chapter listing of some of the key topics that have been included in this edition.

## Chapter 1: An Invitation to Health and Wellness

✔ A history of health promotion and wellness, including visual models

✔ A section on the social determinants of health and current information on the health status of Canadians

✔ A new table on provincial and territorial health and wellness reports, initiatives, and programs

✔ A section on the trans-theoretical model of change (six stages), including a figure on the change process that can be used within the stages

## Chapter 2: Personal Stress Management

✔ A section on the physiological reactions to stress

✔ A current overview of stress levels of Canadian college and university students

✔ A personal interview with a psychologist who encourages reflection about emotional intelligence

✔ A report on a study about test stress and Canadian students

✔ Information on how students can survive stress and a special section on stress reduction strategies

## Chapter 3: Psychological Health

✔ A section on clarifying values, boosting self-esteem, and managing moods

✔ Up-to-date information on how stress and post-traumatic stress disorder affects our physical health

✔ Current research reporting on gender and stress

✔ A special section on options for treatment of mental health disorders

## Chapter 4: Physical Activity for Fitness and Health

✔ An update of present national and provincial active-living programs and initiatives

✔ An introduction to *Canada's Physical Activity Guide*

✔ A section on the principles of exercise; the FIT guidelines for cardiovascular exercise, strength, endurance, and flexibility; and information on how to start and maintain a physical activity program

## Chapter 5: Personal Nutrition

✔ A section on nutrients, including macronutrients (protein, carbohydrates, fats) and micronutrients (vitamins and minerals); includes nutrient data from Health Canada and the Dietitians of Canada

✔ An up-to-date section on Dietary Reference Intakes (DRIs)

✔ Visual models of *Eating Well with Canada's Food Guide*, the *Northwest Territories' Food Guide*, and other food guides from around the world

## Chapter 6: Healthy Eating for Healthy Living

✔ A section on body mass index, waist-to-hip ratio, and waist circumference measurements as they relate to health issues

✔ A section on dietary theories—set point, energy-balance equation, and dietary fat theory

✔ A comprehensive section on disordered eating in college and university students

✔ Current information and research on the dangers of obesity

✔ Updated Canadian Obesity map

## Chapter 7: Communication and Sexuality

✔ Up-to-date information on the sexual behaviour of college and university students, including the findings of a 20-year longitudinal study of students at a Canadian college

✔ A section on "sober sex" and "safer sex"

✔ A new section on gender diversity

✔ A new section on sex in cyberspace

## Chapter 8: Reproductive Choices

✔ Current information on contraceptive methods including effectiveness and level of protection against STIs

✔ A section on abortion methods and information on abortion laws in Canada

✔ A section on the physical and emotional aspects of pregnancy

✔ Current information on infertility that includes information on artificial insemination and infertility treatments

✔ A new section on pro-life choices

## Chapter 9: Protecting Yourself from Infectious Diseases

✔ A user-friendly section on the agents of infection—viruses, bacteria, fungi, and protozoa

✔ A new section on the listeriosis outbreak in Canada

✔ Current information on West Nile virus, BSE (bovine spongiform encephalopathy), avian influenza, and SARS

✔ A comprehensive section on STIs

✔ Updated information on HIV/AIDS in Canada

## Chapter 10: Lowering Your Risk of Major Diseases

✔ New information on healthy-heart diets

✔ A section on lipoprotein profile, a new table on interpreting cholesterol levels, and information on how to reduce cholesterol levels

✔ Expanded coverage of stroke

✔ Current information on heart disease and stroke

✔ The latest information on cancer risks and death rates of Canadians

✔ Up-to-date information on diabetes mellitus in Canada

## Chapter 11: Drug Use, Misuse, and Abuse

✔ An important section about legal and illegal drugs and their effects, including the popular drugs ecstasy and crystal meth

✔ Research on the use of drugs on college and university campuses across Canada

✔ Current information and research on anabolic steroids

✔ An informative section on treating drug dependence and abuse, including federal, provincial, and municipal initiatives such as the Four Pillars Drug Strategy, the All Nations Healing Hospital, and the NAOMI project

## Chapter 12: Alcohol and Tobacco Use, Misuse, and Abuse

✔ Updated sections on the *Criminal Code of Canada* as it relates to drinking and driving, college drinking, and binge drinking

✔ A section on college and university drinking including research from the 2004 *Canadian Campus Survey*

✔ New findings from the 2007 *Canadian Addictions Survey*

✔ An expanded section on the health effects of tobacco use

✔ A new section on smoking and women

✔ Information on marketing techniques used to sell cigarettes

## Chapter 13: Traditional and Complementary Health-Care Approaches

✔ A section on becoming a knowledgeable health-care consumer

✔ Updated information on evaluating online health-care information

✔ Current information about Canada's health-care system and our health-care providers

✔ An updated section on complementary health-care approaches

✔ An updated section on natural-health products

## Chapter 14: Staying Safe: Preventing Injury, Violence, and Victimization

✔ A section on individual risk factors for unintentional injury

✔ An expanded section on road safety, including safe driving and safe cycling

✔ Current research on recreational and sport safety

✔ Updated information on violence in Canada, including hate crimes on college and university campuses

✔ Current research on sexual victimization and violence on college and university students

## Chapter 15: A Lifetime of Health

✔ Current research on aging in Canada

✔ *Canada's Physical Activity Guide to Healthy Active Living for Older Adults*

✔ Information on the aging brain

✔ Up-to-date research on menopause and the Women's Health Initiative

✔ Sexuality and aging

✔ A section on the challenges of aging, including the latest information on osteoporosis and Alzheimer's disease

✔ Information on preparing a will and the emotional responses to dying

## Chapter 16: Working Toward a Healthy Environment

✔ An updated introduction to environmentalists who have made a difference including Al Gore and Andrew Weaver

✔ New information and current research on climate change

✔ An introduction to the First Nations Environmental Network

✔ Strategies for working toward a "well" world

✔ An introduction to Barry Commoner's Four Laws of Ecology

✔ A special section on the Sierra Club BC and the new CERCles initiative

✔ A new section on the "greening" of college and university campuses

✔ A new table that provides examples of green and sustainability initiatives on college and university campuses across Canada

✔ Current research on air and water quality in Canada

## Chapter 17: The Spirit of Health and Wellness

✔ An expansion of this chapter dedicated to the spiritual dimension of health and wellness
✔ New information and current research on the link between spirituality, religion, and health
✔ A special section on First Nations' spirituality
✔ Information on the connection between nature and spirituality
✔ A section describing the major religions of the world
✔ A philosophical discussion on meaning, purpose, and human potential

## Features and Pedagogy

**Human Potential** stories are about Canadians who have faced challenges and made a difference in the lives of others. These stories help to illustrate the link between health, wellness, and human potential.

**FAQs (Frequently Asked Questions)** are found at the beginning of each chapter. These engage students with answers to the most commonly asked health and wellness questions, such as: "What is health?" "How do I overcome a weight problem?" "What causes drug dependence and abuse?" "What can help me relax?" and "What is spirituality?" Page references are included after each question, and each corresponding heading is marked with an icon, signalling where the answer can be found.

**The X & Y Files** are boxes found throughout the text that focus on topics related to gender differences in health. Among the topics covered are differences in susceptibility to cancer, differences in stress vulnerabilities, differences in communication styles, and differences in vulnerability to alcohol and drug abuse.

**Strategies for Change** boxes appear throughout the text and provide practical, checklist-format, behavioural change strategies for achieving better health.

**Strategies for Prevention** boxes appear throughout the text and provide effective, checklist-format, strategies for preventing health problems and reducing health risks.

**Self-Responsibility and Social Responsibility** boxes have been designed to help students reflect on the Stages of Change model and determine at which stage they are with regard to making lifestyle changes and positive health and wellness choices.

**Making This Chapter Work for You** is a study feature that reviews important chapter material by asking ten multiple-choice questions. Answers are provided on page 450.

**CengageNOW™** If your textbook package includes CengageNOW™, students can go to http://west.cengagenow.com/ilrn/ to link to CengageNOW™ to access their understanding of the material. CengageNOW™ is an integrated, online suite of services, including pre-tests, study plans, and post-tests.

**Sites & Bytes** boxes at the end of every chapter include updated interactive websites and InfoTrac® College Edition activities, encouraging students to use the Internet for additional learning resources.

**Learning Objectives** open each chapter and outline the most essential information on which students should focus while reading.

**Key Terms** are boldfaced where they are defined and are listed at the end of each chapter with page references. They are also defined in the Glossary at the end of the book.

**Critical Thinking** questions, included at the end of each chapter, ask the students to consider some applications of the chapter's coverage or weigh in on a health-related controversy.

## Ancillary Package

**Instructor's Resource CD** (0-17-647526-5/978-0-17-647526-0) This CD assembles all the instructor resources in one location for easy accessibility:

- **Instructor's Manual** provides chapter outlines, learning objectives, key terms, discussion questions, instructor's activities, student handouts, suggestions for additional readings, and video and Internet Resources.
- **Test Bank** contains a variety of questions to assess the students' understanding and comprehension of the text: multiple choice, fill in the blank, matching, and essay questions and a mid-term exam with questions covering the first eight chapters of the text.
- **ExamView** can help you create, deliver, and customize tests and study guides (both print and online) in minutes with its easy-to-use assessment and tutorial system. ExamView offers both a Quick Test Wizard and an Online Test Wizard that guide you step by step through the process of creating tests, while it allows you to see the test you are creating on the screen exactly as it will print or display online. Using Exam View's complete word-processing capabilities, you can enter an unlimited number of new questions or edit existing ones.
- **Lecture Presentation in PowerPoint** covers all essential sections presented in each chapter of the text to reinforce major topics. Adopters may adapt or add slides to customize their lectures.

**CengageNOW!™** This online student study resource is where students can take the **Pre-Test** for each chapter to determine their personalized **Study Plan,** then take the **Post-Test** to determine what concepts they have mastered and what they still need work on to succeed.

**Book-Companion Website** (www.health.nelson.com) The accompanying website for *An Invitation to Health* provides an array of teaching and learning resources for instructors and students. This site offers student resources, including quizzes and web links, and instructor resources, including downloadable supplementary resources.

**InfoTrac® College Edition Student Guide for Health** This 24-page booklet offers detailed guidance for students on how to use the InfoTrac® College Edition database, including log-in help, search tips, and a topic list of key word-search terms for health, fitness, and wellness. Available free when packaged with the text.

## Acknowledgments

Thanks must first go to Dianne Hales, the author of *An Invitation to Health,* Brief Third Edition, which was published in the United States and was used as a template for the First Canadian edition of this textbook. Thanks must also go to Paul Fam, Executive Editor–Higher Education, for believing in this textbook and finding a way to make the second edition possible. I continue to be forever grateful to Katherine Goodes, from My Editor Inc., who guides me through the writing process with patience, grace, enthusiasm, and care. From answers to my ongoing questions on just about everything, to the detail work of photo permissions, page counts, generally helpful suggestions, and an inordinate amount of patience and tenacity, this second edition has as much to do with her as me. Thank you as well to Heather Cameron at My Editor Inc. who assisted in the manuscript preparation. I also want to thank Jill Payne, a graduate student of mine who helped with research for the first five chapters. Clare Hall-Patch, a past student, helped update website links and find up-to-date statistics so our textbook would have the most current research and data available. She also lent a helping hand for the chapters on sexual health. Thanks, Clare.

Dianna Little created a wonderful cover for this book: thank you. Imoinda Romain, our senior content production manager, did a great job in keeping us all on track. Wendy Yano, the copy editor, did the meticulous editing of the final manuscript. Wendy's gentle suggestions and wonderful ability to polish the manuscript have made this edition even better than the first. I also am appreciative of Sean Chamberland's marketing efforts. Thank you as well to permissions editor, Nicola Winstanley, who cleared permissions and researched

new photos for this edition. Tiffany Timmerman, project editor, S4Carlisle Publishing Services, also deserves a huge thank you for her efforts in the final production stages of the textbook.

Finally, I would like to thank the reviewers, whose comments were so valuable in the preparation of both the first and second Canadian editions. Their willingness to share ideas and resources has made *An Invitation to Health* a first-class textbook. They are:

Deborah Foster, *Athabasca University*
Mary Anne Yurkiw, *Athabasca University*
Norman Temple, *Athabasca University*
Robert Hawes, *Brock University*
Lorne Adams, *Brock University*
Vineet B. Johnson, *Capilano College*
Judy A. Hurst, *Loyalist College*
Rene Turcotte, *McGill University*
Mark Lund, *Grant McEwan Community College*
Dave Kato, *Grant McEwan Community College*
Cindy Livingstone, *Nova Scotia Community College*
Peter T. Katzmarzyk, *Queen's University*
Barb Pimento, *George Brown College*
Emilio Landolfi, *University College of the Fraser Valley*
Kelly MacKenzie, *University of Alberta*
Simone Longpre, *University of British Columbia*
Twyla Salm, *University of Regina*

—Lara Lauzon

## About the Authors

Dianne Hales, a contributing editor for *Parade*, has written more than 2000 articles for national publications. Her trade books include *Just Like a Woman: How Gender Science Is Redefining What Makes Us Female* and the award-winning compendium of mental health information, *Caring for the Mind: The Comprehensive Guide to Mental Health.* Dianne Hales is one of the few journalists to be honoured with national awards for excellence in magazine writing by both the American Psychiatric Association and the American Psychological Association. She also has won the EMMA (Exceptional Media Merit Award) for health reporting from the National Women's Political Caucus and Radcliffe College, and numerous writing awards from various organizations, including the Arthritis Foundation, California Psychiatric Society, CHAAD (Children and Adults with Attention-Deficit Disorders), Council for the Advancement of Scientific Education, National Easter Seal Society, and the New York City Public Library.

Lara Lauzon is an Assistant Professor at the University of Victoria in British Columbia. Her teaching focus in the

School of Physical Education is human wellness and personal potential. Her research specialty is in teacher wellness. She is also a consultant specializing in workplace wellness and leadership. She has worked for not-for-profit, municipal, provincial, and private health and fitness agencies. She coproduced and hosted an internationally syndicated health and fitness show called *Body Moves* for seven years. She has won many awards, including a Faculty of Education Teaching Excellence Award (University of Victoria), a Graduate Student Award for Teaching Excellence, the Victoria "Y" Women of Distinction Award for the fitness and health category, the B.C. Promotion Plus Leadership Award for promotion of girls and women in fitness and sport, a B.C. Paraplegic Association Award for the production of two fitness videos for persons with disabilities, and a Community Wellness Award for outstanding contribution to the field of community wellness. She has written hundreds of fitness and health columns for newspapers and health magazines and has published a number of fitness and health journal articles. She also has a chapter titled "A Work In Progress" included in a collaborative work called *Wise Women Speak: Changes Along the Path.* She is a popular keynote speaker and continues to present health and wellness workshops in Canada and the United States.

*an invitation to*

# health

Second Canadian Edition

# An Invitation to Health and Wellness

"How are you?" You may hear that question many times each day. "Fine," you answer, without thinking. But how often do you ask yourself how you really are? How do you feel about yourself and your life? Are the lifestyle choices you are making supporting your personal well-being and career goals?

Being healthy and well includes a connection between body, mind, and spirit. Health and wellness are also dependent on the community, society, and environment in which you live. This edition of *An Invitation to Health* is an invitation to embrace a "well" way of living and an opportunity to reflect upon the link between healthy lifestyle choices and your own personal potential.

As you read through this book, you will discover the importance of emotional and physical well-being. You will be encouraged to think about healthy food choices. Drug, alcohol, and tobacco use is discussed as well as such topics as sexuality, reproductive choices, and lowering your risk of major diseases. You will also find out about environmental issues that affect global wellness and the spiritual dimension of holistic living.

Establishing the basis for good health now can support a healthy way of living in your future. We begin with an introduction to health and wellness.

After studying the material in this chapter, you will be able to:

- **Describe** and **discuss** health-promotion and wellness models.
- **Identify** and **describe** the dimensions of health and wellness.
- **List** the factors that influence the development of health behaviours.
- **Discuss** the principles and goals of prevention, and **differentiate** prevention from protection.
- **Apply** a behaviour-change theory to a personal health and wellness action plan.

**????  FREQUENTLY ASKED QUESTIONS**

FAQ: What is health? p. 4

FAQ: What is epidemiology? p. 8

FAQ: What is wellness? p. 9

FAQ: What is the average life expectancy? p. 11

FAQ: How can I begin to make lifestyle changes? p. 16

# Health and Wellness

There has been much discussion among health and wellness advocates as to whether health equals wellness or wellness equals health. For many, being well is essentially the same as being healthy. For others, there is a distinction between the two terms. Many health and wellness programs are based on very similar health risk-reduction strategies. In this section, you will be introduced to definitions of *health* and *wellness*. You will also discover some health-promotion and wellness models. You are encouraged to adopt or adapt whatever terms and models you find meaningful.

Travelling back to ancient Greece, we can discover our earliest and most enduring icon of medicine and health and wellness—that of the Greek god of health and father of medicine, Asklepios, also known by his Roman name, Aesculapius. Two of Asklepios's children also became celebrated healers. His daughter Panacea believed that the best way to help people was to treat illness. Her sister Hygeia believed that it was important to teach people how to live so that they did not become ill.[1] Their legacy is our understanding of the words **panacea,** which means to heal, a remedy for all difficulties, a cure-all, and **hygiene,** meaning healthy, akin to well and to living; a science of the establishment and maintenance of health; conditions or practices conducive to health.[2]

## First Nations Health and Wellness

In Canada, we do not have to return to ancient Greek mythology to be educated or inspired about health and wellness. Instead, we can look to the worldview of Aboriginal people to gain an understanding of health and well-being, in which the emphasis on the interconnectedness between the physical and spiritual world, between the individual and their environment, and between the mind, body, and spirit guided the concept of **holism.**[3]

Kulchyski, McCaskill, and Newhouse (1999) say in their book *In the Words of Elders: Aboriginal Cultures in Transition* that "at the heart of most elders' stories and teachings is the idea that it is important for an individual to attempt to live Bimaadiziwin, 'the way of good life' or 'everyday good living' in accordance with the teachings of the Creator."[4] They go on to suggest that "it is through an understanding of the reciprocal relationship between ourselves and Mother Earth and living in a balanced way that we are provided with the sustenance, both physical and spiritual, necessary for life."[5]

First Nations Medicine Wheels assist in the teaching of Bimaadiziwin. Although there are many different but related versions for Aboriginal groups, they share traditional theology, philosophy, psychology, and the teachings of the Creator (see Figure 1-1). There is an encouragement to balance ourselves through the four aspects of self: physical, mental, emotional,

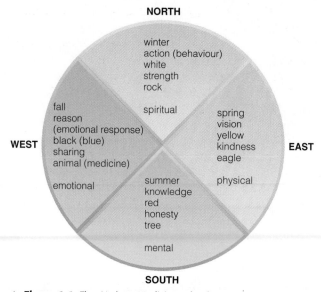

▲ **Figure 1-1** First Nations Medicine Wheel

Source: Redrawn from Illustration of First Nations Medicine Wheel from Kulchyski, P., McCaskill, D., & Newhouse, D. (1999). *In the words of elders: Aboriginal cultures in transition.* Toronto: University of Toronto Press, chapter 1, page 4. Permission granted by University of Toronto Press.

and spiritual. We are asked to live the four fundamental values of kindness, honesty, sharing, and strength. We are reminded that our world is made up of individuals, families, clans, and nations. We are asked to respect nature.

Newhouse believes that the concept of balance within an organism and its environment, along with the Aboriginal idea of holism, forces us to think in a very different manner about health and wellness. He believes the control of decisions regarding health and wellness ". . . must rest with the individual and not with the medical profession. Collective responsibility is also important, but health is not something that one gets from someone else. One needs to have an active role in achieving it."[6]

# Health and Health Promotion

## ???? What Is Health?

Another view of health has its beginnings from the World Health Organization (WHO), an agency that has shaped our understanding of health as many Canadians know it today. The World Health Organization emphasized the importance of the preventative side of health and a declaration was adopted in 1947 that stated that "the enjoyment of the highest attainable standard of health is one of the fundamental rights of every human being."[7] WHO defined **health** as "not merely the absence of disease or infirmity," but "a state of complete physical, mental, and social well-being."[8] This was the beginning of a new era in health care.

In 1974, an important document titled *A New Perspective on the Health of Canadians* presented epidemiological evidence for the focus of lifestyle and environmental factors on health. Often referred to as the Lalonde Report,[9] this breakthrough work presented a conceptual framework called the Health Field Concept, which included four main elements: human biology, environment, lifestyle, and health-care organizations. This report was influential in persuading medical leaders to rethink current medical practices based on treatment-focused medicine. The document acknowledged that while the medical system was supporting the health of Canadians, vast sums of money were also being used to treat diseases that could have been prevented. The full report can be viewed at www.hc-sc.gc.ca/hcs-sss/com/fed/lalonde-eng.php.

The definition of health continued to broaden as we moved from measuring our nation's health status only by **morbidity** (disease) and **mortality** (death) rates to viewing health as a part of everyday living. In 1986, Jake Epp, the federal minister of Health and Welfare at that time, hosted the first International Conference on Health Promotion in Ottawa. It was at this conference, held primarily as a response to growing expectations for a new public health movement around the world, that WHO's definition of health was expanded. Known as the *Ottawa Charter,*[10] this expanded definition became a move toward building healthy public policy through health promotion:

> **Health promotion** is the process of enabling people to increase control over and to improve their health. To reach a state of complete physical, mental, and social well-being, an individual or group must be able to identify and realize aspirations, to satisfy needs, and to change or cope with the environment. Health is, therefore, seen as a resource for everyday life, not the objective of living. Health is a positive concept emphasizing social and personal resources, as well as physical capacities. Therefore, health promotion is not just the responsibility of the health sector, but goes beyond healthy lifestyles to well-being.

A follow-up report titled *Achieving Health for All: A Framework for Health Promotion*[11] identified three national health challenges: reducing inequities, increasing the prevention effort, and enhancing people's capacity to cope. The three mechanisms to health promotion were identified as **self-care**—or the decisions and actions individuals take in the interest of their own health; **mutual aid**—or the actions people take to help each other cope; and **healthy environments**—or the creation of conditions and surroundings conducive to health. Implementation strategies included fostering public participation, strengthening community health services, and coordinating healthy public policy. This health-promotion framework is still used today as a foundation for planning, implementing, and evaluating health-promotion programs and education.

Many more health models have been developed over the past few decades. The Health Belief Model, originated by Hochbaum, Kegels, and Rosenstock in the 1950s, was developed to help explain and predict health behaviour. This model considers social, ecological, and environmental factors that can influence our behaviour.[12] Twenty-five years of work, beginning at the University of Berkeley and later at the University of British Columbia, resulted in the Precede-Proceed Model for Health Promotion Planning and Evaluation.[13] This model helps us to think about our quality of life and health levels; assess our behaviour, lifestyle, and environment; and determine predisposing, reinforcing, and enabling factors for health. It also combines health education and organizational policies that support healthy living (see Figure 1-2).

The Quality of Life Model, developed in Canada at the Quality of Life Research Unit at the University of Toronto, is another helpful tool for individuals or communities wanting to enhance their health and well-being. This model has three life domains—Being, Belonging, and Becoming—with each domain having three subdomains (see Table 1-1). Quality of life is measured as the degree to which a person enjoys the important possibilities of his or her life.[14] The model emphasizes an individual's physical, psychological, and spiritual functioning; the connections with his or her environment; and the opportunities for maintaining and enhancing skills.

Health professionals, researchers, and recreation and school educators working in numerous national, federal, and provincial agencies support the health and well-being of Canadians, too. A short description of just some of these agencies and the programs and services they provide are shared here. You are encouraged to access the websites listed to gain a more in-depth look and understanding of Canadian health initiatives.

The Canadian Institute for Health Information (CIHI) is an independent, not-for-profit organization that provides information about national health indicators and standards, health spending, and current health research. One example of a special project of CIHI is the Canadian Population Health Initiative (CPHI). **Population health** is a way of thinking about the social and economic forces that shape the health of Canadians. It builds upon public health and health promotion but goes beyond our more traditional understanding of the causes of health and illness. You can access CIHI's website at www.cihi.ca.[15]

The Public Health Agency of Canada, is a national agency that works closely with provinces and territories to keep Canadians healthy and reduce health-care costs. Headed by the Chief Public Health Officer, who reports to the Minister of Health, this agency focuses on efforts to prevent chronic diseases and respond to health emergencies and infectious disease outbreaks. Its mission is to renew the public health system in Canada and support a sustainable health-care system.[16]

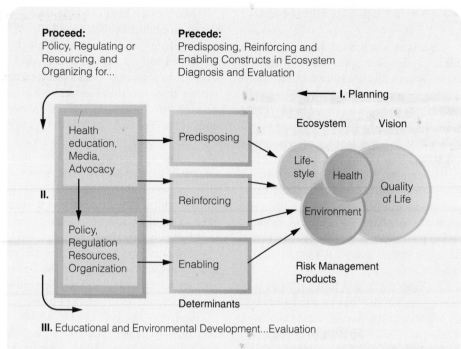

**Proceed:**
Policy, Regulating or Resourcing, and Organizing for...

**Precede:**
Predisposing, Reinforcing and Enabling Constructs in Ecosystem Diagnosis and Evaluation

I. Planning

II.

Health education, Media, Advocacy

Policy, Regulation Resources, Organization

Predisposing

Reinforcing

Enabling

Ecosystem     Vision

Lifestyle    Health

Environment

Quality of Life

Risk Management Products

Determinants

**III.** Educational and Environmental Development...Evaluation

▲ **Figure 1-2** Precede-Proceed Model for Health Promotion Planning and Evaluation

Source: Redrawn from Green, L.W. & Kreuter, M.S. (1999). *Health Promotion and Planning: An Educational and Ecological Approach*, 3rd edition. Mountain View: CA: Mayfield Publishing. Figure from: The Institute of Health Promotion Research, University of British Columbia. http://www.ihpr.ubc.ca/ProcedePrecede.html.

The Canadian Institutes of Health Research (CIHR)[17] is a federal agency that funds health research in Canada. New health knowledge gained from the research is then made available to health, recreation, and school professionals and practitioners so that health services, programs, and products can help to strengthen our health care system. Access their site at www.cihr-irsc.gc.ca/e/193.html.

The First Nations, Inuit & Aboriginal Health branch of Health Canada[18] at www.hc-sc.gc.ca/fniah-spnia/index-eng. php supports the delivery of public health and health-promotion services on reserves and in Inuit communities. Other services are also provided to First Nations and Inuit people in all parts of Canada. Specific information about diabetes; fetal alcohol syndrome; injury prevention; and alcohol, drugs, and tobacco is also available through this agency.

On November 28, 2002, a special commission headed by Roy Romanow delivered its *Final Report: Building on Values: The Future of Health Care in Canada*[19] to Canadians. Sweeping changes to Canada's health-care system were recommended so that Canada's universally accessible, publicly funded health-care system could be sustained for the long term. The report highlights included a collective vision for health care, the suggestion to update the Canada Health Act, and the recommendation that stable and predictable funding be put in place to address health-care issues. Aboriginal health care and the impact of globalization were

also addressed. The full report can be accessed at www. hc-sc.gc.ca/hcs-sss/hhr-rhs/strateg/romanow-eng.php.

For over 30 years, ParticipACTION, an organization created in 1971, attempted to increase the awareness of the benefits of regular physical activity and sustain the active-living movement in Canada. Using a combination of public messaging through the media; social marketing strategies; educational material for schools, workplaces, and fitness and recreation facilities; and partnerships between health, medical, recreation, and sport bodies, ParticipACTION aimed to motivate all Canadians to be more active and to improve general levels of fitness over a lifetime. The success story of ParticipACTION, from its pioneering efforts to its closure in January 2001, has been told in a special supplement of the *Canadian Journal of Public Health*[20] (see Figure 1-3). You can access this document by going to the ParticipACTION Archive Project website at www.usask.ca/ archives/participaction/english/home.html.

A study done in 2005 suggested that 75 percent of adult Canadians had a positive image of ParticipACTION. In 2007, the federal government decided to renew this agency and pledged $5 million over two years to support specific health and fitness initiatives aimed at children 12 and under, seniors, Aboriginal people, and people with disabilities. A new website—Healthy Canadians, available at www.HealthyCanadians.ca—is designed as a one-stop shop

## ▼ Table 1-1 Quality of Life Model

| Being | Who One Is |
|---|---|
| Physical Being | • physical health<br>• personal hygiene<br>• nutrition<br>• exercise<br>• grooming and clothing<br>• general physical appearance |
| Psychological Being | • psychological health and adjustment<br>• cognitions<br>• feelings<br>• self-esteem, self-concept, and self-control |
| Spiritual Being | • personal values<br>• personal standards of conduct<br>• spiritual beliefs |
| **Belonging** | **Connections with One's Environments** |
| Physical Belonging | • home<br>• workplace/school<br>• neighbourhood<br>• community |
| Social Belonging | • intimate others<br>• family<br>• friends<br>• co-workers<br>• neighbourhood and community |
| Community Belonging | • adequate income<br>• health and social services<br>• employment<br>• educational programs<br>• recreational programs<br>• community events and activities |
| **Becoming** | **Achieving Personal Goals, Hopes, and Aspirations** |
| Practical Becoming | • domestic activities<br>• paid work<br>• school or volunteer activities<br>• seeing to health or social needs |
| Leisure Becoming | • activities that promote relaxation and stress reduction |
| Growth Becoming | • activities that promote the maintenance or improvement of knowledge and skills<br>• adapting to change |

Source: Quality of Life Model. Developed at the Centre for Health Promotion. Permission to use the model granted by The Quality of Life Research Unit. Department of Occupational Therapy, 500 University Avenue, Rm. 914, Toronto, Ontario, M5G 1V7. Available at www.utoronto.ca/qol/concepts.htm.

▲ **Figure 1-3** ParticipACTION, The Mouse that Roared: A Marketing and Health Communications Success Story

Source: ParticipACTION: The mouse that roared. A marketing and health communications success story. *Canadian Journal of Public Health, 95,* Supplement 2, May–June 2004. Permission granted by *Canadian Journal of Public Health.*

Canadian Association for Health, Physical Education, Recreation and Dance [CAHPERD])[22] is doing to be helpful and inspiring. This organization, first named the Canadian Physical Education Association (CPEA), was founded in 1933 by Dr. Arthur Lamb of McGill University. Advocating and educating for quality physical and health education programs such as Quality Daily Physical Education (QDPE) and Comprehensive School Health (CSH) in both school and community environments has become its mission. Find resource material, research, and program ideas at www.cahperd.ca.

Many provincial and territorial governments in Canada have also developed health reports and new initiatives and programs. Table 1-2 lists some of them.

The provinces and territories could not support public health, wellness, and physical activity programs and initiatives without the hard work, dedication, and research agendas of individuals working in the health field. There are many people across Canada who deserve recognition for the work they do as active living advocates; one of them is Dr. Joan Wharf Higgins, our Canada Research Chair in Health and Society. The Canada Research Chairs program, established in 2000, has invested $300 million a year to attract and retain some of the world's most accomplished

to provide people with information on health and lifestyle issues.[21]

If you are planning to work with children in a school or recreation setting, you will find the work that the Physical and Health Education Canada (PHE Canada) (formerly called the

▼ **Table 1-2 Provincial and Territorial Health and Wellness Reports, Initiatives, and Programs**

| Province | Initiative | Website |
|---|---|---|
| British Columbia | Act Now BC | www.actnowbc.ca |
| Alberta | The Alberta Centre for Active Living | www.centre4activeliving.ca/index.html |
| Saskatchewan | Action Plan for Saskatchewan Health Care | www.health.gov.sk.ca/hplan_intro.html |
| Manitoba | Manitoba Healthy Living | www.gov.mb.ca/healthyliving/index.html |
| Ontario | Ministry of Health Promotion | www.mhp.gov.on.ca/english/resources.asp |
| Quebec | Health and Social Services | www.msss.gouv.qc.ca/en |
| New Brunswick | New Brunswick Department of Health | www.gnb.ca/0051/index-e.asp |
| Prince Edward Island | Prince Edward Island Strategy for Healthy Living | www.gov.pe.ca/photos/original/hss_hl_strategy.pdf |
| Nova Scotia | Nova Scotia Mi'kmaw Youth, Recreation & Active Circle for Living | http://nsmsrc.tripod.com |
| Newfoundland | Go Healthy | www.gohealthy.ca |
| Yukon | Yukon Health and Social Services | www.hss.gov.yk.ca/programs/health_promotion |
| Northwest Territories | Health and Social Services Initiatives | www.hlthss.gov.nt.ca/Features/Initiatives |
| Nunavut | Health Promotion Programs in Nunavut | www.gov.nu.ca/health/promo.shtml |

and promising researchers. By engaging in specialized research, the chairholders help train future researchers through graduate student supervision, teaching, and collaborative research work.

Wharf Higgins's research, based at the University of Victoria in British Columbia, focuses on people's life choices, chances, and circumstances as it relates to their health. When asked about her research, she describes her philosophy or worldview as this:

✔ **Life choices**. Or our personal decisions about lifestyle and ways of living (e.g., being physically active, eating a healthy diet, being smoke-free, engaging in environmentally friendly practices) are a reflection of and influenced by our life chances and circumstances.

✔ **Chances.** What we were born with and into that frame our health and life choices from an early age. Genes and biology we inherit from our parents. Chances also include things such as our ethnicity, sex, early childhood experiences, and extended family—whether or not we had a chance to play and learn in early life, the opportunities that our parents were able to afford us and provide for us.

✔ **Circumstances**. The neighbourhood we live in, where we work and what we do, and the trust, equity, and respect we feel in these settings. Circumstances also include who we live with and where we live— including animals, the province, country, and provincial and national policies that are in place that support our well-being.

Her understanding of life choices, chances, and circumstances shapes the type of research in which she engages. One example is the Saanich Peninsula Diabetes Prevention Project, where Wharf Higgins was more interested in having people engaged in the life of their community to enhance their own lifestyle than focusing on traditional risk factors, such as reducing blood sugar levels. She suggests that sometimes we assume that if we give people more knowledge about health issues they will translate that knowledge into healthy living. That is not always so. For example, in a heart health project, a number of the mothers involved were already aware of lifestyle risks but often had to sacrifice good nutrition to provide for their children, relying on their smoking habit to curb their appetites. Some participants in Wharf Higgins' research project simply told her that "it's hard to be good when life is so bad." This is a research example of how life choices and circumstances are very real.

## ???? What Is Epidemiology?

**Epidemiology** is the study of how often diseases occur in different groups of people and why. Epidemiological information can be used to evaluate health strategies and prevent certain illnesses. It is also used to guide doctors and health-care providers in the management of patients who are dealing with specific diseases. If you were to engage in epidemiological research, you might find yourself studying in any of the following areas: infectious disease, neuroepidemiology, chronic disease, and epidemiology of aging. Epidemiological research uses a variety of methodological approaches including environmental, clinical, genetic, molecular, social, lifecourse, pharamacoepidemiology, and surveillance epidemiology. Researchers can examine the distribution of disease in a specific population, known as descriptive epidemiology, or investigate a hypothesized causal factor by conducting a study that relates to the exposure of interest to the disease, known as analytical epidemiology. There are many exciting careers in epidemiology. You can find out more at the Canadian Society for Epidemiology and Biostatistics website at www.cseb.ca/en/index.htm.

# Wellness and the Wellness Movement

## ???? What Is Wellness?

**Wellness** can be defined as purposeful, enjoyable living or, more specifically, a deliberate lifestyle choice characterized by personal responsibility and optimal enhancement of physical, mental, and spiritual health. More than freedom from disease, it means taking steps to prevent illness and involves a capacity to live life to the fullest. A healthy and well individual has a greater capacity for personal potential. To understand how the concepts of wellness and health fit together, let's review the history of the wellness movement.

Halbert Dunn, considered a pioneer of the wellness movement, was a physician and chief of the United States National Office of Vital Statistics from 1935 to 1950. He believed health care should be more than the treatment of disease. His definition of wellness was based on that of WHO's; however, he believed that health was *a passive state of homeostasis or balance*, whereas wellness was *a dynamic process of continually moving toward one's potential for optimal functioning*. Wellness, for Dunn, was dependent on three criteria: (1) direction and progress toward a higher potential of functioning; (2) the total individual, which includes physical, mental, emotional, social, and spiritual components; and (3) functioning and adapting for daily living and in times of crisis.[23]

In 1974, while Canadians were moving toward a new perspective on health care, Dr. John Travis, inspired by Halbert Dunn, founded the first Wellness Resource Centre in the United States in 1975. A medical doctor by training, Travis decided to shift his focus from disease care to self-responsibility and prevention. His wellness model, the Illness/Wellness Continuum, is seen in Figure 1-4. Travis suggests that many of us are at the neutral point where we are not ill but have much more potential to be well. His definition of wellness includes the belief that wellness is a choice, a decision you make to move toward optimal health, and a lifestyle you design to achieve your highest potential for well-being.[24] He continues to write about wellness, with a new focus on global wellness, and children and wellness. His website can be accessed at www.thewellspring.com.

Another influential wellness expert, Dr. Bill Hettler, the cofounder and president of the board of directors of the National Wellness Institute, began his work in the wellness field at the University of Wisconsin–Stevens Point in the 1970s. Hettler believed that health care could be improved with health-promotion activities and educational opportunities that encouraged self-care. He created a Lifestyle Assessment Questionnaire (LAQ) that has been redesigned as TestWell, a self-scoring wellness assessment that is available for personal or organizational use.[25] A short version is now available online at www.nationalwellness.org. Click on "Wellness Current—Free Wellness Assessment." There are college and adult versions of this inventory.

Hettler also developed the Six Dimensions of Wellness model (see Figure 1-5). This model has been used in many corporate health and wellness programs and as a basis for a number of health models. A brief overview of the six dimensions is presented here.

## Social Dimension

This dimension encourages a collectivist view of the world—that of contributing to society, helping others, and valuing the concept of interdependence between ourselves and our environment. By embracing the social dimension of wellness, we begin to take an active part in improving

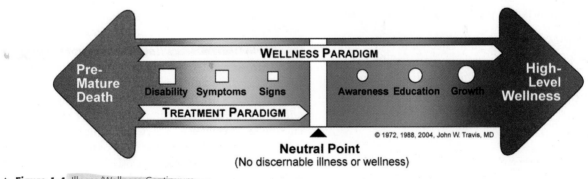

▲ **Figure 1-4** Illness/Wellness Continuum

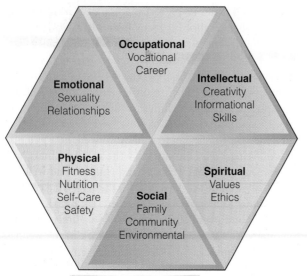

▲ **Figure 1-5** Six Dimensions of Wellness

Source: Hettler, B. (1976, 1979); National Wellness Institute (1993). Testwell, p. i. Copyright 1979 by Hettler, copyright 1993 by National Wellness Institute, Inc., WCB Brown & Benchmark Publishers. Also available at www.nationalwellness.org/index.php?id_tier=2&id_c=25. Permission granted by National Wellness Institute.

our world by living in a healthy way. Actively seeking ways to enhance personal relationships and friendships supports social wellness.[26] The social dimension is especially important in times of crisis. "Ultimately, community helps us heal from trauma," says psychiatrist Robert Ursano.[27]

Health educators are placing a greater emphasis on the social dimension of wellness. Current research shows that people with spouses, friends, and a rich social network may outlive isolated loners by as much as 30 years.[28]

## Occupational Dimension

Finding enrichment through our work or vocation can enhance our well-being. A "well" occupation is consistent with personal values, interests, and beliefs. It is also the attitude we hold about our work. In a well work environment, you share your unique gifts, skills, and talents and enjoy work that is meaningful and rewarding. Occupational wellness follows the tenet that it is healthy to choose a career that supports our personal values, interests, and beliefs.[29]

As you begin to plan for your career or to reflect upon the career choices you have made, an understanding of the importance of occupational wellness can direct you in your choice of profession, ensure job satisfaction, help you to define your career ambitions, and assist you in evaluating your personal performance on the job.

## Spiritual Dimension

Identifying our basic purpose in life; learning how to experience love, joy, peace, and fulfillment; and helping

▲ In every culture, religious rituals play an important role in the lives and health of individuals.

ourselves and others achieve our potential are all aspects of the spiritual dimension. Spiritual wellness also supports the concept that it is better to live in harmony with others and our environment than to live with them in conflict.[30] As we devote ourselves to others' needs, our spiritual development produces a sense of greater meaning in our lives and helps us discover what our personal legacy might be.

Spirituality has been described in many ways. Some definitions include transcendence, connectedness, a power, a force, or energy. Robert Russell[31] states that the spiritual dimension unites all other wellness dimensions. Becoming more spiritual can result in a stronger awareness of our inner selves. It can also mean developing a relationship with what some call a higher being, or the universe.[32]

Spirituality can also mean a connection to a formal religion. Research shows that people who regularly attend religious services are twice as likely to have a very strong feeling of belonging to their community, compared with those who do not attend at all.[33] Believers also recovered from depression earlier[34] and frequent churchgoers have been shown to have lower blood pressure and more rigorous immune systems.[35]

## Physical Dimension

Physical wellness is met through participation in regular physical activity. Aerobic conditioning includes walking, running, cycling, and swimming—activities that help to keep our hearts healthy. Exercises such as strength training and calisthenics help to improve muscle strength and endurance. Stretching exercises keep us flexible.

Being physically active also helps us maintain a healthy body weight or body mass index. Learning about healthy eating habits supports the tenet of physical wellness—that it is better to consume foods and beverages that enhance good health rather than those that impair it.[36]

To be physically well, we also need to avoid harmful behaviours such as tobacco use, drug misuse, and excessive alcohol consumption. As physical wellness is pursued, a heightened awareness of the connection between body, mind, and spirit is experienced.

Dr. Martin Collis,[37] a renowned Canadian wellness expert, began researching the benefits of physical activity and its link to health in the 1970s. Collis's powerful voice encouraged fitness professionals to broaden their vision of wellness to include total fitness, a connection of mind, body, and spirit.

## Intellectual Dimension

Your brain is the only organ capable of self-awareness. Every day you use your mind to gather, process, and act on information; to think through your values; and to make decisions, set goals, and figure out how to handle a problem or challenge. Intellectual wellness refers to your ability to think and learn from life experience, your openness to new ideas, and your capacity to question and evaluate information. Throughout your life, you'll use your critical-thinking skills, including your ability to evaluate health information, to safeguard your well-being.

A well person cherishes intellectual growth and stimulation. When we embrace this dimension of wellness we stretch and challenge our minds with intellectual and creative pursuits and become more productive.[38]

## Emotional Dimension

Emotional wellness includes the degree to which one feels positive and enthusiastic about oneself and life.[39] It also involves awareness and acceptance of a wide range of feelings in oneself and others. When you are emotionally well, you have the capacity to express and manage your own feelings. You make choices and decisions based upon the connection of feelings, thoughts, philosophies, and behaviours. You become aware of limitations and personal and professional stressors but are able to effectively work around those limitations and cope with the stressors.

Emotional wellness also means that we have the capability to work independently but recognize the importance of being able to ask for help or support when needed. An emotionally well individual knows that there are times when there is a benefit to working interdependently with others and celebrating the commitment, trust, and respect that those relationships are based on.[40]

Emotional wellness follows these tenets: It is better to be aware of and accept our feelings than to deny them and to be optimistic in our approach to life.[41] When we adopt or create a personal health and wellness model, we begin the process of self-care; living well can be part of a personal and professional plan of action.

# Health Challenges

## ??? What Is the Average Life Expectancy?

In 1900, the average woman could expect to live to be 50.9 years of age, compared with 47.9 years for a man. Infectious diseases, such as smallpox and tuberculosis, claimed tens of thousands of lives, particularly among the young and the poor. A high percentage of women died during childbirth or shortly afterward.

From 1990 to 2005, the average age at death for both sexes rose. For men, it increased by 3.5 years. For women, by 3.2 years. In 2005, the average age at death for the overall population was 74.2 years. For men, it was 71.1, and for women, 77.4. According to new data from Statistics Canada, the life expectancy has also risen. Men who were 65 years of age in 2005 can expect to live another 17.9 years, and women can expect to live another 21.1 years. (See Table 1-3 and The X & Y Files: "Do Sex and Gender Matter?")

Aside from life-expectancy statistics and gender differences (see also Figure 1-6), there are other health challenges facing Canadians. According to the Chief Public Health Officer's Report on the State of Public Health in Canada,[42]

✔ If recent trends continue, six out of ten people in Canada in 2008 will die of either circulatory diseases, such as heart attacks, heart failure, or stroke, or from cancer.

✔ Research indicates that where we live can have an impact on our life. The potential of years of life lost (PYLL) is greater if you live in the northern regions of Canada. This is mostly due to unintentional injuries and self-inflicted injuries.

✔ There has been a sharp increase in the number of Canadians with diabetes. The vast majority—about 90 percent—have Type 2 diabetes, which is strongly linked to being overweight.

▼ **Table 1-3 Health Canada's Life Expectancy Table**

|  | 1931 | 1961 | 1991 | 2005[1] |
|---|---|---|---|---|
|  |  | years |  |  |
| **Females** |  |  |  |  |
| At birth | 62.1 | 74.2 | 80.9 | 82.7 |
| At 65 | 13.7 | 16.1 | 19.9 | 21.1 |
| **Males** |  |  |  |  |
| At birth | 60.0 | 68.4 | 74.6 | 78.0 |
| At 65 | 13.0 | 13.5 | 15.8 | 17.9 |

Note: See Catalogue no. 84-537-XIE for a complete explanation of the methodology used to produce abridged life tables.
Source: Statistics Canada, CANSIM table 102-0511 and Catalogue no. 84-518-XPE.

[1] Starting with 2005 data, life expectancy is calculated using a 3-year average of age-specific mortality rates.

## The X & Y Files

# Do Sex and Gender Matter?

Sex does matter. That was the conclusion of the Institute of Medicine Committee on Understanding the Biology of Sex and Gender Differences in the first significant review of the status of sex and gender differences in biomedical research.

*Sex,* the committee stated, is "a classification, generally as male or female, according to the reproductive organs and functions that derive from the chromosomal complement." *Gender* refers to "a person's self-representation as male or female, or how that person is responded to by social institutions on the basis of the individual's gender presentation." Rooted in biology, gender is shaped by environment and experience.

The experience of being male or female in a particular culture and society can and does have an effect on physical and psychological well-being. This realization is both new and revolutionary. For centuries, scientists based biological theories solely on a male model and viewed women as shorter, smaller, and rounder versions of men. We now know this simply isn't so. Sex begins in the womb, but sex and gender differences affect behaviour, perception, and health throughout life.

The X & Y Files throughout this book show that virtually every part and organ system of the body differs in men and women (see Figure 1-6). A man's core body temperature runs lower than a woman's; his heart beats at a slower rate. A woman takes 9 breaths a minute; a man averages 12. Her blood carries higher levels of protective immunoglobulin; his has more oxygen-rich hemoglobin. Her ears are more sensitive to sound; his eyes are more sensitive to light. Male brains are 10 percent larger, but certain areas in female brains contain more neurons.

Gender differences persist in sickness as well as in health. Before age 50, men are more prone to lethal diseases, including heart attacks, cancer, and liver failure.

Women show greater vulnerability to chronic but non-life-threatening problems such as arthritis and autoimmune disorders. Women are twice as likely to suffer depression; men have a fivefold greater rate of alcoholism. Women outlive men by approximately five years, yet they are more prone to age-related problems, such as osteoporosis and Alzheimer's disease. Health behaviours—patterns of drinking, smoking, or using seat belts—also are different in men and women.

More women than men have a regular physician. Men have fewer dental as well as medical checkups. They're less likely to seek psychiatric services, to have their cholesterol levels and blood pressure checked regularly, and to undergo some form of screening for colon cancer. More women than men are overweight, and fewer women are physically active. Although college men are among those at highest risk of testicular cancer, three out of four do not know how to perform self-examination. Male undergraduates are much less likely to examine their testicles than female students are to examine their breasts. College-age men also are significantly more likely to engage in risky and physically dangerous behaviours and to suffer more injuries, including fatal ones, as a result.

Recognition of these gender differences is transforming medical research and practice. A new science called *gender-specific medicine* is replacing one-size-fits-all health care with new definitions of what is normal for men and women, more complex concepts of disease, more precise diagnostic tests, and more effective treatments.

Sources: Committee on Understanding the Biology of Sex and Gender Differences. (2001). *Exploring the biological contributions to human health: Does sex matter?* Washington, DC: Institute of Medicine, National Academy of Sciences; Hales, D. (2001). *Just like a woman.* New York: Bantam; Hales, D. (2002, September). Biology shows women and men are different. *Mayo Clinic Women's Healthsource, 6*(9), 1.

---

✔ Hypertension, or high blood pressure, is a major contributor to poor health of Canadians. About 18 percent of Canadians aged 20 years or older report being diagnosed with high blood pressure. For those over the age of 44, it is 31 percent.

✔ Mental health issues are also a concern. Almost 5 percent of Canadians report having experienced symptoms consistent with a major depressive episode over the past year.

## Social Determinants

The overview of health and wellness helps us to understand that personal health and wellness is not only dependent on self-care, but also on many conditions that support self-care.

New research in the area of the **social determinants of health (SDOH)** support the notion that diversity and social exclusion, income inequality, job security and working conditions, housing and food security, and education and care in early life are also very important to health and wellness status.[43]

Canada has been a world leader in research that is related to social determinants of health, but there is evidence that there is a growing inequality in social and economic status between groups of Canadians. According to Wilkinson and Marmot,[44] the larger the gap, the lower the health status of the overall population. We still have much to do to secure and to maintain a healthy Canadian population. A more in-depth look at the social determinants of health is presented in the next section.

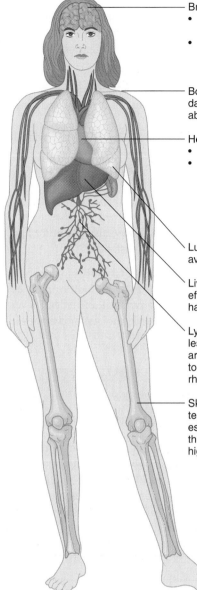

**Brain:**
- Women are twice as likely as men to suffer from depression.
- Some parts of the corpus callosum—the bridge that joins the left and right halves of the brain—are smaller in men than in women.

**Body Temperature:** Temperature varies throughout the day, but a man's body temperature consistently runs about half a degree lower than a woman's.

**Heart and Circulatory System:**
- Men's heart rates tend to be slower than women's.
- Women are less likely than men to develop high blood pressure while they are young because their higher levels of estrogen prevent cholesterol deposits from forming on artery walls. However, as women grow older, their risks for heart disease begin to match those of men.

**Lungs:** Women average 9 breaths per minute; men average 12.

**Liver:** Men metabolize alcohol faster and more efficiently than women, are less likely to suffer hangovers, and are more likely to become alcoholics.

**Lymphatic System:** Men's immune systems respond less forcefully to a cold than do women's. However, men are less likely than women to suffer from diseases linked to malfunctioning highly active immune systems, such as rheumatoid arthritis and lupus erythematosus.

**Skeletal System:** Men's bodies will always produce some testosterone, but women's bodies nearly stop producing estrogen when they go through menopause. Because these hormones maintain bone density, women face a higher risk of brittle bones as they age.

▲ **Figure 1-6** Sex Differences in Health

## Diversity and Social Exclusion

We live in the most diverse nation on Earth and in one that is becoming increasingly diverse. For society, this variety can be both enriching and divisive. Diversity can mean people of different ages or people from different cultural, racial, or ethnic groups. It can also mean individuals of different sexual orientation. Canadians of different educational levels and abilities are sometimes defined as being diverse.[45] Today in Canada, increased disparities are evident as many different groups of Canadians do not have equal access to health care and health and wellness opportunities. Members of minority groups often encounter much difficulty in accessing health-care services in Canada. There are many reasons for this, but two stand at the forefront. One is poverty. Aboriginal people and immigrants are three times as likely as the average Canadian to be unemployed. Some studies show that visible minority immigrants are at a high risk for long-term poverty.

The other is social exclusion based on gender, age, ability, sexual orientation, race, ethnicity, and religious beliefs. Public-health experts are now moving beyond the narrow definition of *minority* to a broader concept of *underserved*. Often, when an individual or a group of individuals is underserved and faces a difficult living situation in one area, they face many more challenges where health inequities become even more evident as one disadvantage causes further disadvantages.

## Income Inequity

Poverty remains a major barrier to health and wellness as the poverty gap has widened over the last decade. Incomes have become more polarized, too.[46] In a report titled *Young People in Canada: Their Health and Well Being*, the significant relationship between income and youth health was revealed. Students in lower income families self-report that they are not as healthy, nor do they experience the same level of life satisfaction as students in families who are relatively affluent.[47]

## Job Security and Working Conditions

Many changes in the workforce have occurred because of globalization—the increased transnational movement of capital, goods, people, and political systems and a rapid turnover of ideas and images through new communication technologies. Globalization has fostered what we might call a standardization of cultural expression around the world.[48] Layoffs; the increase in temporary part-time, casual, contract, and self-employment work situations; and the changes made to employment insurance have also affected Canadian families. Half of working Canadians experience some sort of income and job insecurity. Many of these Canadians are young people with children. They often do not have access to available health care.[49]

## Housing and Food Security

There continues to be a housing crisis among renters in Canada. Low-income families, especially Aboriginal ones, new immigrants, and single-parent families, struggle with housing issues. When rents in many Canadian cities take 30 to 50 percent or more of an individual's income, money is not available for food, health care, or recreation.[50]

Low-income families are also 13 times more likely to report that their children go hungry than higher income families. This is especially so for single mothers. We will see in Chapter 2 that basic human needs include a place to live and enough food to eat.[51]

## Education and Care in Early Life

We do not have enough regulated child-care spaces for children of working parents in Canada. There are numerous studies suggesting that while high-quality, early childhood education has many positive benefits for society, total spending on daycare spaces has dropped. As well, budget cutbacks to public school education endangers the health of Canadians and the well-being of the social structure of our society, according to Ungerleider and Burns.[52] Aboriginal students have lower rates of high school graduation, and their attendance at postsecondary schools is well below the national average.

## Taking Action

All is not doom and gloom in Canada, however. Six key strategies to enhance the social determinants of health have been adopted by a number of health agencies and provincial governments. They are:

1. Adopting a framework for social inclusion.
2. Promoting full employment, job security, and healthy working conditions.
3. Protecting universal access to our high-quality health system.
4. Protecting Canada's high-quality public-education system.
5. Ensuring the right of all Canadians to adequate housing and food.
6. Reducing income disparities by ensuring minimum wages and levels of social assistance.

The health and well-being of Canadians depends on a commitment from individuals to adopt healthy lifestyles in partnership with municipal, provincial, and federal governments to support healthy lifestyle choices for everyone.[53]

## The Health of College and University Students

As one of the nation's 1 047 700 full- or part-time college or university students, you belong to one of the most diverse groups in Canada. In 2005–06, nearly 75 percent of students were enrolled full-time, and women enrolled in record numbers, with their total reaching 604 900, including both undergraduate and graduate students. The largest gain over the previous year was in humanities, while enrollment in the health, parks, recreation, and fitness field surpassed 100 000 for the first time.[54]

With regard to healthy lifestyles, college and university students often engage in behaviours that put them at risk for serious health problems. College-age men are more likely than women to engage in risk-taking behaviours—to use drugs and alcohol; to engage in risky sexual behaviours, such as having multiple partners and having sex while under the influence of alcohol; and to drive dangerously. Men also are more likely to be hospitalized for injuries and to commit suicide. Three-fourths of the deaths in the 15–24 age range are men.[55]

College or university living can be hazardous to your health, too. Dormitories have proven to be breeding grounds for serious infectious diseases such as meningitis. Secondhand smoke can present a long-term threat to smokers' roommates. Binge drinking imperils not only the drinkers, but also those in their immediate environment, including anyone on the road if an intoxicated student gets behind the wheel of a car.[56]

Undergraduates also face risks to their psychological health. In a Canadian survey, college students reported more distress than the general Canadian population, or their peers not enrolled in college.[57] Nearly a third of more than 7500 undergraduates surveyed had significantly elevated psychological distress—women more than men, younger students more than upper-level students.

First year seems to take the greatest toll. In an American study, a survey of 3680 students interviewed at the beginning and end of their first year found significant drops in physical and emotional well-being. As entering freshmen, 51 percent rated their physical health as "above average." At the end of the year, only 41 percent did. The percentage of students reporting above-average emotional health dropped from 52 percent to 45 percent.[58]

However, despite potential health risks, the great majority of students not only survive college and university, but also increase their chances of a long and healthful life. Many risk factors for disease—including high blood pressure, elevated cholesterol, and cigarette smoking—decline steadily as education increases, regardless of how much money people make. Education may be good for the body as well as the mind by influencing lifestyle behaviours, problem-solving abilities, and values. People who earn college and university degrees gain positive attitudes about the benefits of healthy living, learn how to gain access to preventive health services, join peer groups that promote healthy behaviour, and develop higher self-esteem and greater control over their lives.

## Becoming All You Can Be

Your choices and behaviours affect how long and how well you live. What aspects of your life could use some attention and improvement? Use this textbook and course as an opportunity to embrace healthy living and take time to learn about how you can make healthy lifestyle choices. The following sections discuss some of the processes you might go through to make a successful change for the better.

## Understanding Health Behaviour

Behaviours that affect your health include exercising regularly, eating a balanced nutritious diet, seeking care for symptoms, and taking the necessary steps to overcome illness and restore well-being. If you want to improve health behaviour, it is important to realize that change isn't easy. Between 40 and 80 percent of those who try to kick bad health habits lapse back into their unhealthy ways within six weeks. To make lasting beneficial changes, it helps to understand the three types of influences that shape behaviour: predisposing, enabling, and reinforcing factors (see Figure 1-7).

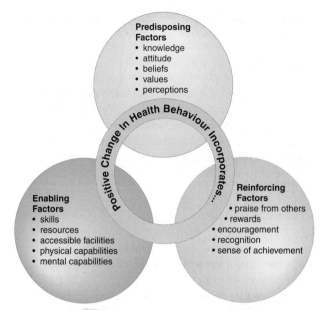

▲ **Figure 1-7** Factors that Shape Positive Behaviour

Source: Hespenheide Design

## Predisposing Factors

Predisposing factors include knowledge, attitudes, beliefs, values, and perceptions. Unfortunately, knowledge isn't enough to cause most people to change their behaviour; for example, people fully aware of the consequences of smoking often continue to puff away. Nor is attitude—one's likes and dislikes—sufficient; an individual may dislike the smell and taste of cigarettes but continue to smoke regardless.

Beliefs are more powerful than knowledge and attitudes, and researchers report that people are most likely to change health behaviour if they hold three beliefs:

✔ **Susceptibility.** They acknowledge they are at risk for the negative consequences of their behaviour.
✔ **Severity.** They believe that they may pay a very high price if they don't make a change.
✔ **Benefits.** They believe that the proposed change will be advantageous to their health.

There can be a gap between stated and actual beliefs, however, because people of all ages, everywhere, often feel invulnerable, that nothing bad can or will happen to them, that if there were a real danger, they would somehow know it. Often it's not until something happens that our behaviours become consistent with our stated beliefs.

The value or importance we give to health also plays a major role in changing behaviour. Many people aren't concerned about their health just for the sake of being healthy. Usually they want to look or feel better, be more productive or competitive, or behave more independently. They're more likely to change and to stick with a change, if they can see that the health benefits also enhance other important aspects of their lives.

## Enabling Factors

Enabling factors include skills, resources, accessible facilities, and physical and mental capabilities. Before you initiate a change, assess the means available to reach your goal. No matter how motivated you are, you'll become frustrated if you keep encountering obstacles. That's why breaking a task or goal down into step-by-step strategies is so important in behavioural change.

## Reinforcing Factors

Reinforcing factors may include praise from family and friends, rewards from teachers or parents, or encouragement and recognition for meeting a goal. Although these help a great deal in the short run, lasting change depends not on external rewards but on an internal commitment and sense of achievement. To make a difference, reinforcement must come from within.

A decision to change a health behaviour should stem from a permanent, personal goal, not from a desire to please or to impress someone else. If you lose weight for a special occasion, you're almost sure to regain pounds afterward. But if you shed extra pounds because you want to feel better about yourself or get into shape, you're far more likely to keep off the weight.

## Making Decisions

Every day you make decisions that have immediate and long-term effects on your health. You decide what to eat, whether to drink or smoke, when to exercise, and how to cope with a sudden crisis. Beyond these daily matters, you decide when to see a doctor, what kind of doctor, and with what sense of urgency. You decide what to tell your doctor and whether to follow the advice given, whether to keep up your immunizations, whether to have a prescription filled and comply with the medication instructions, and whether to seek further help or a second opinion. The entire process of maintaining or restoring health depends on your decisions; it cannot start or continue without them.

The small or large decisions of everyday life can be broken down into manageable steps:

- ✔ **Set priorities.** What matters most to you? What would you like to accomplish in the next week, month, or year? Look at the decision you're about to make in the context of your values and goals.
- ✔ **Inform yourself.** The more you understand, the better you'll be able to make healthy decisions. Gathering information may involve formal research or informal conversations with teachers, counsellors, family members, or friends.
- ✔ **Consider all your options.** List as many options you can think of, along with the advantages and disadvantages of each.
- ✔ **Tune in to your intuitive feelings.** While it's not infallible, your sixth sense can provide valuable feedback. If something just doesn't feel right, listen to this inside

voice. Are there any fears you haven't dealt with? Do you have doubts about taking a certain path?
- ✔ **Consider a worst-case scenario.** When you've come close to a final decision, imagine what will happen if everything goes wrong—the workload becomes overwhelming, your partner betrays your trust, your expectations turn out to be unrealistic. If you can live with the worst consequences of a decision, you're probably making the right choice.

## How Can I Begin to Make Lifestyle Changes?

Change is never easy—even if it's done for the best possible reasons. When you decide to change a behaviour, you have to give up something familiar and easy for something new and challenging. Change always involves risk—and the prospect of rewards.

Researchers have identified various approaches that people use to make beneficial changes. In the *moral model,*

---

### Strategies for Prevention

#### Setting Realistic Goals

Here's a framework for setting goals and objectives, the crucial preliminary step for prevention. The framework is based on the SMART model[59]—your goals and objectives need to be Specific, Measurable, Achievable, Realistic, and Trackable.

- ▲ Determine your goal or objective. Define it in words and on paper. Can you attain your goal and still be the person you want to be?

- ▲ Think in terms of evolution, not revolution. If you want to change the way you eat, start by changing just one meal a week.

- ▲ Identify your resources. Do you have the knowledge, skills, finances, time—whatever it takes? Find out from others who know. Be sure you're ready for the next step.

- ▲ Choose a plan. Think it through, step by step, trying to anticipate what might go wrong and why. Track your lifestyle changes. Keep a nutrition or physical-activity log, make journal entries, or create daybook schedules.

- ▲ Systematically analyze barriers. How can missing resources be acquired? Identify and select alternative plans. List solutions for any obstacles you foresee.

- ▲ Ask yourself what worked and what didn't. Attempt to determine why or why not as you take steps to continue with your lifestyle-change plans.

you take responsibility for a problem (such as smoking) and its solution; success depends on adequate motivation, while failure is seen as a sign of character weakness. In the *enlightenment model,* you submit to strict discipline to correct a problem; this is the approach used in Alcoholics Anonymous. The *behavioural model* involves rewarding yourself when you make positive changes. The *medical model* sees the behaviour as caused by forces beyond your control (a genetic predisposition to being overweight, for example) and employs an expert to provide advice or treatment. For many people, the most effective approach is the *compensatory model,* which doesn't assign blame but puts responsibility on individuals to acquire whatever skills or power they need to overcome their problems.

Before they reach the stage where they can and do take action to change, most people go through a common process. First, they reach a level of accumulated unhappiness that makes them ready for change. Then they have a moment of truth that makes them want to change.

Social and cultural **norms**—behaviours that are expected, accepted, or supported by a group—can make change much harder if they're constantly working against a person's best intentions. You may resolve to eat less, for instance, yet your mother may keep offering you home-made brownies because your family's norm is to show love by making and offering delicious treats. Or you might decide to drink less, yet your friends' norm may be to equate drinking with having a good time.

If you're aware of the norms that influence your behaviour, you can devise strategies either to change them or adapt to them. Another option is to develop relationships with people who share your goals and whose norms can reinforce your behaviour.

## Stages of Change

According to the trans-theoretical model of change, developed by Prochaska, Norcross, and DiClemente, individuals progress through a sequence of stages as they make a change. Certain activities and experiences, called *change processes,* can help individuals progress through these stages[60] (see Figure 1-8). As you read each chapter of this textbook and attempt to make lifestyle changes, refer to this model of change to determine just where you are in the stages of change.

1. **Precontemplation.** Individuals at this stage are often not even aware that they have a problem, whereas others around them might. They have no intention of making a change.
2. **Contemplation.** Individuals in this stage are aware they have a behavioural problem and are considering changing it within the next six months. They may be torn between the positives of the new behaviour and the amount of energy, time, and other resources required to change. They do start to "contemplate."
3. **Preparation.** People in this stage intend to change a problem behaviour within the next month. Some focus on a master plan. They might look into fitness classes or gym memberships. They might start by making small changes, such as walking to classes rather than driving their car.
4. **Action.** People at this stage are modifying their behaviour according to their plan. The stage requires a commitment of time and energy. Changes made during this stage are visible to others. For instance, they might be jogging or working out at the gym three times a week.
5. **Maintenance.** In this stage, individuals have continued to work at changing their behaviour. The change may take up to six months to a lifetime. New exercisers are likely to stop during the first three to six months. Some lapses may be temporary.
6. **Termination.** While it may take two to five years, a behaviour becomes so deeply ingrained that a person can't imagine abandoning it.

# Strategies for Change

## How to Make a Change

▲ Get support from friends, but don't expect them to supply all the reinforcement you need. In the long run, your own commitment to losing weight has to be strong enough to help you keep eating well.

▲ Focus on the immediate rewards of your new behaviour. You may stop smoking so that you'll live longer, but take note of every other benefit it brings you—more stamina, less coughing, more spending money, no more stale tobacco taste in your mouth.

▲ Remind yourself of past successes you've had in making changes. Commend yourself on how well you've done so far and how well you'll continue to do.

▲ Reward yourself regularly. Plan a pleasant reward as an incentive for every week you stick to your new behaviour. Small, regular rewards are more effective in keeping up motivation than one big reward that won't come for many months.

▲ Expect and accept some relapses. The greatest rate of relapse occurs in the first few weeks after making a behaviour change. During this critical time, get as much support as you can. In addition, work hard on self-motivation, reminding yourself daily of what you have to gain by sticking with your new health habit.

| Precontemplation | Contemplation | Preparation | Action | Maintenance | Termination |
| --- | --- | --- | --- | --- | --- |

**Consciousness raising:** Increased knowledge or awareness of a problem—for example, learning about the health risks of obesity (Precontemplation and Contemplation).

**Emotional arousal:** A deeper, more emotional process of increasing awareness (Contemplation and Preparation).

**Self-re-evaluation:** Thoughtful appraisal of what we are like while continuing a problem behavior and what we would be like after changing it (Contemplation and Preparation).

**Commitment:** Accepting personal responsibility for the behavior change (Preparation, Action, and Maintenance).

**Rewards:** Using compliments or small gifts upon reaching a certain goal (Action and Maintenance).

**Countering:** Replacing unhealthful behaviors with more healthful ones (Action and Maintenance).

**Environmental control:** Using the external environment to help make changes (Action and Maintenance).

**Helping relationships:** Seeking support, acceptance, and encouragement from health professionals, friends, and family (Action and Maintenance).

▲ **Figure 1-8** The Stages of Change and Some Change Processes

Source: Reprinted from Petrocelli, J.V. (2000). Table 1: Processes and stages of change: Process of change and their descriptions. *Journal of Counselling and Development, 80*, p. 24. The American Counseling Association. Reprinted with permission. No further reproduction authorized without written permission from the American Counseling Association.

## Successful Change

Some people find it helpful to sign a contract—a written agreement in which they make a commitment to change—with their partner, parent, or health educator. Spelling out what they intend to do, and why, underscores the seriousness of what they're trying to accomplish.

Change also depends on the belief that you can and will succeed. In his research on **self-efficacy,** psychologist Albert Bandura found that the individuals most likely to reach a goal are those who believe they can. The more strongly they feel that they can and will change their behaviour, the more energy and persistence they put into making the change. Other researchers have linked positive health change with optimism.

Another crucial factor is **locus of control.** If you believe that your actions will make a difference in your health, your locus of control is internal. If you believe that external forces or factors play a greater role, your locus of control is external. Individuals with an external locus of control for health are less likely to seek preventive health care and are less optimistic about early treatment.

**Reinforcements,** either positive (a reward) or negative (a punishment), also can play a role. If you decide to set up a regular exercise program, you might reward yourself with a new sweatsuit if you stick to it for three months or you

might punish yourself for skipping a day by doing an extra ten minutes of exercises the following day.

Your **self-talk**—the messages you send yourself—also can play a role. In recent decades, mental health professionals have recognized the conscious use of positive self-talk as a powerful force for changing the way individuals think, feel, and behave. "We have a choice about how we think," explains psychologist Martin Seligman, Ph.D., author of *Learned Optimism.* By learning to challenge automatic negative thoughts that enter our brains and asserting our own statements of self-worth, we can transform ourselves into optimists who see what's right rather than pessimists forever focusing on what's wrong. "Optimism is a learned set of skills," Seligman contends. "Once learned, these skills persist because they feel so good to use. And reality is usually on our side."[61]

## Health and Wellness Education

In the past, health and wellness education focused either on individual or organizational change. Today, many educators are using a framework in which individual behaviour change

## Christopher Bratseth— The Power of Kindness

We open our Human Potential story series in this second edition of *An Invitation to Health* with a past graduate student of mine, Christopher Bratseth. We met many years ago when I did a guest lecture for another colleague. Since then, our paths have crossed many times, the most recent connection with Chris working with me as a research assistant. As you will discover, Chris has faced many challenges along his way, but by reaching out to others, knowing when to ask for help and finding meaning in his work and personal life, he embodies personal health and wellness. Enjoy his story and be inspired.

Sometimes from our darkest moments come our clearest insights about how to live well. During my undergraduate degree, I suffered through periods of depression brought on by test-taking and social anxiety. Although I took part in sports and loved the academic challenge of school, I did not have the resources to cope with the emotional challenges. I still remember one night in my third year when I was overcome by grief and mental anguish. In this moment, I felt like I could empathize fully with the silent suffering of so many people with mental illness. I promised to myself then that if I found a way to overcome this pain, I would work to relieve the suffering of others. This intention would shape my life in more powerful ways than I could ever imagine.

I was fortunate to experience the kindness of strangers when Dr. John Cook, a registered psychologist, began to work with me. He used cognitive and group therapy to empower and educate me about my condition. I spent time in counselling to reduce my fear of public speaking, open up to my family about my depression, and learn how to reduce my anxiety through meditation, physical activity, and cognitive behavioral therapy. Taking these healing steps allowed me to enjoy my last years at university and finish my degree.

After university, I wanted to work in media and find a way to serve others at the same time. It was at this time when I came together with three of my closest friends—Erik Hanson, Val Litwin, and Brad Stokes—to create a web-television show called *Extreme Kindness*. The concept was simple: we would film spontaneous acts of kindness and upload

Brad Stokes, Chris Bratseth, Val Litwin, and Erik Hanson of the Kindness Crew.
© Courtesy of Christopher Bratseth

them to our web site in the hopes that people would be inspired *to be the change they wished to see in the world.* Unfortunately, our forward momentum was slowed by a series of challenging events.

The year 2001 was life-altering for our group, and we struggled to find meaning in the new landscape of our lives. Erik, Val, and myself came together to support our friend Brad and his mother, Judy, after she was diagnosed with ovarian cancer. In the summer, we were there beside Brad and his sister Devon when their mother passed away. During our time with her, Judy taught us about the need to live in the moment and follow our passions for helping others. Only one month later, our world was shaken again in the wake of grief and horror of September 11.

In the aftermath of September 11, we struggled to make sense of how we could have any part in trying to mend the hearts of the millions who were affected by these acts of terrorism. It was in our collective moments of reflection, we found our focus. We began to see how kindness connects all people regardless of their social, economic, and religious background. Kindness was also immediately empowering and accessible to anyone who was suffering. We believed kindness could be an antidote to the disconnection and fear with which people were plagued. Our simple but passion-filled gesture was to build a Kindness Crew—a group committed to connecting the world through kindness—and start a wave of love across the continent.

In the fall of 2002, after a year of planning and garnering support, we embarked on the road trip of a lifetime. We set out across Canada on the Extreme Kindness Tour with a mission to inspire a million acts of kindness. We travelled by motorhome from

*continued*

Victoria, B.C., to St. John's, Newfoundland, connecting with others through compassion. In each community we visited, we staged Kindness Marathons—working from dawn until dusk with schools, non-profits, and businesses on community projects and acts of service.

From staffing soup kitchens in Calgary and roofing homes in Winnipeg to serving the homeless in Toronto, our acts ranged from the mundane to the magnificent. Our highlights included mobilizing the town of Salmon Arm, B.C., to commit over 19 000 random acts of kindness in one day; having the city of Gander, Newfoundland, proclaim November 23 Kindness Day; CNN broadcasting our story across the world; and Catherine Ryan Hyde (the author of the book *Pay it Forward*) flying out to Halifax to join us on our tour. In the end, there was no way to directly measure the impact of the tour; however, as a group we made it our life mission to inspire, educate, and mobilize others toward service.

The tour eventually spawned work with schools, non-profits, First Nations communities, and Fortune 500 companies. One firm, SAS Canada, was inspired to allow all employees four days off per year to volunteer with their charity of choice. We also wrote a book about our journey, titled *Cool to Be Kind— Random Acts and How to Commit Them*, to engage the next generation of do-gooders. Our website, www.extremekindness.com, now serves as a resource for people looking to join the kindness revolution.

Ironically, I have begun to make a living as a speaker and educator. As I reflect on my experience on the tour, I now realize how powerful kindness was in helping me to heal from my anxieties. Without the overarching focus of helping others, I would not have found the inner strength to overcome this challenge.

Kindness has become a central virtue in my life, and I am grounded by the words of Theodore Isaac Rubin who eloquently said, "Kindness is more important than wisdom and the recognition of this is the beginning of wisdom." Kindness is also a starting point for living a healthy life, rich in meaning and joy. Life still ebbs and flows, but now the main current of my life is filled with a richness that leaves me with a feeling of peace and purpose.

You can check out the Kindness Crew's website at www.extremekindness.com.

---

occurs within the context of the environment of a person's life. Its primary themes—prevention of health problems and protection from health threats—can establish the basis for good health now and in the future.

## The Power of Prevention

No medical treatment, however successful or sophisticated, can compare with the power of prevention. Preventive efforts have already proved helpful in increasing physical activity, quitting smoking, reducing dietary fat, preventing sexually transmitted diseases and unwanted pregnancy, reducing intolerance and violence, and avoiding alcohol and drug abuse.

**Prevention** can take many forms. Primary or before-the-fact prevention efforts might seek to reduce stressors and increase support to prevent problems in healthy people. Consumer education provides guidance about how to change our lifestyle to prevent problems and enhance well-being. Other preventive programs identify people at risk and empower them with information and support so they can avoid potential problems. Prevention efforts may target an entire community and try to educate all of its members about the dangers of alcohol abuse or environmental hazards, or they may zero in on a particular group (for instance, seminars on safer sex practices offered to teens) or an individual (one-on-one counselling about substance abuse).

In the past, physicians did not routinely incorporate prevention into their professional practices. But times have changed. Medical schools are providing more training in preventive care. A growing number of studies have demonstrated that prevention saves not only money, but also productivity, health, and lives. Many deaths caused by cardiovascular disease, strokes, and cancer could be avoided or delayed by preventive measures. Eliminating smoking and changes in diet could prevent even more.

## The Potential of Protection

There is a great deal of overlap between prevention and **protection.** Some people might think of immunizations as a way of preventing illness; others see them as a form of protection against dangerous diseases. In many ways, protection picks up where prevention leaves off. You can prevent sexually transmitted infections (STIs) or unwanted pregnancy by abstaining from sex. But if you decide to engage in potentially risky sexual activities, you can protect yourself with condoms and spermicides. Similarly, you can prevent many automobile accidents by not driving when road conditions are hazardous. But if you do have to drive, you can protect yourself by wearing a seat belt and using defensive-driving techniques.

The very concept of protection implies some degree of risk—immediate and direct (for instance, the risk of intentional injury from an assailant or unintentional harm from a fire) or long-term and indirect (such as the risk of heart disease and cancer as a result of smoking). To know how best to protect yourself, you have to be able to realistically assess risks.

## Assessing Risks

We all face a host of risks, from the danger of being the victim of violence to the hazards of self-destructive behaviours like drinking and using illegal drugs. At any age, the greatest health threats stem from high-risk behaviours—smoking, excessive drinking, not getting enough exercise, eating too many high-fat foods, and not getting regular medical checkups, to name just a few. That is why changing unhealthy habits is the best way to reduce risks and prevent health problems.

Environmental health risks also need to be assessed. Every year brings calls of alarm about a new hazard to health: electromagnetic radiation, fluoride in drinking water, hair dyes, silicone implants, radon, lead. Here are some key factors to consider:

✔ Are there possible benefits? Advantages—such as the high salary paid for working with toxic chemicals or radioactive materials—may make some risks seem worth taking.

✔ Is the risk voluntary? All of us tend to accept risks that we freely choose to take, such as playing a sport that could lead to injuries, as opposed to risks imposed on us, such as threats of terrorism.

✔ Is the risk fair? The risk of skin cancer affects us all. We may worry about it and take action to protect ourselves and our planet, but we don't resent it the way we resent living with the risk of violence because the only housing we can afford is in a high-crime area.

✔ Are there alternatives? As consumers, we may become upset about cancer-causing pesticides or food additives when we learn about safer chemicals or methods of preservation.

✔ Are lives saved or lost? Our thinking about risks often depends on how they're presented. For instance, if we're told that a new drug may kill one out of every 100 people, we react differently than if we're told that it may save the lives of 99 percent of those who use it.

## The Future of Health and Wellness

Medical science is moving ahead at an astonishing speed. Every week seems to bring a new discovery or breakthrough. But with all the advances in medical science, it is still important to make healthy lifestyle choices that support all the dimensions of health and wellness.

**CHAPTER 1**

**Making This Chapter Work for You**

1. The components of health include all of the following *except*
   a. supportive friends and family.
   b. high-risk behaviour.
   c. energy and vitality.
   d. a clean environment.

2. Wellness is defined as
   a. purposeful, enjoyable living, characterized by personal responsibility and enhancement of physical, mental, and spiritual health.
   b. a state of complete physical, mental, and social well-being.
   c. attitudes and beliefs that contribute to a healthy state of mind.
   d. the absence of physical or mental illness.

3. Which of the following statements about the dimensions of wellness is true?
   a. Spirituality provides solace and comfort for those who are severely ill, but it has no health benefits.
   b. The people who reflect the highest levels of social health are usually among the most popular individuals in a group and are often thought of as the life of the party.
   c. Intellectual health refers to one's academic abilities.
   d. Optimal physical health requires a nutritious diet, regular exercise, avoidance of harmful behaviours and substances, and self-protection from accidents.

4. Which of the following statements about sex and gender differences is true?
   a. A man's core body temperature runs higher than a woman's.
   b. A man's heart beats at a higher rate than a woman's.
   c. More than half of men between the ages of 18 and 29 do not have a regular physical, compared to one-third of women.
   d. More men than women are overweight.

5. Social determinants of health include
   a. income inequality, job security and working conditions, housing and food security, education and care in early life, and diversity and social exclusion.
   b. medical treatment, new health products, and drug therapy.
   c. depression, sleep problems, and family concerns.
   d. environmental stressors, short- and long-term stressors, and social stressors.

6. Which of the following health hazards faced by college and university students can be avoided?
   a. binge drinking
   b. unprotected sex
   c. smoking
   d. all of the above

7. The development of health behaviours is influenced by all of the following *except*
   a. reinforcing factors, which involve external recognition for achieving a goal.
   b. pre-existing health factors, which take into account the individual's current position on the wellness continuum.
   c. predisposing factors, which include knowledge, attitudes, and beliefs.
   d. enabling factors, which are related to an individual's skills and capabilities to make behaviour changes.

8. If you want to change unhealthy behaviour, which of the following strategies is *least* likely to promote success?
   a. believing that you can make the change
   b. rewarding yourself regularly
   c. during self-talks, reminding yourself about all your faults
   d. accepting that you are in control of your health

9. According to the stages of change in the trans-theoretical model of change, which statement is *incorrect*?
   a. In the maintenance stage, individuals have avoided relapse for six months.
   b. In the contemplation stage, individuals are considering changing a problem behaviour in the next six months.
   c. In the action stage, individuals are actually modifying their behaviour according to their plan.
   d. In the preparation stage, individuals intend to change a problem behaviour in the next six months.

10. Which of the following statements is *incorrect*?
    a. Prevention involves specific actions that an individual can take when participating in risky behaviour to prevent health threats.
    b. You can prevent health problems by educating yourself about them and then avoiding the risky behaviour that may cause them.
    c. An example of a preventive measure is to avoid driving in icy, snowy conditions, and an example of a protective measure is to put chains on your tires.
    d. In assessing risks, two questions to ask are: Is the risk voluntary? Are there alternatives?

Answers to these questions can be found on page 450.

## Self Responsibility

*It seems ludicrous to prepare a student for a lifetime career in their area of interest and not prepare them for the responsibilities of maintaining their life.*[62]

**Dr. Bill Hettler**

Education can be an important step toward making healthy lifestyle changes. As you read through this textbook and debate health and wellness concepts with your classmates, friends, and families, think about ways you might take responsibility for lifestyle changes that will enhance your health and well-being. Then ask

## Social Responsibility

*Start a Kindness Revolution at your school, office, or neighbourhood.*

**Chris Bratseth**

yourself how healthy lifestyle choices might move you closer to realizing your own human potential. Begin by asking yourself what Stage of Change you are in.

Taking care of ourselves allows us to be better able to take care of others. What can you do to make your campus healthy and well?

## Critical Thinking

1. What is the definition of health according to the text? Does your personal definition differ from this? Does it differ from your definition of wellness? If so, in what ways? How would you have defined the terms health and wellness before reading this chapter?

2. Talk to classmates from different racial or ethnic backgrounds than yours about their culture's health attitudes. Ask them what is considered healthy behaviour in their culture. For example, is having a good appetite a sign of health? What kinds of self-care practices did their parents and grandparents use to treat colds, fevers, rashes, and other health problems? What are their attitudes about the health-care system?

3. Where are you on the wellness–illness continuum? What variables might affect your place on the scale? What do you consider your optimum state of health to be?

4. In what ways would you like to change your present lifestyle? What steps could you take to make those changes?

# CENGAGENOW™

If your textbook package includes CengageNOW™, go to http://west.cengagenow.com/ilrn/ to link to CengageNOW™ for Health, your online study tool. First take the **Pre-test** for this chapter to get your personalized **Study Plan,** which will identify topics you need to review and direct you to the appropriate resources. Then take the **Post-test** to determine what concepts you have mastered and what you still need work on.

## SITES & BYTES

### Canadian Institute for Health Information
**www.cihi.ca**

Access information about national health indicators and standards, health spending, current health research, and the Canadian Population Health Initiative (CPHI).

### Public Health Agency of Canada
**www.publichealth.gc.ca**

Find credible and practical e-health information gathered from federal, provincial, and municipal agencies; university libraries; and community groups.

### Canadian Institutes for Health Research
**www.cihr-irsc.gc.ca/e/193.html**

Learn about Canada's lead federal funding agency and funding opportunities for health research in four areas: biomedical, clinical, health systems and services, and population and public health.

### The First Nations, Inuit & Aboriginal Health, Health Canada
**www.hc-sc.gc.ca/fniah-spnia**

Discover public-health and health-promotion services for First Nations and Inuit people in Canada.

### Health Canada
**www.hc-sc.gc.ca**

A federal government website where health information can be found. Check out *The Daily,* a special page that keeps Canadians on top of current health issues.

### Speakwell
**www.speakwell.com**

An award-winning e-wellness website from Speakwell, a health and wellness education company. Check out the WELL newsletter, which is free of charge.

    Please note that links are subject to change. If you find a broken link, use a search engine such as

*continued*

www.google.ca and search for the website by typing in keywords.

### InfoTrac® College Edition Activity

Gieck, D.J., & Olsen, S. (2007). Holistic wellness as a means to developing a lifestyle approach to health behaviour among college students. *Journal of American College Health, 56*(1), 29–35.

1. Describe how the researchers of this study adapted Hettler's Six Dimensions of Wellness model so that data could be collected from college students as a way to measure holistic wellness.

2. Describe two interventions that the researchers used to measure physical activity level throughout the study.

3. What type of health and wellness courses and programs are available on your campus? How might you begin a holistic wellness program this school term?

You can find additional readings relating to personal health with InfoTrac® College Edition, an online library of more than 5000 journals and publications. Follow the instructions for accessing InfoTrac® that were packaged with your textbook, then search for articles using a keyword search.

For additional links and resources, visit our text-specific website at www.health.nelson.com.

## Key Terms

The terms listed here are used within the chapter on the page indicated. Definitions of terms are in the Glossary at the end of the book.

| | | | |
|---|---|---|---|
| **action** 17 | **hygiene** 4 | **panacea** 4 | **self-care** 5 |
| **contemplation** 17 | **locus of control** 18 | **population health** 5 | **self-efficacy** 18 |
| **epidemiology** 8 | **maintenance** 17 | **precontemplation** 17 | **self-talk** 18 |
| **health** 4 | **morbidity** 5 | **preparation** 17 | **social determinants of** |
| **health promotion** 5 | **mortality** 5 | **prevention** 20 | **health (SDOH)** 12 |
| **healthy environments** 5 | **mutual aid** 5 | **protection** 20 | **termination** 17 |
| **holism** 4 | **norms** 17 | **reinforcements** 18 | **wellness** 9 |

## References

1. Leadbetter, R. (2000, January 31). Aesculapius. *Encyclopedia Mythica*. Available at www.pantheon.org/articles/a/asclepius.html.
2. Woolf, H.B. (ed. in chief). (1994). *Webster's new collegiate dictionary*. Toronto: Thomas Allen & Son, Ltd.
3. McKenzie, B., & Morrissette, V. (2003, April). Social work practice with Canadians of Aboriginal background: Guidelines for respectful social work. *Envision: The Manitoba Journal of Child Welfare, 2*(1).
4. Kulchyski, P., McCaskill, D., & Newhouse, D. (1999). Introduction, in P. Kulchyski, D. McCaskill & D. Newhouse (eds.), *In the words of elders: Aboriginal cultures in transition,* pp. xi–xxv. Toronto: University of Toronto Press. p. iv.
5. Ibid., p. xvi.
6. Newhouse, D. (1997, February). Lecture notes for Native studies 1000. Attachment, personal e-mail correspondence, June 2, 2002.
7. World Health Organization Interim Commission. (1947). *Chronicle of the World Health Organization, 1*(1–2), 2. Available at http://whqlibdoc.who.int/hist/chronicles/chronicle_1947.pdf.
8. Constitution of the World Health Organization. (1947). *Chronicle of the World Health Organization*. Geneva, Switzerland: WHO.
9. Lalonde, M. (1974). *A new perspective on the health of Canadians*. Ottawa: Government of Canada. Available at www.hc-sc.gc.ca/hcs-sss/com/fed/lalonde-eng.php.
10. The Ottawa Charter for health promotion. (1986). World Health Organization, Health and Welfare Canada and Canadian Public Health Association. Available at www.who.int/hpr/NPH/docs/ottawa_charter_hp.pdf.
11. Epp, J. (1986). *Achieving health for all: A framework for health promotion*. Ottawa: Minister of Supply and Services Canada. Available at www.hc-sc.gc.ca/hcs-sss/pubs/system-regime/1986-frame-plan-promotion/index-eng.php.
12. Anspaugh, D.J., Dignan, M.B., & Anspaugh, S.L. (2000). Models for health promotion interventions. In *Developing health promotion programs*. Boston: McGraw-Hill.
13. McKenzie, J.F., & Smeltzer, J.L. (2001). *Planning, implementing, and evaluating health promotion programs: A primer,* 3rd ed. Boston: Allyn and Bacon.
14. The quality of life model. (n.d.). Quality of Life Research Unit, University of Toronto. Available at www.utoronto.ca/qol/concepts.htm.
15. Canadian Institute for Health Information. (n.d.). CIHI—Taking health information further. Available at www.cihi.ca.
16. Public Health Agency of Canada. (n.d.). Index. Public Health Agency of Canada. Available at http://publichealth.gc.ca.
17. Canadian Institutes of Health Research. (n.d.). Who we are. Available at www.cihr-irsc.gc.ca/e/193.html.

18. Health Canada. (2008, June 13). First Nations and Inuit Health Branch. Available at www.hc-sc.gc.ca/fniah-spnia.

19. Health Canada. (2004, October 1). *Final report. Commission on the future of health care in Canada.* Available at www.hc-sc.gc.ca/hcs-sss/hhr-rhs/strateg/romanow-eng.php.

20. Edwards, P., et al. (2004, May–June). ParticipACTION: The mouse that roared: A marketing and health communications success story. *Canadian Journal of Public Health, 95,* Supplement 2. Available at www.usask.ca/archives/participaction/english/impact/CPHA.html.

21. $5M to bring back ParticipACTION exercise program. (2007, February 19). CBC News. Available at www.cbc.ca/health/story/2007/02/19/participaction.html.

22. Physical and Health Education Canada. (n.d.). Available at www.cahperd.ca.

23. Dunn, H. (1961). *High-level wellness. A collection of twenty-nine short talks on different aspects of high-level wellness for man and society.* Arlington, VA: R.W. Beatty.

24. Travis, J.W., & Ryan, R.S. (2004). *The wellness workbook,* 3rd ed. Berkeley, California: Celestial Arts: pp. xiv–xv.

25. National Wellness Institute. (n.d.). Testwell. Available at www.nationalwellness.org/index.php?id_tier=91&id_c=55.

26. National Wellness Institute. (n.d.). Six dimensional model. Available at www.nationalwellness.org/index.php?id_tier=2&id_c=25.

27. Ursano, Robert. Personal interview.

28. Roizen, M. (2000). *Real age: Are you as young as you can be?* New York: HarperCollins.

29. National Wellness Institute. (n.d.). Six dimensional model. Available at www.nationalwellness.org/index.php?id_tier=2&id_c=25.

30. Ibid.

31. Russell, R. (1996). Unpublished paper (Carbondale, IL; Southern Illinois University, Health Education Department) as quoted in Mullen, D., McDermott, R., Gold, R., & Belcastro, P. (1996). *Connections for health.* Madison: Brown & Benchmark Publishers.

32. McSherry, W. (1998). Nurses' perceptions of spirituality and spiritual care. *Nursing Standard, 13,* 36–40.

33. Clark, W. (2000, Winter). Patterns of religious attendance. *Canadian Social Trends.* Statistics Canada—Catalogue no. 11-008.

34. Schnittker, J. (2001, September). When is faith enough? *Journal for the Scientific Study of Religion, 40*(3), 393.

35. Garfield, A.M., et al. (2001, October 15). Religion/spirituality, education and physical health in mid-life adults. *Gerontologist,* 160.

36. National Wellness Institute. (n.d.). Six dimensional model. Available at www.nationalwellness.org/index.php?id_tier=2&id_c=25.

37. Collis, M. (2004). Available at www.speakwell.com.

38. National Wellness Institute. (n.d.). Six dimensional model. Available at www.nationalwellness.org/index.php?id_tier=2&id_c=25.

39. Ibid.

40. Covey, S.R. (1989). *The seven habits of highly effective people: Restoring the character ethic.* New York: Simon & Schuster.

41. National Wellness Institute. (n.d.). Six dimensional model. Available at www.nationalwellness.org/index.php?id_tier=2&id_c=25.

42. Public Health Agency of Canada. (2008, June 19). Report on the state of public health in Canada 2008. Available at www.phac-aspc.gc.ca/publicat/2008/cpho-aspc/index-eng.php.

43. Federal/Provincial/Territorial Advisory Committee on Population Health. (1999). *Toward a healthy future. Second report on the health of Canadians.* Ottawa: Health Canada.

44. Wilkinson, R., & Marmot, M. (1998). *Social determinants of health: The solid facts.* Copenhagen: World Health Organization. Available at www.euro.who.int/healthy-cities.

45. McKenzie, J.F., & Smeltzer, J.L. (2001). *Planning, implementing, and evaluating health promotion programs. A primer,* 3rd ed. Boston: Allyn and Bacon.

46. Scott, K. (2002, November). A lost decade: Income equality and the health of Canadians. Paper presented at the Social Determinants of Health across the Life-Span Conference, Toronto.

47. Health Canada. (2004). *Young people in Canada: Their health and well-being.* Report. Available at www.phac-aspc.gc.ca/dca-dea/publications/hbsc-2004/pdf/hbsc_summary_2004_e.pdf.

48. Merriam Webster Online. (n.d.). Available at www.m-w.com.

49. Jackson, A., & Robinson, D. (2002). *Falling behind: The state of working Canada, 2000.* Canadian Centre for Policy Alternatives.

50. National Housing and Homelessness Network (NHHN). (2002, November 22). *More than half the provinces betray commitments: NHHN report card on anniversary of affordable housing framework agreement.* Toronto: National Housing and Homelessness Network.

51. McIntyre, L., Walsh, G., & Connor, S.K. (2001, June). A follow-up study of child hunger in Canada. Working paper W-01-1-2E. Ottawa: Human Resources Development Canada, Applied Research Branch, Strategic Policy.

52. Ungerleider, C., & Burns, T. (2002, November). The state and quality of public elementary and secondary education. A presentation and paper given at the Social Determinants of Health across the Life Span Conference, Toronto.

53. Federal/Provincial/Territorial Advisory Committee on Population Health. (1999). *Toward a healthy future. Second report on the health of Canadians.* Ottawa: Health Canada.

54. Statistics Canada. (2004, July 30). University enrollment. *The Daily.* Available at www.statcan.ca/Daily/English/080207/d080207a.htm.

55. Davies, J., et al. (2000). Identifying male college students' perceived health needs, barriers to seeking help, and recommendations to help men adopt healthier lifestyles. *Journal of American College Health, 48*(5).

56. Keeling, R. (2001, September). Is college dangerous? *Journal of American College Health, 50*(2), 53.

57. Adlaf, E., et al. (2001, September). The prevalence of elevated psychological distress among Canadian undergraduates: Findings from the 1998 Canadian Campus Survey. *Journal of American College Health, 50*(2), 67.

58. Bartlett, T. (2002, February 1). Freshman pay, mentally and physically, as they adjust to life in college. *Chronicle of Higher Education.*

59. Jordan, D.J. (2007). Direct leadership techniques. In *Leadership in leisure services. Making a difference,* 2nd ed. State College, PA: Venture Publishing, Inc.

60. Prochaska, J., Norcross, J., & DiClimente, C. (1994). *Changing for good: The revolutionary program that explains the six stages of change and teachers you how to free yourself from bad habits.* New York: William Morrow and Company, Inc.

61. Martin Seligman. Personal interview.

62. Hettler, W. (1984). Wellness: Encouraging a lifetime pursuit of excellence. *Health Values: Achieving high level wellness, 8*(4), 13–17.

CHAPTER 2

# Personal Stress Management

© Ramzi Hachicho/Shutterstock

You know about stress. You live with it every day: the stress of passing exams, preparing for a career, meeting people, facing new experiences. Everyone—regardless of age, gender, race, or income—has to deal with stress, as an individual and as a member of society.

As researchers have demonstrated, stress has profound effects, both immediate and long term, on our bodies and minds. While stress alone doesn't cause disease, it triggers molecular changes throughout the body that make us more susceptible to many illnesses. Its impact on the mind is no less significant. The burden of chronic stress can undermine the ability to cope with day-to-day hassles and can exacerbate psychological problems such as depression and anxiety disorders.

Yet stress in itself isn't necessarily bad. What matters most is not the stressful situation, but an individual's response to it. By learning to anticipate stressful events, to manage day-to-day hassles, and to prevent stress overload, you can find alternatives to running endlessly on a treadmill of alarm, panic, and exhaustion. As you organize your schedule, find ways to release tension, and build up coping skills, you will begin to experience the sense of control and the confidence that make stress a challenge rather than an ordeal.

**After studying the material in this chapter, you will be able to:**

- **Define** stress and stressors and **describe** how the body responds to stress according to the general adaptation syndrome (GAS) theory.
- **List** the physical changes associated with frequent or severe stress and **discuss** how stress can affect the cardiovascular, immune, and digestive systems.
- **Explain** how stressful events can affect psychological health, including post-traumatic stress disorder.
- **Describe** some personal causes of stress, especially those experienced by students, and **discuss** how their effects can be prevented or minimized.
- **Discuss** the major social issues that can cause stress.
- **Identify** ways of managing time more efficiently.
- **Describe** some techniques to help manage stress.

**??? FREQUENTLY ASKED QUESTIONS**

**FAQ: Is stress hazardous to physical health?** p. 29

**FAQ: Is stress hazardous to psychological health?** p. 31

**FAQ: What can help me relax?** p. 37

**FAQ: How can I better manage my time?** p. 38

## What Is Stress?

People use the word *stress* in different ways: as an external force that causes a person to become tense or upset, as the internal state of arousal, and as the physical response of the body to various demands. Dr. Hans Selye, a pioneer in studying physiological responses to challenge, defined **stress** as "the non-specific response of the body to any demand made upon it."[1] In other words, the body reacts to **stressors**—the things that upset or excite us—in the same way, regardless of whether they are positive or negative.

Stress can be acute, episodic, or chronic, depending on the nature of the stressors or external events that cause the stress response. Acute or short-term stressors, which can range from a pop quiz to a bomb threat in a crowded stadium, trigger a brief but intense response to a specific incident. Episodic stressors such as monthly bills or mid-term and final exams cause regular but intermittent elevations in stress levels. Chronic stressors include everything from rush-hour traffic to a learning disability to living with an alcoholic parent or spouse.

Not all stressors are negative. Some of life's happiest moments—births, reunions, weddings—are enormously stressful. We weep with the stress of frustration or loss; we weep, too, with the stress of love and joy. Selye coined the term **eustress** for positive stress in our lives (*eu* is a Greek prefix meaning "good"). Eustress challenges us to grow, adapt, and find creative solutions in our lives. **Distress** refers to the negative effects of stress that can deplete or even destroy life energy. Ideally, the level of stress in our lives should be just high enough to motivate us to satisfy our needs and not so high that it interferes with our ability to reach our fullest potential.

## What Causes Stress?

Of the many biological theories of stress, the best known may be the **general adaptation syndrome (GAS),** developed by Hans Selye.[2] His research showed that our bodies constantly strive to maintain a stable and consistent physiological state, called **homeostasis.** Stressors, whether in the form of physical illness or a demanding job, disturb this state and trigger a non-specific physiological response. The body attempts to restore homeostasis by means of an **adaptive response.**

Selye's general adaptation syndrome, which describes the body's response to a stressor—whether threatening or exhilarating, consists of three distinct stages:

1. *Alarm.* When a stressor first occurs, the body responds with changes that temporarily lower resistance. Levels of certain hormones may rise; blood pressure may increase (see Figure 2-1). The body quickly makes internal adjustments to cope with the stressor and return to normal activity.

2. *Resistance.* If the stressor continues, the body mobilizes its internal resources to try to sustain homeostasis. For example, if someone you love is seriously hurt in an accident, you initially respond intensely and feel great anxiety. During the subsequent stressful period of recuperation, you struggle to carry on as normally as possible, but this requires considerable effort.

3. *Exhaustion.* If the stress continues long enough, you usually cannot keep up your normal functioning. Even a small amount of additional stress at this point can cause a breakdown.

Among the non-biological theories is the cognitive-transactional model of stress, developed by Richard Lazarus, which looks at the relation between stress and health. Stress, according to Lazarus, is "neither an environmental stimulus, a characteristic of the person, nor a response, but a relationship between demands and the power to deal with them without unreasonable or destructive costs."[3] Thus, an event may be stressful for one person but not for another, or it may seem stressful on one occasion but not on another. For instance, one student may

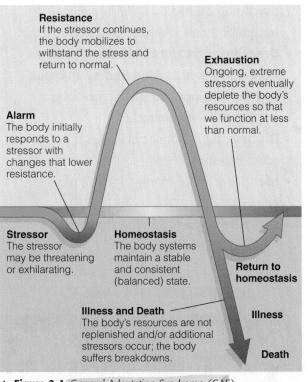

**Resistance**
If the stressor continues, the body mobilizes to withstand the stress and return to normal.

**Exhaustion**
Ongoing, extreme stressors eventually deplete the body's resources so that we function at less than normal.

**Alarm**
The body initially responds to a stressor with changes that lower resistance.

**Stressor**
The stressor may be threatening or exhilarating.

**Homeostasis**
The body systems maintain a stable and consistent (balanced) state.

**Return to homeostasis**

**Illness and Death**
The body's resources are not replenished and/or additional stressors occur; the body suffers breakdowns.

**Illness**

**Death**

▲ **Figure 2-1** General Adaptation Syndrome (GAS)
The three stages of Hans Selye's GAS are alarm, resistance, and exhaustion.

Source: Hespenheide Design

think of speaking in front of the class as extremely stressful, while another relishes the chance to do so—except on days when he or she is not well prepared.

At any age, some of us are more vulnerable to life changes and crises than others. The stress of growing up in families troubled by alcoholism, drug dependence, or physical, sexual, or psychological abuse may have a lifelong impact—particularly if these problems are not recognized and dealt with. Other early experiences, positive and negative, also can affect our attitude toward stress—and our resilience to it. Our general outlook on life, whether we're optimistic or pessimistic, can determine whether we expect the worst and feel stressed or anticipate a challenge and feel confident. The number and frequency of changes in our lives, along with the time and setting in which they occur, have a great impact on how we'll respond.

## Is Stress Hazardous to Physical Health?

These days we've grown accustomed to warning labels advising us of the health risks of substances such as alcohol and cigarettes. Medical researchers speculate that another component of twenty-first century living also warrants a warning: stress.[4] In recent years, an ever-growing number of studies has implicated stress as a culprit in a range of medical problems. Mental stress, according to recent investigations, may even kill. In individuals with heart disease, severe mental stress, which increases oxygen demand by causing elevations in blood pressure and heart rate, can trigger a lack of blood flow to the heart and increase the risk of dying.[5]

Stress triggers complex changes in the body's endocrine, or hormone-secreting, system. When you confront a stressor, your body responds by producing stress hormones that speed up heart rate and blood pressure and prepare the body to deal with the threat. This fight-or-flight response prepares you for quick action: Your heart works harder to pump more blood to your legs and arms. Your muscles tense, your breathing quickens, and your brain becomes extra alert. Because they're nonessential in a crisis, your digestive and immune systems practically shut down.

Cortisol, one of the stress hormones, speeds the conversion of proteins and fats into carbohydrates, the body's basic fuel, so that we have the energy to fight or flee from a threat. This can be a good thing. However, increased amounts of cortisol can also increase the release of more free fatty acids, or disassembled triglycerides, into the blood. This can then cause excessive central or abdominal fat, deep abdominal obesity, and suppression of the immune system,[6] all which heighten the risk of diseases such as diabetes, high blood pressure, and stroke.[7] Even slender, pre-menopausal women faced with increased stress and lacking good coping skills are more likely to accumulate excess weight around their waists, thereby increasing their risk of heart disease and other health problems.[8]

Figure 2-2 illustrates how persistent or repeated increases in stress hormones can be hazardous throughout the body. Very prolonged or severe stress can damage the brain's ability to remember and can actually cause brain cells, or neurons, to atrophy and die.

Hundreds of studies over the last 20 years have shown that stress contributes to approximately 80 percent of all major illnesses: cardiovascular disease, cancer, endocrine and metabolic disease, skin rashes, ulcers, ulcerative colitis, emotional disorders, musculoskeletal disease, infectious ailments, premenstrual syndrome (PMS), uterine fibroid cysts, and breast cysts.

It is important to remember that a number of studies have also shown that participation in regular physical activity can help reduce stress while increasing physical health.[9, 10]

## Stress and the Heart

In the 1970s, cardiologists Meyer Friedman and Ray Rosenman suggested that excess stress could be the most important factor in the development of heart disease. They compared their patients to individuals of the same age with healthy hearts and developed two general categories: Type A and Type B.

Hardworking, aggressive, and competitive, Type As never have time for all they want to accomplish, even though they usually try to do several tasks at once. Type Bs are more relaxed, though not necessarily less ambitious or successful. The degree of danger associated with Type-A behaviour remains controversial, as further studies over the past 30 years resulted in both support for and contradiction to Friedman and Rosenman's findings. However, of all the personality traits linked with Type-A behaviour, the one that has emerged as the most sinister is chronic hostility or cynicism. People who are always mistrustful, angry, and suspicious are twice as likely to suffer blockages of their coronary arteries. Friedman and fellow researchers[11] also found that altering Type-A behaviour, within a controlled experimental design, did reduce cardiac morbidity and mortality in post–myocardial infarction (heart attack) patients.

A major global study, led by Canadian researchers, on the effect of modifiable risk factors associated with myocardial infarction found that the majority of these attacks may be predicted by nine easily measured risk factors. While the two most important factors were cigarette smoking and abnormal ratio of blood lipids, which together predicted two-thirds of the global risk of heart attacks,

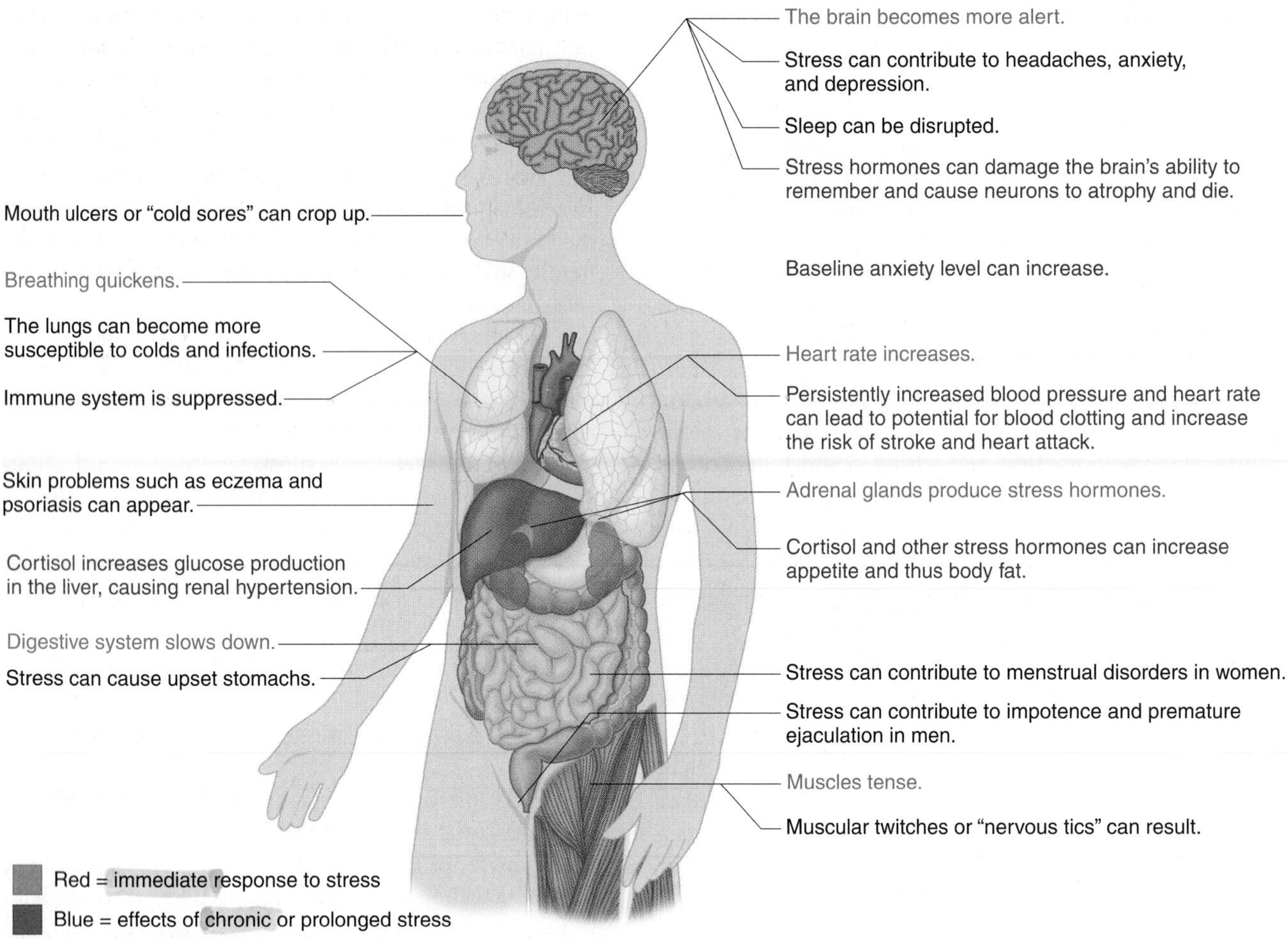

The brain becomes more alert.

Stress can contribute to headaches, anxiety, and depression.

Sleep can be disrupted.

Stress hormones can damage the brain's ability to remember and cause neurons to atrophy and die.

Baseline anxiety level can increase.

Mouth ulcers or "cold sores" can crop up.

Breathing quickens.

The lungs can become more susceptible to colds and infections.

Immune system is suppressed.

Heart rate increases.

Persistently increased blood pressure and heart rate can lead to potential for blood clotting and increase the risk of stroke and heart attack.

Skin problems such as eczema and psoriasis can appear.

Adrenal glands produce stress hormones.

Cortisol and other stress hormones can increase appetite and thus body fat.

Cortisol increases glucose production in the liver, causing renal hypertension.

Digestive system slows down.

Stress can cause upset stomachs.

Stress can contribute to menstrual disorders in women.

Stress can contribute to impotence and premature ejaculation in men.

Muscles tense.

Muscular twitches or "nervous tics" can result.

Red = immediate response to stress

Blue = effects of chronic or prolonged stress

▲ **Figure 2-2** Effects of Stress on the Body

Source: Hespenheide Design

other important risk factors in men and women included hypertension, along with psychosocial factors, abdominal obesity, and diabetes.[12]

## Stress and the Immune System

The powerful chemicals triggered by stress dampen or suppress the immune system—the network of organs, tissues, and white blood cells that defend against disease. Impaired immunity makes the body more susceptible to many diseases, including infections (from the common cold to tuberculosis) and disorders of the immune system itself. Research has shown that traumatic stress, such as losing a loved one through death or divorce, can impair immunity for as long as a year.

Even minor hassles take a toll. Research by Lazarus has shown that the daily hassles a person experiences can be more harmful to our health than significant life changes. He believes that these daily events are damaging to our health because of how frequently they occur.[13]

## Stress and the Digestive System

Do you ever get butterflies in your stomach before giving a speech in class or before a big game? To avoid problems, pay attention to how you eat—eating on the run, gulping food, or overeating results in poorly chewed foods, an overworked stomach, and increased abdominal pressure.

Some simple strategies can help you avoid stress-related stomachaches. By drinking plenty of water, you replenish lost fluids and prevent dehydration. Fibre-rich foods counteract common stress-related problems, such as cramps and constipation. A regular intake of protein and complex carbohydrates is important, especially in times of stress. Try not to skip meals. If you do, you're more likely to feel fatigued and irritable. You will find more in-depth information about healthy food choices in Chapters 5 and 6.

Be wary of overeating under stress. Some people consume more because they eat too quickly. Others reach for snacks to calm their nerves or comfort themselves. Watch out for caffeine. Coffee, tea, and cola drinks can make your strained nerves jangle even more. Also avoid sugary snacks.

They'll send your blood sugar levels on a roller coaster ride—up one minute, down the next.

## Is Stress Hazardous to Psychological Health?

There has been much debate over the years about the impact of stress on our psychological health. Everyone experiences stress. Stress is a normal, everyday experience and within acceptable limits can play a positive role in our lives. Yet there is a difference between everyday stress that has us coping with work demands, family responsibilities, and even playful activities and stress that becomes so great our coping mechanisms begin breaking down and our emotional and mental well-being is compromised.

Stress becomes distress when symptoms such as moodiness, irritability, depression, and anxiety become an everyday occurrence. Some people describe their distress as a feeling of paralysis or numbness. Incapacitating fears can create such an imbalance in our mental health that it has an impact on our relationships with others and our ability to be successful in our careers and home life.[14]

Traumatic events (such as a robbery, assault, or the death of a loved one) take a toll, too. When dealing with traumatic events, it's normal to feel sad, tense, overwhelmed, angry, or incapable of coping with the ordinary demands of daily living. Usually such feelings and behaviours subside with time. The stressful event fades into the past, and those whose lives it has touched adapt to its lasting impact. But sometimes individuals remain extremely distressed and unable to function as they once did. While the majority of individuals who survive a trauma recover, about 12 percent of the population suffers from **posttraumatic stress disorder (PTSD)** and later develop serious symptoms such as depression, anxiety, and panic attacks.[15] A more in-depth discussion of PTSD can be found in Chapter 3.

## Stress and the Student

You've probably heard that these are the best years of your life, but being a student—full-time or part-time, in your late teens, early twenties, or later in life—can be extremely stressful. You may feel pressure to perform well to qualify for a good job or graduate school. To meet tuition payments, you may have to juggle part-time work and coursework. You may feel stressed about choosing a major,

getting along with a difficult roommate, passing a particularly hard course, or living up to your parents' and instructors' expectations. If you're an older student, you may have children, housework, homework, a job, and elder care to balance. Your days may seem so busy and your life so full that you worry about coming apart at the seams. One thing is for certain: you're not alone. Stress levels among college and university students have risen, especially among women (see the X & Y Files: "Men, Women, and Stress").

Surveys of students at colleges and universities around the country and the world show that stress levels are consistently high and stressors are remarkably similar.[16] Among the most common are the following:

- Test pressures
- Academic failure
- Financial problems
- Frustrations, such as delays in reaching goals
- Problems in friendships and dating relationships
- Daily hassles
- Pressures as a result of competition, deadlines, and the like
- Changes, which may be unpleasant, disruptive, or too frequent
- Losses, whether caused by the break-up of a relationship or the death of a loved one

In one Canadian study,[17] researchers found that medical students were stressed because of the need to learn a large quantity of new information, time pressure, loss of opportunities for social activities, and going into debt. Another important finding was the discovery that students who previously did very well academically compared to their peers sometimes found themselves to be in the average category when compared to their medical-student peers. Academic excellence at an institution of higher learning can be quite different from that in a hometown school.

Researchers investigating stress in medical students, law students, and graduate students at McGill University concluded that medical students were not greatly stressed relative to other groups, but that the transition from basic science training to clinical training might have been associated with increased levels of stress.[18] Findings from yet another study on Canadian undergraduate students found that the students felt they experienced too much stress. They believed they knew how to identify strategies to lower their stress, but they did not follow through on an action plan to do so.[19]

Results from the *2004 Canadian Campus Survey* show that those at the greatest risk were first-year students. The study also showed that students living on campus were at slightly higher risk for levels of distress compared to students living off campus.[20]

## The X&Y Files

# Men, Women, and Stress

Women, who make up 58 percent of today's college and university students in Canada, experience higher psychological distress than men.[21] Among medical students, residents, and graduate students, significant gender differences were also found. Women reported higher levels of stress in all three groups. In a study by Campbell and Svenson[22] of undergraduate students, women were significantly more likely to report their lives as stressful, with mature women reporting the highest levels of stress. Older men reported having less stressful lives than younger men. Women, more than men, reported that they needed to reduce stress. The reasons why female and male undergraduate students were stressed also differed. Women were more likely to report lack of time and lack of self-discipline, whereas older men (as compared to younger men and all women) reported lack of self-discipline as the reason for their stress.

Gender differences in lifestyle may help explain why women feel so stressed. One survey revealed that college men spend significantly more time doing things that are fun and relaxing: exercising, partying, watching TV, and playing video games. Women, on the other hand, tend to study more, do more volunteer work, and handle more household and child-care chores.[23]

At all ages, women and men tend to respond to stress differently. While males (human and those of other species) react with the classic fight-or-flight response, females under attack try to protect their children and seek help from other females—a strategy dubbed *tend-and-befriend*. When working mothers studied by psychologists had a bad day, they coped by concentrating on their children when they got home. Stressed-out fathers were more likely to withdraw.[24]

The gender difference in stress responses may be the result of hormones and evolution. While both men and women release stress hormones, men also secrete testosterone, which tends to increase hostility and aggression. For prehistoric women, who were usually pregnant, nursing, or caring for small children, neither fight nor flight was a wise strategy. Smaller and weaker than males, women may long ago have reached out to other women to form a social support system that helped ensure their safety and that of their children.

---

Many students bring complex psychological problems with them to campus, including learning disabilities and mood disorders such as depression and anxiety. Some have grown up in broken homes and bear the scars of family troubles. Others fall into the same patterns of alcohol abuse that they observed for years in their families or suffer lingering emotional scars from childhood physical or sexual abuse. In some First Nations and Inuit communities, young people have dealt with high rates of suicide and grief over multiple losses and disruptions of lifestyle.[25]

Among college and university students, excessive levels of stress have been linked to increased headaches, sleep disturbances, and colds.[26] Students have said that they react to stress physiologically (by sweating, stuttering, trembling, or developing physical symptoms), emotionally (by becoming anxious, fearful, angry, guilty, or depressed), behaviourally (by crying, eating, smoking, or being irritable or abusive), or cognitively (by thinking about and analyzing stressful situations and strategies that might be useful in dealing with them).

Social support, effective time management, forming close friendships, and meditation programs also reduce stress and compensate for the depressive effects of negative experiences, such as failing a test.[27]

Campuses are providing more frontline services than they have in the past, including career-guidance workshops, study skills sessions, and social and recreation programs to help students manage the stress of making the transition from high school or work to college and university life. Brock University offers individual and group counselling sessions for students who are experiencing personal and social difficulties.[28] The University of British Columbia (UBC) has available online a *Wellness Guide*, which discusses stress management strategies and lists health, wellness, and counselling services available on campus.[29] There is also an *At Risk Student Guide*, which lists signs and symptoms of students who might need a referral to deal with stressful issues. Check out your college or university student services department to see what is available to support your emotional and mental health dimensions.

## Test Stress

For many students, mid-terms and final exams are the most stressful times of the year. Results of an Ipsos-Reid survey, conducted on Canadian university students for Kumon Math and Reading Centres,[30] showed that no students described themselves as free of stress, and 40 percent said they experienced high stress levels when studying for exams. Stress levels were the highest in Ontario at 47 percent, Saskatchewan and Manitoba at 52 percent, and the lowest in Quebec at 27 percent.

Some college and university students report that the incidence of colds and flu soar during finals. Some students feel the impact of test stress in other ways—headaches, upset stomachs, skin flare-ups, or insomnia. All of these symptoms were reported by the university students responding to the Ipsos-Reid survey. Additional examples of exam-related stress ranged from feelings of nervousness and anxiety (29 percent), to difficulty sleeping (27 percent), to fatigue and exhaustion (15 percent). Students also reported having difficulty focusing or concentrating (12 percent), feeling irritable (12 percent), having bad moods (11 percent), and even nausea and vomiting (10 percent).[31] Under exam stress, students can also experience a dip in immune function and a higher rate of infections.

## Strategies for Prevention

### Defusing Test Stress

Tips from the University of Ottawa might help you "beat test stress":

▲ Get organized and take your time. Establish short- and long-term goals for yourself. Map out a study schedule for each course. Set aside a small amount of time every day or every other day to review the course materials.

▲ Make your notes work for you. Attend classes. Check for online notes. Complete your assigned readings. Take clear notes. Visit with your professor before the exam.

▲ Maintain a realistic perspective. Consider the bigger picture. How much is your exam worth? Budget your study time well.

▲ Be positive. Picture yourself taking your final exam. Imagine yourself walking into the exam room feeling confident that you have prepared well.

▲ Study in 30- to 60-minute intervals. Take 5- to 10-minute breaks regularly. Get up from your desk, breathe deeply, and stretch. Try mini-meditation breaks and deep breathing. You'll feel more refreshed than you would if you drank another cup of coffee.

▲ Organize a study group with other students. But be sure to study on your own, too.

▲ Get enough sleep. Your brain will perform better.

▲ Be satisfied with doing your best. You can't expect to ace every test; all you can and should expect is your best effort.

The students most susceptible to exam stress are those who believe they'll do poorly and who see tests as extremely threatening. Negative thoughts often become a self-fulfilling prophecy. As their fear increases, they try harder, pulling all-nighters. Fuelled by caffeine and munching on sugary snacks, they become edgy and find it harder and harder to concentrate. By the time it's test day, they're nervous wrecks, scarcely able to sit still and focus on the exam.

Can you do anything to reduce test stress and feel more in control? Yes, you can. One way is to defuse stress through relaxation programs such as controlled breathing, meditation, progressive relaxation, and guided imagery (visualization). Another way is to learn how to transform stress into resilience. Researchers Steinhardt and Dolbier found that students who participated in a four-week resilience education program had significantly higher resilience scores, more effective coping strategies, higher scores on self-esteem and self-leadership factors, and lower scores on depressive symptoms and perceived stress level in the post-intervention than did the wait-list control group.[32] Another strategy is to begin preparing for mid-terms, finals, and papers early. Sixty-eight percent of students report that they only start studying or preparing for exams at most a week in advance, and another 27 percent admit to staying up all night to prepare.[33]

## Other Personal Stressors
### Job Stress

More than ever, many people find that they are working up to 55 or 60 hours per week—and enjoying it less. This exhausting cycle of overwork causes stress, which can make work harder, which leads to more stress. Even the workplace itself can contribute to stress. A noisy, open-office environment can increase levels of stress without workers even realizing it.

Researchers Leontaridi and Ward[34] have found that workers in France, Canada, and Sweden have the highest stress levels in 15 developed countries compared to the most relaxed employees living in Denmark, Switzerland, and the Czech Republic. A national survey of over 9000 employees reveals that in Canada, 41 percent of employees "often" or "always" experience stress at work, while only 1.9 percent of Canadian workers report they never experience stress on the job.

Yet work in itself is not hazardous to health. Attitudes about work and habits related to how we work are the true threats. In fact, a job—stressful or not, enjoyable or not—can be therapeutic.

## Financial Stress

Financing a college or university education can be difficult. Results from the Pan-Canadian Study of First Year College Students shows that obtaining adequate funding to cover tuition, books, accommodation, and food was a major concern. Sixty-eight percent of students relied on personal savings to finance their postsecondary education, while 55 percent depended on loans as a source of funding. Scholarships and awards were an important source (27 percent), while 19 percent received money from grants.[35]

Forty-seven percent of the respondents in this study did report that they were very concerned about the amount of debt they might accrue over their degree program. One-third indicated they were worried about their ability to repay debt once they graduated. To add to the student's stress about finances while attending college, up to 70 percent of students expected to work while attending classes. Twenty-three percent of students worked between ten and twenty hours per week while studying.

There are things you can do to manage the financial obligations that a postsecondary education demands.

✔ Take advantage of financial plans, scholarships, and bursary programs.
✔ Take advantage of your summer vacations. Look for work internship programs that might support your degree.
✔ Make a budget. Attempt to stick to it or revise when necessary. Start by writing down all your regular monthly expenses and miscellaneous spending. Write down your income. Monitor your spending from the beginning of each term. Create an emergency fund.
✔ Use credit cards wisely.
✔ Be resourceful. Use coupons. Share food expenses with friends. Shop wisely.
✔ Make a plan for repayment of student loans before you graduate.
✔ Be frugal—an important part of financial stress management while you are a student.

## Illness and Disability

Just as the mind can have profound effects on the body, the body can have an enormous impact on our emotions. Whenever we come down with the flu or pull a muscle, we feel under par. When the problem is more serious or persistent—a chronic disease such as diabetes, for instance, or a lifelong hearing impairment—the emotional stress of constantly coping with it is even greater. Most colleges and universities have in place a system for special concessions with regard to your academic program should you become ill. Student ancillary services, the counselling unit, or academic advisors can help.

A common source of stress for college and university students is a learning disability. Some students have only one area of difficulty, such as reading or math. Others have problems with attention, writing, communicating, reasoning, coordination, social competence, and emotional maturity—all of which may make it difficult to excel. Many academic institutions now have programs and services available to students who may be faced with learning challenges. Asking for help can alleviate much stress that is linked to disabilities. There are diagnostic tests to evaluate skills and abilities that can help students to determine what type of assistance they may need.

Someone with a learning disability may exhibit the following traits:

✔ Unable to engage in a focused activity such as reading
✔ Extremely distractible, forgetful, or absentminded
✔ Easily frustrated by waiting, delays, or traffic
✔ Disorganized, unable to manage time efficiently and complete tasks on time
✔ Hot tempered, explosive, constantly irritated
✔ Impulsive, making decisions with little reflection or information
✔ Easily overwhelmed by ordinary hassles
✔ Clumsy, with a poor body image and poor sense of direction
✔ Physically restless

## Societal Stressors

Not all stressors are personal. Centuries ago the poet John Donne observed that no man is an island. Today, on an increasingly crowded and troubled planet, these words seem truer than ever. Problems such as discrimination and terrorism can no longer be viewed only as economic or political issues. Directly or indirectly, they affect the well-being of all of us who inhabit the Earth—now and in the future. Even more mundane stressors, such as traffic, can lead to outbursts of anger that have come to be known as *road rage*.[36]

## Discrimination

Discrimination is another form of a societal stressor. It can take many forms—some as subtle as not being included in a conversation or joke, some as blatant as threats scrawled on a wall, and some as violent as brutal beatings and other hate crimes. Because it can be hard to deal with individually, discrimination is a particularly sinister form of stress. By banding together, however, those who experience discrimination can take action to protect themselves, challenge the ignorance and hateful assumptions that fuel bigotry, and promote a healthier environment for all.

In the last decade, there have been reports of greater intolerance among young people and a greater tolerance for overt expressions and acts of hatred on college and university campuses. In a study by Schellenberg, Hirt, and Sears,[37] attitudes toward homosexuals among students at a Canadian university were measured. Their findings showed that (1) attitudes toward gay men were more negative than attitudes toward lesbians; (2) students in the faculties of Arts or Social Science had a more positive attitude than students in Business and Science; (3) women were more positive than men; and (4) attitudes toward gay men also improved with time spent at college, but only for male students.

In a more recent study, researchers found that classroom interventions on college and university campuses must be supported by experiential learning outside the classroom. Brief exposure to gay, bisexual, lesbian and transgendered issues in the classroom was not sufficient to help some students change homophobic beliefs and attitudes.[38]

Discrimination with regard to culture is also an issue on many campuses. Bellegarde, the Chair of the Assembly of First Nations Chiefs' Committee on Education, says that many Aboriginal students don't see themselves or their cultures reflected in the curriculum being offered in schools. Another reason for the lack of Aboriginal student success is that there are not enough positive role models in the education system. But he believes there is hope and that there seems to be signs of shifting attitudes among educators to be more inclusive of First Nations' students.[39]

Many schools have set up programs and classes to educate students about each other's backgrounds and to acknowledge and celebrate the richness diversity brings to campus life. Educators have called on universities to make campuses less alienating and more culturally and emotionally accessible, with programs and policies targeted not only at minority students, but also at the university population as a whole.

## Stress Survival

Sometimes we respond to stress or challenge with self-destructive behaviours such as drinking or using drugs. These responses can lead to psychological problems, such as anxiety or depression, and physical problems, including psychosomatic illnesses.

**Defence mechanisms,** such as those described in Table 2-1, are another response to stress. These psychological devices are mental processes that help us cope with personal problems. Such responses are also not the answer to stress—and learning to recognize them in yourself will enable you to deal with your stress in a healthier way.

The key to coping with stress is realizing that your *perception* of and *response* to a stressor are crucial. Changing the way you interpret events or situations—a skill called *reframing*—makes all the difference. An event such as a move to a new city is not stressful in itself. A move becomes stressful if you see it as a traumatic upheaval rather than an exciting beginning of a new chapter in your life.

Dr. Nancy Wardle, a well-known Canadian stress expert, encourages us to recognize that balance in life is not a still point—rather, it is a process. In order to manage our unique and individual stressors, we need to be willing to recognize what is disruptive and unbalanced and how we feel physically and emotionally when it happens. Finding ways to regain equilibrium when life presents unexpected challenges can help to lower our stress levels.[40]

| ▼ Table 2-1 Common Defence Mechanisms Used to Alleviate Anxiety and Eliminate Conflict | |
|---|---|
| **Defence Mechanism** | **Example** |
| **Denial:** The refusal to accept a painful reality. | You don't accept as true the news that a loved one is seriously ill. |
| **Displacement:** The redirection of feelings from their true object to a more acceptable or safer substitute. | Instead of lashing out at a coach or a teacher, you snap at your best friend. |
| **Projection:** The attribution of unacceptable feelings or impulses to someone else. | When you want to end a relationship, you project your unhappiness onto your partner. |
| **Rationalization:** The substitution of "good," acceptable reasons for the real motivations for our behaviour. | You report a classmate who has been mean to you for cheating on an exam and explain that cheating is unfair to other students. |
| **Reaction formation:** Adopting attitudes and behaviours that are the opposite of what you feel. | You lavishly compliment an acquaintance that you really despise. |
| **Repression:** The way we keep threatening impulses, fantasies, memories, feelings, or wishes from becoming conscious. | You don't "hear" the alarm after a late night, or you "forget" to take out the trash. |

Robert Blank, a registered psychologist, educator, and facilitator who has experience working with students dealing with depression, anxiety, ADD/ADHD, and general stress issues, suggests that another way we can manage our stress is to acknowledge and celebrate our emotional intelligence. In an academic environment, cognitive development is highly valued. While cognitive intelligence can be one of our greatest strengths, our focus on it can also be one of our greatest challenges. It is important to balance our intellect with our emotions. He encourages us to be aware and mindful of the present or "staying in the now." The power of being in the "now" allows us to come back into the moment, to check in with ourselves and discover what we need to support our health and well-being. He talks passionately about education as transformation or a development of "self." Throughout your academic journey, attempt to use your cognitive intelligence to explore your own humanness to find ways to grow emotionally.[41]

In times of stress, the following simple exercises can stop the stress build-up inside your body and help you to regain a sense of calm and control.

- ✔ *Breathing.* Deep breathing relaxes the body and quiets the mind. Draw air deeply into your lungs, allowing your chest to fill with air and your belly to rise and fall. You will feel the muscle tension and stress begin to melt away.
- ✔ *Refocusing.* Thinking about a situation you can't change or control only increases the stress you feel. Force your mind to focus on other subjects. If you're stuck in a long line, distract yourself. In a traffic jam, turn on the car radio to a music station you like.
- ✔ *Serenity breaks.* Build moments of tranquility into your day. Take mini-meditation breaks. Close your eyes and visualize a soothing scene, such as walking in a meadow or along a beach or doing something you like to do.
- ✔ *Stress signals.* Learn to recognize the first signs that your stress load is getting out of hand: Is your back bothering you? Do you have a headache? Do you find yourself speeding or misplacing things? Whenever you spot these early warnings, force yourself to stop and say, "I'm under stress. I need to do something about it."
- ✔ *Reality checks.* To put things into proper perspective, ask yourself: Will I remember what's made me so upset a month from now? If I had to rank this problem on a scale of 1 to 10, with worldwide catastrophe as 10, where would it rate?
- ✔ *Stress inoculation.* Rehearse everyday situations that you find stressful, such as speaking in class. Think of how you might make the situation less tense—for instance, by breathing deeply before you talk or jotting down notes beforehand.
- ✔ *Laughter.* Humour counters stress by focusing on comic aspects of difficult situations and may, as various studies have shown, lessen harmful effects on the immune system and overall health.

- ✔ *Spiritual coping.* Saying a prayer under stress is one of the oldest ways of calming yourself. Other forms of spiritual coping, such as putting trust in God or helping others (for example, volunteering for a local community service centre), can also provide a different perspective on daily hassles and stresses.
- ✔ *Sublimation.* This term refers to the redirection of any drives considered unacceptable into socially acceptable channels. Outdoor activity is one of the best ways to reduce stress through sublimation. For instance, if you're furious with a friend who betrayed your trust, you might go for a walk, long run, or hike to sublimate your anger.
- ✔ *Journalling.* One of the simplest, yet most effective, ways to work through stress is by putting your feelings into words that only you will read. The more honest and open you are as you write, the better. According to the research of psychologist James Pennebaker, students who wrote in their journals about traumatic events felt much better afterward than those who wrote about superficial topics.[42]

## Strategies for Prevention

### Recognize the Warning Signals of Stress Overload

Are you

- ▲ experiencing physical symptoms, including chronic fatigue, headaches, indigestion, diarrhea, and sleep problems?
- ▲ battling frequent illness or worrying about illness?
- ▲ self-medicating, including using non-prescription drugs?
- ▲ having problems concentrating on studies or work? Producing poor quality work or not able to complete tasks?
- ▲ feeling irritable, anxious, or apathetic?
- ▲ working or studying longer and harder than usual?
- ▲ exaggerating, to yourself and others, the importance of what you do?
- ▲ becoming accident-prone?
- ▲ breaking rules, whether it's a curfew at home or a speed limit on the highway?
- ▲ going to extremes, such as drinking too much, overspending, or gambling?

## ???? What Can Help Me Relax?

Relaxation is the physical and mental state that is the opposite of stress. Rather than gearing up for fight or flight, our bodies and minds grow calmer and work more smoothly. We're less likely to become frazzled and more capable of staying in control. The most effective relaxation techniques include progressive relaxation, visualization, meditation, mindfulness, and biofeedback.

**Progressive relaxation** works by intentionally increasing and then decreasing tension in the muscles. While sitting or lying down in a quiet, comfortable setting, you tense and release various muscles, beginning with those of the hand, for instance, and then proceeding to the arms, shoulders, neck, face, scalp, chest, stomach, buttocks, and so on, down each leg to the toes. Relaxing the muscles can quiet the mind and restore internal balance.

**Visualization**, or **guided imagery,** involves creating mental pictures that calm you down and focus your mind. Some people use this technique to promote healing when they are ill. Visualization skills require practice and, in some cases, instruction by qualified health professionals.

**Meditation** has been practised in many forms over the ages, from the yogic techniques of the Far East to the Quaker silence of more modern times. Brain scans have shown that meditation activates the sections of the brain in charge of the autonomic nervous system, which governs bodily functions such as digestion and blood pressure that we cannot consciously control.[43] Although many studies have documented the benefits of meditation for overall health, it may be particularly helpful for people dealing with stress-related medical conditions such as high blood pressure.

Meditation helps a person reach a state of relaxation, but with the goal of achieving inner peace and harmony. There is no one right way to meditate, and many people have discovered how to meditate on their own, without even knowing what it is they are doing. Most forms of meditation have common elements: sitting quietly for 15 to 20 minutes once or twice a day, concentrating on a word or image, and breathing slowly and rhythmically. If you wish

▲ Spending time outdoors is a great way to leave behind daily tensions and gain a new perspective.

▲ Writing in your journal about feelings and difficulties is a simple and very effective way to help control your stress.

to try meditation, it often helps to have someone guide you through your first sessions. There are many tapes and CDs available that provide guided meditation sessions.

**Mindfulness** is a modern form of an ancient Asian technique that involves maintaining awareness in the present moment. You tune in to each part of your body, scanning from head to toe, noting the slightest sensation. You allow whatever you experience—an itch, an ache, a feeling of warmth—to enter your awareness. Then you open yourself to focus on all the thoughts, sensations, sounds, and feelings that enter your awareness. Mindfulness keeps you in the here and now, thinking about what *is* rather than about *what if* or *if only*.

**Biofeedback** is a method of obtaining feedback, or information, about some physiological activity occurring in the body. An electronic monitoring device attached to the body detects a change in an internal function and communicates it back to the person through a tone, light, or meter. By paying attention to this feedback, most people can gain some control over functions previously thought to be beyond conscious control, such as body temperature, heart rate, muscle tension, and brain waves. The goal of biofeedback for stress reduction is a state of tranquility, usually associated with the brain's production of alpha waves, which are slower and more regular than normal waking waves.

## Time Management

We live in what some sociologists call hyper-culture, a society that moves at warp speed. Information constantly bombards us. The rate of change seems to accelerate every year. Our time-saving devices—pagers, cell phones, modems, faxes, palm-sized organizers, laptop computers—have simply extended the boundaries of where and how we work.

As a result, more and more people are suffering from time sickness, a nerve-racking feeling that life has become little more than an endless to-do list. The best antidote is time management—to help us find our way out of the time trap.

### How Can I Better Manage My Time?

Time management involves skills that anyone can learn, but they require commitment and practice to make a difference in your life. It may help to know the techniques that other students have found most useful:

✔ **Schedule your time.** Use a calendar, planner, or a hand-held PDA (personal digital assistant). Beginning the first week of class, mark down deadlines for each assignment, paper, project, and test scheduled that semester. Develop a daily schedule, listing very specifically what you will do the next day, along with the times. Block out times for working out, eating dinner, calling home, and talking with friends as well as for studying.

✔ **Develop a game plan.** Allow at least two nights to study for any major exam. Set aside more time for researching and writing papers. Make sure to allow time to type, edit, and print out a paper—and to deal with emergencies such as a computer breakdown. Set daily and weekly goals. When working on a big project, don't neglect your other courses. Whenever possible, try to work ahead in all your classes.

✔ **Identify time robbers.** For several days keep a log of what you do and how much time you spend doing it. You may discover that disorganization is eating away at your time or that you have a problem getting started. Look for opportunities to save time. An hour spent with a resource librarian familiar with your field of study can save you many hours searching for research or resources on your own.

✔ **Make the most of classes.** Read the assignments before class rather than waiting until just before you have a test. Go to class. Read your lecture notes at the end of each day or at least at the end of each week. We all have different learning styles, so ask yourself how you learn best: are you an auditory, visual, or kinesthetic learner?

✔ **Develop an efficient study style.** Some experts recommend studying for 50 minutes, then breaking for 10 minutes. Small incentives, such as allowing yourself to call or visit a friend during these 10 minutes, can provide the motivation to keep you at the books longer. When you're reading, write notes or questions to yourself in the margins to help you retain more information. Even if you're racing to start a paper, take a few extra minutes to prepare a workable outline.

✔ **Focus on the task at hand.** Rather than worrying about how you did on yesterday's test or how you'll ever finish next week's project, focus intently on whatever you're doing at any given moment. If your mind starts to wander, use any distraction—the sound of the phone ringing or a noise from the hall—as a reminder to stay in the moment.

✔ **Break bigger tasks into smaller ones.** Break down your term paper into a series of steps, such as selecting a topic, identifying sources of research information, taking notes, developing an outline, and so on.

✔ **Keep your workspace in order.** Even if the rest of your room is a shambles, try to keep your desk clear. Piles of papers are distracting, and you can end up wasting lots of time looking for notes you misplaced or an article you have to read by morning. Try to spend the last 10 minutes of the day cleaning up your desk so you will have a fresh start on the new day.

## Rob Dyke—An Epic Journey: Just Say Yes

Consider competing in Ironman competitions, swimming across the Strait of Georgia (the ferry route from Vancouver to Victoria, B.C.), climbing Mount Everest, and attempting to swim around Vancouver Island. Many people would say participating in these events would be very demanding, even nearly impossible. Our human potential story for this chapter is about Rob Dyke, an adventurer. Rob fully embraces what life has to offer and encourages others to put their potential in perspective so that they might fulfill their dreams and visions, too. Here is his story.

I learned about discipline, commitment, and hard work from a long competitive swimming career that took me to the University of Victoria. I also learned that I was swimming for a variety of reasons: for my parents, for my coach, for my education and for my country, for medals and glory. But I was unaware at that moment that I was meant to do more—something else—something meaningful—something for myself without losing sight of other's needs.

After my swimming career at UVic was over, I set out to make a difference. After challenging myself with Olympic-distance triathlons and Ironman competitions, I then took on the challenge of swimming across the Strait of Georgia, from Vancouver to Victoria, when a fellow distance swimmer was unable to attempt a first-ever swim to raise funds for sick children. I gave it my best but was pulled out of the water semi-conscious after eight hours of swimming in the Pacific Ocean. I could have been discouraged and given up, but I decided to learn from my mistakes instead. I became the first person to complete the 52 kilometre swim the following year, in 1996. I did so in 10.5 hours—raising funds for the B.C. Children's Hospital. Further adventures: a six-month journey from the Bay of Bengal to Mount Everest in support of a good friend's dream to summit without oxygen in 2003, attempting a 1400 kilometre swim around Vancouver Island, also in 2003, and another trip up Mount Everest in 2005 as the cook for a British

Rob Dyke swimming 1400 kilometres around Vancouver Island to raise funds for the Canadian Red Cross. His epic journey—The Island Aquathon, June to September, 2005.
Source: Courtesy of Rob Dyke

climbing team are just some of my other accomplishments. Then came another attempt at the almost impossible swim around Vancouver Island in the summer of 2005 for an agency and cause I am passionate about: the Canadian Red Cross. The successful swim continues to raise money for a legacy fund dedicated to reducing the yearly drowning average of 400 across Canada and make remote villages water-safe. The fund has raised more than $150 000 so far.

From all of my adventures, I have learned some powerful life lessons. I consider myself an ordinary man who consistently does extraordinary things. I think that there is a hero in us all, but sometimes it gets hidden under layers of unnecessary caution and common sense, buried by stress, fear of failure, and embarrassment. Preparation for my journeys has been predominantly mental and spiritual. I have spent time in the mountains and with Buddhist monks to find deep inner strength. I have discovered that there is a powerful mind, body, and spiritual connection within all of us, and that when you find something you love to do, you can make doing things you love a habit. Everyone will have their rough days, their stressful times, their doubts and reservations, but when you trust in your abilities, you can do amazing things. Amazing things like swimming with dolphins, meeting people from different cultures, and helping others who might not be able to help themselves.

*continued*

As one student commented after hearing me speak, "Over the past few months I have been doubting those things that I have always wanted to do, stressing out about my marks, student loans, and my future. Today I have learned that self-doubt can stop you from learning about new things, meeting new people, making a difference in this life. If there is something that you want to do mental power and positive thoughts are strong enough to help you exceed your limits. I plan to create an experience that is life changing in my future." And as I have now learned to say, "Just say yes."

Rob now shares his experiences across Canada, owns a company that focuses on wellness as well as a speaking bureau, is recently married, and is preparing for another great adventure: becoming a father. You can check out Rob's Vancouver Island swim at www.islandaquathon.ca. Other stories about Rob's adventures are available at www.speakwell.com.

Many colleges and universities offer time-management courses or workshops. York University has an excellent time-management information package available online at www.yorku.ca/cdc/lsp/skillbuilding/timemanagement.html.[44] You may want to access this site to find out more about the time-management cycle, goal setting, time awareness, and time tracking.

## Overcoming Procrastination

Putting off until tomorrow what should be done today is a habit that creates a great deal of stress for many students. It also takes a surprising toll. In a study of students taking a health psychology course, researchers found that although procrastinating provided short-term benefits, including periods of low stress, the tendency to dawdle had long-term costs, including poorer health and lower grades. Early in the semester, the procrastinators reported less stress and fewer health problems than students who scored low on procrastination. However, by the end of the semester, procrastinators reported more health-related symptoms, more stress, and more visits to health-care professionals than nonprocrastinators.[45] Students who procrastinate also get poorer grades in courses with many deadlines.[46]

The three most common types of procrastination are putting off unpleasant things, putting off difficult tasks, and putting off tough decisions. Procrastinators are most likely to delay by wishing they didn't have to do what they must or by telling themselves they "just can't get started," which means they never do.

To get out of the procrastination trap, keep track of the tasks you're most likely to put off, and try to figure out why you don't want to tackle them. Think of alternative ways to complete these tasks. If you put off library readings, for instance, is the problem getting to the library or doing the reading itself? If it's the trip to the library, arrange to walk over with a friend whose company you enjoy.

Develop daily time-management techniques, such as a to-do list. Rank items according to priorities (A, B, C), and schedule your days to make sure the As get accomplished. Try not to fixate on half-completed projects. Divide large tasks, such as writing a term paper, into smaller ones, and reward yourself when you complete a part.

Do what you like least first. Once you have a major task out of the way, you can concentrate on the tasks you enjoy. Learn to live according to a three-word motto: Just do it!

**CHAPTER**

**2**

**Making This Chapter Work for You**

1. Stress can be defined as
   a. a negative emotional state related to fatigue and similar to depression.
   b. the physiological and psychological response to any event or situation that either upsets or excites us.
   c. the end result of the general adaptation syndrome.
   d. a motivational strategy for making life changes.

2. According to the general adaptation syndrome theory, how does the body typically respond to an acute stressor?
   a. The heart rate slows, blood pressure declines, and eye movement increases.
   b. The body enters a physical state called *eustress* and then moves into the physical state referred to as *distress*.
   c. If the stressor is viewed as a positive event, there are no physical changes.
   d. The body demonstrates three stages of change: alarm, resistance, and exhaustion.

3. Over time, increased levels of stress hormones have been shown to increase a person's risk for which of the following conditions?
   a. diabetes, high blood pressure, memory loss, and skin disorders
   b. stress fractures, male pattern baldness, and hypothyroidism
   c. hemophilia, AIDS, and hay fever
   d. none of the above

4. A person suffering from post-traumatic stress disorder may experience which of the following symptoms?
   a. procrastination
   b. constant thirst
   c. drowsiness
   d. terror-filled dreams

5. Stress levels in college and university students
   a. may be high due to stressors such as academic pressures, financial concerns, learning disabilities, and relationship problems.
   b. are usually low because students feel empowered, living independently of their parents.

   c. are typically highest in fourth-year students because their self-esteem diminishes during the undergraduate years.
   d. are lower in minority students because they are used to stressors such as a hostile social climate and actual or perceived discrimination.

6. Which of the following situations is representative of a societal stressor?
   a. Peter has been told that his transfer application has been denied because his transcripts were not sent in by the deadline.
   b. Nia and Kwame find an unsigned note pinned to the door of their new home, ordering them to move out or face the consequences.
   c. Kelli's boyfriend drives her car after he had been drinking and has an accident.
   d. Joshua, who is the leading basketball player on his college varsity team, has just been diagnosed with diabetes.

7. Which of the following illustrates the defence mechanism of displacement?
   a. You have a beer in the evening after a tough day.
   b. You act as if nothing has happened after you have been laid off from your job.
   c. You start an argument with your sister after being laid off from your job.
   d. You argue with your boss after he lays you off from your job.

8. If you are stuck in a traffic jam, which of the following actions will help reduce your stress level?
   a. deep slow breathing
   b. honking your horn
   c. berating yourself for not taking a different route
   d. getting on your cell phone to reschedule appointments

9. A relaxed, peaceful state of being can be achieved with which of the following activities?
   a. an aerobic exercise class
   b. playing a computer game
   c. meditating for 15 minutes
   d. attending a rap concert

10. To effectively manage your time, which of these techniques should you try?
    a. Use a calendar or planner.
    b. Keep a log of your activities for a week.
    c. Tackle a large task by breaking it down into a series of smaller tasks.
    d. All of the above.

Answers to these questions can be found on page 450.

## Self Responsibility

*If you want to be brave, do not count your fears.*

**Cree wisdom**

During stressful times, it can be difficult to believe in your own possibilities, but possibilities can be healing. If you find your stress levels rising, stop, reflect, seek advice, and quietly find your way. This is the most important time to practise healthy and well ways of living. How can you move yourself from contemplating about your stress to preparing a stress-

## Social Responsibility

*If you find yourself down, the best way to pick yourself up is to do something for somebody else. You can't see your own joy, but you can see someone else's.*

**Nissa**

management plan? How can you move from preparation to action?

When you are feeling down, one of the best ways to lighten your own load is to help someone else. How might you lessen someone's stress today? Make them a meal? Help them with a school project? Take them for a walk? Reaching out to others is a proven stress reducer.

## Critical Thinking

1. Stress levels among college and university students have reached record highs. What reasons can you think of to account for this? Consider possible social, cultural, and economic factors that may play a role.

2. Identify three stressful situations in your life and determine whether they are examples of eustress or distress. Describe both the positive and negative aspects of each situation.

3. Can you think of any ways in which your behaviour or attitudes might create stress for others? What changes could you make to avoid doing so?

4. What advice might you give an incoming first-year student about managing stress in college or university? What techniques have been most helpful for you in dealing with stress? Suppose that this student is from a different ethnic group than you. What additional suggestions would you have for him or her?

# CENGAGENOW™

If your textbook package includes CengageNOW™, go to http://west.cengagenow.com/ilrn/ to link to CengageNOW™ for Health, your online study tool. First take the **Pre-test** for this chapter to get your personalized **Study Plan,** which will identify topics

you need to review and direct you to the appropriate resources. Then take the **Post-test** to determine what concepts you have mastered and what you still need work on.

## SITES & BYTES

**The Canadian Institute of Stress**
www.stresscanada.org

The Canadian Institute of Stress (CIS) was founded by Drs. Hans Selye and Richard Earle. The site offers information on personal stress control, distance education and certification, workplace training and consulting, and research and development innovations.

**The Canadian Mental Health Association**
www.cmha.ca

The mission of the CMHA is to promote mental health for all. Reports, surveys, and briefs about stress research and national initiatives are available at this site.

**First Nations Health—UBC Library**
www.library.ubc.ca/xwi7xwa/health.htm

Links to numerous web pages that support First Nations health issues, including mental health, are available at this site.

Please note that links are subject to change. If you find a broken link, use a search engine such as www.google.ca and search for the website by typing in keywords.

 **InfoTrac® College Edition Activity**
Yorgason, J.B., Linville, D., & Zitzman, B. (2008). Mental health among college students: Do those who need services know about and use them? (Report) (Survey), *Journal of American College Health* 57(2), 173–81.

1. List three factors related to student's knowledge of university mental health services.
2. List and discuss four reasons why students did not use mental health services available on their campus.
3. Discuss ways in which you might help other students know about the mental health services available on your campus.

You can find additional readings relating to stress management with InfoTrac® College Edition, an online library of more than 5000 journals and publications. Follow the instructions for accessing InfoTrac® that were packaged with your textbook; then search for articles using a keyword search.

For additional links and resources, visit our text-specific website at www.health.nelson.com.

## Key Terms

The terms listed here are used within the chapter on the page indicated. Definitions of the terms are in the Glossary at the end of the book.

| | | | |
|---|---|---|---|
| **adaptive response** 28 | **general adaptation syndrome (GAS)** 28 | **mindfulness** 38 | **stressors** 28 |
| **biofeedback** 38 | **guided imagery** 37 | **post-traumatic stress disorder (PTSD)** 31 | **visualization** 37 |
| **defence mechanisms** 35 | **homeostasis** 28 | **progressive relaxation** 37 | |
| **distress** 28 | **meditation** 37 | **stress** 28 | |
| **eustress** 28 | | | |

## References

1. Selye, H. (1974). *Stress without distress.* New York: Lippincott, p. 14.
2. Selye, H. (1974). *Stress without distress.* New York: Lippincott.
3. Lazarus, R., & Launier, R. (1978). Stress-related transactions between person and environment. In *Perspectives in interactional psychology.* New York: Plenum.
4. Senior, K. (2001). Should stress carry a health warning? *Lancet, 357,* 126.
5. Sheps, D., et al. (2002). Mental stress-induced ischemia and all-cause mortality in patients with coronary artery disease: Results from the Psychophysiological Investigations of Myocardial Ischemia Study. *Circulation, 105,* 1780.
6. Stress increases fat's staying power. (2002). *American Medical News, 45*(9), 38.
7. Perticone, F., Ceravolo, R., Candigliota, M., Ventura, G., Iacopino, S., Sinopolo, F., & Mattioli, P.L. (2001). Obesity and body fat distribution induce endothelial dysfunction by oxidative stress. *Diabetes, 50,* 159–65.
8. Epel, E.S., McEwen, B., Seeman, T., Matthews, K., Catellazzo, G., Brownell, K.D., Bell, J., & Ickovics, J.R. (2000). Stress and body shape: Stress-induced cortisol secretion is consistently greater among women with central fat. *Psychosomatic Medicine, 62,* 623–32.
9. Wei, B., Kilpatrick, M., Naquin, M., & Cole, D. (2006). Psychological perceptions to walking, water aerobics and yoga in college students. *American Journal of Health Studies, 21*(3), 142–47.

10. Deckro, G.R., Ballinger, K.M., Hoyt, M., Wilcher, M., Dusek, J., Myers, P., Greenberg, B., Rosenthal, D.S., & Benson, H. (2002). The evaluation of a mind/body intervention to reduce psychological distress and perceived stress in college students. *Journal of American College Health, 50*(6), 281–87.

11. Friedman, M., Thoresen, C.E., Gill, J.J., Ulmer, D., Powell, L.H., Price V.A., Brown, B., Thompson, L., Rabin, D.D., Breall, W.S., Bourg, E., Levy, R., & Dixon, T. (1986). Alteration of type A behavior and its effect on cardiac recurrences in post myocardial infarction patients: Summary results of the Recurrent Coronary Prevention Project. *American Heart Journal, 112,* 653–65.

12. Yusuf, S., Hawken, S., Ounpuu, S., Dans, T., Avezum, A., Lanas, F., McQueen, M., Budaj, A., Pais, P., Varigos, J., & Lisheng, L. (2004). Effect of potentially modifiable risk factors associated with myocardial infarction in 52 countries (the INTERHEART study): Case-control study. *Lancet, 364,* 937–52.

13. Lazarus, R.S., & DeLongis, A. (1983). Psychological stress and coping in aging. *American Psychologist, 38,* 245–54.

14. Canadian Mental Health Association. (2002–3). *Effects of depression and anxiety on Canadian society—Executive summary.* Campus Survey. Available at www.cmha.ca/bins/content_page.asp?cid=5-34-183&lang=1.

15. Saskatchewan Health. (2007). Post-trauma stress. Available at www.health.gov.sk.ca/rr_post_trauma_stress.html.

16. Stressed out on campus. (2000). *Techniques, 75*(3).

17. Enns, M.W., Cox, B.J., Sareen, J., & Freeman, P. (2001). Adaptive and maladaptive perfectionism in medical students: A longitudinal investigation. *Medical Education, 35,* 1034–42.

18. Helmers, K.F., Danoff, D., Steinert, Y., Leyton, M., & Young, S.N. (1997). Stress and depressed mood in medical students, law students and graduate students at McGill University. *Academic Medicine, 72,* 708–14.

19. Campbell, R.L., & Svenson, L.W. (1992). Perceived level of stress among university undergraduate students in Edmonton, Canada. *Perceptual and Motor Skills, 75,* 552–54.

20. Adlaf, M.A., Demers, A., & Gliksman, L. (2005). Canadian campus survey 2004. Toronto, Centre for Addiction and Mental Health. Available at www.camh.net/research/population_life_course.html.

21. Ibid.

22. Campbell, R.L., & Svenson, L.W. (1992). Perceived level of stress among university undergraduate students in Edmonton, Canada. *Perceptual and Motor Skills, 75,* 552–54.

23. How women handle stress: Is there a difference. (2001). *Harvard Mental Health Letter, 17*(10).

24. Women's response to stress. (2002). *Harvard Women's Health Watch, 9*(9).

25. Brown, I. (2003). Aboriginal health and healing. *In Touch (Mental Health and Wellness in Aboriginal Communities), 26.* Available at www.niichro.com/mental%20health/men_1.html.

26. Deckro, G., et al. (2002). The evaluation of a mind/body intervention to reduce psychological distress and perceived stress in college students. *Journal of American College Health, 50,* 281.

27. Oman, D., Shapiro, S.L., Thoresen, C.E., Plante, T.G., & Flinders, T. (2008). Meditation lowers stress and supports forgiveness among college students: a randomized controlled trial. (Report). *Journal of American College Health, 56*(5), 569–79.

28. Student Development Centre, Brock University. (n.d.). Personal counselling services. Available at www.brocku.ca/sdc/counselling.

29. Wellness Centre, University of British Columbia. (n.d.). *Wellness guide.* Available at http://students.ubc.ca/health/guide.cfm.

30. Ipsos-Reid and Kumon Math and Reading Centre. (2005, April 12). Canadian university students on study habits and exam-related stress. Available at www.ipsos.ca.

31. Ibid.

32. Steinhardt, M., & Dolbier, M.S. (2008). Evaluations of a resilience intervention to enhance coping strategies and protective factors and decrease symptomatology. *Journal of American College Health, 54*(4), 445–63.

33. Ipsos-Reid and Kumon Math and Reading Centre. (2005, April 12). Canadian university students on study habits and exam-related stress. Available at www.ipsos.ca.

34. Leontaridi, R., & Ward, M. (2002). Canadian workers among most stressed (brief article). *Worklife Report, 14*(2), 8–10.

35. Dietsche, P., Toneguzzo, A., Larouche, P., & Wilson, D. (2007). Human Resources and Social Development Canada. (2007, August 29). Association of Canadian Community Colleges. Pan-Canadian study of first-year college students—Report 1 student characteristics and the college experience—August 2007. Available at www.hrsdc.gc.ca/en/publications_resources/learning_policy/sp_787_08_07e/page01.shtml.

36. Driving-induced stress in urban college students. (2000). *Perceptual and Motor Skills, 90*(2).

37. Schellenberg, E.G., Hirt, J., & Sears, A. (1999). Attitudes toward homosexuals among students at a Canadian university. *Sex Roles: A Journal of Research, 40*(1), 139.

38. Swank, E., & Raiz, L. (2007). Explaining comfort with homosexuality among social work students: the impact of demographic, contextual, and attitudinal factors. *Journal of Social Work Education, 43*(2), 257–80.

39. Petten. C. (2003). Where are all the Native grads? (Canadian Classroom). *Wind Speaker, 21*(1), 32.

40. Wardle, N. (1999). Balance: A sense of personal artistry and wholeness. Available at http://speakwell.com/well/1999_fall/articles/balance.html.

41. Blank, Robert J., M.A., Registered Psychologist. (2008, October 7). Personal interview. Available at www.bardonet.ca.

42. Pennebaker, J. (1993). Putting stress into words: Health, linguistic and therapeutic implications. *Behavioral Research, 31*(6).

43. Barbar, C. (2001, May). The science of meditation. *Psychology Today,* 54.

44. Counselling and Development Centre, York University. (2002). Time management for university students. Available at www.yorku.ca/cdc/lsp/skillbuilding/timemanagement.html.

45. Procrastinators always finish last, even in health. (1998). *American Psychological Monitor, 20*(1).

46. Tuchman, B. (2002, August 22). Procrastinators. Presentation, American Psychological Association, Chicago.

# Psychological Health

**After studying the material in this chapter, you will be able to:**

- **Identify** the characteristics of emotional, mental, and spiritual health.
- **Discuss** the concepts of emotional and spiritual intelligence.
- **Describe** the relationship of needs, values, self-esteem, a sense of control, and relationships to psychological health.
- **Explain** the differences between mental health and mental illness, and **list** some effects of mental illness on physical health.
- **Describe** the major mental illnesses—anxiety disorders, depressive disorders, attention disorders, and schizophrenia—and the characteristic symptoms of each type.
- **Discuss** some of the factors that may lead to suicide as well as strategies for prevention.
- **Describe** the treatment options available for those with psychological problems.

The process of becoming an adult is challenging in every culture and country. Psychological health can make the difference between facing this challenge with optimism and confidence or feeling overwhelmed by expectations and responsibilities. Returning to college or university as an adult can also be daunting. Attempting to balance work, family commitments, and education can stretch one's ability to stay psychologically well.

There have been numerous studies on psychological health. The findings of these studies indicate that psychologically healthy men and women generally share certain characteristics. They value themselves and strive toward happiness and fulfillment. They establish and maintain close relationships with others. They accept the limitations as well as the possibilities that life has to offer. And they feel a sense of meaning and purpose that makes the gestures of living worth the effort required.

Young adulthood—the years from the late teens to the mid-twenties—is a time when many serious disorders, including bipolar illness (manic depression) and schizophrenia, often develop.

The saddest fact is not that so many feel so bad, but that so few realize they can feel better. Only one of every five men and women who could use treatment ever seeks help. Yet 80 to 90 percent of those treated for psychological problems recover, most within a few months.[1]

By learning about psychological disorders, you may be able to recognize early warning signals so you can deal with potential difficulties or seek professional help for more serious problems.

# What Is Psychological Health?

"A sound mind in a sound body is a short but full description of a happy state in this world," the philosopher John Locke wrote in 1693. More than 300 years later, his statement still rings true. Both physical and psychological well-being are essential to total wellness. However, modern theorists have gone beyond these general requirements to analyze other components of well-being, including coping styles, goals, and adaptation to stress and change.[2]

Psychological health encompasses both our emotional and mental states—that is, our feelings and our thoughts. **Emotional health** generally refers to feelings and moods, both of which are discussed later in this chapter. Characteristics of emotionally healthy persons, identified in an analysis of major studies of emotional wellness, include the following:

✔ Determination and effort to be healthy
✔ Development of a sense of meaning of and affirmation for life
✔ An understanding that the self is not the centre of the universe
✔ Compassion for others
✔ Increased depth and satisfaction in intimate relationships
✔ A sense of control over the mind and body that leads to health-enhancing choices and decisions[3]

**Mental health** describes our ability to perceive reality as it is, to respond to its challenges, and to develop rational strategies for living. The mentally healthy person doesn't try to avoid conflicts and distress, but copes with life's transitions, traumas, and losses in a way that allows for emotional stability and growth. The characteristics of mental health include:

✔ The ability to function and carry out responsibilities
✔ The ability to form relationships
✔ Realistic perceptions of the motivations of others
✔ Rational, logical thought processes
✔ The ability to adapt to change and to cope with adversity[4]

There is considerable overlap between psychological health and **spiritual health,** which involves our ability to identify our basic purpose in life and to experience the fulfillment of achieving our full potential. However, many people consider the two separate. "We like to think that emotional problems have to do with the family, childhood, and trauma—with personal life but not with spirituality," observes Thomas Moore, author of *Care of the Soul.* "Yet it is obvious that the soul, seat of the deepest emotions, can benefit greatly from the gifts of a vivid spiritual life and can suffer when it is deprived of them."[5]

In Canada, we are entering a time when First Nations spirituality is respected and embraced as a living faith tradition and a way of healing. Holst (2004)[6] suggests that the primary reason for this may be that many of us find something lacking in our inherited church communities. Betty Bastien,[7] a Siksikaitsitapi, Sikapinaki (Black Eyes Woman), from the Blackfoot peoples in southern Alberta, says that Ihtsipaitapiiyo'pa—the sacred power, spirit, or Source of Life whose manifestation is the sun—helps her identify the meaning and purpose of her life. Chief Larry Oakes of the Nekaneet First Nation in Saskatchewan focuses on traditional ceremonies, medicines, and healing practices to help people get back in touch with their culture and nature. The elders also talk about the spiritual connection to animals and the environment.[8] A more in-depth discussion of spiritual health and well-being is presented in Chapter 17.

In addition, **culture** helps to define psychological health. In one culture, men and women may express feelings with great intensity, shouting with joy or wailing in grief, while in another culture such behaviour might be considered abnormal or unhealthy. In our diverse society, many cultural influences affect Canadians' sense of who they are, where they came from, and what they believe. Cultural rituals help bring people together, strengthen their bonds, reinforce the values and beliefs they share, and provide a sense of belonging, meaning, and purpose.

## Emotional Intelligence

A person's IQ—intelligence quotient—was once considered the leading determinant of achievement. However, psychologists have determined that another way of knowing, dubbed **emotional intelligence,** may make an even greater difference in a person's personal and professional success. Psychologist Daniel Goleman identifies five components of emotional intelligence (sometimes called *emotional quotient* or *EQ*): self-awareness; altruism; personal motivation; empathy; and the ability to love and be loved by friends, partners, and family members. People who possess high emotional intelligence are the people who truly succeed in work as well as play, building flourishing careers and lasting, meaningful relationships.[9]

Emotional intelligence isn't fixed at birth, nor is it the same as intuition. The emotional competencies that most benefit students are focusing on clear, manageable goals, and identifying and understanding emotions rather than relying on gut feelings.[10]

▲ First Nations powwows and Cl...

© Brent Wong/Shutterstock

*[handwritten note overlay]*
Milton Rokeach:
Instrumental Values =
ways of thinking & acting
that we hold important
Terminal Values : goals,
   achievements
Instrumental Values +
   Terminal Values
make basis for our
attitudes & behaviour

## How Can ... a Fulfilling Life?

What's life all about? We all ask this question sooner or later. Whether dreams come true or fade away, whether we achieve our goals or not, we find ourselves confronting profound questions about the purpose of our time on Earth. Each of us must create life satisfaction on our own.

Psychology, a field that traditionally concentrated on what goes wrong in our lives and in our minds, has shifted its focus to the study of what goes right. *Positive psychology* emphasizes building personal strengths rather than treating weaknesses. One of its key beliefs is that young people who learn to be **optimistic** and resilient are less likely to suffer from mental disorders and more likely to lead happy, productive lives.

Positive attitudes may even prolong life. In a study that has followed 678 Catholic nuns into old age, those who expressed more positive emotions (such as joy, love, hope, and happiness) in autobiographies written in their twenties lived as much as ten years longer than those expressing fewer positive emotions.[11]

### Knowing Your Needs

The humanist theorist Abraham Maslow believed that human needs are the motivating factors in personality development. First we must satisfy basic physiological needs, such as those for food, shelter, and sleep. Only then can we pursue fulfillment of our higher needs—for safety and security, love and affection, and self-esteem. According to Maslow, few individuals reach the state of **self-actualization,** in which one functions at the highest possible level and derives the greatest possible satisfaction from life (see Figure 3-1).

### ...our Values

Your **values**—the criteria by which you evaluate things, people, events, and yourself—represent what's most important to you. In our complex world, values can provide guidelines for making decisions that are right for you. If understood and applied, they help give life meaning and structure.

Social psychologist Milton Rokeach[12] distinguished between two types of values. *Instrumental values* represent ways of thinking and acting that we hold important, such as being loving or loyal. *Terminal values* represent goals, achievements, or ideal states that we strive toward, such as happiness. Instrumental and terminal values form the basis for our attitudes and our behaviour.

There can be a large discrepancy between what people say they value and what their actions indicate about their values. That's why it's important to clarify your own values, making sure you understand what you believe so you can live in accordance with your beliefs. To do so, follow these steps:

1. Carefully consider the consequences of each choice.
2. Choose freely from among all the options.
3. Publicly affirm your values by sharing them with others.
4. Act out your values.

Values clarification is not a once-in-a-lifetime task, but an ongoing process of sorting out what matters most to you. If you believe in protecting the environment, do you shut off lights and walk rather than drive to conserve energy? Do you vote for political candidates who support environmental protection? Do you recycle newspapers, bottles, and cans? Values are more than ideals we'd like to attain; they should be reflected in the way we live day by day.

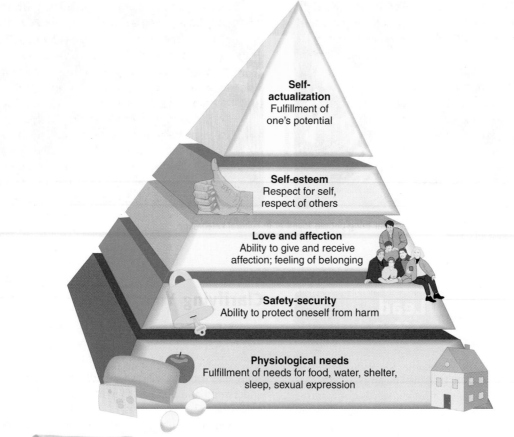

▲ **Figure 3-1** The Maslow Pyramid
To attain the highest level of psychological health, you must first satisfy your needs for safety and security, love and affection, and self-esteem.

Source: Hespenheide Design

## Boosting Self-Esteem

Each of us wants and needs to feel significant as a human being with unique talents, abilities, and roles in life. A sense of **self-esteem,** of belief or pride in ourselves, gives us the confidence to achieve at school or work and to reach out to others to form friendships and close relationships. Self-esteem is the little voice that whispers, "You're worth it. You can do it. You're okay."

Self-esteem is not based on external factors such as wealth or beauty, but on what you believe about yourself. It's not something you're born with; self-esteem develops over time. It's also not something anyone else can give you, although those around you can either help boost or diminish your self-esteem.

The seeds of self-esteem are planted in childhood when parents provide the assurance and appreciation youngsters need to push themselves toward new accomplishments: crawling, walking, and forming words and sentences.

Adults, too, must consider themselves worthy of love, friendship, and success if they are to be loved, make friends, and to achieve their goals. Low self-esteem is more common

in people who have been abused as children and in those with psychiatric disorders, including depression, anxiety, alcoholism, and drug dependence. Feeling neglected as a child can also lead to poor self-esteem. Adults with poor self-esteem may unconsciously enter into relationships that reinforce their negative self-perceptions and may prefer and even seek out people who think poorly of them.

One of the most useful techniques for bolstering self-esteem and achieving your goals is developing the habit of positive thinking and talking. Negative observations, such as constant criticism or reminders of the most minor of faults, can undermine self-image, while positive affirmations—compliments, kudos, encouragements— have proven effective in enhancing self-esteem and psychological well-being. Individuals who fight off negative thoughts fare better psychologically than those who collapse when a setback occurs or who rely on others to make them feel better.

Self-esteem has proven to be one of the best predictors of college and university adjustment. Students with high self-esteem report better personal, emotional, social, and academic adjustment.[13] However, true self-esteem requires an honest sense of your own worth. In a study of students, psychology professors followed self-enhancers who began their first year with an inflated sense of their own academic ability. These students expected to get much higher grades than might be expected based on their high school grades and test scores. While they felt confident and happy for a while, they did no better academically and were no more likely to graduate than their realistic or self-deprecating peers. In fact, their self-esteem and interest in school declined with each passing year.[14]

## Managing Your Moods

Feelings come and go within minutes. A **mood** is a more sustained emotional state that colours our view of the world for hours or days. According to some surveys, bad moods descend upon us an average of three out of every ten days. A few people, about 2 percent, are happy just about every day. About 3 percent report bad moods four out of every five days.[15] Some personality types are prone to longer bad moods, which can lead to health problems.[16]

There are also gender differences in mood management: Men typically try to distract themselves (a partially successful strategy) or use alcohol or drugs (an ineffective tactic); women are more likely to talk to someone (which can help) or to ruminate on why they feel bad (which doesn't help).[17] Learning effective mood-boosting, mood-regulating strategies can help both men and women pull themselves up and out of an emotional slump.

The most effective way to banish sadness or a bad mood is by changing what caused it in the first place—if you can figure out what made you upset and why. "Most bad moods are caused by loss or failure in work or intimate relationships," says Larsen. "The questions to ask are: What can I do to fix the failure? What can I do to remedy the loss? Is there anything under my control that I can change? If there is, take action and solve it." Rewrite the report. Ask to take a make-up exam. Apologize to the friend whose feelings you hurt. Tell your parents you feel bad about the argument you had.

If there's nothing you can do, accept what happened and focus on doing things differently next time. Or think about what happened in a different way and put a positive spin on it. This technique, known as *cognitive reappraisal* or *reframing,* helps you look at a setback in a new light: What lessons did it teach you? What would you have done differently? Could there be a silver lining or hidden benefit?

If you can't identify or resolve the problem responsible for your emotional funk, the next-best solution is to concentrate on altering your negative feelings. Try setting a quick, achievable goal that can boost your spirits with a small success. Clean out a closet; sort through the piles of paper on your desk; write that letter you've been putting off for weeks.

Another good option is to get moving. In studies of mood regulation, exercise consistently ranks as the single most effective strategy for banishing bad feelings. Numerous studies have confirmed that aerobic workouts, such as walking or jogging, significantly improve mood. Even non-aerobic exercise, such as weight lifting, can boost spirits; improve sleep and appetite; reduce anxiety, irritability, and anger; and produce feelings of mastery and accomplishment.

Leisure may also provide people with opportunities to feel empowered to manage challenges that come their way in life. A study by Iwasaki[18] highlights the importance of leisure as a way of coping with stress and maintaining good health and well-being within the context of general coping. His study examined the effects of leisure coping (defined as people's beliefs that their leisure helps them cope with stress) in university students' daily lives. Leisure coping had a significant and positive correlation with psychological well-being. Leisure friendship was also significantly and positively correlated with psychological well-being and perceived stress reduction.

Although it's tempting to pull away from others when you're in a slump, it's better not to withdraw. Friends often can help improve your mood by giving you good feedback. But be wary of seeking out companions solely for a gripe-and-groan session. You might end up feeling worse rather than better. Another option is listening to music, one of the most popular and effective ways of distracting people from their troubles and changing their bad moods.

## Social Responsibility

**Altruism** is an unselfish regard for others. **Social responsibility** is a principle or ethical theory that suggests governments, corporations, organizations, and individuals have a responsibility to contribute to the welfare of society. Research is showing that helping others enhances self-esteem, relieves physical and mental stress, and protects psychological well-being.

Whether you are altruistic on a personal level or participate in a corporate community project, research suggests that people who help other people consistently report a surge of well-being, called *helper's high,* which they describe as a unique sense of calmness, warmth, and enhanced self-worth. Hans Selye, the father of stress research, described cooperation with others for the self's sake as *altruistic egotism,* whereby we satisfy our own needs while helping others satisfy theirs. College students who provided community service reported changes in attitude (a greater degree of thankfulness for personal opportunities) and behaviour (a greater commitment to do more volunteer work).[19]

Service learning has also been shown to help students reflect on the health disparities evident in their own communities and assist them in making healthy lifestyle choices so that they are better prepared to help others.[20] The focus on "others" sometimes helped them move from a focus on self-referral to that of doing something purposeful and meaningful for others. Studies also show that students from business schools are asking for curriculum that helps them understand the financial benefits of social responsibility. They are beginning to understand that working for companies whose business plans align with their own personal values of caring for others will lessen their stress as they move into career-oriented jobs.[21]

The options for volunteerism and giving of yourself are limitless: serve a meal at a homeless shelter; collect donations for a charity auction; teach reading in a literacy program. Volunteer opportunities are often available on college and university campuses. Women's centres, intercultural clubs, peer mentoring, and study groups are just a few options.

Many businesses across Canada and around the world have also adopted a social responsibility mandate as part of their strategic planning process. Industry Canada promotes Corporate Social Responsibility (CSR) because it makes companies more innovative, productive, and competitive. CSR often overlaps with corporate citizenship or sustainability initiatives.[22] Natural Resources Canada is working to address climate change issues and assist companies with environmental sustainability projects that benefit the company and the world at large.[23] As you ponder your own career path, take time to think about ways you might become socially responsible—a concept that is win–win for businesses and individuals.

## Feeling in Control

Although no one has absolute control over destiny, we can do a great deal to control how we think, feel, and behave. By realistically assessing our life situations, we can live in a way that allows us to make the most of our circumstances. By doing so, we gain a sense of mastery. In many surveys, people who feel in control of their lives report greater psychological well-being than those who do not.

Albert Bandura's social cognitive theory of human functioning[24] suggests that **self-efficacy**—our belief that we can produce an effect—is a foundation of human motivation, well-being, and personal accomplishments. He suggests that unless we believe we can produce desired results by our actions we will have little incentive to act or to persevere in the face of difficulties. Efficacy beliefs play a key role in shaping our lives. Our level of self-efficacy influences the types of activities and environments we choose to be in.

## Developing Autonomy

One goal that many people strive for is **autonomy,** or independence. Both family and society influence our ability to grow toward independence. Autonomous individuals are true to themselves. As they weigh the pros and cons of any decision, whether it's using or refusing drugs or choosing a major area of study or a career, they base their judgment on their own values, not entirely on those of others. Those who've achieved autonomy may seek the opinions of others, but they do not allow their decisions to be dictated solely by external influences. Their locus of control—that is, where they view control as originating—is *internal* (from within themselves) rather than *external* (from others).

## Asserting Yourself

Being **assertive** means recognizing your feelings and making your needs and desires clear to others. Unlike aggression, a far less healthy means of expression, assertiveness usually works. You can change a situation you don't like by communicating your feelings and thoughts in non-provocative words, by focusing on specifics, and by making sure you're talking with the person who is directly responsible.

Becoming assertive isn't always easy. Many people have learned to cope by being passive and not communicating their feelings or opinions. Sooner or later they become so irritated, frustrated, or overwhelmed that they explode in an outburst—which they think of as being assertive. Assertiveness doesn't mean screaming or telling someone off. You can communicate your wishes calmly and clearly. Assertiveness is a behaviour that respects your rights and the rights of other people, even when you disagree.

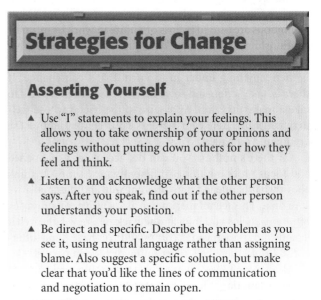

## Strategies for Change

### Asserting Yourself

▲ Use "I" statements to explain your feelings. This allows you to take ownership of your opinions and feelings without putting down others for how they feel and think.

▲ Listen to and acknowledge what the other person says. After you speak, find out if the other person understands your position.

▲ Be direct and specific. Describe the problem as you see it, using neutral language rather than assigning blame. Also suggest a specific solution, but make clear that you'd like the lines of communication and negotiation to remain open.

▲ Don't think you have to be obnoxious in order to be assertive. It's most effective to state your needs and preferences without any sarcasm or hostility.

# Connecting with Others

While developing autonomy is important, connecting with others is just as important. At every age, people who feel connected to others tend to be healthier physically and psychologically.[25] College and university students are no exception: those who have a supportive, readily available network of relationships are less psychologically distressed and more satisfied with life.

Covey[26] says that when we develop autonomy or independence, we can enter into a whole new dimension—that of interdependence. Building rich, enduring relationships with other people allows us to ask for or give help when needed. As we begin to trust in ourselves and others, we begin to think of working or being together as a win–win situation—a mutual benefit.

The opposite of *connectedness* is **social isolation,** a major risk factor for illness and early death. Individuals with few social contacts face two to four times the mortality rate of others. The reason may be that their social isolation weakens the body's ability to ward off disease. Medical students with higher-than-average scores on a loneliness scale had lower levels of protective immune cells.[27] The end of a long-term relationship—through separation, divorce, or death—also dampens immunity.

It is part of our nature as mammals and as human beings to crave relationships. But we invariably end up alone at times. Solitude is not without its own quiet joys—time for introspection, self-assessment, learning from the past, and looking toward the future. Each of us can cultivate the joy of our own company, of being alone without becoming lonely.

## Overcoming Loneliness

According to the *General Social Survey* (GSS), on an average day, Canadians aged 15 and over spent 5.9 hours alone (excluding sleep and personal hygiene). As well, people spent more time alone during both their paid and unpaid work and their leisure activities.[28]

For some individuals, being alone and being lonely are two different things. Not all people who spend time alone are lonely. However, loneliness can cause emotional distress when it is a chronic rather than an episodic condition.[29] Findings in the GSS showed that people who spent a lot of time by themselves were less likely to be very happy with their lives than those who spent little time alone. Forty-eight percent of those who spent less than two hours alone on an average day were very happy, compared with 37 percent of Canadians who spent eight or more hours by themselves.[30]

To combat loneliness, people may join groups or surround themselves with superficial acquaintances. Others avoid the effort of trying to connect, sometimes limiting most of their personal interactions to chat groups on the Internet. However, the Internet may actually make people feel lonelier. Dittman,[31] in a study on undergraduate students, found that loneliness is more prevalent in the students who use the Internet more than 40 hours per week and in those who prefer the Internet over face-to-face interaction or talking on the phone. The use of the Internet did not contribute to loneliness among undergraduates using it for less than 40 hours per week.

In another study of the social and psychological effects of Internet use at home, researchers found that people who spend even a few hours a week online have higher levels of depression and loneliness than those who use the Internet less frequently.[32]

Race and gender can affect the experience of loneliness. Some studies have found that men are lonelier than women. Others find no gender differences in loneliness, but researchers note men, particularly those who score high on measures of masculinity, are more hesitant than women to admit that they're lonely.[33]

The true keys to overcoming loneliness are developing skills to fulfill our own potential and learning to reach out to others. In this way, loneliness can become a means to personal growth and discovery.

## Facing Social Anxieties

Many people are uncomfortable meeting strangers or speaking or performing in public. In some surveys, as many as 40 percent of people describe themselves as shy or socially anxious. Some shy people—an estimated 10 to 15 percent of children—are born with a predisposition to shyness. Others become shy because they don't learn proper social responses or because they experience rejection or shame.

Social anxieties often become a problem in late adolescence. Students may develop symptoms when they are at a social event or are called on in class. Some experience symptoms when they try to perform any sort of action in the presence of others, even such everyday activities as eating in public, using a public restroom, or writing a cheque. About 7 percent of the population could be diagnosed with **social phobia,** a severe form of social anxiety in which individuals typically fear and avoid various social situations.[34] Adolescents and young adults with severe social anxiety are at increased risk of major depression.[35] The key difference between these problems and normal shyness and self-consciousness is the degree of distress and impairment that individuals experience.

If you're shy, you can overcome much of your social apprehensiveness on your own, the same way you might set out to stop smoking or lose weight. For example, you can improve your social skills by pushing yourself to talk with a stranger in one of your classes or to a person attending a meeting or gathering. Gradually you'll acquire a sense of social timing and a verbal ease that will take the worry out of close encounters with others.

Those with more disabling social anxiety may do best with professional guidance, which has proven highly effective. Over time, most people are able to emerge from the walls that shyness has built around them and take pleasure in interacting with others.

## Understanding Mental Health

Mentally healthy individuals value themselves, perceive reality as it is, accept their limitations and possibilities, carry out their responsibilities, establish and maintain close relationships, pursue work that suits their talent and training, and feel a sense of fulfillment that makes the efforts of daily living worthwhile (see Figure 3-2).

According to research conducted by the World Health Organization (WHO), mental disorders affect 400 million people around the world, and these numbers will surge even higher in the coming decades.[36] A Report on Mental Illnesses in Canada published in 2002 calls for increased efforts to recognize, treat, and prevent mental disorders.[37]

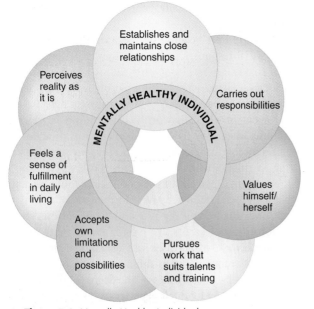

▲ **Figure 3-2** Mentally Healthy Individual
Mental well-being is a combination of many factors.

Source: Hespenheide Design

## What Is a Mental Illness?

While lay people may speak of nervous breakdowns or insanity, these are not scientific terms. The contributors to the *Report on Mental Illnesses* in Canada define **mental illness** as characterized by alterations in thinking, mood, or behaviour (or a combination of these) associated with significant distress and impaired functioning. The symptoms of mental illness vary from mild to severe, depending on the type of mental illness, the individual, the family, and the socioeconomic environment. Mental illness includes mood disorders, schizophrenia, anxiety disorders, personality disorders, and eating disorders.

This report also states that approximately 20 percent of individuals will experience a mental illness during their lifetime and the remaining 80 percent will be affected by an illness in family members, friends, or colleagues.[38] Nearly one in five Canadian adults will personally experience a mental illness during a one-year period.[39] The full report can be viewed at www.cmha.ca/bins/content_page .asp?cid=4-42-215.

In a report on the First Nations' and Inuit health branch (Manitoba region), it was stated that at least 30 to 50 percent of the issues for which people were seeking help from nurses in this region were related to mental health.[40]

## Does Mental Health Affect Physical Health?

Mental illness affects the mind and the body. **Anxiety** can lead to intensified asthmatic reactions, skin conditions, and digestive disorders. Stress can play a role in hypertension, heart attacks, sudden cardiac death, and immune disorders. Individuals with mental illness can develop physical symptoms such as weight loss and blood biochemical imbalances associated with eating disorders.

**Depression** has increasingly been recognized as a serious risk factor for physical illness. According to a review of large-scale studies on depression of more than 36 000 men and women, depressed individuals were 1.5 to 4 times more likely to develop heart problems.[41] In still-unknown ways, depression may increase risk factors for heart disease, such as high blood pressure.[42] Together, depression and heart disease worsen a patient's prognosis more than either condition alone. One in five heart-attack survivors suffers major depression.[43] They are two to five times more likely to die in the first six to twelve months following a heart attack.[44] Since depression can and often does recur, physicians now view it as a chronic illness with lifelong implications for mental and physical health.[45]

By some estimates, as many as 60 percent of those who seek help from physicians suffer primarily from a psychological problem. Treating mental health problems leads not only to improved health, but also to lower health-care costs. Psychiatric treatment reduces hospitalizations, cuts medical expenses, and reduces work disability.

## Diversity and Mental Health

Mental illness affects people in all occupations, educational and income levels, and cultures. However, there are some gender and age differences that can be noted. According to *A Report on Mental Illness in Canada,* data from the Centre for Chronic Disease Prevention and Control, Health Canada, and the Canadian Institute for Health Information show that rates among women were higher than among men in all age groups.[46] (See also The X & Y Files: "Gender and Stress.")

Young people are also at risk. Nearly one-half of all admissions for one of the seven most common mental illnesses involved individuals between the ages of 25 and 44. The seven mental illnesses were anxiety disorders, bipolar disorders, schizophrenia, major depression, personality disorders, eating disorders, and attempted suicide. Rates of hospitalization among young adults between 15 and 24 years of age were almost comparable to those of the 25- to 44-year-old age group.[47]

Cultural assimilation plays a role in mental health, too. Loneliness, isolation, alien religious rituals, suppression of native language, ridicule, harsh punishment, and sexual abuse experienced at residential schools across Canada has been emotionally devastating to many children of First Nations, Inuit, and Métis descent. Many studies show that the high levels of psychological problems in our Aboriginal communities are a direct result of the abuse suffered.[48]

## Anxiety Disorders

**Anxiety disorders** may involve inordinate fears of certain objects or situations (phobias); episodes of sudden, inexplicable terror (panic attacks); chronic distress (generalized anxiety disorder); or persistent, disturbing thoughts and behaviours (obsessive-compulsive disorder). Anxiety disorders affect 12 percent of the Canadian population, causing mild to severe impairment. Hospitalization rates for anxiety disorders in general hospitals are twice as high among women as men.[49]

**Generalized anxiety disorder (GAD),** an excessive or unrealistic apprehension that causes physical symptoms, can last for six months or longer. It usually starts when people are in their twenties.[50] Unlike fear, which helps us recognize and avoid real danger, GAD is an exaggerated, irrational, or unwarranted response to harmless objects or situations. The most common symptoms are faster heart rate, sweating, increased blood pressure, muscle aches, intestinal pains, irritability, sleep problems, and difficulty concentrating.

Chronically anxious individuals worry constantly, about almost everything: their health, families, finances, marriages, and potential dangers. Treatment for GAD may consist of a combination of psychotherapy, behavioural therapy, and anti-anxiety drugs.

Many individuals do not seek treatment for their anxiety. Sometimes the symptoms themselves may interfere with seeking help. Yet most who do get treatment, even for severe and disabling problems, improve dramatically.

## Phobias

**Phobias**—the most prevalent type of anxiety disorder—are out-of-the-ordinary, irrational, intense, persistent fears of certain objects or situations. The most common phobias involve animals, particularly dogs, snakes, insects, and mice; the sight of blood; closed spaces *(claustrophobia);* heights *(acrophobia);* air travel; and being in places or situations from which they perceive it difficult or embarrassing to escape *(agoraphobia).*

Although various medications have been tried, none is effective by itself in relieving phobias. The best approach is behaviour therapy, which consists of gradual, systematic exposure to the feared object (a process called *systematic desensitization).* Numerous studies have proven that exposure to the actual source of the fear rather than simply imagining it—is highly effective. *Medical hypnosis,* the use of induction of an altered state of consciousness, also can help.

The characteristic symptoms of a phobia include:

- Excessive or unreasonable fear of a specific object or situation
- Immediate, invariable anxiety when exposed to the object or situation
- Recognition that the fear is excessive or unreasonable
- Avoidance of the feared object or situation, or enduring it only with intense anxiety or distress
- Inability to function as usual at school or work or in social relationships because of the phobia

## Panic Attacks, Panic Disorder, and Post-traumatic Stress Disorder

Individuals who have had **panic attacks** describe them as the most frightening experiences of their lives. Without reason or warning, their hearts race wildly. They may become light-headed or dizzy. Because they can't catch

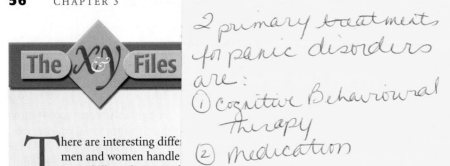

The X & Y Files

*[Handwritten note: 2 primary treatments for panic disorders are: (1) Cognitive Behavioural Therapy (2) medication]*

There are interesting diffe[rences...] men and women handle [...] mental illness between th[...]

- One of the most important rea[...] to stress differently is hormon[...] the hormones cortisol and epi[...] bloodstream in a woman, as th[...] is the release of another horm[...] counters the production of co[...] promotes nurturing and relax[ing emotions...] secrete the hormone oxytocin when they are stressed but in much smaller amounts. Researchers think that this is the reason why when men are stressed they tend toward the fight-or-flight response. They bottle up their stress and escape or they fight back, whereas women reach out to others to protect themselves and reduce stress.[53]

- Women may also be better than men at controlling their emotions due to the make-up of the brain itself. Researchers have found that sections of the brain used to control aggression and anger responses are larger in women than they are in men.[54]

- Relationship loss for women and performance failure for men are often the greatest stressors when comparing sexes.[55]

[...]onds more intensely to emotion. [...]naging studies, the genders [...] emotions, especially sadness, [...]ns in an area eight times larger in [...]

[...]s twice as common in women.[56]

[...]st common women's mental [...]nay be more persistent in women [...]research is needed to confirm this.

- Diagnosis of antisocial personality disorder is three to one for men compared to women.[58]

- There are no marked gender differences in the rates of severe mental disorders, such as schizophrenia and bipolar disorder, which affect less than 2 percent of the population.[59]

- There are gender biases in the treatment of psychological disorders. Doctors are more likely to diagnose depression in women when compared to men, and if you are a female, you are more likely to be prescribed mood-altering psychotrophic drugs than men.[60]

- There is a significantly higher number of women suffering from post-traumatic stress disorder than men.[61]

their breath, they may start breathing rapidly and hyperventilate. Worst of all is the terrible sense that something horrible is about to happen: that they will die, lose their minds, or have a heart attack. Most attacks reach peak intensity within ten minutes. Afterward, individuals live in dread of another one.

**Panic disorder** develops when attacks recur or apprehension about them becomes so intense that individuals cannot function normally. Full-blown panic disorder occurs in about 1.6 percent of all adults in the course of a lifetime and usually develops before age 30. The lifetime risk of panic disorder is about 2.5 times greater in women than men.[51] Parents, siblings, and children of individuals with panic disorders also are more likely to develop them than are others.[52]

The two primary treatments for panic disorder are (1) *cognitive-behavioural therapy*, which teaches specific strategies for coping with symptoms like rapid breathing; and (2) *medication*. Treatment helps as many as 90 percent of those with panic disorder improve significantly or recover completely, usually within six to eight weeks. Individuals who receive cognitive-behavioural therapy as

well as medication are less likely to suffer relapses than those taking medication alone and often can learn to control their symptoms without drugs.[62]

In **post-traumatic stress disorder (PTSD)** individuals re-experience terror and helplessness they have experienced in the past again and again in their dreams or intrusive thoughts. In the past, PTSD was viewed as a psychological response to out-of-the-ordinary stressors, such as captivity or combat. However, other experiences can also forever change the way in which people view themselves and their world. Thousands of individuals experience or witness traumatic events, such as fires or floods. According to recent research, almost half of car accident victims may develop PTSD. Those who were seriously injured are especially vulnerable.[63] Children, in particular, are likely to develop PTSD symptoms if they have witnessed a loved one or friend being assaulted or have been sexually abused.[64]

Those with pre-existing psychological problems may be the most vulnerable. In the brain, stress hormones linked to powerful emotions may help create long-lasting memories of events. The sooner trauma survivors receive psychological

## Simon Ibell—Live Every Day

Sometimes we are fortunate in life to meet remarkable people with amazing stories to tell. One such person is Simon Ibell, an advocate for Human Potential and a Role Model for Persons with Disabilities. Simon has a condition known as MPS II (mucopolysacharridosis) or Hunter Syndrome. MPS II is a rare and progressive disease caused by an enzyme deficiency. It affects most of his major organs and his joints and is both painful and debilitating. However, "debilitating" does not enter into Simon's vocabulary; he refuses to allow this progressive disorder to deter him, and in so doing, he has defied all medical predictions and surpassed all expectations.

Simon received his degree in Leisure Services Administration at the University of Victoria in June 2002. A few weeks into his Master of Arts in Human Kinetics with specialization in Sports Psychology and Human Potential, Simon had to move east to participate in a medical trial at the University of North Carolina–Chapel Hill Medical Center. If successful, this trial and the enzyme replacement therapy treatment would prolong his life and stop the progression of MPS II.

Living with MPS II has taught Simon that every moment of life is precious. Taking a leaf from Gandhi, Simon lives every day like it's his last and learns every day like he will live forever. The weekly trip to North Carolina continued for two years before the enzyme replacement therapy became available in Toronto. Flight cancellations, five hours of infusions, and hours of testing were no deterrent for the man who is well-known for his positive attitude and acceptance of his circumstance. This attitude has been the result of enormous respect from many who have sought his counsel and his friendship.

Friendship and friends helped Simon get one step toward one of his goals. The Ontario government refused to fund Elaprase, the essential new MPS II enzyme replacement drug. Outraged by the government's thoughtless attitude, which was in conflict with Simon's goal to give children with MPS II a chance of a prolonged life, Simon received widespread support from friends from across

Simon Ibell and good friend Steve Nash during an advocacy campaign for MPS.

Source: Courtesy of Simon Ibell

Canada. With lifelong friend and NBA all-star Steve Nash, Simon delivered a strong message, which was played on YouTube and received widespread attention from the Canadian media. The message together with the thousands of signatures and support from friends resulted in the Ontario government agreeing to fund Elaprase.

Simon's vision is to create extensive awareness of his rare but serious condition and to generate funds for research and a cure for MPS II and all MPS diseases. Personally, Simon has already come a long way in achieving his second goal: the perception of the difference and the tendency to automatically earmark that difference as a deficiency. On first meeting Simon there is little doubt of the physical difference, but after that initial meeting, "deficiency" is not a word that ever comes to mind.

*continued*

Whether listening to him on the podium, on the coaching team, or in conversation, all have left feeling better about themselves and richer for the experience.

Simon compares his survival to sport: often competing against the impossible and winning a personal goal. When awarded the Kinsman Foundation's award for courage in Grade 12, Simon said life was like sport: we do not always get the desired result, but if we give our best and play fairly, then we get the opportunity to keep going. Sport has been Simon's lifeline; it is his medicine and his passion. He has inspired hundreds of students and teachers with his courage, determination, compassion, and respect.

A strong believer that differences are not deficiencies, Simon put his belief to the test in the summer of 2002, with his Bike 4 MPS odyssey, which involved cycling the length of Vancouver Island (500 kilometres). A true role model for the role models, Simon was accompanied on his ride by numerous family and friends, such as Steve Nash and Olympic gold medallist Simon Whitfield.

His Bike 4 MPS efforts were recognized and applauded when he was presented the Spirit of Sport Story of the Year Award at the 2003 Canadian Sport Awards. He was also awarded the Queen's Golden Jubilee Commemorative Medal for Her Majesty Queen Elizabeth the Second.

Currently, Simon heads up his Ibellieve Foundation (www.ibellieve.com) and sits on the Board of Directors for the Canadian MPS Society (www.mpssociety.ca). He is also the Athlete Relations & Communications Manager for Right To Play Canada (www.righttoplay.ca).

This story ends with one of Simon's favourite quotations, from Terry Fox, another great Canadian: "I may have a disability but it's not a handicap."

---

help, the better they are likely to fare. Behavioural, cognitive, and psychodynamic therapy can help individuals suffering PTSD; however, new research suggests that trauma produces changes in the brain that impedes a person's ability to think and talk about the events. Traditional therapies can sometimes be debilitating for PTSD sufferers. Belleruth Naparstek, a renowned psychotherapist, suggests that guided imagery uses what is most accessible in the traumatized brain to help with the healing. Often individuals who have PTSD will respond to nonverbal engagement, such as images, symbols, metaphors, drawing, writing, conscious breathing, and movement.[65]

## Obsessive-Compulsive Disorder

Another type of anxiety disorder is known as **obsessive-compulsive disorder** (**OCD**). Some individuals suffer only from an *obsession,* a recurring idea, thought, or image that they realize, at least initially, is senseless. The most common obsessions are repetitive thoughts of violence, contamination, and doubt. Most people with OCD also suffer from a *compulsion,* repetitive behaviour performed according to certain rules or in a stereotyped fashion. The most common compulsions involve hand washing, cleaning, hoarding useless items, counting, or checking (for example, making sure dozens of times that a door is locked).[66]

Individuals with OCD realize that their thoughts or behaviours are bizarre, but they cannot resist or control them. Eventually, the obsessions or compulsions consume a great deal of time and significantly interfere with normal routine, job functioning, social activities, and relationships with others.

OCD is believed to have biological roots. It may be a result of gene abnormalities, head injury, or even an autoimmune reaction after childhood infection with the strep bacteria. Treatment may consist of cognitive therapy to correct irrational assumptions, behavioural techniques such as progressively limiting the amount of time someone obsessed with cleanliness can spend washing and scrubbing, and medication. About 70 to 80 percent of those with OCD improve with treatment.

## Depressive Disorders

Depression, the world's most common mental ailment, affects the brain, the mind, and the body in complex ways. It is the leading cause of years lived with disability.[67] Stress-related events may trigger half of all depressive episodes; great trauma in childhood can increase vulnerability to depression later in life.[68] Approximately 8 percent of Canadian adults will experience major depression at some time in their lives and the onset of depression usually occurs during adolescence.[69] An estimated 15 to 40 percent of college-age men and women (18- to 24-year-olds) may develop depression.[70]

Comparing everyday blues to a **depressive disorder** is like comparing a cold to pneumonia. Major depression can destroy a person's joy for living. Food, friends, sex, or any form of pleasure no longer appeals. It is impossible to concentrate on work and responsibilities. Depressed individuals may fight back tears throughout the day and toss and turn through long, empty nights. Thoughts of death or suicide may push into their minds.

But there is good news: depression is a treatable disease. Psychotherapy is remarkably effective for mild depression. In more serious cases, **antidepressant** medication can lead to dramatic improvement in 40 to 80 percent of depressed patients.

Exercise also is a good way to both prevent and treat psychological problems. Several studies have shown that exercise effectively lifts mild to moderate depression; for some patients with major depression, exercise may be more effective than drug treatment.[71] In a study of 150 individuals diagnosed with major depression, one group was assigned to four months of walking, jogging, or cycling; another took antidepressant medication; and a third both exercised and took medication. At the end of four months, all had improved significantly. Six months later, the exercisers were in better shape physically and mentally—and much less likely to have suffered a relapse. At ten months, the chance of a patient still being depressed was reduced by 50 percent for every 50 minutes of current weekly exercise.[72] Among older adults, low-intensity exercise that included weight training improved overall mood more than aerobic exercise alone.[73]

© iStockphoto.com/Daniel Bobrowsky

▲ A number of factors can contribute to the development of depression during your college or university years, including stressful events, poor academic performance, loneliness, and relationship problems.

## Major Depression

The simplest definition of **major depression** is sadness that does not end. The incidence of major depression has soared over the last two decades, especially among young adults.

The characteristic symptoms of major depression include:

- Feeling depressed, sad, empty, discouraged, tearful
- Loss of interest or pleasure in once-enjoyable activities
- Eating more or less than usual and either gaining or losing weight
- Having trouble sleeping or sleeping much more than usual
- Feeling slowed down, or feeling restless and unable to sit still
- Lack of energy
- Feeling helpless, hopeless, worthless, inadequate
- Difficulty concentrating, forgetfulness, not able to think clearly or make decisions
- Persistent thoughts of death or suicide
- Withdrawal from others, lack of interest in sex
- Physical symptoms (headaches, digestive problems, aches and pains)

Neuroscience, the study of the brain, has revealed that major depression is as physical as diabetes or heart disease. Dozens of brain-imaging studies have revealed abnormalities in the front part of the brain, which is involved in regulating emotions, and the shrinking of certain brain regions during depressive episodes.[74]

Most cases of major depression can be treated successfully, usually with psychotherapy, medication, or both. Psychotherapy alone works in more than half of mild-to-moderate episodes of major depression. Psychotherapy helps individuals pinpoint the life problems that contribute to their depression, identify negative or distorted thinking patterns, explore behaviours that contribute to depression, and regain a sense of control and pleasure in life. Two specific psychotherapies—cognitive-behavioural therapy and interpersonal therapy—have proven as helpful as antidepressant drugs in treating mild cases of depression, although they take longer than medication to achieve results.

Three of four patients treated for depression take antidepressant medications.[75] These prescription drugs generally take three or four weeks to produce significant benefits and may not have their full impact for up to eight weeks.

Newer antidepressants that boost levels of the neurotransmitter serotonin have proven equally effective as older medications, but their side effects are different. Patients report higher rates of diarrhea, nausea, insomnia, and headache.[76] Older drugs are more likely to adversely affect the heart and blood pressure and to cause dry mouth, constipation, dizziness, blurred vision, and tremors. Unfortunately, only one-third of Canadians are aware of new treatment options that are more effective, safe, and tolerable, especially younger Canadians, with 27 percent of those 18 to 34 years old knowing of them, compared to 35 percent of those aged 35 to 44, 42 percent of those aged 45 to 64, and 32 percent of those 65 years of age and older.[77] Younger people are also less likely to believe that treatment can allow sufferers of depression and anxiety to be symptom-free.[78]

Yet, one more study suggests that modest exercise—30 minutes on a treadmill or stationary bicycle three times a week—has proven effective against major depression.[79]

Eighty percent of people who have one episode of depression are likely to have another. Because of this high risk of recurrence, many psychiatrists now view depression as a chronic disease and advise ongoing treatment with antidepressants. However, little is known about the long-term effects of these medications.[80]

For individuals who cannot take antidepressant medications because of medical problems, or who do not improve with psychotherapy or drugs, *electroconvulsive therapy* (ECT)—the administration of a controlled electrical current through electrodes attached to the scalp—remains the safest and most effective treatment. About 50 percent of depressed individuals who do not get better with antidepressant medication and psychotherapy improve after ECT.

## Bipolar Disorder (Manic Depression)

**Bipolar disorder,** or manic depression, consists of mood swings that may take individuals from *manic* states of feeling euphoric and energetic to *depressive* states of utter despair. In episodes of full mania, they may become so impulsive and out of touch with reality that they endanger their careers, relationships, health, or even survival. One percent of the Canadian population suffers from this serious but treatable disorder, which affects both sexes and all races. For bipolar disorder, it is generally accepted that the ratio between men and women is approximately equal.[81] However, research also shows that women are hospitalized for bipolar disorder at significantly higher rates than men.[82]

The characteristic symptoms of bipolar disorder include:

- Mood swings (from happy to miserable, optimistic to despairing)
- Changes in thinking (thoughts speeding through one's mind, unrealistic self-confidence, difficulty concentrating, delusions, hallucinations)
- Changes in behaviour (sudden immersion in plans and projects, talking very rapidly and much more than usual, excessive spending, impaired judgment, impulsive sexual involvement)
- Changes in physical condition (less need for sleep, increased energy, fewer health complaints than usual)

During manic periods, individuals may make grandiose plans or take dangerous risks. But they often plunge from this highest of highs to a horribly low depressive episode, during which they may feel sad, hopeless, and helpless and develop other symptoms of major depression. The risk of suicide is very real.

Professional therapy is essential in treating bipolar disorders. Mood-stabilizing medications are the cornerstone of treatment, although psychotherapy plays a critical role in helping individuals understand their illness and rebuild their lives. Most individuals continue taking medication indefinitely after remission of their symptoms because the risk of recurrence is high.

## Seasonal Affective Disorder (SAD)

**Seasonal affective disorder (SAD)** is a condition that affects one to three percent of the Canadian population. Compared to clinical depression, where people have severe bouts of feeling down all of the time, low energy, problems with sleep and appetite, and have difficulty functioning at home and at work, people with SAD experience these symptoms only during the fall and winter seasons.[83] According to information from the University of British Columbia Mood Disorders Centre,[84] another 15 percent of people have the "winter blues"—similar symptoms to SAD, but not to the point of being diagnosed with clinical depression.

Some research suggests that SAD might result from shorter day lengths, where exposure to sunlight is limited. Treatments for SAD include light therapy or phototherapy. Patients with SAD are exposed to bright, artificial, fluorescent light for as little as 30 minutes a day. Use of these special light boxes have resulted in significant improvements in 60 to 70 percent of SAD patients.[85]

People may experience nausea, headaches, or eye strain when they first begin their treatment. There are no known long-term harmful effects of light therapy, but people with medical conditions such as retinal disease or diabetes should check with their eye doctor before beginning light therapy. People with bipolar disorder should also check with their family physician. Other treatments for SAD include antidepressant medications, counselling, and spending more time outdoors during the winter months.

## Why Are So Many Young People Depressed?

At one time, young people were considered immune to sadness. Now mental health professionals know better. Even preschoolers can develop symptoms of depression, such as irritability, sadness, and withdrawal.[86]

"Depression is the most common emotional problem in adolescence and the single greatest risk factor for teen suicide," says child psychiatrist Peter Jensen, director of the Centre for the Advancement of Children's Mental Health. He also notes that depression rates have been rising over the last half century: "Teens born in the 1980s are more likely to develop depression than those who were born in the 1970s, whose rate of depression is higher than for those born in the 1960s."[87]

No one knows the reason for this steady surge in sadness, but experts point to the breakdown of families, the pressures of the information age, and increased isolation. "Social environment doesn't cause depression," explains psychiatrist John March, M.D., who is heading a nationwide study of therapies for teen depression. "But environmental stress can bring out depression in people who are susceptible. Depression is more than teenage angst. It is an illness of the central nervous system that is common, impairing, and lethal."[88]

A family history of depression greatly increases a young person's vulnerability. In one recent study of high school students diagnosed with depression, family members of depressed adolescents had much higher rates of major depression.[89] Evidence suggests that many different genes may act together and in combination with other factors to cause mood disorders. The exact genetic factors that are involved still remain unknown.[90]

Stress may predispose individuals to an initial episode.[91] Several factors associated with physical illness may contribute to the onset or worsening of depression. These include the psychological impact of disability, decline in quality of life, and the loss of relationships.

Medication side effects may also be a contributing factor. Physical illness may also contribute directly to the onset of depression by affecting physiological mechanisms such as neurotransmitters, hormones, and the immune system.[92]

However, the strongest predictor of depression might be cigarette smoking. Depressed teens may smoke because they think smoking will make them feel better, but nicotine alters brain chemistry and actually worsens symptoms of depression.[93]

Depression can be hard to recognize. Many depressed people don't look or act sad. Rather than crying, young people may snap grouchily at parents or friends or burst into angry tirades. Some turn to alcohol or drugs in hopes of feeling better; others become depressed after they start abusing these substances. As they drop out of activities and pull away from friends, depressed people spend more time alone. Schoolwork or part-time and full-time work suffers, and many people are labelled as underachievers. Those whose anger explodes in public are branded as troublemakers.

## Suicide

Suicidal behaviour is an important and preventable public-health problem in Canada. While not a mental illness, suicidal behaviour is highly correlated with mental illness and can be a tragic consequence of emotional and psychological problems. It usually marks the end of a long road of hopelessness, helplessness, and despair. In Canada, suicide accounts for 2 percent of all deaths. It is also one of the leading causes of death in both men and women from adolescence to middle age, accounting for 24 percent of all deaths among 15- to 24-year-olds and 16 percent among 25- to 44-year-olds.[94]

According to a Report of the Advisory Group on Suicide Prevention—*Acting on What We Know: Preventing Youth Suicide in First Nations,* there is an unprecedented level of concern about First Nations youth suicide where it is estimated to be five to six times higher than that of non-Aboriginal youth.[95]

Suicidal behaviour that does not result in death (attempted suicide) is a sign of serious distress. Individuals between 15 and 44 years of age account for 73 percent of hospital admissions for attempted suicide.[96]

## What Leads to Suicide?

Researchers have looked for explanations for suicide by studying everything from phases of the moon to seasons (suicides peak in the spring and early summer) to birth order in the family.[97] Yet they have found no conclusive answers. A constellation of influences—mental disorders, personality traits, biologic and genetic vulnerability, medical illness, and psychosocial stressors—may combine in ways that lower an individual's threshold of vulnerability. School pressures, social difficulties, confusion about sexual orientation, family problems, and drug and alcohol use and abuse may also be contributors. The risk of suicide is higher in people who live in cities, are single, have a low income, or are unemployed.[98] No one factor in itself may ever explain fully why a person chooses death.

Some specific factors believed to be linked to suicide are listed here:

- More than 95 percent of those who commit suicide have a mental disorder. Suicide also is a risk for those with schizophrenia and other personality disorders.
- Many of those who commit suicide drink beforehand and their use of alcohol may lower their inhibitions. Since alcohol itself is a depressant, it can intensify the despondency suicidal individuals are already feeling.
- Drug abuse also can alter thinking and lower inhibitions against suicide.
- Hopelessness and helplessness may be the most common contributing factors in suicide. When hope dies, individuals expect the worst possible outcomes for their problems.
- One of every four people who attempt suicide has a family member who also tried to commit suicide, although a family history of suicide is not in itself considered a predictor of suicide.
- Investigators have found abnormalities in the brain chemistry of those who complete suicide, especially low levels of a metabolite of the neurotransmitter serotonin. There are indications that individuals with a deficiency of this substance may have as much as a ten times greater risk of committing suicide than those with higher levels.
- Access to guns can add to the risk of suicide.
- Major life crises such as job changes, births, financial reversals, divorce, and recent retirement can increase the risk of suicide.
- Longstanding, intense conflict with family members or other significant people may add to the danger.

## Gender Differences

In Canada, overall mortality rates from suicide among men were nearly four times higher than among women (19.5 versus 5.1 per 1000, respectively). Rates among women show three peaks: the late teens (15 to 19 years), in middle age (45 to 59 years), and among older seniors (80 to 84 years).[99] Medical symptoms, having a friend attempt or

## Strategies for Prevention

### If You Start Thinking About Suicide

At some point, the thought of ending it all—the disappointments, problems, and bad feelings—may cross your mind. This experience isn't unusual. But if the idea of taking your life persists or intensifies, you should respond as you would to other warnings of potential threats to your health—by getting the help you need:

- ▲ *Talk to a mental health professional.* If you have a therapist, call immediately. If not, call a suicide hotline.
- ▲ *Find someone you trust and can talk with honestly about what you're feeling.* If you suffer from depression or another mental disorder, educate trusted friends or relatives about your condition so they are prepared if called upon to help.
- ▲ *Write down your more uplifting thoughts.* A simple record of your hopes for the future and the people you value in your life can remind you of why your own life is worth continuing.
- ▲ *Avoid drugs and alcohol.* Most suicides are the result of sudden, uncontrolled impulses, and drugs and alcohol can make it harder to resist these destructive urges.
- ▲ *Go to the hospital.* Hospitalization can sometimes be the best way to protect your health and safety.

complete suicide, illicit drug use, and a history of mental health problems also increase the risk for females.

For men, mortality rates rise dramatically in the late teens (15 to 19 years) and early twenties (20 to 24 years). They continue to be high until middle age (40 to 44 years) when they start to decrease.[100] Among males, risk factors include carrying a weapon at school, same-sex romantic attraction, a family history of suicide or suicide attempts, and easy household access to guns.

## Suicide Prevention

Researchers also have identified factors that protect us from suicide. Feeling connected to parents and family is important. For females, emotional well-being is also protective. A high grade-point average in school can be an additional protective factor for males. High parental expectations for school achievement, more people living in a household, and religiosity were protective for some of the males, but not for the females. Availability of counselling services at school and parental presence at key times during the day were protective for some females, but not for males.

If someone you know has talked about suicide, behaved unpredictably, or suddenly emerged from a severe depression into a calm, settled state of mind, don't rule out the possibility that he or she may attempt suicide.

✔ Encourage your friend to talk. Ask concerned questions. Listen attentively. Show that you take the person's feelings seriously and truly care.

✔ Don't offer trite reassurances. List reasons to go on living.

✔ Suggest alternative solutions to problems. Encourage positive action, such as getting away for a while to gain a better perspective on a problem.

✔ Don't be afraid to ask whether your friend has considered suicide. The opportunity to talk about thoughts of suicide may be an enormous relief, and—contrary to a longstanding myth—will not fix the idea of suicide more firmly in a person's mind.

✔ Don't think that people who talk about killing themselves never carry out their threat. Most individuals who commit suicide give definite indications of their intent to die.

More than 80 percent of those who commit suicide have seen a physician about a medical complaint within the six months preceding suicide. To help general physicians identify people at risk of suicide, researchers have developed a set of four crucial questions:

✔ Have you ever had a period of two weeks or more when you had trouble falling asleep, staying asleep, waking up too early, or sleeping too much?

✔ Have you ever had two weeks or more during which you felt sad, blue, or depressed, or when you lost interest and pleasure in things you usually cared about or enjoyed?

✔ Has there ever been a period of two weeks or more when you felt worthless, sinful, or guilty?

✔ Has there ever been a period of time when you felt that life was hopeless?

Anyone who answers yes to these questions should be referred immediately to a mental health professional.

The Suicide Prevention Advisory Group has made four key recommendations to address specific factors affecting First Nations youth: (1) increasing knowledge about what works in suicide prevention; (2) developing more integrated health-care service; (3) supporting community-driven approaches; and (4) creating strategies for building youth identity, resilience, and culture.[101] These recommendations might be the building blocks for all suicide-prevention programs.

## Attention Disorders

**Attention deficit/hyperactivity disorder (ADHD)** is a common psychiatric diagnosis of childhood.[102] Its causes are complex and include genetic and biological factors, including differences within the brain. Research has shown that children with ADHD often have smaller overall brain volumes than others, particularly in the right frontal region, an area of the brain associated with the processes of paying attention and focusing concentration.[103]

Between 40 and 70 percent of youngsters with ADHD do not outgrow this condition. Adults with ADHD have one or more of three primary symptoms: hyperactivity, impulsivity, and distractibility. Rather than scooting around a room, they may tap their fingers or jiggle their feet. Some appear calm and organized but cannot concentrate long enough to finish reading a paragraph or follow a list of directions. Others, on a whim, go on buying sprees or take wild dares.

The impairments related to ADHD in college and university students can affect academic success. Findings from a research study suggests that students suffering from ADHD reported more frequent academic problems, had lower grade-point averages, and were likely to be on academic probation. Findings also showed that students with ADHD did not differ in psychosocial problems as compared to students who did not have ADHD.[104]

## Schizophrenia

**Schizophrenia,** a brain disease and one of the most debilitating mental disorders, profoundly impairs an individual's sense of reality.

The symptoms of schizophrenia include:

✔ Hallucinations—seeing or hearing things that do not exist

✔ Delusions—false or irrational beliefs

✔ Inability to think in a logical manner

✔ Talking in rambling or incoherent ways

✔ Making odd or purposeless movements or not moving at all

✔ Repeating others' words or mimicking their gestures

✔ Showing few, if any, feelings; responding with inappropriate emotions

✔ Lacking will or motivation to complete a task or accomplish something

✔ Functioning at a much lower level than in the past at work, in interpersonal relations, or in taking care of themselves

Schizophrenia affects 1 percent of the Canadian population. Fifty-two percent of hospitalizations for schizophrenia in general hospitals are among adults 25 to 44 years of age. Current research shows that hospitalization rates for schizophrenia in general hospitals are increasing among young and middle-aged men.[105]

Schizophrenia has a profound effect on an individual's ability to function effectively in all aspects of life. This includes self-care, family relationships, income, school, employment, housing, community, and social life.[106] Researchers have identified early markers of schizophrenia, including impaired social skills, intellectual ability, and capacity for organization.[107]

Schizophrenia might be the result of a failure in brain development that occurs very early in life. The underlying defect is probably present before birth. Schizophrenia has a strong genetic basis and is not the result of upbringing, social conditions, or traumatic experiences.[108]

The mortality associated with schizophrenia is one of the most distressing consequences of this disorder. Approximately 40 to 60 percent of individuals with schizophrenia attempt suicide, and they are between 15 and 25 times more likely than the general population to die from a suicide attempt.[109]

Minimizing the impact of this serious illness depends mainly on early diagnosis and appropriate treatment and support. A comprehensive treatment program includes antipsychotic medication, education, family support, rehabilitation, cognitive therapy, and integrated addictions programs.[110]

▲ "My Head Is Going Round and Round," a drawing by a patient suffering from schizophrenia, expresses the anxiety and agitation that may occur with this brain abnormality.

*"My Head Is Going Round and Round" from Art As Healing by Edward Adamson/Coventure, Limited*

## Overcoming Problems of the Mind

Mental illness costs our society billions of dollars each year in lost work time and productivity, employee turnover, disability payments, and death.[111] Although in many cases mental illnesses can be treated effectively, the stigma attached presents a serious barrier not only to diagnosis and treatment, but also to acceptance in our communities. The result is stereotyping, fear, embarrassment, anger, and avoidance behaviours. People with mental illnesses often delay seeking health care, avoid following through with recommended treatment when they do ask for assistance, and avoid sharing their concerns with family, friends, and co-workers.[112]

The Canadian Alliance for Mental Illness and Mental Health (CAMIMH) advocates that preventing discrimination against victims of mental illness should be a top priority in improving the mental health of Canadians. Educating the public and the media about mental illness is the first step. Developing and enforcing policies that address discrimination and human rights violations is the next.[113]

## ???? Where Can I Turn for Help?

As a student, your best source for identifying local services may be your college or university's health unit. Medical personnel can tell you about general and mental health counselling available on campus, school-based support groups, community-based programs, and special emergency services.

There are also many new initiatives in Canada that have begun to relieve the burden of mood disorders. They include not only improved recognition and use of effective treatments, but also education for individuals and families and for the community. An important document released by the Canadian Mental Health Association in 2004 called *Your Education—Your Future, A Guide to College and University for Students with Psychiatric Disabilities*[114] is one such document. This resource focuses on particular aspects of college and university experience and how students who are faced with mood disorders and mental illness can improve their level of self-care while studying at an academic institution. The full report is available online at www.cmha.ca/youreducation.

The report includes information about how students can ask for advice on arranging academic accommodations, work out emergency plans, and engage others in advocating on their behalf.

Within the community, you may find help through community mental health centres and local hospitals. Local branches of national service organizations, such as United Way, Alcoholics Anonymous, and other 12-step programs, may also be helpful. You can call the psychiatric or psychological association in your city or province for the names of licensed professionals. Your family doctor may also be able to help.

The telephone directory is another good resource. There you will find listings for crisis intervention, violence prevention, and child-abuse prevention programs; drug treatment information; shelters for battered women; senior citizen centres; and self-help and counselling services. Some services have special hotlines for coping with emergencies.

## Types of Therapists

Only professionally trained individuals who have met federal or provincial licensing requirements are certified as psychiatrists, psychologists, social workers, psychiatric nurses, and marriage and family therapists. Before selecting any of these mental health professionals, be sure to check the person's background and credentials.

- ✔ **Psychiatrists** are licensed medical doctors (M.D.) who have training in various forms of psychotherapy and psychopharmacology. They can prescribe medication.
- ✔ **Psychologists** have completed a university graduate degree program and required licensing. They cannot prescribe medication.
- ✔ **Social workers** are university undergraduates and master's degree graduates. Certification or licensing depends on the province.

Other therapists include pastoral counsellors, stress-management counsellors, psychoanalysts, psychotherapists, and alcohol and drug counsellors.

## Options for Treatment

The term **psychotherapy** refers to any type of counselling based on the exchange of words, guided imagery, or healing work in the context of the unique relationship that develops between a mental health professional and a person seeking help. Most mental health professionals today are trained in a variety of psychotherapeutic techniques and tailor their approach to the problem, personality, and needs of each person seeking their help.

## Psychodynamic Psychotherapy

**Psychodynamic psychotherapy** takes into account the role of early experiences and unconscious influences in *actively* shaping behaviour. Psychodynamic treatments work toward the goal of providing greater insight into problems and bringing about behavioural change. Therapy may consist of a certain number of sessions or may continue for several years. According to current thinking, psychotherapy can actually rewire the network of neurons within the brain in ways that ease distress and improve functioning in many areas of daily life.

## Interpersonal Therapy

**Interpersonal therapy (IPT)** focuses on relationships in order to help individuals deal with unrecognized feelings and needs and improve their communication skills. IPT concentrates on the current problems of getting along with others. Individuals with major depression, chronic difficulties developing relationships, chronic mild depression, or bulimia are most likely to benefit.

## Cognitive-Behavioural Therapy

**Cognitive-behavioural therapy (CBT)** focuses on inappropriate or inaccurate thoughts or beliefs to help individuals break out of a distorted way of thinking. The techniques of CBT include identification of an individual's beliefs and attitudes, recognition of negative thought patterns, and education in alternative ways of thinking. Individuals with major depression or anxiety disorders are most likely to benefit. In a recent study, cognitive therapy proved at least as effective as medication for long-term treatment of severe depression.[115]

**Behaviour therapy** strives to substitute healthier ways of behaving for maladaptive patterns used in the past. Its premise is that distressing psychological symptoms are learned responses that can be modified or unlearned. Some therapists believe that changing behaviour also changes how people think and feel. Behaviour therapies work best for disorders characterized by specific, abnormal patterns of acting, such as alcohol and drug abuse, anxiety disorders, and phobias, and for individuals who want to change bad habits.

## Psychiatric Drug Therapy

Medications that alter brain chemistry and relieve psychiatric symptoms have brought great hope and help to millions of people. Thanks to the recent development of a new generation of more precise and effective **psychiatric drugs,** success rates for treating many common and disabling disorders—depression, panic disorder, schizophrenia, and others—have soared. Often used in conjunction with psychotherapy, sometimes used as the primary treatment, these medications have revolutionized mental health care.[116]

Psychiatric medications affect every aspect of a person's physical, mental, and emotional functioning. Some take effect immediately; others take several weeks to relieve symptoms. A few continue to exert their effects even after an individual discontinues their use. When taken appropriately, psychiatric agents can alleviate tremendous suffering and reduce the financial and personal costs of mental illness by lessening the need for hospitalization and by restoring an individual's ability to function normally, to work, and to contribute to society. But they do have side effects and must be used with care.

## Alternative Mind–Mood Medicine

Increasingly consumers are trying natural products, such as herbs and enzymes, that claim to have psychological effects. Because they are not classified as drugs, they have not undergone the rigorous scientific testing required of psychiatric medications, and some medical professionals are concerned that little is known about their safety or efficacy. "Natural" doesn't mean risk-free. Opium and cocaine are natural substances that have dramatic and potentially deadly effects on the mind.[117]

St. John's wort (named after St. John the Baptist because the yellow flowers of the *Hypericum perforatum* plant bloom in June, the month of his execution) has been used to treat anxiety and depression in Europe for many years. Although more than 24 clinical trials have investigated St. John's wort, many researchers feel that most had significant flaws in design.[118] Health Canada is concerned about this herbal product because new scientific studies suggest that it may interact with certain prescription drugs, when used in combination. Drug interaction can significantly alter or diminish the effectiveness of some prescription medications.[119] Side effects include dizziness, abdominal pain and bloating, constipation, nausea, fatigue, and dry mouth. St. John's wort should not be taken in combination with other prescription antidepressants.

**CHAPTER 3**

**Making This Chapter Work for You**

1. Psychological health is influenced by all of the following *except*
   a. spiritual health
   b. physical agility
   c. culture
   d. a firm grasp on reality

2. Emotional intelligence encompasses which of the following components?
   a. creativity, sense of humour, scholastic achievement
   b. integrity, honesty, and perseverance
   c. piety, tolerance, and self-esteem
   d. empathy, self-awareness, and altruism

3. Which of the following activities can contribute to a lasting sense of personal fulfillment?
   a. becoming a Big Sister or Big Brother to a child from an inner-city single-parent home
   b. using drugs to enhance your sense of comfort at a party
   c. being a regular participant in an Internet chat room
   d. going on a shopping spree

4. Individuals who have developed a sense of mastery over their lives are
   a. skilled at controlling the actions of others.
   b. usually passive and silent when faced with a situation they don't like.
   c. aware that their locus of control is internal, not external.
   d. aware that their locus of control is external, not internal.

5. A mental disorder can be described as
   a. a condition associated with migraine headaches and narcolepsy.
   b. a condition that is usually caused by severe trauma to the brain.
   c. a behavioural or psychological disorder that impairs an individual's ability to conduct one or more important activities of daily life.
   d. a psychological disorder that is easily controlled with medication and a change in diet.

6. Which of the following statements about psychological health is correct?
   a. Individuals with social phobia typically enjoy various social situations.
   b. Mentally healthy individuals value themselves, accept their limitations, and carry out their responsibilities.
   c. A psychologically healthy individual often feels out of control.
   d. A psychologically healthy individual has difficulty managing their moods.

7. Which of the following statements about anxiety disorders is true?
   a. Anxiety disorders are the least prevalent type of mental illness.
   b. An individual suffering from a panic attack may mistake her symptoms for a heart attack.
   c. The primary symptom of obsessive-compulsive disorder is irrational, intense, and persistent fear of a specific object or situation.
   d. Generalized anxiety disorders respond to systematic desensitization behaviour therapy.

8. Some characteristic symptoms of major depression are
   a. difficulty concentrating, lack of energy, and eating more than usual.
   b. exaggerated sense of euphoria and energy.
   c. palpitations, sweating, numbness, and tingling sensations.
   d. talking in rambling ways, inability to think in a logical manner, and delusions.

9. A person may be at higher risk of committing suicide if
   a. he is taking antidepressant medication.
   b. he lives in a rural environment and is married.
   c. he has been diagnosed with hyperactivity disorder.
   d. he has lost his job because of alcoholism.

10. Which of the following statements is true?
   a. Psychiatric medications do not have any known side effects.
   b. Psychiatric medications affect every aspect of a person's physical, mental, and emotional functioning.
   c. Psychologists are usually trained in a variety of psychotherapeutic techniques and are licensed to prescribe psychiatric medications.
   d. Interpersonal therapy focuses on inappropriate or inaccurate thoughts or beliefs.

Answers to these questions can be found on page 450.

## Self Responsibility

*When we learn to manage our emotions long enough to stop and shift our attention to the quieter message of the heart, we can gain a wider perspective on any situation, often saving ourselves from hurt, frustration, and pain.*

It is not always possible to manage stressful situations with skill, energy, and enthusiasm, but you have to start somewhere. Being responsible for lifestyle choices that enhance your well-being is one step. The other—asking for help when you need it—can make an impossible situation or dream seem possible. Today, ask yourself who might provide support for

## Social Responsibility

*When you do nothing, you feel overwhelmed and powerless. But when you get involved, you feel the sense of hope and accomplishment that comes from knowing you are working to make things better.*

**Unknown**

problems you are facing or future visions you have. This would be an example of moving from preparation to action.

If you have energy and time to help others, find an organization or agency that aligns with your values and do something for someone else. You will be making a difference for others and yourself.

## Critical Thinking

1. Would you say that you view life positively or negatively? Would your friends and family agree with your assessment? Ask two of your closest friends for feedback about what they perceive are your typical responses to a problematic situation. Are these indicative of positive attitudes? If not, what could you do to become more psychologically positive?

2. Research has indicated that many homeless men and women are in need of outpatient psychiatric care, often because they suffer from chronic mental illnesses or alcoholism. Presently, in many provinces, health-care dollars are scarce for proper treatment and prevention programs. How do you feel when you pass homeless individuals who seem disoriented or out of touch with reality? Who should take responsibility for their welfare? Should they be forced to undergo treatment at psychiatric institutions?

3. You have been prescribed a psychoactive drug to help alleviate symptoms of a mental disorder. What questions would you ask your family physician or psychiatrist before you begin taking this drug? How could you find out about any reported risks or side effects? How would you know if the medication was working?

# CENGAGENOW™

If your textbook package includes CengageNOW™, go to http://west.cengagenow.com/ilrn/ to link to CengageNOW™ for Health, your online study tool. First take the **Pre-test** for this chapter to get your personalized **Study Plan,** which will identify topics you need to review and direct you to the appropriate resources. Then take the **Post-test** to determine what concepts you have mastered and what you still need work on.

## SITES & BYTES

**Canadian Association of Social Workers (CASW)**
**www.casw-acts.ca**

Find out about social work in Canada and abroad and information about social work regulation.

**Canadian Institute of Stress (CIS)**
**www.stresscanada.org**

The site for the Canadian Institute of Stress, founded in 1979 by Drs. Hans Selye and Richard Earle, offers programs, consultation, and tools for workplaces and individuals, and certification training and distance education for professionals.

**Canadian Mental Health Association**
**www.cmha.ca**

This site has numerous and current reports on mental illness and mental health as well as links to other sites that provide mental health information.

**Canadian Mental Health Association—Your Education Your Future—A Guide to College and University for Students with Psychiatric Disabilities**
**www.cmha.ca/youreducation**

This site provides college and university students with a valuable resource—information gathered from colleges and universities across Canada and from students with psychiatric disabilities. The guide, organized into sections, can help students and families who are interested in finding out more about the rewards and challenges of higher education.

## Canadian Psychological Association
www.cpa.ca

From "Need a Psychologist?" to "Psychology Quick Facts"and "Psychology Works Fact Sheets," you can browse for information about psychology and mental health. There is also information for individuals wanting to discover how to become a psychologist in Canada.

## Centre for Addiction and Mental Health (CAMH)
www.camh.net

The Centre for Addiction and Mental Health is Canada's leading addiction and mental health teaching hospital. This site provides you with information about clinical practice, health promotion, education, and research.

## Public Health Agency of Canada—Mental Health
www.phac-aspc.gc.ca/ccdpc-cpcmc/topics/mental_e.html

This site provides access to a range of online materials that relate to mental health. Selected links to other sites are also provided.

## University of British Columbia Mood Disorders Centre
www.vch.ca/mood

The UBC Hospital Mood Disorders Centre (MDC) is affiliated with the Department of Psychiatry at the University of British Columbia and the Vancouver Hospital and Health Sciences Centre. At this site you can learn about the activities of the MDC, which is educating health professionals and the public about mood disorders. You can also learn about new clinical research in this field.

Please note that links are subject to change. If you find a broken link, use a search engine such as www.google.ca and search for the website by typing in keywords.

**InfoTrac® College Edition Activity** Miller, M.H. (2004, September 13). Colleges reporting more students with mental health problems. (around the nation) *Community College Week, 17*(3), 2–4.

1. Why do you think that there has been a growth in the number of students requiring extra assistance with their mental health over the past five years? What do the authors of this study say?

2. Given that the findings of this study indicate that college students are "wary of the campus programs and services available for students with mental disorders," what suggestions do you have for college and university health-care providers, professors, and administrators who are attempting to deal with the mental health issues of students?

3. Describe some high-stress factors that are common among students attending a two-year college program.

You can find additional readings related to psychological health with InfoTrac® College Edition, an online library of more than 5000 journals and publications. Follow the instructions for accessing InfoTrac® that were packaged with your textbook; then search for articles using a keyword search.

For additional links and resources, visit our text-specific website at www.health.nelson.com.

## Key Terms

The terms listed here are used within the chapter on the page indicated. Definitions of the terms are in the Glossary at the end of the book.

altruism 51
antidepressant 59
anxiety 54
anxiety disorders 55
assertive 52
attention deficit/hyperactivity disorder (ADHD) 63
autonomy 52
behaviour therapy 65
bipolar disorder 60
cognitive-behavioural therapy (CBT) 65
culture 48
depression 54
depressive disorder 59
emotional health 48
emotional intelligence 48
generalized anxiety disorder (GAD) 55
interpersonal therapy (IPT) 65
major depression 59
mental health 48
mental illness 54
mood 51
obsessive-compulsive disorder (OCD) 58
optimistic 49
panic attacks 55
panic disorder 56
phobias 55
post-traumatic stress disorder (PTSD) 56
psychiatric drugs 65
psychiatrists 65
psychodynamic psychotherapy 65
psychologists 65
psychotherapy 65
schizophrenia 63
seasonal affective disorder (SAD) 60
self-actualization 49
self-efficacy 52
self-esteem 50
social isolation 53
social phobia 53
social responsibility 51
social workers 65
spiritual health 48
values 49

# References

1. Satcher, D. (2000). Executive summary: A report of the surgeon general on mental health. *Public Health Reports, 115*(1).
2. Diener, E., et al. (1999). Subjective well-being: Three decades of progress. *Psychological Bulletin, 125*(2).
3. Shapiro, D., & Walsh, R. (1983). *Beyond health and normalcy.* New York: Van Nostrand Reinhold.
4. Satcher, D. (2000). Executive summary: A report of the surgeon general on mental health. *Public Health Reports, 115*(1).
5. Moore, T. (1994). *Care of the soul.* New York: Harper Perennial.
6. Holst, W. (2004). "Native spirituality" gets new respect. [Book review]. *National Catholic Reporter, 41*(7), 20–21.
7. Bastien, B. (2003). The cultural practice of participatory transpersonal visions: An indigenous perspective. *Revision, 26*(2), 41–48.
8. Miller, H.A. (2002). Traditional medicines and spirituality focus of gathering (Health). *Wind Speaker, 20*(4), 26.
9. Goleman, D. (1997). *Emotional intelligence.* New York: Bantam Books.
10. Chatterjee, C. (2000). Emotional ignorance. *Psychology Today, 33*(6), 12.
11. Danner, D., et al. (2001). Positive emotions in early life and longevity: Findings from the nun study. *Journal of Personality & Social Psychology, 80*(5), 804.
12. Rokeach, M. (1960). *The open and closed mind.* New York: Basic Books.
13. Hertel, J. (2003). College students generational status: Similarities, differences, and factors in college adjustment. *The Psychological Record, 52*(1), 3.
14. Robins, R., & Beer, J. (2001). Positive illusions about the self: Short-term benefits and long-term costs. *Journal of Personality & Social Psychology, 80*(2), 340.
15. Larsen, Randy, psychologist. Personal interview.
16. Persistent bad mood leads to poor health. (2002, June 3). *Health & Medicine Week*, p. 4.
17. Larsen, Randy, psychologist. Personal interview.
18. Iwasaki, Y. (2003). Roles of leisure in coping with stress among university students: A repeated assessment field study. *Anxiety, Stress and Coping, 16*(1), 31–57.
19. Jones, S.R., & Hill. K.E. (2003). Understanding patterns of commitment: Student motivation for community service. *Journal of Higher Education, 74*(5), 516–24.
20. Ottenritter, N.W. (2004). Service learning, social justice, and campus health. (Viewpoint). *Journal of American College Health, 52*(4), 189–91.
21. Business Students Practice Philanthropy. (2005, May/June). *BizEd, 4*(4), 6–8.
22. Industry Canada. (2008, July 8). Business Tools and Resources. Corporate and Social Responsibility. Available at www.ic.gc.ca/epic/site/csr-rse.nsf/en/Home.
23. Natural Resources Canada. (2004, March 31). Strategic Policy Branch. Sustainable Development. CSR Publication. Corporate Social Responsibility: Lessons Learned. Available at www.nrcan.gc.ca/sd-dd/pubs/csr-rse/csr_e.html.
24. Bandura, A. (2001). Social cognitive theory: An agentic perspective. *Annual Review Psychology, 52*, 1–26. Available at www.des.emory.edu/mfp/Bandura2001ARPr.pdf.
25. What is the psychiatric significance of loneliness? (2000). *Harvard Mental Health Letter, 16*(10).
26. Covey, S.R. (1989). *The seven habits of highly effective people: Restoring the character ethic.* New York: Simon & Schuster.
27. Schwartz, R. (1997). Loneliness. *Harvard Review of Psychiatry, 5*(2).
28. Clark, W. (2002). Time alone. *Canadian Social Trends, Statistics Canada.* Autumn, Catalogue No 11-008.
29. What is the psychiatric significance of loneliness? (2000). *Harvard Mental Health Letter, 16*(10).
30. Clark, W. (2002). Time alone. *Canadian Social Trends, Statistics Canada.* Autumn, Catalogue No 11-008.
31. Dittman, K.L., & Andrews, U. (2004). A study of the relationship between loneliness and Internet use among university students. *Dissertation Abstracts International: Section B: The Sciences & Engineering, 64*(7–B), 3518.
32. Preboth, M., & Wright, S. (1999). Does the Internet make people unhappy? *American Family Physician, 59*(6).
33. Cramer, K., & Neyedley, K. (1998). Sex differences in loneliness: The role of masculinity and femininity. *Sex Roles: A Journal of Research, 38*(7–8).
34. Stein, M., et al. (2000). Social phobia symptoms, subtypes, and severity. *Archives of General Psychiatry, 57*(11).
35. Government of Canada. (2006). The Human Face of Mental Health and Mental Illness in Canada 2006. Available at www.phac-aspc.gc.ca/publicat/human-humain06/index-eng.php.
36. This year's international mental health agenda: Erasing the stigma of mental illness. (2001, May). *WHO Reports*, p. 24.
37. Health Canada Editorial Board Mental Illnesses in Canada. (2002). *A report on mental illness in Canada.* Ottawa: Health Canada. Available at www.cmha.ca/bins/content_page.asp?cid=4-42-215.
38. Ibid.
39. Ibid.
40. Mignone, J., Neil, J.D., & Wilkie, C. (2003, July). Mental health services review. First Nations and Inuit health branch Manitoba region. *Centre for Aboriginal Health Research, University of Manitoba.* Available at www.umanitoba.ca/centres/centre_aboriginal_health_research/researchreports/mental_health_review_fina_report.pdf.
41. Mounting evidence indicates heart disease link. (2002, July 21). *Medical Letter on the CDC & FDA*, p. 14.
42. Depression doubles risk of later hypertension. (2002). *Family Practice News, 32*(9) 13.
43. Parmet, S. (2002). Depression and heart disease. *Journal of the American Medical Association, 288*, 792.
44. Depression and heart disease. (2001). *Harvard Heart Letter, 11*(8).
45. Andrews, G. (2001). Should depression be managed as a chronic disease? *British Medical Journal, 322*(7283), 419.
46. Health Canada Editorial Board Mental Illnesses in Canada. (2002). *A report on mental illness in Canada.* Ottawa: Health Canada. Available at www.cmha.ca/bins/content_page.asp?cid=4-42-215.
47. Ibid.
48. Corrado, R.R., & Cohen, I.M. (2003). Mental health profiles for a sample of British Columbia's Aboriginal survivors of the Canadian residential school system. Publications. Research Series. Aboriginal Healing Foundation. Available at www.ahf.ca/publications/research-series.
49. Health Canada Editorial Board Mental Illnesses in Canada. (2002). *A report on mental illness in Canada.* Ottawa: Health Canada. Available at www.cmha.ca/bins/content_page.asp?cid=4-42-215.
50. What you should know about generalized anxiety disorders. (2000). *American Family Physician, 62*(7).
51. Rabatin, J., & Buckvar, L. (2002). Generalized anxiety and panic disorder. *Western Journal of Medicine, 176*(3) 164.
52. What are the current treatments for panic disorder? (2000). *Harvard Mental Health Letter, 16*(11).
53. Why men and women handle stress differently. (2005, June 6). WebMD Feature. Available at http://my.webmd.com/content/Article/107/108405.htm.
54. How male and female brains differ. (2005, April 11). WebMD Feature. Available at http://my.webmd.com/content/Article/104/107367.htm.
55. Ibid.
56. World Health Organization. (n.d.). Gender and women's mental health. Available at www.who.int/mental_health/prevention/genderwomen/en.
57. Ibid.
58. Ibid.
59. Ibid.
60. Ibid.

61. Government of Saskatchewan. (n.d.). Post-trauma stress. Brochure. Available at www.health.gov.sk.ca/rr_post_trauma_stress.html.

62. CBT may help patients control panic disorder. (2002). *Mental Health Weekly, 12*(7), 7.

63. Schnyder, U., et al. (2000). Incidence and prediction of posttraumatic stress disorder symptoms in severely injured accident victims. *American Journal of Psychiatry, 158,* 594.

64. Wijma, K., et al. (2000). Prevalence of post-traumatic stress disorder among gynecological patients with a history of sexual and physical abuse. *Journal of Interpersonal Violence, 5*(9), 944.

65. Naparstek, B. (2004). *Invisible heroes: Survivors of trauma and how they heal.* New York: Bantam Books.

66. Obsessive-compulsive disorder: What it is and how to treat it. (2000). *American Family Physician, 61*(5).

67. Health Canada Editorial Board Mental Illnesses in Canada. (2002). *A report on mental illness in Canada.* Ottawa: Health Canada. Available at www.cmha.ca/bins/content_page.asp?cid=4-42-215.

68. Pullen, L., et al. (2000). Adolescent depression: Important facts that matter. *Journal of Child and Adolescent Psychiatric Nursing, 13*(2).

69. Health Canada Editorial Board Mental Illnesses in Canada. (2002). *A report on mental illness in Canada.* Ottawa: Health Canada. Available at www.cmha.ca/bins/content_page.asp?cid=4-42-215.

70. Walling, A. (2000). Depression in young adults. *American Family Physician, 62*(1).

71. Exercise against depression. (2001). *Harvard Mental Health Letter, 7*(19).

72. Babyak, M., et al. (2000). Exercise treatment for major depression: Maintenance of therapeutic benefit at 10 months. *Psychosomatic Medicine, 62,* 633–38.

73. LeTourneau, M. (2001, May–June). Pump up to cheer up. *Psychology Today,* p. 27.

74. Vastag, B. (2002). Decade of work shows depression is physical. *Journal of the American Medical Association, 287*(14), 1787.

75. Olfson, M., et al. (2002). National trends in the outpatient treatment of depression. *Journal of the American Academy of Child and Adolescent Psychiatry, 41*(7), 837.

76. Straton, J., & Cronholm, P. (2002). Are paroxetine, fluoxetine, and sertraline equally effective for depression? *Journal of Family Practice, 51*(3), 285.

77. Canadian Mental Health Association. (2002–3). *Effects of depression and anxiety on Canadian society—Executive summary.* Compas Survey. Available at www.cmha.ca/bins/content_page.asp?cid=5-34-183&lang=1.

78. Ibid.

79. Babyak, M., et al. (2000). Exercise treatment for major depression: Maintenance of therapeutic benefit at 10 Months. *Psychosomatic Medicine, 62,* 633–38.

80. Hales, R.E., & Hales, D. (2001). *The mind-mood pill book.* New York: Bantam.

81. Health Canada Editorial Board Mental Illnesses in Canada. (2002). *A report on mental illness in Canada.* Ottawa: Health Canada. Available at www.cmha.ca/bins/content_page.asp?cid=4-42-215.

82. Ibid.

83. UBC Mood Disorders Centre. (n.d.). Seasonal affective disorder information page. Available at www.ubcsad.ca.

84. Ibid.

85. Ibid.

86. Dubin, J.W. (2001, May–June). More than a mood. *Psychology Today,* p. 26.

87. Jensen, Peter. Personal interview.

88. March, John. Personal interview.

89. Teenage depression shows family ties. (2001). *Science News, 159*(1), 72.

90. Health Canada Editorial Board Mental Illnesses in Canada. (2002). *A report on mental illness in Canada.* Ottawa: Health Canada. Available at www.cmha.ca/bins/content_page.asp?cid=4-42-215.

91. De Marco, R.R. (2000). The epidemiology of major depression: Implications of occurrence, recurrence, and stress in a Canadian community sample. *Canadian Journal of Psychiatry, 45,* 67–74.

92. Health Canada Editorial Board Mental Illnesses in Canada. (2002). *A report on mental illness in Canada.* Ottawa: Health Canada. Available at www.cmha.ca/bins/content_page.asp?cid=4-42-215.

93. Hughes, A., et al. (2000). Depressive symptoms and cigarette smoking among teens. *Journal of the American Medical Association, 284*(23).

94. Health Canada Editorial Board Mental Illnesses in Canada. (2002). *A report on mental illness in Canada.* Ottawa: Health Canada. Available at www.cmha.ca/bins/content_page.asp?cid=4-42-215&lang=1.

95. First Nations and Inuit Health Branch. (2003). *Acting on what we know: Preventing youth suicide in First Nations. The report of the advisory group on suicide prevention.* Available at www.hc-sc.gc.ca/fnih-spni/pubs/suicide/prev_youth-jeunes/index_e.html.

96. Health Canada Editorial Board Mental Illnesses in Canada. (2002). *A report on mental illness in Canada.* Ottawa: Health Canada. Available at www.cmha.ca/bins/content_page.asp?cid=4-42-215.

97. The seasons of suicide. (2000). *Harvard Mental Health Letter, 16*(11).

98. Walling, A. (2000). Which patients are at greatest risk of committing suicide? *American Family Physician, 61*(8), 2487.

99. Health Canada Editorial Board Mental Illnesses in Canada. (2002). *A report on mental illness in Canada.* Ottawa: Health Canada. Available at www.cmha.ca/bins/content_page.asp?cid=4-42-215.

100. Ibid.

101. First Nations and Inuit Health Branch. (2003). *Acting on what we know: Preventing youth suicide in First Nations. The report of the advisory group on suicide prevention.* Available at www.hc-sc.gc.ca/fnih-spni/pubs/suicide/prev_youth-jeunes/index_e.html.

102. Popper, C., & West, S. (1999). Disorders usually diagnosed in infancy, childhood or adolescence. *American Psychiatric Press Textbook of Psychiatry,* 3rd ed. Washington, DC: American Psychiatric Press.

103. Mostofsky, S. (1999, April). *Brain abnormalities in children with ADHD.* Toronto: American Academy of Neurology, Annual Meeting.

104. Heiligenstien, E., Guenther, G., Levy, A., Savino, F., & Fulwiler, J. (1999). Psychological functioning in college students with attention deficit hyperactivity disorder. *Journal of American College Health, 47*(5), 181.

105. Health Canada Editorial Board Mental Illnesses in Canada. (2002). *A report on mental illness in Canada.* Ottawa: Health Canada. Available at www.cmha.ca/bins/content_page.asp?cid=4-42-215.

106. Keks, N., Mazumdar, P., & Shields, R. (2000). New developments in schizophrenia. *Australia Family Physician, 29,* 129–31; 135–36.

107. Harbingers of schizophrenia. (2000). *Harvard Mental Health Letter, 17*(5).

108. How schizophrenia develops: New evidence and new ideas. (2001). *Harvard Mental Health Letter, 17*(8).

109. Radomsky, E., Hass, G.I., Mann, J.J., & Sweeny, J.A. (1999). Suicidal behaviour in patients with schizophrenia and other psychotic disorders. *American Journal of Psychiatry, 156,* 1590–95.

110. Health Canada Editorial Board Mental Illnesses in Canada. (2002). *A report on mental illness in Canada.* Ottawa: Health Canada. Available at www.cmha.ca/bins/content_page.asp?cid=4-42-215.

111. Ibid.

112. Ibid.

113. Ibid.

114. Canadian Mental Health Association. (2004). *Your education—your future. A guide to college and university for students with psychiatric disabilities.* Available at www.cmha.ca/youreducation.

115. Cognitive therapy tops medication. (2002, June 17). *Pain & Central Nervous System Week,* p. 6.

116. Hart, V. (2000). The balance of psychotherapy and pharmacotherapy. *Perspectives in Psychiatric Care, 36*(2).

117. Hales, R.E., & Hales, D. (2001). *The mind-mood pill book.* New York: Bantam.

118. Davidson, J. (2002). Effect of hypericum perforatum (St. John's wort) in major depressive disorder: A randomized controlled trial. *Journal of the American Medical Association, 287*(14), 1807.

119. Health Canada Online. (2000, April 6). Potential drug interactions with St. John's wort. Available at www.hc-sc.gc.ca/dhp-mps/medeff/advisories-avis/prof/_2000/hypericum_perforatum_hpc-cps-eng.php.

# Physical Activity for Fitness and Health

We are designed to move. In ways far more complex than airplanes or cars, our bodies can run, stretch, bend, climb, glide, and stride—day after day and year after year. While machines break down from constant wear and tear, the human body thrives on physical activity. When we use our bodies, we become stronger and healthier.

As you'll see in this chapter, regular physical activity yields immediate rewards: it boosts energy, improves mood, soothes stress, improves sleep, and makes you feel better. In the long term, physical activity slows many of the changes associated with chronological aging, such as loss of calcium and bone density, and lowers the risk of serious chronic illnesses.

You will also discover that to get these benefits, you don't have to turn into a jock or fitness fanatic. An interesting study by Tremblay and Chiasson[1] showed that Canadian college women and men, aged 17 to 20, who were actively fit were not endurance athletes. Instead, they followed a lifestyle that has been promoted by many health agencies and professionals. Their lifestyles included regular daily physical activity and healthy food choices.

What else is in this chapter? There is an introduction to *Canada's Physical Activity Guide*, the principles of exercise, guidelines for becoming more physically fit, and information on how to design aerobic, muscular strength, endurance, and flexibility programs. You will also discover some gender differences with regard to physical fitness and physical activity levels.

**After studying the material in this chapter, you will be able to:**

- **Describe** the components of physical fitness.
- **Describe** the health benefits of regular physical activity.
- **List** the different forms of cardiorespiratory, muscular strength, endurance, and flexibility activities.
- **Design** cardiorespiratory, strength, endurance, and flexibility workouts.
- **List** safety strategies for physically active individuals.
- **Describe** some of the Canadian Active Living initiatives that have been designed to increase the physical-activity level of Canadians.

**?????  FREQUENTLY ASKED QUESTIONS**

**FAQ: Why should I participate in regular physical activity?** p. 74

**FAQ: Can a person be fat and fit?** p. 81

**FAQ: How much exercise is enough?** p. 84

**FAQ: Should I check with my doctor before I get started?** p. 84

**FAQ: How do I design an aerobic workout?** p. 87

**FAQ: How do I design a muscle workout?** p. 89

**FAQ: What is the difference between stretching and warming up?** p. 91

**FAQ: How can I prevent sports injuries?** p. 91

# What Is Physical Activity?

The Physical Activity Unit within Health Canada[2] defines **physical activity** as all leisure and non-leisure body movement produced by the skeletal muscles and resulting in an increase in energy expenditure. **Sport** is a form of leisure-time physical activity that is planned, structured, and competitive. **Active living** is a way of life in which physical activity is valued and integrated into daily living.[3]

# What Is Physical Fitness?

**Physical fitness** is the ability to respond to routine physical demands with enough reserve energy to cope with a sudden challenge. Consider yourself fit if you meet your daily energy needs, can handle unexpected extra demands, and are protecting yourself against potential health problems, such as heart disease.

Fitness is important—for health and optimal living. The health-related components of physical fitness, which this chapter emphasizes, include aerobic or cardiorespiratory endurance, muscular strength and endurance, body composition, and flexibility. Optimal living depends on these components as well as performance and skill-related fitness such as agility, coordination, balance, and speed.

**Cardiorespiratory fitness** refers to the ability of the body to sustain prolonged rhythmic activity. It is achieved through **aerobic exercise**—any activity, such as brisk walking, jogging, running, swimming, or cycling, in which the amount of oxygen taken into the body is slightly more than, or equal to, the amount of oxygen used by the body. In other words, aerobic exercise involves working out strenuously without pushing to the point of breathlessness.

**Muscular fitness** has two components: strength and endurance. **Strength** refers to the force within muscles; it is measured by the absolute maximum weight that a person can lift, push, or press in one effort. **Endurance** is the ability to perform repeated muscular effort; it is measured by counting how many times a person can lift, push, or press a given weight. Both are equally important. It's not enough to be able to hoist a shovelful of snow; you've got to be able to keep shovelling until the entire driveway is clear.

**Body composition** refers to the amount of fat versus the amount of lean tissue in the body. Fat includes both essential and storage fat. Lean tissue includes all tissues exclusive of fat: muscles, bones, organs, and fluid. A high proportion of body fat has serious health implications, including an increased incidence of heart disease, high blood pressure, diabetes, stroke, gall bladder problems, back and joint problems, and some forms of cancer (see The X & Y Files: "Gender Differences: Physical Fitness and Physical Activity Levels").

A combination of regular exercise and good nutrition is the best way to maintain a healthy body composition. Aerobic exercise helps by burning calories and increasing metabolic rate (the rate at which the body uses calories) for several hours after a workout. Strength training increases the proportion of lean body tissue by building muscle mass, which also increases the metabolic rate. You will find more information on body composition in Chapter 6, "Healthy Eating for Healthy Living."

**Flexibility** is the range of motion around specific joints. Flexibility depends on many factors: your age, gender, and posture; bone spurs; and how fat or muscular you are. A gradual loss of joint mobility occurs when muscles and connective tissue, such as tendons and ligaments, shorten and tighten because they are not used through their full range of motion.

Physical **conditioning** (or training) refers to the gradual building up of the body to enhance cardiorespiratory or aerobic fitness, muscular strength and endurance, and flexibility.

# Why Should I Participate in Regular Physical Activity?

If exercise could be packed into a pill, it would be the single most widely prescribed and beneficial medicine in the nation. Stewart, a Canadian health and fitness expert, calls it "the miracle medicine for a long and healthy life."[4]

## Health Benefits from Exercise

- Heart muscles become stronger, and blood is pumped more efficiently.
- Heart rate and resting heart rate slow down.
- Blood pressure may drop slightly.
- Bones thicken and loss of calcium slows.
- Flexibility is increased.
- Digestion and elimination is improved.
- Metabolism is increased so that the body burns more calories and body fat decreases.
- A heightened sensitivity to insulin is attained.
- Enhanced clot-dissolving substances form in the blood.

Here is a summary of the benefits of regular physical activity (see Figure 4-1). (See also Table 4-1.)

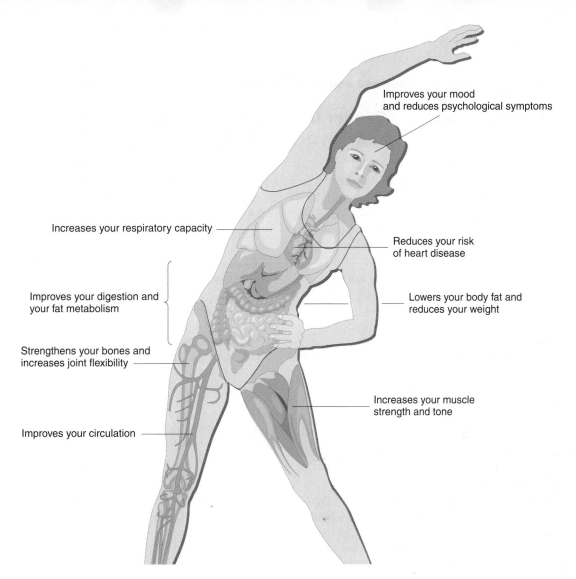

Improves your mood
and reduces psychological symptoms

Increases your respiratory capacity

Reduces your risk
of heart disease

Improves your digestion and
your fat metabolism

Lowers your body fat and
reduces your weight

Strengthens your bones and
increases joint flexibility

Increases your muscle
strength and tone

Improves your circulation

▲ **Figure 4-1** Benefits of Exercise
Regular physical activity enhances your overall health and helps prevent disease.

### ▼ Table 4-1 Why College and University Students Exercise—or Don't

In a sample of 147 graduates, the regular exercisers—92 percent of men and
63.8 percent of women—perceived more benefits than those who didn't exercise.

**Top Exercise Benefits**

1. Exercise increases my level of physical fitness.
2. Exercise improves the way my body looks.
3. My muscle tone is improved with exercise.
4. Exercise gives me a sense of personal accomplishment.
5. Exercise increases my muscle strength.

**Top Exercise Barriers**

1. Exercise tires me.
2. Exercise is hard work for me.
3. I am fatigued by exercise.
4. Exercising takes too much of my time.
5. My family members do not encourage me to exercise.

Source: Grubbs, L. & Carter, J. (2002, July). The relationship of perceived benefits and barriers in college undergraduates.
*Family and Community Health, 255*(2), 76. Reprinted with permission from Lippincott, Williams and Wilkins: www.lww.com.

## The X & Y Files

# Gender Differences: Physical Fitness and Physical Activity Levels

Men and women benefit equally from physical activity and exercise. However, physical activity is generally more prevalent among men than girls and women. Some factors why this is so are listed in a World Health Organization report on physical activity and women:

- Women's income is often lower than men and may limit access to physical activity facilities.

- Agreement may be required from senior members of some households before women can use family financial resources to engage in physical activity.

- Women often have a workload that includes careers and well as care-giving roles for family members, and time available for physical activity is minimal.

- Cultural expectations may limit the participation of women and girls.[5]

From a Canadian perspective there are also gender differences in physical activity levels. According to a Canadian Fitness and Lifestyle Research Institute report (CFLRI)[6] and Statistics Canada[7]:

- Slightly more women (52 percent) than men (47 percent) are physically inactive (see Table 4-2). Inactive means that you would accumulate on average less than 1.5 METS of physical activity daily. This amount of physical activity could be achieved through walking a total of half an hour a day.

- Women are more likely than men to hold strong beliefs about the benefits of physical activity, particularly its potential to reduce stress.

- Men are more likely than women to fully intend to be active in the future.

- Women are more likely than men to cite lack of time, energy, or skill as barriers to an active lifestyle.

- Women are more likely than men to rate advice on scheduling physical activity into daily life and choosing the most important activities as very important in making it easier for them to be physically active.

Physiology needs to be considered, too. On average, men have roughly twice the percentage of muscle mass and half the percentage of body fat. Overall, men are about 30 percent stronger, particularly above the waist. Their lungs take in 10 to 20 percent more oxygen, so they have a greater maximum oxygen uptake. They also pump more blood with each heart beat.

Women's body fat is often distributed around the hips and thighs; men carry more body fat around the waist and stomach. The average woman has a smaller heart, a lower percentage of slow-twitch muscle fibres, and a smaller blood volume than a man. Because women have a lower concentration of red blood cells, their bodies are less effective at transporting oxygen to their working muscles during exercise.

Even though training produces the same relative increases for both genders, a woman's maximum oxygen intake remains about 25 to 30 percent lower than that of an equally well-conditioned man. In elite athletes, the difference is smaller: 8 to 12 percent. Because the angle of the upper leg bone (femur) to the pelvis is greater in a woman, her legs are less efficient at running. However, in some endurance events, such as ultra-marathon running and long-distance swimming, female anatomy and physiology may have some aerobic advantages. The longer a race—on land, water, or ice—the better women perform.

▼ Table 4-2 Level of Leisure-time Physical Activity, Household Population Aged 12 or Older, Canada, 2005

|  | Active | Moderately Active | Active or Moderately Active | Inactive |
|---|---|---|---|---|
| **Total** | **27.1** | **25.1** | **52.2** | **47.8** |
| Men | 30.2* | 24.6* | 54.8* | 45.2* |
| Women† | 24.1 | 25.6 | 49.7 | 50.3 |
| Age 12 to 17 | 50.9 | 22.6 | 73.5 | 26.5 |
| Men | 57.6* | 21.5* | 79.1* | 20.9* |
| Women† | 43.8 | 23.7 | 67.5 | 32.5 |

▼ **Table 4-2 Level of Leisure-time Physical Activity, Household Population Aged 12 or Older, Canada, 2005 (continued)**

| | Active | Moderately Active | Active or Moderately Active | Inactive |
|---|---|---|---|---|
| Age 18 to 24 | 38.3 | 23.5 | 61.8 | 38.2 |
| Men | 43.8* | 22.2* | 66.0* | 34.0* |
| Women† | 32.5 | 24.9 | 57.4 | 42.6 |
| Age 25 to 34 | 26.4 | 26.1 | 52.5 | 47.5 |
| Men | 29.0* | 25.1* | 54.0* | 46.0* |
| Women† | 24.0 | 27.1 | 51.0 | 49.0 |
| Age 35 to 44 | 23.4 | 25.4 | 48.8 | 51.2 |
| Men | 24.0 | 24.9 | 48.9 | 51.1 |
| Women† | 22.7 | 26.0 | 48.8 | 51.3 |
| Age 45 to 54 | 22.0 | 25.6 | 47.6 | 52.4 |
| Men | 22.5 | 25.6 | 48.1 | 51.9 |
| Women† | 21.4 | 25.6 | 47.0 | 53.0 |
| Age 55 to 64 | 22.6 | 26.3 | 48.9 | 51.1 |
| Men | 24.3* | 25.0* | 49.2 | 50.8 |
| Women† | 21.0 | 27.7 | 48.6 | 51.4 |
| Age 65 or older | 18.5 | 24.5 | 43.0 | 57.0 |
| Men | 24.2* | 26.1* | 50.2* | 49.8* |
| Women† | 14.1 | 23.4 | 37.5 | 62.5 |
| **Household income§** | | | | |
| Lowest | 22.7* | 21.6* | 44.3* | 55.7* |
| Low-middle | 23.3* | 23.8* | 47.1* | 52.9* |
| Middle | 26.2* | 26.7* | 52.9* | 47.1* |
| High-middle | 29.0* | 26.4* | 55.4* | 44.6* |
| Highest† | 32.9 | 29.4 | 62.3 | 37.7 |
| **Ethnic origin** | | | | |
| White | 27.2 | 25.9‡ | 53.2‡ | 46.9‡ |
| Black | 28.8 | 18.5‡ | 47.3‡ | 52.7‡ |
| Southeast/East Asian | 21.6‡ | 22.1‡ | 43.7‡ | 56.3‡ |
| Off-reserve Aboriginal | 34.0‡ | 21.9‡ | 56.0‡ | 44.0‡ |
| Other | 27.0 | 21.8‡ | 48.8‡ | 51.2‡ |
| **Immigrant, years in Canada** | | | | |
| 0 to 4 | 21.7‡ | 21.6‡ | 43.3‡ | 56.7‡ |
| 5 to 9 | 24.9 | 19.5‡ | 44.3‡ | 55.7‡ |
| 10 to 14 | 25.1 | 21.0‡ | 46.2‡ | 53.8‡ |
| 15 to 19 | 21.2‡ | 22.0‡ | 43.2‡ | 56.8‡ |
| 20 or more | 23.8‡ | 24.7 | 48.4‡ | 51.6‡ |

Source: Gilmour, H. (2007). "Physically Active Canadians" from *Statistics Canada Health Reports* (Vol. 18, No. 3). Available at www.statcan.ca/english/freepub/82-003-XIE/2006008/articles/physically/physicallyactivecanadians-en.pdf, page 46.

† Reference category
‡ Significantly different from estimate for Canada (p < 0.05)
§ Excludes territories
* Significantly different from estimate for reference group (p < 0.05)

Note: Based on self-reported frequency and duration of participation in leisure-time physical activity in previous 3 months
Source: 2005 Canadian Community Health Survey

## Longer Life

Approximately 1.9 million people around the globe die every year because they are not physically active, according to the World Health Organization.[8] Inactivity increases all causes of mortality, doubles the risk of cardiovascular diseases, diabetes, and obesity, and increases the risk of colon cancer, high blood pressure, osteoporosis, depression, and anxiety.[9]

Capacity for exercise has proven a better predictor of whether a male would die in the next few years than other risk factors, such as high blood pressure, high total cholesterol, or smoking.[10] Formerly sedentary people, even the elderly, who begin to exercise live longer, on average, than those who remain inactive.[11]

## Protection Against Heart Disease and Certain Cancers

Sedentary people are about twice as likely to die of a heart attack as people who are physically active. In Canada, cardiovascular disease (CVD) remains the number-one cause of premature death. It claims the lives of 79 500 Canadians each year and costs the health-care system over $7.3 billion in direct costs. By 2021, the annual growth in deaths due to CVD will be almost four times the population growth.[12] Regular physical activity can reduce the risk of this disease.

In addition to its effects on the heart, exercise makes the lungs more efficient. They take in more oxygen, and their vital capacity (ability to take in and expel air) is increased, providing more energy for you to use. As demonstrated in a 20-year study of almost 4000 men, regular physical activity also makes blood less likely to clot and cause a stroke or heart attack.[13]

Recent studies have shown that physical activity can reduce the risk of colon cancer by as much as 50 percent.[14] This is important research as the Canadian Cancer Society suggests that in 2008, there will be an estimated 21 500 Canadians diagnosed with colorectal cancer and 8900 will die of this disease.[15] Physically fit men are less likely to die of prostate and colon cancer than others.[16] Research also shows that physical activity may protect against breast cancer in women. Dr. Friedenreich (Alberta Cancer Board, Calgary, AB) and Dr. Cust (University of Melbourne, Australia) did an extensive review of the literature examining how timing, type, and level of physical activity affects breast cancer risk. Forty-seven of the sixty-two articles they reviewed indicated that there was a typical 25 to 30 percent reduction in the risk of breast cancer for women if they were physically active. The studies also showed that more exercise increased the benefits[17, 18] by lowering blood levels of estrogen in postmenopausal women.[19]

## Better Bones

Weak and brittle bones are common among people who don't exercise. **Osteoporosis,** a condition in which bones lose their mineral density and become increasingly susceptible to injury, affects a great many older people. Women, in particular, are more vulnerable because their bones are less dense to begin with. Close to 25 percent of women over age 50 and half over age 70 will develop osteoporosis.[20] Researchers estimate that a minimum of two 45-minute exercise sessions per week may protect the bones of postmenopausal women.[21]

## Enhanced Immunity

Moderate exercise correlates with a reduced number of sick days. Exercise may enhance immune function by reducing stress hormones such as cortisol that can dampen resistance to disease. In recent studies, women who walked briskly for 35 to 45 minutes five days a week experienced half the number of sick days with cold symptoms as inactive women. While moderate exercise seems to bolster a person's immune system, heavy training may increase the risk of upper respiratory tract infections for endurance athletes.[22]

## Brighter Mood

Exercise makes people feel good from the inside out. Exercise boosts mood, increases energy, reduces anxiety, improves concentration and alertness, and increases the ability to handle stress. This may be the result of increased levels of mood-elevating brain chemicals called **endorphins.**

## Better Mental Health

Exercise is an effective, but underused, treatment for mild to moderate depression and may help in treating other mental disorders.[23] Regular, moderate exercise, such as walking, running, or lifting weights, three times a week, has proven helpful for depression and anxiety disorders, including panic attacks.[24] It also eases certain symptoms, such as agitation and hallucinations, in schizophrenic patients.[25] In a recent study of people with major depression, exercise proved as effective as medication in improving mood and also helped prevent relapse.[26]

## Lower Weight

Over half (51 percent) of Canadians aged 20 are classified as overweight or obese. This equates to having a body mass index of 25.0 or higher to be considered overweight and 30.0 or higher to be considered obese.[27] Aerobic exercise burns off calories during your workout. As your body responds to the increased demand from your muscles for nutrients, your metabolic rate rises. Moreover, this surge persists after exercise, so you continue to use up more calories even after you've stopped sweating. Called excess post-exercise oxygen consumption (EPOC), this increased metabolism includes oxygen replenishment; lactate removal; and increased ventilation, blood circulation, and body temperature. The body generally takes anywhere from 15 minutes to 48 hours to fully recover to a resting state. The magnitude and duration of EPOC depends on gender and intensity and duration of exercise.[28]

### Lowering Risk of Diabetes

One in 18 Canadians has been diagnosed with diabetes. As we age, the likelihood of diabetes increases—1 percent among those less than 25 years of age to about 13 percent among those 65 years old and older.[29] According to the Canadian Diabetes Association, there is concern for both Type 1 and Type 2 diabetes. In 2006 alone, the federal government spent over $10.5 million in research for Type 1 diabetes and nearly $7 million for Type 2. In addition to these sums, $190 million over five years has been invested to address diabetes in an Aboriginal diabetes initiative.[30] Physical activity can reduce the risk of developing Type 2 diabetes by as much as 50 percent.[31]

### A More Active Old Age

Exercise slows the changes that are associated with advancing age: loss of lean muscle tissue, increases in body fat, and decrease in work capacity. Exercise also helps older adults retain the strength and mobility needed to live independently. It boosts strength and stamina, lessens time in wheelchairs, and improves outlook and the sense of being in control.[32]

## Physical Activity and Health

Alarmed by Canadians' sedentary ways—49.6 percent of Canadians (18 and older) are inactive[33]—health officials have shifted their emphasis from promoting regular and rigorous exercise to urging people to become more active in any way possible. Studies have confirmed that lifestyle activities, such as walking, housecleaning, and gardening, are as effective as a structured exercise program in improving heart function, lowering blood pressure, and maintaining or losing weight.[34] Light exercise—activities that increase oxygen consumption no more than three times the level burned by the body at rest—can produce cardiorespiratory benefits.[35]

The Physical Activity Unit within Health Canada has the lead responsibility for improving the health and well-being of Canadians through regular physical activity. The goals of the Physical Activity Unit are (1) to encourage and assist all Canadians to be physically active; (2) to influence positive social and physical environments and opportunities that facilitate the integration of physical activity into daily life; and (3) to establish partnerships with government and non-governmental agencies to foster physical activity in Canada. These goals have been set because $2.1 billion or about 2.5 percent of the total direct health-care costs can be attributed to physical inactivity. As well, conservative estimates suggest that reducing the prevalence of physical inactivity by 10 percent would save $150 million annually.[36]

A major initiative of this unit has been the development of *Canada's Physical Activity Guide to Healthy Active Living* (see Figure 4-2). The guide, produced by Health Canada[37] in partnership with the Canadian Society for Exercise Physiology (CSEP),[38] helps Canadians make wise choices about physical activity. National organizations such as the College of Family Physicians of Canada, Physical and Health Education Canada (PHE), the Canadian Association for School Health (CASH), and the Canadian Parks and Recreation Association (CPRA) have endorsed the guide.

The guide recommends an accumulation of 60 minutes of light physical activity such as walking every day to reduce the risk of premature death and disease. As your fitness level improves, you can participate in moderate to intense activity for 30 to 60 minutes, four days per week. Muscle-strength exercises are encouraged two to four days per week and gentle stretching activities to improve flexibility are recommended four to seven days per week.

## Physical and Health Education Canada (PHE Canada)

An important organization—Physical and Health Education Canada (PHE Canada) was mentioned in Chapter 1. A brief overview of this agency's Quality Daily Physical Education program is offered here.

Physical and Health Education Canada's primary concern is to influence the development of children and youth by advocating for quality, school-based physical and health education. This agency has renewed its efforts to promote a program called Quality Daily Physical Education (QDPE),[39] a planned program of instruction and physical activity for all students on a daily basis throughout the school year. It is one of the most comprehensive strategies for increasing the physical education levels of Canadian children and youth. This program can include daily curricular instruction such as physical education classes, intramural activities, and school sports.

Research has shown that most schools in Canada offer an average of less than one hour of physical education per week, less than 40 percent of the minimum recommendation set by HPE. The benefits of a QDPE

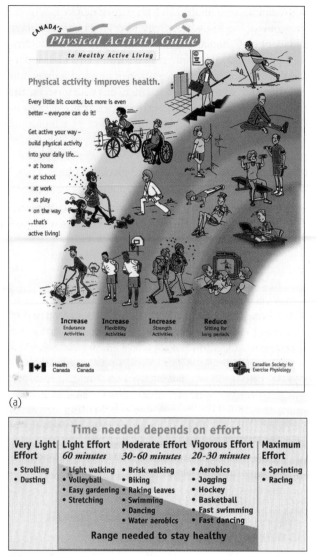

(a)

(b)

▲ **Figure 4-2** Canada's Physical Activity Guide to Healthy Active Living
Use Canada's Physical Activity Guide (www.phac-aspc.gc.ca/pau-uap/paguide/index.html) to create a physical activity plan for your life.

Source: Canada's Physical Activity Guide, Public Health Agency of Canada, 2008. Reproduced with the permission of the Minister of Public Works and Government Services Canada, 2008.

program are many and include improved self-esteem and self-concept, better academic performance, fewer discipline problems, and a lower likelihood of students smoking and using drugs or alcohol. Information on how to deal with issues such as no room in the gym, the budget, or the timetable and no physical education specialist teachers is available from PHE.

## Right to Play

Another organization that believes in the connection of physical activity, sport, and health is Right To Play.[40] This

### Activating Your Lifestyle

▲ Add a physical component to passive activities. Stand while talking on the phone. Stretch during television commercials.

▲ Actively use waiting time. If you have to wait for a delayed appointment, take a quick walk down the hall or up the stairs.

▲ Create opportunities for getting physical. Go dancing instead of to the movies. Shoot hoops instead of sipping coffee.

▲ Right To Play logo.

▲ Adam van Koeverden with Right To Play in Liberia.

international humanitarian organization uses sport and play programs to improve health, develop life skills, and foster peace for children and communities in the most disadvantaged areas of the world. Working in both the humanitarian and development contexts, Right To Play has projects in more than 20 countries across Africa, Asia, and the Middle East. Right To Play takes an active role in driving Sport for Development and Peace research and policy and in supporting children's rights.

Across Canada, Canadian students are supporting Right To Play in various ways, such as joining their university's Right To Play club, volunteering at local Right To Play events, and using Right To Play's School Program "Learning To Play, Playing To Learn" resource in their teacher education training. Many students understand the difference that sport has made in their own lives, and through volunteering and supporting Right To Play, Canadian students are helping children in Right To Play programs to have these same opportunities. For more information on Right To Play, please visit www.righttoplay.ca.

> "Seeing the joy that Right To Play brings to the children and communities I visited in Liberia was an incredible thing to witness and a life-changing experience. Sport and play should be a right for all children, not a privilege."
>
> —Adam van Koeverden, World Champion, Olympic Gold Medalist, and Right To Play Athlete Ambassador

### ???? Can a Person Be Fat and Fit?

Most people assume fitness comes in only one size: small. That's not necessarily so. As we discuss in Chapter 6, there is considerable controversy over how to define a healthy weight. But individuals of every size can improve their physical fitness.

In 10 years of research on 25 000 men and 8000 women, scientists led by Steven Blair, director of research at the Cooper Institute for Aerobics Research, have found that heavier individuals can be just as healthy and physically fit as their leaner counterparts. In their studies, obese people who exercised moderately (30 minutes of daily walking at 3 or 4 miles [5–6 kilometres] per hour) had half the death rate of those who were slimmer but more sedentary. Low cardiorespiratory fitness, regardless of an individual's weight, is as great a risk factor for dying of heart disease or other causes such as diabetes, high blood pressure, and other well-recognized threats such as smoking.[41, 42]

## The Principles of Exercise

Why does exercise work? As you begin working toward fitness, keep in mind the three principles of exercise: the overload principle, the reversibility principle, and the specificity principle.

### Overload Principle

The **overload principle** requires a person exercising to provide a greater stress or demand on the body than it's usually accustomed to handling. For any muscle, including the heart, to get stronger, it must work against a greater-than-normal resistance or challenge. To continue to improve, you need further increases in the demands—but not too much, too quickly. **Progressive overloading** gradually increases physical challenges and provides the benefits of exercise without the risk of injuries.

Although slow and gentle activity can enhance basic health, you need to work harder—that is, at a greater intensity—to improve fitness. Whatever exercise you do, there is a level or threshold at which fitness begins to improve; a target zone, where you can achieve maximum benefits; and an upper level, at which potential risks outweigh any further benefits. The acronym **FIT** sums up the three dimensions of progressive overload: *frequency* (how often you exercise), *intensity* (how hard), and *time* (how long).

### Frequency

To achieve and maintain physical fitness, you need to exercise regularly, but the recommended frequency varies with different types of exercise and with an individual's fitness goals. The minimum frequency recommended by fitness experts is three to five days of cardiovascular or aerobic exercise a week and two to three days of resistance and flexibility training a week.

### Intensity

Exercise intensity varies with the type of exercise and with personal goals. To improve cardiovascular fitness, you need to increase your heart rate to a target zone (the level that produces benefits). To develop muscular strength and

## Human Potential

### Tyler Duncan—Get Smart. Get Active. A Cross-Canada Tour

From: tylerd

Sent: Wednesday, July 04, 2007 5:53 PM

To: llauzon

Subject: Cycling Trip

Hi Lara,

Hope the summer is going really well for you and you have had at least a little time to get out and enjoy the sunshine!

I have an idea that I was hoping to run by you. Recently I have been thinking about riding across Canada, during the summer of '08, and I thought that it might be good to do it as a ride to raise awareness for health and physical education in schools. I would not even know where to start on such a thing, or even if it is feasible with less than a year timeline.

Do you have any thoughts on if this would be a good plan, and if so how I might go about organizing it? I will be in Victoria for the rest of the week, but I have to go to a job in Baja this Saturday for the rest of the summer, so there is no immediate urgency.

All the best,

Tyler Duncan

Student

Physical Education

University of Victoria

And so began a conversation with a past student of mine, Tyler Duncan, about the idea of cycling across Canada and speaking to young people and teachers about the benefits of daily physical education. Crazy idea? Yes, as the timeline was impossible. But as a good friend of mine, Keith Evans, once told me, "Lara, impossible is possible, it just takes a little more time." Here is Tyler's story about his amazing Get Smart. Get Active. tour.

Tyler Duncan on his Get Smart. Get Active. cross-Canada bicycle tour.

© Courtesy of Tyler Duncan

Get Smart. Get Active. logo

© Courtesy of Tyler Duncan

What is the mark I want to leave on the world? That is the question that guides my life. Sure, I'm passionate, but is passion really enough? What is the bigger crime, lacking passion or lacking the will to act on it? My name is Tyler Duncan, I am 24 years old and a physical education student at the University of Victoria.

My journey begins when I was in grade twelve at Whistler Secondary. There I had the opportunity to take an outdoor education class taught by Mitch Sulkers, one of the greatest teachers and mentors that I have ever had. Through Mitch and this class, I gained a burning passion for nature. I have spent my years since high school graduation sharing this passion with children around the world.

After leaving high school the question was: "How can I pursue my passion for the outdoors, and what type of career will give me the best opportunity to make a difference?" I spent the next two years trying to find the answer to this question. It was in Australia, while working as a SCUBA diving instructor and outdoor guide, that I decided that my future was in education and that I wanted to work with young people.

My next stop was in North Carolina, where I worked in an experiential summer education program that uses the outdoor environment to teach life skills and confidence building to youth. I had the good fortune to travel all around the work, gaining experience at every stop. In the Caribbean, I taught sailing and SCUBA diving to high school students. Taking students completely out of their comfort zone and helping them learn and excel is an indescribable experience. As their teacher you get to live every success and every failure with your students.

After two years of gaining valuable experience, my career had progressed as far as it could without further postsecondary education. I then made a decision to attend the University of Victoria to obtain a teaching degree. Unfortunately, it was there that I started to become disillusioned with the task before me. The statistics about young people, obesity levels, and physical inactivity seemed insurmountable. At the same time I was feeling that I was living in a sheltered world, writing lesson plans, and practising on my fellow university student colleagues who always do what they are asked and enjoy anything you present to them.

I needed to do something to inspire people, to fill them with the same passion for activity that I felt. One of my life dreams had been to cycle across Canada. Connecting my dream with my new goal of educating others about the benefits of regular physical activity, *The Get Smart. Get Active. Tour* was

born. My life journey took a whole new turn. The basic concept for the tour was simple enough; I would ride my bike across Canada, from Victoria, B.C., to St. John's, Newfoundland, and stop along the way to talk to students and teachers with the hope of getting them excited about active healthy living. As it turned out, the execution of this concept was anything but simple.

My goal was to complete the entire tour before school was out for the summer, so I was forced to start my ride in the spring of 2008. It just happened that this would be the coldest spring Canada has had for years. I climbed through the Rockies in blizzards and crossed the Prairies in −15°C with 50-kilometre winds blowing in my face. There were days when I could barely sit on my bicycle seat. Five hour rides seemed like an impossible task. During the tour, there were three times that I almost gave up; hours spent alone on a bike weigh heavily on your mind and make you question everything.

In the end, it was the students and teachers I met that kept me going. The looks in the students' faces and the excitement in their eyes at every presentation I gave filled me with a newfound drive to complete the tour. I was very fortunate to meet teachers that love their jobs and commit themselves 100 percent to their students. By the end of the tour, I had spoken to over 7000 students and teachers about the joys of active living. I travelled 6900 kilometres on a bike, dipping my tire in both the Pacific and Atlantic oceans. I had some of the most incredible, life-changing experiences I had ever had, and the tour opened doors that I could not even imagine were there to be opened. Most importantly, however, I didn't sit idly by while my passion ebbed; I went out and set my own path, hopefully inspiring others to do the same.

endurance, you need to increase the amount of weight you lift or the resistance you work against and/or the number of repetitions. For enhanced flexibility, you need to stretch muscles beyond their normal length.

## Time (Duration)

The amount of time, or duration, of your workouts is also important, particularly for cardiovascular exercise. In general, experts[43] have found similar health benefits from a single 30-minute session of moderate exercise as from three 10-minute moderate aerobic sessions throughout the day. Duration and intensity are interlinked. If you're exercising

at high intensity (biking or running at a brisk pace, for instance), you don't need to exercise as long as when you're working at lower intensity (walking or swimming at a moderate pace). For muscular strength and endurance and for flexibility, duration is defined by the number of sets or repetitions rather than total time.

## Reversibility Principle

The **reversibility principle** is the opposite of the overload principle. Just as the body adapts to greater physical demands, it also adjusts to lower levels. If you stop exercising, you can lose as much as 50 percent of your fitness improvements within two months. If you have to curtail your usual exercise routine because of a busy schedule, you can best maintain your fitness by keeping the intensity constant and reducing frequency or duration. The principle of reversibility is aptly summed up by the phrase, "Use it or lose it."

## Specificity Principle

The **specificity principle** refers to the body's adaptation to a particular type of activity or amount of stress placed upon it. Jogging, for instance, trains the heart and lungs to work more efficiently and strengthens certain leg muscles. However, it does not build upper body strength or enhance flexibility.

In other words, the overload principle is specific to each body part and to each component of fitness. Leg exercises develop only the lower limbs; arm exercises, only the upper limbs. This is why you need a comprehensive fitness plan that includes a variety of exercises to develop all parts of the body.

## How Much Exercise Is Enough?

If you're not active at all, any physical exercise will produce some benefits. In the beginning, don't worry about frequency or intensity. You're better off starting slow and small, with just a 10-minute walk or bike ride a few days a week than pushing to do too much and giving up because of injury or discomfort.[44] Although exercising just once or twice a week is not enough to improve cardiorespiratory or aerobic fitness, it does produce benefits. In a study of 45 healthy office workers, even those who exercised just once a week had lower body weights and lower body fat than those who didn't work out at all.[45] Simply walking one hour a week reduced the risk of heart disease for sedentary middle-aged women, even those who were overweight, smoked, or had high cholesterol.[46] However, while some exercise is better than none, fitness and health experts do agree that more exercise is better (see Table 4-3).

## Should I Check with My Doctor Before I Get Started?

If you are unsure about whether or not you should begin a physical activity or exercise program, you might want to complete the Physical Activity Readiness Questionnaire (PAR-Q). This form, developed by the B.C. Ministry of Health in 1978[47] and revised by an Expert Advisory Committee of the Canadian Society for Exercise Physiology in 2002,[48] consists of seven questions that will help you determine if you are ready to begin exercising (see Table 4-4). Also available are the PARmedX, which is used by a physician for individuals who have had positive responses to the PAR-Q, and the PARmedX for Pregnancy, for pregnant women who wish to become more active.

▼ **Table 4-3 Guidelines for Physical Fitness**

|  | Cardiorespiratory | Strength | Flexibility |
|---|---|---|---|
| **Type of Activity** | Aerobic activity that uses large-muscle groups and can be maintained continuously | Resistance activity that is performed at a controlled speed and through a full range of motion | Stretching activity that uses the major muscle groups |
| **Frequency** | A minimum of 4 to 7 days per week | 2 to 4 days per week | A minimum of 4 to 7 days per week |
| **Intensity** | 55 to 90% of maximum heart rate | Enough to enhance muscle strength and improve body composition | Enough to develop and maintain a full range of motion |
| **Time (Duration)** | 30 to 60 minutes | 8 to 12 repetitions of 8 to 10 different exercises (minimum) | 4 repetitions of 10 to 30 seconds per muscle group (minimum) |

Source: Adapted from *Canada's Physical Activity Guide to Healthy Active Living*. Available online at www.hc-sc.gc.ca/hppb/paguide/; and the American College of Sports Medicine. (1998). Position stand: The recommended quantity and quality of exercise for developing and maintaining cardiorespiratory and muscular fitness, and flexibility in healthy adults. *Medicine and Science in Sports and Exercise, 30,* 975–91.

▼ **Table 4-4 Physical Activity Readiness Questionnaire (PAR-Q)**

Physical Activity Readiness
Questionnaire - PAR-Q
(revised 2002)

# PAR-Q & YOU

### (A Questionnaire for People Aged 15 to 69)

Regular physical activity is fun and healthy, and increasingly more people are starting to become more active every day. Being more active is very safe for most people. However, some people should check with their doctor before they start becoming much more physically active.

If you are planning to become much more physically active than you are now, start by answering the seven questions in the box below. If you are between the ages of 15 and 69, the PAR-Q will tell you if you should check with your doctor before you start. If you are over 69 years of age, and you are not used to being very active, check with your doctor.

Common sense is your best guide when you answer these questions. Please read the questions carefully and answer each one honestly: check YES or NO.

| YES | NO | |
|-----|-----|---|
| ☐ | ☐ | **1. Has your doctor ever said that you have a heart condition <u>and</u> that you should only do physical activity recommended by a doctor?** |
| ☐ | ☐ | **2. Do you feel pain in your chest when you do physical activity?** |
| ☐ | ☐ | **3. In the past month, have you had chest pain when you were not doing physical activity?** |
| ☐ | ☐ | **4. Do you lose your balance because of dizziness or do you ever lose consciousness?** |
| ☐ | ☐ | **5. Do you have a bone or joint problem (for example, back, knee or hip) that could be made worse by a change in your physical activity?** |
| ☐ | ☐ | **6. Is your doctor currently prescribing drugs (for example, water pills) for your blood pressure or heart condition?** |
| ☐ | ☐ | **7. Do you know of <u>any other reason</u> why you should not do physical activity?** |

## If you answered

### YES to one or more questions

Talk with your doctor by phone or in person BEFORE you start becoming much more physically active or BEFORE you have a fitness appraisal. Tell your doctor about the PAR-Q and which questions you answered YES.

- You may be able to do any activity you want — as long as you start slowly and build up gradually. Or, you may need to restrict your activities to those which are safe for you. Talk with your doctor about the kinds of activities you wish to participate in and follow his/her advice.
- Find out which community programs are safe and helpful for you.

### NO to all questions

If you answered NO honestly to <u>all</u> PAR-Q questions, you can be reasonably sure that you can:

- start becoming much more physically active – begin slowly and build up gradually. This is the safest and easiest way to go.
- take part in a fitness appraisal – this is an excellent way to determine your basic fitness so that you can plan the best way for you to live actively. It is also highly recommended that you have your blood pressure evaluated. If your reading is over 144/94, talk with your doctor before you start becoming much more physically active.

→ **DELAY BECOMING MUCH MORE ACTIVE:**

- if you are not feeling well because of a temporary illness such as a cold or a fever – wait until you feel better; or
- if you are or may be pregnant – talk to your doctor before you start becoming more active.

**PLEASE NOTE:** If your health changes so that you then answer YES to any of the above questions, tell your fitness or health professional. Ask whether you should change your physical activity plan.

<u>Informed Use of the PAR-Q</u>: The Canadian Society for Exercise Physiology, Health Canada, and their agents assume no liability for persons who undertake physical activity, and if in doubt after completing this questionnaire, consult your doctor prior to physical activity.

Source: Physical Activity Readiness Questionnaire (PAR-Q) © 2002. Used with permission from Canadian Society for Exercise Physiology www.csep.ca.

# Cardiorespiratory or Aerobic Fitness

Since physical activity requires more energy, the heart, lungs, and blood vessels have to work harder to deliver more oxygen to the cells. A person with good cardiorespiratory endurance can engage in a physical activity for a long time without becoming fatigued. The heart of a person who isn't in good condition has to pump more often; as a result, it becomes fatigued more easily.

Unlike muscular endurance, which is specific to individual muscles, cardiorespiratory endurance involves the entire body. The exercises that improve cardiorespiratory endurance are referred to as aerobic because the body uses as much, or slightly more, oxygen than it takes in. Aerobic exercise can take many forms, as noted later in this chapter, but all involve working strenuously without pushing to the point of breathlessness.

In **anaerobic exercise,** the amount of oxygen taken in by the body cannot meet the demands of the activity. This quickly creates an oxygen deficit that must be made up later. Anaerobic activities are high in intensity but short in duration, usually lasting only about ten seconds to two minutes. An example is sprinting 400 metres, which leaves even the best-trained athletes gasping for air.

In non-aerobic exercise, such as bowling, softball, or doubles tennis, there is frequent rest between activities. Because the body can take in all the oxygen it needs, the heart and lungs really don't get much of a workout.

## Your Target Heart Rate

To be sure you're working hard enough to condition your heart and lungs, but not overdoing it, use your pulse, or heart rate, as a guide. One of the easiest places to feel your pulse is in the carotid artery in your neck. Slightly tilt your head back and to one side. Use your middle finger or forefinger, or both, to feel for your pulse. (Do not use your thumb; it has a beat of its own.) To determine your heart rate, count the number of pulses you feel for 10 seconds and multiply that number by 6, or count for 30 seconds and multiply that number by 2. Learn to recognize the pulsing of your heart when you're sitting or lying down. This is your **resting heart rate.**

Start taking your pulse during, or immediately after, exercise, when it's much more pronounced than when you're at rest. Three minutes after heavy exercise, take your pulse again. The closer that reading is to your resting heart rate, the better your condition. If it takes a long time for your pulse to recover and return to its resting level, your body's ability to handle physical stress is poor. As you

continue working out, however, your pulse will return to normal much more quickly.

You don't want to push yourself to your maximum heart rate, but fitness experts recommend you exercise at about 55 to 90 percent of that maximum to get cardiovascular benefits from your training. This range is called your **target heart rate.** If you don't exercise intensely enough to raise your heart rate at least this high, your heart and lungs won't benefit from the workout. If you push too hard and exercise at or near your absolute maximum heart rate, you run the risk of placing too great a burden on your heart. Table 4-5 lists target heart rates for various ages. The following formula can also be used to calculate your maximum and target heart rates (in beats per minute):

1. Estimate your maximum heart rate. Take 220 – your age = ___ (this is your maximum).
2. Determine your lower-limit target heart rate by multiplying your maximum heart rate by 0.55 = ___.
3. Determine your upper-limit target heart rate by multiplying your maximum heart rate by 0.9 = ___.

Your target heart rate range is between your lower and upper limits.

According to the American College of Sports Medicine, for most people, exercising at the lower end of the target heart rate range for a long time is more beneficial than exercising at the higher end of the range for a short time.[49] If your goal is losing weight, exercise at 55 to 70 percent of your maximum heart rate in order to burn fat calories. To improve aerobic endurance and strengthen your heart, work at 70 to 80 percent of your maximum heart rate. A target heart rate of between 40 and 50 percent of maximum is recommended for individuals who are in poor physical condition. Competitive athletes may train at 80 to 100 percent of their maximum heart rate.[50]

| ▼ **Table 4-5 Target Heart Ranges Based on Age** | | | |
|---|---|---|---|
| **Age** | **Average Maximum Heart Rate (100%)** | **Target Heart Rate (55–90%)** | |
| 20 | 200 | 110 | 180 |
| 25 | 195 | 107 | 175 |
| 30 | 190 | 104 | 170 |
| 35 | 185 | 101 | 166 |
| 40 | 180 | 99 | 162 |
| 45 | 175 | 96 | 157 |
| 50 | 170 | 93 | 153 |
| 55 | 165 | 90 | 148 |
| 60 | 160 | 88 | 144 |
| 65 | 155 | 85 | 139 |
| 70 | 150 | 82 | 135 |

## ??? How Do I Design an Aerobic Workout?

Whatever activity you choose, your aerobic workout should consist of several stages, including a warm-up and a cool-down.

### Warm-Up

To prepare your cardiorespiratory system for a workout, speed up the blood flow to your lungs, and increase the temperature and elasticity of your muscles and connective tissue to avoid injury, start by walking briskly for about 5 minutes. This helps your body make the transition from inactivity to exertion. Follow this general warm-up with about 5 minutes of simple stretches of the muscles you'll be exercising most.

### Aerobic Activity

The two key components of this part of your workout are intensity and duration. As described in the previous section, you can use your target heart rate range to make sure you are working at the proper intensity. The current recommendation is to keep moving for at least 30 to 60 minutes, either in one session or several briefer sessions, each lasting at least 10 minutes.

### Cool-Down

Ideally, you should walk for 5 to 10 minutes at a comfortable pace before you end your workout session. When you stand or sit immediately after vigorous exercise, blood can pool in your legs. You need to keep moving at a slower pace to ensure an adequate supply of blood to your heart.

### Your Long-Term Plan

One of the most common mistakes people make is to push too hard, too fast. Often they end up injured or discouraged and quit entirely. If you are just starting an aerobic program, think of it as a series of phases: beginning, progression, and maintenance:

- ✓ *Beginning (4–6 weeks)*. Start slow and low (in intensity). If you're walking, monitor your heart rate and aim for 55 percent of your maximum heart rate. Moving at the right pace is also important. If you can sing as you walk, you're going too slow; if you can't talk, you're going too fast.
- ✓ *Progression (16–20 weeks)*. Gradually increase the duration and/or intensity of your workouts. Add 5 minutes every two weeks to your walking time. Gradually pick up your pace, using your target heart

rate as your guide. Keep a log of your workouts so you can chart your progress until you reach your goal.
- ✓ *Maintenance (lifelong)*. Once you've reached the stage of exercising for an hour every day combine or alternate activities to that you enjoy. This can be a form of *cross-training*.

## Walking

Walking continues to be the most popular physical activity in Canada.[51] The good news for all is that walking may well be the perfect exercise.

Recent research has demonstrated the health benefits of walking for both men and women and for both healthy individuals and those with heart disease. The Women's Health Study, a randomized, controlled trial of aspirin and heart disease, found that even walking one hour per week can lower heart-disease risk among relatively sedentary women.[52] Walking also protects men's hearts, whether they're healthy or have had heart problems. In a recent British study of 772 men, those who regularly engaged in light exercise, including walking, had a risk of death that was 58 percent lower than that of their sedentary counterparts.[53]

Treadmills are another option. They keep you moving at a certain pace. Holding onto the handrails while walking on a treadmill reduces both heart rate and oxygen consumption, so you burn fewer calories. Experts advise slowing the pace if necessary so you can let go of the handrails while working out.[54]

There is a new body of research about "manpo-kei" or 10 000 steps.[55] Some studies suggest that stepping 10 000 steps a day can be a beneficial way to increase heart health, lose weight, and feel healthier. More research is currently being done to determine varying step counts for individuals of different fitness levels. Crouteau (2004) implemented an eight-week pedometer lifestyle-intervention program with 37 college employees. The results of this study indicated that those employees who used pedometers had a significant increase in average daily step counts as compared to those who did not use a pedometer.[56] Tudor-Locke, one of the foremost pedometer researchers, began the First Step Program, a research project funded by the Canadian Diabetic Association. Her findings showed the activity level of older adults in the First Step Program who used pedometers was significantly higher than the activity level of the control group—the participants in the research study who did not use pedometers.[57, 58]

Although a pedometer cannot gauge the intensity of your effort—it counts walking on flat ground the same as hiking up a mountain, and stride length will differ from person to person—the benefits of using a pedometer far outweigh these small limitations.

▲ The H215 pedometer, showing a margin of error in step counting of less than 1 percent can be used to track daily steps.

© Courtesy of Speakwell

## Jogging and Running

The difference between jogging and running is speed. You should be able to carry on a conversation with someone on a long jog or run; if you're too breathless to talk, you're pushing too hard.

If your goal is to enhance aerobic fitness, long, slow, distance running is best. If you want to improve your speed, try *interval training,* which consists of repeated hard runs over a certain distance, with intervals of relaxed jogging in between. Depending on what suits you and what your training goals are, you can vary the distance, duration, and number of fast runs, as well as the time and activity between them.

If you have been sedentary, it's best to launch a walking program before attempting to jog or run. Start by walking for 15 to 20 minutes three times a week at a comfortable pace. When you can handle a brisk 20-minute walk, alternate fast walking with slow jogging. Continue to alternate in this manner until you can jog for 10 minutes without stopping.

## Other Aerobic Activities

Many people prefer different forms of aerobic exercise. All can provide many health benefits. Among the popular options:

✔ *Swimming.* For aerobic conditioning, try to keep up a steady pace for 20 minutes that's fast enough to make you feel pleasantly tired, but not completely exhausted. Your heart will beat more slowly in water than on land, so your heart rate while swimming is not an accurate guide to exercise intensity.

✔ *Cycling.* Bicycling, indoors and out, can be an excellent cardiovascular conditioner, as well as an effective way to control weight. Alternate flat surfaces and hills for an overall workout.

✔ *Spinning™.* Spinning is a cardiovascular workout for the whole body that utilizes a special stationary bicycle. Led by an instructor, a group of bikers listens to music and modifies their individual bike's resistance and their own pace according to the rhythm. An average spinning class lasts 45 minutes.

✔ *Aerobic dance or fitness class.* A typical aerobic class consists of warm-up stretching exercises followed by choreographed movement patterns, often done to music. Some classes include floor exercises such as sit-ups and muscle strength and endurance exercises followed by cool-down exercises.

✔ *Step training or bench aerobics.* "Stepping" combines step or bench climbing with music and choreographed movements. Basic equipment consists of a bench 10 to 30 centimetres high. The fitter you are, the higher the bench—but the higher the bench, the greater the risk of knee injury.

✔ *Stair-climbing.* Stair-climbing machines are a popular piece of fitness equipment in most fitness centres. Exercisers push a pair of pedals up and down, which is much easier on the feet and legs than many other activities. You can also use the stairs in an office building or dormitory as a way of increasing your daily physical activity. A workplace health initiative, launched in Lake Louise in 2002, called Stairway to Health, encouraged employees to take the stairs instead of the elevator. Using the stairs burns twice as many calories as walking and requires no special skill, equipment, or clothing. Climbing just two flights of stairs everyday could result a loss of 2.7 kilograms, or 6 pounds, per year. Six flights a day could help you trim nearly 18 pounds. Adding stairs to your day can

© iStockphoto.com/Eliza Snow

▲ Spinning has become a popular option for aerobic exercise because people of different ages, skills, and fitness levels can participate in the same class.

add years to your life. Studies show that risk of cardio-vascular disease and death is lower among those who are regular stair climbers.[59]

✓ *Inline skating.* Inline skating can increase aerobic endurance and muscular strength and is less stressful on joints and bones than running or high-impact aerobics. Skaters can adjust the intensity of their workout by varying the terrain. Protective gear—including a helmet, knee and elbow pads, and wrist guards—is essential.

# Muscular Strength and Endurance

Muscular strength and endurance workouts are important because they enable muscles to work more efficiently and reliably. Conditioned muscles function more smoothly, and contract more vigorously with less effort. With exercise, muscle tissue becomes firmer and can withstand much more strain—the result of toughening the sheath protecting the muscle and developing more connective tissue within it.

Muscular strength and endurance are critical for handling everyday burdens, such as cramming a heavy suitcase into an overhead luggage bin or hauling textbooks around the campus. Prolonged exercise prepares the muscles for sustained work by improving the circulation of blood in the tissue. The number of tiny blood vessels, called capillaries, increases by as much as 50 percent in regularly exercised muscles, and existing capillaries open wider so that the total circulation increases by as much as 400 percent, thus providing the muscles with a much greater supply of nutrients. This increase occurs after about 8 to 12 weeks in young people, but takes longer in older individuals. Inactivity reverses the process, gradually shutting down the extra capillaries that have developed.

The latest research on burning fat shows that the best way to reduce your body fat is to add muscle-strengthening exercise to your workouts. Muscle tissue is your very best calorie-burning tissue, and the more you have, the more calories you burn, even when you are resting. You don't have to become a serious body builder. Using free weights two or three times a week is enough.

## Exercise and Muscles

Muscles that are not used will atrophy, weaken, or break down. If you use them rigorously and regularly, however, they grow stronger. The only way to develop muscles is by demanding more of them than you usually do. This is called **overloading.** As you train, you have to gradually increase the number of repetitions or the amount of resistance and work the muscle to temporary fatigue.

You need to exercise differently for strength than for endurance. *To develop strength,* do 4 to 8 repetitions with heavy loads. As you increase the weight your muscles must move, you increase your strength. *To increase endurance,* do 8 to 12 repetitions with lighter loads.

Muscles can do only two things: contract or relax. As they do so, skeletal muscles either pull on bones or stop pulling on bones. All exercise involves muscles pulling on bones across a joint. The movement that takes place depends on the structure of the joint and the position of the muscle attachments involved.

In an **isometric** contraction, the muscle applies force while maintaining an equal length. The muscle contracts and tries to shorten but cannot overcome the resistance. An example is pushing against an immovable object, such as a wall, or tightening an abdominal muscle while sitting. The muscle contracts, but there is no movement. Push or pull against the immovable object, with each muscle contraction held for 5 to 8 seconds; repeat 5 to 10 times daily.

An **isotonic** contraction involves dynamic muscle movement against a constant resistance several times. The actual force exerted by the muscle is not constant because at some point in the movement, the position of the joint will produce a mechanical advantage. Contracting the muscle constitutes the **concentric phase** of an isotonic contraction. Lowering the weight to the starting position of the exercise represents the **eccentric phase** of the lift.

True **isokinetic** contraction is a constant speed contraction. Isokinetic exercises require special machines that provide resistance to overload muscles throughout the entire range of motion. Hydraulic strength training equipment used in some fitness centres such as Curves is sometimes called an isokinetic training program.

## ???? How Do I Design a Muscle Workout?

A workout with weights should exercise your body's primary muscle groups, including the *deltoids* (shoulders), *pectorals* (chest), *triceps* and *biceps* (back and front of upper arms), *quadriceps* and *hamstrings* (front and back of thighs), *gluteus maximus* (buttocks), *trapezius* and *rhomboids* (upper back), and *abdomen* (see Figure 4-3). Various machines and free-weight routines focus on each muscle group, but the principle is always the same. Muscles contract as you raise and lower a weight, and you repeat the lift-and-lower routine until the muscle group is tired.

A weight-training program is made up of *reps* (the single performance, or *repetition,* of an exercise, such as lifting 20 kilograms one time) and *sets* (a *set* is the number of repetitions of the same movement, such as a set of 20 push-ups).

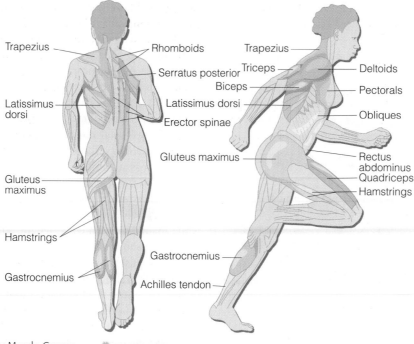

▲ **Figure 4-3** Primary Muscle Groups
Different exercises can strengthen and stretch different muscle groups.

Source: Hespenheide Design

Maintaining proper breathing during weight training is crucial. To breathe correctly, inhale when muscles are relaxed, and exhale when you push or lift. Don't hold your breath, because oxygen flow helps prevent muscle fatigue and injury.

No one type of equipment—free weight or machine—has a clear advantage in terms of building fat-free body mass, enhancing strength and endurance, or improving a sport-specific skill. Each type offers benefits but also has drawbacks.

Free weights offer great versatility for strength training. With dumbbells you can perform a variety of exercises to work specific muscle groups, such as the chest and shoulders. Machines, in contrast, are more limited; most allow only one exercise.

However, strength-training machines have advantages, too. They ensure correct movement for a lift, which helps protect against injury and prevent cheating when fatigue sets in. They isolate specific muscles, which is good for rehabilitating an injury or strengthening a specific body part. Because they offer high-tech options such as varying resistance during the lifting motion, they can tax muscles in ways that a traditional barbell cannot.

Your muscles need sufficient time to recover from a weight-training session. Allow no less than 48 hours but no more than 96 hours between training sessions, so your body can recover from the workout and you avoid overtraining. Two or three 30-minute training sessions a week should be sufficient for building strength and endurance.

Other types of exercise programs such as yoga, Pilates, and the use of exercise balls provide muscle strength and endurance workouts, too. There are many different types of programs to choose from—many offered at colleges and university fitness and recreation centres. Certified instructors can provide you with beginner to advanced classes.

## Flexibility

Flexibility determines the range of motion achievable without injury at a joint or group of joints. There are two types of flexibility: static and dynamic. **Static flexibility** refers to the ability to assume and maintain an extended position at one end point in a joint's range of motion. **Dynamic flexibility** involves movement. It is the ability to move a joint quickly and fluidly through its entire range of motion with little resistance. The static flexibility in the hip joint determines whether you can do a split; dynamic flexibility would enable you to perform a split leap.

Static flexibility depends on the structure of a joint and the tightness of the muscles, tendons, and ligaments attached to it. Dynamic flexibility is influenced by static flexibility but also depends on additional factors, such as strength, coordination, and resistance to movement.

Genetics, age, gender, and body composition all influence how flexible you are. Girls and women tend to be more flexible than boys and men to a certain extent because of hormonal and anatomical differences. Over time, the natural elasticity of muscles, tendons, and joints decreases in both genders, resulting in stiffness.

## The Benefits of Flexibility

Flexibility can make everyday tasks, such as bending over to tie a shoe or reaching up to a high shelf, easier and safer. It can also prevent and relieve the ankle, knee, back, and shoulder pain that many people feel as they get older. If you do other forms of exercise, flexibility lowers your risk of injury and may improve your performance.

✔ *Prevention of injuries.* Flexibility training stretches muscles and increases the elasticity of joints.
✔ *Relief of muscle strain.* Stretching helps relieve muscle tension and enables you to work more effectively.
✔ *Relaxation.* Flexibility exercises are great stress busters that reduce mental strain, slow the rate of breathing, and reduce blood pressure.
✔ *Better athletic performance.* Good flexibility allows for more efficient movement and exertion of more force through a greater range of motion. This is a special benefit for any activity, from gymnastics to golf, where positions beyond the normal range of motion are necessary to perform certain skills.

### What Is the Difference Between Stretching and Warming Up?

Warming up means getting the heart beating, breaking a sweat, and readying the body for more vigorous activity. Stretching is a specific activity intended to elongate the

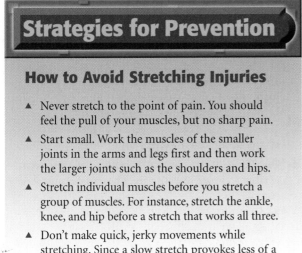

## Strategies for Prevention

### How to Avoid Stretching Injuries

▲ Never stretch to the point of pain. You should feel the pull of your muscles, but no sharp pain.

▲ Start small. Work the muscles of the smaller joints in the arms and legs first and then work the larger joints such as the shoulders and hips.

▲ Stretch individual muscles before you stretch a group of muscles. For instance, stretch the ankle, knee, and hip before a stretch that works all three.

▲ Don't make quick, jerky movements while stretching. Since a slow stretch provokes less of a reaction from the stress receptors, the muscles can safely stretch farther than usual.

muscles and keep joints limber, not simply a prelude to a game of tennis or a 5-kilometre run.

For most sports, light to moderate activity, such as walking at gradually increasing intensity, is a better warm-up than stretching. One of the best times to stretch is after an aerobic workout. Your muscles will be warm, more flexible, and less prone to injury. In addition, stretching after aerobic activity can help a fatigued muscle return to its normal resting length and possibly helps reduce delayed muscle soreness.

## Sports Safety

Whenever you work out, you don't want to risk becoming sore or injured. Starting slowly when you begin any new fitness activity is the smartest strategy. Keep a simple diary to record the time and duration of each workout. Get accustomed to an activity and then begin to work harder or longer. In this way, you strengthen your musculoskeletal system so you're less likely to be injured, you lower the cardiovascular risk, and you build the exercise habit into your schedule.

### How Can I Prevent Sports Injuries?

Both genders are equally likely to suffer an exercise-related injury. An estimated one in four women and one in three men discontinue their exercise programs because of injury.[60] The most common exercise-related injury sites are the knees, feet, back, and shoulders, followed by the ankles and hips. **Acute injuries**—sprains, bruises, and pulled muscles—are the result of sudden trauma, such as a fall or collision. **Overuse injuries** are the result of overdoing a repetitive activity, such as running. When one particular joint is overstressed (such as a tennis player's elbow or a swimmer's shoulder), tendonitis, an inflammation at the point where the tendon meets the bone, can develop. Other overuse injuries include muscle strains and aches and stress fractures, which are hairline breaks in a bone, usually in the leg or foot.

To prevent injuries and other exercise-related problems before they happen, use common sense and take appropriate precautions, including the following:

✔ Get proper instruction and, if necessary, advanced training from knowledgeable instructors.
✔ Make sure that stretching and exercises are preventing, not causing, injuries.
✔ Make sure you have good equipment and keep it in good condition. Always check your equipment prior to each use (especially if you're renting it).

✔ Use reasonable protective measures, including wearing a helmet when cycling, skiing, or skating.

✔ Take each outing seriously. Avoid the unknown under adverse conditions (for example, hiking unfamiliar terrain during poor weather or kayaking a new river when water levels are unusually high or low) or when accompanied by a beginner whose skills may not be as strong as yours.

✔ Never combine alcohol or drugs with any sport.

## Thinking of Temperature

Prevention is the wisest approach to heat problems. Always dress appropriately for the weather and be aware of the health risks associated with temperature extremes.

### Heeding Heat

Always wear as little as possible when exercising in hot weather. Choose loose-fitting, lightweight, white or light-coloured clothes. Never wear rubberized or plastic pants and jackets to sweat off pounds. These sauna suits don't allow your body heat to dissipate, and they can be dangerous. Drink plenty of fluids while exercising (especially water), and watch for the earliest signs of heat problems, including cramps, stress, exhaustion, and heatstroke.

### Coping with Cold

Protect yourself in cold weather (or cold indoor gyms) by covering as much of your body as possible, but don't overdress. Wear one layer less than you would if you were outside but not exercising. Don't use warm-up clothes of waterproof material because they tend to trap heat and keep perspiration from evaporating. Make sure your clothes are loose enough to allow movement and exercise of the hands, feet, and other body parts, thereby maintaining proper circulation. Because 40 percent or more of your body heat is lost through your head and neck, wear a hat, turtleneck, or scarf. Cover your hands and feet, too; mittens provide more warmth and protection than gloves.

### Overtraining

About half of all people who start an exercise program drop out within six months. One common reason is that they **overtrain,** pushing themselves to work too intensely, too frequently. Signs of overdoing it include persistent muscle soreness, frequent injuries, unintended weight loss, nervousness, and an inability to relax. Overtraining for endurance sports such as marathon running can damage the lungs and intensify asthma symptoms. If you're pushing too hard, you may find yourself unable to complete a normal workout or to recover after a normal workout. Rest is just as important as your training program.

**CHAPTER**

**4**

**Making This Chapter Work for You**

1. Mary Ann takes a step aerobics class three times a week. Which component of physical fitness does her exercise routine emphasize?
   a. muscular strength and endurance
   b. flexibility
   c. cardiorespiratory fitness
   d. body composition

2. The benefits of regular physical activity include
   a. decreased bone mass.
   b. lowered risk of shin splints.
   c. enhanced immune response.
   d. altered sleep patterns.

3. In *Canada's Physical Activity Guide to Healthy Active Living,* which activity would be considered a moderate-effort activity?
   a. sprinting
   b. dusting
   c. hockey
   d. swimming for 30 to 60 minutes

4. The three principles of exercise are
   a. overload, specificity, and duration.
   b. overload, reversibility, and specificity.
   c. overload, progressive overloading, and FIT.
   d. frequency, intensity, and time.

5. To receive the cardiovascular benefits of exercise, at what percentage of your target heart rate must you exercise?
   a. 60 to 65
   b. 55 to 90
   c. 80 to 90
   d. 90 to 100

6. Which of the following best describes the primary benefit of aerobic exercise?
   a. It improves cardiorespiratory endurance.
   b. It helps condition your muscles, enabling them to work efficiently and reliably.
   c. It can enhance weight loss.
   d. It increases the range of motion of your joints.

7. An aerobic workout may consist of
   a. 5 minutes of brisk walking, 30 minutes of flexibility exercises, 5 minutes of brisk walking.
   b. 15 minutes of resistance exercises followed by 10 minutes of stretching.
   c. 10 minutes of sprints, 5 minutes of slow jogging, 5 minutes of stretching, 10 minutes of sprints.
   d. 5 minutes of stretching, 5 minutes of brisk walking, 45 minutes of jogging, 5 minutes of slow walking, 5 minutes of stretching.

8. Which statement is true about isometric, isotonic, and isokinetic exercises?
   a. Isokinetic exercises usually involve pushing on an object, isometric exercises involve pulling on an object, and isotonic exercises involve lifting an object.
   b. Isometric and isokinetic exercises can be done with free weights, but isotonic exercises require special resistance machines.
   c. Weight lifting is an isotonic exercise, pushing against the wall is an isometric exercise, and isokinetic exercises require special machines that move muscles through their range of motion.
   d. Isotonic exercises are much more effective at contracting muscles than isometric or isokinetic.

9. A regular flexibility program provides which of the following benefits?
   a. stronger heart and lungs
   b. relief of muscle strain and soreness
   c. increased strength and endurance
   d. increased bone mass and leaner muscles

10. To stay safe when exercising in hot weather, which of these is *not* a good idea?
    a. wear loose-fitting, lightweight clothes
    b. carry a damp towel or cloth to cool yourself down
    c. drink plenty of fluids, especially water
    d. wear one layer more than you would if you were not exercising

Answers to these questions can be found on page 450.

## Self Responsibility

*Clarify, adjust, and take it to completion.*

**Mark Allen, six-time winner of the Hawaii Ironman**

Beginning or maintaining a regular physical activity program takes time, commitment, and energy. You don't have to be an elite athlete like Mark Allen, but you can use his words of advice to get started or to keep going. If you are trying to "get back on track," clarify: ask yourself what is stopping you. Do you prefer group fitness classes or walks or runs on your own? Do you need some instruction from a fitness expert to get you started? Once you figure out what is preventing you from participating in regular physical activity, then adjust. Check out your daily schedule. Find ways to "fit fitness in." Remember, you do not have to spend hours at a fitness facility to realize fitness benefits.

## Social Responsibility

*Look after yourself. Look after one another.*

**Right To Play**

Once you have begun or rejuvenated your fitness program, take it to completion. Ask yourself what success will look like. Will you plan to compete in an 8-kilometre run or does attendance at a regular yoga program mean success to you? The wonderful thing about a physical-activity program is that you can start one—anytime—even if you have stopped in the past. Prochaska's Stages of Change support Mark Allen's model: You contemplate, prepare, take action, and then maintain.

If you have ever thought about doing some volunteer work, consider volunteering for *Right To Play*. This organization encourages and supports young adults who want to make a difference through physical activity and sport.

## Critical Thinking

1. Allison knows that exercise is good for her health, but she figures she can keep her weight down by dieting and worry about her heart and health when she gets older. "I look good. I feel okay. Why should I bother exercising?" she asks. What would you reply?

2. When he started working out, Jeff simply wanted to stay in shape. But he felt so pleased with the way his body looked and responded that he kept doing more. Now he runs 15 kilometres a day, lifts weights, works out on exercise equipment almost every day, and plays racquetball or squash whenever he gets a chance. Is Jeff getting too much of a good thing? Is there any danger in his fitness program? What would be a more reasonable approach?

## CENGAGENOW™

If your textbook package includes CengageNOW™, go to http://west.cengagenow.com/ilrn/ to link to CengageNOW™ for Health, your online study tool. First take the **Pre-test** for this chapter to get your personalized **Study Plan,** which will identify topics you need to review and direct you to the appropriate resources. Then take the **Post-test** to determine what concepts you have mastered and what you still need work on.

## SITES & BYTES

### Canadian Fitness and Lifestyle Research Institute
**www.cflri.ca**

This national research agency advises, educates, and informs Canadians about the importance of healthy, active lifestyles.

### Canada's Physical Activity Guide
**www.phac-aspc.gc.ca/pau-uap/paguide**

Health Canada and the Canadian Society for Exercise Physiology worked in partnership to develop this physical-activity guide.

### Canada's Physical Activity Guide Handbook
**www.phac-aspc.gc.ca/pau-uap/fitness/order.html**

The *Physical Activity Guide Handbook* provides additional information to help you make the best use of the one-page guide.

### Canadian Society for Exercise Physiology
**www.csep.ca**

You can find current information on exercise physiology, exercise biochemistry, and fitness and health from CSEP's site. Also available is information about health and fitness certifications and health-screening forms.

### Health Canada—Healthy Living Unit
**www.phac-aspc.gc.ca/pau-uap/fitness/about.html**

Visit this site to learn about the Healthy Living Unit within Health Canada. You can also access information about the role of physical activity for the prevention of chronic disease.

### Speakwell
**www.speakwell.com**

Check out this award-winning fitness and wellness site. Current research on healthy living and an interactive pedometer tracking site are just some of the things you will find.

Please note that links are subject to change. If you find a broken link, use a search engine such as www.google.ca and search for the website by typing in keywords.

### InfoTrac® College Edition Activity

Jackson, E.M., & Howton, A. (2008). Increasing walking in college students using a pedometer intervention: Differences according to body mass index. *Journal of American College Health, 57*(2), (Sept.–Oct.) 159–64.

1. The authors of this study found some unexpected results after they analyzed their data collected to determine if body mass of students made a difference in the number of steps taken throughout the day, tracked by the use of a pedometer. What were these surprise findings?

2. Discuss how you might use an interactive intervention such as pedometers to help you increase your daily physical activity levels. What barriers might you face? What benefits might you realize?

You can find additional readings relating to fitness with InfoTrac® College Edition, an online library of more than 5000 journals and publications. Follow the instructions for accessing InfoTrac® that were packaged with your textbook; then search for articles using a keyword search.

For additional links and resources, visit our text-specific website at www.health.nelson.com.

## Key Terms

The terms listed here are used within the chapter on the page indicated. Definitions of the terms are in the Glossary at the end of this book.

| | | | |
|---|---|---|---|
| **active living** 74 | **dynamic flexibility** 90 | **muscular fitness** 74 | **progressive** |
| **acute injuries** 91 | **eccentric phase** 89 | **osteoporosis** 78 | **overloading** 81 |
| **aerobic exercise** 74 | **endorphins** 78 | **overload principle** 81 | **resting heart rate** 86 |
| **anaerobic exercise** 86 | **endurance** 74 | **overloading** 89 | **reversibility principle** 83 |
| **body composition** 74 | **FIT** 81 | **overtrain** 92 | **specificity principle** 84 |
| **cardiorespiratory** | **flexibility** 74 | **overuse injuries** 91 | **sport** 74 |
| **fitness** 74 | **isokinetic** 89 | **physical activity** 74 | **static flexibility** 90 |
| **concentric phase** 89 | **isometric** 89 | **physical fitness** 74 | **strength** 74 |
| **conditioning** 74 | **isotonic** 89 | | **target heart rate** 86 |

## References

1. Tremblay, A., & Chiasson, L. (2002). Physical fitness in young college men and women. *Canadian Journal of Applied Physiology, 27,* 563–74.
2. Health Canada. (2003, October 8). Physical activity unit. Available at www.phac-aspc.gc.ca/pau-uap/fitness/about.html.
3. Fitness and Amateur Sport, Government of Canada. (1992). Active living tool kit. Secretariat of Focus on Active Living.
4. Stewart, G.S. (1995). *Active living: The miracle medicine for a long and healthy life.* Windsor, ON: Human Kinetics, xi.
5. World Health Organization. (2004). Physical Activity and Women. Global Strategy on Diet, Physical Activity and Health. Available at www.who.int/dietphysicalactivity/factsheet_women/en/index.html.
6. Craig, C.L., & Cameron, C. (2004). *Increasing physical activity: Assessing trends from 1998–2003.* Ottawa, ON: Canadian Fitness and Lifestyle Research Institute.
7. Statistics Canada. (2003). Canadian community health survey (CCHS)—Cycle 1.1. Available at www.statcan.ca/english/concepts/health/index.htm.
8. World Health Organization. (2004). Diet and physical activity: A public health priority. Global Strategy on Diet, Physical Activity and Health. Available at www.who.int/dietphysicalactivity/en/index.html.
9. Tufts University. (2002). How fit you are determines your life span. *Tufts University Health & Nutrition Letter, 20*(5), 6.
10. Palatini, P., et al. (2002). Exercise capacity and mortality. *New England Journal of Medicine, 347*(4), 288.
11. Roberts, S. (2002). Why exercise matters. *Diabetes Forecast, 55*(8), 73.
12. Foot, D., Curnew, G., & Pearson, L. (2005). *The shape of things to come: A national report on heart disease and the challenges ahead.* Toronto: Commissioned by Becel. Available at www.becel.ca/pdf/shapeofthings_en.pdf.

13. Harvard University. (2002). Heart beat—Activity keeps the blood flowing. *Harvard Heart Letter, 12*(11).

14. Lee, I.-M., Paffenberger, R.S. Jr., & Hsieh, C.-C. (1991). Physical activity and risk of developing colorectal cancer among college alumni. *Journal of the National Cancer Institute, 83,* 1324–29.

15. Canadian Cancer Society. (2008, August 17). About Cancer. Colorectal Cancer Stats. Available at www.cancer.ca/Canada-wide/About%20cancer/Cancer%20statistics/Stats%20at%20a%20glance/Colorectal%20cancer.aspx?sc_lang=en.

16. Tufts University (2002). Regular physical exertion may fight cancer as well as heart disease. *Tufts University Health & Nutrition Letter, 18*(7).

17. Canada.com. (2008). Home. Topics. News. Physical activity on breast cancer varies. Available at www.canada.com/topics/news/story.html?id=582d0af9-135b-4028-ab74-37e9ed7d6e76.

18. Harris, S. (2007). Moderate physical activity prevents breast cancer recurrence. *Healthy Living, 5*(3). Available at www.abreastinthewest.ca/active2.cfm?Num=53.

19. Exercise lowers levels of blood estrogen. (2002, August 8). *Women's Health Weekly,* 10.

20. Goeree, R., O'Brien, B., Pettit, D., Cuddy, L., Ferraz, M., & Adachi, J. (1996). An assessment of the burden of illness due to osteoporosis in Canada. *Journal SOCG Supplement,* 15–24.

21. Yonclas, P., et al. (2002). Osteoporosis: How much exercise is enough for bone health? *Consultant, 42*(7), 829–34.

22. Exercise and illness. (2002). *JOPERD—The Journal of Physical Education, Recreation & Dance, 73*(6), 19.

23. Exercise against depression. (2001). *Harvard Mental Health Letter, 17*(19).

24. LeTourneau, M. (2001, May–June). Pump up to cheer up. *Psychology Today,* 27.

25. Exercise as psychotherapy. (2000). *Harvard Mental Health Letter, 17*(3).

26. Babyak, M., et al. (2000). Exercise treatment for major depression: Maintenance of therapeutic benefit at 10 months. *Psychosomatic Medicine, 62*(5), 633–38.

27. Tjepkema, M. (2005). Adult Obesity in Canada: Measured Height and Weight. Available at www.statcan.ca/Daily/English/050706/d050706a.htm.

28. Vella, C., & Kravitz, L. (2004, November/December). Exercise afterburn—A research update: What effect do intensity, mode, duration and other factors have on calorie burning after exercise? *Idea Fitness Journal, 5,* 42–46.

29. Public Health Agency of Canada (2008). Diabetes in Canada: Highlights from the National Diabetes Surveillance System, 2004–2005. Available at www.phac-aspc.gc.ca/ccdpc-cpcmc/ndss-snsd/english/index_e.html.

30. Clement, Tony (2006, October). Minister of Health's Speech. Presented at the 10th Annual Canadian Diabetes Association/Canadian Society of Endocrinology & Metabolism Professional Conference. Available at www.hc-sc.gc.ca/ahc-asc/minist/speeches-discours/2006_10_19-eng.php.

31. Manson, J.E., Rimm, E.B., Stampfer, M.J., et al. (1991). Physical activity and the incidence of non-insulin dependent diabetes in women. *Lancet, 338,* 774–78.

32. *National blueprint: Increasing physical activity among adults age 50 and older.* (2001, May 1). Washington, DC: National Center for Chronic Disease Prevention and Health Promotion.

33. Gilmour, H. (2007). Physically active Canadians. *Statistics Canada Health Reports, 18*(3), 45–65. Available at www.statcan.ca/Daily/English/070822/d070822b.htm.

34. Heart lines—Walking and gardening beneficial for heart disease patients. (2001). *Harvard Heart Letter, 11*(8).

35. Easy ways to reduce the risk of heart disease. (2001, April). *Health Facts.*

36. Health Canada. (2003, October 8). Our mission. Physical activity unit. Available at www.phac-aspc.gc.ca/pau-uap/fitness/about.html.

37. Health Canada. (2007, March 3). Over 40 national organizations endorse new physical activity guide. News Release. Available at www.phac-aspc.gc.ca/pau-uap/fitness/partners.html.

38. Canadian Society for Exercise Physiology. (2008). Home. Available at www.csep.ca.

39. Physical and Health Education Canada. (PHE). (2008). Quality daily physical education. Available at www.cahperd.ca/eng/physicaleducation/about_qdpe.cfm.

40. Right To Play. (2008). Home. Available at www.righttoplay.com/site/PageServer?pagename=canada.

41. Wei, M, et al. (1999). Relationship between low cardiorespiratory fitness and mortality in normal-weight, overweight, and obese men. *Journal of the American Medical Association, 282*(16), 1547.

42. Heart and Stroke Foundation. (2008). Heart disease. General info—Incidence of cardiovascular disease. Available at www.heartandstroke.com.

43. Blair, S., Kohl, H.W. III, & Gordon, N.F. (1992). Physical activity and health: A lifestyle approach. *Medicine, Exercise, Nutrition, and Health. 1,* 54–57.

44. Don't sweat over how much or what type of exercise, just do it. (2001). *American Family Physician, 63,* 1899.

45. Ramadan, J., et al. (2001). Low-frequency physical activity insufficient for aerobic conditioning is associated with lower body fat than sedentary conditions. *Nutrition, 17,* 225.

46. Lee, I-Min, et al. (2001). Physical activity and coronary heart disease in women: Is "no pain, no gain" passé? *Journal of the American Medical Association, 285*(11).

47. Chisholm, M.D., Collis, M.L., Kulak, L.L., Davenport, W., Gruber, N., & Steward, G.W. (1978). *PAR-Q* validation report: The evaluation of a self-administered pre-exercise screening questionnaire for adults.* British Columbia Ministry of Health and Health and Welfare Canada.

48. Canadian Society for Exercise Physiology. (2002). PAR-Q screening forms. Available at www.csep.ca/main.cfm?cid=574&nid=5110.

49. American College of Sports Medicine. (2007). Home. Available at www.acsm.org.

50. Burke, E. (2002). Heart rate ABCs. *Better Nutrition, 64*(8), 48.

51. Canadian Fitness and Lifestyle Research Institute. (CFLRI). (2000). 2000 physical activity monitor. Available at www.cflri.ca/eng/statistics/surveys/pam2000.php.

52. Lee, I-Min, et al. (2001). Physical activity and coronary heart disease in women: Is "no pain, no gain" passé? *Journal of the American Medical Association, 285*(11).

53. Heart lines—Walking and gardening beneficial for heart disease patients. (2001). *Harvard Heart Letter, 11*(8).

54. Welch, G. (2001). Learning to let go. *American Fitness, 9*(4), 61.

55. Hatano, Y. (1993). Use of pedometers for promoting daily walking exercise. *Journal of the International Council for Health, Physical Education and Recreation, 29*(4), 4–8.

56. Croteau, K.A. (2004). A preliminary study on the impact of a pedometer-based intervention on daily steps. *Health Promotion, 18*(3), 217–20.

57. Tudor-Locke, C.E., & Myers, A.M. (2001). Methodological considerations for researchers and practitioners using pedometers to measure physical (ambulatory) activity. *Research Quarterly for Exercise and Sport, 72*(1), 1–12.

58. Tudor-Locke, C.E. (2001). First step program. *Canadian Diabetes Care, 24*(4).

59. Health Canada. (2007, February 26). Welcome to the stairway to health. Physical activity unit. Available at www.phac-aspc.gc.ca/sth-evs/english/index.htm.

60. Hootman, J., et al. (2002). Epidemiology of musculoskeletal injuries among sedentary and physically active adults. *Medicine and Science in Sports and Exercise, 34,* 838.

# CHAPTER
# 5

# Personal Nutrition

We are what we eat—and it shows in everything from our stamina and strength to the sheen in our hair and the health of our skin. Eating well helps us live and feel well. As demonstrated by the science of **nutrition,** the field that explores the connections between our bodies and the foods we eat, our daily diet affects how long and how well we live. Sensible eating can provide energy for our daily tasks, protect us from many chronic illnesses, and may even extend longevity.

Many foods can serve as the building blocks of a healthy lifestyle. However, making good food choices isn't easy. Faced with a bewildering array of food products and a blitz of advertising claims, you may well find it hard to select the foods that not only taste good, but also are good for you. This chapter can help. It translates the latest information on good nutrition into specific advice that you can use to nourish yourself and enjoy eating well.

You will learn about nutrients, vitamins, and serving sizes. You will be introduced to a variety of food guides and culturally diverse diets. There is also information on dietary reference intakes and nutrition labelling. The chapter will conclude with a section on food safety.

**After studying the material in this chapter, you will be able to:**

- **List** the basic nutrients necessary for a healthy body and **describe** their functions.
- **Describe** *Eating Well with Canada's Food Guide* and **explain** its significance.
- **Explain** current recommendations for food portions and servings.
- **Discuss** the purpose of the Dietary Reference Intakes and **explain** how to interpret the nutritional information provided on the food labels.
- **Compare** the advantages and disadvantages of various alternative diets and ethnic foods.
- **List** the food-safety hazards and describe prevention measures.

# What You Need to Know About Nutrients

Every day your body needs certain **essential nutrients** that it cannot manufacture for itself. They provide energy, build and repair body tissues, and regulate body functions. The six classes of essential nutrients, which are discussed in this section, are water, protein, carbohydrates, fats, vitamins, and minerals (see Table 5-1).

Water makes up about 60 percent of our body and is essential for health and survival. Besides water, we also need energy to live, and we receive our energy from the carbohydrates, proteins, and fats in the foods we eat. These three essential nutrients are called **macronutrients** because they are the nutrients required by the human body in the greatest amounts. The amount of energy that can be derived from the macronutrients is measured in **calories.** There are nine calories in every gram of fat and four calories in every gram of protein or carbohydrate. The other two essential nutrients—the vitamins and minerals—are called **micronutrients** because our bodies need them in only very small amounts.

An individual's need for macronutrients depends on how much energy he or she expends. Because fats, carbohydrates, and protein can all serve as sources of energy, they can, to some extent, substitute for one another in providing calories. In the latest report of the National Academy of Sciences, the agency that establishes nutrient intake recommendations for the United States and Canada,[1] adults should get 45 to 65 percent of calories from carbohydrates, 20 to 35 percent from fat, and 10 to 35 percent from protein. Children's fat intake should be slightly higher: 25 to 40 percent of their caloric intake.

## Water

Water, which makes up 85 percent of blood, 70 percent of muscles, and about 75 percent of the brain, performs many essential functions: It carries nutrients, maintains temperature, lubricates joints, helps with digestion, rids the body of waste through urine, and contributes to the production of sweat, which evaporates from the skin to cool the body. Research has correlated high fluid intake with a lower risk of kidney stones, colon cancer, and bladder cancer.

You lose about 2 to 2.5 litres of water a day—the equivalent of 8 to 10 cups (1 cup equals 250 millilitres)—through perspiration, urination, bowel movements, and normal exhalation. You lose water more rapidly if you exercise, live in a dry climate or at a high altitude, drink a lot of caffeine or alcohol (which increase urination), skip a meal, or become ill. To ensure adequate water intake, we need a minimum of approximately 2.7 to 3.7 litres (8 to 12 cups) of fluid each day. Water, 4 to 8 percent carbohydrate-containing sports drinks, and unsweetened juices are good

▼ **Table 5-1   The Essential Nutrients**

| | Functions | Sources |
|---|---|---|
| **Water** | Carries nutrients and removes waste; dissolves amino acids, glucose, and minerals; cleans body by removing toxins; regulates body temperature | Liquids, fruits, and vegetables |
| **Proteins** | Help build new tissue to keep hair, skin, and eyesight healthy; build antibodies, enzymes, hormones, and other compounds; provide fuel for body | Meat, poultry, fish, eggs, beans, nuts, cheese, tofu, vegetables, some fruits, pasta, breads, cereal, and rice |
| **Carbohydrates** | Provide energy | Grains, cereal, pasta, fruits, vegetables, nuts, milk, and sugars |
| **Fats** | | |
| **Saturated Fats** | Provide energy; trigger production of cholesterol | Red meat, dairy products, egg yolks, and coconut and palm oils |
| **Unsaturated Fats** | Also provide energy, but trigger more "good" cholesterol production and less "bad" cholesterol production | Some fish; avocados; olive, canola, and peanut oils; shortening (not made with beef tallow or other animal sources); stick margarine; baked goods |
| **Vitamins** | Facilitate use of other nutrients; involved in regulating growth, maintaining tissue, and manufacturing blood cells, hormones, and other body components | Fruits, vegetables, grains, some meat and dairy products (see Table 5-2) |
| **Minerals** | Help build bones and teeth; aid in muscle function and nervous system activity; assist in various body functions including growth and energy production | Many foods (see Table 5-3) |

beverage selections to prevent dehydration and to re-hydrate. Alcoholic and caffeinated beverages (coffee, tea, cola) can contribute to total fluid consumption but are not recommended since they may have diuretic effects which can leave you less hydrated.[2]

We can only survive a few days without water, whereas deficiencies of other nutrients may take weeks, months, or possibly years to develop.

## Protein

Critical for growth and repair, **proteins** form the basic framework for our muscles, bones, blood, hair, and finger-nails. Supplying four calories per gram, they are made of combinations of 20 **amino acids,** nine of which we must get from our diet because the human body cannot produce them. These are called *essential amino acids.*

Animal proteins—meat, fish, poultry, and dairy products—are **complete proteins** that provide the nine essential amino acids. Grains, dry beans, and nuts are **incomplete proteins** that may have relatively low levels of one or two essential amino acids but fairly high levels of others. Combining incomplete proteins, such as beans and rice, ensures that the body gets sufficient protein.

Based on the latest data, the recommended level of protein intake for adults is 0.8 grams per kilogram of body weight. The recommended intake of protein during pregnancy has been increased to provide an additional 25 grams a day above non-pregnant intake. Because of conflicting or inadequate data on the health risks of high-protein diets, the National Academy of Sciences has not set a tolerable upper intake level, although it does warn about this potential danger. The Executive Summary can be found at http://books.nap.edu/execsumm_pdf/10490.pdf.

You can also find age-based requirements for all nine of the essential amino acids found in dietary protein.

## Carbohydrates

**Carbohydrates** are organic compounds that provide our brain—our only truly carbohydrate-dependent organ—and body with *glucose,* their basic fuel. Carbohydrates can be classified according to the number and type of simple sugar units present. Monosaccharides (glucose, fructose, galactose), known as simple sugars or simple carbohydrates, consist of one simple sugar unit. Disaccharides (sucrose, lactose, maltose, table sugar) contain two sugar units linked by a chemical bond, while polysaccharides (starches and glycogen), known as complex carbohydrates, have more than 10 units of sugar. Fibre is also classified as a carbohydrate.

Most digestible carbohydrates are broken down to monosaccharides in the intestine. Monosaccharides that are

▲ Protein comes in many different forms.

absorbed in the small intestine may be metabolized and stored as glycogen in the liver or muscle cells or oxidized to give metabolically usable energy. All provide four calories per gram. Health Canada[3] recommends that both adults and children consume at least 130 grams of non-dietary fibre and non-sugar alcohol carbohydrate per day based on the glucose needs of the brain. Pregnant women should consume 175 grams per day in order to ensure adequate glucose provision to the fetal brain in addition to meeting the needs of the mother. To ensure the replacement of the carbohydrate secreted in human milk, lactating women should consume 210 grams of carbohydrates each day.

### Simple Carbohydrates

**Simple carbohydrates** include *natural sugars,* such as the lactose in milk and the fructose in fruit, and *added sugars,* including candy, soft drinks, fruit drinks, pastries, and other sweets. Added sugars should make up no more than 25 percent of total calories consumed.[4] Those whose diets are higher in added sugars typically have lower intakes of other essential nutrients. Other nutritional advocacy groups have challenged this recommendation and suggest 8 percent of calories, or about 40 grams of added sugar a day, for a person consuming 2000 calories.[5]

### Complex Carbohydrates

**Complex carbohydrates** are the foundation of a healthy diet and include grains, cereals, vegetables, beans, and nuts. Many Canadians, however, get most of their complex carbohydrates from refined grains, which have been stripped of fibre and many nutrients.

Far more nutritious are whole grains, which are made up of all components of the grain: the *bran* (or fibre-rich outer layer), the *endosperm* (middle layer), and the *germ* (the nutrient-packed inner layer).[6] Several health organizations have joined in recommending that Canadians increase their consumption of whole-grain foods to 5 to 12 servings a day. Individuals who eat whole-grain products each day have about a 15 to 25 percent reduction in death from all causes, including heart disease and cancer.[7]

## Fibre

**Dietary fibre** is the non-digestible form of carbohydrates occurring naturally in plant foods, such as leaves, stems, skins, seeds, and hulls. **Functional fibre** consists of isolated, non-digestible carbohydrates that may be added to foods and that provide beneficial effects in humans. Total fibre is the sum of both.

The various forms of fibre enhance health in different ways. They slow the emptying of the stomach, which creates a feeling of fullness and aids weight control. They interfere with absorption of dietary fat and cholesterol, which lowers the risk of heart disease and stroke. In addition, fibre helps prevent constipation and diverticulosis (a painful inflammation of the bowel). The link between fibre and colon cancer is complex. Some studies have indicated that increased fibre intake reduces risk, but a large-scale study of almost 90 000 women found no such correlation.[8]

The federal report on macronutrients set the first-ever recommendations for daily intake levels of total fibre (dietary plus functional fibre): 38 grams of total fibre for men and 25 grams for women. For men and women over 50 years of age, who consume less food, the recommendations are, respectively, 30 and 21 grams.[9]

Good fibre sources include wheat and corn bran (the outer layer); leafy greens; the skins of fruits and root vegetables; oats, beans, and barley; and the pulp, skin, and seeds of many fruits and vegetables, such as apples and strawberries. Because sudden increases in fibre can cause symptoms like bloating and gas, experts recommend gradually adding more fibre to your diet with an additional serving or two of vegetables, fruit, or whole-wheat bread.[10]

## Glycemic Index

According to the Dietitians of Canada, the term **glycemic index (GI)** is a new buzzword in many of the latest diet books.[11] What does GI mean?

Researchers developed the GI as a measure of how much a carbohydrate-containing food is likely to raise your blood sugar. According to the GI, foods can be divided into high, medium, and low glycemic values. A food with a high GI will raise your blood sugar more than a food with a low GI.

Studies have found that low glycemic index foods have health benefits such as the prevention of Type 2 diabetes,

control of blood sugar levels, and control of blood cholesterol levels. Use of the glycemic index is recommended in meal planning for people with diabetes or those at high risk of developing Type 2 diabetes. Some studies have also found that including low-GI foods in your diet may result in short-term weight loss. However, there have been no studies to date that have determined whether or not low-GI foods can lead to long-term weight loss.

Foods that have a high GI are found in the grain products food group. They include bread, cereal, pasta, rice, and potatoes. There are some low GI choices within this food group, and they include some types of bread such as pumpernickel, 100 percent stone-ground whole-wheat breads and cereals (such as oatmeal and bran), sweet potatoes, and converted rice.

For more information about low-, medium-, and high-GI choices, you can view a GI resource developed by the Canadian Diabetes Association and released in September 2008, at www.diabetes.ca/for-professionals/resources/nutrition/glycemic-index.

## Fats

Fats, although generally thought of as something to be avoided in our diet, are actually an important nutrient. Fats carry the fat-soluble vitamins A, D, E, and K; aid in these vitamins' absorption in the intestine; protect organs from injury; regulate body temperature; and play an important role in growth and development. They provide nine calories per gram—more than twice the amount of calories in carbohydrates or proteins.

## Forms of Fat

**Saturated fats** and **unsaturated fats** are distinguished by the type of fatty acids in their chemical structures. Unsaturated fats, such as oils, are likely to be liquid at room temperature; saturated fats, such as butter, are likely to be solid. In general, vegetable and fish oils are unsaturated, and animal fats are saturated.

Olive, soybean, canola, cottonseed, corn, and other vegetable oils are unsaturated fats. Olive oil is considered a good fat and one of the best vegetable oils for salads and cooking and has been correlated with a lower incidence of heart disease, including strokes and heart attacks. The *omega-3 fatty acids* in deep-water fish like salmon are unsaturated and may help lower the risk of cardiovascular disease.[12]

In contrast, saturated fats can increase the risk of heart disease and should be avoided as much as possible. In response to consumer and health professionals' demand for less saturated fat in the food supply, many manufacturers switched to partially hydrogenated oils.

The process of hydrogenation creates unsaturated fatty acids called **trans-fatty acids.** They are found in some margarine products and most foods made with partially hydrogenated oils, such as baked goods and fried foods. Even though trans-fatty acids are unsaturated, they behave like saturated fats in terms of raising cholesterol levels. Epidemiological studies have suggested a possible link between cardiovascular-disease risk and high intakes of trans-fatty acids, and researchers have concluded that they are, gram for gram, twice as damaging as saturated fat. There is no safe level for trans-fatty acids, which occur naturally in meats as well as in foods prepared with partially hydrogenated vegetable oils.

In 2007, the federal government announced that Health Canada would adopt the twofold recommendations of the Trans Fat Task Force: the trans-fat content of vegetable oils and soft, spreadable margarines would be limited to 2 percent of the total fat content and that for all other foods, the limit of trans-fat content would be 5 percent. The food industry has been given two years to achieve these limits. Monitoring of the food industry will be done through the Trans Fat Monitoring program. Canada is the first country to monitor and publish this type of data.[13]

To cut down on both saturated and trans-fatty acids, choose soybean, canola, corn, olive, safflower, and sunflower oils, which are naturally free of trans-fatty acids and lower in saturated fats. Look for reduced-fat, low-fat, fat-free, and trans-fatty-acid-free versions of baked goods, snacks, and other processed foods.

### ???? How Much Fat Is Okay?

The government's recommended range for fat intake is 20 to 35 percent of total calories. High-fat diets can lead to obesity and its related health dangers, which are discussed in Chapter 6. However, low-fat diets can be unhealthy, too. When people eat very low levels of fat and very high levels of carbohydrates, their levels of high-density lipoproteins (HDLs), sometimes called *good cholesterol,* declines. **Cholesterol,** a form of fat manufactured by our bodies that circulates in our blood is made up of HDLs and low-density lipoproteins (LDLs). The HDLs help to transport cholesterol to our livers for metabolism and elimination. The LDLs transport cholesterol to our body's cells, but they can accumulate on the inner walls of our arteries. This build up is known as **plaque.** With lower levels of HDLs and higher levels of LDLs, our bodies are at risk for strokes and heart attacks.

### ???? Why Should I Eat Fish?

Unsaturated fats known as omega-3 fatty acids make more molecules such as the prostaglandins that have proven beneficial for heart health. Because they are rich in omega-3 fatty acids, fish oils improve healthy blood lipids (fats), prevent blood clots, ward off age-related macular degeneration, and may lower blood pressure, especially in people with hypertension or atherosclerosis.

While servings of fatty fish, such as salmon, tuna, and sardines, are recommended as part of a healthy diet, some nutritionists do not recommend the use of fish-oil supplements. They can increase bleeding time, interfere with wound healing, worsen diabetes, and impair immune function. Often made from fish skins and livers, the supplements also may contain environmental contaminants.

## Vitamins and Minerals

**Vitamins,** which help put proteins, fats, and carbohydrates to use, are essential to regulating growth, maintaining tissue, and releasing energy from foods. Together with the enzymes in the body, they help produce the right chemical reactions at the right times. They're also involved in the manufacture of blood cells, hormones, and other compounds.

The body produces some vitamins, such as Vitamin D, which is manufactured in the skin after exposure to sunlight. Other vitamins must be ingested. Vitamins A, D, E, and K are fat soluble; they are absorbed through the intestinal membranes and stored in the body. The B vitamins and Vitamin C are water soluble; they are absorbed directly into the blood and then used up or washed out of the body in urine and sweat. They must be replaced daily. Table 5-2 summarizes key information about vitamins.

Carbon, oxygen, hydrogen, and nitrogen make up 96 percent of our body weight. The other 4 percent consists of **minerals** that help build bones and teeth, aid in muscle function, and help our nervous system transmit messages. Every day we need about a tenth of a gram (100 milligrams) or more of the major minerals: sodium, potassium, chloride, calcium, phosphorus, and magnesium. We also need about a hundredth of a gram (10 milligrams) or less of each of the trace minerals: iron (premenopausal women need more), zinc, selenium, molybdenum, iodine, copper, manganese, fluoride, and chromium. See Table 5-3 for a summary of mineral information.

## Other Substances in Food

### Antioxidants

**Antioxidants** are substances that prevent the harmful effects caused by oxidation within the body. They include Vitamins C, E, and beta-carotene (a form of

▼ **Table 5-2 Key Information about Vitamins**

| Vitamin | Significant Sources | Chief Functions | Signs of Severe, Prolonged Deficiency | Signs of Extreme Vitamin Excess |
|---------|---------------------|-----------------|---------------------------------------|---------------------------------|
| **Fat-Soluble** | | | | |
| Vitamin A | Fortified milk, cheese, cream, butter, fortified margarine, eggs, liver, spinach and other dark, leafy greens, broccoli, deep orange fruits (apricots, cantaloupes), vegetables (squash, carrots, sweet potatoes, pumpkins) | Antioxidant, needed for vision, health of cornea, epithelial cells, mucous membranes, skin health, bone and tooth growth, hormone synthesis and regulation, immunity | Anemia, painful joints, cracks in teeth, tendency toward tooth decay, diarrhea, depression, frequent infections, night blindness, keratinization, corneal degeneration, rashes, kidney stones | Nosebleeds, bone pain, growth retardation, headaches, abdominal cramps and pain, nausea, vomiting, diarrhea, weight loss, over-reactive immune system, blurred vision, pain in calves, fatigue, irritability, loss of appetite, dry skin, rashes, loss of hair, cessation of menstruation |
| Vitamin D | Fortified milk or margarine, eggs, liver, sardines, exposure to sunlight | Promotes calcium and phosphorus absorption | Abnormal growth, misshapen bones (bowing of legs), soft bones, joint pain, malformed teeth | Raised blood calcium, excessive thirst, headaches, irritability, loss of appetite, weakness, nausea, kidney stones, stones in arteries, mental and physical retardation |
| Vitamin E | Margarine, salad dressings, shortenings, green leafy vegetables, wheat germ, whole-grain products, nuts, seeds | Antioxidant, needed for stabilization of cell membranes, regulation of oxidation reactions | Red blood-cell breakage, anemia, muscle degeneration, weakness, difficulty walking, leg cramps, fibrocystic breast disease | Augments the effects of anti-clotting medication; general discomfort |
| Vitamin K | Liver, green leafy vegetables, cabbage-type vegetables, milk | Needed for synthesis of blood-clotting proteins and a blood protein that regulates blood calcium | Hemorrhage | Interference with anticlotting medication; jaundice |
| **Water-Soluble** | | | | |
| Vitamin $B_6$ | Green and leafy vegetables, meats, fish, poultry, shellfish, legumes, fruits, whole grains | Part of a coenzyme needed for amino acid and fatty acid metabolism, helps make red blood cells | Anemia, smooth tongue, abnormal brain-wave pattern, irritability, muscle twitching, convulsions | Depression, fatigue, impaired memory, irritability, headaches, numbness, damage to nerves, difficulty walking, loss of reflexes, weakness, restlessness |
| Vitamin $B_{12}$ | Animal products (meat, fish, poultry, milk, cheese, eggs) | Part of a coenzyme used in new cell synthesis, helps maintain nerve cells | Anemia, smooth tongue, fatigue, nervous system degeneration progressing to paralysis, hypersensitivity | None reported |
| Vitamin C | Citrus fruits, cabbage-type vegetables, dark-green vegetables, cantaloupe, strawberries, peppers, lettuce, tomatoes, potatoes, papayas, mangoes | Antioxidant, collagen synthesis (strengthens blood vessel walls, forms scar tissue, matrix for bone growth), amino acid metabolism, strengthens resistance to infection, aids iron absorption | Anemia, pinpoint hemorrhages, frequent infections, bleeding gums, loosened teeth, muscle degeneration and pain, hysteria, depression, bone fragility, joint pain, rough skin, blotchy bruises, failure of wounds to heal | Nausea, abdominal cramps, diarrhea, excessive urination, headache, fatigue, insomnia, rashes, aggravation of gout symptoms; deficiency symptoms may appear at first on withdrawal of high doses |

▼ **Table 5-2 Key Information about Vitamins (continued)**

| Vitamin | Significant Sources | Chief Functions | Signs of Severe, Prolonged Deficiency | Signs of Extreme Vitamin Excess |
|---|---|---|---|---|
| Thiamin (B$_1$) | Pork, ham, bacon, liver, whole grains, legumes, nuts; occurs in all nutritious foods in moderate amounts | Part of a coenzyme needed for energy metabolism, normal appetite function, and nervous system | Edema, enlarged heart, abnormal heart rhythms, heart failure, nerve/muscle degeneration, wasting, weakness, pain, low morale, difficulty walking, loss of reflexes, mental confusion, paralysis | None reported |
| Riboflavin (B$_2$) | Milk, yogurt, cottage cheese, meat, leafy vegetables, whole-grain or enriched breads and cereals | Part of a coenzyme needed for energy metabolism, supports normal vision and skin health | Cracks at corner of mouth, magenta tongue, hypersensitivity to light, reddening of cornea, skin rash | None reported |
| Niacin (B$_3$) | Milk, eggs, meat, poultry, fish, whole-grain and enriched breads and cereals, nuts, and all protein-containing foods | Part of a coenzyme needed for energy metabolism, supports skin health, nervous system, and digestive system | Diarrhea, black smooth tongue, irritability, loss of appetite, weakness, dizziness, mental confusion, flaky skin rash on areas exposed to sun | Diarrhea, heartburn, nausea, ulcer irritation, vomiting, fainting, dizziness, painful flush and rash, sweating, abnormal liver function, low blood pressure |
| Folate (B$_9$) | Green leafy vegetables, legumes, seeds, liver, enriched bread, cereal, pasta, and grains | Part of a coenzyme needed for new cell synthesis | Anemia, heartburn, diarrhea, constipation, frequent infections, smooth red tongue, depression, mental confusion, fainting | Masks Vitamin B$_{12}$ deficiency |
| Panothenic acid | Widespread in foods | Part of a coenzyme used in energy metabolism | Vomiting, intestinal distress, insomnia, fatigue | Water retention (rare) |
| Biotin | Widespread in foods | Used in energy metabolism, fat synthesis, amino acid metabolism, and glycogen synthesis | Abnormal heart action, loss of appetite, nausea, depression, muscle pain, weakness, fatigue, dry facial skin, rash, hair loss | None reported |

Source: Adapted from Sizer, F., & Whitney, E. (2000). *Nutrition: Concepts and controversies,* eighth edition. Belmont, CA: Wadsworth.

Vitamin A), as well as compounds such as carotenoids and flavonoids. All share a common enemy: renegade oxygen cells called *free radicals,* which are released by normal metabolism as well as by pollution, smoking, radiation, and stress.

Diets high in antioxidant-rich fruits and vegetables have been linked with lower rates of esophageal, lung, colon, and stomach cancer. But there continues to be conflicting findings in scientific studies. To date there is not conclusive evidence that any specific antioxidant, particularly in supplement form, can prevent cancer, and a 2005 report has shown that increased levels of Vitamin E might actually increase the risk of cardiovascular morbidity.[14]

## Phytochemicals

**Phytochemicals,** compounds that exist naturally in plants, serve many functions, including helping a plant protect itself from bacteria and disease. Flavonoids, found in apples, strawberries, grapes, onions, green and black tea, and red wine, may decrease atherosclerotic plaque and DNA damage related to cancer developments. Phytochemicals are associated with a reduced risk of heart disease, certain cancers, age-related macular degeneration, adult-onset diabetes, stroke, and other diseases. However, research has yet to show a cause-and-effect relationship between consumption of phytochemicals and prevention of a specific disease.

▼ **Table 5-3  Key Information about Essential Minerals**

| Mineral | Significant Sources | Chief Functions | Signs of Severe, Prolonged Deficiency | Signs of Extreme Excess |
|---|---|---|---|---|
| **Major Minerals** | | | | |
| Sodium | Foods processed with salt, cured foods (corned beef, ham, bacon, pickles, sauerkraut), table and sea salt, bread, milk, cheese, salad dressing | Needed to maintain acid-base balance in body fluids, helps regulate water in blood and body tissues, needed for muscle and nerve activity | Weakness, apathy, poor appetite, muscle cramps, headache, swelling | High blood pressure, kidney disease, heart problems |
| Potassium | Plant foods (potatoes, squash, lima beans, tomatoes, bananas, oranges, avocados), meats, milk and milk products, coffee | Needed to maintain acid-base balance in body fluids, helps regulate water in blood and body tissues, needed for muscle and nerve activity | Weakness, irritability, mental confusion, irregular heartbeat, paralysis | Irregular heartbeat, heart attack |
| Chloride | Foods processed with salt, cured foods (corned beef, ham, bacon, pickles, sauerkraut), table and sea salt, bread, milk, cheese, salad dressing | Aids in digestion, needed to maintain acid-base balance in body fluids, helps regulate water in the body | Muscle cramps, apathy, poor appetite, long-term mental retardation in infants | Vomiting |
| Calcium | Milk and milk products, broccoli, dried beans | Component of bones and teeth, needed for muscle and nerve activity, blood clotting | Weak bones, rickets, stunted growth in children, convulsions, muscle spasms, and osteoporosis | Drowsiness; calcium deposits in kidneys, liver, and other tissues; suppression of bone remodelling; decreased zinc absorption |
| Phosphorus | Milk and milk products, meats, seeds, nuts | Component of bones and teeth, energy formation, needed to maintain the right acid-base balance of body fluids | Loss of appetite, nausea, vomiting, weakness, confusion, loss of calcium from bones | Loss of calcium from bones, muscle spasms |
| Magnesium | Plant foods (dried beans, tofu, peanuts, potatoes, green vegetables) | Component of bones and teeth, nerve activity, energy and protein formation | Stunted growth in children, weakness, muscle spasms, personality changes | Diarrhea, dehydration, impaired nerve activity |
| **Trace Minerals** | | | | |
| Iron | Liver, beef, pork, dried beans, iron-fortified cereals, prunes, apricots, raisins, spinach, bread, pasta | Aids in transport of oxygen, component of myoglobin, energy formation | Anemia, weakness, fatigue, pale appearance, reduced attention span, lowered resistance to infection, developmental delays in children | "Iron poisoning," vomiting, abdominal pain, blue coloration of skin, shock, heart failure, diabetes, decreased zinc absorption |
| Zinc | Meats, grains, nuts, milk and milk products, cereals, bread | Protein reproduction, component of insulin | Growth failure, delayed sexual maturation, slow wound healing, loss of taste and appetite; in pregnant women, low-birth-weight infants and preterm delivery | Nausea, vomiting, weakness, fatigue, susceptibility to infection, copper deficiency, metallic taste in mouth |
| Selenium | Meats and seafood, eggs, grains | Acts as an antioxidant in conjunction with Vitamin E | Anemia, muscle pain and tenderness, Keshar disease (a potentially fatal form of cardiomyopathy or cardiac muscle degeneration), heart failure | Hair and fingernail loss, weakness, liver damage, irritability, garlic or metallic breath |
| Molybdenum | Dried beans, grains, dark green vegetables, liver, milk and milk products | Aids in oxygen transfer from one molecule to another | Rapid heartbeat and breathing, nausea, vomiting, coma | Loss of copper from the body, joint pain, growth failure, anemia, gout |

▼ **Table 5-3 Key Information about Essential Minerals (continued)**

| Mineral | Significant Sources | Chief Functions | Signs of Severe, Prolonged Deficiency | Signs of Extreme Excess |
|---|---|---|---|---|
| Iodine | Iodized salt, milk and milk products, seaweed, seafood, bread | Component of thyroid hormones that helps regulate energy production and growth | Goitre, cretinism in newborns (mental retardation, hearing loss, growth failure) | Pimples, goitre (just as too little iodine can cause a sweeling of the thyroid gland, so can a prolonged intake of iodine cause the formation of a goitre, which decreases the thyroid function) |
| Copper | Bread, potatoes, grains, dried beans, nuts and seeds, seafood, cereals | Component of enzymes involved in the body's utilization of iron and oxygen; functions in growth, immunity, cholesterol, and glucose utilization; brain development | Anemia, seizures, nerve and bone abnormalities in children, growth retardation | Wilson's disease (excessive accumulation of copper in the liver and kidneys); vomiting, diarrhea, tremors, liver disease |
| Manganese | Whole grains, coffee, tea, dried beans, nuts | Formation of body fat and bone | Weight loss, rash, nausea and vomiting | Infertility in men, disruptions in the nervous system, muscle spasms |
| Fluoride | Fluoridated water, foods, and beverages; tea; shrimp; crab | Component of bones and teeth (enamel) | Tooth decay and other dental diseases | Fluorosis, brittle bones, mottled teeth, nerve abnormalities |
| Chromium | Whole grains, liver, meat, beer, wine | Glucose utilization | Poor blood-glucose control, weight loss | Kidney and skin damage |

Source: Adapted from Brown, J.E. (2002). *Nutrition Now,* 3rd ed. Belmont, CA: Wadsworth.

# Eating for Good Health

No one food can provide all the nutrients we need. To make sure you consume a healthful variety, Health Canada suggests that you follow *Eating Well With Canada's Food Guide* (see Figure 5-1).[15] Canada's first food guide, the *Official Food Rules,* was introduced in July 1942. This guide acknowledged wartime food rationing while endeavouring to prevent nutritional deficiencies and to improve the health of Canadians. Since 1942, the food guide has been changed many times. A document on the evolution of the food guide, titled *Canada's Food Guides from 1942 to 1992,*[16] is available on the Health Canada website at www.hc-sc.gc.ca/ fn-an/food-guide-aliment/context/hist-eng.php.

 **What Is a Serving Size?**

## Food Portions and Servings

Consumers often are confused by what a *serving* actually is, especially since many Canadian restaurants have supersized the amount of food they put on their customers' plates. The average bagel has doubled in size in the last 10 to 15 years.[17] The average size of a hamburger has increased from 42.5 grams (1.5 ounces) to 130 grams (4.5 ounces), the average size of pop from 236 millilitres (8 ounces) to 946 millilitres (32 ounces).

Today's *Food Guide,* which suggests a way of eating for people over the age of four, has two parts. The rainbow side of the guide places foods into four groups: vegetables and fruit, grain products, milk and alternatives, and meat and alternatives. It also illustrates the kinds of foods to choose for healthy eating.

The bar side of the *Food Guide* provides the recommended number of food guide servings per day.

The *Food Guide* is based on guidelines from Health Canada that encourage us to enjoy a variety of foods and limit salt, alcohol, and caffeine. It also gives us advice on how to choose foods. You can create your own personal food guide using Health Canada's interactive website at www.hc-sc.gc.ca/fn-an/food-guide-aliment/myguide-menuguide/index-eng.php.

✔ Enjoy a variety of foods from each group each day.
✔ Choose lower-fat foods more often.
✔ Choose whole-grain and enriched products more often.
✔ Choose dark green and orange vegetables and orange fruit more often.

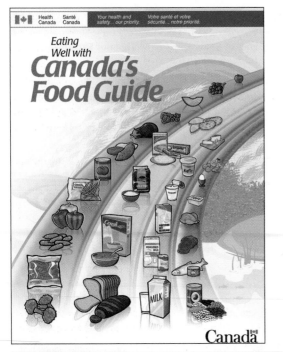

▲ **Figure 5-1** Eating Well with Canada's Food Guide
This graphic demonstrates the daily food choices that make up a healthy diet: modest amounts of meat, dairy products, and fats and a larger number of servings of foods containing grains, cereals, fruits, and vegetables.

Source: Eating Well with Canada's Food Guide (2007), Health Canada. Available at www. healthcanada.gc.ca/foodguide. Reproduced with the permission of the Minister of Public Works and Government Services Canada, 2009.

✔ Choose lower-fat milk products more often.
✔ Choose leaner meats, poultry, and fish, as well as dried peas, beans, and lentils more often.

There is a range of servings recommended for each of the four food groups. The number of servings you need every day from the four food groups and other foods depends on your age, sex, body size, activity level, and if you are pregnant or breast-feeding. People who will need to have more than the lower number of servings are pregnant and breast-feeding women, male teenagers, and highly active people. (See also The X & Y Files: "Do Men and Women Have Different Nutritional Needs?")

## Vegetables and Fruit

Naturally low in fat and high in fibre, vegetables provide crucial vitamins (such as A and C) and minerals (such as iron and magnesium). Seven to eight servings per day are recommended for females ages 19–50. Eight to ten servings are recommended for men the same age. One serving of vegetables consists of 125 millilitres (½ cup) of fresh, frozen, or canned vegetables or fresh salad. It also equals one medium-sized carrot or potato. Dark green vegetables are good sources of vitamins and minerals. Collards, kale, turnip, and mustard provide calcium and iron. Winter squash, carrots, broccoli, cabbage, kohlrabi, and cauliflower (the **crucifers**) are high in fibre, rich in vitamins, and are excellent sources of **indoles,** chemicals that help lower cancer risk.

Fruits are excellent sources of vitamins, minerals, and fibre. Along with vegetables, fruits may protect against cancer. One serving consists of a medium apple, banana, or orange; 125 millilitres (½ cup) of chopped, cooked, or canned fruit; or 125 millilitres (½ cup) of fruit juice.

Try the following suggestions to get more vegetables and fruit into your daily diet.

✔ Make or order sandwiches with extra tomatoes or other vegetable toppings.
✔ Add extra vegetables whenever you're preparing soups and sauces.
✔ Use raw vegetables for dipping, instead of chips.
✔ Carry a banana, apple, or package of dried fruit with you as a healthy snack.
✔ Start the day with a "daily double": a glass of juice and a banana or other fruit on cereal.
✔ Add citrus fruits (such as slices of grapefruit, oranges, or apples) to green salads, rice, or grains and to chicken, pork, or fish dishes.

## Grain Products

Breads, cereals, rice, and pasta are the foundation of a healthy diet because they are a good source of complex carbohydrates. For females aged 19–50, six to seven servings a day are recommended; for men: eight servings. Both simple and complex carbohydrates (starches) have four calories per gram. The sugars in simple carbohydrates provide little more than a quick spurt of energy, whereas complex carbohydrates are rich in vitamins, minerals, and other nutrients.

One serving in this category might be one slice of bread, 30 grams of cold cereal, or 175 millilitres (¾ cup) of hot cereal. Two servings would be one bagel, pita, or bun or 250 millilitres (1 cup) of pasta or rice. Although many people think of these foods as fattening, it's the butter on a roll or cream sauce on pasta that adds extra calories.

To get more grains in your diet:

✔ Add brown rice or barley to soups.
✔ Check labels of rolls and bread, and choose those with at least 2 to 3 grams of fibre per slice.
✔ Choose pasta—it has 210 calories per cooked 250 millilitres (1 cup) and only nine calories from fat. Whole-grain pastas may provide more nutrients than those made with refined flour.

## Milk and Alternatives

Most milk products—milk, yogurt, and cheese—are high in calcium, riboflavin, protein, and Vitamins A and $B_{12}$. Dairy products, such as milk and yogurt, are the best calcium sources, but be sure you choose products that are low fat or, preferably, non-fat. Recommended daily amounts for both females and males ages 19–50 are 2 servings; pregnant and breast-feeding women: 3 to 4 servings. A serving in this category consists of 250 millilitres (1 cup) of milk, 185 millilitres (¾ cup) of plain yogurt, or 50 grams (2 ounces) of hard cheese.

A growing concern is the problem of lactose intolerance, or the inability to digest milk products. In people who do not produce adequate amounts of the intestinal enzyme lactase, milk products travel through the stomach undigested and ferment in the small bowel, causing gas, cramps, and diarrhea. Over-the-counter medicines such as oral lactase supplements can help, and many dairy products such as lactose-hydrolyzed milk are available for the lactose-intolerant. Some lactose-intolerance experts suggest that smaller quantities of milk, taken with meals or other foods spread throughout the day, or yogurt with active cultures might help to slowly increase lactose tolerance.

To make sure you get more milk with less fat, try the following:

✔ Gradually switch from whole milk to 2% fat (reduced fat) milk, to 1% fat (low-fat) milk, and then to skim (non-fat) milk.
✔ Substitute fat-free sour cream or non-fat plain yogurt for sour cream.
✔ Use part-skim or low-fat cheeses whenever possible.

## Meat and Alternatives

Foods in the meat and bean group include meat, poultry, fish, tofu, dry beans (lentils, soy, kidney, black, etc.), and nuts. Two servings a day are recommended for females ages 19–50, and three servings are recommended for men the same age. A serving in this category consists of 50 to 100 grams of lean, cooked meat, fish, or poultry (roughly the size of an average hamburger or the amount of meat on a chicken drumstick). An egg or 125 to 250 millilitres of cooked dry beans can substitute for one serving of lean meat. Thirty millilitres (2 tablespoons) of peanut butter count as one serving of meat. Thus, one day's total protein intake might include an egg at breakfast; a serving of beans, meat, or 30 millilitres of peanut butter in a sandwich at lunch; and 50 to 100 grams of fish for dinner.

To pick the best protein, follow these recommendations:

✔ Choose the leanest meats, such as beef round or sirloin, pork tenderloin, or veal. Broil or roast instead of fry. Trim fat before cooking, which can lower the fat content of the meat you eat by more than 10 percent.
✔ Cook stews, boiled meat, or soup stock ahead of time; refrigerate; and remove the hardened fat before using. Drain fat from ground beef after cooking.
✔ Watch out for processed chicken and turkey products; for example, bolognas and salamis made from turkey can contain 45 to 90 percent fat.

## Oils and Fats

A small amount of unsaturated fat—30 to 45 millilitres (2 to 3 tablespoons)—can be included each day. This would include oils that you would use for cooking, making salad dressing, or spreading on bread or food. Try to use vegetable oils such as olive, soybean, or canola oil. If you choose soft margarines, be sure to look for ones that are low in saturated and trans-fats. Limit your intake of butter, hard margarine, lard, and shortening.

## Nutritional Supplements

Choosing foods according to *Eating Well With Canada's Food Guide* can provide all of the vitamins and minerals needed for good health for most Canadians. Yet many Canadians regularly use nutritional supplements—vitamins, minerals, and botanical and biological substances.

Prior to January 1, 2004, natural health products (NHPs), defined as vitamins and minerals, herbal remedies, homeopathic medicines, traditional medicines, probiotics, and other products such as amino acids and essential fatty acids, were sold as either drugs or foods under the Food and Drugs Act and Regulations because there was no other category under which to classify them. As more Canadians began to use these products, it was felt that a new policy that would address the unique nature of NHPs was needed. Canadians can now access *The Natural Health Products Regulations*[18] at www.hc-sc.gc.ca/dhp-mps/prodnatur/index-eng.php to learn more about this new policy.

## Do Men and Women Have Different Nutritional Needs?

Men and women do not need to eat different foods, but their nutritional needs are different. Because most men are bigger and taller than most women, they consume more calories. Eating more means it's easier for them to get the nutrients they need.

Women, particularly those who restrict their caloric intake or are chronically dieting, are more likely to develop specific deficiencies. Calcium is one example. Women drink less milk than men, and many do not consume the recommended 800 to 1200 milligrams of calcium daily. This deficiency increases the risk of bone-weakening osteoporosis. Calcium supplementation can help individuals who are lactose intolerant.

Many women also get too little iron. Even in adolescence, girls are more prone to iron deficiency than boys; some suffer memory and learning impairments as a result. In adult women, menstrual blood loss and poor eating habits can lead to low iron stores, which puts them at risk for anemia. Women can increase their iron intake by eating meat (iron from animal sources is absorbed better than that from vegetable sources) or a combination of meat and vegetable iron sources together (for example, a meat and bean burrito). Women who are low in iron should consult a physician. Because large doses of iron can be toxic, iron supplements should be taken only with medical supervision.

Women who could become pregnant should take a multivitamin with 400 micrograms of folic acid, which helps prevent neural-tube defects such as spina bifida. Folic acid is also useful to men because it may cut the risk of heart disease, stroke, and colon cancer.

Both men and women should increase their fruit and vegetable intake to ensure that they are getting adequate amounts of vitamins and fibre in their daily diet.

---

These new regulations will be phased in over a six-year period with all manufacturers, importers, packagers, and labellers employing good manufacturing practices and attaining site licences over the first two years and all NHPs having a NHP or DIN-HM (homeopathic medicine) number by the sixth year.[19]

Under the regulations, there must be good scientific evidence for the effectiveness of the product and the products must be safe for consideration as an over-the-counter (OTC) product. Natural health products will be available for self-care and self-selection and will not require a prescription to be sold. Vitamins and minerals will be regulated under this policy because they are considered to be natural health products.

One example of a supplement that has put many Canadians at risk is ephedra/ephedrine. Although found in traditional medicines, which have regulated standard dosages of 8 milligrams or 32 mg/day, many unregulated and unapproved products, marketed for appetite suppression, weight loss, metabolic enhancement, or increased wakefulness, include higher doses. It is sometimes combined with stimulants such as caffeine, which can increase its action. This substance aggravates conditions such as heart disease, hypertension, thyroid disease, diabetes, anxiety, and glaucoma. It should not be used during pregnancy or lactation. Adverse effects of ephedra/ephedrine can include dizziness, headache, gastrointestinal distress, irregular heartbeat, tachycardia, hypertension, stroke, seizures, psychosis, and death.[20]

A health advisory and recall was issued in 2001; however, a continuing demand for these products despite the warnings from Health Canada has ensured that they remain on the shelves of many stores. The new regulations should assist in tracking products such as these, which pose health risks to Canadians.

## Dietary Reference Intakes

Since 1938, Health Canada has been reviewing nutrition research and defining nutrient needs for healthy people. Since 1995, scientists in Canada and the United States have been working together to develop nutrient recommendations based on current research. The new recommendations are called **Dietary Reference Intakes (DRIs)**.[21] The DRIs replace the 1990 Recommended Nutrient Intakes (RNIs) in Canada and the 1989 Recommended Dietary Allowances in the United States.

Dietary Reference Intakes is an umbrella term that describes four types of reference values:

- *Estimated Average Requirement (EAR)*—the median usual intake value that is estimated to meet the requirement of half of the healthy individuals in a life stage and gender group.
- *Recommended Dietary Allowance (RDA)*—the average daily dietary intake level that is sufficient to meet the nutrient requirement of nearly all (97–98 percent) healthy individuals in a particular life stage and gender group.
- *Adequate Intake Level (AL)*—the adequate nutritional intake level that includes normal growth and other aspects of nutritional well-being or general health.

✔ *Tolerable Upper Intake Level (UL)*—the highest level of continuing daily nutrient intake that is likely to pose no risk in almost all individuals in the life-stage group for which it has been designed.

It is important to note that DRIs are standards for apparently healthy people and are not meant to be applied for anyone who has an acute or chronic disease. The DRI approach has helped harmonize nutrient recommendations for Canada and the United States. A series of published reports are available, some of which outline DRIs for many vitamins and minerals.[22]

Another important finding in developing these nutrient-reference values was the importance of regular daily physical activity with regard to overall health levels.[23]

### Should I Take Vitamin Supplements?

Many health experts feel that if you rely on vitamin/mineral pills and fortified foods to make up for poor nutrition, you may shortchange yourself. It's unlikely that changing any one nutrient will in itself produce great benefits—and may, by interfering with the complex balance of nutrients, do harm.

In particular, the fat-soluble vitamins, primarily A and D, can build up in our bodies and cause serious complications, such as damage to the kidneys, liver, or bones. Side effects of doses of Vitamin E greater than 400 units a day and long-term use can include blurred vision, diarrhea, headaches, nausea or stomach cramps, and unusual tiredness or weakness.

Large doses of water-soluble vitamins, including the B vitamins, may also be harmful. Excessive intake of Vitamin B$_6$ (pyridoxine), often used to relieve premenstrual bloating, can cause neurological damage, such as numbness in the mouth and tingling in the hands. High doses of Vitamin C can produce stomachaches and diarrhea. Niacin, often taken in high doses to lower cholesterol levels, can cause jaundice, liver damage, and irregular heartbeats as well as severe, uncomfortable flushing of the skin. Table 5-2 provides more information about the effects of vitamin excess.

There are certain situations in which specific vitamin or mineral supplements are recommended. The evidence is clear that the use of supplements containing folic acid substantially reduces the risk of occurrence of birth defects known as neural-tube defects (NTDs). All women who could become pregnant should take a multivitamin containing 0.4 milligrams of folic acid every day, in addition to the amount of folate found in a healthy diet.

If you eat a balanced diet and get outside in the sunshine at least 1.5 to 2 hours a week, you should be getting all the Vitamin D you need.[24] If you live in an area of Canada where the amount of sunshine is limited during specific times of the year, you might benefit from supplements.

If you are considering a multivitamin or multivitamin-mineral supplement, talk to your health care provider to find the best supplement for you. See Table 5-4 for the minimum and maximum daily dosages suggested by Health Canada.

## Knowing What You Eat

Canadian consumers now know much more about the food they eat because of nutrition-labelling requirements that were published on January 1, 2003. These regulations require most food labels on almost all prepackaged foods to carry a mandatory Nutrition Facts table listing calories and 13 key nutrients. They also contain science-based health claims and defined nutrient-content claims. The aim of these regulations is to give Canadians the information they need to make informed food choices and compare products. They are also designed to increase our understanding of the links between nutritional health and well-being.[25]

In evaluating food labels and product claims, keep in mind that while individual foods vary in their nutritional value, what matters is your total diet. If you eat too much of any one food—regardless of what its label states—you may not be getting the variety and balance of nutrients that you need.

### What Should I Look for on Nutrition Labels?

As Figure 5-2 shows, the Nutrition Facts on food labels present a wealth of information—if you know what to look for. The Nutrition Facts table[26] will show calories, the amount of fat including saturated and trans fats, cholesterol, sodium, carbohydrate, fibre, sugars, protein, calcium, iron, and Vitamins A and C in a specified amount of food. The nutrients chosen were those that consumers, health professionals, and scientists consider important to the health of Canadians.

✔ *Calories.* Calories are the measure of the amount of energy that can be derived from food. Science defines a *calorie* as the amount of energy required to raise the temperature of one gram of water by one degree Celsius. In the laboratory, the caloric content of food is measured in 1000-calorie units called *kilocalories*. The calorie referred to in everyday usage is actually the equivalent of the laboratory kilocalorie.

The Nutrition Facts label lists two numbers for calories: calories per serving and calories from fat per

▼ **Table 5-4 Dietary Reference Intakes Reference Values for Vitamins**

| Unit | Vitamin A[1,2] µg/day (RAE) | | | IU/day (RAE) | | | Vitamin D µg/day | | IU/day | | Vitamin E[5] mg/day | | | Vitamin K µg/day | |
|---|---|---|---|---|---|---|---|---|---|---|---|---|---|---|---|
| | EAR | RDA/AI | UL[3] | EAR | RDA/AI | UL[3] | AI[4] | UL | AI[4] | UL | EAR | RDA/AI | UL[6] | AI | UL[7] |
| **Infants** | | | | | | | | | | | | | | | |
| 0–6 months | ND | 400* | 600 | ND | 1333* | 2000 | 5* | 25 | 200* | 1000 | ND | 4* | ND | 2.0* | ND |
| 7–12 months | ND | 500* | 600 | ND | 1667* | 2000 | 5* | 25 | 200* | 1000 | ND | 5* | ND | 2.5* | ND |
| **Children** | | | | | | | | | | | | | | | |
| 1–3 y | 210 | 300 | 600 | 700 | 1000 | 2000 | 5* | 50 | 200* | 2000 | 5 | 6 | 200 | 30* | ND |
| 4–8 y | 275 | 400 | 900 | 917 | 1333 | 3000 | 5* | 50 | 200* | 2000 | 6 | 7 | 300 | 55* | ND |
| **Males** | | | | | | | | | | | | | | | |
| 9–13 y | 445 | 600 | 1700 | 1483 | 2000 | 5667 | 5* | 50 | 200* | 2000 | 9 | 11 | 600 | 60* | ND |
| 14–18 y | 630 | 900 | 2800 | 2100 | 3000 | 9333 | 5* | 50 | 200* | 2000 | 12 | 15 | 800 | 75* | ND |
| 19–30 y | 625 | 900 | 3000 | 2083 | 3000 | 10 000 | 5* | 50 | 200* | 2000 | 12 | 15 | 1000 | 120* | ND |
| 31–50 y | 625 | 900 | 3000 | 2083 | 3000 | 10 000 | 5* | 50 | 200* | 2000 | 12 | 15 | 1000 | 120* | ND |
| 51–70 y | 625 | 900 | 3000 | 2083 | 3000 | 10 000 | 10* | 50 | 400* | 2000 | 12 | 15 | 1000 | 120* | ND |
| >70 y | 625 | 900 | 3000 | 2083 | 3000 | 10 000 | 15* | 50 | 600* | 2000 | 12 | 15 | 1000 | 120* | ND |
| **Females** | | | | | | | | | | | | | | | |
| 9–13 y | 420 | 600 | 1700 | 1400 | 2000 | 5667 | 5* | 50 | 200* | 2000 | 9 | 11 | 600 | 60* | ND |
| 14–18 y | 485 | 700 | 2800 | 1617 | 2333 | 9333 | 5* | 50 | 200* | 2000 | 12 | 15 | 800 | 75* | ND |
| 19–30 y | 500 | 700 | 3000 | 1667 | 2333 | 10 000 | 5* | 50 | 200* | 2000 | 12 | 15 | 1000 | 90* | ND |
| 31–50 y | 500 | 700 | 3000 | 1667 | 2333 | 10 000 | 5* | 50 | 200* | 2000 | 12 | 15 | 1000 | 90* | ND |
| 51–70 y | 500 | 700 | 3000 | 1667 | 2333 | 10 000 | 10* | 50 | 400* | 2000 | 12 | 15 | 1000 | 90* | ND |
| >70 y | 500 | 700 | 3000 | 1667 | 2333 | 10 000 | 15* | 50 | 600* | 2000 | 12 | 15 | 1000 | 90* | ND |
| **Pregnancy** | | | | | | | | | | | | | | | |
| < 18 y | 530 | 750 | 2800 | 1767 | 2500 | 9333 | 5* | 50 | 200* | 2000 | 12 | 15 | 800 | 75* | ND |
| 19–30 y | 550 | 770 | 3000 | 1833 | 2567 | 10 000 | 5* | 50 | 200* | 2000 | 12 | 15 | 1000 | 90* | ND |
| 31–50 y | 550 | 770 | 3000 | 1833 | 2567 | 10 000 | 5* | 50 | 200* | 2000 | 12 | 15 | 1000 | 90* | ND |
| **Lactation** | | | | | | | | | | | | | | | |
| < 18 y | 885 | 1200 | 2800 | 2950 | 4000 | 9333 | 5* | 50 | 200* | 2000 | 16 | 19 | 800 | 75* | ND |
| 19–30 y | 900 | 1300 | 3000 | 3000 | 4333 | 10 000 | 5* | 50 | 200* | 2000 | 16 | 19 | 1000 | 90* | ND |
| 31–50 y | 900 | 1300 | 3000 | 3000 | 4333 | 10 000 | 5* | 50 | 200* | 2000 | 16 | 19 | 1000 | 90* | ND |

This table presents *Estimated Average Requirements (EARs) in italics,* **Recommended Dietary Allowances (RDAs) in bold type,** and Adequate Intakes (AIs) in ordinary type followed by an asterisk (*). Tolerable Upper Intake Levels (ULs) are in shaded columns.

[1] As Retinol Activity Equivalents (RAE). See conversion factors for more details.
[2] No DRIs are established for beta-carotene or other carotenoids. However, existing recommendations for consumption of carotenoid-rich fruits and vegetables are supported.
[3] UL as preformed vitamin A only. Beta-carotene supplements are advised only to serve as a provitamin A source for individuals at risk of vitamin A deficiency.
[4] AI values are based on the absence of adequate exposure to sunlight.
[5] EAR and RDA/AI as alpha-tocopherol (2R-stereoisomeric forms) only. See conversion factors for more details.
[6] The UL for vitamin E applies only to synthetic vitamin E (all isomeric forms) obtained from supplements, fortified foods, or a combination of the two.
[7] Due to lack of suitable data, a UL could not be established for vitamin K. This does not mean that there is no potential for adverse effects resulting from high intakes.

Note: These are reference values for normal, apparently healthy individuals eating a typical mixed North American diet. An individual may have physiological, health, or lifestyle characteristics that may require tailoring of specific nutrient values.

## ▼ Table 5-4 Dietary Reference Intakes Reference Values for Vitamins (continued)

| Unit | Vitamin C[8] mg/day | | | Thiamin mg/day | | | Riboflavin mg/day | | | Niacin[10] mg/day(NE) | | | Vitamin B6 mg/day | | |
|---|---|---|---|---|---|---|---|---|---|---|---|---|---|---|---|
| | EAR | RDA/AI | UL | EAR | RDA/AI | UL[9] | EAR | RDA/AI | UL[9] | EAR | RDA/AI | UL[11] | EAR | RDA/AI | UL |
| **Infants** | | | | | | | | | | | | | | | |
| 0–6 months | *ND* | 40* | ND | *ND* | 0.2* | ND | *ND* | 0.3* | ND | *ND* | 2*[a] | ND | *ND* | 0.1* | ND |
| 7–12 months | *ND* | 50* | ND | *ND* | 0.3* | ND | *ND* | 0.4* | ND | *ND* | 4* | ND | *ND* | 0.3* | ND |
| **Children** | | | | | | | | | | | | | | | |
| 1–3 y | *13* | **15** | 400 | *0.4* | **0.5** | ND | *0.4* | **0.5** | ND | *5* | **6** | 10 | *0.4* | **0.5** | 30 |
| 4–8 y | *22* | **25** | 650 | *0.5* | **0.6** | ND | *0.5* | **0.6** | ND | *6* | **8** | 15 | *0.5* | **0.6** | 40 |
| **Males** | | | | | | | | | | | | | | | |
| 9–13 y | *39* | **45** | 1200 | *0.7* | **0.9** | ND | *0.8* | **0.9** | ND | *9* | **12** | 20 | *0.8* | **1.0** | 60 |
| 14–18 y | *63* | **75** | 1800 | *1.0* | **1.2** | ND | *1.1* | **1.3** | ND | *12* | **16** | 30 | *1.1* | **1.3** | 80 |
| 19–30 y | *75* | **90** | 2000 | *1.0* | **1.2** | ND | *1.1* | **1.3** | ND | *12* | **16** | 35 | *1.1* | **1.3** | 100 |
| 31–50 y | *75* | **90** | 2000 | *1.0* | **1.2** | ND | *1.1* | **1.3** | ND | *12* | **16** | 35 | *1.1* | **1.3** | 100 |
| 51–70 y | *75* | **90** | 2000 | *1.0* | **1.2** | ND | *1.1* | **1.3** | ND | *12* | **16** | 35 | *1.4* | **1.7** | 100 |
| >70 y | *75* | **90** | 2000 | *1.0* | **1.2** | ND | *1.1* | **1.3** | ND | *12* | **16** | 35 | *1.4* | **1.7** | 100 |
| **Females** | | | | | | | | | | | | | | | |
| 9–13 y | *39* | **45** | 1200 | *0.7* | **0.9** | ND | *0.8* | **0.9** | ND | *9* | **12** | 20 | *0.8* | **1.0** | 60 |
| 14–18 y | *56* | **65** | 1800 | *0.9* | **1.0** | ND | *0.9* | **1.0** | ND | *11* | **14** | 30 | *1.0* | **1.2** | 80 |
| 19–30 y | *60* | **75** | 2000 | *0.9* | **1.1** | ND | *0.9* | **1.1** | ND | *11* | **14** | 35 | *1.1* | **1.3** | 100 |
| 31–50 y | *60* | **75** | 2000 | *0.9* | **1.1** | ND | *0.9* | **1.1** | ND | *11* | **14** | 35 | *1.1* | **1.3** | 100 |
| 51–70 y | *60* | **75** | 2000 | *0.9* | **1.1** | ND | *0.9* | **1.1** | ND | *11* | **14** | 35 | *1.3* | **1.5** | 100 |
| >70 y | *60* | **75** | 2000 | *0.9* | **1.1** | ND | *0.9* | **1.1** | ND | *11* | **14** | 35 | *1.3* | **1.5** | 100 |
| **Pregnancy** | | | | | | | | | | | | | | | |
| < 18 y | *66* | **80** | 1800 | *1.2* | **1.4** | ND | *1.2* | **1.4** | ND | *14* | **18** | 30 | *1.6* | **1.9** | 80 |
| 19–30 y | *70* | **85** | 2000 | *1.2* | **1.4** | ND | *1.2* | **1.4** | ND | *14* | **18** | 35 | *1.6* | **1.9** | 100 |
| 31–50 y | *70* | **85** | 2000 | *1.2* | **1.4** | ND | *1.2* | **1.4** | ND | *14* | **18** | 35 | *1.6* | **1.9** | 100 |
| **Lactation** | | | | | | | | | | | | | | | |
| < 18 y | *96* | **115** | 1800 | *1.2* | **1.4** | ND | *1.3* | **1.6** | ND | *13* | **17** | 30 | *1.7* | **2.0** | 80 |
| 19–30 y | *100* | **120** | 2000 | *1.2* | **1.4** | ND | *1.3* | **1.6** | ND | *13* | **17** | 35 | *1.7* | **2.0** | 100 |
| 31–50 y | *100* | **120** | 2000 | *1.2* | **1.4** | ND | *1.3* | **1.6** | ND | *13* | **17** | 35 | *1.7* | **2.0** | 100 |

This table presents *Estimated Average Requirements (EARs) in italics,* **Recommended Dietary Allowances (RDAs) in bold type,** and Adequate Intakes (AIs) in ordinary type followed by an asterisk (*). Tolerable Upper Intake Levels (ULs) are in shaded columns.

[8] Because smoking increases oxidative stress and metabolic turnover of vitamin C, the requirement for smokers is increased by 35 mg/day.
[9] Due to lack of suitable data, ULs could not be established for thiamin and riboflavin. This does not mean that there is no potential for adverse effects resulting from high intakes.
[10] As Niacin Equivalents (NE). See conversion factors for more details.
[11] The UL for niacin applies only to synthetic forms obtained from supplements, fortified foods, or a combination of the two.
[a] As preformed niacin, not NE, for this age group.

Note: These are reference values for normal, apparently healthy individuals eating a typical mixed North American diet. An individual may have physiological, health, or lifestyle characteristics that may require tailoring of specific nutrient values.

*continued*

## ▼ Table 5-4 Dietary Reference Intakes Reference Values for Vitamins (continued)

| Unit | Folate[12] µg/day (DFE) | | | Vitamin B$_{12}$ µg/day | | | Pantothenic Acid mg/day | | Biotin µg/day | | Choline[15] mg/day | |
|---|---|---|---|---|---|---|---|---|---|---|---|---|
| | EAR | RDA/AI | UL[13] | EAR | RDA/AI | UL[14] | AI | UL[14] | AI | UL[14] | AI | UL |
| **Infants** | | | | | | | | | | | | |
| 0–6 months | *ND* | 65* | ND | *ND* | 0.4* | ND | 1.7* | ND | 5* | ND | 125* | ND |
| 7–12 months | *ND* | 80* | ND | *ND* | 0.5* | ND | 1.8* | ND | 6* | ND | 150* | ND |
| **Children** | | | | | | | | | | | | |
| 1–3 y | *120* | **150** | 300 | *0.7* | **0.9** | ND | 2* | ND | 8* | ND | 200* | 1000 |
| 4–8 y | *160* | **200** | 400 | *1.0* | **1.2** | ND | 3* | ND | 12* | ND | 250* | 1000 |
| **Males** | | | | | | | | | | | | |
| 9–13 y | *250* | **300** | 600 | *1.5* | **1.8** | ND | 4* | ND | 20* | ND | 375* | 2000 |
| 14–18 y | *330* | **400** | 800 | *2.0* | **2.4** | ND | 5* | ND | 25* | ND | 550* | 3000 |
| 19–30 y | *320* | **400** | 1000 | *2.0* | **2.4** | ND | 5* | ND | 30* | ND | 550* | 3500 |
| 31–50 y | *320* | **400** | 1000 | *2.0* | **2.4** | ND | 5* | ND | 30* | ND | 550* | 3500 |
| 51–70 y | *320* | **400** | 1000 | *2.0* | **2.4**$^d$ | ND | 5* | ND | 30* | ND | 550* | 3500 |
| > 70 y | *320* | **400** | 1000 | *2.0* | **2.4**$^d$ | ND | 5* | ND | 30* | ND | 550* | 3500 |
| **Females** | | | | | | | | | | | | |
| 9–13 y | *250* | **300** | 600 | *1.5* | **1.8** | ND | 4* | ND | 20* | ND | 375* | 2000 |
| 14–18 y | *330* | **400**$^b$ | 800 | *2.0* | **2.4** | ND | 5* | ND | 25* | ND | 400* | 3000 |
| 19–30 y | *320* | **400**$^b$ | 1000 | *2.0* | **2.4** | ND | 5* | ND | 30* | ND | 425* | 3500 |
| 31–50 y | *320* | **400**$^b$ | 1000 | *2.0* | **2.4** | ND | 5* | ND | 30* | ND | 425* | 3500 |
| 51–70 y | *320* | **400** | 1000 | *2.0* | **2.4**$^d$ | ND | 5* | ND | 30* | ND | 425* | 3500 |
| >70 y | *320* | **400** | 1000 | *2.0* | **2.4**$^d$ | ND | 5* | ND | 30* | ND | 425*$^d$ | 3500 |
| **Pregnancy** | | | | | | | | | | | | |
| < 18 y | *520* | **600**$^c$ | 800 | *2.2* | **2.6** | ND | 6* | ND | 30* | ND | 450* | 3000 |
| 19–30 y | *520* | **600**$^c$ | 1000 | *2.2* | **2.6** | ND | 6* | ND | 30* | ND | 450* | 3500 |
| 31–50 y | *520* | **600**$^c$ | 1000 | *2.2* | **2.6** | ND | 6* | ND | 30* | ND | 450* | 3500 |
| **Lactation** | | | | | | | | | | | | |
| < 18 y | *450* | **500** | 800 | *2.4* | **2.8** | ND | 7* | ND | 35* | ND | 550* | 3000 |
| 19–30 y | *450* | **500** | 1000 | *2.4* | **2.8** | ND | 7* | ND | 35* | ND | 550* | 3500 |
| 31–50 y | *450* | **500** | 1000 | *2.4* | **2.8** | ND | 7* | ND | 35* | ND | 550* | 3500 |

This table presents *Estimated Average Requirements (EARs) in italics*, **Recommended Dietary Allowances (RDAs) in bold type**, and Adequate Intakes (AIs) in ordinary type followed by an asterisk (*). Tolerable Upper Intake Levels (ULs) are in shaded columns.

Source: Dietary Reference Intakes. Health Canada (2006, June 2009) Available at www.hc-sc.gc.ca/fn-an/nutrition/reference/table/ref_vitam_tbl-eng.php. Reproduced with the permission of the Minister of Public Works and Government Services Canada, 2008.

[12] As Dietary Folate Equivalents (DFE). See conversion factors for more details.
[13] The UL for folate applies only to synthetic forms obtained from supplements, fortified foods, or a combination of the two.
[14] Due to lack of suitable data, ULs could not be established for vitamin B$_{12}$, pantothenic acid, or biotin. This does not mean that there is no potential for adverse effects resulting from high intakes.
[15] Although AIs have been set for choline, there are few data to assess whether a dietary supply of choline is needed at all stages of the life cycle, and it may be that the choline requirement can be met by endogenous synthesis at some of these stages.
$^b$ In view of evidence linking the use of supplements containing folic acid before conception and during early pregnancy with reduced risk of neural tube defects in the fetus, it is recommended that all women capable of becoming pregnant take a supplement containing 400 µg of folic acid every day, in addition to the amount of folate found in a healthy diet.
$^c$ It is assumed that women will continue consuming 400 µg folic acid from supplements until their pregnancy is confirmed and they enter prenatal care. The critical time for formation of the neural tube is shortly after conception.
$^d$ Because 10 to 30 percent of older people may malabsorb food-bound vitamin B$_{12}$, it is advisable for those older than 50 years to meet the RDA mainly by consuming foods fortified with vitamin B$_{12}$ or a supplement containing vitamin B$_{12}$.

Note: These are reference values for normal, apparently healthy individuals eating a typical mixed North American diet. An individual may have physiological, health, or lifestyle characteristics that may require tailoring of specific nutrient values

# Dr. Stanley Zlotkin—Sprinkles Global Health Initiative: Creative Thought, Creative Purpose

As a college or university student, you may at times have wondered if research does make a difference. Our Human Potential story for this chapter suggests that it can. Dr. Stanley Zlotkin, M.D., Ph.D., FRCPC, at the Hospital for Sick Children, Division of Gastroenterology and Nutrition, at the University of Toronto, is a researcher who has used his academic knowledge and research skills to combat the most prevalent nutrition problem in the developing world today—iron-deficiency anemia in infants and young children.

The health issues linked to anemia during childhood and infancy include impaired mental and cognitive development and the capacity to learn. One common strategy used to prevent and treat iron deficiencies in young children is the use of iron drops. However, some studies have demonstrated that because of the metallic taste of the drops, a strong odour, and gastric irritation, many children stop taking the drops. There are also cultural beliefs to honour and the expense of administering the iron drops to consider.

With creative thought and purpose, Dr. Zlotkin and his group of researchers have developed an alternative micronutrient delivery system for infants and toddlers, called Sprinkles. Lipid-encapsulated iron (soy-lipid) and other essential micronutrients, including Vitamins A, C, and D, B vitamins, folic acid, and zinc, are packaged in powder form into individual packets as a single daily dose. The Sprinkles can be mixed into a bowl of any infant-weaning foods. There is no metallic aftertaste or change of colour, smell, or texture to the foods. No special measuring is required and the cost of this product is not prohibitively high.

The development of this product is admirable. Dr. Zlotkin could have stopped there. But what made his work special was his ongoing commitment to field test the Sprinkles through research

Dr. Stanley Zlotkin, creator of Sprinkles, is committed to reducing micronutrient deficiencies among infants and young children in developing countries.

studies in Afghanistan, Bangladesh, Bolivia, China, Cambodia, Indonesia, Guyana, Ghana, India, Mongolia, Pakistan, Vietnam, and Benin and First Nation and Inuit communities in Canada. This is no small task and takes tenacity, commitment, and patience to deal with the many complex operational issues associated with the introduction of any new health intervention, especially when trying to reach some of the most at-risk people in the world. His research group has made significant progress in this regard, and Sprinkles has been widely accepted as a solution to treat and prevent iron-deficiency anemia in young children worldwide.

There is not space in this textbook to describe all of the amazing work Dr. Zlotkin and his group are doing in countries around the world. Some examples include work with the French humanitarian relief agency Action Contre Le Faim (ACF) in regions in Afghanistan; the Helen Keller Indonesia (a large international NGO) in Cambodia and Indonesia; the Ministry of Health, Health Research

*continued*

Facility in Kintampo, Central Ghana; and Health Canada's First Nations, Inuit & Aboriginal Health branch in northern communities such as Attawapiskat, Fort Albany, and Igloolik. For the full scope of their projects, you can access the Sprinkles Global Initiative website at www.sghi.org. There *is* space, however, to report that the research is ongoing, the commitment strong, and the results of some of the field tests promising. One of the studies in Ghana demonstrated that Sprinkles were as effective in treating iron-deficiency anemia in infants as the standard treatment of oral iron drops, do not conflict with breast-feeding practices, can be mixed into complementary weaning foods including homemade foods by the child's caregiver, are inexpensive, and can be mixed with other vitamins and minerals to improve nutritional status. More research abstracts and articles are available at www.sghi.org/research_publication/index.html.

If you are considering a research career, start asking yourself how you might use your knowledge and research skills to help others. Research can and does make a difference—as seen through the work and vision of people such as Dr. Zlotkin.

serving. This allows consumers to calculate how many calories they'll consume and to determine the percentage of fat in an item.

- ✔ *Serving size.* You will find the specific amount of food listed under the Nutrition Facts title. All nutrient information is based on this amount of food and will be listed in common measures that you use at home. You will be able to compare this to the amount you eat and Canada's *Food Guide.*

The nutrient information is based on a specified amount of food. Compare this to the amount you eat.

This number is the amount of the nutrient in the specified quantity of food.

The *Nutrition Facts* table will include this list of Calories and 13 nutrients.

The % Daily Value gives a context to the amount of the nutrient in the specified amount of food. The Daily Values are based on recommendations for healthy eating.

| **Nutrition Facts** Per 125 mL (87 g) | | | |
|---|---|---|---|
| **Amount** | | | **% Daily Value** |
| **Calories** 80 | | | |
| **Fat** 0.4 g | | | 1 % |
| **Saturated** 0 g + **Trans** 0 g | | | 0 % |
| **Calories** 80 | | | |
| **Sodium** 0 mg | | | 0 % |
| **Carbohydrate** 18 g | | | 6 % |
| **Fibre** 2 g | | | 8 % |
| **Sugars** 2 g | | | |
| **Protein** 3 g | | | |
| **Vitamin A** | 2 % | **Vitamin C** | 10 % |
| **Calcium** | 0 % | **Iron** | 2 % |

The **horizontal format** may only be used when there is not enough room for the standard format.

| **Nutrition Facts Valeur nutritive** | **Amount / Teneur** | % DV / % VQ | **Amount / Teneur** | % DV / % VQ |
|---|---|---|---|---|
| | **Fat / Lipides** 13 g | **20 %** | **Carbohydrates / Glucides** 23 g | **8 %** |
| Per 1 bar (40 g) pour 1 barre (40 g) | Saturated / saturés 5 g + Trans / trans 3.5 g | **42 %** | Fibre / Fibres 0 g | **0 %** |
| | | | Sugars / Sucres 20 g | |
| **Calories** 220 | **Cholesterol / Cholestérol** 10 mg | | **Protein / Protéines** 3 g | |
| | **Sodium / Sodium** 70 mg | **3 %** | | |
| * DV = Daily Value | Vitamin A / Vitamine A | 2 % | Vitamin C / Vitamine C | 0 % |
| VQ = valeur quotidienne | Calcium / Calcium | 6 % | Iron / Fer | 4 % |

The **linear format** may appear on smaller packages.

**Nutrition Facts** per 1 cup (204 g) **Calories** 200 **Fat** 13 g (20 %) **Saturated Fat** 3 g + **Trans Fat** 2 g (25 %) **Cholesterol** 30 mg **Sodium** 660 mg (28 %) **Carbohydrates** 31 g (10 %) **Fibre** 0 g (0 %) **Sugars** 5 g **Protein** 5 g **Vit A** (4 %) **Vit C** (2 %) **Calcium** (15 %) **Iron** (4 %) % = % Daily Value

▲ **Figure 5-2** Understanding Nutrition Labels
The Nutrition Facts label lists the essential nutrient content of packaged food as well as the amount of potentially harmful substances such as fat and sodium.

Source: Information Sheet on Nutrition Facts. (2003). Health Canada. Office of Nutrition Policy and Promotion. Education. Available at www.hc-sc.gc.ca/fn-an/label-etiquet/nutrition/cons/cr_tearsheet-cr_fiche-eng.php. Reproduced with the permission of the Minister of Public Works and Government Services Canada, 2008.

- ✔ *Daily Values (DVs).* The Daily Values are based on recommendations for a healthy diet. The % Daily Value makes comparing foods easier because it puts all nutrients on the same scale (0%–100% Daily Value). For example, a food that has a % Daily Value of 5% or less for fat, sodium, or cholesterol would be low in these nutrients. A food that has a % Daily Value of 15% or more for calcium, Vitamin A, or fibre would be high in these nutrients.

  Look for higher % Daily Value next to nutrients you are trying to increase in your diet such as fibre, Vitamins A and C, calcium, and iron. Look for lower % Daily Value for nutrients you are trying to decrease, such as saturated and trans fats, cholesterol, and sodium. If you eat double the amount that is listed, you must double the value for calories and nutrients.
- ✔ *Calories per gram.* The Nutrition Facts lists the number of calories per gram for fat, carbohydrates, and protein. Among the useful items to check are the following:
  - *Calories from fat.* Get into the habit of calculating the percentage of fat calories in a food before buying or eating it.
  - *Total fat.* It's easy to overload on fat. Saturated fat is a figure worthy of special attention because of its reported link to several diseases.
  - *Cholesterol.* Cholesterol is made by and contained in products of animal origin only. Many high-fat products, such as potato chips, contain 0 percent cholesterol because they're made from plants and are cooked in vegetable fats. However, the vegetable fats they contain can be processed and made into saturated fats that are more harmful to the heart than cholesterol.

- *Fibre.* A high-fibre food has 5 or more grams of fibre per serving. A good source of fibre provides at least 2.5 grams.
- *Calcium.* High equals 200 milligrams or more per serving. Good means at least 100 milligrams.
- *Sodium.* Since many foods contain sodium, most of us routinely get more than we need. Read labels carefully to avoid excess sodium, which can be a health threat.
- *Vitamins.* A Daily Value of 10% of any vitamin makes a food a good source; 20% qualifies it as high in a certain vitamin.

Nutrition labelling is not required for fresh fruits and vegetables, raw meat and poultry (except ground meat and poultry), raw fish and seafood, foods that are sold only in retail establishments where they are prepared or processed, and individual servings of food intended for immediate consumption.[27]

If you are planning to work as a nutrition educator you might find the following resources helpful:

✔ Nutrition Labelling Toolkit for Educators, available at www.hc-sc.gc.ca/fn-an/label-etiquet/nutrition/educat.[28]

✔ Nutrition Labelling Toolkit for Educators—First Nations and Inuit Focus, available at www.hc-sc.gc.ca/fn-an/label-etiquet/nutrition/fni-pni/nutri-kit-trousse.[29]

An investigation also took place at the University of Saskatchewan to measure the reported use of nutrition information on food labels by university students. There were approximately equal numbers of label users and nonusers among males, while label users outnumbered nonusers by almost four to one among females. The only consistently observed difference between label users and nonusers (male and female) was that users believed in the importance of nutrition information on food labels while nonusers did not.[30]

## The Way We Eat

### Dietary Diversity

Whatever your cultural heritage, you have probably sampled Chinese, Mexican, First Nations, Italian, or Japanese foods. If you belong to any of these ethnic groups, you may eat these cuisines regularly. Each type of ethnic cooking has its own nutritional benefits and potential drawbacks, yet all recommend eating more carbohydrate-rich grains, vegetables, and fruits, and less high-protein meat and dairy (see Figure 5-3).

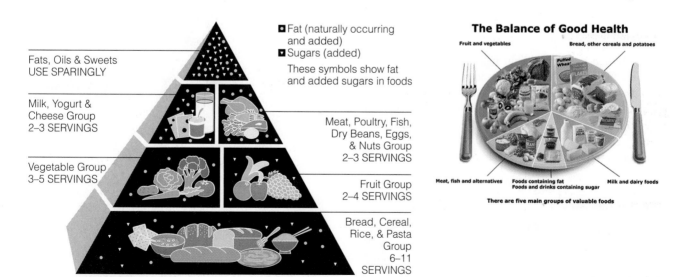

▲ **Figure 5-3** Shapes of Food Guides
Some countries use images other than a rainbow to present recommendations to eat more carbohydrate-rich grains, vegetables, and fruits. The United Kingdom and Mexico use plates. China and Korea use pagodas. The United States uses a pyramid.

## Chinese Diet

The Mainland Chinese diet—plant-based, high in carbohydrates, and low in fats and animal protein—is considered one of the healthiest in the world. The Food Guide Pagoda recommends plenty of cereals, vegetables, fruits, and beans, with physical activity balancing food intake.[31] However, Chinese food prepared in Canada contains more meat and sauces. According to laboratory tests of typical take-out dishes from Chinese restaurants, many have more fats and cholesterol than hamburger or egg dishes from fast-food outlets.

Try selecting boiled, steamed, or stir-fried dishes; mix entrées with steamed rice. If you are prone to high blood pressure, watch out for the high sodium content of soy and other sauces and the seasoner MSG (monosodium glutamate).

## French Diet

Traditional French cuisine, which includes rich, high-fat sauces and dishes, has never been considered healthful. Yet nutritionists have been stumped to explain the so-called French paradox. Despite a diet high in saturated fats, the French have had one of the lowest rates of coronary artery disease in the world.

However, fat consumption in France has risen as the French have begun eating more meat and fast foods, snacking more, eating fewer relaxed meals, exercising less, and drinking less wine.[32] They've also been getting fatter. The French diet increasingly resembles the Canadian and American diet, but French portions tend to be one-third to one-half the size of Canadian or American portions.

## Indian Diet

Many Indian dishes highlight healthful ingredients such as vegetables and legumes (beans and peas). However, many also use *ghee* (a form of butter) or coconut oil; both are rich in saturated fats. Good choices include *daal* or *dal* (lentils), *karbi* or *karni* (chickpea soup), and *chapati* (tortilla-like bread). Hold back on *bhatura* (fried bread), coconut milk, and *samosas* (fried meat or vegetables in dough).

## Japanese Diet

The traditional Japanese diet is very low in fat, which may account for the low incidence of heart disease in Japan. Dietary staples include soybean products, fish, vegetables, noodles, rice, and fruits. However, Japanese cuisine is high in salted, smoked, and pickled foods. Watch out for deep-fried dishes such as tempura and salty soups and sauces. Ask for broiled entrées or non-fried dishes made with tofu, which has no cholesterol.

## Mediterranean Diet

Research has confirmed that heart disease is much less common in countries along the Mediterranean than in other western nations. No one knows exactly why. It could be that the plant-based Mediterranean diet, which is rich in fruits, vegetables, legumes, cereal, wine, and olive oil, may be the reason (see Figure 5-4).

## Mexican Diet

The cuisine served in Mexico features rice, corn, and beans, which are low in fat and high in nutrients. However, the dishes many Canadians think of as Mexican are far less healthful. Burritos, especially when topped with cheese and sour cream, are very high in fat. Nutritious choices include rice, beans, and shrimp or chicken tostadas on unfried cornmeal tortillas.

## Southeast Asian Diet

A rich variety of bamboo shoots, bok choy, cabbage, mangoes, papayas, and cucumbers provides a sound nutritional basis for this diet. In addition, most foods are broiled or stir-fried, which keeps fat low. However, coconut oil and milk, used in many sauces, are high in fat. The use of MSG and pickled foods means the sodium content is high. At Thai or Vietnamese restaurants, choose salads (*larb* is a chicken salad with mint) or seafood soup (*po tak*).

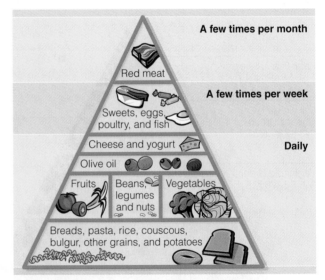

▲ **Figure 5-4** Mediterranean Food Pyramid
The Mediterranean diet relies heavily on fruits, vegetables, grain, and potatoes and includes considerable olive oil.

Source: Oldways Preservation & Exchange Trust. Reprinted by permission of the *New York Times*. All rights reserved.

## Aboriginal Diet

The Northwest Territories Health and Social Services System Action Plan 2002–2005 has led to many health initiatives that encourage Aboriginal people to embrace traditional ways of living to build healthy communities. The *Northwest Territories Food Guide*,[33] one of those initiatives (see Figure 5-5), is similar to *Eating Well with Canada's Food Guide* in that it recommends a variety of foods from each of the four food groups. Note the differences though—bannock, bread, and cereal, as well as caribou, duck and char, birds, eggs, and all edible parts of these animals, are included in the guide.

Researchers Receveur, Boulay, and Kuhnlein[34] evaluated the influence of traditional food on diet differences in dietary intake for adult Dene-Métis in 16 communities of the Northwest Territories. Although the Dene-Métis traditional food system is still used extensively, there is a trend toward decreasing use in the younger generations. The implications for health include higher levels of fat and saturated fat and lower intakes of calcium, Vitamin A, and dietary fibre.

## 100-Mile Diet

By now you have probably heard about the 100-mile diet.[35] Alisa Smith and J.B. McKinnon, long-time vegetarians, were moved to make a change in their own personal eating habits when they discovered that the food eaten by the average North American must travel over 1500 miles (2400 kilometres) from the farm to the grocery store. Their book, *The 100-Mile Diet: A Year of Local Eating*, is a story of their experience attempting to spend an entire year eating food grown within a 100-mile (160-kilometre) radius of their Vancouver apartment.

People from around the world have gone on to adopt this philosophy, and 100-mile diet groups have sprung up in small towns and large cities. Susan Cosier, a science, health, and environment reporter from Brooklyn, New York, was inspired to try the diet, and although she no longer eats a 100-mile diet exclusively, she does try to incorporate foods that are purchased close to home in her meals. There is a movement growing. People are beginning to understand that supporting local food producers helps not only the local economy, but also the world at large. Eating more

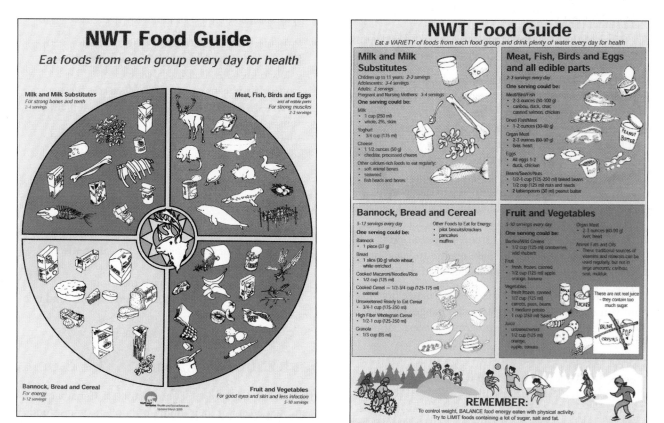

▲ **Figure 5-5** Northwest Territories Food Guide
The *Northwest Territories Food Guide* includes four food groups. Traditional foods recommended include bannock, fish heads and bones, and caribou, duck, and char.

Source: *Northwest Territories Food Guide*. Available at www.hlthss.gov.nt.ca. Northwest Territories Health & Social Services, © 2000 Government of the Northwest Territories.

seasonally, reducing greenhouse gases by reducing the distances food is shipped, and connecting with your own local community are all part of healthy living strategies.[36]

## Meal Exchange

In every community, people are faced with rising food costs and feeding their families. Food banks are the norm in many cities and towns. Another innovative program called Meal Exchange, a national student-founded, student-driven, registered charity, is also assisting people in need.[37] Meal Exchange began in 1993, when Rahul Raj found he had money left over from his university meal plan. To honour his grandmother's commitment to the poor people in India, Rahul began donating and delivering food to local social agencies. In 1998, Meal Exchange was incorporated and is now run through over fifty campuses across Canada.

This organization has generated over $2 million since the program began. The vision of this organization is to eliminate the root causes of hunger and poverty by engaging students in volunteer work. Students who become involved in Meal Exchange help to donate food, educate others about the causes of hunger, create volunteer opportunities that address hunger-related issues, and identify and implement student solutions.

Some of the Meal Exchange core successful programs include:

✔ Trick or Eat®—a Halloween event where students collect non-perishable food items for local food assistance programs.
✔ Skip-A-Meal®—a program that allows student meal plan holders an opportunity to donate a meal from their campus meal plan to purchase food at wholesale prices for donation to a local food program.
✔ Clear the Shelves—a program that encourages students to donate excess food, clothing, and furniture to local community members at the end of the academic year.
✔ Meal Exchange All-Star—a student recognition program for students who have made a tremendous effort to help the organization and social change.

To find out more about the Meal Exchange organization, you can check out www.mealexchange.com. There may even be a Meal Exchange program on your campus.

## ???? What Should I Know about Vegetarian Diets?

According to a report by the American Dietetic Association and Dieticians of Canada, approximately 2.5 percent of adults in the United States and 4 percent of adults in Canada follow a vegetarian diet.[38]

There are several types of vegetarian diets:

✔ **Vegan** or total vegetarian diet—consume only foods of plant origin, no animal products of any type
✔ **Lacto-vegetarian** includes dairy products, but no eggs
✔ **Lacto-ovo vegetarian** includes both dairy products and eggs
✔ **Semivegetarian**—no red meat but includes poultry and fish with plant foods, dairy products, and eggs

Vegetarian diets can be healthful and nutritionally adequate when planned well. You can use the vegetarian food guide rainbow to help you meal plan. It is available at www.dietitians.ca/news/downloads/vege_guide(EN).pdf.[39]

Serving sizes are small, so a meal or snack may easily include several servings from a group. Calcium-set tofu and fortified soymilk are included in the legumes, nuts, and other protein-rich foods group and are calcium-rich, too.

Vegetarian diets have proven health benefits. Studies show that vegetarians' cholesterol levels are low, they are seldom overweight, and they're less apt to be candidates for heart disease. They also have lower incidences of breast, colon, and prostate cancer; high blood pressure; and osteoporosis. When combined with exercise and stress reduction, vegetarian diets have helped reverse the build-up of harmful plaque within the blood vessels of the heart.

Pay special attention to the following:

✔ Protein—vary your sources of dietary protein. Soy protein has been shown to be equal in nutritional value to proteins of animal origin.
✔ Iron—dried beans, spinach, enriched products, brewer's yeast, and dried fruits are all good plant sources of iron.
✔ Vitamin $B_{12}$—comes naturally only from animal sources, so vegans should look for fortified breakfast cereals, fortified soy beverages, veggie meats, or Vitamin $B_{12}$ supplement.
✔ Calcium and Vitamin D—dairy products provide calcium as do soymilk, rice milk, and orange juice. Certain green vegetables such as broccoli, kale, bok choy, and Chinese cabbage as well as almonds, figs, and blackstrap molasses are also good sources of calcium. Sunlight enables us to make our own Vitamin D, and cow's milk, fortified soymilk, and rice milk have Vitamin D.

## Fast Food: Nutrition on the Run

"Burger and fries to go." Sound familiar? Canadians now spend 40 percent of their dining-out dollars on fast food.[40] Fast service and cheap prices keep consumers buying quick and easy meals. However, there is a growing feeling that there is a real cost to our fast-food purchases—and that might be a nutritional one.[41]

Fast foods can contribute protein, carbohydrates, vitamins, and minerals. Some fast-food restaurants now offer healthier food options that are lower in fat and calories. There are even fruit and vegetable choices, too. But there are many problems with fast food.

✔ While many fast-food meals give you half of your daily energy requirements, they give you only one-quarter of your vitamin and mineral daily requirements.

✔ Almost half of the calories in typical fast-food meals come from fat. The fat content of many items is extremely high. A Burger King Whopper with cheese contains 723 calories and 48 grams of fat, 18 grams from saturated fat. A McDonald's Sausage McMuffin with Egg has 517 calories and 33 grams of fat, 13 grams from saturated fat.[42]

✔ Recommended sodium intake is about 2000 mg/day. A typical fast-food meal with regular fries and a small shake gives you about 1500 milligrams of sodium.

## Food Safety

Increasingly, Canadians are concerned not just about whether the food they eat is nutritious, but also whether it's safe. Many unsuspected safety hazards have been identified by **food toxicologists**—specialists who detect toxins (potentially harmful substances) in our food and treat the conditions they produce.

### Pesticides, Irradiation, and Genetic Engineering

Plants and animals naturally produce compounds that act as pesticides to aid in their survival. The vast majority of the pesticides we consume are therefore natural—that is, not added by farmers or food processors. The problem lies with commercial pesticides, chemical wonders that save billions of dollars of valuable crops from pests, but endanger human health and life.

Many consumers are now purchasing **organic** foods. *Organic* refers to foods produced without the use of commercial chemicals at any stage. Independent groups now certify foods before they can be labelled organic. Foods that are truly organic have much lower levels of residues than standard commercial produce. There's no guarantee that the organic produce you buy at a grocery or health-food store is more nutritious than other produce. Organic food can also be more expensive. However, buying organic foods is one way in which you can work toward a healthier environment.

**Irradiation** is the use of radiation, either from radioactive substances or from devices that produce X-rays, on food. It doesn't make the food radioactive. Its primary benefit is to prolong the shelf life of food. Like the heat in canning, irradiation can kill all the microorganisms that might grow in a food, and the sterilized food can then be stored for years in sealed containers at room temperature without spoiling. Low-dose irradiation can inhibit the sprouting of vegetables such as potatoes and onions and delay the ripening of some fruits, such as bananas and tomatoes.

Nutritional studies have shown no significant decreases in the quality of the foods, but high-dose treatments may cause vitamin losses similar to those that occur during canning. It's also possible that the ionizing effect of radiation creates new compounds in foods that may be mutagenic or carcinogenic.

In Canada, several federal agencies are involved in regulating aspects of the food-irradiation process. The Health Products and Food Branch of Health Canada, through the *Food and Drugs Act,* is responsible for establishing standards related to the safety of foods sold to the Canadian consumer; the Canadian Food Inspection Agency (CFIA) is responsible for all enforcement and compliance issues relating to irradiated foods; and the Radiation Protection Bureau (RPB) of Health Canada is responsible for investigating, communicating, and reducing health risks to Canadians from exposure to ionizing and non-ionizing radiation. Food irradiation facilities must comply with these regulations.[43]

**Genetically modified organisms (GMOs),** custom built to improve quality or remove unwanted traits, may become an important part of our diets in the future. By modifying the genetic makeup of plants, engineers will be able to produce apples that resist insects, raspberries that last longer, and potatoes that absorb less fat in cooking.

Concern from consumer and environmental groups around the world about the potential hazards of GMOs has resulted in mandatory labelling of such foods in many European countries, Australia, New Zealand, Japan, Korea, and Hong Kong.[44] In Canada, labelling is necessary only if the modification has resulted in potential health or safety concerns, such as a nutritional or compositional change or an increase in potential allergenicity.[45] The CFIA is considering a voluntary approach to labelling of GMO products. Currently, the Canadian General Standards Board is developing the standard for voluntary labelling.

Will GMOs be as tasty and healthful as foods grown the old-fashioned way? Will they have unforeseen health hazards? That's yet to be seen.

### Additives: Risks versus Benefits

**Additives** are substances added to foods to lengthen storage time, change taste in a way the manufacturer thinks is better, alter colour, or otherwise modify them to make them more appealing.

Additives provide numerous benefits. Sodium and calcium propionate, sodium benzoate, potassium sorbate, and sulfur dioxide prevent the growth of bacteria, yeast, and mould in baked goods. BHA (butylated hydroxyanisole), BHT (butylated hydroxytoluene), propyl gallate, and Vitamin E protect against the oxidation of fats (rancidity). Other additives include leavening agents, emulsifiers, stabilizers, thickeners, dough conditioners, and bleaching agents.

Some additives can pose a risk to eaters. Nitrites, used in bacon, sausages, and lunch meats to inhibit spoilage, prevent botulism, and add colour, can react with other substances in your body or in food to form potentially cancer-causing agents called *nitrosamines*. Sulfites, used to prevent browning, can produce severe, even fatal, allergic reactions in sensitive individuals. Labelling of sulfites in packaged foods is now mandatory.

## ???? What Causes Food Poisoning?

*Salmonella* is a bacterium that contaminates many foods, particularly undercooked chicken, eggs, and, sometimes, processed meat. Eating contaminated food can result in salmonella poisoning, which causes diarrhea and vomiting. Another bacterium, *Campylobacter jejuni*, may cause even more stomach infections than salmonella. Found in water, milk, and some foods, Campylobacter poisoning causes severe diarrhea and has been implicated in the growth of stomach ulcers.

Bacteria can also cause illness by producing toxins in food. *Staphylococcus aureus* is the most common culprit. When cooked foods are cross-contaminated with the bacteria from raw foods and not stored properly, staph infections can result, causing nausea and abdominal pain anywhere from 30 minutes to 8 hours after ingestion.

An uncommon but sometimes fatal form of food poisoning is **botulism,** caused by the *Clostridium botulinum* organism. Improper home canning procedures are the most common cause of this potentially fatal problem.

## Food Allergies

Cow's milk, eggs, seafood, wheat, soybeans, nuts, seeds, and chocolate have all been identified as common triggers of food allergies. The symptoms they produce vary. One person might sneeze if exposed to an irritating food; another might vomit or develop diarrhea; and others might suffer headaches, dizziness, hives, or a rapid heartbeat. Symptoms may not develop for up to 72 hours, making it hard to pinpoint which food was responsible. If you suspect that you have a food allergy, see a physician with specialized training in allergy diagnosis.

## Strategies for Prevention

### Protecting Yourself from Food Poisoning

▲ Clean food thoroughly. Wash produce thoroughly. Wash utensils, plates, cutting boards, knives, blenders, and other cooking equipment with very hot water and soap after preparing raw meat, poultry, or fish to avoid contaminating other foods or the cooked meat.

▲ Drink only pasteurized milk.

▲ Don't eat raw eggs—they can be contaminated with salmonella.

▲ Cook chicken thoroughly. About one-third of all poultry sold contains harmful organisms.

▲ Cook pork thoroughly to kill a parasite called *trichina* occasionally found in the muscles of pigs.

▲ Know how to store foods. Don't leave food out for more than two hours in the temperature danger zone—4° Celsius (40° Fahrenheit) and 50° Celsius (140° Fahrenheit). After that time, throw the food away.

▲ Stored food doesn't last forever. Refrigerate leftovers as soon as possible and use them within three days. If frozen, use leftovers within two to three months.

**CHAPTER 5**

**Making This Chapter Work for You**

1. The classes of essential nutrients include which of the following?
   a. amino acids, antioxidants, fibre, and cholesterol
   b. proteins, calcium, calories, and folic acid
   c. carbohydrates, minerals, fat, and water
   d. iron, whole grains, fruits, and vegetables

2. Which type of fat is *not* considered a threat to heart health?
   a. omega-3 fatty acids
   b. trans-fatty acids
   c. cholesterol
   d. saturated fats

3. Antioxidants
   a. are nutrients important in the production of hemoglobin.
   b. are substances added to foods to make them more flavourful or physically appealing.
   c. are suspected triggers of food allergies.
   d. are substances that prevent the harmful effects of free radicals.

4. Which of the following is true about *Eating Well with Canada's Food Guide*?
   a. It advises that, on a daily basis, you eat the same amounts of food from each of the food groups represented in guide.
   b. It recommends that oils and fats are a major part of a healthy diet.
   c. According to the guide, one should eat 6 to 11 servings of meat and alternatives every week.
   d. The guide advises 8 servings of grain products and 8 to 10 servings of vegetables and fruit for males ages 19–50.

5. Which statement about essential nutrients is *false*?
   a. Carbohydrates provide body cells with glucose.
   b. Fats are necessary for the growth and repair of body cells.
   c. Water is an essential nutrient but doesn't provide any energy.
   d. Vitamins are necessary for the body to manufacture blood cells and hormones.

6. Food labels on packaged food include all of the following *except*
   a. total recommended servings.
   b. total amount of nutrients contained in the food.
   c. the percentage of nutrient Daily Values provided in the food.
   d. serving size.

7. Which of the following statements is true?
   a. The Chinese diet, which is high in fats and low in carbohydrates, leads to a high incidence of obesity and heart disease.
   b. The French diet is considered to be healthful because the food is high in saturated fats.
   c. The Mediterranean diet is rich in fruits, vegetables, wine, and olive oil and may help prevent heart disease.
   d. Mexican recipes often include MSG, which is unhealthy for people with high blood pressure.

8. Some vegetarians may
   a. include chicken and fish in their diets.
   b. avoid Vitamin $B_{12}$ supplements if they eat only plant foods.
   c. eat only legumes or nuts because these provide complete proteins.
   d. have high cholesterol levels because of the saturated fats in fruits and vegetables.

9. Food hazards include all the following *except*
   a. nitrites.
   b. raw eggs.
   c. pesticides.
   d. refrigerated leftovers used within three days.

10. Common causes of food-borne infections include which of the following?
    a. influenza virus
    b. salmonella and *E. coli* bacteria
    c. additives
    d. irradiation

Answers to these questions can be found on page 450.

## Self Responsibility

*Fresh food for a fresh attitude.*

**Julie Patterson**

Many of us want to change the way we eat, but are stuck in the contemplation stage—thinking about making changes, but not doing much about it. How might you get started? Think about the type of diet you would like to try. You can lower the fat content in your diet, try a vegetarian approach to eating, find out more about ethnic food, or simply eat more fruits and vegetables. You could try the 100-mile diet. Check out

## Social Responsibility

*There is hunger for ordinary bread, and there is hunger for love, for kindness, for thoughtfulness; and this is the great poverty that makes people suffer so much.*

**Mother Teresa**

your local library or bookstore or find a reputable website to find more about healthy nutrition. What can you do to move from contemplation to preparation and then to action?

Find out more about food bank programs on your campus. Many colleges and universities are setting up student food banks. There are many opportunities to help out through your academic year.

## Critical Thinking

1. Which alternative or ethnic diet do you think has the best-tasting food? Which is the most healthy? Why?

2. Is it possible to meet nutritional requirements on a limited budget? Have you ever been in this situation? What would you recommend to someone who wants to eat healthfully on $75 a week?

3. Consider the number of times a week you eat fast food. How much money would you have saved if you had eaten home-prepared meals? Which fast foods could you have selected that would have provided more nutritional value?

CENGAGENOW™

If your textbook package includes CengageNOW™, go to http://west.cengagenow.com/ilrn/ to link to CengageNOW™ for Health, your online study tool. First take the **Pre-test** for this chapter to get your personalized **Study Plan,** which will identify topics

you need to review and direct you to the appropriate resources. Then take the **Post-test** to determine what concepts you have mastered and what you still need work on.

# SITES & BYTES

**Canadian Council of Food and Nutrition**
www.ccfn.ca

The CCFN is an organization committed to nutrition advocacy and communications. You can access science-based food and nutrition policy and information.

**Dietitians of Canada**
www.dietitians.ca

The Dietitians of Canada website is an excellent source for comprehensive information that includes dietary guidelines, *Canada's Food Guide to Healthy Eating,* information about nutritional supplements, healthy diets, and current nutrition news.

**Eating+Activity Tracker—EATracker.ca**
www.dietitians.ca/public/content/eat_well_live_well/
english/eatracker

EATracker lets you track your day's food and activity choices and compares them to guidelines set out by Health Canada. Assess your food choices, receive personalized feedback on your total intake of energy and essential nutrients, and compare your results to what is recommended for your age, gender, and activity level. You can also determine your body mass index. To get "tracking," click on Take the Assessment.

**Food Guide Serving Sizes for 1–5 Years**
www.healthyalberta.com/Documents/Food_Serving_
Sizes_1_to_5_Yr_2008.pdf

Did you know that 125 millilitres (1/2 cup) of fresh or soft vegetable slices equals the size of 1 hockey puck? If you have ever wondered just what a food guide serving looks like, you can access this pdf file from Healthy Alberta to find out more.

**Office of Nutrition Policy and Promotion**
www.hc-sc.gc.ca/ahc-asc/branch-dirgen/hpfb-dgpsa/
onpp-bppn/

The ONPP at Health Canada promotes the nutritional health and well-being of Canadians by acting as a hub for current, reliable nutrition information. Check out all of their reports and keep up to date on nutrition recommendations for Canadians.

Please note that links are subject to change. If you find a broken link, use a search engine such as www.google.ca and search for the website by typing in keywords.

**InfoTrac® College Edition Activity**
Trautmann, J., Rau, S.I., Wilson, M.A., & Walters, C. (2008). Vegetarian students in their first year of college: Are they at risk for restrictive or disordered eating behaviours? (Report). *College Student Journal, 42*(2), 340–48.

1. What were the two main reasons college students decided to become vegetarians?
2. Describe the purpose of this study. What were the researchers trying to determine?
3. What were the limitations of this study?
4. Based on the findings of this study, what recommendations would you make to first-year college and university students who are considering a vegetarian lifestyle?

You can find additional readings related to nutrition with InfoTrac® College Edition, an online library of more than 5000 journals and publications. Follow the instructions for accessing InfoTrac® that were packaged with your textbook, and then search for articles using a keyword search.

For additional links and resources, visit our text-specific website at www.health.nelson.com.

## Key Terms

The terms listed here are used within the chapter on the page indicated. Definitions of the terms are in the Glossary at the end of this book.

additives 121
amino acids 101
antioxidants 103
botulism 122
calories 100
carbohydrates 101
cholesterol 103
complete proteins 101
complex carbohydrates 101
crucifers 108

dietary fibre 102
Dietary Reference Intake (DRI) 110
essential nutrients 100
food toxicologists 121
functional fibre 102
genetically modified organism (GMO) 121
glycemic index (GI) 102
incomplete proteins 101

indoles 108
irradiation 121
lacto-ovo vegetarian 120
lacto-vegetarian 120
macronutrients 100
micronutrients 100
minerals 103
nutrition 99
organic 121
phytochemicals 105

plaque 103
proteins 101
saturated fats 102
semivegetarian 120
simple carbohydrates 101
trans-fatty acids 103
unsaturated fats 102
vegan 120
vitamins 103

## References

1. Panel on Micronutrients, Subcommittees on Upper Reference Levels of Nutrients and Interpretation and Uses of Dietary Reference Intakes, and the Standing Committee on the Scientific Evaluation of Dietary Reference Intakes. (2002). *Dietary reference intakes for energy, carbohydrates, fiber, fat, protein and amino acids.* Washington, DC: National Academy of Sciences Press. Available at www.nap.edu.

2. Panel on Dietary Reference Intakes for Electrolytes and Water, Standing Committee on the Scientific Evaluation of Dietary Reference Intakes (2004). *Dietary Reference Intakes for Water, Potassium, Sodium, Chloride, and Sulfate.* Washington, DC: National Academy of Sciences Press. Available at www.nap.edu.

3. Health Canada. (2005). Dietary Reference Intakes tables. Available at. www.hc-sc.gc.ca/fn-an/nutrition/reference/table/index-eng.php.

4. Ibid.

5. Center for Science in the Public Interest. (n.d.). Health, nutrition and diet. Available at http://cspinet.org/nutrition.

6. Harder, B. (2002). Wholesome grains: Insulin effects may explain healthful diet. *Science News, 61*(20), 308.

7. Webb, D. (2001). Whole grains boast phytochemicals (not just fiber) to fight diseases. *Environmental Nutrition, 24*(2), 1.

8. Panel on Micronutrients, Subcommittees on Upper Reference Levels of Nutrients and Interpretation and Uses of Dietary Reference Intakes, and the Standing Committee on the Scientific Evaluation of Dietary Reference Intakes. (2002). *Dietary reference intakes for energy, carbohydrates, fiber, fat, protein and amino acids.* Washington, DC: National Academy of Sciences Press. Available at www.nap.edu.

9. Ibid.

10. Eating more fiber doesn't have to be uncomfortable. (2002). *Tufts University Health & Nutrition Letter, 20*(5), 7.

11. Dietitians of Canada. (2004). Glycemic index: The new buzz word, but what is it really? Available at www.dietitians.ca/resources/resourcesearch.asp?fn=view&contentid=2671.

12. Evidence for fish/heart health connection strengthens even more. (2002). *Tufts University Health & Nutrition Letter, 20*(4), 3.

13. Health Canada. (2008, July 15). Food and nutrition. Trans fat. Available at www.hc-sc.gc.ca/fn-an/nutrition/gras-trans-fats.

14. The HOPE and HOPE-TOO Trial Investigators. (2005). Effects of long-term Vitamin E supplementation on cardiovascular events and cancer: A randomized controlled trial. *Journal of the American Medical Association, 293,* 1138–1347.

15. Health Canada. (2007, December 12.). *Eating well with Canada's Food Guide.* Available at www.hc-sc.gc.ca/fn-an/food-guide-aliment/.

16. Health Canada. (2007, February 05). *Canada's food guides from 1942 to 1992.* Available at www.hc-sc.gc.ca/fn-an/food-guide-aliment/context/hist-eng.php.

17. Glanz, K. (2000). Reducing chronic diseases risk through nutrition. *Facts of Life: Issue Briefing for Health Reporters, 5*(9), 2.

18. Natural Health Products Directorate. (2004). *Natural health products regulations.* Health Canada. Available at www.hc-sc.gc.ca/dhp-mps/prodnatur/index-eng.php.

19. Ibid.

20. Health Canada. (2008, March 11). Health Canada reminds Canadians not to use Ephedra/ephedrine products. Available at www.hc-sc.gc.ca/ahc-asc/media/advisories-avis/_2008/2008_41-eng.php.

21. Office of Nutrition Policy and Promotion. (2004, January 1). A consumer's guide to the DRIs (dietary reference intakes). Health Products and Food Branch, Health Canada. Available at www.hc-sc.gc.ca/fn-an/nutrition/reference/cons_info-guide_cons-eng.php.

22. Ibid.

23. Ibid.

24. Medline Plus. (2008, March 1). Herbs and supplements: Vitamin D. U.S. National Library of Medicine and the National Institutes of Health. Available at www.nlm.nih.gov/medlineplus/druginfo/natural/patient-vitamind.html.

25. Office of Nutrition and Promotion. (2008, January 17). Nutrition labelling. Health Canada. Available at www.hc-sc.gc.ca/fn-an/label-etiquet/nutrition/cons/index-eng.php.

26. Office of Nutrition and Promotion. (2008, January 17). Nutrition facts table. Health Canada. Available at www.hc-sc.gc.ca/fn-an/label-etiquet/nutrition/index-eng.php.

27. Health Canada. (2003, March 27). Frequently asked questions about nutrition labelling. Available at www.hc-sc.gc.ca/fn-an/label-etiquet/nutrition/educat/te_quest-eng.php.

28. Office of Nutrition and Promotion. (2008, January 17). Nutrition labelling toolkit for educators Health Products and Food Branch, Health Canada. Available at www.hc-sc.gc.ca/fn-an/label-etiquet/nutrition/educat.

29. Office of Nutrition and Promotion. (2004, October 1). Nutrition labelling toolkit for educators: First Nations and Inuit focus. Health

Products and Food Branch, Health Canada. Available www.hc-sc .gc.ca/fn-an/label-etiquet/nutrition/fni-pni/nutri-kit-trousse.

30. Smith, S.C., Taylor, J.G., & Stephen, A.M. (2000). Use of food labels and beliefs about diet-disease relationships among university students. *Public Health Nutrition, 3*(2), 175–82.

31. Dietary guidelines and the food guide pagoda. (2000). *Journal of the American Dietetic Association, 100*(8).

32. de Lorgeril, M., & Salen, P. (1999). Wine, ethanol, platelets, and mediterranean diet. *Lancet, 353*(9158).

33. Northwest Territories Health and Social Services. (2005, March). *Northwest Territories food guide.* Available at www.hlthss.gov.nt.ca/ english/publications/subject/publications_healthy_eating_and_ acitve_living.asp.

34. Receveur, O., Boulay, M., & Kuhnlein, H.V. (1997). Decreasing traditional food use affects diet quality for adult dene/metis in 16 communities of the Canadian Northwest Territories. *Journal of Nutrition, American Society for Nutritional Sciences, 127,* 2179–86.

35. Giese, R. (2007, April 11). Home cooking. Alisa Smith and J.B. McKinnon talk about the 100-mile diet. CBC Arts/ Books. Available at www.cbc.ca/arts/books/100_mile_diet.html.

36. Cosier, S. (2007). The 100 mile diet. *E-The Environmental Magazine, 18*(5), 42–43.

37. Meal Exchange. (2006). Home. Available at www.mealexchange. com.

38. Vegetarianism—A meatless eating experience. (2004). Agriculture, Food and Rural Development, Government of Alberta. Available at www1.agric.gov.ab.ca/$department/deptdocs.nsf/all/sis8739.

39. Messina, V., Melena, V., & Mangels, A.R. (2003). A new food guide for North American vegetarians. *Canadian Journal of Dietetic Practice Research, 64*(2), 82. Available at www.dietitians.ca/news/ downloads/vege_guide(EN).pdf.

40. Surviving the fast food circuit. (2006, September). *Nutrition Matters.* York Region Health Services Department. Available at www.york.ca/NR/rdonlyres/qcvldhy3lbr6oewyifjjsbretqak76nsxf 5ns23jyggzatntw63xrj3rqaqgpmknsmfsheztynqjgwjxdlixuotg3c/ Surviving+the+Fast+Food+Circuit+new+letterhead07.pdf.

41. Schlosser, E. (2001). *Fast food nation.* New York: Simon & Schuster.

42. Spurlock, M. (2005). *Don't eat this book: Fast food and the supersizing of America.* New York: G. P. Putnam's Sons.

43. Frequently asked questions regarding food irradiation. (2002, November 25). Health Products and Food Branch Home. Available at www.hc-sc.gc.ca/fn-an/securit/irridation/ index-eng.php.

44. Food Safety Network. (2001, June 1). Labelling of genetically modified foods: International approaches AGCare backgrounder. Available at www.foodsafetynetwork.ca/en/news-details. php?a=3&c=29&sc=220&id=51044.

45. Chaitoo, R., & Hart, M. (2000). Labelling of GMO products: Strategic trade policy considerations for Canada. A report prepared for the Canadian Biotechnology Advisory Committee (CBAC). Available at http://cbac-cccb.ca/epic/site/cbac-cccb.nsf/en/ ah00451e.html.

# Healthy Eating for Healthy Living

After studying the material in this chapter, you should be able to:

- **Define** body mass index (BMI) and **describe** the different methods of estimating body composition.
- **Identify** several factors that influence food consumption.
- **Identify** and **describe** the symptoms and dangers associated with eating disorders.
- **Define** obesity and **describe** its relationship to genetics, lifestyle, and major health problems.
- **Assess** various approaches to weight loss.

About a billion people worldwide are now considered overweight or obese. In Canada, 8.6 million people over the age of 18 are overweight. Another 5.5 million are obese. Together, this represents 59 percent of the Canadian adult population.[1] The growing body of research dedicated to children's health and nutrition patterns is also setting off alarm bells. Health issues linked to diets too high in calories and fat are discussed repeatedly in academic journals.[2, 3] Health and education professionals concur with the dire warnings being made by the Heart and Stroke Foundation of Canada[4]—that the increasing number of overweight and obese Canadians now poses one of the greatest threats ever to public health in our country.

Ironically, as average weights have increased,[5] the quest for thinness has become a national obsession. In a society where slimmer is seen as better, anyone who is less than lean may feel like a failure. Individuals who are overweight or embarrassed by their appearance often assume that they would be happier, sexier, or more successful in thinner bodies.[6] So they diet. Each year millions of Canadians go on diets, but no matter how much they lose, 90 to 95 percent regain extra pounds within five years.

This chapter examines unhealthy eating patterns and eating disorders; explains body mass index (BMI); explores our preoccupation with slimness; tells what obesity is and why excess pounds are dangerous; shows why fad diets don't work; and offers guidelines for how to control weight safely, sensibly, and permanently.

????  **FREQUENTLY ASKED QUESTIONS**

FAQ: What should I weigh? p. 130

FAQ: How many calories do I need? p. 131

FAQ: Who develops eating disorders? p. 135

FAQ: What causes obesity? p. 140

FAQ: How can I overcome a weight problem? p. 142

FAQ: Do high-protein, low-carbohydrate diets work? p. 144

# Body Image

Throughout most of history, bigger was better. The great beauties of centuries past, as painted by such artistic masters as Rubens and Renoir, were soft and fleshy, with rounded bellies and dimpled thighs. Culture often shapes views of beauty and health. Many developing countries still regard a full figure, rather than a thin one, as the ideal.

Not so in North America, where, influenced by the media and the need to belong or conform, many young women are attempting to become slimmer while young men are attempting to become more muscular. In a study of high school girls, those who regularly read women's health and fitness magazines, which may present unrealistic physical ideals, were more likely to go on low-calorie diets, take pills to suppress their appetites, use laxatives, or force themselves to vomit after eating.[7] In other research, girls who watched a lot of television and expressed concern about slimness and popularity were more dissatisfied with their bodies than girls involved in sports.[8] Boys' body images also are influenced by media images depicting super strong, highly muscular males.[9, 10]

Other studies have shown that college students of different ethnic and racial backgrounds, including Asians, express as much—and sometimes more—concern about their body shape and weight as whites.[11] As shown in The X & Y Files (page 136), men and women are prone to different distortions in body image.

# ???? What Should I Weigh?

Many factors determine what you weigh: heredity, eating behaviour, food selection, and amount of daily exercise. For any individual of a given height, there is no single best weight, but a range of healthy weights. Health Canada has replaced ideal-weight tables with a weight classification system that includes body mass index, waist circumference, and waist-to-hip ratio.

## Body Mass Index

**Body mass index (BMI),**[12] a ratio between weight and height, is a mathematical formula that correlates with body fat. The BMI numbers apply to both men and women (see Table 6-1).

You calculate your body mass index by dividing your weight in kilograms by your height in metres$^2$. The formula is BMI = weight (kg)/height (m$^2$). A body mass index calculator is available at www.heartandstroke.bc.ca/site/c .kpIPKXOyFmG/b.3644813/k.6A38/Assess_Your_Weight_ BMI.htm.

Doctors, health professionals, and personal trainers use BMI to identify weight-related health risks in populations and individuals. It is intended for use among Canadian adults age 18 and older. Health risks associated with the underweight category, or a BMI under 18.5, include under

---

▼ **Table 6-1 Body Mass Index Nomogram**

This BMI nomogram is not intended for use with:

- those under 18 years of age; and
- pregnant and lactating women.

You can calculate your BMI using this formula: BMI = weight (kg)/height (m$^2$)

**Health Risk Classification According to Body Mass Index (BMI)**

| Classification | BMI Category (kg/m$^2$) | Risk of Developing Health Problems |
|---|---|---|
| Underweight | < 18.5 | Increased |
| Normal weight | 18.5–24.9 | Least |
| Overweight | 25.0–29.9 | Increased |
| Obese class I | 30.0–34.9 | High |
| Obese class II | 35.0–39.9 | Very high |
| Obese class III | ≥ 40.0 | Extremely high |

Source: Body Mass Index (BMI) Nomogram. *Office of Nutrition Policy and Promotion. Health Products and Food Branch, Health Canada.* Available at www.hc-sc.gc.ca/fn-an/ nutrition/weights-poids/guide-ld-adult/bmi_chart_java-graph_imc_java-eng.php. Reproduced with permission of the Minister of Public Works and Government Services, 2008.

---

Note: For persons 65 years and older the "normal" range may begin slightly above BMI 18.5 and extend into the "overweight" range. To clarify risk for each individual, other factors such as lifestyle habits, fitness level, and presence or absence of other health risk conditions also need to be considered.

nutrition, osteoporosis, and infertility. Health risks associated with overweight and obesity, or a BMI of 25 or higher, include Type 2 diabetes, hypertension, coronary heart disease, sleep apnea, and certain cancers.

However, using BMI as an assessment tool has limitations. Muscular individuals, including athletes and body builders, may be incorrectly categorized as overweight or obese because they have greater lean muscle mass. BMI also does not reliably reflect body fat, an independent predictor of health risk, and is not useful for growing children, women who are pregnant or nursing, or the elderly.

## Waist Circumference

**Waist circumference**[13] **(WC)** is used along with body mass index as a practical indicator of risk that is associated with excess abdominal fat. Where you carry your weigh is even more important than how much weight you carry. People who have apple-shaped bodies (weight around the waist) are more likely than those with pear-shaped bodies (weight on hips and thighs) to have high cholesterol levels, high blood pressure, and an increased risk of diabetes. Cut-off points for both men and women have been established by Health Canada. A waist circumference above these cut-off points is associated with increased risk of coronary heart disease, Type 2 diabetes, and hypertension.

- ✔ For Caucasion men: WC ≥ 102 cm (40.2 inches)
- ✔ For Asian men: WC ≥ 90 cm (35.4 inches)
- ✔ For Caucasion women: WC ≥ 88 cm (34.6 inches)
- ✔ For Asian women: WC ≥ 80 cm (31.5 inches)

A helpful tool and video clip for calculating waist circumference is available at the British Columbia site for the Canadian Heart and Stroke Foundation. Go to: www.heartandstroke.bc.ca/site/c.kpIPKXOyFmG/b.4018791/k.8708/Healthy_Waists.htm.

## Waist-to-Hip Ratio

To determine your **waist-to-hip ratio (WHR),** divide your waist circumference by your hip circumference.[14] A WHR greater than 1.0 for men or 0.85 for women is considered a signal of high risk for disease; a WHR of 0.90 to 1.0 for men or 0.80 to 0.85 for women indicates moderately high risk; and a WHR less than 0.90 for men or less than 0.80 for women indicates lower risk.

## Body-Composition Assessment

Ideal body-fat percentages for men range from 7 to 25 percent and for women from 16 to 35 percent. Methods of assessing body composition include:

- ✔ **Skinfold fat measurement.** A calliper is used to measure the amount of skinfold. Various sites on the body are measured, depending on different skinfold tests. The sites can include triceps, biceps, subscapular, iliac crest, chest, abdomen, suprailiac, and thigh. Equations determine body fat percentage. Calculations take into account age, gender, race, and other factors. Limitations include lack of precision in taking skinfold measurements at exact sites.[15]
- ✔ **Hydrostatic (underwater) weighing.** This method, also known as hydrodensitometry, measures the weight of displaced fluid. Muscle has a higher density than water, and fat has a lower density. Thus fat people tend to displace less water than lean people. The limitations include expensive and complex testing methods and the inability for some people to be lowered under the water and exhale fully.
- ✔ **Bioelectrical Impedance Analysis.**[16] This rapid, non-invasive method uses a BIA analyzer where a low-level electrical current is passed through the body and the impedance (Z) or opposition to the flow of current is measured. The resistance to current flow will be greater in individuals with large amounts of body fat because adipose tissue is a poor conductor of electrical current due to its relatively low water content. Limitations include following strict pre-test protocol such as not exercising or drinking water prior to the test.
- ✔ **Dual-energy X-ray absorptiometry (DXA).** X-rays are used to quantify the skeletal and soft-tissue components of body mass. The test requires 10 to 20 minutes, and radiation dosage is low (800 to 2000 times lower than a typical chest X-ray). Some researchers believe that DXA will supplant hydrostatic testing as the standard for body composition assessment. Limitations are the expense and availability of equipment, few trained technicians, and concern about radiation.

## How Many Calories Do I Need?

**Calories** are the measure of the amount of energy that can be derived from food. How many calories you need depends on your gender, age, body-frame size, weight, percentage of body fat, and your **basal metabolic rate (BMR)**—the number of calories needed to sustain your body at rest. Your activity level also affects your calorie requirements. The Dietitians of Canada has defined our daily caloric needs as EER—or Estimated Energy Requirement. See Table 6-2 for energy estimates for different ages and activity levels.

The average Canadian adult consumes 2921 calories per day.[17] A low active woman (20–30 years old) needs

▼ **Table 6-2 Estimated Energy Requirements (EER) for Different Ages and Activity Levels**

| | Males | | | Females* | | |
|---|---|---|---|---|---|---|
| Age | Sedentary | Low Active | Active | Sedentary | Low Active | Active |
| 14–18 | 2200 | 2400–2800 | 2800–3200 | 1800 | 2000 | 2400 |
| 20–30 | 2400 | 2600–2800 | 3000 | 2000 | 2000–2200 | 2400 |
| 35–50 | 2200 | 2400–2600 | 2800–3000 | 1800 | 2000 | 2200 |
| 55–70 | 2000 | 2200–2400 | 2600–2800 | 1600 | 1800 | 2000–2200 |
| 75–80 | 2000 | 2200 | 2400–2600 | 1600 | 1800 | 2000 |

The Estimated Energy Requirement (EER) is defined as the dietary energy intake that is predicted to maintain energy balance in a healthy adult of a defined age, gender, weight, height, and level of physical activity consistent with good health.

**Activity Levels Defined**

**Sedentary:** If <60 minutes total in low-intensity activities and 0 minutes in moderate-intensity plus 0 minutes vigorous activity. *Sedentary* means a lifestyle that includes only physical activity of independent living.

**Low Active:** If ≥60 minutes total of low-intensity activities and <30 minutes of moderate-intensity activity and 0 minutes vigorous intensity activities. *Low active* means a lifestyle that includes physical activity equivalent to walking about 5 to 6.5 kilometres (1.5–3 miles) per day at 5 to 6.5 kilometres (3–4 miles) per hour, in addition to the activities of independent living.

**Active:** If ≥60 minutes total of low-intensity activities and ≥30 minutes moderate-intensity activity and vigorous intensity activity. *Active* means a lifestyle that includes physical activity equivalent to walking more than 5 kilometres (3 miles) per day at 5 to 6.5 kilometres (3–4 miles) per hour, in addition to the activities of independent living.

Source: The Food and Nutrition Board, Institute of Medicine. Dietary reference intakes for energy, carbohydrate, fiber, fat, fatty acids, cholesterol, protein, and amino acids. 2002. References are calculated by gender, age and activity level for reference-size individuals. Reprinted with permission from the National Academies Press, Copyright 2002, National Academies of Sciences.

* • Pregnancy: second trimester: Add 340 calories
  • Pregnancy: third trimester: Add 452 calories
  • Breastfeeding: Add 330 calories

about 2000–2200 calories a day, and a man (20–30 years old) about 2600–2800. If we compare the daily caloric needs of women and men to a fast-food meal, we can begin to understand why overweight and obese Canadians are becoming the norm. A double cheeseburger, large fries, and a large soft drink contain about 1800 calories. That is just one meal!

Regardless of whether you consume fat, protein, or carbohydrates, if you take in more calories than required to maintain your size and don't work them off in some sort of physical activity, your body will convert the excess to fat.

## Hunger and Satiety

More than a dozen different signals may influence our **hunger,** our physiological drive to consume food. Researchers at the National Institutes of Health have discovered appetite receptors within the hypothalamus region of the brain that specifically respond to hunger messages carried by chemicals. Hormones, including insulin and stress-related epinephrine (adrenaline), may also stimulate or suppress hunger. Recent studies show that hunger activates parts of the brain involved with emotions,

thinking, and feeling. Even the size of our fat cells may affect how hungry we feel.

**Appetite**—the psychological desire to eat—usually begins with the fear of the unpleasant sensation of hunger. We learn to avoid hunger by eating a certain amount of food at certain times of the day, just as dogs in a laboratory learn to avoid electric shocks by jumping at the sound of a warning bell. We stop eating when we feel satisfied; this is called **satiety,** a feeling of fullness and relief from hunger.

But appetite is easily led into temptation. Biologists speculate that creamy, buttery, or greasy foods, which human beings seem to crave, may override our natural feeling of fullness and encourage overeating, causing internal changes that increase appetite and, consequently, weight.

## Dietary Theories

There are numerous dietary theories, all supported by research, yet none are conclusive about why some people gain weight, why others don't, and why, for some, weight loss is a lifelong challenge. Presented here are just a few of the current theories.

## Set-Point Theory

According to the **set-point theory,** each individual has an unconscious control system in the brain for regulating appetite and satiety to keep body fat at a predetermined level, or *set point.* Many studies have attempted to discover if our set point can be altered. Other studies have found that most overweight individuals cannot lose weight permanently. A recent study followed 24 overweight women for a four-year period to evaluate their metabolic changes after dieting. After losing an average of 30 pounds, the candidates stopped dieting. On average, the women returned to their initial overweight level by the four-year follow-up, and their metabolic rate increased, comparable to that of women who were never overweight.

The lead author Dr. Weinsier says that our metabolic rate falls when we cut back on calories because this is nature's way of preventing starvation. However, after people lose weight and then stop restricting calories, their metabolic rate returns to normal.[18] It may be that a well-designed weight-loss program that includes a healthy caloric intake and regular physical activity is the only way to work with personal set points.

## The Energy-Balance Equation Theory

The **energy-balance equation theory** suggests that our weight will remain constant if our caloric input (energy in) and caloric output (energy out) is balanced. Any calories consumed in excess of what our body uses will be converted to fat tissue. If we do not take in enough calories, the result will be weight loss. For many people, this approach to weight management works.

The key to this theory is maintaining the balance of energy in and energy out, not just lowering caloric intake. A group of scientists in Britain have noted that the average recorded energy intake (food) has declined substantially, whereas obesity rates have climbed. The findings of this study suggest that physical activity levels might have declined even faster.[19] Decreasing food intake must still be balanced with the maintenance of regular physical activity.

## The Dietary Fat Theory

Some studies have shown that consuming a diet high in fat calories will result in being overweight or obese.[20] The **dietary fat theory** differs from the energy-balance equation theory in that it suggests that all calories are not the same. Weight-control intervention studies that focused on low-fat diets have found promising results.

However, the science of dietary fat is not as simple as it once appeared. There is some evidence that a high-fat diet overrides normal satiety mechanisms, which leads to increased total caloric consumption.[21] There is also concern that eating less fat might have a profound effect on our bodies, some which might be harmful. Fat is the primary component of cell membranes. A change in types of fat humans ingest might change the fat composition of the membranes, which in turn, might change their permeability, "which controls the transport of everything from glucose, signalling proteins, and hormones to bacteria, viruses, and tumour-causing agents into and out of the cell. The relative saturation of fats in the diet could also influence cellular aging as well as the clotting ability of blood cells."[22]

More research continues. In the meantime, healthy food choices and regular physical activity seem to be our best bet for weight management and disease prevention.

## Unhealthy Eating Behaviour

Unhealthy eating behaviour takes many forms, ranging from not eating enough to eating too much too quickly. Its roots are complex. In addition to media and external pressures, a family history can play a role, as can stress and culture.[23] In this section, you will learn about disordered eating, extreme dieting, and compulsive overeating. The next section, Eating Disorders, will discuss anorexia nervosa, bulimia, and binge eating disorder (BED).

At certain times in life or in certain situations, many people don't eat the way they should. They may skip meals, thereby increasing the likelihood that they'll end up with more body fat, a higher weight, and a higher blood cholesterol level. They may live on diet foods but consume so much of them that they gain weight anyway. Some people engage in more extreme eating behaviour. Dissatisfied with almost all aspects of their appearance, they continuously go on and off diets or eat compulsively.[24] Such behaviours can be warning signs of potentially serious eating disorders that should not be ignored.

## Disordered Eating in College and University Students

College and university students can be at risk for unhealthy eating behaviours. The most common weight-related problem on campuses may be gaining weight, particularly in the first year. Weight gain can occur for many reasons. Moving away from home, settling into residence or off-campus living, academic responsibilities, a lack of space to cook, or the availability of fast food or restaurants are just a few. According to one study, 44 percent of college students surveyed ate out at a restaurant (including fast food) at least once a week. The same number of students brought snack foods, including chips, pretzels, or crackers, to class or to the campus.[25]

Several studies have documented changes in both weight and body fat. In one study, the average weight gain was 1.4 kilograms (3.08 pounds).[26] Another study found that first-year students gained an average of 1.9 kilograms (4.2 pounds) during their first 12 weeks at college.[27] Twenty percent of this significant weight gain was attributed to the all-you-can-eat breakfast and lunch eating facilities. Other factors were the number of evening snacks, the number of meals eaten on weekends, the consumption of "junk" food, and constant dieting.

Some college and university campuses are attempting to help students monitor the amount of food they are eating by removing plastic dinner trays from their cafeterias. University officials are noticing that students are eating less. Instead of filling trays with numerous plates, bowls, and several glasses, students are taking one plate of food and a drink. Other positive outcomes of the tray take-away initiatives are a decrease in food waste and conserving water and energy used in cleaning the trays. Many students are not happy with the removal of cafeteria dinner trays, but others believe it may help them eat less. Aramark, a food service provider at 500 colleges in the United States predicts that 50 to 60 percent of the campuses it serves will go trayless in 2008. It also predicts that food waste will be reduced by 34 to 51 grams (1.2 to 1.8 ounces) per person at each meal.[28]

In a study of Australian male undergraduates, one in four men worried about shape and weight; one in five displayed attitudes and behaviours characteristic of disordered eating and eating disorders. None ever sought treatment, even if the students recognized they had a problem. The reason, the researchers theorized, may be that the young men hesitated to seek treatment for an illness stigmatized as a problem that affects only women.[29]

One study that followed more than 100 undergraduate women through their first year found that those who reported the most body dissatisfaction and unhealthy eating patterns at the beginning of the first semester were most likely to experience more eating problems, such as losing control of their eating when feeling strong emotions. The strongest predictor that eating symptoms would get worse over the first year was not BMI or weight, but body dissatisfaction.[30] Foreign students, who had incorporated foods high in fat, salt, and sugar into their diets, gained about 1 kilogram (3 pounds) on average, and their percentage of body fat rose by about 5 percent.[31]

## Extreme Dieting

Extreme dieters go beyond cutting back on calories or increasing physical activity. They become preoccupied with what they eat and weigh. Although their weight never falls below 85 percent of normal, their weight loss is severe enough to cause uncomfortable physical consequences, such as weakness and sensitivity to cold, and they are at increased risk for anorexia nervosa.

Extreme dieters may think they know a great deal about nutrition, yet many of their beliefs about food and weight are misconceptions or myths. They may eat only protein because they believe complex carbohydrates, including fruits and breads, are fattening. When they're anxious, angry, or bored, they focus on food and their fear of fatness. Dieting and exercise become ways of coping with any stress in their lives.

Sometimes nutritional education alone can help change this eating pattern. However, many avid dieters who deny that they have a problem with food may need counselling to correct dangerous eating behaviours and prevent further complications.

## Compulsive Overeating

People who eat compulsively cannot stop putting food in their mouths. They eat fast, and they eat a lot. They eat even when they're full. They may eat around the clock rather than at set meal times, often in private because of embarrassment over how much they consume.

Some mental health professionals describe compulsive eating as a food addiction that is much more likely to develop in women. According to Overeaters Anonymous (OA), an international 12-step program, many women who eat compulsively view food as a source of comfort against feelings of inner emptiness, low self-esteem, and fear of abandonment.

The following behaviours may signal a potential problem with compulsive overeating:

- ✔ Turning to food when depressed or lonely, when feeling rejected, or as a reward.
- ✔ A history of failed diets and anxiety when dieting.
- ✔ Thinking about food throughout the day.
- ✔ Eating quickly and without pleasure.
- ✔ Continuing to eat even when no longer hungry.
- ✔ Frequent talking about food or refusing to talk about food.
- ✔ Fear of not being able to stop eating once starting.

Recovery from compulsive eating can be challenging because people with this problem cannot give up entirely the substance they abuse. However, they can learn new eating habits and ways of dealing with underlying emotional problems. An OA survey found that most of its members joined to lose weight but later felt the most important effect was their improved emotional, mental, and physical health.

# Eating Disorders

Eating disorders involve a serious disturbance in eating behaviour. In addition to either eating too much or too little, individuals who suffer from eating disorders have great concerns over body size and shape. For some people, the concern develops into a compulsion of unhealthy eating behaviours and lifestyles.

Individuals with **eating disorders**[32] display a broad range of symptoms that occur along a continuum. Those with anorexia nervosa refuse to maintain a minimally normal body weight and have an intense fear of gaining weight and a distorted perception of the shape or size of their body. Those with bulimia nervosa binge eat and then use vomiting, excessive exercise, or laxatives to purge the food eaten. A diagnosis of binge eating disorder (BED) is made when binge eating is not followed by purging. This disorder is often associated with obesity.

## Who Develops Eating Disorders?

Most people with eating disorders are young (ages 14 to 25), white, female, and affluent, with perfectionist personalities. However, despite past evidence that eating disorders were primarily problems for white women, they are increasing among men and members of different ethnic and racial groups[33] (see Table 6-3 for major risk factors, and The X & Y Files: "Men, Women, and Weight").

In a survey at a large, public, rural university, eating disorders did not discriminate, equally affecting women of different races, religions, athletic involvement, and living arrangements. Although the students viewed eating disorders as both mental and physical problems and felt that individual therapy would be most helpful, all said that they would first turn to a friend for help.[34] In another study of 1620 students, almost 11 percent of the women and 4 percent of the men were at risk for eating disorders. About 17 percent of the women and 10 percent of the men said concerns about weight interfered with their academic work.[35]

Male and female athletes are also vulnerable to eating disorders because of the pressure to maintain ideal body weight or to achieve a weight that might enhance their performance. Many athletes, particularly those participating in sports or activities that emphasize leanness (such as gymnastics, distance running, diving, figure skating, and classical ballet), have subclinical eating disorders that could undermine their nutritional status and energy levels. However, there is often little awareness or recognition of their disordered eating.[36] Athletes competing in weight-class sports such as rowing or boxing are also under pressure to lose weight to "make class."

### Table 6-3 Major Risk Factors for Eating Disorders

**Biological**
Dieting
Obesity/overweight/pubertal weight gain

**Psychological**
Body image/dissatisfaction/distortions
Low self-esteem
Obsessive-compulsive symptoms
Childhood sexual abuse

**Family**
Parental attitudes and behaviours
Parental comments regarding appearance
Eating-disordered mothers
Misinformation about ideal weight

**Sociocultural**
Peer pressure regarding weight/eating
Media: TV, magazines
Distorted images: toys
Elite athletes as an at-risk group

Source: White, J. (2000, April). The prevention of eating disorders: A review of the research on risk factors with implications for practice. *Journal of Child and Adolescent Psychiatric Nursing, 13*(2). Reprinted with permission of Blackwell Publishers.

If someone you know has an eating disorder, let him or her know you're concerned and that you care. Don't criticize or make fun of eating habits. Encourage discussion about other problems and feelings and suggest that he or she see a counsellor or someone at the mental health centre, the family doctor, or another trusted adult. Offer to go along if you think that will make a difference. See Table 6-4 for the physiological and psychological repercussions of eating disorders.

## Anorexia Nervosa

Although *anorexia* means "loss of appetite," most individuals with **anorexia nervosa** are, in fact, hungry all the time. For them, food is an enemy—a threat to their sense of self, identity, and autonomy. In the distorted mirror of their mind's eye, they see themselves as fat or flabby even at a normal or below-normal body weight. Some simply feel fat; others think that they are thin in some places and too fat in others, such as the abdomen, buttocks, or thighs.

The incidence of anorexia nervosa has increased in the last three decades in most developed countries. An estimated 0.5 to one percent of young women in their late teens and early 20s develop anorexia.[39] Not everyone who has a low weight is anorexic, but there is a risk of anorexia nervosa when anyone is 15 percent below their ideal weight or under 18.5 BMI.

## The X & Y Files

# Men, Women, and Weight

Women have long been bombarded by the media with idealized images of female bodies that bear little resemblance to the way most women look. Increasingly, more advertisements and men's magazines are featuring idealized male bodies. Sleek, strong, and sculpted, they too do not resemble the bodies most men inhabit. The gap between reality and ideal is getting bigger for both genders.

Women are more prone to unhealthy eating and eating disorders than men, but the incidence among men is increasing. Anorexia nervosa and bulimia predominantly affect young women. A Canada-wide study found that 5 percent of men ages 15 and over and 8 percent of women showed symptoms of an eating disorder.[37] Men and women with these problems share many psychological similarities and experience similar symptoms. However, men are more likely to have other psychiatric disorders and are less likely to seek professional treatment. Some feel that eating disorders fall under the category of "women's diseases." Others may not recognize the symptoms because eating disorders have long been assumed to plague only women.

Men are more likely to be affected by binge-eating disorder than by other eating disorders. In many cases, BED starts during adolescence or young adulthood.

We also know that hospitalizations for eating disorders across Canada have increased. In 2006, 10.7 per 100 000 women and 0.7 per 100 000 men were treated for an eating disorder, with British Columbia having the highest hopsitalization for women at 15.9 per 100 000.[38]

---

### ▼ Table 6-4 Physiological and Psychological Repercussions from Eating Disorders

**Sufferers may not have all symptoms**
**Physiological Repercussions**
Excessive facial or body hair because of inadequate protein in diet
Abnormal weight loss
Sensitivity to cold
Absent or irregular menstruation
Hair loss
Intestinal ulcers
Dehydration
Ruptured stomach
Serious heart, kidney, and liver damage
Tooth and gum erosion
Tears of the esophagus
Shortness of breath
Chest pain
Stunted bone growth
Toxicity to heart with use of laxatives, diuretics, or emetics
Reduced bone strength

**Psychological Repercussions**
Depression
Low self-esteem
Shame and guilt
Impaired family and social relationships
Mood swings
Perfectionism
"All or nothing" thinking
Listlessness
Difficulty concentrating

Source: National Association of Anorexia Nervosa and Associated Disorders www.anad.org.

▲ Anorexia nervosa and bulimia nervosa are complex disorders. Treatment usually requires medical, nutritional, and behavioural therapies.

© iStockphoto.com/Aldo Murillo

In the *restricting* type of anorexia, individuals lose weight by avoiding any fatty foods and by dieting and fasting. They may eat only a couple hundred calories per day or just drink water. Many of them start fasting and exercising as well. Others start smoking as a way of controlling their weight; it is difficult when you are starving not to eat. Some anorexics, although eating very little, feel that even a cookie or a normal meal is too much food. When they eat something they feel they should not have, they may purge, similar to bulimics.

Obsessed with an intense fear of fatness, anorexics may weigh themselves several times a day, measure various parts of their body, check mirrors to see if they look fat, and try on different items of clothing to see if they feel tight.[40]

## Bulimia Nervosa

Individuals with **bulimia nervosa** go on repeated eating binges and rapidly consume large amounts of food. Those with *purging* bulimia induce vomiting or take large doses of laxatives to relieve guilt and control their weight. In *nonpurging* bulimia, individuals use other means, such as fasting or excessive exercise, to compensate for binges.

An estimated 1 to 3 percent of women develop bulimia. Some experiment with bingeing and purging for a few months and then stop when they change their social or living situation. Others develop longer-term bulimia. Among males, this disorder is about one-tenth as common. The average age for developing bulimia is 18.[41]

## Binge Eating Disorder

**Binge eating disorder (BED)**—the rapid consumption of an abnormally large amount of food in a relatively short time— often occurs in compulsive eaters. Individuals who binge eat may feel a lack of control over eating and binge at least twice a week for at least a six-month period.[42] During most of these episodes they often eat alone because they are embarrassed by how much they eat and by their eating habits.

As their weight climbs, they become depressed, anxious, or troubled by other psychological symptoms to a much greater extent than others of comparable weight. Treatment includes education, behavioural approaches, cognitive therapy, and psychotherapy.[43]

## Being Overweight or Obese

Health Canada has developed guidelines that have changed the definition of what it means to be overweight or obese by focusing on body composition. The guidelines shift

## Strategies for Prevention

### Do You Have an Eating Disorder?

Physicians have developed a simple screening test for eating disorders, consisting of the following questions:

▲ Do you make yourself sick because you feel uncomfortably full?

▲ Do you worry you have lost control over how much you eat?

▲ Do you believe yourself to be fat when others say you are too thin?

▲ Would you say that food dominates your life?

Score one point for every "yes." A score of two or more is a likely indication of anorexia nervosa or bulimia nervosa.

focus away from body weight—the numbers on the scale—to body mass index (BMI), waist circumference, waist-to-hip-ratio, and individual risk factors for diseases and conditions associated with obesity (as described earlier in this chapter).

The guidelines define **overweight** as a BMI of 25 to 29.9 and **obesity** as a BMI of 30 and above (see Table 6-1). As noted earlier, very muscular people may have a high BMI yet not be overweight or obese.

The risk for cardiovascular and other diseases rises significantly in individuals with BMIs above 25; the risk of premature death increases when BMI reaches 30 or above. As BMI levels rise, average blood pressure and total cholesterol levels increase, while high-density lipoprotein, the "good" form of cholesterol, decreases. Men in the highest obesity category have more than twice the risk of hypertension, high blood cholesterol, or both compared with men whose BMIs are in the healthy range. Women in the highest obesity category have four times the risk. Obesity affects all racial and ethnic groups.

## Distribution of Fat and Weight

The waist-to-hip ratio, which considers the distribution of weight and the location of excess fat, is important. Excess weight around the abdominal area, creating an apple-shaped silhouette, is associated with increased cardiovascular risk

## Human Potential

### Thea Maguire—A Message of Hope

Thea Maguire, a graduate in a recreation and health education program, is now living in Dubai, United Arab Emirates, with her fiancé. She is excited about her current career in real estate and hopeful about what the future holds for her. However, the story she would like to share is one that began in high school.

Thea was very active in sports and dance. There was also musical theatre, the leadership club, and community youth groups. She is convinced that the pressure to "do everything" came from within. "My achievements and success began to form my identity."

One year she also grew nine inches. She comes from a family that is genetically tall and thin; however, she did not think of family genes when she heard comments such as "Do you have a hollow leg?" and "You are a human coat hanger!" said in joking ways by people of all ages. As Thea says, when you grow that fast no amount of healthy eating is going to prevent you from being "skinny." Then there were the mixed messages. While attending a professional ballet school, she was told she had the perfect body type to be a ballerina but was asked to withdraw for growing too tall as there was no partner available for someone her height. That is when she began drinking coca-cola to stunt her growth.

Quitting dancing, entering into an outdoor education school, and physically maturing during her grade 11 and 12 years resulted in major changes in her outward body appearance. With the changes came comments such as "You are finally filling out" and "You look so different—not a skinny Thea anymore." "It was a loss of identity. It had a huge impact on me. If I wasn't skinny Thea, then who was I?"

She remembers the day when she read about a diet in a magazine—a diet that would soon go wrong. Thea is convinced that the media played a role in her eating disorder. The models were people she looked up to. She began restricting food and overexercising. New comments started right away—"You're so thin again," "Skinny Thea is back."

Thea's parents were concerned and sent her to a nutritionist. She went to "get them off my back." She

Thea Maguire, a young woman who faced the despair of eating disorders now encourages others with a message of hope.

was thin but managed to convince them she was recovering. She also graduated the top of her class. After graduation she took a summer job away from home. She clung to her eating disorder losing thirteen more kilograms (30 lbs). At her lowest weight, she was 45 kilograms (100 lbs), still 183 centimetres (6 ft) tall. She lost control of her emotions and began crying all of the time. "Lying was my survival. Much of the deceit is meant for you. You don't even realize that you are lying. Anorexia became my life, all consuming. I did not care about anything except how much I ate and how much I exercised."

It was a visit from her brother—his shock at seeing her, his care and compassion, that helped Thea realize, for the first time, that something was very wrong. She returned home and started on the road of recovery. Initially, the recovery began for her family. Then it shifted to her. Thea says that "ultimately the recovery has to be for yourself." It was a two steps forward, one step back process. She feels that for some individuals, this is the way it will be, no matter what interventions are used. "You must reprogram your brain to think outside the disorder's reality. It can be a very long and painful process."

During her recovery, there was still much deceit. She had to learn to separate herself from the disorder. She credits an amazing team of professionals—a pediatrician, nutritionist, psychiatrist, family, and friends, for helping her in her recovery process. "You just can't expect help from one person, and you can't expect all the healing to come from yourself." She is in her seventh year of recovery now, and her life is completely different. Dealing with an eating disorder has changed her life. She discovered that she has strength and power that can be used in positive ways. She has found her experience to be humbling and healing. She has developed a much greater understanding of herself and others. Recovering from anorexia nervosa required a huge leap of faith on Thea's part. It required letting go of a control mechanism that made her feel safe, whereas in reality it was killing her slowly.

Her advice for students: "Know that you are not alone. Do what you can to convince yourself that you can ask for help. This is about you, and you have the power to be sick or to get better." Her advice for parents and friends: "Know your role—you are not their doctor. Your job is to be honest, find professional help, and be there for support. Know that you will be met with great resistance. Find strength to do what you know needs to be done." Her advice for teachers: "Be brave. Be honest. Be interested in your students. You might save a life."

Thea now speaks to student and parent groups about eating disorders. Her presentations have already made a difference. She still struggles at times, but the good times far outweigh the bad. She has a newfound trust in herself and her own strength and no longer relies on the opinions of others for validation.

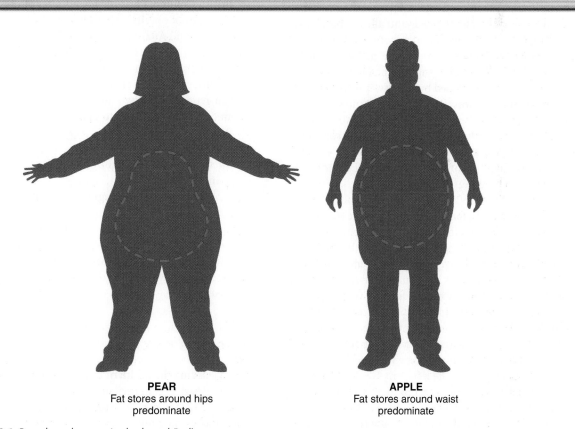

**PEAR**
Fat stores around hips
predominate

**APPLE**
Fat stores around waist
predominate

▲ **Figure 6-1** Pear-shaped versus Apple-shaped Bodies

for both men and women (see Figure 6-1). A waist circumference higher than the recommended cut off point described on page 131 signifies an increased risk in those with BMIs over 25.

Many women accumulate excess weight in their hips and thighs, giving them a pear shape. This fat, stored primarily for special purposes such as pregnancy and nursing, is more difficult to lose.

When men and women diet, men lose more visceral fat located around the abdominal area. This weight loss produces more cardiovascular benefits for men, including a decrease in triglycerides (fats circulating in the blood) and an increase in the "good" form of cholesterol, high-density lipoprotein (HDL).[44]

## ???? What Causes Obesity?

Are some people fated to be fat? Scientists have identified a gene for a protein that signals the brain to halt food intake or to step up metabolic rate to make use of extra calories. If this gene is defective or malfunctions, it could contribute to weight problems. The discovery of a genetic predisposition to excess weight could explain, at least in part, why children with obese parents tend to be obese themselves, especially if both parents are obese.[45]

A protein named *leptin* also may play a role. When laboratory mice are injected with high doses of leptin, they initially decrease their food intake, increase their metabolic rate, and become much thinner. Eventually, the body adapts to the high levels of leptin and becomes resistant to its effects. However, human studies have had contradictory results.[46] Some researchers suggest that increased leptin does not cause, but is caused by, obesity. A hormone called *ghrelin,* secreted primarily from the stomach, is also believed to play a role in the long-term regulation of body weight. The concentration of ghrelin in a person's blood rises rapidly before a meal and falls once food is eaten.[47]

Scientists now realize that obesity is a complex disorder with multiple causes, including:

✔ **Developmental factors.** Some obese people have a high number of fat cells, others have large fat cells, and the most severely obese have both a high number and large fat cells. Whereas the size of fat cells can increase at any time in life, the number is set during childhood, possibly the result of genetics or overfeeding at a young age.

✔ **Social determinants.** In affluent countries, people in lower socioeconomic classes tend to be more obese. For reasons unknown, those in the upper classes, who can afford as much food as they want, tend to be leaner. Education may be a factor.

✔ **Physical activity.** Obesity tends to go with a sedentary lifestyle. In countries where many people tend to work at physically demanding jobs, obesity is rare.

✔ **Emotional influences.** Emotions can play a role in weight problems. Some people cope with stressful situations by overeating, bingeing, or purging.

✔ **Lifestyle.** People who watch more than three hours of TV a day are twice as likely to be obese as those who watch less than an hour. Even those who log between one and two hours are fatter than those who watch just one.

## Canadian Overweight and Obesity Trends

Being overweight or obese can be a major health threat that increases the risk of many chronic diseases such as Type 2 diabetes and heart disease. This is a concern as the 2007 Canadian Community Health Survey reports that 4 million people (16 percent) aged 18 and over were in the obese category. A further 8 million (32 percent) were classified as overweight. The good news is that although the percentage of Canadians who were overweight or obese rose dramatically between 1985 and 1995, between 2005 and 2007 these rates did not change much.[48] Currently, we have a Canadian obesity map for the years 1985–2004 (see Figure 6-2). For males, the obesity rate is not only higher, but has also risen faster than females.

Overweight and obesity rates vary with demographic characteristics such as age, income, education, and geography.[49, 50]

✔ British Columbia had the lowest rates of obesity. The rates of obesity were highest in Saskatchewan, Alberta, and Atlantic Canada.

✔ 11 pecent of adults were obese in British Columbia; 18 percent in Alberta, and 22 percent in Newfoundland Labrador.

✔ Self-reported obesity rates were generally highest among people aged 45 to 64.

✔ Rates of both obesity and overweight were lowest among people aged 18 to 24.

✔ Men's rates of overweight/obesity increase with a rise in income.

✔ Women with a higher degree of education seem to be less likely to be overweight or obese. The pattern is less obvious for men—the overweight/obesity rate appears to be equally distributed among groups of different education, except those with some postsecondary education, who are less likely to be overweight or obese.

## Dangers of Obesity

While tracking the health of middle-aged men and women over the past decade, scientists have discovered that the incidence of diabetes, gallstones, hypertension, heart disease, and colon cancer has increased with the degree of overweight in both sexes. Those with BMIs of 35 or more were approximately 20 times more likely to develop diabetes. Women who were overweight but not obese, with BMIs between 25 and 29.9, were significantly more likely than leaner women to develop gallstones, high blood pressure, high cholesterol, and heart disease.[51] Overweight men were also more likely to suffer strokes.

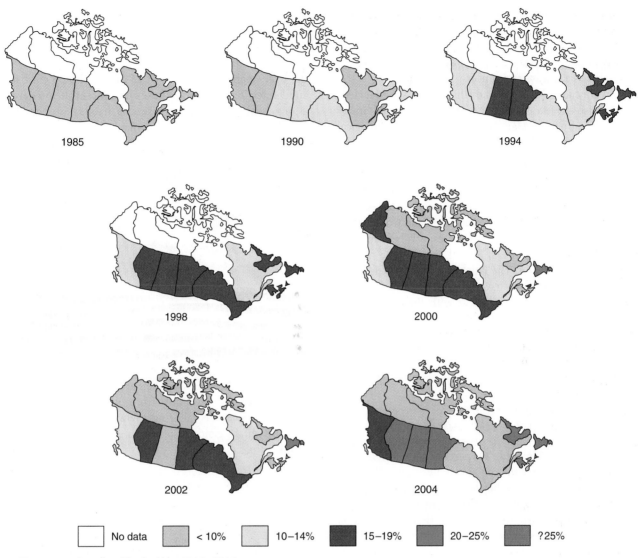

▲ **Figure 6-2** Canadian Obesity Map, 1985–2004

Note: Prevalence of obesity among Canadian adults in 1985, 1990, 1994, 1998, 2000, 2002, and 2004. Weighted prevalence was calculated from self-reported heights and weights from the 1985 and 1990 Health Promotion Surveys and the 1994 and 1998 national population Health Surveys. According to recent guidelines, adults are classified as being of normal weight with a body mass index (BMI) of 18.5–24.5 kg/m², overweight with a BMI of 25.0–29.9 kg/m², and obese with a BMI ≥ 30 kg/m².

Source: 1985—Katzmarzyk, P.T. (2002). *Can Med Assoc J 166*, 1039–40. Obesity Trends* Among Canadian Adults HPS, 1985 (*BMI ≥ 30, or ~ 30 lbs overweight for 5′4″ woman); 1990—Katzmarzyk, P.T. (2002). *Can Med Assoc J 166*, 1039–40; 1994—Katzmarzyk, P.T. (2002). *Can Med Assoc J 166*, 1039–40; 1998—Katzmarzyk, P.T. (2000). *Can Med Assoc J 166*, 1039–40; 2000—Statistics Canada. Health Indicators, May, 2002; 2002—Statistics Canada. CCHS 2002; 2004—Statistics Canada. CCHS 2004.

Overweight individuals who have surgery are more likely to develop complications. Even relatively small amounts of excess fat—as little as 2.3 kilograms (5 pounds)—can add to the dangers in those already at risk for hypertension and diabetes. According to a new study supported by the National Heart, Lung, and Blood Institute, being overweight, even if not obese, increases the risk of heart failure.[52] Obesity also causes alterations in various measures of immune function.[53]

Obesity now is considered a greater threat to a healthy heart than smoking. People who both smoke and are obese are at especially high risk of cardiovascular disease. Although some smokers have felt that they couldn't lose weight until they stopped smoking, researchers have found that weight loss among smokers is possible and beneficial, leading to a reduction in other risk factors, such as lower blood pressure and lower cholesterol.[54] Health educators also are targeting teenage dieters, who are more likely to begin smoking—often to help control their weight.[55]

Researchers estimate that the effects of obesity on health are the equivalent of 20 years of aging.[56] However, as discussed in Chapter 4, activity levels are critically important. Fat-and-fit people who exercise regularly are at less risk of dying prematurely than leaner sedentary men and women. Unfortunately, many heavy Canadians are inactive and in increased danger of dying of all causes, particularly heart disease and cancer.

In our calorie-conscious and thinness-obsessed society, obesity also affects quality of life, including sense of vitality and physical pain.[57] Many see it as a heavy psychological burden, a sign of failure, laziness, or inadequate willpower. In fact, the psychological problems once considered the cause of obesity may be its consequence.

Does obesity lead to a shorter life? The answer is far from clear—and intensely controversial. Studies have shown that overweight middle-aged men and women have a higher risk of dying from all causes, especially from heart disease and certain cancers, than those who are normal weight or underweight. The risk rises if they develop diabetes.[58] Among men who have smoked, the risk of dying is almost two times higher for those with the highest body weight than for those with the lowest body weight. Researchers have found a correlation between greater body mass index and higher death rates.[59]

### ???? How Can I Overcome a Weight Problem?

Each year an estimated 70 percent of women and 35 percent of men are dieting at any given time,[60] but no matter how much weight they lose, 95 percent gain it back within five years. Most dieters cut back on food not because they want to feel better, but because they want to look better. Those who drastically reduce their food intake and make weight loss a major part of their lives may be jeopardizing their physical and psychological well-being.

The best approach to a weight problem depends on how overweight a person is. For extreme obesity—a BMI higher than 40 (or higher than 35 for those with other conditions)—medical treatments such as surgery to reduce the volume of their stomachs and to tighten the passageway from the stomach to the intestine is performed. Others opt for a gastric bubble, a soft, polyurethane sac placed in the stomach to make the person feel full while following a low-calorie diet. It is not yet clear whether people who lose weight with this bubble will be able to keep it off. It is important to note that these medical procedures also have inherent risks to them.

For people who are moderately or mildly obese—individuals with a BMI of 30 to 39—doctors recommend a six-month trial of lifestyle therapy, including a supervised diet and exercise. The initial goal should be a 10 percent reduction in weight, an amount that reduces obesity-related risks. With success and if warranted, individuals can attempt to lose more weight. The keys to overcoming

obesity are addressing individual differences, altering unrealistic expectations, setting limits, and learning coping skills to provide self-nurturing without relying on food.[61]

Rather than going on a low-calorie diet, people who are overweight—with BMIs of 25 to 29—should cut back moderately on their food intake and concentrate on developing healthy eating and exercise habits. Support for healthy eating can be found in many communities across Canada. The Dietitians of Canada[62] offer information about finding nutrition professionals. You can access their database at www.dietitians.ca/find/index.html.

## Practical Guide to Weight Management

No diet—high-protein, low-fat, or high-carbohydrate—can produce permanent weight loss. Successful weight management requires a lifelong commitment to healthful lifestyle behaviours emphasizing sustainable and enjoyable eating practices and daily physical activity.[63] Studies have shown that successful dieters were highly motivated, monitored their food intake, increased their activity, set realistic goals, and received social support from others. Another key to long-term success is tailoring any weight-loss program to an individual's gender, lifestyle, and cultural, racial, and ethnic values.

## Customize Your Weight-Loss Plan

"If there's one thing we've learned in decades of research into weight management, it's that the one-diet-fits-all approach doesn't work," says clinical psychologist David Schlundt.[64] The key is recognizing the ways you tend to put on weight and developing strategies to overcome them. Here are some examples.

✔ Do you simply like food and consume lots of it? If so, keep a diary of everything you put in your mouth and tally up your daily total in calories and fat grams. Look for the source of most of the calories—probably high-fat foods such as whole milk, cookies, fried foods, potato chips, steaks—and cut down on how much and how often you eat them. Also watch portion sizes.

✔ Do you eat when you're bored, sad, frustrated, or worried? "People get in the habit of using food to soothe bad feelings or cope with boredom," says Schlundt. "Sometimes the real issue is a self-esteem or body-image problem." Dealing with these concerns is generally more helpful in the long run than dieting.

✔ Do you graze, nibbling on snacks rather than eating regular meals? If so, limit yourself to low-calorie, low-fat foods, such as carrots, celery, or grapes. Drink water regularly. Try to eat in the same place, preferably while seated. This helps you break the habit of putting food in your mouth without thinking.

You can also track your day's food and activity choices and compare them to the guidelines laid out by Health Canada with the Dietitians of Canada EATracker.[65] EATracker assesses your food choices and provides personalized feedback on your total intake of energy (calories) and essential nutrients and compares this to what is recommended for your age, sex, and activity level. It also determines your BMI and provides information to help you achieve and maintain a healthy weight.

You can also review your progress over time. Go to www.dietitians.ca and click on EATracker; then click on "Take the Assessment" and see how you measure up.

## Avoid Diet Traps

There are many diet plans that promise quick, easy results. These almost invariably turn into dietary dead ends. If the diet seems too good to be true, it probably is. Four common traps to avoid are diet foods, the yo-yo diet, the very low-calorie diet, and diet pills.

### Diet Foods

When choosing "diet foods," don't be fooled. Many companies advertise their food products as "lite" or "low calorie." What some people don't realize is that many foods that are low in fat are still high in sugar and calories. Refined carbohydrates, rapidly absorbed into the bloodstream, raise blood glucose levels. As they fall, appetite increases.

Nutritionists caution us to use artificial sweeteners and fake fats that appear in many products in moderation. One such product is Olestra, originally created in 1968 by Proctor and Gamble researchers as sucrose polyester, a synthetic product to help increase premature babies' intake of fat. When it was discovered that it didn't work very well, Olestra was then offered as a fat substitute. It tastes like fat, but the molecules are so large they cannot be digested, so they pass through the digestive track without leaving any calories behind.[66] This product seemed ideal for diet foods and has been used in snack foods such as chips, crackers, and tortilla chips in the United States. However, Health Canada has rejected Olestra as a food additive based on its own research and the fact that the U.S. Food and Drug Administration (FDA) received more than 18 000 adverse-reactions reports of gastrointestinal distress.[67] Products that contain Olestra must still carry a warning label.

Foods made with fat substitutes may have fewer grams of fat, but they don't necessarily have significantly fewer calories. Many people who eat more of the low- or no-fat foods actually end up with higher daily-calorie intake.

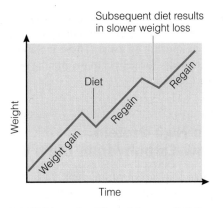

▲ **Figure 6-3** Weight-cycling Effect of Repeated Dieting
Each round of dieting is typically followed by a rebound leading to a greater weight gain.

### The Yo-Yo Syndrome

On-and-off-again dieting, especially by means of very low-calorie diets (under 800 calories a day), can be self-defeating and dangerous. Some studies have shown that weight cycling may make it more difficult to lose weight or keep it off (see Figure 6-3). Repeated cycles of rapid weight loss followed by weight gain may even change food preferences. Chronic crash dieters often come to prefer foods that combine sugar and fat.

You can avoid the yo-yo syndrome and overcome its negative effects by exercising. Some researchers have found that when overweight women who also exercised went off a very low-calorie diet, their metabolism did not stay at a low level but bounced back to the appropriate level for their new, lower body weight. The reason may be exercise's ability to preserve muscle tissue. The more muscle tissue you have, the higher your metabolic rate.

### Very Low-Calorie Diets

Any diet that promises to take pounds off fast can be dangerous. For reasons that scientists don't fully understand, rapid weight loss is linked with increased mortality. Most risky are very low-calorie diets that provide fewer than 800 calories a day. Whenever people cut back drastically on calories, they immediately lose several pounds because of a loss of fluid. As soon as they return to a more normal way of eating, they regain this weight.

On a very low-calorie diet, as much as 50 percent of the weight you lose may be muscle (so you'll actually look flabbier). Because your heart is a muscle, it may become so weak that it no longer can pump blood through your body. Your blood pressure may plummet, causing dizziness, lightheadedness, and fatigue. You may develop nausea and abdominal pain. You may lose hair. If you're a woman, your menstrual cycle may become irregular, or you may stop menstruating altogether. As you lose more water, you also lose essential vitamins, and your metabolism slows down. Even reaction time slows, and crash dieters may not be able to respond as quickly as usual. These metabolic changes may make it harder for people to maintain a reduced body weight after dieting.

### Do High-Protein, Low-Carbohydrate Diets Work?

High-protein, low-carbohydrate diets, such as the Atkins diet, have emerged as a diet fad of the twenty-first century. These diets appeal to many people because they can eat as much protein as they want, including steaks, eggs, and fatty foods they'd long been told to shun, as long as they strictly limit their carbohydrates.

The Dietitians of Canada, the American College of Sports Medicine, the American Dietetic Association, and other professional groups have challenged these diets. As they note, no scientific evidence proves that a diet providing more than the 10 to 15 percent protein recommended by federal guidelines enhances health or athletic performance. Scientific advisory warnings that high-protein diets are potentially dangerous because they may increase the risk of heart diseases, diabetes, stroke, kidney and liver disease, and cancer have been made recently.[68] Although it is possible to lose weight on a high-protein diet, the reason is the same as with other quick weight-loss diets: low calorie count.

### Diet Pills and Products

In their search for a quick fix to weight problems, millions of people have tried often-risky remedies. In the 1920s, some women swallowed patented weight-loss capsules that turned out to be tapeworm eggs. In the 1960s and 1970s, addictive amphetamines were common diet aids. In the 1990s, appetite suppressants known as fen-phen (*fen* referring to fenfluramine [Pondimin] or dexfenfluramine [Redux], appetite depressants, and *phen* referring to phentermine, a type of amphetamine) became popular. They were taken off the market after being linked to heart-valve problems.

More weight-loss drugs, including Meridia® (sibutramine) and Xenical® (orlistat), both intended only for people with a BMI of at least 30 or a BMI of 27 with additional risk factors and available only by prescription, are now being marketed over the Internet to anyone who fills out a computerized form reviewed by a company doctor. As a result, many people are taking this medication without medical supervision. Such misuse could cause health risks.

The search for the perfect diet drug continues—with plenty of economic incentives for drugmakers. Diet products are also big business. If used appropriately—as actual replacements rather than supplements to regular meals and snacks—they can be a useful strategy for weight loss. Yet people who use these products aren't necessarily sure to slim down. In fact, people who consume such products often gain weight because they think that they can afford to add high-calorie treats to their diet.

## Exercise: The Best Solution

You may think that exercise will make you want to eat more. Actually, it has the opposite effect. The combination of exercise and cutting back on calories may be the most effective way of taking weight off and keeping it off. According to a number of research studies, most successful weight losers both restrict how much they eat and increase their physical activity.

Exercise has other benefits: it increases energy expenditure, builds up muscle tissue, burns off fat stores, and stimulates the immune system. Exercise also may reprogram metabolism so that more calories are burned during and after a workout as mentioned in Chapter 4.

Moderate physical activity also can help control weight. Recent studies have found that everyday activities, such as walking, gardening, and heavy household chores, are as effective as a structured exercise program in maintaining or losing weight. Once you start an exercise program, keep it up. People who've started an exercise program during or after a weight-loss program are consistently more successful in keeping off most of the pounds they've shed.

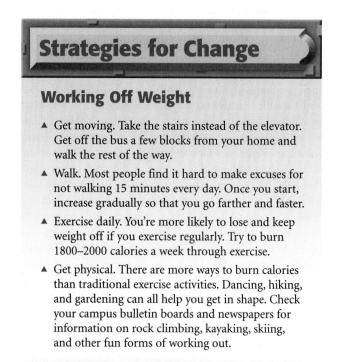

## Strategies for Change

### Working Off Weight

▲ Get moving. Take the stairs instead of the elevator. Get off the bus a few blocks from your home and walk the rest of the way.

▲ Walk. Most people find it hard to make excuses for not walking 15 minutes every day. Once you start, increase gradually so that you go farther and faster.

▲ Exercise daily. You're more likely to lose and keep weight off if you exercise regularly. Try to burn 1800–2000 calories a week through exercise.

▲ Get physical. There are more ways to burn calories than traditional exercise activities. Dancing, hiking, and gardening can all help you get in shape. Check your campus bulletin boards and newspapers for information on rock climbing, kayaking, skiing, and other fun forms of working out.

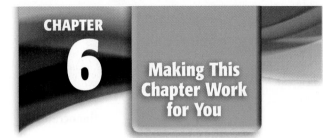

**CHAPTER 6**

**Making This Chapter Work for You**

1. The best way to determine whether you are at a healthy weight is to
   a. stand on a scale.
   b. calculate your body-fat percentage.
   c. check ideal weight tables.
   d. calculate your body mass index.

2. Body composition estimates can be obtained with which of the following methods?
   a. weighing yourself using a scale
   b. skin fold measurement
   c. height-weight charts
   d. basal metabolic rate measurement

3. According to the set-point theory,
   a. the physiological drive to consume food is stimulated by hormones.
   b. body fat is maintained at a predetermined level by an unconscious control system.
   c. the psychological desire to eat is determined by the size of the hypothalamus.
   d. fat cells cannot increase in number beyond a genetically determined point.

4. Which of the following statements about body weight is *not* true?
   a. BMI is a mathematical formula that correlates with body fat.
   b. Daily energy requirements depend on your activity level.
   c. Only women have body weight and shape concerns.
   d. If your BMI is high, you may be at increased risk of heart disease.

5. Which of the following eating behaviours may be a warning sign of a serious eating disorder?
   a. vegetarianism
   b. compulsive food washing
   c. binge eating
   d. weight gain during the first year of college or university

6. Individuals with anorexia nervosa
   a. believe they are overweight even if they are extremely thin.
   b. typically feel full all the time, which limits their food intake.
   c. usually look overweight even though their body mass index is normal.
   d. have a reduced risk for heart-related abnormalities.

7. Bulimia nervosa is
   a. characterized by excessive sleeping followed by periods of insomnia.
   b. found primarily in older women who are concerned with the aging process.
   c. associated with the use of laxatives or excessive exercise to control weight.
   d. does not have serious health consequences.

8. Which of the following statements is *not* true?
   a. Obesity is a greater threat to heart health than smoking.
   b. Men who accumulate fat around their waist are at increased risk for cardiovascular risk.
   c. Individuals who are obese are neither more nor less psychologically troubled than people of normal weight.
   d. Children with an obese parent are more likely to be thin because of their embarrassment about the parent's appearance.

9. Weight-management strategies that work include which of the following?
   a. Increase your activity level and eat less, aiming for a weekly weight loss of about 0.7 kilograms.
   b. Ask friends for recommendations for methods that helped them lose weight quickly.
   c. Practise good eating habits about 50 percent of the time so that you can balance your cravings with healthy food.
   d. Try a number of weight-loss diets to find the one that works best for you.

10. Which of the following statements is true?
    a. Very low-calorie diets increase metabolism, which helps burn calories more quickly.
    b. An individual eating low-calorie or fat-free foods can increase the serving sizes.
    c. High-protein, low-carbohydrate diets may increase the risk of heart disease.
    d. Yo-yo dieting works best for long-term weight loss.

Answers to these questions can be found on page 450.

## Self Responsibility

*Believe in yourself! Have faith in your abilities! Without a humble but reasonable confidence in your own powers, you cannot be successful or happy.*

**Norman Vincent Peale**

Changing eating habits is not an easy thing to do. Recognizing that change takes time is helpful. Knowing that people follow certain stages—such as Prochaska's stages of change—can help. What would it take to move you from contemplation to preparation? From preparation to action? From action to maintenance? Friends, family, books, websites, and

## Social Responsibility

*The wise man (woman) should consider that health is the greatest of human blessings. Let food be your medicine.*

**Hippocrates**

professional health experts can all be part of your change process. You have to start with the belief that you can make a change.

Making healthy food choices can also be considered part of social responsibility. The more people eat in a healthy way, the less we will be paying for health-care costs later.

## Critical Thinking

1. Do you think you have a weight problem? If so, what makes you think so? Is your perception based on your actual BMI measurement or on how you believe you look? If you found out that your BMI is within the ideal range, would that change your opinion about your body? Why or why not?

2. Different cultures have different standards for body weight and attractiveness. Within our society, men and women often seem to follow different

standards. What influences have shaped your personal feelings about desired weight?

3. Suppose one of your roommates appears to have symptoms of an eating disorder. You have told him or her of your concerns, but your roommate has denied having a problem and brushed off your fears. What can you do to help this individual? Should you contact his or her parent? Why or why not?

If your textbook package includes CengageNOW™, go to http://west.cengagenow.com/ilrn/ to link to CengageNOW™ for Health, your online study tool. First take the **Pre-test** for this chapter to get your personalized **Study Plan,** which will identify topics

you need to review and direct you to the appropriate resources. Then take the **Post-test** to determine what concepts you have mastered and what you still need work on.

## SITES & BYTES

**Canadian Guidelines for Body Weight Classification in Adults**

www.hc-sc.gc.ca/fn-an/nutrition/weights-poids/guide-ld-adult

This technical report describes a body-weight classification system for Canadian adults. Use this system to identify weight-related health risks in populations or for yourself.

**Health Canada, Food and Nutrition, Healthy Weights**

www.hc-sc.gc.ca/fn-an/nutrition/weights-poids/index-eng.php

Calculate your body mass index (BMI) using this interactive BMI Nomogram. Find out more about BMI by accessing the Question and Answer section on weight classification and weight and health.

**National Eating Disorders Association**

www.nedic.ca

The National Eating Disorder Information Centre (NEDIC) is a Toronto-based, non-profit organization that provides information and resources on eating disorders and weight preoccupation.

**A Report on Mental Illnesses in Canada— Chapter 6, Eating Disorders**

www.cmha.ca/bins/content_page.asp?cid=4-42-215

This comprehensive report includes a special chapter on eating disorders and includes information on the impact, causes, and treatment of eating disorders.

**St. Paul's Hospital Eating Disorders Program**

www.stpaulseatingdisorders.ca

Visit British Columbia's designated program for the treatment of adults with anorexia nervosa and bulimia nervosa. Information about research activities and links to other websites are also available.

Please note that links are subject to change. If you find a broken link, use a search engine such as www.google.ca and search for the website by typing in keywords.

**InfoTrac® College Edition Activity**

Jung, M.E., Bray, S.R., & Ginis, K.A.M. (2008). Behavior change and the freshman 15: Tracking physical activity and dietary patterns. *Journal of American College Health, 56*(5), 523–30.

1. Describe the changes in body-fat measures of the participants in this study over the 12-month period of data collection.

2. Compare the dietary behaviour and physical activity behaviour of the participants in this study over the 12-month period of data collection.

3. What type of physical activity and nutrition programs do you think would benefit first-year college and university students to help prevent weight gain?

You can find additional readings relating to eating patterns and problems with InfoTrac® College Edition, an online library of more than 5000 journals and publications. Follow the instructions for accessing InfoTrac® that were packaged with your textbook; then search for articles using a keyword search.

For additional links and resources, visit our text-specific website at www.health.nelson.com.

## Key Terms

The terms listed here are used within the chapter on the page indicated. Definitions of the terms are in the Glossary at the end of the book.

# References

1. Canadian Community Health Survey. (2007). *The Daily*, June 18, 2008. Available at www.statcan.gc.ca/daily-quotidien/080618/dq080618a-eng.htm.

2. Tremblay, M.S., & Willms, J.D. (2000). Secular trends in the body mass index of Canadian children. *Canadian Medical Association Journal, 163*, 1429–33.

3. Nielsen, S., & Popkin, B. (2003). Patterns and trends in food portion sizes, 1977–1998. *Journal of the American Medical Association, 289*, 450–53.

4. Heart and Stroke Foundation of Canada. (2003). The growing burden of heart disease and stroke in Canada. Available at ww2.heartandstroke.ca/images/English/Heart_Disease_EN.pdf.

5. Katzmarzyk, P.T. (2002). The Canadian obesity epidemic, 1985–1998. Commentary. *Canadian Medical Association Journal, 166*(8). Available at www.cmaj.ca/cgi/content/full/166/8/1039.

6. Kitsantas, A.M., Gilliagan, T.D., & Kamata, A. (2003). College women with eating disorders: Self-regulation, life satisfaction, and positive/negative effect. *Journal of Psychology, 137*, 381–96.

7. Magazine ideals wrong. (2001). *Journal of the American Medical Association, 286*, 409.

8. Tiggeman, M. (2001). The impact of adolescent girls' life concerns and leisure activities on body dissatisfaction, disordered eating, and self-esteem. *Journal of Genetic Psychology, 162*(2), 133.

9. Cohane, G., & Pope, H. (2001). Body image in boys: A review of the literature. *International Journal of Eating Disorders, 29*(4).

10. Berry, T., & Lauzon, L. (2004). A content analysis of fitness magazines. *Avante, 9*(1), 25–33.

11. Arriaza, C., & Mann, T. (2001). Ethnic differences in eating disorders among college students: The confounding role of body mass index. *Journal of American College Health, 49*(6), 309.

12. Office of Nutrition Policy and Promotion. (2003, September 19). Body mass index (BMI) nomogram. Health Products and Food Branch, Health Canada. Available at www.hc-sc.gc.ca/fn-an/nutrition/weights-poids/guide-ld-adult/bmi_chart_java-graph_imc_java-eng.php.

13. Office of Nutrition Policy and Promotion. (2003, March 13). Health risk classification according to waist circumference (WC). For use among adults age 18 and older. Health Products and Food Branch, Health Canada. Available at www.hc-sc.gc.ca/fn-an/nutrition/weights-poids/guide-ld-adult/weight_book-livres_des_poids-03-table2-eng.php.

14. Office of Nutrition Policy and Promotion. (2002, November 14). Are you an apple or a pear? What's your waist to hip ratio? Health Products and Food Branch, Health Canada. Available at www.hc-sc.gc.ca/fn-an/nutrition/weights-poids/vitalit/apple_pear-pomme_poire-eng.php.

15. Canadian Society for Exercise Physiology. (CSEP). 2006. Certified personal trainer's examiner's manual. Ottawa, Ontario.

16. Heyward, V. (1998). Practical body composition assessment for children, adults, and older adults. *International Journal of Sport Nutrition, 8*, 285–307.

17. You are what you eat—Unfortunately. For something that's so central to our survival, it seems few of us get our intake of food right. (2002). *Canada and the World Backgrounder, 67*(5), 10–16.

18. Weinsier, R.T., Nagy, T.R., Hunter, G.R., Darnell, B.E., Hensrud, D.D., & Weiss, H.L. (2000). Do adaptive changes in metabolic rate favour weight gain in weight-reduced individuals? An examination of the set-point theory. *American Journal of Clinical Nutrition, 72*, 1088–94.

19. Prentice, A.M., & Jebb, S.A. (1995). Obesity in Britian: Gluttony or sloth? *British Medical Journal, 311*, 437–39.

20. Bessessen, D.H., Bull, S., & Cornier, M.A. (2008). Trafficking of dietary fat and resistance to obesity. *Physiology and Behavior, 94*(5), 681–88.

21. Goris, A, H.C., & Westerterp, K.R. (2008). Physical activity, fat intake and body fat. *Physiology and Behavior, 94*(2), 164–68.

22. Taubes, G. (2001). Nutrition: The soft science of dietary fat. *Science, 291*(5513), 2536–45.

23. McCaffree, J. (2001). Eating disorders: All in the family? *Journal of the American Dietetic Association, 101*, 622.

24. Body image concerns. (2000). *Nutrition Research Newsletter, 9*(5).

25. Combating the infamous freshman 15! Tupperware poll shows more than half of those who attend college change eating habits. (2003, August 19). *PR Newswire*.

26. Jung, M.E., Bray, S.R., & Ginis, K.A. (2008). Behavior change and the freshman 15: Tracking physical activity and dietary patterns in first-year university women. (Report). *Journal of American College Health, 56*(5), 523–30.

27. Holmes, L. (2003, July 28). Freshmen weight gain may contribute to college eating problems. *Your Guide to Mental Health Resources Newsletter*.

28. Cohen, J.S. (2008, September 7). Friendly to planet, rude to diners: In one of the quirkiest attempts to go green, colleges are removing trays from cafeterias. *Chicago Tribune* (Chicago, IL).

29. O'Dea, J., & Abraham, S. (2002). Eating and exercise disorders in young college men. *Journal of American College Health, 50*(4), 273.

30. Cooley, E., & Toray, T. (2001). Disordered eating in college freshman women: A prospective study. *Journal of American College Health, 49*(5), 229.

31. Holben, D. (2000, October 18). International students gain fat and weight from American diet. Presentation, American Dietetic Association.

32. Eating disorder glossary. (2004). Toronto: The National Eating Disorder Information Centre. Available at www.nedic.ca.

33. Woodside, D.B., Garfinkel, P.E., Lin, E., Goering, P., Kaplan, A.S., Goldbloom, D.S., et al. (2001). Comparisons of men with full or partial eating disorders, men without eating disorders, and women with eating disorders in the community. *American Journal of Psychiatry, 158*, 570–74.

34. Prouty, A., et al. (2002). College women: Eating behaviours and help-seeking preferences. *Adolescence, 37*(146), 353.

35. Ibid.

36. Young female athletes at risk, say U.S. experts. (2000). *Lancet, 356*(9234).

37. Statistics Canada. (2002). Canadian community health survey, mental health and well-being, 2002. Release date: (2004, September 9). Available at www.statcan.ca/bsolc/english/bsolc?catno=82-617-X.

38. Here to Help. (2006). Eating disorders and body image. BC Partners for Mental Health and Addictions. Available at www.heretohelp.bc.ca/publications/factsheets/eating-disorders.

39. Sadovsky, R. (2002). A review of anorexia nervosa in primary care. *American Family Physician, 65*(3), 478.

40. Ibid.

41. Bulimia Anorexia Nervosa Association. (n.d.). Home. Available at www.bana.ca.

42. Nutrient Intake of Binge Eaters. (2001). *Nutrition Research Newsletter, 20*(3), 3.

43. Wilson, T., et al. (2002). Cognitive-behavioural therapy for bulimia nervosa: Time course and mechanisms of change. *Journal of Consulting and Clinical Psychology, 70*(2), 267.

44. Gender difference in weight reduction. (1999). *Nutrition Research Newsletter, 18*(2).

45. Magid, B. (1995). Is biology destiny after all? *Journal of Psychotherapy Practice & Research, 4*(1).
46. Heymsfield, S., et al. (1999). Recombinant leptin for weight loss in obese and lean adults. *Journal of the American Medical Association, 282*(16).
47. Cummings, D., et al. (2002). Plasma ghrelin levels after diet-induced weight loss or gastric bypass surgery. *New England Journal of Medicine, 346*(21), 1623.
48. Canadian Community Health Survey. (2007). *The Daily,* June 18, 2008. Available at www.statcan.gc.ca/daily-quotidien/080618/dq080618a-eng.htm.
49. Ibid.
50. Alberta Agriculture, Food, and Rural Development. (2004). Canadian consumer trends in obesity and food consumption: Economics and competitiveness. Available at www.agric.gov.ab/ca/app21/rtw/index.jsp.
51. Overweight, obesity threaten U.S. health gains. (2002). *FDA Consumer, 36*(2), 8.
52. National Heart, Lung, and Blood Institute. (n.d.). Home. Available at www.nhlbi.nih.gov.
53. Dangers are overlooked. (2001, August 12). *Medical Letter on the CDC & FDA.*
54. Wilson, K., et al. (2001). Impact on smoking status on weight loss and cardiovascular risk factors. *Journal of Epidemiology & Community Health, 55*(3), 213.
55. Austin, S.B., & Grotmaker, S. (2001). Dieting and smoking initiation in early adolescent girls and boys: A prospective study. *American Journal of Public Health, 91*(3), 446.
56. Sturm, R. et al. (2002). Datawatch: The effects of obesity, smoking and drinking on medical problems and costs. *Journal of Health Affairs, 21*(2).
57. Weight change affects quality of life. (2000). *JOPERD—The Journal of Physical Education, Recreation & Dance, 71*(2).
58. Keeping diabetes at bay. (2001). *Nutrition Action Healthletter, 28*(6), 11.
59. Weight loss can decrease mortality risk. (2000, November 26). *Medical Letter on the CDC & FDA.*
60. The National Eating Disorder Information Centre. (n.d.). Home. Available at www.nedic.ca.
61. Murphy, D. (2001). Fit or fad: A dieting decision. *Current Health 27*(7), 16.
62. Dietitians of Canada. (n.d.). Find a nutrition professional. Available at www.dietitians.ca/find/index.html.
63. Ibid.
64. Schlundt, David. Personal interview.
65. Dietitians of Canada. (n.d.). EATracker. Available at www.dietitians.ca/public/content/eat_well_live_well/english/eatracker.
66. Centre for Science in the Public Interest. (n.d.). A brief history of Olestra. Available at www.cspinet.org/olestra/history.html.
67. Centre for Science in the Public Interest. (2000, June 22). Health Canada rejects olestra as a food additive. Available at www.cspinet.org/canada/olestra.html.
68. Secrets of successful dieters. (2002). *Harvard Women's Health Watch, 9*(9).

# Communication and Sexuality

We are born social. From our first days of life, we reach out to others, struggle to express ourselves, and strive to forge connections. People make us smile, laugh, cry, hope, dream, and pray. The fabric of our personalities and lives becomes richer as others weave through it the threads of their experiences.

We are also innately sexual. Our biological maleness or femaleness is an integral part of who we are, how we see ourselves, and how we relate to others. Among all of our involvements with others, sexual intimacy, or physical closeness, can be the most rewarding. Although sexual expression and experience can provide intense joy, they also can involve great emotional turmoil.

You are ultimately responsible for your sexual health and behaviour. You make decisions that affect how you express your sexuality, how you respond sexually, and how you give and receive sexual pleasure. Yet most sexual activity involves another person. Therefore, your decisions about sex—more so than those you make about nutrition, drugs, or exercise—affect other people. Recognizing this fact is the key to responsible sexuality.

Sexual responsibility means learning about your relationships, your body, your partner's body, your sexual development and preferences, and the health risks associated with sexual activity. This chapter will help you explore sexual issues in today's world.

**After studying the material in this chapter, you will be able to:**

- **Describe** the role verbal and nonverbal communication plays in forming and maintaining relationships.
- **Define** friendship and **explain** how friendship grows.
- **Discuss** the behaviour and emotional expectations for friendship, dating, and intimate relationships.
- **Compare** and **contrast** romantic love and mature love.
- **Identify** the problems likely to affect long-term relationships, and **explain** how they can be prevented.
- **Describe** the male and female reproductive systems and the functions of the individual structures of each system.
- **Describe** conditions or issues unique to women's and men's sexual health.
- **Define** sexual orientation and **give examples** of sexual diversity.
- **List** the range of sexual behaviours practised by adults.

# Personal Communication

Getting to know someone is one of life's greatest challenges and pleasures. When you find another person intriguing—as a friend, a teacher, a colleague, or a possible partner—you want to find out more about him or her. Roommates may talk for endless hours. Friends may spend years getting to know each other. Partners in committed relationships may delight in learning new things about each other.

Communication stems from a desire to know and a decision to tell. Each of us chooses what information about ourselves we want to disclose and what we want to conceal or keep private. But in opening up to others, we increase our own self-knowledge and understanding.

## Talking and Listening

A great deal of daily communication focuses on facts: on who, what, where, when, and how. Information is easy to convey and comprehend. Emotions are not. Some people have great difficulty saying "I appreciate you" or "I care about you," even though they are genuinely appreciative and caring. Others find it hard to know what to say in response and how to accept such expressions of affection.

Some people feel relationships shouldn't require any effort, that there's no need to talk of responsibility between people who care about each other. Yet responsibility is implicit in our dealings with anyone or anything we value—and what can be more valuable than those with whom we share our lives? Friendships and other intimate relationships always demand an emotional investment, but the rewards they yield are great.

Sometimes people convey strong emotions with a kiss or a hug, a pat or a punch, but such actions aren't precise enough to communicate exact thoughts. Stalking out of a room and slamming the door may be clear signs of anger, but they don't explain what caused the anger or suggest what to do about it. As two people build a relationship, they must sharpen their communication skills so they can discuss all the issues they may confront. They must learn how to communicate anger as well as affection, sadness as well as joy—and they must listen as carefully as they speak.

Listening involves more than waiting for the other person to stop talking. Listening is an active process of trying to understand the other person's feelings and motivation. Effective listeners ask questions when they're not sure they understand the other person and prompt the other person to continue.

## Nonverbal Communication

More than 90 percent of communication may be nonverbal. The most common elements of nonverbal communication include the use of space or proximity, touch, eye contact, facial expressions, gestures, posture, physical appearance, and paraverbal language—sounds made by people that are not distinguishable by words, such as um, uh, or uh huh.[1]

Learning to interpret what people *don't* say can reveal more than what they *do* say. "Understanding nonverbal communication is probably the best tool there is for a good life of communicating, be it personally or professionally," says Marilyn Maple, a university educator. "It's one of the most practical skills you can develop. When you can consciously read what others are saying unconsciously, you can deal with issues before they become problems."[2]

Culture has a great deal of influence over body language. In some cultures, establishing eye contact is considered hostile or challenging; in others, it conveys friendliness. A person's sense of personal space—the distance from others at which he or she feels most comfortable—varies in different societies.

Nonverbal messages also reveal something important about the individual. "Nonverbal messages come from deep inside of you, from your own sense of self-esteem," says Maple. "To improve your body language, you have to start from the inside and work out. If you're comfortable

## Strategies for Change

### How to Enhance Communication

▲ Use "I" statements. Describe what's going on with you. Say "I worry about being liked" or "I get frustrated when I can't put my feelings into words." Avoid generalities such as "You never think about my feelings" or "Nobody understands me."

▲ Gently ask how the other person feels. If your friend or partner describes thoughts rather than feelings, ask for more adjectives. Was he or she sad, excited, angry, hurt?

▲ Become a good listener. When another person talks, don't interrupt, ask why, judge, or challenge. Nod your head. Use your body language and facial expression to show you're eager to hear more.

▲ Respect confidences. Treat a friend or partner's secrets with the discretion they deserve. Consider them a special gift entrusted to your care.

with yourself, it shows. People who have good self-esteem, who give themselves status and respect, who know who they are, have a relaxed way of talking and moving."

## Forming Relationships

As children we first learn how to relate in our families. Our relationships with parents and siblings change dramatically as we grow toward independence. In college or university, students can choose to spend their leisure time socializing or engaging in solitary activities. Relationships between friends also change as they move or develop different interests; between lovers, as they come to know more about each other; between spouses, as they pass through life together; and between parents and children, as youngsters develop and mature. But throughout life, close relationships, tested and strengthened by time, allow us to explore the depths of our souls and the heights of our emotions.

### I, Myself, and Me

The way each of us perceives himself or herself affects all the ways we reach out and relate to others. If we feel unworthy of love, others may share that opinion. Self-esteem provides a positive foundation for our relationships with others. Self-esteem doesn't mean vanity or preoccupation with our own needs; rather, it is a genuine concern and respect for ourselves so that we remain true to our own feelings and beliefs. We can't know or love or accept others until we know and love and accept ourselves, however imperfect we may be.

If we're lacking in self-esteem, our relationships may suffer. According to research on college students, individuals with negative views of themselves seek out partners (friends, roommates, dates) who are critical and rejecting—and who confirm their low opinion of their own worth.[3]

### Friendship

Friendship has been described as "the most holy bond of society." Every culture has prized the ties of respect, tolerance, and loyalty that friendship builds and nurtures. Friends can be a basic source of happiness, a connection to a larger world, a source of solace in times of trouble. Although we have different friends throughout life, often the friendships of adolescence and young adulthood are the closest we ever form. They ease the normal break from parents and the transition from childhood to independence.

Both teenage boys and girls see their same-sex friendships as important. However, girls rate the quality of their friendships more positively, express more positive emotions toward friends, share power more equally, and show less jealousy, particularly in friendships they describe as "satisfying" rather than "unsatisfying." From middle childhood into adulthood, girls and women continue to show more responsive and supportive behaviour toward their female friends, disclose more, and disagree less than male friends.[4]

In the past, many people believed that men and women couldn't become close friends without getting romantically involved. But as the genders have worked together and come to share more interests, this belief has changed. Yet, unique obstacles arise in male-female friendships, such as distinguishing between friendship and romantic attraction and dealing with sexual tension. However, men and women who overcome such barriers and become friends benefit from their relationship—but in different ways.

For men, a friendship with a woman offers support and nurturance. What they report liking most is talking and relating to women, something they don't do with their male buddies. Women view their friendships with men as more light-hearted and casual, with more joking and less fear of hurt feelings. They especially like gaining insight into what men really think.[5]

Friendship transcends all boundaries of distance and differences and enhances feelings of warmth, trust, love, and affection between two people. It is a common denominator of human existence that cuts across major social categories—in every country, culture, and language, human beings make friends. Friendship is both a universal and a deeply satisfying experience.

"Wishing to be friends," Aristotle wrote, "is quick work, but friendship is a slowly opening fruit." The qualities that make a good friend include honesty, acceptance, dependability, empathy, and loyalty. To sustain a close friendship, both people must be able to see the other's perspective, anticipate each other's needs, and take each other's viewpoint into account.[6] More than anything else, good friends are there when we need them. They see us at our worst but never lose sight of our best. They share our laughter and tears, our triumphs and tragedies.

### Dating

A date is any occasion during which two people share their time. It can be dancing at a club, a bicycle ride, a dinner for two, or a walk in the park. Friends and lovers go on dates; so do complete strangers. Some men date other men; some women date other women; and some people date both men and women. We don't expect to love, or even like, everyone we date.

While in school, you may go out with people you meet in class or on campus. Some students form close relationships; others connect only for a one-time sexual encounter that might involve anything from kissing to intercourse. With more people remaining single longer, the search for a date has become more complex. While bars and clubs are still popular places for college and university students to meet, cafés, health clubs, and bookstores have become acceptable as places to meet new people, too. Personal ads and cyberspace are alternative ways to meet potential dates.

Dating can do more than help you meet people. Dating helps you learn how to make conversation, helps you get to know more about others, and provides you with an opportunity to share feelings, opinions, and interests. In adolescence and young adulthood, dating also provides an opportunity for exploring sexual identity. Some people date for months and never share more than a kiss. Others have sex before they fall in love or even "like."

Separating your emotional feelings about someone you're dating from your sexual desire is often difficult. The first step to making responsible sexual decisions is respecting your sexual values and those of your partner. If you care about the other person—not just his or her body—and the relationship you're creating, sex will be an important, but not the all-important, factor.

Dating has potential dangers. As discussed in Chapter 14, many young women are physically and/or sexually abused by a dating partner.[7] Authors of a study where 3642 female students from six universities across Ontario were surveyed found that 24 percent of female students reported being physically assaulted and 15 percent reported being sexually assaulted during the previous year.[8] The assaults were associated with year of study, marital status, alcohol consumption, illicit drug use, prescription drug use, unhealthy eating and stress behaviours, and less time spent on academics.

Most longitudinal studies on dating relationships have shown that love has been found to increase for individuals who advance to a deeper, more long-lasting commitment. A four-year study of romantic couples, all dating as the study began, found that those who remained together perceived that their love, satisfaction, and commitment had grown.[9]

▲ Romantic attraction is characterized by a high level of emotional arousal, reciprocal liking, and mutual sexual desire.

## What Causes Romantic Attraction?

What draws two people to each other and keeps them together: chemistry or fate, survival instincts, or sexual longings? "Probably it's a host of different things," reports sociologist Edward Laumann, coauthor of a landmark survey of 3432 men and women conducted by the National Opinion Research Center.[10] "But what's remarkable is that most of us end up with partners much like ourselves—in age, race, ethnicity, socioeconomic class, education."

Why? "You've got to get close for sexual chemistry to occur," says Laumann. "Sparks may fly when you see someone across a crowded room, but you only see a pre-selected group of people—people enough like you to be in the same room in the first place. This makes sense because initiating a sexual relationship is very uncertain. We all have such trepidations about ourselves not being desirable. We try to lower the risk of rejection by looking for people more or less like us."

Scientists have tried to analyze the combination of factors that attracts two people to each other. In several studies, predictors ranked as the most important reasons for attraction: warmth and kindness, desirable personality, something specific about the person, and reciprocal liking.[11]

In his cross-cultural research, psychologist David Buss, author of *The Evolution of Desire,* found that men in 37 sample groups drawn from Africa, Asia, Europe, North and South America, Australia, and New Zealand rated youth and attractiveness as more important in a possible mate than did women. Women placed greater value on

© iStockphoto.com/Martin Purmensky

potential mates who were somewhat older, had good financial prospects, and were dependable and hardworking.[12]

The reason for this gender difference could be evolutionary. Throughout time, men have sought fertile females of "high reproductive value." Two outward signs of female fertility are youth and a more subtle factor: waist-to-hip ratio. When researchers analyzed the physical dimensions of the women considered most attractive by men, those with the slimmest waists and roundest hips were consistently rated as most desirable. Women have had to look for mates who could provide greater security for their offspring. For them, a man's power, wealth, and status—which require more time to assess—mattered more than appearance (see The X & Y Files: "Men, Women, and Marital Preferences").

## Intimate Relationships

The term **intimacy**—the open, trusting sharing of close, confidential thoughts and feelings—comes from the Latin word for *within*. Intimacy doesn't happen at first sight or in a day or a week or a number of weeks. Intimacy requires time and nurturing; it is a process of revealing rather than hiding, of wanting to know another and to be known by that other (see Figure 7-1 for the elements of love). Although intimacy doesn't require sex, an intimate relationship often includes a sexual relationship, heterosexual or homosexual.

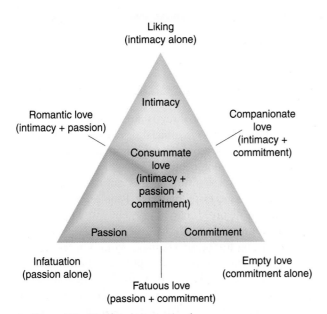

▲ **Figure 7-1** Sternberg's Love Triangle
The three components of love are intimacy, passion, and commitment. The various kinds of love are composed of different combinations of the three components.

All of our close relationships, whether they're with parents or friends, have a great deal in common. We feel we can count on these people in times of need. We feel they understand us and we understand them. We give and receive loving emotional support. We care about their happiness and welfare. However, when we choose one person above all others, there is something even deeper and richer—something we call *mature love*.

## Mature Love

Social scientists have distinguished between *passionate love* (characterized by intense feelings of elation, sexual desire, and ecstasy) and *companionate love* (characterized by friendly affection and deep attachment). Often relationships begin with passionate love and evolve into a more companionate love. Sometimes the opposite happens and two people who know each other well discover that their friendship has caught fire and the sparks have flamed an unexpected passion.

A romantic relationship shows promise if:

✔ You feel at ease with your new partner.
✔ You feel good about your new partner when you're together and when you're not.
✔ Your partner is open with you about his or her life—past, present, and future.
✔ You can say no to each other without feeling guilty.
✔ You feel cared for, appreciated, and accepted as you are.
✔ Your partner really listens to what you have to say.

Mature love is a complex combination of sexual excitement, tenderness, commitment, and—most of all—an overriding passion that sets it apart from all other love relationships in one's life. This passion isn't simply a matter of orgasm, but also entails a crossing of the psychological boundaries between oneself and one's lover. You feel as if you're becoming one with your partner while simultaneously retaining a sense of yourself.

## When Love Ends

Breaking up is indeed hard to do. Sometimes two people gradually grow apart, and both of them realize that they must go their separate ways. More often, one person falls out of love first. It hurts to be rejected; it also hurts to inflict pain on someone who once meant a great deal to you. In surveys, college and university students say it's more difficult to initiate a break-up than to be rejected. Those who decided to end a relationship reported greater feelings of guilt, uncertainty, discomfort, and awkwardness than those with whom they broke up. However, rejected students with

## Men, Women, and Marital Preferences

In a national survey of more than 13 000 adults, researchers asked how willing they would be to marry an individual based on education, income, age, and other factors. As shown in the following table, the women were significantly more willing than men to marry someone who was older, better educated, would earn more, and was not good-looking. The men were more willing than women to marry someone who had less education, was younger, wasn't likely to hold a steady job, and who would earn less. There were minor differences on items related to prior marriages, religion, and already having children.

| How Willing Would You Be to Marry Someone Who: | Women | Men |
| --- | --- | --- |
| had more education than you? | 5.82 | 5.22 |
| had less education than you? | 4.08 | 4.67 |
| was older than you by five or more years? | 5.29 | 4.15 |
| was younger than you by five or more years? | 2.80 | 4.54 |
| was not good-looking? | 4.42 | 3.41 |
| was not likely to hold a steady job? | 1.62 | 2.73 |
| would earn much less than you? | 3.76 | 4.60 |
| would earn much more than you? | 5.93 | 5.19 |
| had been married before? | 3.44 | 3.35 |
| was of a different religion? | 4.31 | 4.24 |
| already had children? | 3.11 | 2.84 |

Note: These responses are based on a seven-point scale, ranging from one ("not at all") to seven ("very willing").
Source: Crooks, Robert, and Karla Baur. *Our Sexuality,* 8th ed. Pacific Grove, CA: Wadsworth, 2002, p. 190.

high levels of jealousy are likely to feel a desire for vengeance that can lead to aggressive behaviour.[13]

Research suggests people do not end their relationships because of the disappearance of love. Rather, a sense of dissatisfaction or unhappiness develops, which may then cause love to stop growing. The fact that love does not dissipate completely may be one reason why break-ups are so painful. While the pain does ease over time, ending a relationship in a way that shows kindness and respect can help both parties. Your basic guideline should be to think of how you would like to be treated if someone were breaking up with you. Would it hurt more to find out from someone else? Would it be more painful if the person you cared for lied to you or deceived you, rather than admitted the truth?

Admitting that "I don't feel the way I once did about you; I don't want to continue our relationship" is hard, but it's also honest and direct.

## Is Living Together a Good Idea?

Although couples have always shared homes in informal relationships without any official ties, "living together," or **cohabitation,** has become more common in the last two decades. Often young people live together to see whether they're compatible—although this does not necessarily lead to a more successful marriage. People who have been married and divorced may be content just sharing their lives with one another.

According to Statistics Canada, common-law-couple families grew most quickly since 2001, reflecting the greater social acceptance of this family structure. The number of common-law-couple families grew 18.9 percent (1 376 900) between 2001 and 2006.[14] For many young adults, particularly children of divorced parents, living together seems like a good way to achieve some of the benefits of marriage as they get to know each other and find out if they're suited to each other. According to a Canadian survey[15] of never-married or previously married individuals, 48 percent said they would live common-law and 52 percent said they would not.

However, cohabitation can have its drawbacks. Cohabiters were more than twice as likely to have affairs as married people. As well, living together in a common-law relationship, as opposed to marriage, sharply increases the probability of the relationship ending in separation. Children of common-law unions are at a higher risk of experiencing family breakdown and are also more likely to see this happen at an early age.[16]

Researchers also found that these unions, in comparison to marriages, tend to have more episodes of domestic violence toward women and more physical and sexual abuse of children. Unmarried couples also report lower levels of happiness and well-being than married couples. Annual rates of depression among unmarried couples are more than three times those of married couples. The divorce rate among couples who eventually marry is also higher.[17]

The longer two people live together without marrying, the more likely they are to have problems. The reason, the researchers suggest, is that individuals develop a *low-commitment ethic* that is the opposite of what is required for a successful marriage.[18] Of course, this is not necessarily so for all couples who cohabitate.

Multiple living-together experiences also have a negative impact, both for an individual's own sense of well-being and for the likelihood of establishing a strong, lifelong partnership. Rather than teaching people to have better relationships, repeated cohabiting is a strong predictor of the failure of future relationships.

## Committed Relationships

Even though men and women today may have more sexual partners than in the past, most still yearn for an intense, supportive, exclusive relationship, based on mutual commitment and enduring over time. In our society, many such relationships take the form of heterosexual or homosexual marriages, but same-sex or heterosexual partners who never marry also sustain long-lasting, deeply committed relationships. These couples create homes, cope with problems, celebrate special occasions, and plan for the future.

## Marriage

In 2006, the census counted 6 105 900 married-couple families, up only 3.5 percent from 2001.[19] This represents 68.6 percent of all census families in 2006, down from 70.5 percent since 2001. With the passing of Bill C-38, the 2006 census included statistics on marriages between gay and lesbian couples and counted 15 000 persons living as same-sex married couples.[20] Yet, fewer people are getting married. In a recent report, researchers found that more couples are choosing to live together outside of marriage or are putting off vows until later in life.[21]

Not too long ago, marriage was often a business deal, a contract made by parents for economic or political reasons when the spouses-to-be were still very young. In some countries, arranged marriages are still culturally acceptable. Even in Canada, certain ethnic groups plan marriages for their children. In such arrangements, the marriage partners are likely to have similar values and expectations, but they start out as strangers who may not even know whether they like—or love—each other.

## Preparing for Marriage

With more than half of all marriages ending in divorce, there's little doubt that modern marriages aren't made in heaven. Are some couples doomed to divorce even before they swap "I do's"? Could counselling before a marriage increase its odds of success? According to recent research findings, the answer to both questions is yes.

## Finding Mr. or Ms. Right

Generally, men and women marry people from the geographical area they grew up in and from the same social background. However, in our culturally diverse society, interracial, cross-cultural, and same-sex marriages are becoming more common and accepted. Although there have been studies that show the odds of failure are greater for long-term relationships that blend race and culture, many couples say that it enriches their relationship, too.

Some of the traits that appeal to us in a date become less important when we select a mate; others become key ingredients in the emotional cement holding two people together. According to psychologist Robert Sternberg, the crucial ingredients for commitment are the following:

✔ Shared values.
✔ A willingness to change in response to each other.
✔ A willingness to tolerate flaws.
✔ A match in religious beliefs.
✔ The ability to communicate effectively.

The single best predictor of how satisfied one will be in a relationship, according to Sternberg, is not how one feels toward a lover, but the difference between how one would like the lover to feel and how the lover actually feels. Feeling that the partner you've chosen loves too little or too much is, as he puts it, "the best predictor of failure."[22]

▲ A relationship is as alive as the individuals who create it. With caring, it grows; with emotional nourishment, it blossoms; with commitment, it endures.

## Premarital Assessments

There are scientific ways of predicting marital happiness. Some premarital-assessment inventories identify strengths and weaknesses in many aspects of a relationship: realistic expectations, personality issues, communication, conflict resolution, financial management, leisure activities, sex, children, family and friends, egalitarian roles, and religious orientation. Couples who become aware of potential conflicts by means of such inventories can sometimes resolve them through discussion or professional counselling. In other cases, reflection and reconsideration about the relationship occurs.

Other common predictors of marital discord, unhappiness, and separation are:

✔ A high level of arousal during a discussion.
✔ Defensive behaviours such as making excuses and denying responsibility for disagreements.

By looking for such behaviours, researchers have been able to predict with better than 90 percent accuracy whether a couple will separate within the first few years of marriage.

## What Is the Current Divorce Rate?

About half of all marriages end in divorce, but the odds of a first marriage lasting are slightly better. In 2001, 7.7 percent of Canadians were divorced. Data from the 2006 Census shows that 8.1 percent of the population 15 years and over was divorced. It is interesting to note that in 1986, only 3.5 percent of individuals aged 15 and over were divorced.[23] Since 1986, the average age at divorce has increased by 4.1 years for men and by 4.2 years for women. In 2002, the average age at divorce for men was 43.1 and for women, 40.5 years.

Even after their hopes for happiness with one spouse end, many men and women still yearn to marry. Eighty percent of divorced men and women remarry. The remarriage rate after a second divorce is 90 percent; after a third divorce, it's even higher. However, more second, third, and fourth marriages fail than original unions.[24]

### When to Think Twice About Getting Married

Don't rush into marriage if:

▲ You or your partner is constantly asking the other such questions as "Are you sure you love me?"

▲ You spend most of your time together disagreeing and quarrelling.

▲ You're both still very young (under the age of 20).

▲ Your boyfriend or girlfriend has behaviours (such as non-stop talking), traits (such as bossiness), or problems (such as drinking too much) that really bother you and that you're hoping will change after you're married.

▲ Your partner wants you to stop seeing your friends, quit a job you enjoy, or change your life in some other way that diminishes your overall satisfaction.

## Family Ties

Canadian families are changing. More than 84 percent of Canadians form a "census" family—living with other people, generally as a spouse, partner, parent, or child. The 2006 Census enumerated 8 896 800 census families in Canada, which is a 6.3 percent increase since 2001. Lone-parent families also increased 7.8 percent from 2001 to 1 414 100 in 2006. Lone-father families rose more than twice as fast (+14.6 percent) compared to lone-mother families (+6.3 percent).

Data also showed that 42.7 percent of census families were couples who did not have children. This compares with 41.4 percent of families who were couples with children. Looking back 20 years ago, over half of census families were couples with children (52.0 percent) whereas only 35.3 percent were couples without children.[25]

If we look at age group differences, the 2006 Census found that only 17.9 percent of young adults between the ages of 20 to 24 were in couples in 2006, down from 19.6 percent in 2001 and 28.4 percent from 1986. For young adults from 25 to 29 years of age, 48.5 percent lived as part of a couple in 2006, compared to 51 percent in 2001 and 62.3 percent in 1986. Some researchers suggest that young people in their twenties may be delaying a couple union to pursue higher education or become more financially independent.[26]

Yet, census data also showed that more young people are living in common-law relationships. The increase of the proportion of common-law partners in their early twenties (20–24 years of age) rose from 9.3 percent to 12.6 percent between 1986 and 2006. For those between 25 and 29, the increase of common-law unions more than doubled from 10.2 percent to 22.6 percent between 1986 and 2006.[27]

Data from a report called *Couples Living Apart*[28] concluded that 1 in 12 Canadians live in separate homes from their partners. In 2001, 8 percent of the Canadian population aged 20 and over were part of such relationships. Fifty-six percent of these people were young adults in their 20s, 19 percent were in their 30s, 14 percent in their 40s, and 11 percent were age 50 and over.

You might expect that since it is more expensive to maintain two households that this type of living arrangement would be chosen by people who are well off financially. Not so, according to the research. Forty percent of those in this type of relationships had annual personal incomes below $20 000, and another 34 percent earned between $20 000 and $40 000. Couples lived apart for a number of reasons such as work availability and family responsibilities.

## Diversity within Families

The 2001 Census[29] was the first to provide data on same-sex partnerships. The number of same-sex common-law couples increased from 34 200 in 2001 to 37 885 in 2006. There were more male same-sex common-law couples than female. The 2006 Census counted 15 000 persons living as same-sex married couples.[30]

Legalization of gay and lesbian marriage in Canada is very recent, with Parliament passing Bill C-38 on June 28, 2005.[31] Its passing ended a long, controversial debate, and Canada has now joined Belgium, the Netherlands, and Spain as countries granting same-sex couples the same benefits as heterosexual couples. The controversy surrounding this issue has been ongoing for many years. In 1967, then-Justice Minister Pierre Trudeau proposed amendments be made to the Criminal Code that would relax the laws against homosexuality. They passed in 1969, and homosexuality was decriminalized. Quebec became the first province to include sexual orientation in its Human Rights Code, in 1977. In 1979, the Human Rights Commission in Canada recommended that sexual orientation be added to the Canadian Human Rights Act.

It would not be until 2000, with the passing of Bill C-23, that same-sex couples who had lived together for more than a year would gain the same benefits and obligations as common-law couples. Yet the definition of marriage would still include the "lawful union of one man and one woman to the exclusion of all others." Two same-sex couples were married in Ontario in 2001, but the government refused to register them. At the same time, the B.C. NDP government

issued legal proceedings against the federal government, seeking the right to marry same-sex couples.

In 2002, the Ontario Superior Court ruled that prohibiting gay couples from marrying was unconstitutional and violated the Charter of Rights and Freedoms. It gave Ontario two years to extend marriage rights to same-sex couples. In June 2003, Toronto began issuing marriage licences to same-sex couples after a ruling by the Court of Appeal for Ontario, whereby couples from anywhere could now marry—no residency limitations were required. In 2004, Quebec's appellate court ruled that same-sex marriage would be legal in the province. Michael Hendricks and René LeBoeuf became the first Quebec same-sex couple to marry (see the Human Potential story, in this chapter). For a more detailed history of gay and lesbian rights in Canada, you can access the Equal Marriage website at www.equalmarriage.ca.

Debate continues about this law. Whether you believe in same-sex marriage or not, Alex Munter with the group Canadians for Equal Marriage says we are living in a country that has put equality and human rights at the centre of its law.[32]

## Women's Sexual Health

Only recently has medical research devoted major scientific investigations to issues in women's health. Until about a decade ago, scientists routinely excluded women from experimental studies because of concerns about menstrual cycles and pregnancy. In clinical settings and with identical complaints, women are more likely than men to have their symptoms dismissed as psychological and not to be referred to a specialist.

## Female Sexual Anatomy

As illustrated in Figure 7-2A, the **mons pubis** is the rounded, fleshy area over the junction of the pubic bones. The folds of skin that form the outer lips of a woman's genital area are called the **labia majora.** They cover soft flaps of skin (inner lips) called the **labia minora.** The inner lips join at the top to form a hood over the **clitoris,** a small elongated erectile organ and the most sensitive spot in the entire female genital area. Below the clitoris is the **urethral opening,** the outer opening of the thin tube that carries urine from the bladder. Below that is a larger opening, the mouth of the **vagina,** the canal that leads to the primary internal organs of reproduction. The **perineum** is the area between the vagina and the anus (the opening to the rectum and large intestine).

At the back of the vagina is the **cervix,** the opening to the womb, or **uterus** (see Figure 7-2B). The uterine walls

## Michael Hendricks and René LeBoeuf—A Celebration of Same-Sex Marriage

Have you ever found yourself thinking that everything in your life seems to be in place, then something you learn about changes you and in a moment you know that you have to be courageous and fight for what you believe in? Michael Hendricks and René LeBoeuf are one such couple. They are famous for launching (in 1998) and winning (in 2004) an almost six-year legal battle for the right to marry like heterosexual couples. They are the first same-sex couple to marry in Quebec—their wedding date was April 1, 2004. However, they had not planned to become famous nor, as Michael says, "travel down the yellow brick road to full civil rights for homosexuals via civil marriage." A short version of their story is presented here. You can access Equal Marriage for Same-Sex Couples at www.equalmarriage.ca for a longer story.

Michael and René have lived together for 33 years. They have been married (at the time of the writing of this textbook) for four years and eight months. They met, like many other couples meet, at a party. This "highly unlikely encounter" changed their lives. After two years of seeing each other, they purchased a house, worked, helped each other through numerous career transitions, cooked dinner, and fed the dog. Their relationship worked because of the "complicity and shared activities." They were socialists, René active in the labour movement and Michael in the film business. You might say they were living happily ever after, with the regular ups and downs that long-term committed relationships experience.

Then came the AIDS epidemic. As their friends were dying, Michael and René began to notice that the health-care system discriminated against gays and lesbians. They weren't HIV-positive, but they felt that they had to do something to help others. They joined an association called ACT UP-Montreal, founded after the fifth World Aids Conference in Montreal, where people with AIDS were allowed to speak for themselves for the first time. They were both deeply impressed. They organized public

Michael Hendricks and René LeBoeuf, the first same-sex couple to legally marry in Quebec, April 1, 2004.

© Courtesy of René LeBoeuf and Michael Hendricks

hearings sponsored by the Quebec Human Rights Commission to address discrimination and violence against gays and lesbians.

Another event that changed their way of thinking was a presentation they heard by a law professor who suggested that gays and lesbians would never have social recognition unless there was a recognition of their conjugal rights as a "family."

"We latched on to that. We started to politely agitate for that, but it didn't work. The symbolic aspects of marriage are extremely important in society, so we decided to file our first suit, Hendricks vs. Quebec." Up until that time they had not considered marriage. They had never used the judicial courts before, but when they read the Canadian Charter of Rights and Freedoms, they knew there was space for them there.

It would take endless years of work, finding family lawyers who could talk about defending the right of marriage for everyone, remortgaging their house to pay for legal fees, and dealing with publicity, but they knew they "were going to stick with it."

But the real reason they filed their suit was that they didn't want anyone to have to go through what they had gone through during their lifetime. The behind-the-scenes story is one of two men who knew they were gay at a young age, but did not know where to turn for support or understanding. There was the suicide attempt by Michael, who woke up to find himself in a mental hospital. He was in law school, but at that time homosexuals could not be lawyers. René had to deal with prejudice and misunderstanding about who he was and coming out at a time when homosexuality was still a criminal offence.

On March 19, 2004, same-sex marriage became legal in Quebec through a ruling by the Quebec Court of Appeal in the case of Hendricks vs. Quebec. June 28, 2005 marked the day when Bill C-38 legalized gay and lesbian marriages in Canada. It is in part due to Michael and René and their desire to make the world a better place—not just for gays and lesbians, but for everyone—that

we have moved in our country toward a celebration of differences and a deeper level of tolerance toward others.

They borrowed their slogan from Ché Guevera—*Be realistic, demand the impossible.* Their advice is to "Live with yourself. Get ready. There are many years ahead, and if you are not true to yourself, then you will become the victim." Their hope is "that adolescents do not have to question whether or not there is a place for them. Happiness does not depend on sexual orientation." Thank you Michael and René—for being brave and sharing your story.

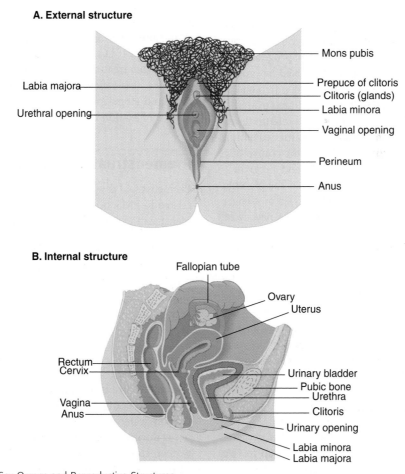

**A. External structure**

Mons pubis

Labia majora

Urethral opening

Prepuce of clitoris
Clitoris (glands)
Labia minora

Vaginal opening

Perineum

Anus

**B. Internal structure**

Fallopian tube

Ovary
Uterus

Rectum
Cervix

Vagina
Anus

Urinary bladder
Pubic bone
Urethra

Clitoris

Urinary opening

Labia minora
Labia majora

▲ **Figure 7-2** Female Sex Organs and Reproductive Structures

Source: Hespenheide Design

are lined by a layer of tissue called the **endometrium.** Two **ovaries**—about the size and shape of almonds, with one on the left of the uterus and one on the right—contain egg cells called **ova** (singular, **ovum**). Extending outward and back from the upper uterus are the **fallopian tubes,** the canals that transport ova from the ovaries to the uterus. When an egg is released from an ovary, the fingerlike ends of the adjacent fallopian tube catch the egg and direct it into the tube.

## What Is the Menstrual Cycle?

As shown in Figure 7-3, the hypothalamus monitors hormone levels in the blood and sends messages to the pituitary gland to release follicle-stimulating hormone (FSH) and luteinizing hormone (LH). In the ovaries, these hormones stimulate the growth of a few of the immature eggs stored in every woman's body. Usually, only one ovum matures completely during each monthly cycle. As it does, the ovaries increase production of the female sex hormone **estrogen,** which in turn triggers the release of a larger surge of LH.

At mid-cycle, the increased LH hormone levels trigger **ovulation,** the release of the ovum from the ovary. Estrogen levels drop, and the remaining cells of the follicle then enlarge, change character, and form the **corpus luteum,** or yellow body. In the second half of the menstrual cycle, the corpus luteum secretes estrogen and larger amounts of **progesterone.** The endometrium (uterine lining) is stimulated by progesterone to thicken and become more engorged with blood in preparation for nourishing an implanted, fertilized ovum.

If the ovum is not fertilized, the corpus luteum disintegrates. As the level of progesterone drops, **menstruation** occurs—the uterine lining is shed during the course of a menstrual period. If the egg is fertilized and pregnancy occurs, the cells that eventually develop into the placenta secrete *human chorionic gonadotropin* (HCG), a messenger hormone that signals the pituitary not to start a new cycle. The corpus luteum then steps up its production of progesterone. It is important to note that the visual representation of a woman's menstrual cycle in Figure 7-3 uses 28 days as the average duration. Many women have cycles that vary and can be as short as 21 days or as long as 32 days. Some women also ovulate more than once a month.

Many women experience physical or psychological changes, or both, during their monthly cycles. Usually the changes are minor, but more serious problems can occur.

### Premenstrual Syndrome

Women with **premenstrual syndrome (PMS)** experience bodily discomfort and emotional distress for up to two weeks, from ovulation until the onset of menstruation. Some women develop very severe symptoms. In some studies, as many as 40 to 45 percent of women have reported at least one PMS symptom.

Once dismissed as a psychological problem, PMS has been recognized as a very real physiological disorder that may be caused by a hormonal deficiency: abnormal levels of thyroid hormone, an imbalance of estrogen and progesterone, and changes in brain chemicals. Social and environmental factors, particularly stress, also play a part. The most common symptoms of PMS are mood changes, anxiety, irritability, difficulty concentrating, forgetfulness, impaired judgment, tearfulness, digestive symptoms (diarrhea, bloating, constipation), hot flashes, palpitations, dizziness, headache, fatigue, changes in appetite, cravings (usually for sweets or salt), water retention, breast tenderness, and insomnia.

Treatments for PMS depend on specific symptoms. Diuretics (drugs that speed up fluid elimination) can relieve water retention and bloating. Relaxation techniques have led to a 60 percent reduction in anxiety symptoms. Sleep deprivation, or the use of bright light to adjust a woman's circadian or daily rhythm, also has proven beneficial. Behavioural approaches, such as regular physical activity have helped. Charting cycles helps by letting women know when they're vulnerable.

Low doses of medications known as *selective serotonin-reuptake inhibitors* (SSRIs), such as fluoxetine (marketed as Prozac, Sarafem, and in generic forms), provide relief for symptoms such as tension, depression, irritability, and mood swings.[33] Calcium supplements also may be beneficial.[34] Other treatments with some reported success include vitamins; less caffeine, alcohol, salt, and sugar; acupuncture; and stress-management techniques such as meditation or relaxation training.[35]

### Premenstrual Dysphoric Disorder

**Premenstrual dysphoric disorder (PMDD),** which is not related to PMS, occurs in an estimated 3 to 5 percent of all menstruating women.[36] It is characterized by regular symptoms of depression (depressed mood, anxiety, mood swings, diminished interest or pleasure) during the last week of the menstrual cycle. Women with PMDD cannot function as usual at work, school, or home. They feel better a few days after menstruation begins. Medications used to treat PMS also are effective in relieving symptoms of PMDD.[37]

### Menstrual Cramps

**Dysmenorrhea** is the medical name for the discomforts—abdominal cramps and pain, back and leg pain, diarrhea, tension, water retention, fatigue, and depression—that can occur during menstruation. About half of all menstruating women suffer from dysmenorrhea. The cause seems to be an overproduction of bodily substances called *prostaglandins,* which typically rise during menstruation.

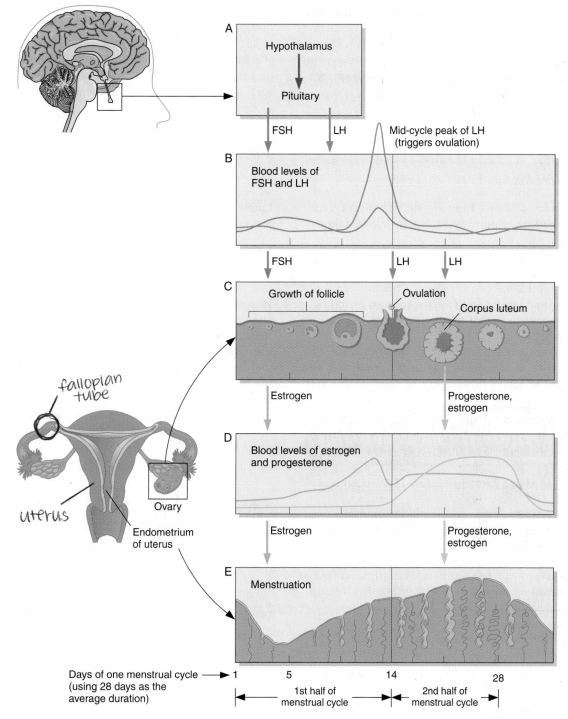

▲ **Figure 7-3** Menstrual Cycle

Levels of the hormones FSH and LH rise and then fall to stimulate the cycle. These changes affect the levels of the hormones estrogen and progesterone, which in turn react with LH and FSH. As a result of the increase in estrogen, the ovarian follicle matures and then ruptures, releasing ova (eggs) into the fallopian tubes. The progesterone helps prepare the lining of the uterus to receive a fertilized egg. If a fertilized egg is deposited into the uterus, pregnancy begins. But if the egg is not fertilized, progesterone production decreases, and the uterine lining is shed (menstruation). At this point, both estrogen and progesterone levels have dropped, so the pituitary responds by producing FSH, and the cycle begins again.

Source: Hespenheide Design

Women who produce excessive prostaglandins have more severe menstrual cramps. During a cramp, the uterine muscles may contract too strongly or frequently and temporarily deprive the uterus of oxygen, causing pain. Medications that inhibit prostaglandins can reduce menstrual pain, and exercise can also relieve cramps.

## Amenorrhea

Women may stop menstruating—a condition called **amenorrhea**—for a variety of reasons, including a hormonal disorder, drastic weight loss, or a change in the environment. Distance running and strenuous exercise also can lead to amenorrhea. The reason may be a drop in body fat from the normal range of 18 to 22 percent to a range of 9 to 12 percent. A woman is considered to have amenorrhea if her menstrual cycle is typically absent for three or more consecutive months. Prolonged amenorrhea can have serious health consequences, including a loss of bone density that may lead to stress fractures or osteoporosis.

In recent years, scientists have discovered that the menstrual cycle actually begins in the brain with the production of gonadotropin-releasing hormone (GnRH).

## Strategies for Prevention

### Preventing Premenstrual Problems

▲ Get plenty of exercise. Physically fit women usually have fewer problems both before and during their periods.

▲ Eat frequently and nutritiously. In the week before your period, your body doesn't regulate the levels of sugar, or glucose, in your blood as well as it usually does.

▲ Swear off salt. If you stop using salt at the table and while cooking, you may gain less weight premenstrually, feel less bloated, and suffer less from headaches and irritability.

▲ Cut back on caffeine. Coffee, colas, diet colas, chocolate, and tea can increase breast tenderness and other symptoms.

▲ Don't drink or smoke. Some women become so sensitive to alcohol's effects before their periods that a glass of wine hits with the impact of several stiff drinks. Nicotine worsens low blood-sugar problems.

▲ Watch out for sweets. Premenstrual cravings for sweets are common. Sugar may pick you up, but later you'll feel worse than before.

Each month a surge of GnRH sets into motion the sequence of steps that lead to ovulation, the potential for conception, and, if conception doesn't occur, menstruation. This understanding has led to the development of chemical mimics, or analogues, of GnRH—usually administered by nasal spray—that trigger ovulation in women who don't ovulate or menstruate normally.

## Toxic Shock Syndrome

This rare, potentially deadly bacterial infection primarily strikes menstruating women under the age of 30 who use tampons. Both *Staphylococcus aureus* and group A *Streptococcus pyogenes* can produce **toxic shock syndrome (TSS).** Symptoms include a high fever; a rash that leads to peeling of the skin on the fingers, toes, palms, and soles; dizziness; dangerously low blood pressure; and abnormalities in several organ systems (the digestive tract and the kidneys) and in the muscles and blood. Treatment usually consists of antibiotics and intense supportive care; intravenous administration of immunoglobulins that attack the toxins produced by these bacteria also may be beneficial.

To reduce the risk of TSS, menstruating women should use sanitary napkins instead of tampons. If tampons are used, they should be changed every four to eight hours and a switch to less-absorbent tampons should be made as the menstrual flow decreases.[38]

## Men's Sexual Health

Because the male reproductive system is simpler in many ways than the female, it's often ignored—especially by healthy young men. However, just like women, men should perform regular self-exams, including checking their penises, testes, and breasts as part of their routine.

## Male Sexual Anatomy

The visible parts of the male sexual anatomy are the **penis** and the **scrotum,** the pouch that contains the **testes** (see Figure 7-4). The testes manufacture **testosterone,** the hormone that stimulates the development of a male's secondary characteristics, and **sperm,** the male reproductive cells. Immature sperm are stored in the **epididymis,** a collection of coiled tubes adjacent to each testis.

The penis contains three hollow cylinders loosely covered with skin. The two major cylinders, the *corpora cavernosa,* extend side by side through the length of the penis. The third cylinder, the *corpus spongiosum,* surrounds the **urethra,** the channel for both seminal fluid and urine (see Figure 7-4).

## A. External structure

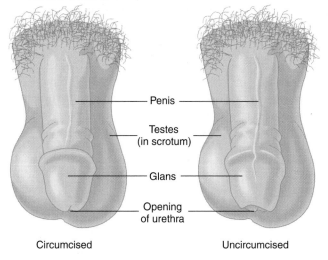

Penis

Testes
(in scrotum)

Glans

Opening
of urethra

Circumcised                Uncircumcised

## B. Internal structure

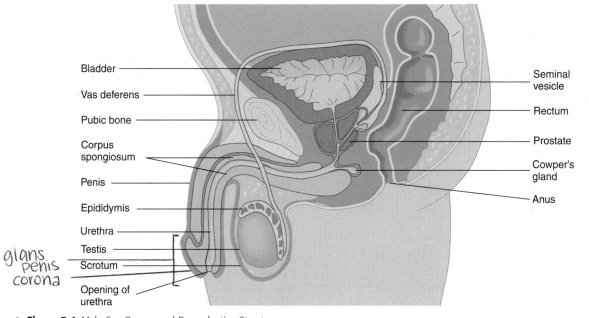

Bladder

Vas deferens

Pubic bone

Corpus
spongiosum

Penis

Epididymis

Urethra

*glans.
penis
corona*

Testis

Scrotum

Opening of
urethra

Seminal
vesicle

Rectum

Prostate

Cowper's
gland

Anus

▲ **Figure 7-4** Male Sex Organs and Reproductive Structures

Source: Hespenheide Design

When hanging down loosely, the average penis is about 9 centimetres long. During erection, its internal cylinders fill with so much blood that they become rigid, and the penis stretches to an average length of 15 centimetres. About 90 percent of all men have erect penises measuring between 12 and 18 centimetres in length. A woman's vagina naturally adjusts during intercourse to the size of her partner's penis.

Inside the body are several structures involved in the production of seminal fluid, or **semen,** the liquid in which sperm cells are carried out of the body during ejaculation. The **vas deferens** are two tubes that carry sperm from the epididymis into the urethra. The **seminal vesicles,** which make some of the seminal fluid, join with the vas deferens to form the **ejaculatory ducts.** The **prostate gland** produces some of the seminal fluid, which it secretes into the urethra during ejaculation. The **Cowper's glands** are two pea-sized structures on either side of the urethra (just below where it emerges from the prostate gland) and connected to it via tiny ducts. When a man is sexually aroused, the Cowper's glands often secrete a fluid that appears as a droplet at the tip of the penis. This fluid is not semen, although it occasionally contains sperm.

## ???? What Is Circumcision?

In its natural state, the tip of the penis is covered by a fold of skin called the *foreskin*. Global estimates in 2006 suggest that about 30 percent of males worldwide undergo **circumcision,** the surgical removal of the foreskin. In Canada in 1996–97, circumcision was performed as common procedure on about 20 percent of Canadian male neonates. By 2005, it was 9.2 percent.[39]

Reasons vary from religious traditions to preventative health measures. However, increasingly more parents are opting not to circumcise their sons.

Until the last half century, scientific evidence to support or repudiate routine circumcision was limited. A review of 40 years of data concluded that although there are potential medical benefits, the data are not strong enough to recommend routine neonatal circumcision.[40] However, other experts, challenging this view, argue that lack of circumcision increases the risk of sexually transmitted infections, including HIV and syphilis.[41]

## Sexual Behaviour

From birth to death, we are sexual beings. Our sexual identities, needs, likes, and dislikes emerge in adolescence and become clearer as we enter adulthood, but we continue to change and evolve throughout our lives. In men, sexual interest is most intense at age 18; in women, it reaches a peak in the 30s. Although age brings changes in sexual responsiveness, we never outgrow our sexuality.

## ???? How Sexually Active Are College and University Students?

Most unmarried college and university students are sexually active. In a national survey of youth,[42] the majority of young people between the ages of 15 and 24 considered sexual health a "very big concern" for their age group. Thirty-seven percent of those 15 to 17 years old and 80 percent of those 18 to 24 reported having sexual intercourse. They also said they wanted more information on sexual health. Another study reported that young people turn to parents and guardians for sexual health education, while others reported friends and sex-education classes were the prime sources for "a lot" of sex-related information.[43]

Findings of a 20-year longitudinal study[44] that analyzed changes in sexual behaviour among students at a Canadian college showed that there were differences between males and females; there were changes in sexual behaviour; and there were trends in sexual safety.

Differences between Males and Females (2000):

✔ Males had significantly higher levels of sexual behaviour and significantly more permissive sexual attitudes than females.
✔ More males had engaged in sexual intercourse.
✔ Sexually experienced males had more partners in their lifetime (7.1 vs. 4.5) and in the current year of the study (1.8 vs. 1.4).
✔ Males were more likely to have sex with strangers (34 percent vs. 14 percent).

Changes in Sexual Behaviour (1980 to 2000):

✔ There were no gender differences in age; men and women had their first experience at 17 years of age.
✔ Throughout the two decades, there was a steady increase in the commitment level of students' premarital sexual relationships. The proportion of committed relationships rose and casual sex declined.

Trends in Sexual Safety (1990 to 2000):

✔ Students became more cautious about sex between 1990 and 2000. Among unmarried, sexually experienced students in 1990, more females than males were asking new partners about their pasts (80 percent vs. 13 percent). Ten years later, about half the males were also doing so, whereas 77 percent of females were asking about their partners' pasts.
✔ Reflecting the North American trend, there was an increase in condom use; sexually experienced students who usually or always used a condom rose from 30 percent in 1990 to 52 percent in 2000.

Students' sexual activity, particularly unsafe practices, often correlate with other risky behaviours. Researchers have found that students who have had multiple sexual partners are more likely to report binge drinking, drinking and driving, physical fighting, thinking about suicide, and marijuana use.[45]

A substantial proportion of college students—male and female—report that they engage in unwanted sexual activity. Sometimes this is the result of sexual coercion or alcohol use.[46] However, some students admit to feigning desire and consenting to an unwanted sexual activity for various reasons, including satisfying a partner's needs, promoting intimacy, and avoiding relationship tension.

College and university students do not always take precautions to reduce the risk of sexually transmitted infections (STIs). Often they believe that HIV and other infections simply couldn't happen to them, or they use misleading criteria in assessing risk. Men especially rely too much on a potential partner's physical attractiveness and give less consideration to sexual history. Women tend to insist on safe-sex practices with a new partner, but as they become more seriously involved, they use protection less often—a potentially dangerous practice since knowing someone better doesn't make sex safer. Netting and Burnett[47] found that only 27 percent of the students at a Canadian college had ever asked their partner to be tested for any sexually transmitted infection. Condom use was universally low among monogamists, suggesting that they were still at risk due to the long incubation period of AIDS.

A study of 61 homosexual college men found considerable concern about HIV infection. More than a quarter of the men had not engaged in homosexual activity. Of the 72 percent who had, some made dramatic changes in their sexual behaviour because of their fear of HIV: 7 percent became celibate, and 14 percent no longer engaged in anal intercourse. About half limited the number of people with whom they had sex and reported being more selective in choosing partners; 36 percent refused to have sex without a condom.

Some research has also been done to explore potential differences between cultures and their attitudes about sex. Asian-Canadian university students were significantly more conservative in attitudes toward sexual behaviour. Asian students were also more tolerant of rape myths and more accepting of sexual harassment, although they demonstrated a decrease in tolerance as their residency in Canada lengthened.[48]

## Sexual Diversity

Human beings are diverse in all ways—including sexual preferences and practices. Physiological, psychological, and social factors determine whether we are attracted to members of the same sex or the other sex. This attraction is our **sexual orientation.** Sigmund Freud argued that we all start off **bisexual,** or attracted to both sexes. But by the time we reach adulthood, most males prefer female sexual partners, and most females prefer male partners. **Heterosexual** is the term used for individuals whose primary orientation is toward members of the other sex. In virtually all cultures, some men and women are **homosexuals,** preferring partners of their own sex.

In Canadian society, we tend to view heterosexuality and homosexuality as very different. In reality, these orientations are opposite ends of a spectrum of sexual preferences. Sex researcher Alfred Kinsey devised a seven-point continuum representing sexual orientation. At one end of the continuum are those exclusively attracted to members of the other sex; at the opposite end are people exclusively attracted to members of the same sex. In between are varying degrees of homosexual, bisexual, and heterosexual orientation.[49]

In First Nations culture, some of the Elders taught that "two-spirited" people—gays and lesbians—were special, to be respected and honoured. They had specific duties and responsibilities to perform, including counselling, healing, and being visionaries. After colonization, many two-spirited First Nations peoples came to be ostracized from their own communities. There is a movement to reclaim traditions and a rightful place in the Aboriginal community. The 2 Spirited People of the 1st Nations is a non-profit social service organization, located in Toronto. Membership consists of Aboriginal gay, lesbian, bisexual, and transgendered people. This agency is attempting to provide a space where Aboriginal two-spirited people can come together as a community. A 2 Spirited People of the 1st Nations information guide provides educators culturally sensitive information on the history, teachings, and spirituality of two-spirited people.[50]

## Bisexuality

Bisexuality—sexual attraction to both males and females—can develop at any point in one's life. In some cultures, bisexual activity is considered part of normal sexual experimentation. Among the Sabmia Highlanders in Papua New Guinea, for instance, boys perform oral sex on one another as part of the rites of passage into manhood.[51]

Some people identify themselves as bisexual even if they don't behave bisexually. Some are *serial* bisexuals—they are sexually involved with same-sex partners for a while and then with partners of the other sex, or vice versa.

Fear of HIV infection has sparked great concern about bisexuality, particularly among heterosexual women who worry about becoming involved with a bisexual man. About 20 to 30 percent of women with AIDS were infected by bisexual partners, and health officials fear that bisexual men who hide their homosexual affairs could transmit HIV to many more women.

## Homosexuality

Homosexuality—social, emotional, and sexual attraction to members of the same sex—exists in almost all cultures. Men and women homosexuals are commonly referred to as *gay;* women homosexuals are also called *lesbians.*

Homosexuality threatens and upsets many people, perhaps because homosexuals are viewed as different or perhaps because no one understands why some people are heterosexual and others homosexual. *Homophobia* has led to an increase in *gay bashing* (attacking homosexuals) in many communities, including college and university campuses. Some blame the emergence of AIDS as a societal danger. However, researchers have found that fear of AIDS has not created new hostility but has simply given bigots an excuse to act out their hatred.

## Roots of Homosexuality

Most mental health experts agree that nobody knows what causes a person's sexual orientation. Research has discredited theories tracing homosexuality to troubled childhoods or abnormal psychological development. Sexual orientation probably emerges from a complex interaction that includes biological and environmental factors.

For decades, behavioural and medical specialists have debated whether homosexuality is biologically or socially determined. Some say that sexual orientation is genetically determined. Others contend that prenatal hormones influence sexual preference. Today, questions and controversies persist about the roots and nature of sexual orientation.

## Homosexual Lifestyles

Extensive studies of male and female homosexuals have shown that only a minority have problems coping with their homosexuality. The happiest and best adjusted tend to be those in close-couple relationships, the equivalent of stable heterosexual partnerships. Gays and lesbians have conceived children in heterosexual relationships; others have become parents through adoption or artificial insemination. Their families are much like any other, and studies of lesbian mothers have found that their children are essentially no different from children of heterosexual couples in self-esteem, gender-related issues and roles, sexual orientation, and general development.[52]

## Gender Diversity

Just as people can have diverse sexual orientations, a broad spectrum of gender identities also exists. **Gender identity** refers to a person's self-identified sense of being male, female, neither, or both.[53] How a person feels about and expresses their gender determines gender identity; physical characteristics do not necessarily define one's gender. A person may identify their gender in a wide number of ways, such as the following:

- ✔ Male
- ✔ Female
- ✔ **Intersexed** (Refers to people who were born with both male and female anatomy, or ambiguous genitalia)
- ✔ **Transgendered** (Refers to people whose gender identity is different than the sex they were assigned at birth; alternately, can be used as a general term to describe individuals whose gender identity differs from traditional gender roles)
- ✔ **Androgynous** (Refers to people who neither identify as male nor female)

Many other definitions of gender identity are possible, and some individuals choose to not label their gender at all.

Sexual orientation and gender identity can exist in any combination: any individual can identify as gay, lesbian, bisexual, asexual (not having sexual feelings for others), or have other definitions to describe what kind of people they are attracted to.

## Sexual Activity

Part of learning about your own sexuality is having a clear understanding of human sexual behaviours. Understanding frees us from fear and anxiety, so that we may accept ourselves and others as the natural sexual beings we all are.

## Celibacy

A celibate person does not engage in sexual activity. Complete **celibacy** means that the person doesn't masturbate (stimulate himself or herself sexually) or engage in sexual activity with a partner. In partial celibacy, the person masturbates but doesn't have sexual contact with others. Just as every person has the right to decide for themselves what degree of sexual activity they are comfortable with, a person's choice to not be sexually active at all must be respected. To some people, choosing to be celibate is an important part of their identity, faith, or belief system. Many people decide to be celibate at certain times of their lives. Some don't have sex because of concerns about pregnancy or STIs; others haven't found a partner for a permanent, monogamous relationship. Many simply have other priorities, such as finishing school or starting a career, and believe that sex outside of a committed relationship does not support their physical and psychological well-being.

## Abstinence

**Abstinence** means different things to different people. For some people, it means no genital or sexual contact. For others, abstinence may mean some sexual stimulation, but no intercourse.[54] Limited data are available on college and university students' perceptions of what is meant by sexual activity or abstinence.[55]

Increasing numbers of adolescents and young adults are choosing to abstain from sex. For some, abstinence is important as a way to express commitment to their religion or traditional culture. Family values or personal beliefs can also be important reasons for an individual to choose abstinence, just as these can be reasons for choosing celibacy. Many people who were sexually active in the past also are choosing abstinence because the risk of medical complications associated with STIs increases with the number of sexual partners a person has. Abstinence is the safest option for many. However, there is confusion about what it means to abstain, and individuals who think they are abstaining may still be engaging in behaviours that put them at risk for HIV and STIs.

## Sex in Cyberspace

The Internet, designed for communication of very different sorts, has become a new medium for relationships, including those that might be described as sexual. In certain chat rooms, individuals can share explicit sexual fantasies or engage in the cyberspace equivalent of mutual fantasizing. Individuals can assume any name, gender, race, or personality and can pretend to lead lives entirely different from their actual existences.

Many see cyberspace as a harmless way of adding an extra erotic charge to their daily lives. In some cases, individuals who meet in cyberspace develop what they come to think of as a meaningful relationship and arrange to meet in person. Sometimes these meetings are awkward; sometimes they do lead to a real-life romance. Flirting and erotic activities on the Internet can build unrealistic expectations in the real world. When couples do meet in person, they often discover they are not physically or emotionally attracted to each other, and the relationship comes to an end.[56]

The use of the Internet for sexual exploration can also lead, for some, to online sexual affairs, or cyber affairs. These romantic or sexual relationships, maintained through virtual contact, can be intrusive and detrimental to a primary relationship with a partner or spouse.[57] Researchers have discovered that both men and women consider online sexual interactions, whether sexual or emotional infidelity, a form of betrayal.[58, 59]

In other cases, the Internet can help to kindle new romances because people feel more comfortable expressing themselves. The anonymity factor provides a sense of personal space while allowing intimate communication. This effect is especially important for individuals who are shy, inhibited, or socially anxious in person, as it gives them a chance to get to know someone and share information about themselves with that person before actually meeting.[60]

If you take part in cybersex or Internet dating, remember to protect yourself; people you meet online may not always be what they appear. In one study of Internet intimacy, 77 percent of men and 46 percent of women reported lying about themselves online, mostly about their age and physical appearance.[61] In another study, individuals who had sexual intercourse with partners they met through the Internet had a greater risk for sexually transmitted infections.[62]

Don't give out personal information over the Internet, such as your address or home phone number, and if you

## Strategies for Change

### How to Say No to Sex

▲ First of all, recognize your own values and feelings. If you believe that sex is something to be shared only by people who've already become close in other ways, be true to that belief.

▲ If you're feeling pressured, let your date know that you're uncomfortable. Be simple and direct. Watch out for emotional blackmail. If your date says, "If you really like me, you'd want to make love," point out that if he or she really likes you, he or she wouldn't try to force you to do something you don't want to do.

▲ If you're a woman, monitor your sexual signals. Men impute more sexual meaning to gestures (such as casual touching) that women perceive as friendly and innocent.

▲ Communicate your feelings to your date sooner rather than later. It's far easier to say, "I don't want to go to your apartment," than to fight off unwelcome advances once you're there.

▲ Remember that if saying no to sex puts an end to a relationship, it wasn't much of a relationship in the first place.

▲ If you are unsure you want to have sex with someone, give yourself time to think. It is all right to wait until you determine what your feelings are for that person. If your date wants to have sex and you are not sure you want to, it is all right to end the date without having sex. You can make plans for sex another time if you feel like seeing that person again.

decide to meet someone in person, make sure you meet in public and let a friend know who you are going out with, what your plans are, and when you plan to return.[63]

## Masturbation

Not everybody masturbates, but most people do. Kinsey estimated that 7 out of 10 women and 19 out of 20 men masturbate (and admit they do). Their reason is simple: It feels good. **Masturbation** produces the same physical responses as sexual activity with a partner and can be an enjoyable form of sexual release.

Masturbation has been described as immature, unsocial, tiring, frustrating, and a cause of hairy palms, warts, blemishes, and blindness. None of these myths are true.

Even Freud felt that masturbation was normal for children. Sex educators recommend masturbation to adolescents as a means of releasing tension and becoming familiar with their sexual organs. Throughout adulthood, masturbation often is the primary sexual activity of individuals not involved in a sexual relationship and can be particularly useful when illness, absence, divorce, or death deprives a person of a partner.

Individuals with a higher level of education are more likely to masturbate than those with less schooling, and people living with sexual partners masturbate more than those who live alone.

## Intercourse

Vaginal **intercourse,** or *coitus,* refers to the penetration of the vagina by the penis. This is the preferred form of sexual intimacy for most heterosexual couples, who may use a wide variety of positions. The most familiar position for intercourse in our society is the missionary position, with the man on top, facing the woman. An alternative is the woman on top, either lying down or sitting upright. Other positions include lying side by side; lying with the man on top of the woman in a rear-entry position; and kneeling or standing. Many couples move into several different positions for intercourse during a single episode of lovemaking; others may have a personal favourite or may choose different positions at different times.

Sexual activity, including intercourse, is possible throughout a woman's menstrual cycle. However, some women prefer to avoid sex while menstruating because of uncomfortable physical symptoms, such as cramps, or concern about bleeding or messiness. Since different cultures have different views on intercourse during a woman's menstrual period, partners should discuss their own feelings and try to respect each other's views.

Vaginal intercourse, like other forms of sexual activity involving an exchange of bodily fluids, carries a risk of sexually transmitted infections, including HIV. In many other parts of the world, in fact, heterosexual intercourse is the most common means of HIV transmission.

## Oral-Genital Sex

Our mouths and genitals give us some of our most intense pleasures. Though it might seem logical to combine the two, some people are very uncomfortable with oral-genital sex. Some even consider it a perversion; it is a sin in some religions. However, others find it normal and acceptable.

The formal terms for oral sex are **cunnilingus,** which refers to oral stimulation of the woman's genitals, and **fellatio,** oral stimulation of the man's genitals. For many couples, oral-genital sex is a regular part of their lovemaking. For others, it's an occasional experiment. Oral sex with a partner carrying a sexually transmitted infection, such as herpes or HIV, can lead to infection, so a condom should be used (with cunnilingus, a condom cut in half to lay flat can be used).

## Anal Stimulation and Intercourse

Because the anus has many nerve endings, it can produce intense erotic responses. Stimulation of the anus by the fingers or mouth can be a source of sexual arousal; anal intercourse involves penile penetration of the anus. As with oral-genital sex, not everyone feels comfortable with anal stimulation and anal intercourse. An estimated 25 percent of adults have experienced anal intercourse at least once. However, anal sex involves important health risks, such as damage to sensitive rectal tissues and the transmission of various intestinal infections, hepatitis, and STIs, including HIV.

## Sexual Concerns

Many sexual concerns stem from myths and misinformation. There is no truth behind these misconceptions: men are always capable of erection, sex always involves intercourse, partners should experience simultaneous orgasms, and people who truly love each other always have satisfying sex lives.

Cultural and childhood influences can affect our attitudes toward sex. Even though Canadians' traditionally puritanical values have eased, our society continues to convey mixed messages about sex. Some children, repeatedly warned of the evils of sex, never accept the sexual dimensions of their identity. Others, especially young boys, may be exposed to macho attitudes toward sex and feel a need to prove their virility. Young girls may feel confused by media messages that encourage them to look and act provocatively and a double standard that blames them for leading boys on. In addition, virtually everyone has individual worries. A woman may feel self-conscious about the shape of her breasts; a man may worry about the size of his penis; or both partners may fear not pleasing the other.

The concept of sexual normalcy differs greatly in different times, cultures, or racial and ethnic groups. In certain times and places, only sex between a husband and wife has been deemed normal. In other circumstances, "normal" has been applied to any sexual behaviour that does not harm others or produce great anxiety and guilt.

## Safer Sex

Having sex is never completely safe; the only 100 percent risk-free sexual choice is abstinence. If you choose to be sexually active, you can greatly reduce your risk by restricting sexual activity to the context of a mutually exclusive, monogamous relationship in which both partners know, on the basis of laboratory testing, that neither has HIV antibodies or a sexually transmitted infection. Sober sex, in which both partners are not under the influence of drugs or alcohol, is more likely to be safer sex.

The only way of knowing for certain that a prospective partner doesn't have a STI or is not infected with HIV is through laboratory testing. Sex educators and health-care professionals strongly encourage couples to abstain from any sexual activity that puts them at risk for STIs until they both undergo medical examinations and testing for STIs.

This process greatly reduces the danger of disease transmission and can also help foster a deep sense of mutual trust and commitment.

Talking to a potential partner is the first step toward safer sex. Professionals offer advice on how to discuss a topic that makes many people uncomfortable: Choose a time and place that is relaxed and comfortable. Arm yourself with facts so you can answer any questions or objections your partner raises. Start on a positive note—for instance, by saying how much you care for your partner and saying that this is the reason you want to discuss something important. This is the time for you to be honest about any STIs you might have had or still carry. Give your partner time to take in what you've said. If you find out about a partner's STI, you may feel a range of emotions. You also will need to acquire information about symptoms, treatment, and how the disease is spread.[64]

**CHAPTER 7**

**Making This Chapter Work for You**

1. In friendships and other intimate relationships, which of the following is *not* true?
   a. Friends can communicate feelings as well as facts.
   b. Listening is just as important as talking.
   c. Emotional investment is required but the rewards are great.
   d. There is no need to pay attention to nonverbal communication.

2. A characteristic of a good relationship is
   a. trust.
   b. financial stability.
   c. identical interests.
   d. physical attractiveness.

3. When looking for a mate, the crucial ingredients for commitment include which of the following?
   a. shared values and a willingness to tolerate flaws
   b. desire to make the relationship work and a financial plan
   c. cohabitation and happiness
   d. a verbal commitment and discussion

4. Partners in successful marital relationships
   a. are generally from the same social and ethnic background.
   b. usually lived together before marrying.
   c. were usually very young at the time of their marriage.
   d. have premarital agreements.

5. Which of the following statements about divorce is *false*?
   a. The older the bride, the more likely the chance that the marriage will endure.
   b. The chances of a first marriage lasting are better than a second marriage.
   c. About 25 percent of all marriages end in divorce.
   d. The majority of divorced men and women remarry, even after multiple divorces.

6. Which of the following statements about menstruation and the menstrual cycle is true?
   a. Prolonged amenorrhea is not a concern.
   b. Premenstrual syndrome is a physiological disorder that usually results in amenorrhea.
   c. Ovulation occurs at the end of the menstrual cycle.
   d. Distance running can lead to amenorrhea.

7. Which statement about male anatomy is *incorrect*?
   a. The testes manufacture testosterone and sperm.
   b. Sperm cells are carried in the liquid semen.
   c. Cowper's glands secrete semen.
   d. Circumcision is the surgical removal of the foreskin of the penis.

8. Young Canadians learn about relationships and sexuality primarily from which of the following?
   a. their parents, friends, and sex-education classes
   b. the Internet
   c. the media
   d. all of the above

9. Which of the following statements is true about sexual orientation?
   a. Most individuals who identify themselves as bisexual are really homosexual.
   b. Homosexuality is caused by a poor family environment.
   c. Homosexual behaviour is found only in affluent and well-educated cultures.
   d. Homosexuality exists in almost all cultures.

10. Abstinence can be defined as
    a. refraining from oral sex.
    b. refraining from all sexual activities that involve vaginal, anal, and oral intercourse.
    c. having sexual intercourse with only one partner.
    d. refraining from drinking alcohol before sexual activity.

Answers to these questions can be found on page 450.

## Self Responsibility

*The Law of Giving—*
*Every relationship is one of give and take, if you stop the flow of either, you interfere with nature's intelligence.*

**Deepak Chopra**

Building relationships takes time, energy, and commitment. In Prochaska's Stages of Change model, maintenance also demands care and attention to avoid a relapse. If you are in a relationship that is lacking in enthusiasm and energy, commitment and caring, it may

## Social Responsibility

*Go out into the world today and love the people you meet. Let your presence light new light in the hearts of people.*

**Mother Teresa**

be time to re-evaluate why this is so. What can you do to rejuvenate this relationship—Spend more time together? Seek out new adventures? Make a change in lifestyle habits that encourage healthy lifelong living? Take time to give and take.

## Critical Thinking

1. While our society has become more tolerant, marriages between people of different religious and racial groups still face special pressures. What issues might arise if you marry someone from another culture? How could these issues be resolved? What are your own feelings about mixed marriages? Would you date someone of a different religion or race? Why or why not?

2. What are your personal criteria for a successful relationship? Develop a brief list of factors you

consider important, and support your choices with examples or experiences from your own life.

3. Bill told his girlfriend, Anita, that he has never taken any sexual risks. But when she suggested that they get tested for STIs, he became furious and refused. Anita doesn't want to take any risks, but she doesn't want to lose him either. What would you advise her to say or do? What would you advise Bill to say or do?

If your textbook package includes CengageNOW™, go to http://west.cengagenow.com/ilrn/ to link to CengageNOW™ for Health, your online study tool. First take the **Pre-test** for this chapter to get your personalized **Study Plan,** which will identify topics you need to review and direct you to the appropriate resources. Then take the **Post-test** to determine what concepts you have mastered and what you still need work on.

## SITES & BYTES

### Aboriginal Canada Portal
**www.aboriginalcanada.gc.ca**

Access this site, then search for sexuality education. Many links to articles, programs, and services for First Nations in Canada are available.

### Sex Information and Education Council of Canada
**www.sieccan.org**

SIECCAN, a national non-profit educational organization, provides both the public and professionals with human sexuality education.

### Sexuality and U
**www.sexualityandu.ca**

This site provides up-to-date information and education on sexual and gender orientation, STIs, and contraception FAQs.

### International Association for Relationship Research
**www.iarr.org**

This site contains links to professional organizations and publications that support research about relationships.

### The Vanier Institute of the Family
**www.vifamily.ca**

This site has many interesting articles on family facts and family issues. Lists of publications and links to other professional organizations are also available.

Please note that links are subject to change. If you find a broken link, use a search engine such as www.google.ca and search for the website by typing in keywords.

**InfoTrac® College Edition Activity**  Knox, D., Zusman, M., & McNeely, A. (2008). University students' beliefs about sex: Men vs. women. (Report). *College Student Journal, 42*(1), 181–85.

1. Describe four important findings of this study on university students' beliefs about sex—men versus women.

2. Discuss the implications of the findings of this study for men and women with regard to expectations within relationships.

3. Discuss how the findings of this study might help you reflect upon your personal beliefs about sex.

You can find additional readings related to communication and to sexuality with InfoTrac® College Edition, an online library of more than 5000 journals and publications. Follow the instructions for accessing InfoTrac® that were packaged with your textbook; then search for articles using a keyword search.

For additional links and resources, visit our text-specific website at www.health.nelson.com.

## Key Terms

The terms listed here are used within the chapter on the page indicated. Definitions of the terms are in the Glossary at the end of the book.

| | | | |
|---|---|---|---|
| abstinence 168 | endometrium 162 | menstruation 162 | semen 165 |
| amenorrhea 164 | epididymis 164 | mons pubis 159 | seminal vesicles 165 |
| androgynous 168 | estrogen 162 | ovaries 162 | sexual orientation 167 |
| bisexual 167 | fallopian tubes 162 | ovulation 162 | sperm 164 |
| celibacy 168 | fellatio 170 | ovum (ova) 162 | testis (testes) 164 |
| cervix 159 | gender identity 168 | penis 164 | testosterone 164 |
| circumcision 166 | heterosexual 167 | perineum 159 | toxic shock syndrome |
| clitoris 159 | homosexual 167 | premenstrual dysphoric | (TSS) 164 |
| cohabitation 156 | intercourse 170 | disorder (PMDD) 162 | transgendered 168 |
| corpus luteum 162 | intersexed 168 | premenstrual syndrome | urethra 164 |
| Cowper's glands 165 | intimacy 155 | (PMS) 162 | urethral opening 159 |
| cunnilingus 170 | labia majora 159 | progesterone 162 | uterus 159 |
| dysmenorrhea 162 | labia minora 159 | prostate gland 165 | vagina 159 |
| ejaculatory ducts 165 | masturbation 169 | scrotum 164 | vas deferens 165 |

## References

1. Jordan, D.J. (2007). *Leadership in leisure services: Making a difference*, 2nd ed. State College, PA: Venture Publishing, Inc.
2. Maple, Marilyn. Personal interview.
3. Swann, W., et al. (1992). Socialization patterns of depressed and non-depressed college students. *Journal of Abnormal Psychology, 104.*
4. Brendgen, M., et al. (2001). The relations between friendship quality, ranked-friendship preference, and adolescents' behaviour with their friends. *Merrill-Palmer Quarterly, 47*(3), 395.
5. Chatterjee, C. (2001, September–October). Can men and women be friends? *Psychology Today,* 61.
6. Gard, C. (2000). The secrets to making lasting friendships. *Current Health 2, 27*(2).
7. Silverman, J., et al. (2001). Dating violence against adolescent girls and associated substance use, unhealthy weight control, sexual risk behaviour, pregnancy, and suicidality. *Journal of the American Medical Association, 286,* 572.
8. Newton-Taylor, B., DeWit, D., & Gliksman, L. (1998). Prevalence and factors associated with physical and sexual assault of female university students in Ontario. *Health Care for Women International, 19*(2).
9. Sprecher, S. (1998). Insiders' perspectives on reasons for attraction to a close other. *Social Psychology Quarterly, 61*(4).
10. Laumann, Edward. Personal interview.
11. Fisher, H. (2007). The laws of chemistry: Whom you are most attracted to reflects the biology of your brain as much as the heat of your heart. It may not have to do with us—it's all about the kids. (Cover story). *Psychology Today, 40*(3), 76–81.
12. Buss, D. (1994). *The evolution of desire.* New York: Basic Books.
13. Sommers, J., & Vodanovich, S. (2000). Vengeance scores among college students: Examining the role of jealousy and forgiveness. *Education, 121*(1).
14. Statistics Canada. (2008, February 13). Census. 2006 Census: Analysis Series. Findings. Family portrait: Continuity and change in Canadian families and households in 2006: National portrait census families. Available at www12.statcan.ca/english/census06/analysis/famhouse/cenfam1.cfm.
15. Statistics Canada. (2002, October 22). 2001 census: Marital status, common-law status, families, dwellings and households. *The Daily.* Available at www.statcan.ca/Daily/English/021022/d021022a.htm.
16. Le Bourdais, C., Neil, G., & Turcotte, P. (2000, Spring). The changing face of conjugal relationships. *Social Trends.* Ottawa: Statistics Canada, Cat. No. 11-008, p. 15. Available at www.statcan.gc.ca/pub/11-008-x/11-008-x1999004-eng.pdf
17. Jabusch, W. (2000). The myth of cohabitation: Cohabiting couples lack both specialization and commitment in their relationships. *America, 183*(10).
18. Ibid.
19. Statistics Canada. (2008, February 13). Census. 2006 Census: Analysis Series. Findings. Family portrait: Continuity and change in Canadian families and households in 2006: National portrait census families. Available at www12.statcan.ca/english/census06/analysis/famhouse/cenfam1.cfm.
20. Statistics Canada. (2007, September 5). Census. 2006 Census: Reference Material. 2006 Census information on same-sex common-law and married couples. Available at www12.statcan.ca/english/census06/reference/same_sex_common_law.cfm.
21. Popenoe, D. (2000). *The state of our unions: The social health of marriage in America.* Piscataway, NJ: Rutgers.
22. Sternberg, Robert. Personal interview.
23. Milan, A., Vézina, M., and Wells, C. (2007). Statistics Canada. Family portrait: Continuity and change in Canadian families and households in 2006, 2006 Census. Families and households, 2006 Census. Catologue No. 97-553-XIE. Ministry of Industry. Available at www12.statcan.ca/english/census06/analysis/famhouse/pdf/97-553-XIE2006001.pdf.
24. Popenoe, D. (2000). *The state of our unions: The social health of marriage in America.* Piscataway, NJ: Rutgers.
25. Milan, A., Vézina, M., and Wells, C. (2007). Statistics Canada. Family portrait: Continuity and change in Canadian families and households in 2006, 2006 Census. Families and households, 2006

Census. Catolugue No. 97-553-XIE. Ministry of Industry. Available at www12.statcan.ca/english/census06/analysis/famhouse/pdf/97-553-XIE2006001.pdf.

26. Ibid.

27. Ibid.

28. Milan, A., & Peters, A. (2003, Summer). Couples living apart. *Canadian Social Trends.* Available at www.statcan.ca/english/studies/11-008/feature/star2003069000s2a02.pdf.

29. Statistics Canada. (2007, September 5). Census. 2006 Census: Reference material. 2006 Census information on same-sex common-law and married couples. Available at www12.statcan.ca/english/census06/reference/same_sex_common_law.cfm.

30. Ibid.

31. Equal Marriage for Same Sex Couples. (2003, June 11). The morning after—A new reality. Available at www.samesexmarriage.ca/legal/ontario_case/appeal/June102003.htm.

32. Canadians for Equal Marriage. (2006, December 7). Harper's motion to re-open equal marriage defeated. Prime Minister says the issue is settled. Available at www.equal-marriage.ca.

33. Dimmock, P., et al. (2000). Efficacy of selective serotonin-reuptake inhibitors in premenstrual syndrome: A systematic review. *Lancet, 356*(9236).

34. Calcium for PMS, Bone Health. (2001). *Contemporary OB/GYN, 46*(5), 151.

35. New treatment approved for severe premenstrual symptoms. (2000). *FDA Consumer, 34*(5).

36. Steiner, M. (2000). Recognition of premenstrual dysphoric disorder and its treatment. *Lancet, 356*(9236).

37. Premenstrual mood disturbance. (2001). *Harvard Medical Health Letter, 17*(12).

38. Swayze, S. (2001). Preventing problems from tampon use. *Nursing, 31*(7), 28.

39. The Circumcision Reference Library. (2008, September 13). Canadian circumcision statistics. Available at www.cirp.org/library/statistics/Canada.

40. Neonatal circumcision revisited. Fetus and Newborn Committee, Canadian Paediatric Society. (1996). *Canadian Medical Association Journal, 154,* 796–80.

41. Schoen, E., et al. (2000). New policy on circumcision—Cause for concern. *Pediatrics, 105*(3).

42. *The sexual health of adolescents and young adults.* (2002). Menlo Park, CA: Henry J. Kaiser Family Foundation.

43. Sexuality and u.ca. (2006). Sex facts in Canada 2006. The Society of Obstetricians and Gynaecologists of Canada. Available at www.sexualityandu.ca/media-room/pdf/Sex-Stats-Fact-Sheet_e.pdf.

44. Netting, N.S., & Burnett, M.L. (2004). Twenty years of student sexual behaviour: Subcultural adaptations to a changing health environment. *Adolescence, 30*(153), 19–20.

45. Ogletree, R., et al. (2001). Associations between lifetime sexual partners and health risk behaviors in a representative sample of United States college students. *Research Quarterly for Exercise and Sport, 72*(1).

46. Ullman, S., et al. (1999). Alcohol and sexual assault in a national sample of college women. *Journal of Interpersonal Violence, 14*(6).

47. Netting, N.S., & Burnett, M.L. (2004). Twenty years of student sexual behaviour: Subcultural adaptations to a changing health environment. *Adolescence, 30*(153), 19–20.

48. Kennedy, M.A., & Gorzalka, B.B. (2002). Asian and non-Asian attitudes toward rape, sexual harassment, and sexuality. *Sex roles: A journal of research, 227,* 12.

49. Kinsey's heterosexual-homosexual rating scale. (n.d.). The Kinsey Institute. Available at www.indiana.edu/~kinsey/research/ak-hhscale.html.

50. 2 Spirits.com. (2005). About 2 Spirits.com 2 spirited people of the 1st Nations. Information guide. Available at www.2spirits.com.

51. Crooks, R., & Baur, K. (2002). *Our sexuality,* 8th ed. Pacific Grove, CA: Wadsworth.

52. Baugher, S. (2000). Same sex relationships. *Journal of Family and Consumer Sciences, 92*(3).

53. Youthline. (n.d.). Definitions. Gender. Available at www.youthline.ca/definitions/gender.html.

54. Canadian Federation of Sexual Health. (2008, June 25). Abstinence. Sexual health info. Available at www.cfsh.ca/Sexual_Health_Info/Contraception-and-Safer-Sex/Contraception-and-Birth-Control/Abstinence.aspx.

55. Remez, L. (2000). Special report: Oral sex among adolescents: Is it sex or is it abstinence? *Family Planning Perspectives, 32*(6), 298–304.

56. Levine, D. (2000). Virtual attraction: What rocks your boat. *CyberPsychology & Behavior, 3*(4), 565–73.

57. Millner, V.S. (2008). Internet infidelity: A case of intimacy with detachment. *The Family Journal: Counseling Therapy for Couples and Families, 16*(1), 78–92.

58. Whitty, M. (2004). Cybercheating. *Counseling and Psychotherapy Journal,* 15, 38–39.

59. Whitty, M. (2008). Liberating or debilitating? An examination of romantic relationships, sexual relationships and friendships on the Net. *Computers in Human Behavior, 24,* 1837–50.

60. McKenna, K.Y., Green, A.S., & Gleason, M.E. (2002). Relationship formation on the Internet: What's the big attraction? *Journal of Social Issues, 58*(1), 9–31.

61. McCown, J. A., Fischer, D., Page, R., & Homant, M. (2001). Internet relationships: People who meet people. *Cyber Psychology & Behaviour, 4*(5), 593–96.

62. Toomey, K., & Rothenberg, R. (2000). Sex and cyberspace—Virtual networks leading to high-risk sex. *Journal of the American Medical Association, 284,* 484–87.

63. Match.com. (2008). The do's and don'ts of dating on and off line. Available at http://match.com/matchus/help/safetytips.aspx.

64. *It's your (sex) life.* (2002). Menlo Park, CA: Henry J. Kaiser Family Foundation.

CHAPTER

# 8

# Reproductive Choices

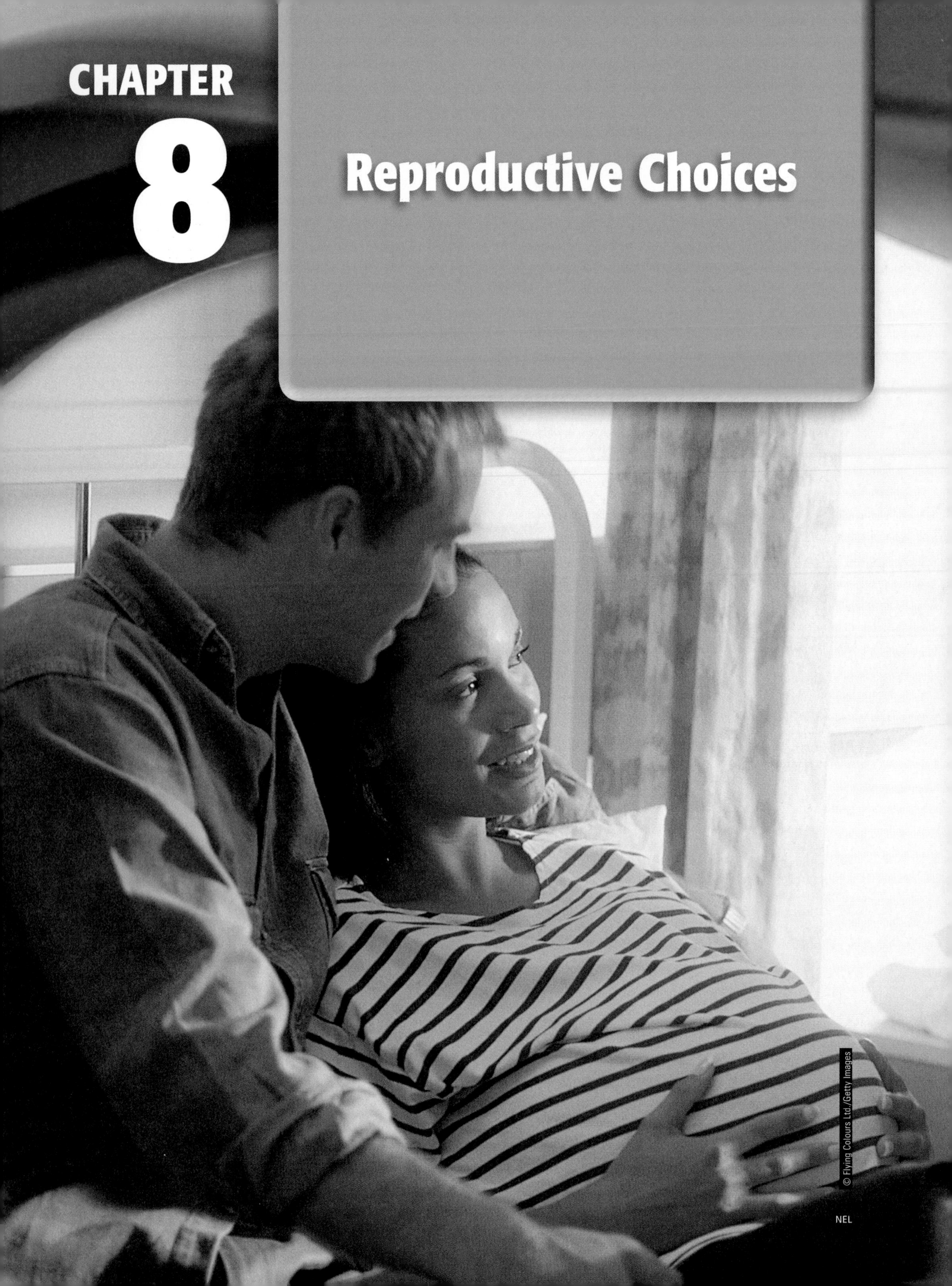

As human beings, we have a unique power: the ability to choose to conceive or not to conceive. No other species on Earth can separate sexual activity and pleasure from reproduction. However, simply not wanting to get pregnant is never enough to prevent conception nor is wanting to have a child always enough to get pregnant. Both desires require individual decisions and actions.

Anyone who engages in vaginal intercourse must be willing to accept the consequences of that activity—the possibility of pregnancy and responsibility for the child who might be conceived—or take action to avoid those consequences. Although many people are concerned about the risks associated with contraception, using birth control is safer and healthier than not using it. According to the Canadian Federation for Sexual Health,[1] the use of contraceptives, including oral contraceptives, saves millions of lives each year. Some forms of contraception also reduce the risk of sexually transmitted infections.

This chapter provides information on conception, birth control, abortion, infertility, and the processes by which a new human life develops and enters the world.

**After studying the material in this chapter, you will be able to:**

- **Describe** the process of human conception.
- **List** the major options available for contraception and **identify** the advantages and risks of each.
- **Describe** the commonly used abortion methods.
- **Discuss** the physiological effects of pregnancy on a woman and **describe** fetal development.
- **Describe** the three stages of labour and the birth process.
- **Give examples** of infertility treatments.

**????** **FREQUENTLY ASKED QUESTIONS**

**FAQ: How do I choose a birth control method? p. 179**

**FAQ: What is emergency contraception? p. 190**

**FAQ: What is the psychological impact of abortion? p. 195**

**FAQ: What is childbirth like? p. 200**

# Conception

The equation for making a baby is quite simple: One sperm plus one egg equals one fertilized egg, which can develop into an infant. But the processes that affect or permit **conception** are quite complicated. The creation of sperm, or **spermatogenesis,** starts in the male at puberty, and the production of sperm is regulated by hormones (see Figure 8-1). Sperm cells form in the seminiferous tubules of the testes and are passed into the epididymis, where they are stored until ejaculation; a single male ejaculation may contain 500 million sperm. Each sperm released into the vagina during intercourse moves on its own, propelling itself toward its target, an ovum.

To reach its goal, the sperm must move through the acidic secretions of the vagina, enter the uterus, travel up the fallopian tube containing the ovum, then fuse with the nucleus of the egg (**fertilization**). Just about every sperm produced by a man in his lifetime fails to accomplish its mission.

There are far fewer human egg cells than there are sperm cells. Each woman is born with her lifetime supply of ova, and between 300 and 500 eggs eventually mature and leave her ovaries during ovulation. Every month, one or the other of the woman's ovaries releases an ovum to the nearby fallopian tube. It travels through the fallopian tube until it reaches the uterus, a journey that takes three to four days. An unfertilized egg lives for about 24 to 36 hours, disintegrates, and, during menstruation, is expelled along with the uterine lining.

Even if a sperm, which can survive in the female reproductive tract for two to five days, meets a ripe egg in a fallopian tube, its success is not assured. It must penetrate the layer of cells and a jellylike substance that surround each egg. Every sperm that touches the egg deposits an enzyme that dissolves part of this barrier. When a sperm bumps into a bare spot, it can penetrate the egg membrane and merge with the egg (see Figure 8-2). The fertilized egg travels down the fallopian tube, dividing to form a tiny clump of cells called a **zygote.** When it reaches the uterus, about a week after fertilization, it burrows into the endometrium, the lining of the uterus. This process is called **implantation.**

Conception can be prevented by **contraception.** Some contraceptive methods prevent ovulation or implantation, and others block the sperm from reaching the egg. Some methods are temporary; others permanently alter one's fertility.

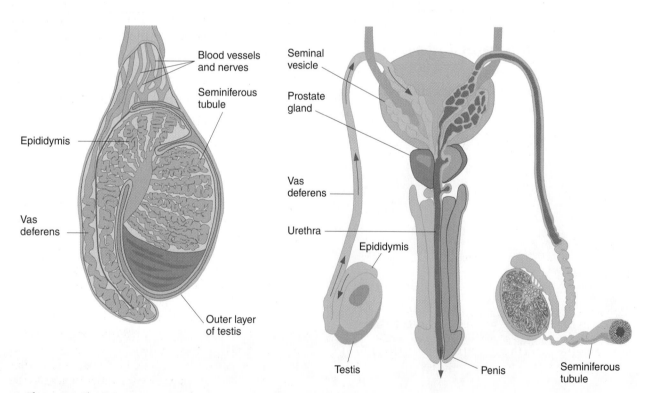

▲ **Figure 8-1** The Testes
Spermatogenesis takes place in the testes. Sperm cells form in the seminiferous tubules and are stored in the coils of the epididymis. Eventually, the sperm drain into the vas deferens, ready for ejaculation.

Source: Hespenheide Design.

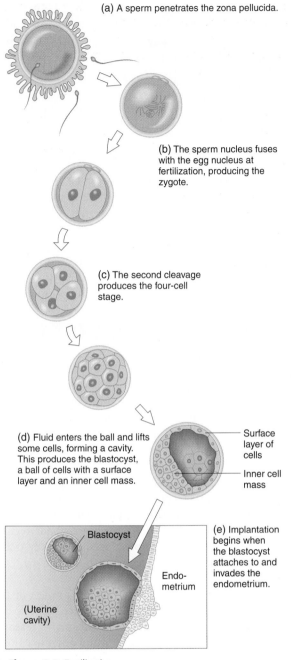

(a) A sperm penetrates the zona pellucida.

(b) The sperm nucleus fuses with the egg nucleus at fertilization, producing the zygote.

(c) The second cleavage produces the four-cell stage.

(d) Fluid enters the ball and lifts some cells, forming a cavity. This produces the blastocyst, a ball of cells with a surface layer and an inner cell mass.

Surface layer of cells

Inner cell mass

Blastocyst

Endo-metrium

(Uterine cavity)

(e) Implantation begins when the blastocyst attaches to and invades the endometrium.

▲ **Figure 8-2** Fertilization
(a) The efforts of hundreds of sperm may allow one to penetrate the ovum's corona radiata, an outer layer of cells, and then the zona pellucida, a thick inner membrane. (b) The nuclei of the sperm and the egg cells merge, and the male and female chromosomes in the nuclei come together, forming a zygote. (c) The zygote divides into two cells, then four cells, and so on. (d) As fluid enters the ball, cells form a ball of cells called a blastocyst. (e) The blastocyst implants itself in the endometrium.

Source: Hespenheide Design.

# Birth Control Basics

A heterosexual woman in a Western country spends 90 percent of her reproductive years trying to prevent pregnancy and 10 percent of these years trying to become or being pregnant. Today birth control is safer, more effective, and more convenient than in the past—yet none of today's contraceptives is 100 percent safe, 100 percent effective, or 100 percent convenient.

Ideally, two partners should decide together which form of birth control to use. However, female methods account for 63 percent of all contraceptive methods reported by women between the ages of 15 and 44.[2] Another barrier to birth control is cost. In some provinces, health insurers have not covered the cost of reversible methods of birth control. However, even when birth control is affordable and available, many college and university students do not use it consistently.[3]

If you are engaging in sexual activity that could lead to conception, you have to be realistic about your situation. This may mean assuming full responsibility for your reproductive ability, whether you're a man or a woman. The more you know about contraception, the more likely you are to use birth control. You also have to recognize the risks associated with various methods of contraception. If you're a woman, the risks are chiefly yours. Although most women never experience any serious complications, it's important to be aware of the potential for long-term risks. Risks that are acceptable to others may not be acceptable to you.

In one recent study, undergraduates were more likely to report "almost always" using a reliable, proven method of birth control after completing an introductory health course.[4]

## How Do I Choose a Birth Control Method?

When it comes to deciding which form of birth control to use, there's no one "right" decision. One study found that women who had a history of sexually transmitted infections and younger, more educated women were more likely to use methods that prevent both pregnancy and disease.[5]

Good decisions are based on sound information. You should consult a physician if you have questions or want to know how certain methods might affect existing or familial medical conditions, such as high blood pressure or diabetes. Table 8-1 presents some contraceptive choices. As the table indicates, contraception doesn't always work. When you evaluate any contraceptive, always consider its *effectiveness* (the likelihood that it will indeed prevent pregnancy). The **failure rate** refers to the number of pregnancies

▼ **Table 8-1 Contraceptive Choices**

| Type of Birth Control | Success Rate |
|---|---|
| **Permanent (also called sterilization)** | |
| • Tubal ligation (female) | 99.9% |
| • Vasectomy (male) | 99.9% |
| **Available with a prescription** | |
| • "The pill" (oral contraceptive) | 98.0% |
| • Intrauterine device (IUD) | 95.0% |
| • Contraceptive patch | 97.0% |
| • Diaphragm with spermicide (foam or jelly) | 81.0% |
| **Available without a prescription** | |
| • Condom with spermicide | 95.0% |
| • Condom alone | 90.0% |
| • Contraceptive sponge | 90.0% |
| • Emergency contraception pill (ECP) | 98.0% |
| **Natural family planning** | |
| • Withdrawal | 77.0% |
| • Rhythm method | 76.0% |

Source: sexualityandU.ca. Contraception. Contraception methods. June 12, 2007. Available at www.sexualityandu.ca/adults/contraception-2.aspx.

## Strategies for Prevention

### Choosing a Contraceptive

Your contraceptive needs may change throughout your life. To decide which method to use now, you need to know:

▲ How well will it fit into your lifestyle?

▲ How convenient will it be?

▲ How effective will it be?

▲ How safe will it be?

▲ How affordable will it be?

▲ How reversible will it be?

▲ Will it protect against sexually transmitted infections?

Source: Courtesy of Planned Parenthood Federation of America, Inc.

that occur per year for every 100 women using a particular method of birth control.

The reliability of contraceptives in actual, real-life use is much lower than those reported in surveys or clinical trials. In general, failure rates are highest among cohabiting and other unmarried women, very poor families, adolescents, and women in their 20s. Unmarried adolescent women who are living with a partner have an average failure rate of about 31 percent in the first year of contraceptive use, regardless of method of birth control, compared with a failure rate of 7 percent among married women aged 30 and older.

Some couples use withdrawal or **coitus interruptus,** removal of the penis from the vagina before ejaculation, to prevent pregnancy, even though this is not a reliable form of birth control. About half the men who have tried coitus interruptus find it unsatisfactory, either because they don't know when they're going to ejaculate or because they can't withdraw quickly enough. Also, the Cowper's glands, two pea-sized structures located on each side of the urethra, often produce a fluid that appears as drops at the tip of the penis any time from arousal and erection to orgasm. This fluid can contain active sperm and, in infected men, the human immunodeficiency virus (HIV).

Millions of unintentional pregnancies each year in Canada are the result of contraceptive failure, either from problems with the drug or device itself or from improper use. Partners can lower the risk of unwanted pregnancy by using backup methods—that is, more than one form of contraception simultaneously. Emergency contraception

(ECP), sometimes referred to the morning-after pill, is a safe and effective way to prevent pregnancy. Recent findings have shown that it can reduce the risk of pregnancy within five days after failed contraception or unprotected intercourse.[6] The sooner you take it, the better it works. If seven days have passed since you had unprotected sex and you do not get your menstrual period on time, you should take a pregnancy test or see your family physician. It is important to remember that ECP is not a replacement for regular contraception, nor does it protect against sexually transmitted infections. Once a pregnancy has occurred, ECP will not work.

Often college and university students aware of the risks associated with unprotected sexual intercourse do not practise safe-sex behaviours. There are many reasons, ranging from the influence of alcohol and drugs to embarrassment about buying condoms. A recent survey of college students found that a significant percentage of both men and women either tried to dissuade a potential partner from condom use or had a sexual partner who had tried to discourage condom use. Both men and women generally used the same arguments against condoms: that sex felt better without them, that the woman wouldn't get pregnant, and that neither would get a sexually transmitted infection.[7]

The bottom line is that it takes two people to conceive a baby, and two people should be involved in deciding *not* to conceive a baby. In the process, they can also enhance their skills in communication, critical thinking, and negotiating.

## Abstinence and Outercourse

The contraceptive methods discussed in this chapter are designed to prevent pregnancy as a consequence of vaginal intercourse. Couples who choose abstinence make a very different decision—to abstain from vaginal intercourse and other forms of sexual activity (any in which ejaculation occurs near the vaginal opening) that could result in conception.

For many individuals, abstinence represents a deliberate choice regarding their bodies, minds, spirits, and sexuality. People choose abstinence for various reasons, including waiting until they are ready for a sexual relationship or until they find the "right" partner, respecting religious or moral values, enjoying friendships without sexual involvement, recovering from a break-up, or preventing pregnancy and sexually transmitted infections.

Abstinence is the only form of birth control that is 100 percent effective and risk-free. It is also an important, increasingly valued lifestyle choice. A growing number of individuals, including some who have been sexually active in the past, are choosing abstinence until they establish a relationship with a long-term partner.

Abstinence offers special health benefits for women. Those who abstain until their twenties and engage in sex with fewer partners during their lifetime are less likely to get sexually transmitted infections, to suffer infertility, or to develop cervical cancer.

Individuals who choose abstinence from vaginal intercourse often engage in activities sometimes called *outercourse,* such as kissing, hugging, sensual touching, and mutual masturbation. Outercourse is nearly 100 percent effective as a contraceptive measure, but pregnancy is possible if there is genital contact. If the man ejaculates near the vaginal opening, sperm can swim up into the vagina and fallopian tubes to fertilize an egg. Except for oral-genital and anal sex, outercourse also may lower the risk of contracting sexually transmitted infections. However, because some STIs, such as herpes and HPV (genital warts), can be transmitted through skin-to-skin contact even when no bodily fluids are exchanged, outercourse cannot be considered "safe" sex.

## Prescription Contraceptives

The most effective and most widely used methods of birth control in Canada include oral contraceptives, the intrauterine device, the diaphragm, and the cervical cap. The newest prescription contraceptives are the contraceptive ring and the contraceptive patch. All are available only from health-care professionals by prescription. All are reversible.

## Birth Control Pill

*The pill*—the popular term for **oral contraceptives**—is the method of birth control used by about 100 million women all over the world.[8] It is also the preferred method of birth control by unmarried women and by those under age 30, including college and university students. Women 18 to 24 years old are most likely to choose oral contraceptives. In use for 40 years, the pill is one of the most researched, tested, and carefully followed medications in medical history—and one of the most controversial.[9] The impact of the pill has been enormous. By virtually eliminating the risk of pregnancy, the pill encouraged women's careers. It also altered the marriage market by enabling young men and women to delay marriage while not having to delay sex.[10]

Although many women incorrectly think that the risks of the pill are greater than those of pregnancy and childbirth, long-term studies show that oral contraceptive use does not increase mortality rates. Oral contraceptives significantly reduce the risk of ovarian and endometrial cancer and produce no increase in serious disease, including breast cancer, diabetes, multiple sclerosis, rheumatoid arthritis, and liver disease.[11] There is an increased risk of blood clots and pulmonary embolism for smokers and women who used earlier types of oral contraceptives.[12]

Three types of oral contraceptives are widely used in Canada: the constant-dose combination pill, the multiphasic pill, and the progestin-only pill. The **constant-dose combination** or **monophasic pill** releases two hormones, synthetic estrogen and progestin, which play important roles in controlling ovulation and the menstrual cycle, at constant levels throughout the menstrual cycle.

The **multiphasic pill** mimics normal hormonal fluctuations of the natural menstrual cycle by providing different levels of estrogen and progesterone at different times of the month. Multiphasic pills reduce total hormonal dose and side effects. Both constant-dose combination and multiphasic pills block the release of hormones that would stimulate the process leading to ovulation. They also thicken and alter the cervical mucus, making it more hostile to sperm, and they make implantation of a fertilized egg in the uterine lining more difficult. Multiphasic pills may heighten a woman's sex drive.

The **progestin-only pill,** or **minipill,** contains a small amount of progestin and no estrogen. Unlike women who take constant-dose combination pills, those using minipills probably ovulate at least occasionally. The minipills make the mucus in the cervix so thick and tacky, however, that sperm can't enter the uterus. Minipills also may interfere with implantation by altering the uterine lining.

**Advantages** Birth control pills have several advantages: They are extremely effective. Among women who miss no pills, only 1 in 1000 becomes pregnant in the first year of use. They are reversible, so a woman can easily stop using them. They do not interrupt sexual activity. Women on the pill have more regular periods, less cramping, and fewer tubal, or ectopic, pregnancies. After five years of use, the pill halves the risk of endometrial and ovarian cancer.

In a major study in 2002, scientists at the Centers for Disease Control and Prevention and the National Institutes of Health in the United States looked at more than 9200 women ages 35 to 64 and found that the pill does not raise the risk of breast cancer, even among women who started taking it early or who have close relatives with the disease.[13] This held true regardless of a woman's race or weight or whether she had started taking contraceptives before age 20, took the early higher-dose oral contraceptives, or had a family history of breast cancer.[14] The pill also reduces the risk of benign breast lumps, ovarian cysts, iron-deficiency anemia, and pelvic inflammatory disease (PID). In actual use, the failure rate is 1 to 5 percent for estrogen/progesterone pills and 3 to 10 percent for minipills. Some physicians suggest that in the future women may use the pill to regulate their menstrual cycle.[15]

**Disadvantages** The pill does not protect against HIV infection and other sexually transmitted infections, so condoms should also be used.[16] Some pills are time sensitive, and pregnancy can result if the pills are not taken at the same time each day.[17] In addition, the hormones in oral contraceptives may cause various side effects, including spotting between periods, weight gain or loss, nausea and vomiting, breast tenderness, and decreased sex drive. Some women using the pill report emotional changes, such as mood swings and depression. Oral contraceptives can interact with other medications which can make the birth control pill less effective or alter the effect of the other medication. Women should inform any physician providing medical treatment that they are taking the pill.[18]

Current birth control pills contain much lower levels of estrogen than early pills. As a result, the risk of heart disease and stroke among users is much lower than it once was; the danger may be lowest with the minipill. Yet a risk of cardiovascular problems is still associated with use of the pill, primarily for women over 35 who smoke and those with other health problems, such as high blood pressure. Heart attacks strike an estimated one in 14 000 pill users between the ages of 30 and 39 and one in 1500 between the ages of 40 and 44. Strokes occur five times more frequently among women taking oral contraceptives, and clots in the veins develop in one of every 500 previously healthy women.

## Before Using Oral Contraceptives

Before starting on the pill, you should undergo a thorough physical examination that includes the following tests:

- ✔ Routine blood pressure test
- ✔ Pelvic exam, including a Pap smear
- ✔ Breast exam
- ✔ Blood test
- ✔ Urine sample

Let your doctor know about any personal or family incidence of high blood pressure or heart disease; diabetes; liver dysfunction; hepatitis; unusual menstrual history; severe depression; sickle-cell anemia; cancer of the breast, ovaries, or uterus; high cholesterol levels; or migraine headaches.

## How to Use Oral Contraceptives

An estimated two million women worldwide become unintentionally pregnant every year because they do not use the pill as directed.[19] The pill usually comes in 28-day packets: 21 of the pills contain the hormones, and 7 are "blanks," included so that the woman can take a pill every day, even during her menstrual period. If a woman forgets to take one pill, she should take it as soon as she remembers. However, if she forgets during the first week of her cycle or misses more than one pill, she should rely on another form of birth control until her next menstrual period.

Even if you experience no discomfort or side effects while on the pill, see a physician at least once a year for an examination, which should include a blood pressure test, a pelvic exam, and a breast exam. Notify your doctor at once if you develop severe abdominal pain, chest pain, coughing, shortness of breath, pain or tenderness in the calf or thigh, severe headaches, dizziness, faintness, muscle weakness or numbness, speech disturbance, blurred vision, a sensation of flashing lights, a breast lump, severe depression, or yellowing of your skin.

Generally, when a woman stops taking the pill, her menstrual cycle resumes the next month, but it may be irregular for the next couple of months. However, 2 to 4 percent of pill users experience prolonged delays. Women who become pregnant during the first or second cycle after discontinuing use of the pill may be at greater risk of miscarriage; they also are more likely to conceive twins. Most physicians advise women who want to conceive to change to another method of contraception for three months after they stop taking the pill.

## Contraceptive Ring

The first contraceptive vaginal ring, the NuvaRing®, became available in 2002 in the United States. It is now available in Canada.[20] Once in place, the NuvaRing® releases a low dose of estrogen and progestin into the surrounding tissue. The ring contains a lower amount of hormones than birth control pills.

The flexible plastic two-inch ring compresses so a woman can easily insert it. Each ring stays in place for three

▲ The NuvaRing® releases estrogen and progestin, preventing ovulation.

*Source: Organon USA*

weeks, then is removed for the fourth week of the menstrual cycle. Like the pill and the patch, the ring works by preventing ovulation.

**Advantages** Women have no need for a daily pill, a fitting by a doctor, or the use of a spermicide. A woman's ability to become pregnant returns quickly once she stops using the ring.

**Disadvantages** There were increased complaints of vaginal discharge, irritation, or infection. Women cannot use oil-based vaginal medicine to treat yeast infections while the ring is in place or a diaphragm or cervical cap for a backup method of birth control. Women who cannot take the birth control pill for medical reasons cannot use the ring either. This includes women who have had a blood clot, heart attack, stroke, or breast cancer, as well as women with active liver disease or women over 35 who smoke.[21]

## Contraceptive Patch

The contraceptive patch (Evra®) is a new method of birth control that has been available in Canada since January 2004.[22] It is a four-square-centimetre beige patch that sticks to the skin and continuously releases estrogen and a progestin (two female hormones) into the bloodstream. It can be applied to the skin of the upper arm, abdomen, back, or buttocks.

Rather than taking a daily pill, a woman replaces the patch every seven days for three consecutive weeks. The fourth week is patch-free. In clinical studies, about 5 percent of women had at least one patch detach from their skin; about 2 percent discontinued use because of skin irritation.[23]

Clinical studies have shown that the patch is as effective as the low-dose birth control pill in preventing pregnancy and less likely to cause breakthrough bleeding or spotting.[24]

**Advantages** Like the pill, the patch is also more than 99 percent effective at preventing pregnancy when used perfectly, with about a 3 percent failure rate for typical users. A woman does not have to remember to take a daily pill and can become pregnant quickly once she stops its use.

**Disadvantages** Users have an increased risk of blood clots, heart attack, and stroke. Reports from the U.S. Food and Drug Administration indicate that in 2004 the risk of dying or suffering a survivable blood clot while using the patch was about three times higher than while using birth control pills.[25] Smoking increases the risk of serious cardiovascular side effects. The patch may be less effective in women who weigh more than 89.8 kilograms or 198 pounds.[26] Wearers of contact lenses may experience a change in vision or be unable to continue to wear lenses.

## Contraceptive Injectables

One injection of Depo-Provera®—hormonal birth control method that contains a progestin, a synthetic version of the natural hormone progesterone—provides three months of contraceptive protection. This long-acting hormonal contraceptive raises levels of progesterone, thereby simulating pregnancy. The pituitary gland doesn't produce FSH and LH, which normally cause egg ripening and release. The endometrial lining of the uterus thins, preventing implantation of a fertilized egg.

**Advantages** The main advantage is that women do not need to take a daily pill. Because Depo-Provera® contains only progestin, it can be used by women who cannot take oral contraceptives containing estrogen (such as those who've had breast cancer). Depo-Provera® also may have some protective action against endometrial and ovarian cancer.

**Disadvantages** Injectable contraceptives provide no protection against HIV and other STIs. Depo-Provera® causes menstrual irregularities in most users, and in a small percentage of users, it causes a delayed return of fertility, excessive endometrial bleeding, and other side effects, including decreased libido, depression, headaches, dizziness, weight gain, frequent urination, and allergic reactions. Weight gain was another concern. The average weight gain

*Ortho-McNeil Pharmaceutical*

▲ The hormones in Evra® are slowly released when the patch is applied to the skin.

in the first year of use is approximately 2.26 kilograms (5 pounds).[27]

In June 2005, new safety information was released by Pfizer Canada, in consultation with Health Canada, stating that new clinical studies with premenopausal adult women (25–35 years of age) and with adolescent women (12–18 years of age) indicated that women who used Depo-Provera™ for conception control might lose significant bone-mineral density. These studies also showed that the longer the contraceptive was used, the more bone-mineral density was lost. Of special concern was the finding that bone-mineral density might not return completely once the use of Depo-Provera® had been discontinued and that cases of osteoporosis and fracture were associated with the use of the product.[28]

## Intrauterine Device

The **intrauterine device (IUD)** is a small T-shaped device with a nylon string attached that is inserted into the uterus through the cervix. It prevents pregnancy by interfering with implantation. Once widely used, IUDs became less popular after most brands were removed from the market because of serious complications such as pelvic infection and infertility. The currently available IUDs have not been shown to increase the risk of such problems for women in mutually monogamous relationships (see Figure 8-3).

The IUD is effective and cost-efficient for preventing pregnancy, although some women may expel the device. The IUD does not offer protection against STIs.

In Canada, there are two types of IUDs available, the Nova-T and the Mirena®.[29] The Nova-T is a polyethylene T-shaped frame with a coil of copper wire on the outside. A thin string attached to the IUD hangs down through the cervix into the top of the vagina to allow you to check to see that it is in place. Copper acts as an effective spermicide

to destroy sperm. It is suggested that women change this IUD after 30 months, but the effective lifespan is five years.[30] It fails in only one out of 100 users per year.[31]

The newest IUD, the Mirena® intrauterine system, launched in Canada in 2001,[32] also consists of a polyethylene T-shaped device, but it is surrounded by a sleeve containing the progestin levonorgestrel, which is released directly to the lining of the uterus. Mirena® contains no estrogen and is 99 percent effective in preventing pregnancy for up to five years.[33]

**Advantages**   The advantages of IUDs are many—they are safe, highly effective, estrogen-free, rapidly reversible, convenient, and practical and have a long duration of use.[34] The IUD should not alter the timing of a woman's period, and women who use an IUD have a lower rate of ectopic pregnancy than women who do not use any birth control.[35] The hormonal IUD Mirena® decreases the amount of menstrual bleeding and may decrease menstrual cramping.[36]

IUDs were long believed to increase the risk of pelvic inflammatory disease, which can lead to scarring and infertility. More recent research has shown that although IUD users are more likely to develop PID than nonusers, it is an uncommon complication. The greatest risk of PID occurs during the first two weeks following insertion; it falls at about 20 days.[37]

**Disadvantages**   Many gynaecologists recommend other forms of birth control for childless women who someday may want to start a family. Women who have never given birth and have used an IUD for an extended period of time may find it more difficult to conceive after discontinuing its use.[38] In addition, women with many sexual partners, who are at highest risk of PID, are not good candidates for this method.[39] Some women are allergic to copper or have adverse effects from hormones.

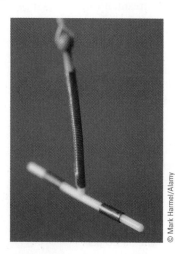

▲ **Figure 8-3** Intrauterine Device (IUD)
The IUD is placed in the uterus.

Source: Hespenheide Design.

▲ Copper T

© Mark Harmel/Alamy

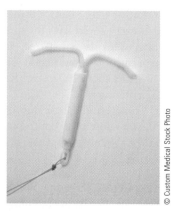

▲ IUD Mirena®

© Custom Medical Stock Photo

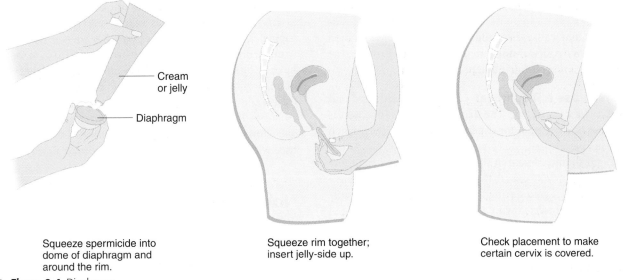

Cream
or jelly

Diaphragm

Squeeze spermicide into
dome of diaphragm and
around the rim.

Squeeze rim together;
insert jelly-side up.

Check placement to make
certain cervix is covered.

▲ **Figure 8-4** Diaphragm
When used correctly and consistently and with a spermicide, the diaphragm is effective in preventing pregnancy and STIs. It must be fitted by a health-care professional.

Source: Hespenheide Design.

During insertion of an IUD, women may experience discomfort, cramping, bleeding, or pain, which may continue for a few days or longer. Women using the Nova-T IUD may find that their periods are heavier and that they experience more menstrual cramping, while users of the Mirena IUD often find that their periods become quite light and sometimes disappear entirely. For either type, an estimated 5 to 10 percent of users expel an IUD within a year of insertion.

If a woman using an IUD does become pregnant, the IUD is removed to reduce the risk of miscarriage (which can be as high as 50 percent).

**How to Use an IUD**   A physician inserts an IUD into a woman's uterus through the cervix and trims the IUD strings so that they can be felt at the entrance to the cervix. An IUD can be inserted during a woman's period or at other times in her menstrual cycle. An IUD can be removed by a doctor at any point if a woman no longer wants to use it. The strings should be checked regularly, particularly after each menstrual cycle, since IUDs can be expelled. Antibiotics may be prescribed to lower any risk of infection.

## Diaphragm

The **diaphragm** is a bowl-like rubber cup with a flexible rim that is inserted into the vagina to cover the cervix and prevent the passage of sperm into the uterus during sexual intercourse (see Figure 8-4). When used with a spermicide, the diaphragm is both a physical and a chemical barrier to

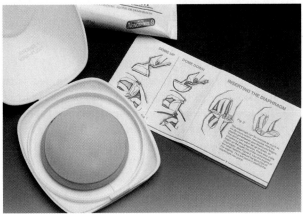

sperm. The effectiveness of the diaphragm in preventing pregnancy depends on strong motivation to use it faithfully and a precise understanding of its use. If diaphragms with spermicide are used consistently and carefully, they can be 92–96 percent effective.[40] Without a spermicide, the diaphragm is not effective. However, the spermicide nonoxynol-9, while effective as a microbicide, has been questioned lately and recent data indicate that it may actually increase the risk of STI and HIV transmission.[41]

**Advantages**   Diaphragms have become increasingly popular, most likely because of concern about the side effects of hormonal contraceptives. It offers women privacy and control because they can insert it before sex.

**Disadvantages**   Some people find that the diaphragm is inconvenient and interferes with sexual spontaneity. The spermicidal cream or jelly is messy, detracts from oral-genital sex, and can cause irritation. A poorly fitted diaphragm may cause discomfort during sex; some women report bladder discomfort, urethral irritation, or recurrent cystitis as a result of diaphragm use.

**How to Use a Diaphragm**  Diaphragms are fitted and prescribed by a doctor. The diaphragm's main function is to serve as a container for a spermicidal foam or jelly, which is available at pharmacies without a prescription. A diaphragm should remain in the vagina for at least six hours after intercourse to ensure that all sperm are killed. If intercourse occurs again during this period, additional spermicide must be inserted with an applicator tube.

A doctor should check the diaphragm's fit and condition every year when the woman has her annual Pap smear. It needs to be refitted if a woman loses or gains up to 4.5 kilograms (9 pounds 14 ounces) or after pregnancy.

The key to proper use of the diaphragm is having it available. A sexually active woman should keep it in the most accessible place—her purse, bedroom, or bathroom. Before every use, a diaphragm should be checked for tiny leaks (hold up to the light or place water in the dome). Oil-based lubricants will deteriorate the latex of the diaphragm and should not be used.

## Cervical Cap

Like the diaphragm, the **cervical cap**, combined with spermicide, serves as both a chemical and physical barrier blocking the path of the sperm to the uterus. The rubber or plastic cap is smaller and thicker than a diaphragm and resembles a large thimble that fits snugly around the cervix. It is about 87–90 percent effective, but the failure rate is higher in women who have already had a baby.[42]

**Advantages**  Women who cannot use a diaphragm because of pelvic-structure problems or loss of vaginal muscle tone can often use the cap. Also, the cervical cap is less messy and does not require additional applications of spermicide if intercourse occurs more than once within several hours.

**Disadvantages**  A cervical cap is more difficult to insert and remove than a diaphragm, and using it requires a woman to be comfortable with touching her vagina and cervix. Users of the cervical cap also need to plan ahead, since the cap must be inserted at least half an hour prior to intercourse. Some women find it uncomfortable to wear or cannot get the right fit, or their partners are able to feel the cervical cap during sex. The cervical cap does not protect against STIs, and an allergy to latex can prevent some women from using the cap.[43]

**How to Use a Cervical Cap**  Like the diaphragm, the cervical cap must be fitted by a doctor. For use, the woman fills it one-third to two-thirds full with spermicide and inserts it by holding its edges together and sliding it into the vagina. The cup is then pressed onto the cervix. (Most women find it easiest to do so while squatting or in an upright sitting position.) The cap can be inserted up to six hours prior to intercourse and should not be removed for at least six hours afterward. It can be left in place for up to 24 hours. Pulling on one side of the rim breaks the suction and allows easy removal. Oil-based lubricants should not be used with the cap because they can deteriorate the latex.

# Non-prescription Contraceptives

As their name implies, **barrier contraceptives** block the meeting of egg and sperm by means of a physical barrier (a condom, a diaphragm, or a cervical cap) or a chemical one (vaginal spermicide in jellies, foams, creams, suppositories, or film). Some of these forms of birth control are available without a prescription and have become increasingly popular because they can do more than prevent conception—they can also help reduce the risk of STIs.

## Male Condom

The male **condom** covers the erect penis and catches the ejaculate, thus preventing sperm from entering the woman's reproductive tract (see Figure 8-5). Most are made of thin surgical latex; an alternative type is made of polyurethane, which is thinner, stronger, and more heat-sensitive. Polyurethane condoms can also be safely used by individuals who are sensitive to latex.

Condoms are 86 to 97 percent effective.[44] The condom can be torn during the manufacturing process or during its use; testing by the manufacturer may not be as strenuous as it could or should be. Careless removal can also decrease the effectiveness of condoms. However, the major reason that condoms have such a low actual effectiveness rate is that couples don't use them each and every time they have sex.

Condoms are second only to the pill in popularity among college- and university-age adults. Condom use has increased in the last decade. Approximately one in five women ages 15 to 44 that use contraception rely on their partner's use of condoms as their primary method of birth control.[45]

However, there are reports that condom use decreases as teens get older, with fewer males ages 18 and 19 using condoms than those 15 to 17 years old. Teenage girls report less frequent use of condoms than males.[46] (See also The X & Y Files: "Sex, Lies, and Condom Use.") Research also shows that Canadian adolescents may be putting themselves at unnecessary risk of STIs by choosing oral contraceptives for the prevention of pregnancy while remaining at risk through unprotected sex.[47]

For girls, being from an intact family and having a mother with higher educational achievement are associated with greater condom use at first intercourse. Teens with more educated parents and teens that were older at first intercourse also had greater condom use. The less similar adolescents are to their partners—whether because of a difference in age, grade, or school—the less likely adolescents are to use condoms and other contraceptive methods.[48]

There are common misconceptions about condoms. Some people believe that there is no space at the tip of a condom or think that Vaseline® can be used with condoms; some say that lambskin protects against HIV better than latex. None of these is true.

**Advantages** Condoms made of latex or polyurethane can help reduce the risk of certain STIs, including syphilis, gonorrhea, chlamydia, and herpes. They appear to lower a woman's risk of pelvic inflammatory disease (PID) and may protect against some parasites that cause urinary tract and genital infections. Public health officials view condoms as the best available defence against HIV infection. They are available without a prescription or medical appointment, and their use does not cause harmful side effects. Some men appreciate the slight blunting of sensation they experience when using a condom because it helps prolong the duration of intercourse before ejaculation.

**Disadvantages** Condoms are not 100 percent effective in preventing pregnancy or STIs, including infection with HIV. For anyone, heterosexual or homosexual, not in a monogamous relationship with a mutually exclusive, healthy partner, condoms can reduce the risks of sexual involvement, but they cannot eliminate them. Condoms may have manufacturing defects, such as pin-size holes, or they may break or slip off during intercourse. Health Canada is also warning about the use of condoms with the spermicidal lubricant (nonoxynol-9). The best STI and HIV barrier is a latex condom without N-9.

The main objections to condoms include odour, lubrication (too much or too little), rips or breaks, access, disposal, feel, taste, and difficulty opening the packages. Some couples feel that putting on a condom interferes with sexual spontaneity; others incorporate it into their sex play. Some men dislike the reduced penile sensitivity or will not use

## The X & Y Files

## Sex, Lies, and Condom Use

In a series of focus groups with 92 sexually active, young, ethnically and racially diverse individuals, ages 15 to 20, researchers focused on their views and motivations for sex and for condom use. Most found it difficult to believe that people their age used condoms every single time they had sex. Although they acknowledged that everyone is at risk for sexually transmitted infections, the young people saw their own risk as minimal.

The genders had different motives both for engaging in sex and for using condoms. In the interviews, young women said they engaged in sexual relations because of a desire for physical intimacy and a committed relationship. They generally reported having sex only with men they cared for and deeply trusted and expected that these men would be honest and forthright about their sexual history. This trust played a significant role in their decision whether to insist on condom use.

In contrast, few of the young men said relationships were an important dimension of their sexual involvements. Their primary motivation was a desire for physical and sexual satisfaction. Most said they were not interested in commitment and viewed emotional expectations as a complication of becoming sexually involved with a woman. The young men also admitted to making judgments about women.

Which partner determined whether a couple would use a condom? In these interviews, the answer was the women—if they chose to do so. Regardless of race or ethnicity, many of the young women were adamant in demanding that their partners use condoms—and many young men said they would not challenge such a demand out of fear of losing the opportunity for sex. Men often expected potential partners to want to use condoms and described themselves as "suspicious" of women who did not.

The young people were most strongly motivated to use condoms when they did not know a potential sexual partner well or were at the earliest stages of sexual involvement with others. Nearly all said they solicited information about a potential partner's sexual history from this person or from friends. Rather than directly asking about the number of past partners, they more often relied on feelings and visual observations. Some admitted to lying when asked about their own sexual experience in order to avoid being seen as promiscuous. Once a couple had sex without a condom, both partners—but especially women—found it awkward to resume condom use because doing so would imply a lack of trust.

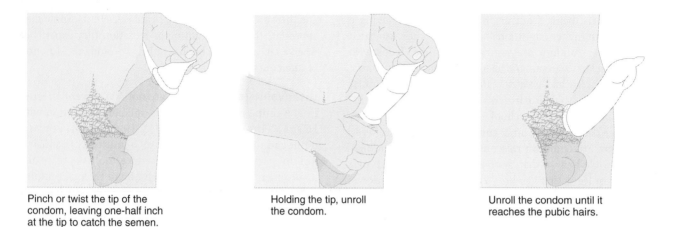

Pinch or twist the tip of the condom, leaving one-half inch at the tip to catch the semen.

Holding the tip, unroll the condom.

Unroll the condom until it reaches the pubic hairs.

▲ **Figure 8-5** Male Condom
Condoms effectively reduce the risk of pregnancy as well as STIs. Using them consistently and correctly are important factors.

Source: Hespenheide Design.

them because they believe they interfere with sexual pleasure. Others cannot sustain an erection while putting on a condom. A small number are allergic to latex condoms.

**How to Use a Condom**   Most physicians recommend prelubricated, latex, or polyurethane condoms, not membrane condoms ("natural" or "sheepskin"). Before using a condom, check the expiration date, and make sure it's soft and pliable. If it's yellow or sticky, throw it out. Don't check for leaks by blowing up a condom before using it; you may weaken or tear it.

The condom should be put on at the beginning of sexual activity, before genital contact occurs (see Figure 8-5). There should be a little space at the top of the condom to catch the semen. Any vaginal lubricant should be water-based. Petroleum-based creams or jellies (such as Vaseline®, baby oil, massage oil, vegetable oils, or oil-based hand lotions) can deteriorate the latex. After ejaculation, the condom should be held firmly against the penis so that it doesn't slip off or leak during withdrawal. Couples engaging in anal intercourse should use a water-based lubricant as well as a condom, but should never assume the condom will protect them from HIV infection or other STIs.

## Female Condom

The female condom, made of polyurethane, consists of two rings and a polyurethane sheath and is inserted into the vagina with a tampon-like applicator (see Figure 8-6). Once in place, the device loosely lines the walls of the vagina. Internally, a thickened rubber ring keeps it anchored near the cervix. Externally, another rubber ring, two inches in diameter, rests on the labia and resists slippage.[49]

Although not widely used in the West, the female condom is gaining acceptance in Africa, Asia, and Latin

## Strategies for Prevention

### Eight Steps of Correct Male Condom Use

▲ Check the expiry date on the condom before use. Use condoms that have not passed the expiry date.

▲ Use a new condom at each act of intercourse.

▲ Handle the condom carefully to avoid damage from fingernails, teeth, or other sharp objects.

▲ Put on condom after penis is erect and before any genital contact with a partner.

▲ Pinch the tip of the condom when putting it on to make sure no air is trapped in the tip.

▲ Ensure adequate lubrication during intercourse.

▲ Use only water-based lubricants with latex condoms.

▲ Withdraw the penis while it is still erect to prevent slippage. Hold the condom firmly against the base of the penis during withdrawal.

America. Properly used, it is believed to be as good as or better than the male condom for preventing infections, including HIV, because it is stronger and covers a slightly larger area.[50] However, it is slightly less effective at preventing pregnancy.

**Advantages**   The female condom gives women more control in reducing their risk of pregnancy and STIs. It does not require a prescription or medical appointment. One size fits all.

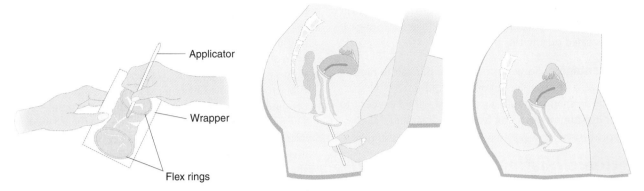

▲ **Figure 8-6** Female Condom
This device is less effective than the male condom for preventing pregnancy and STIs (since no spermicide is used). Like the male condom, this method does not require a prescription.

Source: Hespenheide Design.

© Joel Gordon Photography

**Disadvantages**   The failure rate for the female condom is higher than for other contraceptives. Twelve out of every 100 women using the device could expect to get pregnant during a six-month period. In clinical trials, the actual failure rate was even higher—20.6 percent. Women have complained that the condom is difficult to use.

**How to Use a Female Condom**   As illustrated in Figure 8-6, a woman removes the condom and applicator from the wrapper and inserts the condom slowly by gently pushing the applicator toward the small of the back. When properly inserted, the outer ring should rest on the folds of skin around the vaginal opening, and the inner ring (the closed end) should fit against the cervix. The condom should be used with a water-based lubricant.

## Vaginal Spermicide

The various forms of **vaginal spermicide** include chemical foams, creams, jellies, vaginal suppositories, and gels. Some creams and jellies are made for use with a diaphragm; others can be used alone. In general, failure rates for vaginal suppositories are as high as 10 to 25 percent.[51]

**Advantages**   Conscientious use of a spermicide together with another method of contraception, such as a condom, can provide safe and effective birth control and reduce the risk of some vaginal infections, pelvic inflammatory disease, and STIs. The side effects of vaginal spermicides are minimal. Again, remember Health Canada's caution about products that have in them the spermicide nonoxynol-9.

**Disadvantages**   Even though spermicides can be applied in less than a minute, couples may feel that they interfere with sexual spontaneity. Some people are irritated by the chemicals in spermicides, but often a change of brand solves this problem. Others find foam spermicides messy or feel they interfere with oral-genital contact.

**How to Use a Vaginal Spermicide**   The various types of spermicide come with instructions that should be followed carefully for maximum protection. Contraceptive vaginal suppositories take about 20 minutes to dissolve and cover the vaginal walls. Foam, inserted with an applicator, goes into place much more rapidly. You must apply additional spermicide before each additional intercourse. After sex, women should shower rather than bathe to prevent the spermicide from being rinsed out of the vagina, and they should not douche for at least six hours.

## Contraceptive Sponge

The soft, disposable polyurethane sponge containing spermicide is placed at the cervix.

**Advantages**   This barrier method provides 12-hour protection and it is not necessary to change the sponge if sex is repeated during this time.

**Disadvantages**   Some women find it difficult to remove the sponge, or forget to take it out, or are allergic to the spermicide. The sponge should also be used with a condom to ensure maximum protection from pregnancy and STIs.[52]

## Periodic Abstinence and Fertility Awareness Methods

Awareness of a woman's cyclic fertility can help in both conception and contraception. The different methods of birth control based on a woman's menstrual cycle are sometimes referred to as *natural family planning* or *fertility awareness methods*. They include the cervical-mucus method, the calendar method, and the basal-body-temperature method. New fertility monitors that use saliva for testing can improve the accuracy of these methods.[53]

**Advantages**   Birth-control methods based on the menstrual cycle involve no expense, no side effects, and no need for prescriptions or fittings. On the days when the couple can have intercourse, there is nothing to insert, swallow, or check. In addition, abstinence during fertile periods complies with the teachings of some religions.

**Disadvantages**   During times of possible fertility (usually eight or nine days a month), couples must abstain from vaginal intercourse or use some form of contraception. Conscientious planning and scheduling are essential. Women with irregular cycles may not be able to rely on the calendar method. Others may find the mucus or temperature methods difficult to use. Women must also make sure that their partner will cooperate with them. For all these reasons, this approach to birth control is less reliable than many others. In theory, the overall effectiveness rate for the various fertility awareness methods is 80 percent. In practice, of every 100 women using one of these methods for a year, 24 become pregnant. However, using a combination of the basal-body-temperature method and the cervical-mucus method may be 90 to 95 percent effective in preventing pregnancy (see Figure 8-7). It is important to note here that Figure 8-7 is based on a 28-day cycle. Many women have shorter or longer cycles; therefore, this visual representation of a menstrual cycle may not be accurate for all women.

### Cervical-Mucus Method

This method, also called the **ovulation method,** is based on the observation of changes in the consistency of the mucus in the vagina. In the first days after menstruation, the vagina feels dry because of a decline in hormone production,

indicating a safe period for unprotected intercourse. Within a few days, estrogen levels rise, and the mucus begins to thin out and becomes less cloudy: the fertile period begins. At peak estrogen levels, the mucus is smooth, stretchable, and slippery (like raw egg white) and very clear. Mucus with these characteristics is usually observed within 24 hours of ovulation and lasts one to two days, signalling maximum fertility. The mucus becomes sticky and cloudy again three days thereafter, and the second safe period begins. Most women using this method have to refrain from unprotected intercourse for about nine days of each 28-day menstrual cycle.

### Calendar Method

This approach, often called the **rhythm method,** involves counting the days after menstruation begins to calculate the estimated day of ovulation. The first day of menstruation is day one. A woman counts the number of days until the last day of her cycle, which is the day before menstrual flow begins. To determine the starting point of the period during which she should avoid unprotected intercourse, she subtracts 18 from the number of days in her shortest cycle. For instance, if her shortest cycle was 28 days, day 10 would be her first high-risk day. To calculate when she can again have unprotected intercourse, she subtracts 10 from the number of days in her longest cycle. If her longest cycle is 31 days, she could resume intercourse on day 21. Other forms of sexual activity can continue from day 10 to day 21. This method requires careful timing to avoid the possible meeting of a ripe egg and active sperm in the woman's fallopian tube.

### Basal-Body-Temperature Method

In this method the woman measures her **basal-body temperature,** the body temperature upon waking in the morning, using a specially calibrated rectal thermometer, which is more precise than an oral one. She records her temperature on a chart (see Figure 8-7). The basal-body temperature remains relatively constant from the beginning of the menstrual cycle to ovulation. After ovulation, however, the basal-body temperature rises by more than 1.75 degrees Celsius (approx 0.5 degrees Fahrenheit). The woman knows that her safe period has begun when her temperature has been elevated for three consecutive days. After 8 to 10 months, she should have a sense of her ovulatory pattern, in addition to knowing her daily readings.

 ## What Is Emergency Contraception?

**Emergency contraception (EC)** is the use of a method of contraception to prevent unintended pregnancy after unprotected intercourse or the failure of another form of

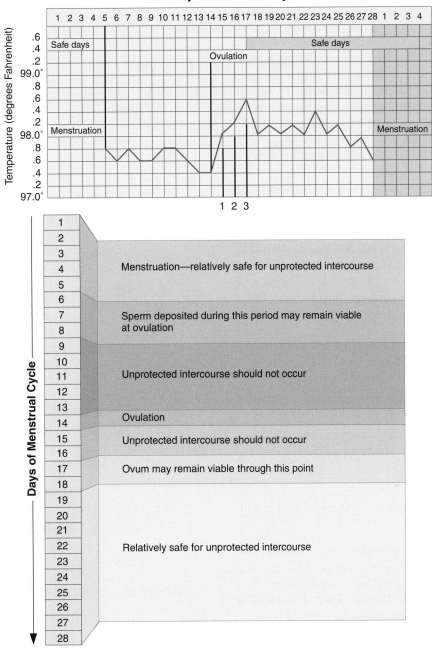

**Days of Menstrual Cycle**

▲ **Figure 8-7** Fertility Awareness Methods
These methods are based on a woman's menstrual cycle and involve charting basal-body temperature (top), careful calculation of the menstrual cycle (bottom), or careful observations of cervical mucus. Use of other contraceptive methods during fertile days or periods of abstinence are a necessary part of these methods. Figure is based on a 28-day cycle. Note that cycles can vary from 21 to 32 days.

Source: Hespenheide Design.

contraception, such as a condom breaking or slipping off. As briefly discussed in the "How Do I Choose a Birth Control Method?" section, emergency contraception is sometimes referred to as the morning-after pill. Medical researchers do not fully understand how ECPs work. They may inhibit or delay ovulation, prevent union of sperm and ovum, or alter the endometrium so a fertilized ovum cannot implant itself. The copper-bearing intrauterine device (IUD) is also an EC option.[54]

It is not necessary to wait until the morning after to take ECPs. A woman can start right away or up to five days after unprotected sex.[55] Therapy is more effective the earlier it is initiated. If taken within 24 hours of having unprotected sex, it can be 95 percent effective in preventing an unintended pregnancy. If taken within 72 hours, it is 85 percent effective; however, it will not have an impact if the pregnancy is already established. Most women can safely use them, even if they cannot use birth control pills as their regular method of birth control. (Although ECPs use the same hormones as birth control pills, not all brands of birth control pills can be used for emergency contraception.) Some women may experience spotting or a full menstrual period a few days after taking ECPs, depending on where they were in their cycle when they began therapy. Most women have their next period at the expected time.

As of April 2005, in Canada, ECP became available without a doctor's prescription. Plan B—Canada's only approved emergency contraceptive—is now available from a pharmacist.[56, 57]

Another alternative is the copper IUD, which can be inserted by a physician up to five days after ovulation to prevent pregnancy. IUDs are more effective at preventing pregnancy than hormonal ECPs and reduce the risk of pregnancy by 99 percent. However, they are not used as commonly as hormonal methods for EC.

## Sterilization

The most popular method of birth control among married couples is **sterilization** (surgery to end a person's reproductive capability).

**Advantages**    Sterilization has no effect on sex drive in either men or women. Many couples report that their sexual activity increases after sterilization because they're free from the fear of pregnancy or the need to deal with contraceptives.

**Disadvantages**    Sterilization should be considered permanent and should be used only if both individuals are sure they do not want any more children. Although sterilization doesn't usually create psychological or sexual problems, it can worsen existing problems, particularly marital ones.

## Male Sterilization

In men, the cutting of the vas deferens, the tube that carries sperm from one of the testes into the urethra for ejaculation, is called **vasectomy**. During the 15- to 20-minute office procedure, done under a local anesthetic, the doctor makes small incisions in the scrotum, lifts up each vas deferens, cuts them, and ties off the ends to block the flow of sperm (see Figure 8-8). Sperm continue to form, but they are broken down and absorbed by the body.

The man usually experiences some local pain, swelling, and discolouration for about a week after the procedure. More serious complications, including the formation of a

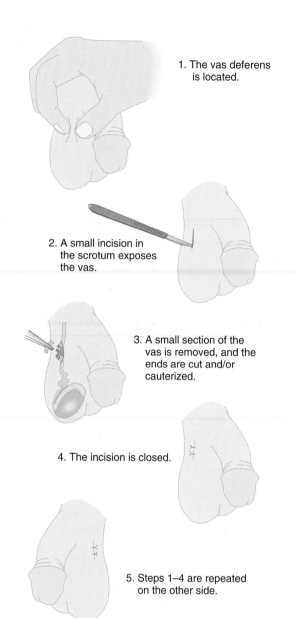

1. The vas deferens is located.

2. A small incision in the scrotum exposes the vas.

3. A small section of the vas is removed, and the ends are cut and/or cauterized.

4. The incision is closed.

5. Steps 1–4 are repeated on the other side.

▲ **Figure 8-8** Male Sterilization, or Vasectomy

Source: Hespenheide Design.

blood clot in the scrotum (which usually disappears without treatment), infection, and an inflammatory reaction, occur in a small percentage of cases. In a 15-year follow-up study of nearly 5000 men, researchers found that sterilization poses no increased danger of heart disease, even decades after the procedure. The pregnancy rate among the wives of men who've had vasectomies is about 15 in 10 000 women per year. Most result from a couple's failure to wait several weeks after the operation, until all sperm stored in each vas deferens have been ejaculated, before having unprotected sex.

Although anyone who chooses to have a vasectomy should consider it permanent, surgical reversal (*vasovasostomy*) is sometimes successful. New microsurgical techniques have led to annual pregnancy rates for the wives of men undergoing vasovasostomies of about 50 percent, depending on such factors as the doctor's expertise and the time elapsed since the vasectomy.

## Female Sterilization

Female sterilization procedures modify the fallopian tubes, which each month normally carry an egg from the ovaries to the uterus. These operations may soon surpass the pill as the first contraceptive choice among women. The two terms used to describe female sterilization are **tubal ligation** (the cutting or tying of the fallopian tubes) and **tubal occlusion** (the blocking of the tubes). The tubes may be cut or sealed with thread, a clamp, or a clip, or by coagulation (burning) to prevent the passage of eggs from the ovaries (see Figure 8-9). They can also be blocked with bands of silicone.

The procedures used for sterilization are laparotomy, laparoscopy, and colpotomy. **Laparotomy** involves making an abdominal incision about two inches long and cutting the tubes. A laparotomy usually requires a hospital stay and up to several weeks of recovery. It leaves a scar and carries the same risks as all major surgical procedures: the side effects of anaesthesia, potential infection, and internal scars. In a **minilaparotomy,** an incision about an inch long is made just above the pubic hairline. The tubes may be tied, cut, plugged, or sealed by electrical coagulation. The operation can be performed by a skilled physician in 10–30 minutes, usually under local anesthesia, and the woman can generally go home the same day. The failure (pregnancy) rate is only one in 1000.

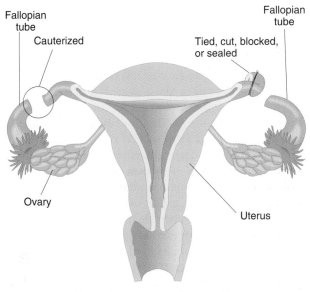

▲ **Figure 8-9** Female Sterilization, or Tubal Ligation

Source: Hespenheide Design.

Tubal ligation or occlusion can also be performed with the use of **laparoscopy,** commonly called *belly-button* or *band-aid surgery.* This procedure is done on an outpatient basis and takes 15–30 minutes. A lighted tube called a *laparoscope* is inserted through a half-inch incision made right below the navel, giving the doctor a view of the fallopian tubes. Using surgical instruments that may be inserted through the laparoscope or through other tiny incisions, the doctor then cuts or seals the tubes, most commonly by electrical coagulation. The possible complications are similar to those of minilaparotomy, as is the failure rate.

In a **colpotomy,** the fallopian tubes are reached through the vagina and cervix. This procedure leaves no external scar but is somewhat more hazardous and less effective. A **hysterectomy** (removal of the uterus) is a major surgical procedure that is too dangerous to be used as a method of sterilization, unless there are other medically urgent reasons for removing the uterus.

## Abortion

More than half of unintended pregnancies end in induced abortions. Abortion rates vary greatly around the world. In many nations with fewer unwanted pregnancies and lower abortion rates, contraceptives are generally easier and cheaper to obtain, and early sex education strongly emphasizes their importance.

Induced abortion rates in Canada have declined among women in every age group except women aged 35 to 39, where it has remained the same. A total of 96 815 abortions were performed on Canadian women in 2005. This was a 3.2 percent drop (100 039) from 2004.[58]

Induced abortions continue to be most common among young women in their twenties. On average, 28 women out of every 1000 aged 20 to 24 obtain an abortion. No woman in any country ever elects to be in a situation where she has to consider abortion. But if faced with an unwanted pregnancy, many women consider *elective abortion* as an option.

Women who have abortions do not fit neatly into any particular category. About 80 percent are unmarried. Most—70 percent—intend to have children, but not at this point in time. Many cannot afford a baby. Some feel unready for the responsibility; others fear that another child would jeopardize the happiness and security of their existing family.

## Thinking through the Options

A woman faced with an unwanted pregnancy can find it extremely difficult to decide what to do. There is the political debate over the right to life. There is also the practical and emotional matters, such as the quality of her relationship with the baby's father, their capacity to provide for the child, the impact on any children she already has, and other important life issues.

Giving up her child for adoption is an option for women who do not feel abortion is right for them. Advocates of adoption reform are pressing for mandatory counselling for all pregnant women considering abortion and for extending the period of time during which a new mother can change her mind about giving up her child for adoption.

In deciding whether or not to have an abortion, women report asking themselves many questions, including the following:

- ✔ How do I feel about the man with whom I conceived this baby? Do I love him? Does he love me? Is this man committed to staying with me?
- ✔ What sort of relationship, if any, have we had or might we have in the future?
- ✔ Who can help me gain perspective on this problem?
- ✔ Have I thought about adoption? Do I think I could surrender custody of my baby? Would it make a difference if the adoption process were open and I could know the adoptive parents?
- ✔ If I keep my child, can I properly care for him or her?
- ✔ How would the birth of another baby affect my other children?
- ✔ Do I have marketable skills, an education, an adequate income? Would I be able to go to school or keep my job if I have a child? Who would help me?
- ✔ Would this child be born with serious abnormalities? Would it suffer or thrive?
- ✔ How does each option fit with what I believe is morally correct? Could I emotionally handle each option?

Answering these questions honestly and objectively may help women as they think through the realities of their situation.

## Medical Abortion

The term **medical abortion** describes the use of drugs, also called *abortifacients*, to terminate a pregnancy. In 2000, the abortion pill mifepristone (Mifeprex®), formerly known as RU-486, became available. Mifepristone, which is 97 percent effective in inducing abortion, blocks progesterone, the hormone that prepares the uterine lining for pregnancy. Two days after taking this compound, a woman takes a prostaglandin pill to increase uterine contractions. The uterine lining is expelled along with the fertilized egg.[59] Women have compared the discomfort of this experience to severe menstrual cramps. Common side effects include excessive bleeding, nausea, fatigue, abdominal pain, and dizziness. About one woman in 100 requires a blood transfusion.

Other agents used in medical abortion are methotrexate, widely used to treat certain cancers and arthritis, and misoprostol (Cytotec®). Methotrexate interferes with the ability of cells to multiply and divide, which halts development of an embryo or placenta. Misoprostol causes the uterus to contract, which helps expel a fertilized egg. Although misoprostol has been used in combination with mifespristone, researchers are investigating whether it can be used alone to terminate pregnancy.[60]

Although condemned by right-to-life advocates, abortion medications may in time lower the public profile of pregnancy termination. They are not painless, cheap, or equally available to all, but they do offer women a chance to carry through on their personal choice in greater privacy and safety. In a recent study, women who had a medical abortion reported a significantly higher level of satisfaction than those undergoing a surgical abortion.[61]

Medical abortion does not require anesthesia, can be performed very early in pregnancy, and may feel more private. However, women experience more cramping and bleeding during medical abortion than during surgical abortion, and bleeding lasts for a longer period.

## Other Abortion Methods

More than half of all abortions (54 percent) are performed within the first eight weeks of pregnancy. Medically, first-trimester abortion is less risky than childbirth. However, the likelihood of complications increases when abortions are performed in the second trimester (the second three-month period) of pregnancy.[62]

The vast majority of abortions performed are surgical. **Suction curettage,** usually done from 6 to 14 weeks after the last menstrual period, involves the gradual dilation (opening) of the cervix, by inserting and removing a dilator (tapered rods of increasing diameter) into the cervix. Some women feel pressure or cramping at this time. Once the cervix has dilated, the physician inserts a suction tip into the cervix, and the uterine contents are drawn out via a vacuum system (see Figure 8-10). A *curette* (a spoon-shaped surgical instrument used for scraping) is used to check for complete removal of the contents of the uterus. This procedure is called *dilation and curettage* (D&C). With suction curettage, the risks of complication are low. Major complications, such as perforation of the uterus, occur in less than one in 100 cases.[63]

For early second-trimester abortions, physicians generally use a technique called **dilation and evacuation (D&E),** in which they open the cervix and use medical instruments to remove the fetus from the uterus. D&E procedures are performed under local or general anesthesia.

To induce abortion from week 15 to week 19, prostaglandins (natural substances found in most body tissues) are administered as vaginal suppositories or injected into the amniotic sac by inserting a needle through the

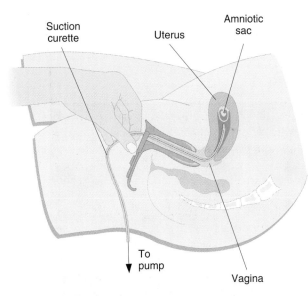

Suction curette    Uterus    Amniotic sac

To pump

Vagina

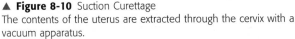

▲ **Figure 8-10** Suction Curettage
The contents of the uterus are extracted through the cervix with a vacuum apparatus.

Source: Hespenheide Design.

abdominal wall. They induce uterine contractions, and the fetus and placenta are expelled within 24 hours. Injecting saline or urea solutions into the amniotic sac can also terminate the pregnancy by triggering contractions that expel the fetus and placenta. Vaginal suppositories or drugs that help the uterus contract can also be used. Sometimes the physician will use suction as in first-trimester abortions, as well as forceps to remove additional fetal tissue. Complications from abortion techniques that induce labour include nausea, vomiting, diarrhea, tearing of the cervix, excessive bleeding, and possible shock and death.

**Hysterotomy** involves surgically opening the uterus and removing the fetus. This is generally done from week 16 to week 24 of the pregnancy, primarily in emergency situations when the woman's life is in danger or when other methods of abortion are considered too risky. However, late-pregnancy abortions increase the risk of spontaneous abortion or premature labour in subsequent pregnancies and should be avoided if possible.

 ## What Is the Psychological Impact of Abortion?

Many people assume that abortion must be psychologically devastating and that women who abort a fetus sooner or later develop what some have termed *post-abortion trauma syndrome.* In her studies, psychiatrist Nada Stotland found otherwise. The primary emotion of women who have just had an abortion, she discovered, is relief. Although many women also express feelings of sadness or guilt, their

anxiety levels eventually drop until they are lower than they were immediately before the abortion.[64]

The best predictor of psychological well-being after abortion is a woman's emotional well-being prior to pregnancy. At highest risk are women who have had a psychiatric illness, such as an anxiety disorder or clinical depression, prior to an abortion and those whose abortions occurred among complicated circumstances (such as a rape or coercion by parents or a partner). The vast majority of women manage to put the abortion into perspective as one of many life events.

## Politics of Abortion

Abortion is one of the most controversial political, religious, and ethical issues of our time. The issues of when life begins, a woman's right to choose, and an unborn child's right to survival are divisive.

Pressure to liberalize Canada's abortion law began in the 1960s and came from medical and legal associations and various women's and social justice groups such as the Humanist Fellowship of Montreal, headed at that time by Dr. Henry Morgentaler. In 1969, a law was passed in Canada to regulate abortion under the Criminal Code. Abortion would still be illegal, but women could apply for special permission from a therapeutic abortion committee (TAC). Ongoing problems resulted from this new law. Many hospitals did not set up TACs since they were not required to do so by law. Where abortions were available, the application process sometimes took six to eight weeks. Some hospitals imposed a quota system. A 1988 Supreme Court of Canada decision found this process unconstitutional. The 1969 law was rendered unenforceable and found to violate section seven of the Charter of Rights and Freedoms. Abortion was decriminalized.[65]

As of March 1998, women could obtain an abortion in all provinces and territories in Canada, except Prince Edward Island, where the government does not provide any abortion services whatsoever, although it will pay for hospital abortions in other provinces for women willing to travel. In British Columbia, Alberta, Ontario, Newfoundland, and most facilities in Quebec, hospital fees or clinic fees are paid by the province. In the remaining provinces and territories, only abortions performed in hospitals are funded; abortion clinics require private payment. First Nations women have the highest rates of abortion in Canada, but many of them must often travel to access abortion services.

The debate over abortion continues to stir passionate emotions, with pro-life supporters arguing that life begins at conception and that abortion is therefore immoral and pro-choice advocates countering that an individual woman should have the right to make decisions about her body and health. The controversy over abortion has at times become violent: physicians who performed abortions have been shot in British Columbia, Ontario, and Manitoba.

## Human Potential

# Dr. Henry Morgentaler—The Right to Choose

"Canada has a fascinating and unique history around abortion, because a single lone figure— one doctor—stands out as a great Canadian hero, a pioneer who forged the way in the struggle for safe, legal abortion on demand," says Joyce Arthur, in an article she wrote called "Abortion in Canada, History, Law and Access" (www. prochoiceactionnetwork-canada.org). That pioneer is Dr. Henry Morgentaler—someone who spent over 37 years fighting for the full rights of women to self-determination and reproductive freedom.

Dr. Morgentaler was born in Lodz, Poland, on March 19, 1923. He is a survivor of the Holocaust. After living through Auschwitz, he went to medical school in Germany on a United Nations scholarship that was offered to Jewish survivors. He began his medical practice in Montreal, where he worked as a general practitioner until 1969, when he gave up his family practice and began openly performing abortions, which at that time were illegal in Canada. Why would someone who had a successful medical practice decide to take such great risks? Why would someone defy the law of the land on behalf of women he did not know? In his address to the graduation class of June 2005 at the University of Western Ontario, Dr. Morgentaler suggests why:

> I am a survivor of the Nazi Holocaust, that orgy of cruelty and inhumanity of man to man. I have personally experienced suffering, oppression, and injustice inflicted by men beholden to a racist, dogmatic, and irrational ideology. To have had the opportunity to diminish suffering and injustice has been very important to me. Reproductive freedom and good access to medical abortion means that women will be able to give life to wanted babies at a time when they can provide love, care, and nurturing. Well-loved children grow into adults who do not build concentration camps; do not rape and do not murder. They are more likely to enjoy life, to love and care for each other and the larger society.

Abortion had been illegal in Canada since 1869. In 1967, Dr. Morgentaler lobbied the Canadian government to change the abortion law. As the president of the Humanist Fellowship in Montreal, he presented a brief to the House of Commons where he shared his belief that women had a basic right to abortion. Various women's groups and people interested in social justice

Dr. Henry Morgentaler, Holocaust survivor, Canadian medical doctor, humanist, and activist for the rights of women to reproductive freedom.

also joined in on the fight. The result was a liberalizing of the law in 1969. Abortion was still illegal, but women could apply for an abortion at hospitals where therapeutic abortion committees (TACs) were set up. Dr. Morgentaler did not support this new law. Some hospitals imposed abortion quotas. Members of the TACs were given the right to deny access to an abortion if they did not feel the woman's health was at risk. Access to abortions was especially difficult for poor women and those who lived outside major cities.

He then made a choice—one that would put his career, health, and family at risk. He began openly performing illegal abortions at his own clinic. In 1970 he was arrested in Quebec. In court, once again in 1973, he was acquitted by a jury, but the ruling was overturned and Morgentaler went to prison. Then there was an appeal, a heart attack in prison and another acquittal. Throughout his lifetime he would struggle with four jury trials, all ending in acquittals. He is the only Canadian in history who spent time in jail as a result of a decision by a higher court in spite of a jury acquittal. A result of his first trial is what is called the Morgentaler Amendment in the Criminal Code, which no longer allows a higher court to substitute a guilty verdict without a trial.

Finally, on January 28, 1988, the Supreme Court of Canada declared that the abortion law was unconstitutional. Since then, Dr. Morgentaler has opened abortion clinics in many provinces, although he still faced many challenges where some provincial governments were anti-choice. In 1992, he survived a bombing of his clinic in Toronto. At 82 years of age, he is still working on behalf of women and reproductive choices. His focus has switched to abortion clinic funding. He is personally suing the government of New Brunswick, which refuses to fund abortions at his clinic in Fredericton. He is also involved in a class-action suit against the Quebec government, which also refuses to fund clinic abortions.

On June 16, 2005, he received an Honourary Doctor of Laws degree from the University of Western Ontario. Also in 2005, CTV produced a movie documenting Dr. Morgentaler's life and practice. On October 10, 2008, in the Citadel in Quebec City, he was bestowed the Order of Canada. Controversy over abortion rights continues in Canada as a handful of protestors gathered at the event and some past Order of Canada recipients returned their insignia because of Dr. Morgentaler's award.

The right to choose is what Dr. Morgentaler has worked for his entire life. His concluding remarks at the graduation ceremony at the University of Western Ontario are an example of his determination, commitment, and compassion for others:

> By fighting for reproductive freedom and making it possible, I have made a contribution to a safer and more caring society where people have a great opportunity to realize their potential. Having known myself the depth of human depravity and cruelty, I have done what I could to build a society where hate would be replaced by love; cruelty with kindness and irrationality with reason.

Courage is part of reaching our human potential. Dr. Morgentaler lives his values. His life is an example of someone who made a difference. To find out more about Dr. Morgentaler's work, go to www.morgentaler.ca.

## Pro-Life

**Pro-life** is a term that is used to refer to the opposition to abortion and support of fetal rights. This term is based on the political and ethical understanding that fetuses and embryos are human beings. Some pro-life supporters believe that human life should be valued either from the moment of conception or implantation until one's natural death. Individuals working on behalf of the pro-life movement are committed to restoring legal protection to embryos and fetuses. Certain forms of birth control, such as birth control pills or the emergency conception pill (EPC), are often opposed to as well.[66]

Many college and university students on campuses across Canada support the pro-life viewpoint. There are right-to-life groups such as the National Campus Life Network[67] and clubs that host debates, run educational booths, and provide educational pro-life materials to students. There is also a movement by some students to encourage health centres to refer students to crisis pregnancy centres instead of abortion facilities.

Pro-life students are challenging those working in academe to be fair and accurate when lecturing on pro-life issues. Planned Parenthood groups on college and university campuses support students who do not choose abortion as a way to deal with an unexpected pregnancy. What is important to remember about the pro-choice/pro-life debate is that every individual has certain values and beliefs. Honouring and celebrating "differences" is important when it comes to making healthy lifestyle choices.

## Pregnancy

In the last half century, pregnancy rates have generally declined, although the absolute number of births has risen. The average age of mothers has risen, but about 70 percent of babies are still born to women in their twenties. Mothers are now averaging slightly fewer than two children each. Not every married couple is opting for parenthood.

Of course, you don't have to be part of a couple to want or to conceive a child. The number of never-married, college and university-educated, career women who are becoming single parents has risen dramatically. They want children—with or without an ongoing relationship with a man—and may feel that, because of their age, they can't delay getting pregnant any longer.

### Preconception Care: A Preventive Approach

The time *before* a child is conceived can be crucial in ensuring that an infant is born healthy, full-size, and full-term. Women who smoke, drink alcohol, take drugs, eat poorly, are too thin or too heavy, suffer from unrecognized infections or illnesses, or are exposed to toxins at work or home may start pregnancy with one or more strikes against them and their unborn babies. **Preconception care**—the enhancement of a woman's health and well-being prior to conception in order to ensure a healthy pregnancy and baby—includes risk assessment (evaluation of medical, genetic, and lifestyle risks), health promotion (such as good nutrition), and interventions to reduce risk (such as treatment of infections and other diseases and assistance in quitting smoking or drug use).

## How a Woman's Body Changes During Pregnancy

The 40 weeks of pregnancy transform a woman's body. At the beginning of pregnancy, the woman's uterus becomes slightly larger, and the cervix becomes softer and bluish due to increased blood flow. Progesterone and estrogen trigger changes in the milk glands and ducts in the breasts, which increase in size and feel somewhat tender. The pressure of the growing uterus against the bladder causes a more frequent need to urinate. As the pregnancy progresses, the woman's skin stretches as her body shape changes, her centre of gravity changes as her abdomen protrudes, and her internal organs shift as the baby grows (see Figure 8-11). Pregnancy is typically divided into three-month periods called trimesters.

## How a Baby Grows

Silently and invisibly, over a nine-month period, a fertilized egg develops into a human being. When the zygote reaches the uterus, it's still smaller than the head of a pin. Once nestled into the spongy uterine lining, it becomes an **embryo.** The embryo takes on an elongated shape, rounded at one end. A sac called the **amnion** envelops it (see photo). As water and other small molecules cross the amniotic membrane, the embryo floats freely in the absorbed fluid, cushioned from shocks and bumps. At nine weeks the embryo is called a **fetus.**

A special organ, the **placenta,** forms. Attached to the embryo by the umbilical cord, it supplies the growing baby with fluid and nutrients from the maternal bloodstream and carries waste back to the mother's body for disposal.

## Emotional Aspects of Pregnancy

Almost all prospective parents worry about their ability to care for a newborn. By talking openly about their feelings and fears, however, they can strengthen the bonds between them, so that they can work together as parents as well as partners. Psychological problems, such as depression, can occur during pregnancy. Social support and other resources for coping with stress can make a great difference in the potential impact of emotional difficulties.

The physiological changes of pregnancy can affect a woman's mood. In early pregnancy, she may feel weepy,

irritable, or emotional. As the pregnancy continues, she may become calmer and more energetic. Men, too, feel a range of intense emotions about the prospect of having a child: pride, anxiety, hope, fears for their unseen child and for the woman they love. The more involved fathers become in preparing for birth, the closer they feel to their partners and babies afterward.

## Complications of Pregnancy

In about 10 to 15 percent of all pregnancies, there is increased risk of some problem, such as a baby's failure to grow normally. **Perinatology,** or maternal-fetal medicine, focuses on the special needs of high-risk mothers and their unborn babies. Several of the most frequent potential complications of pregnancy are discussed following.

### Ectopic Pregnancy

In an **ectopic pregnancy,** the fertilized egg remains in the fallopian tube instead of travelling to the uterus. Ectopic, or tubal, pregnancies have increased dramatically in recent years. STIs, particularly chlamydia infections, have become a major cause of ectopic pregnancy. Other risk factors include previous pelvic surgery, particularly involving the fallopian tubes; pelvic inflammatory disease; infertility; and use of an IUD.

### Miscarriage

About 10 to 20 percent of pregnancies end in **miscarriage,** or spontaneous abortion, before the twentieth week of gestation. Major genetic disorders may be responsible for 33 to 50 percent of pregnancy losses. The most common cause is an abnormal number of chromosomes.[68] About 0.5 to 1 percent of women suffer three or more miscarriages, possibly because of genetic, anatomic, hormonal, infectious, or autoimmune factors.[69] An estimated 70 to 90 percent of women who miscarry eventually become pregnant again.

### Infections

The infectious disease most clearly linked to birth defects is **rubella** (German measles). All women should be vaccinated against this disease at least three months prior to conception to protect themselves and any children they may bear. The most common prenatal infection today is *cytomegalovirus.* This infection produces mild flu-like symptoms in adults but can cause brain damage, retardation, liver disease, cerebral palsy, hearing problems, and other malformations in unborn babies.

STIs, such as syphilis, gonorrhea, and genital herpes, can be particularly dangerous during pregnancy if not

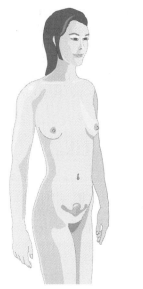
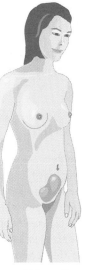

Before conception        At 4 months

### First Trimester

Increased urination because of hormonal changes and the pressure of the enlarging uterus on the bladder.

Enlarged breasts as milk glands develop.

Darkening of the nipples and the area around them.

Nausea or vomiting, particularly in the morning.

Fatigue.

Increased vaginal secretions.

Pinching of the sciatic nerve, which runs from the buttocks down through the back of the legs, as the pelvic bones widen and begin to separate.

Irregular bowel movements.

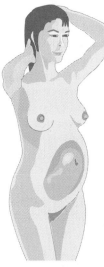

### Second Trimester

Thickening of the waist as the uterus grows.

Weight gain.

Increase in total blood volume.

Slight increase in size and change in position of the heart.

Darkening of the pigment around the nipple and from the navel to the pubic region.

Darkening of the face.

Increased salivation and perspiration.

Secretion of colostrum from the breasts.

Indigestion, constipation, and hemorrhoids.

Varicose veins.

At 7 months

At 9 months

### Third Trimester

Increased urination because of pressure from the uterus.

Tightening of the uterine muscles (called Braxton-Hicks contractions).

Shortness of breath because of increased pressure by the uterus on the lungs and diaphragm.

Heartburn and indigestion.

Trouble sleeping because of the baby's movements or the need to urinate.

Descending ("dropping") of the baby's head into the pelvis about two to four weeks before birth.

Navel pushed out.

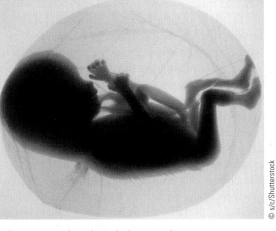

© s/c/Shutterstock

▲ **Figure 8-11** Physiological Changes of Pregnancy

Source: Hespenheide Design.

recognized and treated. If a woman has a herpes outbreak around the date her baby is due, her physician will deliver the baby by caesarean section to prevent infecting the baby. HIV infection endangers both a pregnant woman and her unborn baby, and all pregnant women and new mothers should be aware of the risks to themselves and their babies.

## Premature Labour

Approximately 10 percent of all babies are born too soon (before the 37th week of pregnancy). According to researchers, prematurity is the main underlying cause of stillbirth and infant deaths within the first few weeks after birth. Bed rest, close monitoring, and, if necessary, medications for at-risk women can buy more time in the womb for their babies. But women must recognize the warning signs of **premature labour**—dull, low backache; a feeling of tightness or pressure on the lower abdomen; and intestinal cramps, sometimes with diarrhea. Low-birthweight premature babies face the highest risks.

# Childbirth

Today parents can choose from an array of birthing options that include hospital births attended by a physician and possibly a midwife, to home births.

When interviewing physicians or midwives, look for the following:

- ✔ Experience in handling various complications
- ✔ Extensive prenatal care
- ✔ A commitment to be at the mother's side for the entire labour in order to quickly spot complications and provide assistance
- ✔ A compatible philosophy toward childbirth and medical interventions

## Preparing for Childbirth

The most widespread method of childbirth preparation is **psychoprophylaxis,** or the **Lamaze method.** Fernand Lamaze, a French doctor, instructed women to respond to labour contractions with pre-learned, controlled breathing techniques. As the intensity of each contraction increases, the labouring woman concentrates on increasing her breathing rate in a prescribed way. Her partner coaches her during each contraction and helps her cope with discomfort.

Women who have had childbirth-preparation training tend to have fewer complications and require fewer medications. However, painkillers or anesthesia are always an option if labour is longer or more painful than expected. The lower body can be numbed with an **epidural block,** which involves injecting an anesthetic into the membrane around the spinal cord, or a **spinal block,** in which the injection goes directly into the spinal canal. General anesthesia is usually used only for emergency caesarean births.

## ???? What Is Childbirth Like?

There are three stages of **labour.** The first starts with *effacement* (thinning) and *dilation* (opening up) of the cervix. Effacement is measured in percentages and dilation in centimetres or finger-widths. Around this time, the amniotic sac of fluids usually breaks, a sign that the woman should call her doctor or midwife.

The first contractions of the early, or *latent,* phase of labour are usually not uncomfortable; they last 15–30 seconds, occur every 15–30 minutes, and gradually increase in intensity and frequency. The most difficult contractions come after the cervix is dilated to about 8 centimetres, as the woman feels greater pressure from the fetus. The first stage ends when the cervix is completely dilated to a diameter of 10 centimetres (or five finger-widths) and the baby is ready to come down the birth canal (see Figure 8-12). For women having their first baby, this first stage of labour averages 12–13 hours. Women having another child often experience shorter first-stage labour.

When the cervix is completely dilated, the second stage of labour occurs, during which the baby moves into the vagina, or birth canal, and out of the mother's body. As this stage begins, women who have gone through childbirth-preparation training often feel a sense of relief from the acute pain of the transition phase and at the prospect of giving birth.

This second stage can take up to an hour or more. Strong contractions may last 60–90 seconds and occur every two to three minutes. As the baby's head descends, the mother feels an urge to push. By bearing down, she helps the baby complete its passage to the outside.

As the baby's head appears, or *crowns,* the doctor may perform an *episiotomy*—an incision from the lower end of the vagina toward the anus to enlarge the vaginal opening. The purpose of the episiotomy is to prevent the baby's head from causing an irregular tear in the vagina, but routine episiotomies have been criticized as unnecessary. Women may be able to avoid this procedure by trying different birthing positions or having an attendant massage the perineal tissue.

Usually the baby's head emerges first, then its shoulders, then its body. With each contraction, a new part is born. However, the baby can be in a more difficult position, facing up rather than down, or with the feet or buttocks first (a **breech birth**), and a caesarean birth may then be necessary.

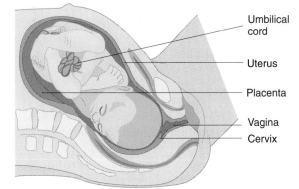

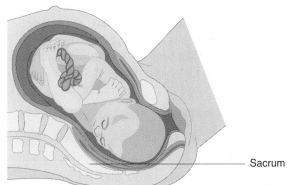

Umbilical
cord

Uterus

Placenta

Vagina

Cervix

Sacrum

1. The cervix is partially dilated, and the
   baby's head has entered the birth canal.

2. The cervix is nearly completely dilated. The baby's head
   rotates so that it can move through the birth canal.

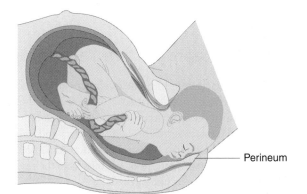

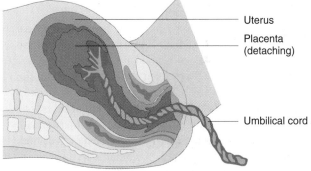

Perineum

Uterus

Placenta
(detaching)

Umbilical cord

3. The baby's head extends as it reaches
   the vaginal opening, and the head and the rest
   of the body pass through the birth canal.

4. After the baby is born, the placenta detaches from
   the uterus and is expelled from the woman's body.

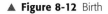

▲ **Figure 8-12** Birth

Source: Hespenheide Design.

In the third stage of labour, the uterus contracts firmly after the birth of the baby and, usually within five minutes, the placenta separates from the uterine wall. The woman may bear down to help expel the placenta, or the doctor may exert gentle external pressure. If an episiotomy has been performed, the doctor sews up the incision. To help the uterus contract and return to its normal size, it may be massaged manually, or the baby may be put to the mother's breast to stimulate contraction of the uterus.

## Caesarean Birth

In a **caesarean delivery** (also referred to as a *caesarean section*), the doctor lifts the baby out of the woman's body through an incision made in the lower abdomen and uterus. The most common reason for caesarean birth is *failure to progress,* a vague term indicating that labour has gone on too long and may put the baby or mother at risk. Other reasons include the baby's position (if

feet or buttocks are first) and signs that the fetus is in danger.

About 36 percent of caesarean sections are performed because the woman has had a previous caesarean birth. However, four of every five women who have had caesarean births *can* have successful vaginal deliveries in subsequent pregnancies.

Caesarean birth involves abdominal surgery, so many women feel more physical discomfort after a caesarean than a vaginal birth, including nausea, pain, and abdominal gas. Women who have had a caesarean section must refrain from strenuous activity, such as heavy lifting, for several weeks.

## After the Birth

Hospital stays for new mothers are shorter than in the past. In some provinces, the average length of stay is now one day after vaginal delivery and four days after a caesarean birth. A primary reason has been the pressure to reduce medical costs. Obstetricians have voiced concern that the rush to release new mothers may jeopardize their well-being and the health of their babies, who are more likely to require emergency care for problems such as jaundice.

# Infertility

The World Health Organization defines **infertility** as the failure to conceive after one year of unprotected intercourse. Western societies regard infertility as a medical rather than social problem. The main causes of infertility are ovulation problems, tubal damage, or sperm dysfunction. Less common causes are endometriosis, cervical factors, or coital difficulties. Even after intensive investigation, 10 to 20 percent of couples have unexplained infertility in which no cause can be demonstrated.

The percentage of women seeking infertility services has risen in the past decade. It is estimated that up to one in eight or 12.5 percent of Canadian couples experiences infertility.[70] Infertility is a problem of the couple, not of the individual man or woman. A thorough diagnostic workup can reveal a cause for infertility in 90 percent of cases.

In women, the most common causes of infertility are age, abnormal menstrual patterns, suppression of ovulation, and blocked fallopian tubes. A woman's fertility peaks between ages 20 and 30 and then drops quickly: by 20 percent after 30, by 50 percent after 35, and by 95 percent after 40.

Male infertility is usually linked to either the quantity or the quality of sperm, which may be inactive, misshapen, or insufficient (less than 20 million sperm per millilitre of semen in an ejaculation of 3 to 5 millilitres). Sometimes the problem is hormonal or a blockage of a sperm duct. Some men suffer from the inability to ejaculate normally or from retrograde ejaculation, in which some of the semen travels in the wrong direction, back into the body of the male.

Infertility can have an enormous emotional impact. For some women the ability to become pregnant touches on a core aspect of femininity. Some feel a great loss if they cannot conceive. Women in their thirties and forties fear that their biological clock is running out of time. Men may be confused and surprised by the intensity of their partner's emotions.

The treatment of infertility has become a multibillion-dollar-a-year enterprise. The odds of achieving a successful pregnancy range from 30 to 70 percent, depending on the specific cause of infertility.[71] One result of successful infertility treatments has been a boom in multiple births, including quintuplets and sextuplets. Some obstetricians have urged less aggressive treatment for infertility to avoid such high-risk multiple births.

## Artificial Insemination

**Artificial insemination** is the introduction of viable sperm into the vagina by artificial means. There are variations of artificial insemination. One is intrauterine insemination (IUI), which usually includes ovarian stimulation and preparation of the semen. Another variation is donor insemination (DI). Sperm from a donor is used to achieve pregnancy when the husband or partner has few or no sperm, sperm of poor quality, or might risk passing on an inherited disease.[72]

## Assisted Reproductive Technology

New approaches to infertility include microsurgery, sometimes with lasers, to open destroyed or blocked egg and sperm ducts; new hormone preparations to induce ovulation; and the use of balloons, inserted through the cervix and inflated, to open blocked fallopian tubes (a procedure called *balloon tuboplasty*). Less than 1 percent of live births are the result of artificial reproductive technology (ART).[73]

Among the most well-known techniques to overcome fertility problems is *in vitro fertilization (IVF),* which involves removing ova from a woman's ovary and placing the woman's egg and her mate's sperm in a laboratory dish for fertilization. If the fertilized egg cell shows signs of development, within several days it is returned to the woman's uterus, the egg cell implants itself in the lining of the uterus, and the pregnancy continues as normal. The success rate varies but is generally less than 20 percent, and the costs are high.

In Canada, there is much debate about assisted human reproduction; however, in March 2004, the Assisted Human Reproduction Act received Royal Assent and became law. This Act ensures that Canada has one of the most comprehensive legislative frameworks in the world. It prohibits human cloning while protecting the health and safety of Canadians who use AHR. An Assisted Human Reproduction Agency of Canada will be responsible for licensing, inspecting, and enforcing activities controlled under this Act.[74]

1. Conception occurs
   a. when a fertilized egg implants in the lining of the uterus.
   b. when sperm is blocked from reaching the egg.
   c. when a sperm fertilizes the egg.
   d. after the uterine lining is discharged during the menstrual cycle.

2. Factors to consider when choosing a contraceptive method include all of the following *except*
   a. cost.
   b. failure rate.
   c. effectiveness in preventing sexually transmitted infections.
   d. preferred sexual position.

3. When used correctly, which is the most effective nonhormonal contraceptive method?
   a. Nova-T Intrauterine Device (IUD)
   b. condom
   c. spermicide
   d. diaphragm

4. Which of the following contraceptive choices offers the best protection against STIs?
   a. condom
   b. IUD
   c. abstinence
   d. withdrawal

5. Which statement about prescription contraceptives is *false*?
   a. Prescription contraceptives do not offer protection against STIs.
   b. Some prescription contraceptives contain estrogen and progestin, and some contain only progestin.
   c. The contraceptive ring must be changed every week.
   d. IUDs prevent pregnancy by preventing or interfering with implantation.

6. Which of the following statements is true about sterilization?
   a. In women, the most frequently performed sterilization technique is hysterectomy.
   b. Many couples experience an increase in sexual encounters after sterilization.
   c. Vasectomies are easily reversed with surgery.
   d. Sterilization is recommended for single men and women who are unsure about whether they want children.

7. In many nations with fewer unwanted pregnancies and lower abortion rates,
   a. the population of women older than 30 is high.
   b. the majority of women are affluent.
   c. the majority of women are poor.
   d. birth control education begins early and contraceptives are generally easier and cheaper to obtain.

8. In the third trimester of pregnancy,
   a. the woman experiences shortness of breath as the enlarged uterus presses on the lungs and diaphragm.
   b. the embryo is now called a fetus.
   c. the woman should begin regular prenatal checkups.
   d. the woman should increase her activity level to ensure that she is fit for childbirth.

9. During childbirth,
   a. breech birth can be prevented by practising the Lamaze method.
   b. the cervix thins and dilates so that the baby can exit the uterus.
   c. the intensity of contractions decreases during the second stage of labour.
   d. the placenta is expelled immediately before the baby's head appears.

10. Which of the following statements is true about infertility?
    a. Infertility is most often caused by female problems.
    b. In men, infertility is usually caused by a combination of excess sperm production and an ejaculation problem.
    c. In vitro fertilization involves introducing sperm into the vagina with a long needle.
    d. Less than 1 percent of live births are the result of artificial reproductive technology.

Answers to these questions can be found on page 450.

## Self Responsibility

*Knowing is not enough; we must apply. Willing is not enough; we must do.*

**Goethe**

When we have reproductive choices, we also have the responsibility to contemplate and prepare for those choices. Self-responsibility becomes responsibility between two people. On the Stages of Change model continuum, where are you? Are you prepared for both the joys of positive sexual relations as well as the inherent risks of having sex? If you are not ready to

## Social Responsibility

*Making the decision to have a child is momentous. It is to decide forever to have your heart go walking around outside your body.*

**Elizabeth Stone**

have sex with your partner, do you have an action plan in place so you are not pressured to do so? If you are not ready to have children, are you using birth control? Do you protect yourself and your partner against STIs? Planning and protecting yourself now can prevent many unnecessary problems in the future.

## Critical Thinking

1. After reading about the various methods of contraception, which do you think would be most effective for you? What factors enter into your decision (convenience, risks, effectiveness, etc.)?

2. As the debate over abortion continues, with pro-life supporters on one side and pro-choice advocates on the other, what is your opinion about a woman's right to make decisions about her own body? What about a man's right to participate in the decision-making process along with his partner if an unexpected pregnancy happened?

3. Suppose that you and your partner were told that your only chance of having a child is by using fertility drugs. After taking the drugs, you and your partner are informed that there are seven fetuses. Would you carry them all to term? What if you knew that the chances of them all surviving were very slim and that eliminating some of them would improve the odds for the others? What ethical issues do cases like these raise?

CENGAGENOW™

If your textbook package includes CengageNOW™, go to http://west.cengagenow.com/ilrn/ to link to CengageNOW ™ for Health, your online study tool. First take the **Pre-test** for this chapter to get your personalized **Study Plan,** which will identify topics you need to review and direct you to the appropriate resources. Then take the **Post-test** to determine what concepts you have mastered and what you still need work on.

## SITES & BYTES

### Canadian Federation for Sexual Health
www.cfsh.ca

This site features current health information pertaining to family planning, including emergency contraception, as well as pregnancy, sexually transmitted diseases, safer sex, and political action. A comprehensive publication—*Sexual Health in Canada Baseline 2007*—is available.

### National Campus Life Network
www.ncln.ca/index.php

This national student organization provides support for pro-life students on Canadian college and university campuses. Check out resources, articles and news, information on a national symposium, and training opportunities.

### Sexuality and U
www.sexualityandu.ca

This site has an excellent section on the different types of contraception.

Please note that links are subject to change. If you find a broken link, use a search engine such as www.google.ca and search for the website by typing in keywords.

### InfoTrac® College Edition Activity
Lesorogol, C.K. (2008). Setting themselves apart: Education, capabilities and sexuality among Samburu women in Kenya. (Report). *Anthropological Quarterly, 81*(3), 551–78.

1. What are three advantages and disadvantages of formal sexual health education for young women in Samburu, Kenya, Africa?
2. Discuss the ethics of providing a "Western sexual health education" curriculum for young women born and raised in Africa.
3. Describe one way young educated girls are challenging Samburu ideals with regard to female sexuality and marriage.

You can find additional readings related to contraception and reproduction with InfoTrac® College Edition, an online library of more than 5000 journals and publications. Follow the instructions for accessing InfoTrac® College Edition that were packaged with your textbook; then search for articles using a keyword search.

For additional links and resources, visit our text-specific website at www.health.nelson.com.

## Key Terms

The terms listed here are used within the chapter on the page indicated. Definitions of the terms are in the Glossary at the end of the book.

amnion 198
artificial insemination 202
barrier contraceptives 186
basal-body temperature 190
breech birth 200
caesarean delivery 201
cervical cap 186
coitus interruptus 180
colpotomy 193
conception 178
condom 186
constant-dose combination pill 181
contraception 178
diaphragm 185

dilation and evacuation (D&E) 194
ectopic pregnancy 198
embryo 198
emergency contraception (EC) 190
epidural block 200
failure rate 179
fertilization 178
fetus 198
hysterectomy 193
hysterotomy 195
implantation 178
infertility 202
intrauterine device (IUD) 184

labour 200
Lamaze method 200
laparoscopy 193
laparotomy 193
medical abortion 194
minilaparotomy 193
minipill 181
miscarriage 198
monophasic pill 181
multiphasic pill 181
oral contraceptives 181
ovulation method 190
perinatology 198
placenta 198
preconception care 197
premature labour 200

progestin-only pill 181
pro-life 197
psychoprophylaxis 200
rhythm method 190
rubella 198
spermatogenesis 178
spinal block 200
sterilization 192
suction curettage 194
tubal ligation 193
tubal occlusion 193
vaginal spermicide 189
vasectomy 192
zygote 178

# References

1. Canadian Federation for Sexual Health. (2008, July 29). Home. Available at www.cfsh.ca/Sexual_Health_Info/Your-Sexual-Health.
2. Darroch, J. (2000). The pill and men's involvement in contraception. *Family Planning Perspective, 32*(2).
3. The Sex Information and Education Council of Canada. (2004). Adolescent sexual and reproductive health in Canada: A report card in 2004. *The Canadian Journal of Human Sexuality, 13,* 67–81.
4. Murray, S., & Miller, J.L. (2000). Birth control and condom usage among college students. *Research Quarterly for Exercise and Sport, 71*(1).
5. Wyatt, G., et al. (2000, April). Factors affecting HIV contraceptive decision-making among women. *Sex Roles: A Journal of Research.*
6. Canadian Federation of Sexual Health. (2008, July 22). Sexual Health. Emergency contraception. Available at www.cfsh.ca/Sexual_Health_Info/Contraception-and-Safer-Sex/Emergency-Contraception.
7. Oncale, R., & King, B. (2001). Comparisons of men's and women's attempts to dissuade sexual partners from the couple using condoms. *Archives of Sexual Behavior, 30*(4), 379.
8. Sexualityandu.ca. (2007, February 27). Home. Adults. Contraception. Contraceptive Methods. Oral contraceptive pill (a.k.a. the Pill). Available at www.sexualityandu.ca/adults/contraception-2-1.aspx.
9. Hormonal contraception forty years after approval of "the Pill." (2002, June). *Kaiser Family Foundation Issue Update, 1.*
10. Goldin, C., & Katz, L. (2002). The power of the pill: Oral contraceptives and women's career and marriage decisions. *Journal of Political Economy, 110*(4), 730.
11. Kemmeren, J., et al. (2001). Third generation oral contraceptives and risk of venous thrombosis: Meta-analysis. *British Medical Journal, 323,* 7305.
12. Ibid.
13. Davidson, N., & Helzsouer, K. (2002). Good news about oral contraceptives. *New England Journal of Medicine, 346,* 2078.
14. Marchbanks, P., et al. (2002). Oral contraceptives and the risk of breast cancer. *New England Journal of Medicine, 346,* 2025.
15. Nelson, A. (2000). Whose pill is it anyway? *Family Planning Perspectives, 32*(2).
16. Sexualityandu.ca. (2007, February 27). Home. Adults. Contraception. Contraceptive Methods. Oral contraceptive pill (a.k.a. the Pill). Available at www.sexualityandu.ca/adults/contraception-2-1.aspx.
17. Ibid.
18. Ibid.
19. Helping women use the pill. (2000). *Population Reports, 28*(2).
20. Sexualityandu.ca. (2007, January 23). Home. Adults. Contraception. Contraceptive Methods. Vaginal ring (NuvaRing™). Available at www.sexualityandu.ca/adults/contraception-2-4.aspx.
21. Ibid.
22. Sexualityandu.ca. (2006, September 5). Home. Adults. Contraception. Contraceptive Methods. Contraceptive patch. Available at www.sexualityandu.ca/adults/contraception-2-2.aspx.
23. First contraceptive skin patch is applied only once weekly. (2002). *RN, 65*(2), 85.
24. Ditrich, R., et al. (2002). Transdermal contraception. *American Journal of Obstetrics and Gynecology, 186*(1), 15.
25. Mendoza, M. (2005, July 17). Birth-control patch linked to clots, death. Associated Press as reported in the *Calgary Herald,* Section A.
26. Does weight play a role in effectiveness? (2002). *Contraceptive Technology Update, 23*(7), 81.
27. Sexualityandu.ca. (2006, September 6). Home. Adults. Contraception. Contraceptive Methods. Injection (Depo-Provera®). Available at www.sexualityandu.ca/adults/contraception-2-3.aspx.
28. Health Canada. (2005, June 30). Public advisory: Endorsed important safety information on DEPO-PROVERA (medroxyprogesterone acetate). Available at www.hc-sc.gc.ca/dhp-mps/medeff/advisories-avis/prof/_2004/depo-provera_hpc-cps-eng.php.
29. Options for Sexual Health. (2008). Birth Control and Pregnancy. Birth Control Options. Intrauterine devices (IUD). Available at www.optionsforsexualhealth.org/birth-control-pregnancy/birth-control-options/iuds.
30. Richardson, K. (2002, April). A new look at the IUD. CTC Communications. Obstetrics & Gynaecology Canada. Available at www.ctccomm.com/Publishing/obgyn/obgynss0202IUD.htm.
31. Sexualityandu.ca. (2006, October 26). Home. Adults. Contraception. Contraceptive Methods. Intrauterine contraceptive device (the copper IUD). Available at www.sexualityandu.ca/adults/contraception-2-6.aspx.
32. Sexualityandu.ca. (2006, September 5). Hormonal IUD (Mirena). Available at www.sexualityandu.ca/adults/contraception-2-5.aspx.
33. Ibid.
34. Richardson, K. (2002, April). A new look at the IUD. CTC Communications. Obstetrics & Gynaecology Canada. Available at www.ctccomm.com/Publishing/obgyn/obgynss0202IUD.htm.
35. Sexualityandu.ca. (2006, October 26). Home. Adults. Contraception. Contraceptive Methods. Intrauterine contraceptive device (the copper IUD). Available at www.sexualityandu.ca/adults/contraception-2-6.aspx.
36. Sexualityandu.ca. (2006, September 5). Home. Adults. Contraception. Contraceptive Methods. Hormonal IUD (Mirena). Available at www.sexualityandu.ca/adults/contraception-2-5.aspx.
37. Richardson, K. (2002, February). A new look at the IUD. CTC Communications. Obstetrics & Gynaecology Canada. Available at www.ctccomm.com/Publishing/obgyn/obgynss0202IUD.htm.
38. Hirozawa, A. (2001). A first pregnancy may be difficult to achieve after long-term use of an IUD. *Family Planning Perspectives, 33*(4), 181.
39. Hollander, D. (2002). IUD ifs, ands and buts. *Family Planning Perspectives, 34*(2), 60.
40. Sexualityandu.ca. (2006, September 5). Home. Adults. Contraception. Contraceptive Methods. Diaphragm. Available at www.sexualityandu.ca/adults/contraception-2-10.aspx.
41. Centre for Infectious Disease Prevention and Control. (2003, April). HIV/AIDS Epi update. Public Health Agency of Canada. Available at www.phac-aspc.gc.ca/publicat/epiu-aepi/hiv-vih/nonoxynol-eng.php.
42. Sexualityandu.ca. (2006, September 5). Home. Adults. Contraceptions. Contraceptive Methods. Cervical cap. Available at www.sexualityandu.ca/adults/contraception-2-11.aspx.
43. Ibid.
44. McKay, A. (2007). The effectiveness of latex condoms for prevention of STI/HIV. *The Canadian Journal of Human Sexuality, 16*(1/2), 57–61.
45. Michaels Opinion Research. (2001, June). *In the heat of the moment.* Menlo Park, CA: Henry J. Kaiser Family Foundation.
46. Condom use by adolescents. (2001). *Pediatrics, 107*(6), 463.
47. McKay, A. (2004). Adolescent sexual and reproductive health in Canada: A report card in 2004. *The Canadian Journal of Human Sexuality, 13*(2), 67–81. Available at http://web.ebscohost.com/ehost/pdf?vid=5&hid=12&sid=2a265511-d55a-4ddc-a77a-f399e4c1deb4%40sessionmgr2.

48. Ford, K., et al. (2001). Characteristics of adolescents' sexual partners and their association with use of condoms and other contraceptive methods. *Family Planning Perspectives, 33*(3), 100.

49. Sexualityandu.ca. (2006, November 13). Home. Adults. Contraception. Contraceptive Methods. Female condom. Available at www.sexualityandu.ca/adults/contraception-2-8.aspx.

50. Study of female condom aims to combat AIDS worldwide. (2000, November 13). *AIDS Weekly.*

51. Sexualityandu.ca. (2006, September 5). Adults. Contraception. Contraceptive Methods. Spermicide. Available at www.sexualityandu.ca/adults/contraception-2-17.aspx.

52. Sexualityandu.ca. (2006, September 5). Adults. Contraception. Contraceptive Methods. Contraceptive sponge. Available at www.sexualityandu.ca/adults/contraception-2-9.aspx.

53. Sexualityandu.ca. (2007, October 15). Home. Adults. Contraception. Contraceptive Methods. Natural Family Planning. Natural birth control methods. Available at www.sexualityandu.ca/adults/contraception-2-16.aspx.

54. Grimes, D., et al. (2001). New approaches to emergency contraception. *Contemporary OB/GYN, 46*(6), 89.

55. Plan B The Morning After Pill. (n.d.). FAQ's Available at www.planb.ca/faq.html.

56. Canadian Federation of Sexual Health. (2008, May 22). News and Events. Emergency contraception now approved for over the counter purchase. Available at www.cfsh.ca/About_CFSH/News-and-Events/news05220802.aspx.

57. Pancham, A., & Dunn, S. (2007). Emergency contraception in Canada: An overview and recent developments, *The Canadian Journal of Human Sexuality, 16*(3/4), 129–33.

58. Statistics Canada. (2008). Publications. Free Internet Publications. Induced abortion statistics. 2005. Catalogue no. 82-223-X. Minister of Industry. Minister responsible for Statistics Canada. Available at www.statcan.ca/english/freepub/82-223-XIE/82-223-XIE2008000.pdf.

59. Kensington Clinic. (2007). Home. Medical abortion. Available at www.kensingtonclinic.com/services.php?service=medical.

60. Ibid.

61. Hollander, D. (2000). Most abortion patients view their experience favorably, but medical abortion gets a higher rating than surgical. *Family Planning Perspectives, 32*(5).

62. Chemical abortion vs. surgical. (2001). *Insight on the News, 17*(4), 16.

63. Kensington Clinic. (2007). Home. Surgical abortion. Available at www.kensingtonclinic.com/services.php?service=medical.

64. Stotland, N. (1998). *Abortion: Facts and feelings.* Washington, DC: American Psychiatric Press.

65. CBC News. (2006, May 24). In Depth. Abortion rights: A timeline of development. Available at www.cbc.ca/news/background/abortion.

66. Life Canada. (n.d.). Organization. Mission statement and objectives. Available at www.lifecanada.org/html/organization/mission.html.

67. National Campus Life Network. (n.d.). Home. Available at www.ncln.ca/index.php.

68. Cohen, J. (2002). Sorting out chromosome errors. *Science, 296,* 2164.

69. Moore, P. (1997). Tackling autoantibody-linked pregnancy loss. *Lancet, 350*(9073); Cowchock, S. (1997). Autoantibodies and pregnancy loss. *New England Journal of Medicine, 337*(3).

70. Health Canada. (2004, October 1). Healthy Living. Assisted Human Reproduction. Assisted human reproduction procedures covered by the Act. Available at www.hc-sc.gc.ca/hl-vs/reprod/hc-sc/legislation/proc-tech-eng.php.

71. Ibid.

72. Ibid.

73. Centers for Disease Control and Prevention. (2002). Use of assisted reproductive technology. *Journal of the American Medical Association, 287*(12), 1521.

74. Health Canada. (2008, February 1). Healthy Living. Assisted Human Reproduction at Health Canada. Introduction to assisted human reproduction (AHR). Available at www.hc-sc.gc.ca/hl-vs/reprod/hc-sc/index-eng.php.

# Protecting Yourself from Infectious Diseases

Throughout history, infectious diseases have claimed more lives than any military conflict or natural disaster. Although modern medicine has won many victories against the agents of infection, we remain vulnerable to a host of infectious illnesses. Drug-resistant strains of tuberculosis and *Staphylococcus* bacteria challenge current therapies. Scientists are also warning of the potential danger of new emerging viruses.

As well, some of today's most common and dangerous infectious illnesses are spread primarily through sexual contact, and their incidence has skyrocketed. Many of these diseases cannot be prevented in the laboratory. However, we can, by our behaviour, prevent and control many of them.

This chapter is a lesson in self-defence against many forms of infection. You will find information about agents of infection, some common infectious diseases, how to protect yourself from sexually transmitted infections, and where to seek help when needed.

**After studying the material in this chapter, you will be able to:**

- **Explain** how the different agents of infection spread disease.
- **Describe** how your body protects itself from infectious disease.
- **List** and **describe** some common infectious diseases, such as the common cold, hepatitis, meningitis, and SARS.
- **Identify** the sexually transmitted diseases and the symptoms and treatment for each.
- **Define** HIV infection and **describe** its symptoms.
- **List** the methods of HIV transmission.
- **Explain** some practical methods for preventing HIV infection and other sexually transmitted infections.

**???? FREQUENTLY ASKED QUESTIONS**

# Understanding Infection

We live in a sea of microbes. Most of them don't threaten our health or survival; some, such as the bacteria that inhabit our intestines, are actually beneficial. Yet in the course of history, disease-causing microorganisms have claimed millions of lives. Infection is a complex process, triggered by various **pathogens** (disease-causing organisms) and countered by the body's own defenders. Physicians explain infection in terms of a **host** (either a person or a population) that contacts one or more agents in an environment. A **vector**—a biological or physical vehicle that carries the agent to the host—provides the means of transmission.

## Agents of Infection

The types of microbes that can cause infection are viruses, bacteria, fungi, protozoa, and helminths (parasitic worms).

### Viruses

**Viruses** are tough, tiny pathogens. (See Figure 9-1(a).) These small infectious organisms, 10 to 100 times smaller than bacteria and much smaller than fungi, consist of a bit of nucleic acid (DNA or RNA, but never both) with a protein coat. A virus may or may not have an outermost spiky layer called the *envelope*. Unlike bacteria, which can grow on nonliving surfaces, a virus is unable to reproduce on its own, so it must invade a living cell (plant or animal) to reproduce. It then instructs the cell to produce new viral particles. Usually the infected cell dies because it can no longer perform its normal functions. But before it dies, the cell releases new viruses, which are then released to enter other cells.

Some viruses do not kill the cells that they infect. Instead, they alter the cell's functions. If the cell loses control over normal cell division, it can become cancerous. Other viruses leave their genetic material in a host cell where it can remain dormant for an extended period of time. When the cell is disturbed, the virus sometimes begins growing again and causes disease.[1]

Usually, viruses infect one particular type of cell. A cold virus would infect the cells of the upper respiratory tract. Some viruses only infect a few species of plants or animals, whereas some only infect people. They are transmitted in a number of ways. Sometimes we swallow viruses or sometimes we inhale them. Some viruses are transmitted by the bites of insects or other parasites—mosquitoes and ticks are two examples. Human viruses don't grow on food, but food can act as a method of transportation, moving a virus from one host to another and causing foodborne illnesses.[2]

The most common viruses are:

✔ *Rhinoviruses* and *adenoviruses,* which get into the mucous membranes and cause upper respiratory tract infections and colds.

✔ *Influenza viruses,* which cause the flu, can change their outer protein coats so dramatically that individuals resistant to one strain cannot fight off a new one.

✔ *Herpes viruses,* which take up permanent residence in the cells and periodically flare up.

✔ *Papillomaviruses,* which cause few symptoms in women and almost none in men, but may be responsible, at least in part, for a rise in the incidence of cervical cancer among younger women.

✔ *Hepatitis viruses,* which cause several forms of liver infection, ranging from mild to life-threatening.

✔ *Slow viruses,* which give no early indication of their presence but can produce fatal illnesses within a few years.

✔ *Retroviruses,* which are named for their backward (*retro*) sequence of genetic replication compared to other viruses. One retrovirus, human immunodeficiency virus (HIV), causes acquired immune deficiency syndrome (AIDS).

✔ *Filoviruses,* which resemble threads and are extremely lethal.

✔ *Noroviruses,* part of a family called *caliciviruses,* which cause gastroenteritis in people.

The problem in fighting viruses is that it's difficult to find drugs that will harm the virus but not the cell it has commandeered. **Antibiotics** (drugs that inhibit or kill bacteria) have no effect on viruses. **Antiviral drugs** don't completely eradicate a viral infection, although they can decrease its severity and duration. Because viruses multiply very quickly, antiviral drugs are most effective when taken before an infection develops or in its early stages.

### Bacteria

Simple one-celled organisms, **bacteria**, have a rigid cell wall and a thin, rubbery cell membrane that surrounds fluid (cytoplasm) inside the cell. Bacteria are complex compared to viruses because they contain all of the genetic information they need to make copies of themselves (DNA), in a structure called a *chromosome.* They also have *ribosomes,* which are tools necessary for copying the DNA so they can reproduce.[3] Some even have *flagella*—threadlike structures that they use to move. Bacteria are the most plentiful microorganisms as well as the most pathogenic.

Most kinds of bacteria don't cause disease; some, like *Escherichia coli* that aid in digestion, play important roles within our bodies. Even friendly bacteria, however, can get out of hand and cause acne, urinary tract infections, vaginal infections, and other problems. (See Figure 9-1(b).)

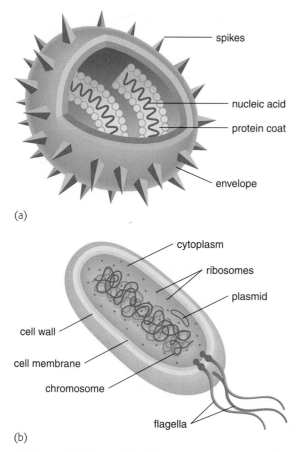

(a)

(b)

▲ **Figure 9-1** Virus and Bacterium
(a) A virus consists of a bit of nucleic acid (DNA or RNA, but never both) with a protein coat. A virus may or may not have an outermost spiky layer called the envelope. (b) Bacteria have a rigid cell wall and a thin, rubbery cell membrane that surrounds fluid (cytoplasm) inside the cell. They contain genetic information they need to make copies of themselves (DNA) in a structure called a chromosome.

Source: Illustration © Eric MacDicken LLC.

Bacteria that harm the body do so by releasing either enzymes that digest body cells or toxins that produce the specific effects of such diseases as diphtheria or toxic shock syndrome. In self-defence, the body produces specific proteins (called *antibodies*) that attack and inactivate the invaders. Tuberculosis, tetanus, gonorrhea, scarlet fever, and diphtheria are examples of bacterial diseases.

Because bacteria are sufficiently different from the cells that make up our bodies, antibiotics can kill them without harming our cells. Antibiotics work only against specific types of bacteria. Tests of your blood, pus, sputum, urine, or stool can identify particular bacterial strains.

## Fungi

**Fungi** are eukaryotic organisms that come in a variety of shapes and sizes. They can be single-celled (yeasts) or consist of long chains of cells that can stretch for miles (moulds or mushrooms). Fungi are basically static, but they can spread by reproductive spores or by growing threadlike fibres. They do not make their own food from the sunlight because they lack chlorophyll. Instead, they absorb nutrients from organic material, which may include human tissue.[4]

Fungi can be helpful to us. Many antibiotics are made from natural compounds that fungi produce. Yeast makes bread rise and helps to brew beer. Fungi break down dead plants and animals.[5] They can also be a nuisance to humans. Fungi release enzymes that digest cells and can attack hair-covered areas of the body, including the scalp, beard, groin, and external ear canals. They also cause athlete's foot. Treatment consists of antifungal drugs. Fungi also affect fruits and vegetables.

## Protozoa

These single-celled, microscopic animals release enzymes and toxins that destroy cells or interfere with their function. Diseases caused by **protozoa** are not a major health problem in our country, primarily because of public-health measures. Around the world, however, some 2.24 billion people (more than 40 percent of the world's population) are at risk for acquiring *malaria*—a protozoan-caused disease. Up to three million people die from this disease annually. Many more come down with amoebic dysentery. Treatment for protozoa-caused diseases consists of general medical care to relieve the symptoms, replacement of lost blood or fluids, and drugs that kill the specific protozoan.

The most common disease caused by protozoa in Canada is *giardiasis,* an intestinal infection caused by microorganisms in human and animal feces. It has become a threat at daycare centres, as well as among campers and hikers who drink contaminated water. Symptoms include nausea, lack of appetite, gas, diarrhea, fatigue, abdominal cramps, and bloating. Many people recover in a month or two without treatment. However, in some cases the microbe causes recurring attacks over many years. Giardiasis can be life-threatening in small children and the elderly, who are especially prone to severe dehydration from diarrhea. Treatment usually consists of antibiotics.

## Helminths (Parasitic Worms)

Small parasitic worms that attack specific tissues or organs and compete with the host for nutrients are called **helminths.** One major worldwide health problem is *schistosomiasis,* a disease caused by a parasitic worm, the fluke, which burrows through the skin and enters the circulatory system. Infection with another helminth, the tapeworm, may be contracted from eating undercooked beef, pork, or fish containing larval forms of the tapeworm. Helminthic diseases are treated with appropriate medications.

## How Do You Catch an Infection?

The major vectors, or means of transmission, for infectious disease are animals and insects, people, food, and water.

### Animals and Insects

House pets, livestock, and wild animals can transmit disease. Insects also spread a variety of diseases. The housefly may spread dysentery, diarrhea, typhoid fever, or trachoma (an eye disease rare in Canada, but common in other parts of the world). Other insects, including mosquitoes, ticks, mites, fleas, and lice, can transmit such diseases as malaria, yellow fever, encephalitis, dengue fever (a growing threat in Mexico), and Lyme disease.

A threat in Canada is West Nile virus (WNV), a virus mainly transmitted to people through the bite of an infected

---

### Strategies for Prevention

#### Protecting Yourself from Insect-Borne Diseases

▲ Consider staying indoors at dawn, dusk, and in the early evening, which are peak mosquito-biting times.

▲ When outdoors, apply insect repellent containing DEET (N, N-diethyl-meta-toluamide), which provides the longest-lasting protection against bites.

▲ Follow all of the label directions, including restrictions for use on young children and the maximum number of applications allowed per day.

▲ Wear long-sleeved clothes and long pants treated with repellents containing permethrin or DEET, since mosquitoes may bite through thin clothing. Do not apply repellents containing permethrin directly to exposed skin. If you spray your clothing, there is no need to spray repellent containing DEET on the skin under your clothing.

▲ Avoid breathing spray mists and never apply sprays inside a tent. Use only in well-ventilated areas. Do not use near food.

▲ Limit the number of places available for mosquitoes to lay their eggs by eliminating standing water sources from around your home.

Source: Saftey Tips on Using Personal Insect Repellents, Health Canada. http://www.hc-sc.gc.ca/cps-spc/pubs/pest/_fact-fiche/deet/index-eng.php. Reproduced with the permission of the Minister of Public Works and Government Services Canada, 2009.

---

mosquito. Mosquitoes transmit the virus after becoming infected themselves by feeding on the blood of birds that carry the virus. Canada had its first confirmed cases of West Nile virus in 2002.[6] As of October 29, 2004, 416 of 6232 dead birds tested for WNV in Canada were positive.[7] Crows and blue jays are very sensitive to WNV.[8] Transmission of WNV also occurs through transplanted organs and possibly from blood products.

While WNV interferes with normal central nervous system functioning and causes inflammation of brain tissue, many people infected with WNV do not have any symptoms and do not get sick. Others experience mild to severe symptoms. Symptoms, which usually appear within 2 to 15 days, include fever, body aches, brain swelling, coma, and paralysis. Less than 1 percent of those infected with WNV develop severe illness. Among these, 3 to 15 percent die, with the highest mortality rate among the elderly. People with chronic diseases such as cancer, diabetes, alcoholism, or heart disease are also at a higher risk for serious health risks from WNV.[9]

We do not yet understand the long-term effects of West Nile virus. Scientists continue to study why some people recover fully, while others suffer long-term health problems. Presently, there is no specific treatment, medication, or cure for West Nile virus. The National Institute of Allergy and Infectious Diseases (NIAID) in the United States is supporting research to develop a WNV vaccine, which will need Food and Drug Administration (FDA) approval. If approved in the United States, Canadians will only have access to such a vaccine if approved by Health Canada.

The Public Health Agency of Canada has coordinated a national surveillance plan and is working closely with Health Canada, the Pest Management Regulatory Agency, and other government departments on a national response to WNV.[10]

### People

The people you are closest to can transmit pathogens through the air, touch, or sexual contact. To avoid infection, stay out of range of anyone who is coughing, sniffling, or sneezing, and don't share food or dishes. Carefully wash your dishes, utensils, and hands, and abstain from sex or make self-protective decisions about sexual partners.

### Food

Every year foodborne illnesses strike many Canadians, sometimes with fatal consequences. Bacteria account for two-thirds of foodborne infections. Thousands of suspected cases of infection with *Escherichia coli* bacteria in undercooked or inadequately washed food are reported annually. *E. coli* infections are now an important public-health problem worldwide.[11] Symptoms include mild to severe diarrhea with no blood to high levels of blood in the stools. Most people recover without antibiotic treatment within 5 to 10 days after exposure; however, young children under five years of age and older adults are susceptible to HUS—hemolytic uremic syndrome. This is a condition where the red blood cells are destroyed and the kidneys fail. HUS can be life-threatening and often requires intensive care, blood transfusions, and kidney dialysis.

Adults are capable of transmitting the infection for one week or less (as long as the bacteria are present in stools). In 33 percent of infected children, transmission can occur for up to three weeks.[12]

Every year approximately 6 000 to 12 000 cases of salmonella are reported in Canada. However, because milder cases are often not reported or diagnosed, the actual number of infections is estimated at many more.[13] Diarrhea, fever, and abdominal cramps are typical symptoms, which occur 12 to 72 hours after being infected. These usually last four to seven days, and many people recover without specific treatment. However, these infections can be serious enough to require hospitalization and can lead to arthritis, neurological problems, and even death. You can greatly reduce your risk of salmonella infections by proper handling, cooking, and refrigeration of raw meat, eggs, and poultry. Proper washing of fresh fruits and vegetables is also important. Exotic pets are also another source—so wash your hands after contact.[14]

A deadly food disease, *botulism,* is caused by certain bacteria that grow in improperly canned foods. Although its occurrence is rare in commercial products, botulism is a danger in home canning.[15] Infant botulism can affect healthy children who are under one year old. Sources of the bacterium, called *Clostridium botulinum,* are soil, dust, and honey. Parents and caregivers can help to prevent infant botulism by not adding honey to baby food or using honey on a soother.[16]

Another uncommon threat is *trichinosis,* caused by the larvae of a parasitic roundworm in uncooked meat. This infection, which causes nausea, vomiting, diarrhea, fever, thirst, profuse sweating, weakness, and pain, can be avoided by thoroughly cooking meat.

In the summer of 2008, an outbreak of *Listeria monocytogenes,* commonly know as listeria, occurred in Canada. Health officials confirmed that the outbreak began at the Maple Leaf Foods plant in Ontario, a result of contaminated slicing equipment.[17] Listeria is a type of bacterium found in food, soil, vegetation, water, sewage, and in the feces of humans and animals. Listeria is unlike most other bacteria in that it can survive and sometimes even grow on foods that are stored in your refrigerator, although it can be killed if you properly cook your food. Many people carry listeria, but not many actually develop **listeriosis,** a serious and sometimes life-threatening disease. Pregnant women, the elderly, and people with weakened immune systems are at risk.[18]

Although a relatively rare disease in Canada, at least 18 people died of this disease, and many more were taken ill. The mild form of listeriosis begins as soon as one day after eating contaminated food, whereas the incubation period of the more serious form of the disease can be up to 90 days.

BSE (bovine spongiform encephalopathy), often called *mad cow disease,* has become a concern in the past two decades in places such as the United Kingdom, Canada, the United States, and Japan. It is a disease that affects the central nervous system, especially in cows. Infected animals become aggressive, sometimes lack coordination, and find it difficult to stand. You can only determine if an animal has BSE by examining its brain after it dies. The brains of animals afflicted with this disease look spongy because holes have developed in the nerve cells. As well, a deposit of fibrous protein is also apparent in the brain tissue.[19]

There is still much mystery surrounding this disease. It has been suggested that a human form of BSE, variant Creutzfeldt-Jakob disease (vCJD), has been linked to eating beef products that have come from animals infected with BSE. Presently, there is no proof as to how BSE is transmitted, but scientists believe that **prions**, infectious self-reproducing protein structures, might be the cause. What is known for sure is that prions are not viruses, bacteria, fungi, or parasites. What is unclear is how prions seem to have the ability to reproduce themselves by changing the shape of an apparently normal protein found within a cell—a change that results in the clogging up of infected brain cells that don't work properly or die.[20] Scientists are even more concerned that it appears that prions might have the ability to jump from one species to another, causing deadly diseases such as vCJD in humans. Research continues.

## Water

Dr. Albert J. Schumacher, the president of the Canadian Medical Association, reminds us that, worldwide, water is a scarce commodity. In his article "Safe Drinking Water: An Urgent Global Public Health Issue," Schumacher reports that, according to the United Nations, there are currently 1.2 billion people in the world who lack access to safe drinking water and 2.4 billion people without proper sanitation facilities.[21] We are fortunate in Canada to have the distinction of being third in the world for our supply of renewable fresh water, behind Brazil and Russia.

Health problems result from the shortage of safe drinking water. There are 3 300 000 deaths each year from diarrheal diseases caused by *E. coli*, salmonella, and cholera bacterial infections as well as parasites such as Giardia and Cryptosporidium. In the developing world, 80 percent of illnesses are due to water-related diseases.[22]

In Canada, we have recently been reminded that water quality and safety are not just developing-country issues. An *E. coli* outbreak in Walkerton, Ontario, in May 2000, caused seven deaths, made more than 2000 people ill, and had an estimated direct economic impact of more than $64.5 million.[23] A combination of a lack of training and expertise of the Walkerton Public Utilities Commission (PUC) operators, years of improper operating practices, and the provincial government's budget restrictions (which led to the discontinuation of government-laboratory testing for municipalities in 1996) were just some of the reasons this tragedy occurred.[24] Public health depends on reliable systems and integrity in monitoring those systems. A special inquiry into Walkerton was called by the government of Ontario to ensure the future safety of the water supply in the province.[25]

Because of reduced confidence in tap water, many people now drink bottled water. According to a Canadian Broadcasting Corporation (2000) file, the bottled-water industry has grown by approximately 10 percent a year during the last decade, making it the fastest-growing product in the Canadian beverage industry.[26] Yet research is showing that bottled water is not necessarily safer. Warburton reports that bottled water and municipal water may contain the same microorganisms, since both can originate from the same sources.[27] More research on the surveillance of the bottled-water industry is needed, and regulations should be developed and enforced.[28] Environmental concerns about bottled water are discussed in Chapter 16.

### The Canadian Science Centre for Human and Animal Health

Canada is now one of a few countries worldwide that can undertake laboratory research on some of the world's most dangerous infectious diseases. The National Microbiology Laboratory and the National Centre for Foreign Animal Diseases are both housed within the Canadian Science Centre for Human and Animal Health—the first facility in the world to accommodate both human and animal health facilities at the highest level of biocontainment. Located in Winnipeg, Manitoba, and operated jointly by Health Canada and the Canadian Food Inspection Agency, it contains Canada's only biosafety Level 4 laboratories. Researchers can now collaborate as they study established and emerging diseases in human and animal populations.[29]

### The Process of Infection

If someone infected with the flu sits next to you and coughs or sneezes, tiny viral particles may travel into your nose and mouth. Immediately the virus finds or creates an opening in a cell membrane, and the infection process begins. During the **incubation period,** the time between invasion and the first symptom, you're unaware of the pathogen multiplying inside you. Incubation may go on for months, even years; for most diseases, it lasts several days or weeks.

The early stage of the battle between your body and the invaders is called the *prodromal period.* As infected cells die, they release chemicals that help block the invasion. Other chemicals, such as *histamines,* cause blood vessels to dilate, thus allowing more blood to reach the battleground. During all of this, you feel mild, generalized symptoms, such as headache, irritability, and discomfort. You're also highly contagious. At the height of the battle—the typical illness period—you cough, sneeze, sniffle, ache, feel feverish, and lose your appetite.

Recovery begins when the body's forces gain the advantage. With time, the body destroys the last of the invaders and heals itself. However, the body is not able to develop long-lasting immunity to certain viruses, such as colds, flu, or HIV.

## How Your Body Protects Itself

Various parts of your body safeguard you against infectious diseases by providing **immunity,** or protection, from these health threats. Your skin, when unbroken, keeps out most potential invaders. Your tears, sweat, skin oils, saliva, and mucus contain chemicals that can kill bacteria. Cilia, the tiny hairs lining your respiratory passages, move mucus, which traps inhaled bacteria, viruses, dust, and foreign matter, to the back of the throat, where it is swallowed; the digestive system then destroys the invaders.

When these protective mechanisms can't keep you infection-free, your body's immune system, which is on constant alert for foreign substances that might threaten the body, swings into action. The immune system includes structures of the lymphatic system—the spleen, thymus gland, lymph nodes, and lymph vessels—that help filter impurities from the body (see Figure 9-2). More than a dozen different types of white blood cells are concentrated in the organs of the lymphatic system or patrol the entire body by way of the blood and lymph vessels. The two basic types of immune mechanisms are humoral and cell-mediated.

**Humoral immunity** refers to the protection provided by antibodies—proteins derived from white blood cells called *B lymphocytes* or B cells. Humoral immunity is most effective during bacterial or viral infections. An *antigen* is any substance that enters the body and triggers production of an antibody. Once the body produces antibodies against

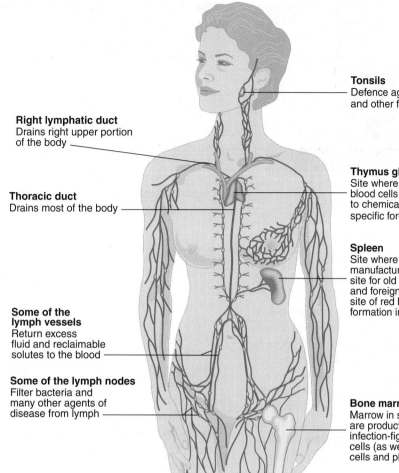

**Tonsils**
Defence against bacteria
and other foreign agents

**Right lymphatic duct**
Drains right upper portion
of the body

**Thoracic duct**
Drains most of the body

**Thymus gland**
Site where certain white
blood cells acquire means
to chemically recognize
specific foreign invaders

**Spleen**
Site where antibodies are
manufactured; disposal
site for old red blood cells
and foreign debris;
site of red blood cell
formation in the embryo

**Some of the
lymph vessels**
Return excess
fluid and reclaimable
solutes to the blood

**Some of the lymph nodes**
Filter bacteria and
many other agents of
disease from lymph

**Bone marrow**
Marrow in some bones
are production sites for
infection-fighting blood
cells (as well as red blood
cells and platelets)

▲ **Figure 9-2** The Human Lymphatic System and Its Functions
The lymphatic system helps filter impurities from the body.

Source: Hespenheide Design

a specific antigen—the mumps virus, for instance—you're protected against that antigen for life. If you're again exposed to mumps, the antibodies previously produced prevent another episode of the disease.

But you don't have to suffer through an illness to acquire immunity. Inoculation with a vaccine containing synthetic or weakened antigens can give you the same protection. The type of long-lasting immunity in which the body makes its own antibodies to a pathogen is called *active immunity*. Immunity produced by the injection of **gamma globulin**, the antibody-containing part of the blood from another person or animal that has developed antibodies to a disease, is called *passive immunity*.

The various types of T cells are responsible for **cell-mediated immunity.** T cells are lymphocytes manufactured in the bone marrow and carried to the thymus for maturation. Cell-mediated immunity mainly protects against parasites, fungi, cancer cells, and foreign tissue.

Thousands of different T cells work together to ward off disease. Different T cells have differing functions, including the activation of other immune cells, help in antibody-mediated responses and the suppression of lymphocyte activity.

## Immune Response

Attacked by pathogens, the body musters its forces and fights. Together, the immune cells work like an internal police force. When an antigen enters the body, the T cells aided by *macrophages* (large scavenger cells with insatiable appetites for foreign cells, diseased and run-down red blood cells, and other biological debris) engage in combat with the invader. Meanwhile, the B cells churn out antibodies, which rush to the scene and join in the fray. Also busy at surveillance are natural killer cells that, like the elite

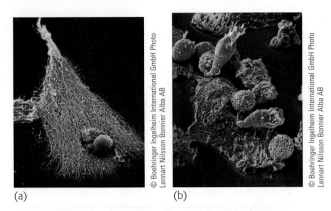

© Boehringer Ingelheim International GmbH Photo
Lennart Nilsson Bonnier Alba AB

© Boehringer Ingelheim International GmbH Photo
Lennart Nilsson Bonnier Alba AB

(a)                    (b)

▲ Types of lymphocytes. (a) B cell covered with bacteria.
The B cells function in humoral immunity by producing antibodies.
(b) T cells attack a cancer cell. The T cells function
in cell-mediated immunity.

forces of a SWAT team, seek out and destroy viruses and cancer cells.

The **lymph nodes,** or glands, are small tissue masses in which some protective cells are stored. If pathogens invade your body, many of them are carried to the lymph nodes to be destroyed. This is why your lymph nodes often feel swollen when you have a cold or the flu.

If the microbes establish a foothold, the blood supply to the area increases, bringing oxygen and nutrients to the fighting cells. Tissue fluids, as well as antibacterial and anti-toxic proteins, accumulate. You may develop redness, swelling, local warmth, and pain—the signs of **inflammation.** As more tissue is destroyed, a cavity, or **abscess,** forms, and fills with fluid, battling cells, and dead white blood cells (pus). If the invaders aren't killed or inactivated, the pathogens are able to spread into the bloodstream and cause what is known as **systemic disease.** The toxins released by the pathogens cause fever, and the infection becomes more dangerous.

## Immunity and Stress

Stress affects the body's immune system in different ways, depending on two factors: the controllability or uncontrollability of the stressor and the mental effort required to cope with the stress. An uncontrollable stressor that lasts longer than 15 minutes may interfere with *cytokine interleukin-6,* which plays an essential role in activating the immune defences. Uncontrollable stressors also produce a high level of the hormone *cortisol,* which suppresses immune system functioning. The mental efforts required to cope with high-level stressors produce only brief immune changes that appear to have little consequence for health. However, stress has been shown to slow pro-inflammatory cytokine production, which is essential for wound healing.

## Immunization: The Key to Prevention

A success story of modern medicine has been the development of vaccines that provide protection against many infectious diseases. Immunization is a process that helps your body fight off diseases caused by certain viruses and bacteria by exposing your body to vaccines. These are usually in the form of injections or shots. The vaccines contain tiny amounts of material that make your immune system produce certain substances called *antibodies.* These antibodies attack and destroy viruses and bacteria.

Your immune system stores this information on how to make these antibodies. Even many years later when your body is exposed to the same virus or bacteria it remembers how to make these antibodies. Your body then produces those antibodies again, stopping the virus or bacteria from making you sick.[30]

Immunization has reduced cases of measles, mumps, tetanus, whooping cough, and other life-threatening illnesses by more than 95 percent. The World Bank suggests that immunization should be an important public-health initiative in which we should invest. Research has shown that the cost-effectiveness of vaccinations—the cost to prevent just one undesired incident such as death, hospitalization, infection, or complications from infections—is relatively low.[31]

The World Health Organization's (WHO) position on vaccines is that by inducing immunity, suffering, disability, and death are avoided. Immunization averted about two million deaths in 2002.[32] Less strain on the health-care system results in savings that can be used for other health services.

New vaccines being developed that will help people in developing countries include vaccines for rotavirus diarrhea, which kills 300 000 to 600 000 children under the age of five every year; human papillomavirus, a leading cause of cervical cancer, which afflicts some 500 000 women each year, 80 percent of them in developing countries; and pneumococcal disease, which causes a large fraction of the world's two million annual deaths from childhood pneumonia.[33]

A comprehensive document, the *Canadian Immunization Guide* (2002), contains up-to-date information on changes that have been made in the immunization field.[34] The National Advisory Committee on Immunization (NACI) recommends that children be immunized against diphtheria, tetanus, acellular Peruses (whooping cough), polio, HIB infection, measles, mumps, German measles (rubella), hepatitis B, pneumoccal pneumonia, and meningococcal C.[35]

The NACI also recommends that adults continue their immunization program. Prevention of infection by immunization is a lifelong process. What immunizations are recommended for adults? Tetanus, diphtheria, hepatitis B, and pneumococcal vaccines are on the list. Influenza vaccines are recommended for anyone 65 and over or for those who are at greatest risk of influenza-related complications, such as health-care workers.

A second dose of a measles (MMR) vaccine is also highly recommended for health-care workers, college and university students, and travellers to areas where measles is epidemic. Mumps vaccine (given as MMR) is recommended for young adults with no history of mumps. Rubella vaccine is recommended for all female adolescents and women of childbearing age unless they have documented evidence of vaccination.[36]

If you're uncertain about your past immunizations, check with family members or your doctor. If you can't find answers, a blood test can show whether you carry antibodies to specific illnesses.

If you're pregnant or planning to get pregnant within the next three months, do not get a measles, mumps, rubella, or oral polio vaccination. If you're allergic to neomycin, consult your doctor before getting a measles, mumps, rubella, or intramuscular polio vaccination. Those with egg allergies should also check with a doctor before getting a measles, mumps, or flu vaccination. Also, never get a vaccination when you have a high fever.

Although statistics show that minor side effects such as mild fevers or soreness at the injection site are common, severe allergic reactions from vaccinations are very rare. However, some people are concerned about getting their children or themselves vaccinated. Reports that vaccines are linked to chronic diseases, sudden infant death syndrome (SIDS), autism, inflammatory bowel disease, brain damage, or asthma have not been proven through rigorous scientific studies according to the Public Health Agency of Canada.[37] The use of the preservative thimerosal, which contains mercury and was used in some vaccines, has been reduced or discontinued in most vaccines. In Canada, the only routine vaccine for children that contained thimerosal was the Hepatitis B vaccine. A new formula for this vaccine that does not include thimerosal is now available.[38]

## Infectious Diseases

An estimated 500 microorganisms cause disease; no effective treatment exists for about 200 of these illnesses. Although infections can be unavoidable at times, the more you know about their causes, the more you can do to protect yourself.

## Who Is at Highest Risk of Infectious Diseases?

Among the most vulnerable are the following groups:

- ✔ **Children and their families.** Youngsters get up to a dozen colds annually; adults average two a year. When a flu epidemic hits a community, about 40 percent of school-aged boys and girls get sick, compared with only 5 to 10 percent of adults. Parents get up to six times as many colds as other adults.

- ✔ **The elderly.** People over 65 who get the flu have a 1 in 10 chance of being hospitalized for pneumonia or other respiratory problems and a 1 in 50 chance of dying from the disease.

- ✔ **The chronically ill.** Lifelong diseases, such as diabetes, kidney disease, or sickle-cell anemia, decrease an individual's ability to fend off infections. Individuals taking medications that suppress the immune system, such as steroids, are more vulnerable to infections, as are those with medical conditions that impair immunity, such as infection with HIV.

- ✔ **Smokers and those with respiratory problems.** Smokers are a high-risk group for respiratory infections and serious complications, such as pneumonia. Chronic breathing disorders, such as asthma and emphysema, also greatly increase the risk of respiratory infections.

- ✔ **Those who live or work in close contact with someone who is sick.** Health-care workers who treat high-risk patients, nursing-home residents, and others living in close quarters—such as students in dormitories—face greater odds of catching others' colds and flus.

- ✔ **Residents or workers in poorly ventilated buildings.** Building technology has helped spread certain airborne illnesses, such as tuberculosis, via recirculated air. Indoor air quality can be closely linked with disease transmission in winter, when people spend a great deal of time in tightly sealed rooms.

## Common Cold

There are more than 200 distinct cold viruses, or rhinoviruses. Although in a single season you may develop a temporary immunity to one or two, you may then be hit by a third. Colds can strike in any season, but different cold viruses are more common at different times of years. Rhinoviruses cause most spring, summer, and early fall colds and tend to cause more symptoms above the neck (stuffy nose, headache, runny eyes). Adenoviruses, parainfluenza viruses, corona viruses, influenza viruses, and others that strike in the winter are more likely to get into the bronchi and trachea (the breathing passages) and cause more fever and bronchitis.

Cold viruses are spread by coughs, sneezes, and touch. Cold sufferers who sneeze and then touch a doorknob or countertop leave a trail of highly contagious viruses behind them. The best preventive tactics are frequent handwashing, replacing toothbrushes regularly, and avoiding stress overload. New research shows that people who feel unable to deal with everyday stresses have an exaggerated immune reaction that may intensify cold or flu symptoms once they've contracted a virus.

Until scientists develop truly effective treatments, experts advise against taking acetylsalicylic acid (Aspirin®) and acetaminophen (Tylenol®), which may suppress the antibodies the body produces to fight cold viruses and increase symptoms such as nasal stuffiness. A better alternative for cold "aches" is ibuprofen (brand names include Motrin®, Advil®, and Nuprin®), which doesn't seem to affect immune response. Children, teenagers, and young adults should never take Aspirin® for a cold or flu because of the danger of Reye's syndrome, a potentially deadly disorder that can cause convulsions, coma, swelling of the brain, and kidney damage.

The main drawback of *antihistamines,* the most widely used cold remedy, is drowsiness, which can impair a person's ability to safely drive or operate machinery. Another ingredient, *pseudoephedrine,* can open and drain sinus passages without drowsiness but can speed up heart rate and cause complications for individuals with high blood pressure, diabetes, heart disease, or thyroid disorders. Decongestant nasal sprays can clear a stuffy nose, but they invariably cause a rebound effect. The use of a saline nasal spray is not addictive and can be used to loosen mucus in the nose and help to wash it out. It is also helpful during dry weather to keep the mucous membranes moist.

## The X & Y Files

## Gender Differences in Susceptibility

When the flu hits a household, the last one left standing is likely to be Mom. The female immune system responds more vigorously to common infections, offering extra protection against viruses, bacteria, and parasites. But this enhanced immunity doesn't apply to sexually transmitted infections (STIs). A woman who has unprotected sex with an infected man is more likely to contract a STI than a man who has sex with an infected woman. Symptoms of STIs also tend to be more "silent" in women, so they often go undetected and untreated, leading to potentially serious complications.

The sexes also differ in their vulnerability to allergies and **autoimmune disorders.** Although both men and women frequently develop allergies, allergic women are twice as likely to experience potentially fatal anaphylactic shock. A woman's robust immune system also is more likely to overreact and turn on her own organs and tissues. On average, three of four people with autoimmune disorders, such as multiple sclerosis, Hashimoto's thyroiditis, and scleroderma, are women. Another autoimmune disease, lupus, affects nine times as many women as men.

Autoimmune disorders often follow a different course in men and women. Women with multiple sclerosis develop symptoms earlier than men, but the disease tends to progress more quickly and be more severe in men. In lupus, women first show symptoms during their childbearing years, while men develop the illness later in life.

Scientists believe that the sex hormones have a great impact on immunity. Through a woman's child-bearing years, estrogen, which protects heart, bone, brain, and blood vessels, also bolsters the immune system's response to certain infectious agents. Women produce greater numbers of antibodies when exposed to an antigen; after immunization, they show increased cell-mediated immunity.

In contrast, testosterone may dampen this response—possibly to prevent attacks on sperm cells, which might otherwise be mistaken as alien invaders. When the testes are removed from mice and guinea pigs, their immune systems become more active. Pregnancy dampens a woman's immune response, probably to ensure that her natural protectors don't attack the fetus as a foreign invader. This impact is so great that pregnant women with transplanted kidneys may require lower doses of drugs to prevent organ rejection. Pregnant women with multiple sclerosis and rheumatoid arthritis typically experience decreased symptoms during the nine months of gestation, then return to their prepregnancy state after giving birth. Oral contraceptives also can diminish symptoms of multiple sclerosis and rheumatoid arthritis. Neither pregnancy nor birth control pills has such an impact on lupus.

Other hormones, such as prolactin and growth hormones, may affect autoimmune diseases. Women have higher levels of these hormones, which may act directly on immune cells through interactions with receptors on the surface of cells. These hormones also may affect the complex interworkings of the hypothalamus, pituitary, and adrenal glands.

Fluids (especially chicken soup) help, but dairy products can contribute to congestion. Mild exercise boosts immunity, but once you're sick, it's better not to work out strenuously. In general, doctors recommend treating specific symptoms—headache, cough, chest congestion, sore throat—rather than taking a multi-symptom medication.

For a cough, the ingredient to look for in any suppressant is *dextromethrophan,* which turns down the brain's cough reflex. In expectorants, the only medicine deemed effective is *guaifenesin,* which helps liquefy secretions so you can bring up mucus from the chest. Unless you're coughing up green or foul yellow mucus (signs of a secondary bacterial infection), antibiotics won't help. They have no effect against viruses and may make your body more resistant to such medications when you develop a bacterial infection in the future.

Many Canadians try alternative remedies for colds. One of the most popular herbal remedies is an extract of the Echinacea plant. Echinacea is believed to increase the number and efficiency of white blood cells, components of the immune system that battle infection. Some evidence indicates that taking Echinacea several times a day at the first sign of sniffles diminishes the symptoms or shortens the duration of an oncoming cold. Most experts recommend only limited use of Echinacea, since long-term use can actually suppress the immune system.[39]

Zinc lozenges, although a popular alternative treatment, do not have consistent research results indicating their effectiveness. Some studies have found no benefits, while others have. Almost all have been criticized for various reasons, such as the size of the sample or the formulation of zinc used. The compound zinc gluconate does seem to have a modest effect in shortening cold symptoms, but zinc acetate has not been shown to have a benefit.[40]

Research and clinical trials have determined that a Canadian product called COLD-fX® decreases the incidence of colds and flu. It is an extract from North American Ginseng and is being touted as a safe, strong, all-natural remedy that strengthens the immune system by enhancing the effects of human pathogen resistors.[41] International Olympic Committee (IOC) protocol testing was conducted on athletes who used this product, and it showed no induced or produced banned substances.[42]

Although sore throats are caused by viruses, many people seek treatment with antibiotics, which are effective only against bacteria. An estimated 5 to 17 percent of sore throats in adults are caused by bacteria *(Group A streptococci).*[43]

Your own immune system can do something modern science cannot: cure a cold. All it needs is time, rest, and plenty of fluids. Warmth also is important because the aptly named "cold" viruses replicate at lower temperatures. Hot soups and drinks (particularly those with a touch of something pungent, such as lemon or ginger) raise body temperature and help clear the nose. Taking it easy reduces demands on the body, which helps speed recovery.

## Influenza

Although similar to a cold, **influenza**—the flu—causes more severe symptoms that last longer. WHO estimates that seasonal influenza epidemics result in up to five million cases of severe illness and up to 500 000 deaths a year in industrialized countries. In Canada, the annual number of deaths directly due to influenza ranges from 500 to 1500. Many more deaths occur due to complications of influenza, such as pneumonia.[44]

Flu viruses, transmitted by coughs, sneezes, laughs, and even normal conversation, are extraordinarily contagious, particularly in the first three days of the disease. The usual incubation period is two days, but symptoms can hit hard and fast. Two varieties of viruses—influenza A and influenza B—cause most flus. In recent years, the deadliest flu epidemics have been caused by various forms of influenza A viruses.[45]

The National Advisory Committee on Immunization (NACI) provides Health Canada with scientific and public-health advice on immunizations. The *Statement on Influenza Vaccination for the 2004–2005 Season*[46] recommends a yearly flu shot for people older than 65; residents of long-term care facilities; adults and children with chronic

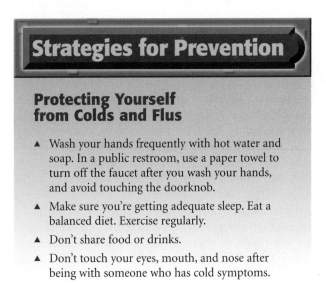

## Strategies for Prevention

### Protecting Yourself from Colds and Flus

▲ Wash your hands frequently with hot water and soap. In a public restroom, use a paper towel to turn off the faucet after you wash your hands, and avoid touching the doorknob.

▲ Make sure you're getting adequate sleep. Eat a balanced diet. Exercise regularly.

▲ Don't share food or drinks.

▲ Don't touch your eyes, mouth, and nose after being with someone who has cold symptoms.

▲ Use tissues rather than cloth handkerchiefs, which may harbour viruses for hours or days.

▲ Don't smoke. Smoking destroys protective cells in the airways and worsens any cough.

▲ Limit your intake of alcohol, which depresses white blood cells and increases the risk of bacterial pneumonia in flu sufferers.

illnesses or weakened immune systems; and, when feasible, young, otherwise healthy children between the ages of 6 and 23 months.

The Health Services departments of the University of Waterloo,[47] Ontario, and the University of Victoria, British Columbia, also encourage students to get flu shots.[48] Influenza contributes to the disruption of academic progress for significant numbers of students each year.

The only individuals who should steer clear are those allergic to eggs, since the inactivated flu viruses are grown in chick embryos.

The recommended time for influenza immunization is between October and mid-November. It is believed that immunity after the administration of a flu shot lasts under one year. For older adults, the protective levels of the vaccine may fall below protective levels within four months.[49]

A new alternative to flu shots is an intranasal spray containing a live, attenuated influenza virus (LAIV) vaccine. Researchers have found that the aerosol vaccine significantly reduces flu severity, days lost from work, health-care visits, and the use of over-the-counter medication. Children who received the vaccine and still got the flu had milder symptoms, were less likely to have a fever, and recovered faster than the children given the placebo.[50]

The approval by the U.S. Food and Drug Administration allows for the use of this nasal spray in the United States in healthy children and adolescents aged 5 to 17 years and healthy adults aged 18 to 49.[51] At the time of writing, this vaccine had not been approved in Canada. Concerns about the vaccine have also surfaced from a study by Mutsch et al.,[52] where researchers discovered that the intranasal vaccine significantly increased the risk of Bell's palsy in adults.

Antiviral drugs such as zanamivir (Relenza™) and oseltamivir (Tamiflu™) are the next best line of defence. These *neuraminidase inhibitors* are designed to block a protein (neuraminidase) that allows the flu virus to escape from one cell and infect others.[53] A small handheld oral inhaler, used twice a day for five days, delivers zanamivivir (Relenza™) to the surface of the lungs, the primary site of flu infection. Oral oseltamivir (Tamiflu™), taken twice a day for five days, comes in pill form. These agents act against both influenza A and influenza B viruses and cause few side effects. In research trials, they shortened the duration of flu by up to two days and decreased the likelihood of complications such as bronchitis, sinusitis, and ear infections. However, to be effective, treatment with either medication must begin within 36 to 48 hours of the first flu symptom. Although approved only for use as a treatment, antiviral drugs also can prevent flu from spreading through a family, workplace, or school.

As with any new agents used to fight infections, there appears to be a growing concern about these new antivirals. A report from the Public Health Agency of Canada reminds us that the misdiagnosis of influenza A can create a health risk for a patient. A 61-year-old Canadian male, thought to have influenza A and prescribed Relenza™, reacted negatively to the antiviral drug. This was especially problematic due to his history of Type 2 diabetes. Further testing showed that he was suffering from Group B streptococcus and needed penicillin instead.[54]

Since mid-December 2003, eight Asian countries—the Republic of Korea, Vietnam, Japan, Thailand, Cambodia, China, Indonesia, and Laos—have confirmed outbreaks of another type of flu—**avian influenza**, a contagious infection that also comes from a virus. This type of flu can infect many kinds of birds and other animals. Wild waterfowl act as a natural reservoir for the virus and may be spreading it to domestic poultry flocks, which are especially vulnerable. Pigs might also become infected because of outdoor breeding programs, such as exist in the United Kingdom. Migrating wild birds could possibly bring avian influenza from other parts of the world, although researchers suggest that at this time this risk is low.

The new strain—H5N1—has caused serious sickness and death in humans. This strain changes quickly or mutates by borrowing genes from other viruses. Health officials then have difficulty making a vaccine that protects against this flu.[55] In British Columbia, two people were infected with another strain—H5N3. Both individuals had close contact with infected poultry. Both recovered fully.[56] As of August 5, 2005, WHO had confirmed a total of 112 human cases of avian influenza. Fifty-seven people had died.[57]

These outbreaks are unprecedented in their scope and geographic and economic impact. It is anticipated that human cases of avian influenza will continue to be detected in countries where outbreaks in poultry are occurring. Research continues to determine the avian–human connection.

## What Is Severe Acute Respiratory Syndrome (SARS)?

**Severe acute respiratory syndrome (SARS)** is a respiratory illness caused by a previously unknown type of coronavirus. Normally, coronaviruses cause mild to moderate upper respiratory symptoms, such as a common cold. SARS can progress from a cough, shortness of breath, difficulty in breathing, and a fever higher than 30°C to severe pneumonia or respiratory failure.[58] Presently, the known risk factors for developing SARS are recent travel to an area where SARS is spreading locally and recent close contact with someone who is ill and either has SARS or has been to an area where SARS is spreading locally. It does appear that people with SARS are not contagious until they develop symptoms, which may take up to 10 days from the time they were in close contact with someone affected by SARS.[59]

According to Health Canada reports, it is important to keep the SARS outbreak in perspective. The flu causes up to an estimated 500 000 deaths worldwide each year. Five hundred to 1500 Canadians, many of them seniors, die annually from pneumonia due to the flu. During the global SARS outbreak in 2003, there were 774 deaths from SARS worldwide and 44 deaths in Canada.[60]

## Meningitis

**Meningitis,** an infection of the fluid and membranes around the brain and spinal cord, can be caused by three kinds of germs: bacteria, viruses, or fungi. The two most common forms of bacteria are *Neisseria meningitidis,* which causes meningococcal meningitis, and *Streptococcus pneumoniae*, which causes pneumococcal meningitis. The symptoms, which are similar in all types of meningitis, include fever, drowsiness or confusion, severe headache, stiff neck, and nausea and vomiting. Meningitis progresses rapidly, often in as little time as 12 hours. If untreated, it can lead to permanent hearing loss, brain damage, seizures, or death. If it is caught early and treated with antibiotics, it is usually curable. There are an estimated 1000 cases of bacterial meningitis in Canada each year.[61] Peak incidence for bacterial meningitis is November to March.

Most common in the first year of life, the incidence of bacterial meningitis rises in young people between the ages of 15 and 24.[62] College and university students are generally not at greater risk, except when they live in dormitories.[63]

Viral meningitis is more common, but usually less serious. Fungal meningitis is usually quite rare. It can cause meningitis in premature babies with very low birth weights or in people with disorders of the immune system such as AIDS, cancer, or diabetes. Antifungal drugs are used in treatment.[64]

### Meningitis Vaccination

The National Advisory Committee on Immunization (NACI) recommends that all children under the age of five be vaccinated against meningococcal and pneumooccal infection.[65] Meningitec®, a vaccine that protects against meningococcus, is now available in Canada. It is a conjugate vaccine approved for children under two years of age.[66] Prevnar® is a conjugage vaccine that protects infants and young children from pneumococcal disease. It was approved by Health Canada in June 2001.[67]

Research into the success of meningococcal vaccination programs on college campuses has shown that women are more likely than men to be vaccinated. Students majoring in science-oriented fields have higher vaccination rates than those majoring in the humanities. More younger students living on campus than older ones get vaccinations, possibly because of greater parental influence or because they see themselves as being at higher risk.[68] Public acceptance is also an important factor. A study done in the Sherbrooke Region of Quebec found that although the effectiveness of meningitis vaccines was agreed upon, 35.9 percent of college students surveyed doubted the safety of the vaccine.[69]

## Hepatitis

In Canada, May is Hepatitis Awareness Month, a campaign that advises Canadians of the potential for hepatitis outbreaks. At least five different viruses, referred to as hepatitis A, B, C, Delta, and E, target the liver, the body's largest internal organ. Newly identified viruses also may be responsible for some cases of what is called "non-A, non-B" hepatitis.

Symptoms of **hepatitis** include headaches, fever, fatigue, stiff or aching joints, nausea, vomiting, and diarrhea. The liver becomes enlarged and tender to the touch; sometimes the yellowish tinge of jaundice develops. Treatment consists of rest, a high-protein diet, and the avoidance of alcohol and drugs that may stress the liver. Alpha interferon, a protein that boosts immunity and prevents viruses from replicating, may be used for some forms.

As many as 10 percent of those infected with hepatitis B and up to two-thirds of those with hepatitis C become carriers of the virus for several years or even life. Some have persistent inflammation of the liver, which may cause mild or severe symptoms and increase the risk of liver cancer. Fatigue and other symptoms can also linger.

Hepatitis A, a less serious form, is the most frequently reported vaccine-preventable disease in North America. The low prevalence of hepatitis A in Western countries has resulted in an overall decrease in population immunity. The result is a low prevalence of hepatitis A antibodies (HAV antibody seroprevalence) in many Canadians. A study by a group of researchers on Canadian and immigrant university students in Toronto supports other Canadian HAV seroprevalence studies.[70] HAV seroprevalence was significantly lower in the young, urban Canadian-born students than the immigrant students. This was true in each age group. The findings suggest that there is the potential for outbreaks of HAV infection.

Hepatitis A is generally transmitted by poor sanitation, primarily fecal contamination of food or water.

Among those at highest risk in Canada are children and staff at daycare centres, residents of institutions, sanitation workers, and workers who handle primates such as monkeys. In Canada, hepatitis A vaccine is currently recommended by the National Advisory Committee for Immunization (NACI) for individuals at increased risk.

Hepatitis B is a potentially fatal disease transmitted through the blood and other bodily fluids. There are approximately 700 cases a year in Canada. The rate is higher among males than females. People aged 30 to 39 are at most risk, followed by those aged 15 to 29.[71] The major risk factors include injection drug use, having multiple heterosexual partners and sex with HBV-infected individuals, drug snorting, blood transfusions, and male homosexual activity.[72]

Vaccination can prevent hepatitis B and is recommended for children, teens, and adults at high risk. Since the early 1990s, a school-based, universal hepatitis B vaccination program, which targets 9- to 13-year-olds, has been implemented in all provinces and territories.[73] Some provinces also have an infant vaccination program.

Hepatitis C virus (HCV) is four times as widespread as HIV. However, many people do not realize they are infected.[74] Hepatitis C, which can lead to chronic liver disease, cirrhosis, and liver cancer, is the leading reason for liver transplantation.

Tattooing and body piercing are creating a new concern for medical professionals. Some studies show that these forms of body art are playing a role in transmitting various infections, including hepatitis. Mayers et al.[75] report that 25 percent of female college students now have tattoos and 60 percent have body piercings. Mele et al.[76] suggest that there is a cause-and-effect relationship between body piercing and HBV infection. Holsen et al.[77] have found that tattooing appears to play a role in transmitting HBV, HCV, as well as syphilis and HIV.

## Mononucleosis

You can get **mononucleosis** through kissing—or any other form of close contact. "Mono" is a viral disease that's most common among people 15 to 24 years old; its symptoms include a sore throat, headache, fever, nausea, and prolonged weakness. The spleen is swollen and the lymph nodes are enlarged. You may also develop jaundice or a skin rash similar to German measles.

The major symptoms usually disappear within two to three weeks, but weakness, fatigue, and often depression may linger for at least two more weeks. The greatest danger is from physical activity that might rupture the spleen, resulting in internal bleeding. The liver may also become inflamed. A blood test can determine whether you have mono. However, there's no specific treatment other than rest.[78]

## Reproductive and Urinary Tract Infections

Reproductive and urinary tract infections are very common. Many are not spread exclusively by sexual contact, so they are not classified as sexually transmitted infections.

## Vaginal Infections

The most common vaginal infections are trichomoniasis, candidiasis, and bacterial vaginosis.

Protozoa *(Trichomonas vaginalis)* that live in the vagina can multiply rapidly, causing itching, burning, and discharge—all symptoms of **trichomoniasis.** Male carriers usually have no symptoms, although some may develop urethritis or an inflammation of the prostate and seminal vesicles. Anyone with this infection should be screened for syphilis, gonorrhea, Chlamydia, and HIV. Sexual partners must be treated with oral medication (metronidazole, known as Flagyl™), even if they have no symptoms, to prevent reinfection.

Populations of a yeast called *Candida albicans*—normal inhabitants of the mouth, digestive tract, and vagina—are usually held in check. Under certain conditions, however, the microbes multiply, causing burning, itching, and a whitish discharge and producing what is commonly known as a yeast infection. Common sites for **candidiasis** are the vagina, vulva, penis, and mouth. The women most likely to test positive for candidiasis have never been pregnant, use condoms for birth control, have sexual intercourse more than four times a month, and have taken antibiotics in the previous 15 to 30 days. Stress can also be a factor. Vaginal medications, such as GyneLotrimin and Monistat, are non-prescription drugs that provide effective treatment. Male sexual partners may be advised to wear condoms during outbreaks of candidiasis. Women should keep the genital area dry and wear cotton underwear.

**Bacterial vaginosis (BV)** is characterized by alterations in the microorganisms that live in the vagina, including depletion of certain bacteria and overgrowth of others. It typically causes a white or grey vaginal discharge with a strong odour similar to that of trichomoniasis. Its underlying cause is unknown, although it occurs most frequently in women with multiple sex partners. Long-term dangers include pelvic inflammatory disease and pregnancy complications. BV is diagnosed based on symptoms, a pelvic examination, and sometimes a Whiff test, where drops of a potassium hydroxide (KOH) solution are added to a sample of vaginal discharge. A fishy odour on the whiff test suggests BV.[79] Metronidazole (Flagyl™), either in the form of a pill or a vaginal gel, is the primary treatment.

Treatment for male sex partners appears to be of little benefit, but some health practitioners recommend treatment for both partners in cases of recurrent infections.

## Urinary Tract Infections

A urinary tract infection (UTI) can be present in any of the three parts of the urinary tract: the urethra, the bladder, or the kidneys. An infection involving the urethra is known as **urethritis.** If the bladder is also infected, it's called **cystitis.** If it reaches the kidneys, it's called **pyelonephritis.**

More women than men develop UTIs. Bacteria, the major cause of UTIs, have a shorter distance to travel up the urethra to infect a woman's bladder and kidneys. Conditions that can set the stage for UTIs include irritation and swelling of the urethra or bladder as a result of pregnancy, bike riding, irritants (such as bubble bath, douches, or a diaphragm), urinary stones, enlargement in men of the prostate gland, vaginitis, and stress. Early diagnosis is critical because infection can spread to the kidneys and, if unchecked, result in kidney failure. Symptoms include frequent burning, painful urination, chills, fever, fatigue, and blood in the urine.

Recurrent UTIs, a frequent problem among young women, have been linked with a genetic predisposition, sexual intercourse, and the use of diaphragms. Frequent recurrence of symptoms may not be caused by infection but by interstitial cystitis, a little-understood bladder inflammation that affects mostly women.

## Sexually Transmitted Infections

Venereal diseases (from the Latin *venus,* meaning *love* or *lust*) are more accurately called **sexually transmitted infections (STIs)** or sexually transmitted diseases (STDs). Around the world, some 50 million cases of curable STIs occur each year (not including HIV and herpes).[80] The highest rates of sexually transmitted infections occur among 16- to 24-year-olds, particularly older teenagers.[81] STIs are much more widespread in developing nations because of the lack of adequate health standards, prevention practices, and access to treatment.[82]

STIs are the major cause of preventable sterility. STIs have tripled the rate of ectopic (tubal) pregnancies, which can be fatal if not detected early. STI complications include miscarriage, premature delivery, and uterine infections after delivery. Moreover, infection with a STI greatly increases the risk of HIV transmission. Unborn and newborn children can be affected by STIs in the womb or during birth.

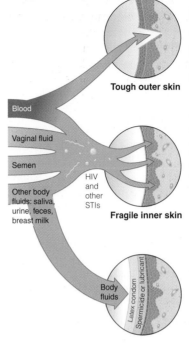

**Tough outer skin**
covers the outside of your body, including hands and lips. Viruses and bacteria enter when skin is chapped or through a hangnail, cut, scrape, sore, or needle puncture.

**Fragile inner skin**
lines the inside of your vagina or penis, anus, and mouth. Viruses and bacteria can enter when skin is torn during sexual contact that involves rubbing, stretching, or not enough lubrication (wetness).

**Barrier protection**
made of latex helps prevent body fluids from entering your body. Latex condoms are recommended for intercourse to lower the risk of the spread of STIs. They also reduce friction, so are less likely to break.

▲ **Figure 9-3** How HIV Infection and Other STIs Are Spread Most STIs are spread by viruses or bacteria carried in certain body fluids.

Source: Hespenheide Design

Although each STI is a distinct disease, all STI pathogens like dark, warm, moist body surfaces, particularly the mucous membranes that line the reproductive organs (see Figure 9-3); they hate light, cold, and dryness. It is possible to catch or have more than one STI at a time. Curing one doesn't necessarily cure another, and treatments don't prevent another bout with the same STI (see Table 9-1).

Many STIs, including early HIV infection and gonorrhea in women, may not cause any symptoms. As a result, infected individuals may continue their usual sexual activity without realizing that they're jeopardizing others' well-being.

## STIs in Adolescents and Young Adults

The college and university years are a prime time for contracting STIs. In one study of college-age women, cases of human papillomavirus (HPV) infections increased from 26 percent to 43 percent over a three-year period. Contracting STIs may increase the risk of being infected with HIV, and half of new HIV infections occur in people under age 25.[83] Because college and university students have more opportunities to have different sexual partners and may use drugs and alcohol more often before sex, they

▼ **Table 9-1 Common Sexually Transmitted Infections (STIs): Mode of Transmission, Symptoms, and Treatment**

| STI | Transmission | Symptoms | Treatment |
|---|---|---|---|
| Chlamydia | The *Chlamydia trachomatis* bacterium is transmitted primarily through sexual contact. It can also be spread by fingers from one body site to another. | In women, PID (pelvic inflammatory disease) caused by Chlamydia may include disrupted menstrual periods, pelvic pain, elevated temperature, nausea, vomiting, headache, infertility, and ectopic pregnancy. In men, Chlamydia infection of the urethra may cause a discharge and burning during urination. Chlamydia-caused epididymitis may produce a sense of heaviness in the affected testicle(s), inflammation of the scrotal skin, and painful swelling at the bottom of the testicle. | Doxycycline, azithromycin, or ofloxacin |
| Gonorrhea ("clap") | The *Neisseria gonnorheae* bacterium ("gonococcus") is spread through genital, oral-genital, or genital-anal contact. | Common symptoms in men are a cloudy discharge from the penis and burning sensations during urination. If disease is untreated, complications may include inflammation of scrotal skin and swelling at base of the testicle. In women, some green or yellowish discharge is produced but often remains undetected. Later, PID may develop. | Dual therapy of a single dose of ceftriaxone, cefixime, ciprofloxacin, or ofloxacin plus doxycycline for seven days or a single dose of azithromycin |
| Non-gonococcal urethritis (NGU) | Primary causes are believed to be the bacteria *Chlamydia trachomatis* and *Ureaplasma urealyticum,* most commonly transmitted through coitus. Some NGU may result from allergic reactions or from *Trichomonas* infection. | Inflammation of the urethral tube. A man has a discharge from the penis and irritation during urination. A woman may have a mild discharge of pus from the vagina but often shows no symptoms. | A single dose of azithromycin or doxycycline for seven days |
| Syphilis | The *Treponema pallidum* bacterium ("spirochete") is transmitted from open lesions during genital, oral-genital, or genital-anal contact. | *Primary stage:* A painless chancre appears at the site where the spirochetes entered the body. *Secondary stage:* The chancre disappears, and a generalized skin rash develops. *Latent stage:* There may be no visible symptoms. *Tertiary stage:* Heart failure, blindness, mental disturbance, and many other symptoms occur. Death may result. | Benzathine penicillin G, doxycycline, erythromycin, or ceftriaxone |
| Herpes simplex | The genital herpes virus (HSV–2) seems to be transmitted primarily by vaginal, anal, or oral-genital intercourse. The oral herpes virus (HSV–1) is transmitted primarily by kissing. | Small, painful red bumps (papules) appear in the genital region (genital herpes) or mouth (oral herpes). The papules become painful blisters that eventually rupture to form wet, open sores. | No known cure. A variety of treatments may reduce symptoms; oral or intravenous acyclovir (Zovirax) promotes healing and suppresses recurrent outbreaks. |
| Chancroid | The *Haemophilus ducrevi* bacterium is usually transmitted by sexual interaction. | Small bumps (papules) in genital regions eventually rupture and form painful, soft, crater-like ulcers that emit a foul-smelling discharge. | Single doses of either ceftriaxone or azithromycin, or seven days of erythromycin |
| Human papillomavirus (HPV) (genital warts) | The virus is spread primarily through vaginal, anal, or oral-genital sexual interaction. | Hard and yellow-grey on dry skin areas; soft, pinkish-red, and cauliflower-like on moist areas | Freezing; application of topical agents such as trichloroacetic acid or podofilox; cauterization, surgical removal, or vaporization by carbon dioxide laser |

▼ **Table 9-1 Common Sexually Transmitted Infections (STIs): Mode of Transmission, Symptoms, and Treatment (continued)**

| STI | Transmission | Symptoms | Treatment |
|---|---|---|---|
| Pubic lice ("crabs") | *Phthirus pubis,* the pubic louse, is spread easily through body contact or through shared clothing or bedding. | Persistent itching. Lice are visible and may often be located in pubic hair or other body hair. | 1% permethrin cream for body areas; 1% Lindane shampoo for hair |
| Scabies | *Sarcoptes scabiei* is highly contagious and may be transmitted by close physical contact, sexual and nonsexual. | Small bumps and a red rash that itch intensely, especially at night. | 5% permethrin lotion or cream |
| Acquired immune deficiency syndrome (AIDS) | Blood and semen are the major vehicles for transmitting HIV, which attacks the immune system. It appears to be passed primarily through sexual contact or needle sharing among injection drug users. | Vary with the type of cancer or opportunistic infections that afflict an infected person. Common symptoms include fevers, night sweats, weight loss, chronic fatigue, swollen lymph nodes, diarrhea and/or bloody stools, atypical bruising or bleeding, skin rashes, headache, chronic cough, and a whitish coating on the tongue or throat. | Commence treatment early after a positive HIV test with a combination of three or more antiretroviral drugs (HAART) plus other specific treatment(s), if necessary, of opportunistic infections and tumours. |
| Viral hepatitis | Hepatitis A seems to be primarily spread via the fecal-oral route, but oral-anal sexual contact is a common mode for transmission. The hepatitis B virus can be transmitted in blood, semen, vaginal secretions, and saliva. Manual, oral, or penile stimulation of the anus are strongly associated with the spread of this virus. | Varies from nonexistent to mild, flu-like symptoms, to an incapacitating illness characterized by high fever, vomiting, and severe abdominal pain. | No specific therapy for A and B types; treatment generally consists of bed rest and adequate fluid intake. Combination therapy with interferon and ribavarin may be effective for hepatitis C infections. |
| Bacterial vaginosis | The most common causative agent, the *Gardnerella vaginalis* bacterium, is sometimes transmitted through coitus. | In women, a fishy- or musty-smelling thin discharge, like flour paste in consistency and usually grey. Most men are asymptomatic. | Metronidazole (Flagyl) by mouth or intravaginal applications of topical metronidazole gel or clindamycin cream |
| Candidiasis (yeast infection) | The *Candida albicans* fungus may accelerate growth when the chemical balance of the vagina is disturbed; it may also be transmitted through sexual interaction. | White, "cheesy" discharge; irritation of vaginal and vulval tissues | Vaginal suppositories or topical cream, such as clotrimazole and miconazole, or oral fluconazole |
| Trichomoniasis | The protozoan parasite *Trichomonas vaginalis* is usually passed through genital sexual contact. | White or yellow vaginal discharge with an unpleasant odour; vulva is sore and irritated. | Metronidazole (Flagyl™) for both women and men |

Source: Crooks, Robert L., and Karla Baur. *Our Sexuality,* 8th ed. Pacific Grove, CA: Wadsworth, 2002.

are at greater risk. More than half of 13- to 24-year-old women with HIV are infected heterosexually.[84]

Even when high school and college students have generally accurate knowledge about STIs, they don't necessarily practise safe sex. According to research, those students with the greatest number of sexual partners are least likely to use condoms. While college and university students admit to engaging in behaviours that put them at risk of HIV and other STIs, they believe that other students do so much more often.[85]

Various factors put young people at risk of STIs, including:

✔ **Feelings of invulnerability.** These lead to risk-taking behaviour. Even though well informed of the risks, adolescents may remain unconvinced that anything bad can or will happen to them.

✔ **Multiple partners.** In surveys of students, a significant minority report having had four or more sexual partners during their lifetime.

✔ **Failure to use condoms.** Among those who reported having had sexual intercourse in the previous three months, fewer than half reported condom use. Students who had had four or more sexual partners were significantly less likely to use condoms than those who had fewer partners.

✔ **Substance abuse.** Teenagers who drink or use drugs are more likely to engage in sexually risky behaviours, including sex with partners whose health status and history they do not know and unprotected intercourse.[86]

Although young adulthood is the age of greatest risk for acquiring STIs, results from the 2003 Canadian Youth, Sexual Health and HIV/AIDS study indicate that 12 percent of boys and 16 percent of girls in Grade 11 did not know where to go to get condoms. As well, 27 percent of Grade 7 students and 14 percent of Grade 9 and 11 students had not received any instruction about HIV/AIDS between 2001 and 2003. Seventeen percent of Grade 7 students, 8 percent of Grade 9 students, and 11 percent of Grade 11 students reported that they had not had any instruction about human sexuality, puberty, or birth control over the past two years.[87]

## Prevention and Protection

Abstinence is the only guarantee of sexual safety—and an option that some people are choosing as a way to safeguard their physical health, their fertility, and their future.

## Strategies for Change

### What to Do If You Have a STI

▲ If you suspect that you have a STI, don't feel too embarrassed to get help through a physician's office or a clinic. Treatment relieves discomfort, prevents complications, and halts the spread of the disease.

▲ Following diagnosis, take oral medication (which may be given instead of or in addition to shots) exactly as prescribed.

▲ Try to figure out from whom you got the STI. Be sure to inform that person, who may not be aware of the problem.

▲ If you have a STI, never deceive a prospective partner about it. Tell the truth—simply and clearly. Be sure your partner understands exactly what you have and what the risks are.

For men and women who are sexually active, a mutually faithful sexual relationship with just one healthy partner is the safest option. For those not in such relationships, safer-sex practices are essential for reducing risks. However, no "protection" is 100 percent "safe." For instance, nononxynol-9, the most widely used spermicide in the world, does not protect women from gonorrhea or chlamydia, according to a study of more than 1200 women being treated for sexually transmitted diseases.[88] As discussed in Chapter 8, recent evidence suggests that frequent use of N-9 may actually increase the risk of infection by HIV by causing disruptions and lesions in the genital mucosal lining.[89]

You can't tell if someone you're dating or hope to date has been exposed to a STI. Ideally, before engaging in any such behaviour, both of you should talk about your prior sexual history (including number of partners and sexually transmitted diseases) and other high-risk behaviour, such as the use of injection drugs. If you know someone well enough to consider having sex with that person, you should be able to talk about STIs. If the person is unwilling to talk, you shouldn't have sex.

## Chlamydia

The most widespread sexually transmitted infection in Canada is *Chlamydia trachomatis*—**Chlamydia**. Although the rates of Chlamydia were in decline for many years, rates have risen steadily since 1997.[90] Those at greatest risk of chlamydial infection are individuals 25 years old or younger who engage in sex with more than one new partner within a two-month period and women who use birth control pills or other nonbarrier contraceptive methods.

As many as 75 percent of women and 50 percent of men with chlamydia have no symptoms or symptoms so mild that they don't seek medical attention. Without treatment, up to 40 percent of cases of Chlamydia can lead to pelvic inflammatory disease, a serious infection of the woman's fallopian tubes that can also damage the ovaries and uterus.[91] Also, women infected with Chlamydia may have three to five times the risk of getting infected with HIV if exposed. Babies exposed to Chlamydia in the birth canal during delivery can be born with pneumonia or with an eye infection called conjunctivitis, both of which can be dangerous unless treated early with antibiotics. Men can develop scarring of the urethra, making urination difficult.

## Pelvic Inflammatory Disease

Infection of a woman's fallopian tubes or uterus, called **pelvic inflammatory disease (PID),** is not actually a STI, but rather a complication of STIs. About one in every seven women of reproductive age has PID; half of all adult women may have had it.

Ten to 20 percent of initial episodes of PID lead to scarring and obstruction of the fallopian tubes severe enough to cause infertility. Other long-term complications are ectopic pregnancy and chronic pelvic pain. Smoking also may increase the likelihood of PID. Two bacteria—gonococcus (the culprit in gonorrhea) and Chlamydia—are responsible for one-half to one-third of all cases of PID.

Women may learn that they have PID only after discovering that they cannot conceive or after they develop an ectopic pregnancy. PID causes an estimated 15 to 30 percent of all cases of infertility every year and about half of all cases of ectopic pregnancy. Most women do not experience any symptoms, but some may develop abdominal pain, tenderness in certain sites during pelvic exams, or vaginal discharge.

## Gonorrhea

**Gonorrhea** (sometimes called "the clap") is another common STI. The incidence is highest among teenagers and young adults. Sexual contact, including oral-genital sex, is the primary means of transmission.

Most men who have gonorrhea know it. Thick, yellow-white pus oozes from the penis and urination causes a burning sensation. These symptoms usually develop two to nine days after the sexual contact that infected them. Men have a good reason to seek help: it hurts too much not to. Women also may experience discharge and burning on urination. However, as many as eight out of ten infected women have no symptoms.

Gonococcus, the bacterium that causes gonorrhea, can live in the vagina, cervix, and fallopian tubes for months, even years, and continue to infect the woman's sexual partners.

If left untreated in men or women, gonorrhea spreads through the urinary–genital tract. In women, the inflammation travels from the vagina and cervix, through the uterus, to the fallopian tubes and ovaries. The pain and fever are similar to those caused by stomach upset, so a woman may dismiss the symptoms. Eventually these symptoms diminish, even though the disease spreads to the entire pelvis. Pus may ooze from the fallopian tubes or ovaries into the peritoneum (the lining of the abdominal cavity), sometimes causing serious inflammation. However, this, too, can subside in a few weeks. Gonorrhea, the leading cause of sterility in women, can cause PID. In pregnant women, gonorrhea becomes a threat to the newborn. It can infect the infant's external genitals and cause a serious form of conjunctivitis, an inflammation of the eye that may lead to blindness. As a preventive step, newborns may have penicillin dropped into their eyes at birth.

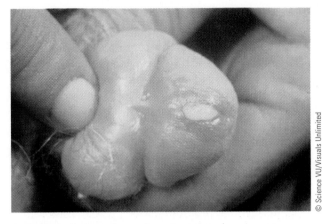

▲ A cloudy discharge is symptomatic of gonorrhea.

In men, untreated gonorrhea can spread to the prostate gland, testicles, bladder, and kidneys. Among the serious complications are urinary obstruction and sterility caused by blockage of the vas deferens (the excretory duct of the testis). In both sexes, gonorrhea can develop into a serious, even fatal, bloodborne infection that can cause arthritis in the joints and meningitis, attack the heart muscle and lining, and attack the skin and other organs.

Although a blood test has been developed for detecting gonorrhea, the tried-and-true method of diagnosis is still a microscopic analysis of cultures from the male's urethra, the female's cervix, and the throat and anus of both sexes.

## Nongonococcal Urethritis

The term **nongonococcal urethritis (NGU)** refers to any inflammation of the urethra that is not caused by gonorrhea. NGU is the most common STI in men. Three microorganisms—*Chlamydia trachomatis*, *Ureaplasma urealyticum*, and *Mycoplasma genitalium*—are the primary causes; the usual means of transmission is sexual intercourse. Other infectious agents, such as fungi or bacteria, allergic reactions to vaginal secretions, or irritation by soaps or contraceptive foams or gels may also lead to NGU.

NGU is more common in men than gonoccocal urethritis. The symptoms in men are similar to those of gonorrhea, including discharge from the penis (usually less than with gonorrhea) and mild burning during urination. Women frequently develop no symptoms or very mild itching, burning during urination, or discharge. Symptoms usually disappear after two or three weeks, but the infection may persist and cause cervicitis or PID in women and in men may spread to the prostate, epididymis, or both. Treatment usually consists of doxycycline and should be given to both sexual partners after testing. For men, a single oral dose of azithromycin has proven as effective as a standard seven-day course of doxycycline.

# Syphilis

A corkscrew-shaped, spiral bacterium called *Treponema pallidum* causes **syphilis.** This frail microbe dies in seconds if dried or chilled but grows quickly in the warm, moist tissues of the body, particularly in the mucous membranes of the genital tract. Entering the body through any tiny break in the skin, the germ burrows its way into the bloodstream. Sexual contact, including oral sex or intercourse, is a primary means of transmission. Genital ulcers caused by syphilis may increase the risk of HIV infection, while individuals with HIV may be more likely to develop syphilis.

Infectious syphilis is the least commonly reported bacterial sexually transmitted infection. The rate of infectious syphilis is increasing in both males and females in Canada—more so in males, however.[92]

Syphilis has clearly identifiable stages: primary, secondary, early latent (asymptomatic syphilis, within the first year), late latent (asymptomatic syphilis, after one year), and tertiary syphilis.[93] During the latent stage, highly contagious lesions of the skin or mucous membranes become evident. They may recur for two to four years. After four years, there is a loss of infectiousness. Until this stage of the disease, however, a pregnant woman can pass syphilis to her unborn child. If the fetus is infected in its fourth month or earlier, it may be disfigured or even die. If infected late in pregnancy, the child may show no signs of infection for months or years after birth but may then become disabled with the symptoms of tertiary syphilis.

In the tertiary stage, 10–20 years after the beginning of the latent stage, the most serious symptoms of syphilis emerge, generally in the organs in which the bacteria settled during latency. Syphilis that has progressed to this stage has become increasingly rare. Victims of tertiary syphilis may die of a ruptured aorta or of other heart damage or may have progressive brain or spinal cord damage, eventually leading to blindness, insanity, or paralysis.

Early diagnosis of syphilis can lead to a complete cure. Penicillin is the drug of choice for treating primary, secondary, and latent syphilis. The earlier treatment begins, the more effective it is. Those allergic to penicillin may be treated with doxycycline, ceftriaxone, or erythromycin. An added danger of not getting treatment for syphilis is an increased risk of HIV transmission.

 ## What Is Herpes?

Herpes (from the Greek word that means *to creep*) collectively describes some of the most common viral infections in humans. **Herpes simplex virus (HSV)** transmission occurs through close contact with mucous membranes or abraded skin. Herpes simplex exists in several varieties. *Herpes simplex virus 1 (HSV-1)* generally causes cold sores and fever blisters around the mouth. *Herpes simplex virus 2 (HSV-2)* may cause blisters and lesions on the penis, inside the vagina, on the cervix, in the pubic area, on the buttocks, or on the thighs.[94] However, both forms of the virus can infect any of these areas. With the increase of oral-genital sex, some doctors report finding type 2 herpes lesions in the mouth and throat.

HSV is not a reportable disease in Canada. Many individuals do not realize they carry the virus because they never develop genital lesions, or they experience only very subtle symptoms. Men and women aged 20 to 29 have higher rates of infection than other age groups.

Most people with herpes contract it from partners who were not aware of any symptoms or of their own contagiousness. Standard methods of diagnosing genital herpes in women, which rely primarily on physical examination and viral cultures, may miss as many as two-thirds of all cases. Newly developed blood tests are more effective in detecting unrecognized infections with HSV-2.

In the past, patients and most doctors thought people with herpes could not pass on the infection when they did not have any symptoms. Research shows, however, that the herpes virus is present in genital secretions and can also be transmitted from skin-to-skin contact even when no bodily fluids are exchanged. This means that even when a person does not show any signs of infection, they are still at risk for spreading HSV to a sex partner. It is estimated that in 70 percent of cases, genital herpes is transmitted by sexual contact from a person who is asymptomatic.[95] There is also growing evidence that genital herpes promotes the spread of HIV.[96]

When herpes sores are present, the infected person is highly contagious and should avoid bringing the lesions into contact with someone else's body through touching, sexual interaction, or kissing.

A newborn can be infected with genital herpes while passing through the birth canal, and the frequency of mother-to-infant transmission seems to be increasing. Most infected infants develop typical skin sores, which should be cultured to confirm a herpes diagnosis. Because of the risk of severe damage and possible death, caesarean delivery may be advised for a woman with active herpes lesions.

The virus that causes herpes never entirely goes away; it retreats to nerves near the lower spinal cord, where it remains for the life of the host. Herpes sores can return without warning weeks, months, or even years after their first occurrence, often during menstruation or times of stress or with sudden changes in body temperature.

Antiviral drugs, such as acyclovir (Zovirax), have proven effective in treating and controlling herpes. Infection with herpes viruses resistant to acyclovir is a growing problem, especially in individuals with immune-suppressing disorders. Clinical trials of an experimental vaccine to protect people from herpes infections are underway.[97]

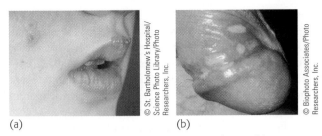

(a)                (b)

© St. Bartholomew's Hospital/Science Photo Library/Photo Researchers, Inc.

© Biophoto Associates/Photo Researchers, Inc.

▲ (a) Herpes simplex virus (HSV-1) as a mouth sore (b) Herpes simplex virus (HSV-2) as a genital sore.

## Human Papillomavirus

Infection with **human papillomavirus (HPV),** a pathogen that can cause *genital warts,* is the most common viral STI. A wide number of different strains of the virus exist, and some of these viral strains can lead to cervical cancer in women. A vaccine which prevents infection of the four of the most common forms of HPV was approved for use in Canada in July 2006. Health Canada supports the HPV vaccine use as "safe and effective." The vaccine is currently approved for use in females ages 9 to 26 and is administered as three doses given over the course of six months (at 0, 2, and 6 months).[98]

The HPV vaccine is not without controversy, however. Canadian researchers have raised many questions about the efficacy of the vaccine and the value of focusing on widespread vaccination for HPV as a routine part of sexual health treatment. Because the HPV vaccine is relatively new, it's not clear for how long the vaccine will be effective or if a booster shot will be required in later years. Research results are also not yet available on the effectiveness of the HPV vaccine when given at the same time as other immunizations. Finally, because cervical cancer is relatively rare, some sexual health experts are concerned that focus on and funding for HPV immunizations may take resources away from preventing other, more widespread, sexually transmitted infections.[99]

Regardless of whether or not you or your partner have had the HPV vaccine, it is vital to remember that a vaccine is just one step in the actions necessary to prevent genital warts or cervical cancer. The Canadian Federation for Sexual Health notes that the HPV vaccination should not be used as a replacement for cervical cancer screening such as Pap tests, nor a replacement for prevention strategies such as condom use.[100]

Young women who engage in sexual intercourse at an early age are more likely than those with later sexual debuts to become infected with HPV. Their risk also increases if they have multiple sexual partners or a history of a sexually transmitted disease, use drugs, smoke, use oral contraceptives, or have sex with partners with a history of HPV.

HPV is transmitted primarily through vaginal, anal, and oral-genital sex. More than half of HPV-infected

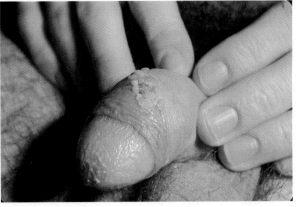

© Marazzi/Photo Researchers, Inc.

▲ Human papillomavirus, which causes genital warts, is the most common viral STI.

individuals do not develop any symptoms. After contact with an infected individual, genital warts may appear from three weeks to 18 months, with an average period of about three months. The warts are treated by freezing, cauterization, chemicals, or surgical removal. Recurrences are common because the virus remains in the body.

HPV infection may invade the urethra and cause urinary obstruction and bleeding. It greatly increases a woman's risk of developing a precancerous condition called *cervical intraepithelial neoplasia,* which can lead to cervical cancer. There also is a strong association between HPV infections and cancer of the vagina, vulva, urethra, penis, and anus.

Women who have had a HPV infection should examine their genitals regularly and get an annual Pap smear. However, this diagnostic test for cervical cancer doesn't identify HPV infection. A newer, more specific test can recognize HPV soon after it enters the body. Women who test positive should undergo checkups for cervical changes every 6 to 12 months. If precancerous cells develop, surgery or laser treatment can prevent further growth.

HPV may also cause genital warts in men and increase the risk of cancer of the penis. HPV-infected men, who may not develop any symptoms, can spread the infection to their partners. People with visible genital warts also may have asymptomatic or subclinical HPV infections that are extremely difficult to treat.

No form of therapy has been shown to completely eradicate HPV, nor has any single treatment been uniformly effective in removing warts or preventing their recurrence.

## Chancroid

A **chancroid** is a soft, painful sore or localized infection caused by the bacterium *Haemophilus ducrevi* and usually acquired through sexual contact. Half of the cases heal by themselves. In other cases, the infection may spread to the lymph glands near the chancroid, where large amounts of pus can accumulate and destroy much of the local tissue. The incidence of this STI, widely prevalent in Africa and tropical and semitropical regions, is rapidly increasing. Chancroids, which may increase susceptibility to HIV infection, are believed to be a major factor in the heterosexual spread of HIV. This infection is treated with antibiotics (ceftriaxone, azithromycin, or erythromycin) and can be prevented by keeping the genitals clean and washing them with soap and water in case of possible exposure.

## Pubic Lice and Scabies

These infections are sometimes, but not always, transmitted sexually. *Pubic lice* (or "crabs") are usually found in the pubic hair, although they can migrate to any hairy areas of the body. Lice lay eggs called *nits* that attach to the base of the hair shaft. Irritation from the lice may produce intense itching. Scratching to relieve the itching can produce sores. *Scabies* is caused by a mite that burrows under the skin, where they lay eggs that hatch and undergo many changes in the course of their life cycle, producing great discomfort, including intense itching.

Lice and scabies are treated with applications of permethrin cream and Lindane shampoo to all the areas of the body where there are concentrations of body hair (genitals, armpits, scalp). You must repeat treatment in seven days to kill any newly developed adults. Wash or dry-clean clothing and bedding.

## HIV

HIV is a global disease of terrible proportions. HIV robs society of the untapped potential of millions of people each year, causing distress and suffering for victims living with the disease and those who care for them. What frustrates health experts is the knowledge that the transmission of HIV is preventable.

Thirty years ago, no one knew about **human immunodeficiency virus (HIV)** nor had they heard of *acquired immune deficiency syndrome (AIDS)*. Once seen as an epidemic affecting primarily gay men and injection-drug users, HIV has taken on a very different form. Today, heterosexuals in developing countries have the highest rates of infection and mortality. HIV infection continues to spread, doubling every 10 years. According to estimates from the Joint United Nations Program on HIV/AIDS (UNAIDS), 33.2 million people are living with HIV infection worldwide, with 2.5 million people becoming newly infected in 2007. Globally, an estimated 2.1 million people

died of AIDS-related illnesses in 2007. The region that has been most affected is sub-Saharan Africa.[101] The epidemic appears to be gathering momentum in other parts of the world too, notably in Eastern Europe and Asia. The mortality rate for AIDS is declining, but HIV infection rates are increasing in certain groups, including women, children, Aboriginal peoples, and ethnic minorities.

In Canada, the HIV epidemic continues to grow. The Public Health Agency of Canada (PHAC) estimates that an estimated 62 561 people in Canada were living with HIV infection (including AIDS) at the end of 2006. This represents an increase from the 2002 estimate of 50 000. An estimated 2558 new HIV infections occurred in 2006 compared with 2491 in 2002.[102]

There has been progress in lowering the rates of HIV transmission through measures such as reducing the incidence of unprotected intercourse and the number of sex partners, delaying sexual initiation, decreasing the incidence of other STIs, directing injection-drug users into drug treatment programs, and reducing needle sharing. Screening the blood supply has reduced the rate of transfusion-associated HIV transmission by 99.9 percent.

Treatment with antiretroviral drugs during pregnancy and birth has reduced transmission by about 90 percent in optimal conditions. Among drug users in some settings, programs that combine addiction treatment and needle exchange reduced the incidence of HIV infection by 30 percent. Even in developing nations, such as Thailand and Uganda, national prevention programs, such as free distribution of condoms and needle-exchange programs, have reduced HIV prevalence by as much as 50 percent.

## The Spread of HIV

In a United Nations AIDS release, Dr. Peter Piot, the executive director of the Joint United Nations Programme on HIV/AIDS, suggested that it was inconceivable that AIDS would spread so rapidly.[103] The reality of HIV is that in many parts of the world it is still in its early stages. HIV is characterized by a relatively long gap between infection and resulting major illnesses.

Several factors—including frequent sexual activity with multiple, anonymous partners and high-risk sexual practices, such as anal intercourse—may have caused its quick spread through homosexual communities in the 1980s. HIV also spread among injection-drug users who, by sharing contaminated needles, injected the virus directly into their bloodstream as well as through heterosexual contact.

The most affected group of Canadians continues to be men who have sex with men (MSM). Approximately 20 percent of infections are related to injection-drug users (IDU). Women, youth, and Aboriginal injection-drug users are particularly at risk of HIV infection. Youth are at risk because many young people perceive that HIV is not a threat to them and do not adopt and maintain behaviours that protect them against infection.

## Reducing the Risk of HIV Transmission

Although no one is immune to HIV, you can reduce the risk if you abstain from sexual activity, remain in a monogamous relationship with an uninfected partner, and do not inject drugs. If you're not in a long-term monogamous relationship with a partner you're sure is safe and you're not willing to abstain from sex, there are things you can do to lower your risk of HIV infection. Remember that the risk of HIV transmission depends on sexual behaviour, not sexual orientation. Whether homosexual, heterosexual, or bisexual, you need to know about HIV transmission and the kinds of sexual activity that increase your risk:

✔ Casual contact does *not* spread HIV infection. You cannot get HIV infection from drinking from a water fountain, contact with a toilet seat, or touching an infected person. Compared to other viruses, HIV is extremely difficult to get.

✔ HIV can live in blood, semen, vaginal fluids, and breast milk.

✔ You cannot tell visually whether a potential sexual partner has HIV. A blood test is needed to detect the antibodies that the body produces to fight HIV, thus indicating infection.

✔ HIV can be spread in semen and vaginal fluids during a single instance of anal, vaginal, or oral sexual contact between heterosexuals, bisexuals, or homosexuals. The risk increases with the number of sexual encounters with an infected partner.

✔ Teenage girls may be particularly vulnerable to HIV infection because the immature cervix is easily infected.

✔ Anal intercourse is an extremely high-risk behaviour because HIV can enter the bloodstream through tiny breaks in the lining of the rectum. HIV transmission is much more likely to occur during unprotected anal intercourse than vaginal intercourse.

✔ Other behaviours that increase the risk of HIV infection include having multiple sexual partners, engaging in sex without condoms, sexual contact with persons known to be at high risk (for example, prostitutes or injection-drug users), and sharing injection equipment for drugs.

✔ Individuals are at greater risk if they have an active sexual infection. Sexually transmitted diseases, such as herpes, gonorrhea, and syphilis, facilitate transmission of HIV during vaginal or rectal intercourse.

✔ No cases of HIV transmission by deep kissing have been reported, but it could happen. Studies have found blood in the saliva of healthy people after kissing; other lab studies have found HIV in saliva. Social (dry) kissing is safe.

✔ Oral sex can lead to HIV transmission. The virus in any semen that enters the mouth could make its way into the bloodstream through tiny nicks or sores in the mouth. A man's risk in performing oral sex on a woman is smaller because an infected woman's genital fluids have much lower concentrations of HIV than does semen.

✔ HIV infection is not widespread among lesbians, although there have been documented cases of possible female-to-female HIV transmission. In each instance, one partner had sex with a bisexual man or male injection-drug user or had injected drugs herself.

Education can help you adopt and maintain behaviours that are protective against HIV. Hawa et al.[104] suggest that knowledge and motivation are the strongest influences on first-year Canadian college and university students' sexual behaviour when reducing HIV-related risk. Their research indicates that prevention programs should emphasize skills that help college and university students resist peer pressure, as well as techniques that make youth aware of the social pressures that work against HIV-preventative behaviour.

The type of education is important, however. Findings from the Canadian Youth, Sexual Health and HIV/AIDS Study indicate that television and the Internet were common sources of information for students, but when it was their main source, they were more likely to have low knowledge scores about the risks of HIV/AIDS.[105]

## HIV Infection

HIV infection refers to a spectrum of health problems that results from immunologic abnormalities caused by the virus when it enters the bloodstream. In theory, the body may be able to resist infection by HIV. In reality, in almost all cases, HIV destroys the cell-mediated immune system, particularly the CD41 T-lymphocytes (also called *T4 helper cells*). The result is greatly increased susceptibility to various cancers and opportunistic infections (infections that take hold because of the reduced effectiveness of the immune system).

Researchers now know that HIV triggers a state of all-out war within the immune system. Almost immediately following infection with HIV, the immune system responds aggressively by manufacturing enormous numbers of CD41 cells. It eventually is overwhelmed, however, as the viral particles continue to replicate, or multiply. The intense war between HIV and the immune system indicates that the virus itself, not a breakdown in the immune system, is responsible for disease progression.

Shortly after becoming infected with HIV, individuals may experience a few days of flu-like symptoms, which most ignore or attribute to other viruses. Some people develop a more severe mononucleosis-type syndrome. After this stage, individuals may not develop any signs or symptoms of disease for a period ranging from weeks to more than 12 years.

HIV symptoms, which tend to increase in severity and number the longer the virus is in the body, may include any of the following:

✔ Swollen lymph nodes
✔ Fever, chills, and night sweats
✔ Diarrhea
✔ Weight loss
✔ Coughing and shortness of breath
✔ Persistent tiredness
✔ Skin sores
✔ Blurred vision and headaches
✔ Development of other infections, such as certain kinds of pneumonia

HIV infection is associated with a variety of HIV-related diseases, including different cancers and dangerous infections. HIV-infected individuals may develop persistent generalized lymphadenopathy, enlargement of the lymph nodes at two or more different sites in the body. This condition typically persists for more than three months without any other illness to explain its occurrence. Diminished mental function may appear before other symptoms. Tests conducted on infected but apparently healthy men have revealed impaired coordination, problems in thinking, or abnormal brain scans.

## HIV Testing

As of May 1, 2003, HIV infection became legally notifiable in all provinces and territories. In most testing situations, laboratories and physicians are responsible for reporting HIV infection; however, this varies in each province or territory. Notification to the Centre for Infectious Disease Prevention at the national level is still voluntary, but all provinces and territories have been reporting positive HIV and AIDS cases. This information is considered important for designing and targeting intervention programs.

All HIV tests measure antibodies, cells produced by the body to fight HIV infection. A negative test indicates no exposure to HIV. It can take three to six months for the body to produce the telltale antibodies; however, so a negative result may not be accurate, depending on the timing of the test.

There are three types of HIV testing available in Canada:[106]

✔ Nominal/name-based HIV testing:
  • Available at health clinics or the office of a health-care provider.
  • The person ordering the tests knows the identity of the person being tested for HIV, and the HIV test is ordered using the name of the person being tested.
  • Patient information such as age, gender, city of residence, name of diagnosing health-care provider, country of birth, HIV-related risk factors, and laboratory data is collected.
  • If the HIV test result is positive, the person ordering the test is legally obligated to notify public-health officials.
  • The test result is recorded in the health-care record of the person being tested.

✔ Non-nominal/non-identifying HIV testing:
  • As above, but the HIV test is ordered using a code name or the initials of the person being tested.

✔ Anonymous testing:
  • The HIV test is carried out using a code. The person ordering the HIV test and the laboratory carrying out the testing on the blood sample do not know to whom the code belongs.
  • Test results are not recorded on the health-care record of the person being tested.
  • If someone tests positive for HIV infection through anonymous testing, that person may subsequently decide to give his or her name and include the HIV test result in the medical record.

Newly developed blood tests can determine how recently a person was infected with HIV and distinguish between longstanding infections and those contracted within the previous four to six months. Health officials recommend HIV testing for the following individuals:

✔ Men who have had sex with other men, regardless of whether they consider themselves homosexual.
✔ Anyone who uses injection drugs or has shared needles.
✔ Anyone who has had sex with someone who uses injection drugs or has shared needles.
✔ Women who have had sex with bisexual men.
✔ Anyone who has had sex with someone from an area with a high incidence of HIV infection.
✔ Individuals who have had sex with people they do not know well.
✔ Anyone who received blood transfusions or blood products between 1978 and 1985, their sexual partners, and, if they are new mothers, their infants.

## AIDS

In Canada a person is diagnosed with **acquired immune deficiency syndrome (AIDS)** if (1) they have undergone testing for HIV and received a positive result and (2) they have one or more of the clinical illnesses or indicator diseases that characterize AIDS.[107] Forty-eight countries of the WHO European Region, Australia, and New Zealand also follow this definition of AIDS diagnosis. In the United States, individuals must also have a CD4T–lymphocyte count of less than 200 cells per cubic millimetre of blood in order to meet the definition of AIDS.

People with AIDS also may experience persistent fever, diarrhea that persists for more than one month, or involuntary weight loss of more than 10 percent of normal body weight. Generalized lymphadenopathy may persist. Neurological disease—including dementia (confusion and impaired thinking) and other problems with thinking, speaking, movement, or sensation—may occur. Secondary infectious diseases that may develop in people who have had AIDS for a long time include *Pneumocystis carinii* pneumonia, tuberculosis, or oral candidiasis (thrush). Secondary cancers associated with HIV infection include Kaposi's sarcoma and cancer of the cervix. For individuals diagnosed in the last ten years, prophylactic medications have lowered the incidence of these diseases.

## Saleema Noon—The Best Job in the World

Our human potential story for this chapter is about Saleema Noon, a sexual health educator. Her job is to make sexual health easy to talk about. This can be a difficult task, but Saleema finds her work to be both meaningful and challenging. Her story is unique, one that might inspire you to not only take care with regard to your own sexual health, but also encourage you to find ways to include sexual health education in the work you might do in the future.

Her entry into this field came by way of a Masters degree at the University of British Columbia in an area called Family Studies. Her work as a teaching assistant for a course called Human Sexuality 316 taught her that that many university students had not been educated about sexual health. Findings from her graduate research with grade 10 students supported what she had discovered in her university classes— that students wanted more sexual education, they wanted it earlier, and they wanted it to be more relevant to their lives.

After graduation she had many jobs while she was building her business. They included being a house sitter, bank teller, daycare worker, and dog sitter. She laughs and says, "Unfortunately, there are not many want ads for sexual health educators!" She also worked as a family support worker with pregnant and parenting teens. The girls taught her about

Saleema Noon, a sexual health educator and workshop leader.

the value of accurate information in making smart decisions about sex.

A turning point for Saleema with regard to her career choice was a conversation she had with a grade 8 student upon returning from a doctor's appointment where the young girl's pregnancy had been confirmed. The conversation went something like this: "Saleema, I don't get it, how could this be happening?" Saleema responded, "Well, did you have sex?" The young woman replied, "Yes." Saleema asked, "Then why are you surprised?" The young woman replied, "But I had it on a Tuesday." Saleema was to learn later that this young girl had been told by a friend that as long as she didn't have sex on the weekend, she didn't need to worry about getting pregnant.

*continued*

Saleema knew then that she had to do whatever she could to help young people get the information they needed about sex education. She now works in schools, workplaces, and recreation centres. She speaks enthusiastically about seeing the excited faces of kindergarten children as they learn to be body scientists and the "grossed out" faces of grade 4 children who are beginning to learn about sex. She provides workshops and seminars for educators, health-care professionals, counsellors, and social workers. She also runs Go Girl! Empowerment Programs for girls aged 10 to 13.

Is this work easy? Not at all, but Saleema says she takes a moment each day to be grateful for a job she loves. She travels a lot. She must be enthusiastic when she is educating and performing for an entire school day. Spare moments find her replying to requests that come in through her website, www.saleemanoon.com. She must also deal with some parents who are convinced that sexual education might harm their children. However, the pros outweigh the cons, and she continues to enjoy work that is rewarding, fun, and inspirational—"the best job in the world!"

Her success did not come easy. She volunteered for many years. She also thanks her mentor, Meg Hickling, a renowned sexual health educator, for teaching her so much. She will be proud if she can accomplish a fraction of what Meg has done.

Advice she gives students about sexual health—be aware, become educated, protect yourself from STIs, unwanted pregnancies, and unhealthy relationships.

Advice on career choices—ask yourself what you are passionate about, what motivates you, and what type of job you see yourself doing. Be realistic, but be creative, too. She also suggests volunteering because: "In today's world you can have a dozen letters behind your name, but if you don't have experience you won't get very far."

## What Progress Has Been Made in Treating HIV/AIDS?

New forms of therapy have been remarkably effective in boosting levels of protective T cells and reducing *viral load*—the amount of HIV in the bloodstream. People with high viral loads are more likely to progress rapidly to AIDS than people with low levels of the virus.

The current "gold-standard" approach to combating HIV is known as HAART (Highly Active AntiRetroviral Therapies), which dramatically reduces viral load even though it does not eradicate the virus. This complex regimen uses one of 250 different combinations of three or more antiretroviral drugs. Since the development of HAART, the number of deaths among persons with AIDS has declined substantially, and the number of those living with AIDS has risen.

A drawback to the treatment is serious side effects, including anemia, mouth ulcers, diarrhea, respiratory difficulties, digestive problems, liver damage, and skin rashes. There also is concern about emerging resistance to some antiretroviral medications. Some Canadian medical experts suggest that drug resistance among individuals receiving treatment is on the rise. Further study is needed to develop guidelines for initial therapy of this disease and to help us understand and prevent the transmission of resistant variants.

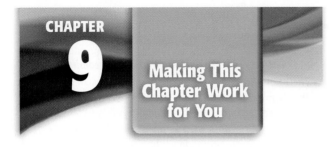

**CHAPTER 9**

**Making This Chapter Work for You**

1. Which of the following statements about disease-causing microbes is *false*?
   a. Helminths cause malaria, one of the major worldwide diseases.
   b. AIDS is caused by a retrovirus.
   c. In Canada, the most common protozoan disease is giardiasis.
   d. Salmonella and botulism are foodborne illnesses caused by bacteria.

2. Which of the following statements about the immune system is *false*?
   a. The immune system has two types of white blood cells: B cells, which produce antibodies that fight bacteria and viruses, and T cells, which protect against parasites, fungi, and cancer cells.
   b. Immune-system structures include the spleen, tonsils, thymus gland, and lymph nodes located throughout the body.
   c. Inoculation with a vaccine confers active immunity.
   d. The effect of stress on the human immune system depends on whether you can control the stressor and on the mental effort required to cope.

3. Before you have a vaccination it is important that you consider which of the following?
   a. if you are pregnant
   b. if you are allergic to eggs
   c. if you have a fever
   d. all of the above

4. Which of the following statements about the common cold and influenza is true?
   a. Influenza is just a more severe form of the common cold.
   b. Aspirin should be avoided by children and young adults who have a cold or influenza.
   c. The flu vaccine is also effective against most of the viruses that cause the common cold.
   d. Antibiotics are appropriate treatments for colds but not for influenza.

5. Which of the following statements about specific infectious diseases is *false*?
   a. Yeast infections can be treated with non-prescription drugs.
   b. Symptoms of UTIs include burning urination, chills, fever, and blood in the urine.
   c. Hepatitis A is usually transmitted through contaminated needles, transfusions, and sexual contact.
   d. College freshmen are at higher risk for contracting meningitis than the general population of young people between the ages of 18 and 23.

6. Sexually transmitted infections
   a. are the major cause of preventable sterility in Canada.
   b. can result in a severe kidney disease called pylonephritis.
   c. have declined in incidence in developing nations due to improving health standards.
   d. do not increase the risk of being infected with HIV.

7. Bacterial agents cause all of the following STIs *except*
   a. genital warts.
   b. syphilis.
   c. Chlamydia.
   d. gonorrhea.

8. Viral agents cause all of the following STIs *except*
   a. herpes.
   b. genital warts.
   c. hepatitis B.
   d. candidiasis.

9. Which of the following statements about HIV transmission is true?
   a. Individuals are not at risk for HIV if they are being treated for Chlamydia or gonorrhea.
   b. HIV can be transmitted between lesbians.
   c. Heterosexual men who do not practise safe sex are at less risk for contracting HIV than homosexual men who do practise safe sex.
   d. HIV cannot be spread in a single instance of sexual intercourse.

10. A person with AIDS
    a. has a low viral load and a high number of T4 helper cells.
    b. can no longer pass HIV to a sexual partner.
    c. may suffer from secondary infectious diseases and cancers.
    d. will not respond to treatment.

Answers to these questions can be found on page 450.

## Self Responsibility

*As to diseases, make a habit of two things—to help, or at least, to do no harm.*

**Hippocrates**

Becoming more aware of the ways you can protect yourself from infectious diseases is a step toward becoming self-responsible. It is also a way of supporting a healthy lifestyle. What stage are you at according to Prochaska's Stages of Change model? Did reading this chapter move you from Pre-contemplation to Contemplation? How might you prepare for the flu season or sexual relationships?

## Social Responsibility

*The global HIV/AIDS epidemic is an unprecedented crisis that requires an unprecedented response. In particular it requires solidarity—between the healthy and the sick, between rich and poor, and above all, between richer and poorer nations. We have 30 million orphans already. How many more do we have to get, to wake up?*

**Kofi Annan**

What does the maintenance stage mean to you when you think about infectious diseases? How does protecting yourself from infectious diseases support your "human potential"?

What can you do to help educate others about sexual health? Volunteer at a sexual health centre? Join a movement such as Stephen Lewis Foundation? Reach out if you can.

## Critical Thinking

1. Before you read this chapter, describe what you did to avoid contracting an infectious disease. Now that you have read the chapter, will you be making any changes in your practices? Briefly explain the convenience, advantages, and disadvantages of each practice that you have and/or will be using to prevent infection.

2. Some employers are now screening personnel for HIV. Some insurance companies test for HIV before selling a policy. Do you believe that an individual has the right to refuse to be tested for HIV? Should a physician be able to order a HIV test without a patient's consent? Can a surgeon refuse to operate on a HIV-infected patient or one who refuses HIV testing? Do patients have the right to know if their doctors, dentists, or nurses are HIV-positive?

3. A man who developed herpes sued his former girlfriend. A woman who became sterile as a result of pelvic inflammatory disease (PID) took her ex-husband to court. A woman who contracted HIV infection from her dentist, who had died of AIDS, filed suit against his estate. Do you think that anyone who knowingly transmits a STI should be held legally responsible? Do you think such an act should be a criminal offence?

## SITES & BYTES

### Canadian Aboriginal Aids Network
**www.caan.ca**

This non-profit coalition of individuals and organizations provides leadership, support, and advocacy for Aboriginal people living with and affected by HIV/AIDS.

### The Canadian AIDS Treatment Information Exchange (CATIE)
**www.catie.ca**

At this site you can access treatment information as well as information about AIDS service organizations. CATIE is a leading source of HIV/AIDS treatment information for Canadians living with the virus and their caregivers.

### Canadian Immunization Guide, (2006) Seventh Edition
**www.phac-aspc.gc.ca/publicat/cig-gci**

Recommendations by the National Advisory Committee on Immunization (NACI) on the use of vaccines in Canada are contained in this guide.

### Sexuality and U
**www.sexualityandu.ca/home_e.aspx**

This comprehensive site has information about many sexually transmitted infections, contraception, sexuality, and reproductive health issues.

### Travel Health
**www.phac-aspc.gc.ca/tmp-pmv/index-eng.php**

If you are travelling outside Canada, this site is a must. Find up-to-date information on international disease outbreaks, immunization recommendations for international travel, and general health advice for travelling.

Please note that links are subject to change. If you find a broken link, use a search engine such as www.google.ca and search for the website by typing keywords.

### InfoTrac® College Edition Activity
Ottenritter, N.W. (2004). Service learning, social justice, and campus health. (Viewpoint). *Journal of American College Health, 52*(4), 189–91.

1. Describe service learning.
2. Discuss how service learning can enhance a college or university education.
3. Based on the information presented in this article, discuss two ways you might become involved in a service learning project on your campus.

You can find additional readings related to infectious diseases with InfoTrac® College Edition, an online library of more than 5000 journals and publications. Follow the instructions for accessing InfoTrac® that were packaged with your textbook; then search for articles using a keyword search.

For additional links and resources, visit our text-specific website at www.health.nelson.com.

## Key Terms

The terms listed here are used within the chapter on the page indicated. Definitions of the terms are in the Glossary at the end of this book.

abscess 216

acquired immune
deficiency syndrome
(AIDS) 233

antibiotics 210

antiviral drugs 210

autoimmune disorders 218

avian influenza 220

bacteria 210

bacterial vaginosis
(BV) 222

candidiasis 222

cell-mediated
immunity 215

chanchroid 229

Chlamydia 226

cystitis 223

fungus 211

gamma globulin 215

gonorrhea 227

helminths 211

hepatitis 221

herpes simplex virus
(HSV) 228

host 210

human immunodeficiency
virus (HIV) 230

human papillomavirus
(HPV) 229

humoral immunity 214

immunity 214

incubation period 214

inflammation 216

influenza 219

listeriosis 213

lymph nodes 216

meningitis 221

mononucleosis 222

nongonococcal urethritis
(NGU) 227

pathogen 210

pelvic inflammatory
disease (PID) 226

prions 213

protozoa 211

pyelonephritis 223

severe acute respiratory
syndrome (SARS) 220

sexually transmitted
infection (STI) 223

syphilis 228

systemic disease 216

trichomoniasis 222

urethritis 223

vector 210

virus 210

## References

1. Viruses. (2007, February). The Merck Manual of Medical Information. Available at www.merck.com/mmhe/sec17/ch198/ch198a.html.

2. Sproutnet. (n.d.). Virus. Available at www.sproutnet.com/Reports/viruses.htm.

3. American Society for Microbiology. (2006). Meet the Microbes. Virus or bacterium? Available at www.microbeworld.org/microbes/virus_bacterium.aspx.

4. American Society for Microbiology. (2006). Meet the Microbes. Types of Microbes. Fungi. Available at www.microbeworld.org/microbes/fungi/default.aspx.

5. Ibid.

6. Health Canada. (2005, August). Healthy Living. It's Your Health. West Nile virus. Available at www.hc-sc.gc.ca/hl-vs/iyh-vsv/diseases-maladies/wnv-vno-eng.php.

7. Public Health Agency of Canada. (2004). Dead birds submitted for West Nile virus: Diagnosis by health region, Canada as of October 20, 2004. Available at http://dsol-smed.phac-aspc.gc.ca/wnv/map600_e.phtml?0.

8. Environmental Health Services. (n.d.). West Nile virus brochure. DuPage County Health Department. Available at www.dupagehealth.org/ehs/wnv/brochure.asp.

9. Health Canada. (2005, May 15). Infectious Diseases. West Nile virus—Protect yourself! Safety tips on using personal insect repellents. Available at www.phac-aspc.gc.ca/wn-no/index-eng.php.

10. Ibid.

11. Public Health Agency of Canada. (2003, December 11). Notifiable Diseases on-line. Verotoxic E. coli. Available at http://dsol-smed.phac-aspc.gc.ca/dsol-smed/ndis/diseases/ecol_e.html.

12. Ibid.

13. Health Canada. (2008, August 29). About Health Canada. Media Room. Information Update. Health Canada reminds Canadians of steps they can take to protect themselves from Salmonella prevention. Available at www.hc-sc.gc.ca/ahc-asc/media/advisories-avis/_2008/2008_149-eng.php.

14. Ibid.

15. Botulism in Canada. (2001). Canadian Medical Association Journal, 164(4), 538. Available at http://collection.nlc-bnc.ca/100/201/300/cdn_medical_association/cmaj/vol-164/issue-4/0538.htm.

16. Health Canada. (December 8, 2006). Infant botulism. Available at www.hc-sc.gc.ca/hl-vs/iyh-vsv/diseases-maladies/botu-eng.php.

17. CTV.ca. (2008, September 19). Canada. Top Stories. Number of Listeria deaths in Canada reaches 18. Available at www.ctv.ca/servlet/ArticleNews/story/CTVNews/20080919/Listeria_toll_080919?s_name=&no_ads=.

18. Health Canada. (2008, August 28). Healthy Living. It's Your Health. Listeria and food safety. Available at www.hc-sc.gc.ca/hl-vs/iyh-vsv/food-aliment/listeria-eng.php.

19. CBC News Online. (2003, December 29). Indepth: Mad cow. Science and symptoms. Available at www.cbc.ca/news/background/madcow/science.html.

20. Guyer, R.L. (n.d.). Prions: Puzzling infectious proteins. National Institutes of Health. Available at http://science.education.nih.gov/home2.nsf/Educational+Resources/Topics/Science+in+the+News/D07612181A4E785B85256CCD0064857B.

21. Schumacher, A.J. (n.d.). Safe drinking water: An urgent global public health issue. Canadian Medical Association. Available at www.cma.ca/index.cfm/ci_id/43233/la_id/1.html.

22. Ibid.

23. Sullivan, P. (2004, October 18). Safety of drinking water remains a crucial health issue, CMA president says. Canadian Medical Association. Available at www.cma.ca/index.cfm/ci_id/10013192/la_id/1.html.

24. O'Connor, D.R. (Hon.). (2002, January 18). Part one: A summary report of the Walkerton inquiry: The events of May 2000 and related issues. Ontario Ministry of the Attorney General. Toronto: Publications Ontario. Available at www.attorneygeneral.jus.gov.on.ca/english/about/pubs/walkerton/part1.

25. Ibid.

26. CBC. (2000, February 8). Marketplace files: Bottled water. Available at http://cbc.ca/consumers/market/files/food/bottledwater.

27. Warburton, D.W. (2000). The microbiological safety of bottled waters. In Farber, J.M., & Todd, E.C.D. (eds). *Safe handling of foods.* New York: Marcel Dekker, Inc.

28. Li, W.M.K., Lacroix, B., & Powell, D.A. (2001). *The microbiological safety of bottled water in Canada.* Available at www. foodsafetynetwork.ca/articles/468/micro_sfty_bottled_water_ canada.pdf.

29. National Microbiology Laboratory (Winnipeg level 4 lab). (2002, March 14). Information. News release. Health Canada Online. Available at www.nml-lnm.gc.ca/overview-apercu-eng.htm.

30. BC Health Guide. (2008, May 23). Health Information. Immunizations. Available at www.bchealthguide.org/kbase/topic/ special/immun/sec1.htm.

31. Fox-Rushby, J.A., Kaddar, M., Levine, R., & Brenzel, L. (2004). The economics of vaccination in low and middle income countries. *Bulletin of the World Health Organization, 82*(9), 640. Available at www.who.int/bulletin/volumes/82/9/640.pdf.

32. Ibid.

33. World Health Organization. (2005, March). Immunization against diseases of public health importance. Fact sheet No. 288. Available at www.who.int/mediacentre/factsheets/fs288/en/index.html.

34. Public Health Agency of Canada. (2006). *Canadian immunization guide,* seventh edition. Available at www.phac-aspc.gc.ca/publicat/ cig-gci.

35. Public Health Agency of Canada. (2007, March 16). Immunization and Vaccines. Immunization schedules. Recommendations from the National Advisory Committee on Immunization (NACI). Available at www.phac-aspc.gc.ca/im/is-cv/index-eng.php.

36. Ibid.

37. Public Health Agency of Canada. (2008, January 8). Immunizations and Vaccines. Vaccine safety. Available at www.phac-aspc.gc.ca/im/ vs-sv/index-eng.php.

38. Ibid.

39. Cold-fighting echinacea. (2000, March). *Psychology Today,* p. 40.

40. Kirchner, J. (2001). A final look at oral zinc for the common cold. *American Family Physician, 63*(9), 1851.

41. Wang, M., et al. (2004). A proprietary extract from North American ginseng (Panax quinquefolium) enhances IL-2 and IFN-y productions in murine spleen cells induced by Con-A. *International Immunopharmacology, 4*(2), 311–15.

42. Goel, D.P., Geiger, J.D., Shan, J.J., Kriellaars, D., & Pierce, G.N. (2004). Doping-control urinalysis of a ginseng extract, Cold-FX, in athletes. *International Journal of Sport Nutrition and Exercise Metabolism, 14*(4), 473–80.

43. Linder, J., & Stafford, R. (2001). Antibiotic treatment of adults with sore throat by community primary care physicians. *Journal of the American Medical Association, 286*(10), 1181.

44. Committee to Advise on Tropical Medicine and Travel. (2005, March 15). Statement of travel, influenza, and prevention. *Canada Communicable Disease Report, 31*(ACS-2). Available at www .phac-aspc.gc.ca/publicat/ccdr-rmtc/05vol31/asc-dcc-2/index.html.

45. Flu season 2000–01. (2000, June 22). Centers for Disease Control and Prevention, Division of Media Relations.

46. National Advisory Committee on Immunization (NACI). (2004, June 15). Statement on influenza vaccination for the 2004–2005 season. *Canada Communicable Disease Report, 30*(ACS-3). Available at www.phac-aspc.gc.ca/publicat/ccdr-rmtc/04vol30/acs-dcc-3/ index.html.

47. University of Waterloo, Health Services. (2005, October 24). Daily Bulletin. Time for flu shots and other notes. Available at www. bulletin.uwaterloo.ca/2005/oct/24mo.html.

48. University of Victoria, Health Services. (2008, May 12). Letter to students from Dr. William Dyson, director of health services. Available at http://health.uvic.ca/news/index.html.

49. National Advisory Committee on Immunization (NACI). (2004, June 15). Statement on influenza vaccination for the 2004–2005 season. *Canada Communicable Disease Report, 30*(ACS-3). Available at www.phac-aspc.gc.ca/publicat/ccdr-rmtc/04vol30/acs-dcc-3/ index.html.

50. Luce, B., et al. (2001). Cost-effectiveness analysis of an intranasal influenza vaccine for the prevention of influenza in healthy children. *Pediatrics, 108*(2), 456.

51. Food and Drug Administration, Department of Health and Human Services. (2003, June 17). First nasal mist flu vaccine approved. FDA News, P03–45. Available at www.fda.gov/bbs/topics/NEWS/2003/ NEW00913.html.

52. Mutsch, M., et al. (2004). Use of inactivated intranasal influenza vaccine and the risk of Bell's Palsy in Switzerland. *The New England Journal of Medicine, 350*(9), 896–903. Available at http://content. nejm.org/cgi/content/short/350/9/896.

53. Flu drugs (antiviral). (2000, June 22). Centers for Disease Control and Prevention, Division of Media Relations.

54. Influenza and the new antivirals: Potential for misdiagnosis and possible misuse of antivirals. (2000, December 1). *Canada Communicable Disease Report, 26-23.* Available at www.phac-aspc .gc.ca/publicat/ccdr-rmtc/00vol26/dr2623ec.html.

55. Public Health Agency. (2006, October 27). Infectious Diseases. Avian influenza. Available at www.phac-aspc.gc.ca/influenza/ avian-eng.php.

56. World Health Organization. (2005, August 5). Avian influenza. Communicable Disease Surveillance and Response (CSR). Available at www.who.int/csr/disease/avian_influenza/country/en/.

57. Public Health Agency of Canada. (2006, October 27). Global reporting on avian influenza. Available at www.phac-aspc.gc.ca/ influenza/avian-eng.php.

58. Health Canada. (2006, December 7). Search A–Z index: Influenza; SARS. Available at www.hc-sc.gc.ca/hl-vs/iyh-vsv/diseases-maladies/ sars-sras-eng.php.

59. Ibid.

60. Ibid.

61. Meningitis Research Foundation of Canada. (n.d.). What is meningitis? Available at www.meningitis.ca/en/what_is_meningitis/ overview.shtml.

62. Harrison, L., & Pass, M. (2001). Invasive meningococcal disease in adolescents and young adults. *Journal of the American Medical Association, 286*(6).

63. Bruce, M., et al. (2001). Risk factors for meningococcal disease in college students. *Journal of the American Medical Association, 286*(6), 286.

64. Meningitis Research Foundation of Canada. (n.d.). What is meningitis? Available at www.meningitis.ca/en/what_is_meningitis/ overview.shtml.

65. National Advisory Committee on Immunization (NACI). (2005, April 15). Update on meningococcal C conjugate vaccines. *Canada Communicable Diseases Report, 31*(ACS 3). Available at www. phac-aspc.gc.ca/publicat/ccdr-rmtc/05vol31/asc-dcc-3/index.html.

66. Ibid.

67. Ibid.

68. Paneth, N., et al. (2000). Predictors of vaccination rates during a mass meningococcal vaccination program on a college campus. *Journal of American College Health, 49*(1).

69. Is vaccination against meningitis useful? The findings of an investigation in the Sherbrooke region, Quebec. (2002, April 15). *Canada Communicable Disease Report, 28-08.* Available at www. phac-aspc.gc.ca/publicat/ccdr-rmtc/02vol28/dr2808ea.html.

70. Levy, I., Chen, D., Sherman, M., Smith, D., & Krajden, M. (2001, June 1). Hepatitis a virus seroprevalence in 1000 university students in Toronto. Reported in *Canada Communicable Disease Report,*

*27-11*. Available at www.phac-aspc.gc.ca/publicat/ccdr-rmtc/ 01vol27/dr2711ea.html.

71. Zhang, J., Zou, S., & Guilivi, A. (2001, September). Hepatitis B in Canada. *Canada Communicable Disease Report, 27S3,* September 2001. Available at www.phac-aspc.gc.ca/publicat/ccdr-rmtc/ 01vol27/27s3/27s3e_e.html.

72. Ibid.

73. Ibid.

74. Hepatitis C fact sheet. (2008, June 27). Available at www.cdc.gov/ hepatitis.

75. Mayer, L.B., et al. (2002). Prevalance of body art (body piercing and tattooing) in university undergraduates and incidence of medical complications. *Mayo Clinic Proc, 77,* 29–34.

76. Mele, A., et al. (1995). Beauty treatments and risk of parenterally transmitted hepatitis: Results from the hepatitis surveillance system in Italy. *Scandinavian Journal of Infectious Disease, 27,* 441–44.

77. Holsen, D.S., Harthug, S., & Myremel, H. (1993). Prevalence of antibodies to hepatitis C virus and association with intravenous drug abuse and tattooing in a national prison in Norway. *European Journal of Clinical Microbiology Infectious Diseases, 12,* 673–76.

78. Riccio, N. (2000). When mono strikes. *Current Health 2, 26*(7), 16.

79. Weir, E. (2004). Bacterial vaginosis: More questions than answers. *Canadian Medical Association Journal, 171*(5), 448. Available at www.cmaj.ca/cgi/content/full/171/5/448.

80. Panchaud, C., et al. (2000) Sexually transmitted diseases among adolescents in developed countries. *Family Planning Perspectives, 32*(1).

81. Catchpole, M. (2001). Sexually transmitted infections: Control strategies. *British Medical Journal, 322*(7295), 1135.

82. Celentano, D., et al. (2002, February 28). Preventive intervention to reduce sexually transmitted infections. *Archives of Internal Medicine, 160*(4).

83. Stephenson, J. (2002). Youth ignorance of HIV/AIDS. *Journal of the American Medical Association, 288*(6), 689.

84. Bon, R., et al. (2001). Normative perceptions in relation to substance use and HIV-risky sexual behaviours of college students. *Journal of Psychology, 135*(2), 165.

85. Buunk, B., et al. (2002). The double-edge sword of providing information about safer sex. *Journal of Applied Social Psychology, 32*(4), 684.

86. O'Connor, M.L. (2000). Social factors play major role in making young people sexual risk-takers. *Family Planning Perspectives, 32*(1).

87. Boyce, W., Doherty, M., Fortin, C., & McKinnon, D. (2003). Canadian youth, sexual health and HIV/AIDS study. Council of Ministers of Education and Canadian Strategy on HIV/AIDS of Health Canada. Available at www.cmec.ca/publications/aids.

88. Nonoxynol-9 found ineffective against STDs. (2002). *Contemporary OB/GYN, 47*(7), 33.

89. Public Health Agency of Canada. (2004, May). Nonoxynol-9 and the risk of HIV transmission. HIV/AIDS Epi Update—May 2004. Available at www.phac-aspc.gc.ca/publicat/epiu-aepi/epi_update_ may_04.

90. Health Canada. (2006, December 6). Chlamydia. Available at www. hc-sc.gc.ca/hl-vs/iyh-vsv/diseases-maladies/chlamyd-eng.php.

91. Ibid.

92. Public Health Agency of Canada. (2002, February 11). Infectious syphilis in Canada. STI–Epi Update. Available at www.phac-aspc. gc.ca/publicat/epiu-aepi/std-mts/infsyph-eng.php.

93. Ibid.

94. Health Canada. (2005, August 9). Genital herpes. Available at www.hc-sc.gc.ca/hl-vs/iyh-vsv/diseases-maladies/herpes-eng.php.

95. Herpes Guide.ca (2007, August 01). Herpes Simplex Virus facts. HSV-2 infections. Available at www.herpesguide.ca/facts/hsv_2_ infections.html.

96. Armstrong, G., et al. (2001). Herpes. *American Journal of Epidemiology, 153*(912).

97. Wald, A., et al. (2000). Reactivation of genital herpes simplex virus type 2 infection in asymptomatic seropositive persons. *New England Journal of Medicine, 343*(12).

98. Public Health Agency. (2007, June 16). Infectious Diseases. Sexual Health. Human papillomavirus (HPV) prevention and HPV vaccine: Questions and answers. Available at www.phac-aspc.gc.ca/ std-mts/hpv-vph/hpv-vph-vaccine-eng.php.

99. Lippman A., Melnychuk R., Shimmin C., & Boscoe M. (2007). Human Papillomavirus, vaccines and women's health: Questions and cautions. *Canadian Medical Association Journal, 177*(5), 484–87.

100. Canadian Federation for Sexual Health. (2008, May 28). Human Papillomavirus position statement. Available at www.cfsh.ca/ About_CFSH/Position-Statements/HPV-Vaccine.aspx.

101. *2007 AIDS Epidemic Update.* (2007). UNAIDS/World Health Organization. Available at http://data.unaids.org/pub/ EPISlides/2007/2007_epiupdate_en.pdf.

102. Public Health Agency of Canada. (2008, March 13). HIV and AIDS in Canada. Surveillance report to December 31, 2006. Surveillance and Risk Assessment Division, Centre for Infectious Disease Prevention and Control. Available at www.phac-aspc.gc.ca/ aids-sida/publication/survreport/index-eng.php.

103. Public Health Agency of Canada. (2008, July 10). Government of Canada Report to the Secretary General of the United Nations on the United Nations General Assembly Special Session on HIV/ AIDS Declaration of Commitment on HIV/AIDS. January 2006– December 2007. Available at www.phac-aspc.gc.ca/aids-sida/ publication/ungass07/index-eng.php.

104. Hawa, R., Munro, B.E., & Doherty-Poririer, M. (1998). Information, motivation and behaviour as predictors of AIDS risk reduction among Canadian first-year university students. *The Canadian Journal of Human Sexuality, 7*(1), 9–19.

105. Boyce, W., Doherty, M., Fortin, C., & McKinnon, D. (2003). Canadian youth, sexual health and HIV/AIDS study. Council of Ministers of Education and Canadian Strategy on HIV/AIDS of Health Canada. Available at www.cmec.ca/publications/aids.

106. Public Health Agency in Canada. Infectious Diseases. (2004. December 1). HIV/AIDS. Reports and Publications. HIV/AIDS EPI Update, May 2004. HIV Testing and Infection Reporting in Canada. Available at www.phac-aspc.gc.ca/publicat/epiu-aepi/epi_ update_may_04/3-eng.php.

107. Public Health Agency of Canada. (2006, September 27). AIDS diagnosis. A guide to HIV/AIDS epidemiological and surveillance terms. Available at www.phac-aspc.gc.ca/publicat/haest-tesvs/a-eng. php.

# CHAPTER 10

## Lowering Your Risk of Major Diseases

© Andresr/Shutterstock

W hether or not you will get a serious disease at some time in your life may seem to be a matter of odds. Genetic tendencies, environmental factors, and luck affect your chances of having to face many health threats. However, you do have some control over such risks, and even if a major illness may be inevitable, you can often prevent or delay it for years, even decades.

Cardiovascular disease—the term for all disorders of the heart and blood vessels—is one example. While the rate of cardiovascular disease has declined 25 percent over the past 10 years, it remains the leading cause of death in Canada claiming the lives of more than 72 000 Canadians in 2004—31 percent of all male deaths and 33 percent of all female deaths. Cardiovascular disease also costs the Canadian economy more than $18 billion every year in physician services, hospital costs, lost wages, and decreased productivity.[1] However, lifestyle changes, such as quitting smoking and making dietary changes that lower blood pressure and cholesterol levels, can make a positive difference in preventing cardiovascular disease.

Some people mistakenly think of heart disease, cancer, and other disorders as illnesses of middle and old age. But the events leading up to these diseases often begin in childhood, develop in adolescence, and become a health threat to men and women in their thirties to fifties. This chapter provides information about the risk factors, silent dangers, and medical advances that can improve your chances of leading a healthier, longer life.

**After studying the material in this chapter, you will be able to:**

- **Explain** how the heart functions.
- **Identify** the risk factors for cardiovascular disease that you can control and those you cannot control.
- **Define** hypertension and **explain** its cause, prevention, and treatment.
- **List** the risk factors for cancer, and **describe** practical ways to reduce the risk.
- **Identify** the risk factors for diabetes (Type 1 and Type 2).

**???? FREQUENTLY ASKED QUESTIONS**

FAQ: What kind of diet is best for a healthy heart? p. 246

FAQ: Why should I worry about heart disease? p. 247

FAQ: What is a healthy cholesterol reading? p. 251

FAQ: What is a healthy blood pressure? p. 252

FAQ: What happens during a heart attack? p. 254

FAQ: What causes a stroke? p. 255

FAQ: Who is at risk for developing cancer? p. 257

FAQ: How can I reduce my cancer risk? p. 260

FAQ: Who is at risk for developing diabetes? p. 267

# How the Heart Works

The heart is a hollow, muscular organ with four chambers that serve as two pumps (see Figure 10-1). It is about the size of a clenched fist. Each pump consists of a pair of chambers formed of muscles. The upper two—each called an **atrium**—receive blood, which then flows through valves into the lower two chambers, the **ventricles,** which contract to pump blood out into the arteries through a second set of valves. A thick wall divides the right side of the heart from the left side; even though the two sides are separated, they contract at almost the same time. Contraction of the ventricles is called **systole;** the period of relaxation between contractions is called **diastole.** The heart valves, located at the entrance and exit of the ventricular chambers, have flaps that open and close to allow blood to flow through the chambers of the heart.

The *myocardium* (heart muscle) consists of branching fibres that enable the heart to contract or beat. The average adult heart beats between 70 and 80 times per minute. A "fit" or well-conditioned heart may beat between 50 and 60 beats per minute. With each beat, the heart pumps about 56 millilitres of blood. This may not sound like much, but it adds up to approximately 4.72 litres of blood pumped by the heart in one minute, or about 283 litres per hour.

The heart is surrounded by the *pericardium,* which consists of two layers of a tough membrane. The space between the two contains a lubricating fluid that allows the heart muscle to move freely. The *endocardium* is a smooth membrane lining the inside of the heart and its valves.

Blood circulates through the body by means of the pumping action of the heart, as shown in Figure 10-2. The right ventricle (on your own right side) pumps blood, via the *pulmonary arteries,* to the lungs, where it picks up oxygen (a gas essential to the body's cells) and gives off carbon dioxide (a waste product of metabolism). The blood returns from the lungs via the *pulmonary veins* to the left side of the heart, which pumps it, via the **aorta,** to the arteries in the rest of the body.

The *arteries* divide into smaller and smaller branches, and finally into **capillaries,** the smallest blood vessels of all (only slightly larger in diameter than a single red blood cell). The blood within the capillaries supplies oxygen and nutrients to the cells of the tissues and takes up various waste products. Blood returns to the heart via the veins: The blood from the upper body (except the lungs) drains into the heart through the *superior vena cava,* while blood from the lower body returns via the *inferior vena cava.*

The *workings* of this remarkable pump affect your entire body. If the flow of blood to or through the heart or to the rest of the body is reduced or if a disturbance occurs

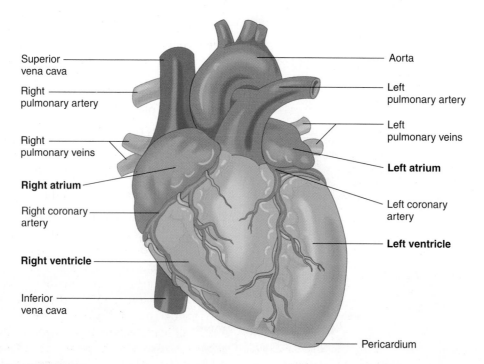

▲ **Figure 10-1** The Healthy Heart
The heart muscle is nourished by blood from the coronary arteries, which arise from the aorta. The pericardium is the outer covering of the heart.

Source: Hespenheide Design

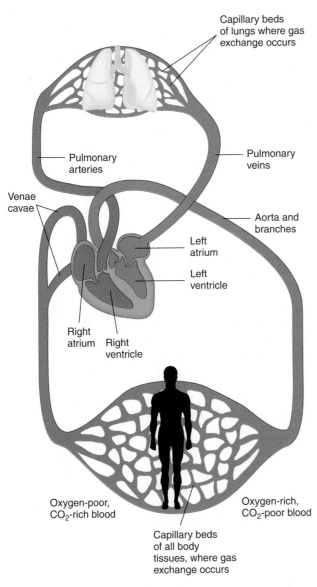

Capillary beds of lungs where gas exchange occurs

Pulmonary arteries

Pulmonary veins

Venae cavae

Aorta and branches

Left atrium

Left ventricle

Right atrium

Right ventricle

Oxygen-poor, $CO_2$-rich blood

Oxygen-rich, $CO_2$-poor blood

Capillary beds of all body tissues, where gas exchange occurs

▲ **Figure 10-2** The Path of Blood Flow
Blood is pumped from the right ventricle through the pulmonic valve into the pulmonary arteries, which lead to the lungs, where gas exchange ($O_2$ for $CO_2$) occurs. Oxygenated blood returning from the lungs drains into the left atrium and is pumped into the left ventricle through the mitral valve. It then passes through the aortic valve to the aorta and its branches. The oxygenated blood flows through the arteries, which extend to all parts of the body. Gas exchange occurs in the body tissues; oxygen is "dropped off" and carbon dioxide "picked up." Deoxygenated blood enters the right atrium through the inferior and superior vena cava, then to the right ventricle through the tricuspid valve. The photo depicts a computer-enhanced image of a healthy heart.

in the small bundle of highly specialized cells in the heart that generate electrical impulses to control heartbeats, the result may at first be too subtle to notice. However, without diagnosis and treatment, these changes could develop into a life-threatening problem.

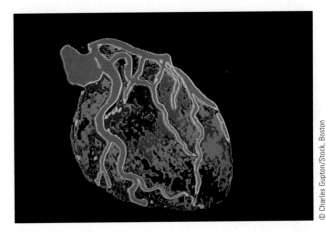

© Charles Gupton/Stock, Boston

Perhaps the biggest breakthrough in the field of cardiology has been not a test or a treatment, but a realization: *Heart disease is not inevitable.* We can keep our hearts healthy for as long as we live, but the process of doing so must start early and continue throughout life.

## Preventing Heart Problems

Risk factors related to lifestyle include smoking, physical inactivity, high blood cholesterol, and raised blood pressure.[2] The best way to protect your heart is by making positive changes in your lifestyle, such as not smoking, exercising, controlling your weight, and limiting saturated fat in your diet.[3] A new Canadian resource—*The Healthy Heart Kit*[4]—cosponsored by Health Canada and the Heart and Stroke Foundation of Canada, provides some helpful suggestions for individuals wanting to implement lifestyle changes. There is also a physician's guide that outlines strategies that can be used for health-care providers. This section might be of interest to students planning on becoming doctors or working in the health-promotion field.

## Physical Activity

For years we've known that regular exercise reduces the risk of heart attack, helps maintain a healthy body weight, lowers blood pressure, and improves metabolism. If rigorous and frequent enough, it also may increase longevity. But you don't have to head to a gym or hit the bike path to keep your heart healthy. As recent studies have confirmed, lifestyle activities, such as walking, housecleaning, and gardening are also effective in improving heart function, lowering blood pressure, and maintaining or losing weight.[5] (See Chapter 4 for a complete discussion of the benefits of regular physical activity.)

For heart health, aerobic endurance activities are the most important. Health Canada recommends accumulating 30 to 60 minutes of moderate aerobic physical activity four to seven days a week to stay healthy. You can add up activities in periods of at least 10 minutes each.[6]

## What Kind of Diet Is Best for a Healthy Heart?

There is so much nutritional information available through many sources—the media, Internet, brochures, pamphlets, and books—that it is sometimes a challenge to plan a heart-healthy diet. A balanced, low-saturated-fat diet that includes a variety of foods is still the best recipe for a healthy heart. In addition to regular physical activity, you can lower your risk of heart disease and stroke by eating well. An introduction to healthy eating was presented in Chapter 5. The following information will provide a nutrition review with specific emphasis on heart health.

### Fat—Good and Bad

Saturated fat is one dietary villain in the development of heart disease. Saturated fats raise our levels of blood cholesterol or LDL (low-density lipoproteins), a "bad" cholesterol that leaves plaque deposits on the artery walls. Foods containing saturated fats come from animal sources. They include fatty meat, poultry with skin, higher-fat dairy products, and butter. Palm and coconut oils also contain saturated fats. Fast foods are notorious for saturated fats as are many ready-made or prepared foods. Watch out as well for foods made with hydrogenated vegetable oil.[7] As discussed in Chapter 5, a low-fat eating plan means about 30 percent of one day's calories come from fat. For a woman this means about 65 grams of fat, for men about 90 grams of fat. To put this amount in perspective, one jelly doughnut provides 15–20 grams of fat.[8]

Not all fats are bad for us. Monounsaturated and polyunsaturated fats, found in vegetable oils, nuts, and fish, can help to reduce LDL cholesterol levels. Unfortunately, they are high in calories, so it is important to consume in moderation. Safflower, sunflower, canola, corn, and olive oil, and non-hydrogenated margarines are good choices. Dry roasted and raw nuts are also recommended because they contain mainly monounsaturated fats. Almonds are high in vegetable protein, whereas walnuts are a good source of omega-3 fatty acids, believed to have heart-healthy benefits.[9]

Recent research has shown that the most damaging kind of fat is trans fat. Found in foods made with shortening, partially hydrogenated vegetable oil, snack foods, baked goods, fast foods, and many prepared foods, these fats raise LDL cholesterol while lowering HDL (high-density lipoproteins), the "good" cholesterol that takes away excess "bad" cholesterol from the body.[10] (See "Risk Factors You Can Control," pages 247–250, for a more in-depth discussion of cholesterol.)

### Fish

Eating fish improves cardiovascular health in a number of ways. All fish, but especially salmon, mackerel, herring, trout, and sardines, contains omega-3 fatty acids, which help reduce the stickiness of your blood. Fish may also prevent erratic heart rhythms, a common cause of sudden cardiac death.[11] The recommendation for eating fish is two to three times per week.

### Vegetables and Fruit

According to the Heart and Stroke Foundation of Canada, when it comes to vegetables and fruit, more is good. They are an excellent source of Vitamins C and A, beta carotene, fibre, folic acid, potassium, and plant chemicals called phytochemicals, all of which reduce your risk of developing heart disease and stroke.[12]

### Fibre and Whole Grains

A daily intake of between 25 and 30 grams of soluble fibre each day has been shown to lower blood cholesterol levels. You can find this type of fibre in oatmeal, oat bran, lentils, legumes, and fruits such as apples and strawberries. Flax, a healthy heart food, has been shown to be rich in omega-3 fatty acids. Flax can also significantly lower cholesterol blood levels and reduce the development of blood clots.[13] When increasing your fibre intake, try to drink up to two litres of water per day.[14] Whole grains are a better choice than refined carbohydrates when it comes to heart health.

### Soy

Soy protein is found in soy beans and other products such as tofu, tempeh, and soy beverages. Consuming soy products may help to reduce elevated levels of LDL cholesterol.

### B Vitamins

$B_6$, $B_{12}$, and folic acid help to regulate blood levels of homocysteine, an amino acid produced by the body and believed to damage the lining of the artery walls, which can lead to a build-up of plaque and in turn increases your risk of heart attack or stroke. You can find $B_6$ in whole grain cereals, potatoes, bananas, chicken, milk, and tuna. Vitamin $B_{12}$ is found in meat, fish, poultry, dairy products, eggs, and some fortified cereals. Sources of folate include dark leafy green vegetables such as lettuce and broccoli.

## Moderate Alcohol Consumption

Some research suggests that moderate consumption of alcoholic beverages is good for heart health—among women aged 40 or older. The reported benefits for men are mixed, with some research suggesting that benefits for men the same age were not significant, while other studies indicated that a protective effect of moderate drinking is beneficial for both sexes.[15] However, as will be discussed in Chapter 12, there are other ways to protect your heart health besides drinking alcohol. These include regular physical activity and managing your stress levels.

# Risk Factors for Cardiovascular Disease

Many people don't realize that they're at risk of heart disease; one-quarter of heart-attack victims have no prior symptoms.[16] The best way of identifying individuals in potential danger is by looking for risk factors. About 19 percent of Canadian adults between the ages of 20 and 59 years have no elevated risk factors and can be categorized as low risk. Eighty percent of Canadians have at least one risk factor, 30 percent have two risk factors, and 11 percent have three or more risk factors[17] (see Table 10-1). You can take a personal heart and stroke assessment by using an online interactive tool on the Canadian Heart and Stroke Foundation's website. The assessment tool is free, confidential, and only takes about five to seven minutes. Access this feature at www.heartandstroke.com/site/c. ikIQLcMWJtE/b.3484475/ and click on *create a personalized action plan.*

A study done by Green, et al.[18] to determine the risk perception of heart disease in college students revealed some important findings. Sixty-five percent of the respondents in the study viewed their risk of a heart attack as lower or much lower than that of their peers and underestimated their risk of heart attacks. Also, many of these students did not recognize the risks that menopause, diabetes, and a family history of heart disease pose to cardiovascular health.

## Why Should I Worry about Heart Disease?

Although many people think of it as a threat to older individuals, behaviours that endanger a heart's health begin in adolescence and early adulthood, including tobacco use, high-saturated-fat diets, sedentary lifestyles, and high stress.

Even students who indicate that they're aware of cardiovascular risks often behave in ways that do not reflect their knowledge. In one recent study of 226 students at a college, half or more ate a high saturated-fat diet or reported moderate to severe stress. Many did not exercise frequently; some already had high cholesterol or high blood pressure.[19]

## Risk Factors You Can Control

A recent study by the World Health Organization (WHO) has identified physical inactivity, tobacco smoking, high blood pressure, high cholesterol, diabetes, high body mass index, and low intake of fruits and vegetables as the top seven contributors to cardiovascular disease in developed countries. The Heart and Stroke Foundation of Canada lists similar risk factors[20] (see Table 10-2). You can choose to avoid these potential risks for the sake of your heart's health.

▼ **Table 10-1 Combined Risk Factors for Cardiovascular Disease (self-reported) among Adults Aged 20–59 Years (2000)**

| Number of Risk Factors | Risk Factors (% of population) |
| --- | --- |
| No Risk Factors | 19.8 |
| At Least 1 Risk Factor | 80.2 |
| 1 Risk Factor | 39.1 |
| 2 Risk Factors | 30.0 |
| 3 or More Risk Factors | 11.1 |

Source: From The Growing Burden of Heart Disease and Stroke in Canada, 2003, prepared in collaboration with Centre for Chronic Disease Prevention and Control, Health Canada, Canadian Cardiovascular Society and Heart and Stroke Foundation of Canada. © Reproduced with the permission of the Heart and Stroke Foundation of Canada, 2008. www.heartandstroke.ca.

▼ **Table 10-2 Modifiable Risk Factors (self-reported) among Adults Aged 20–59 (2000)**

| Risk Factor | Proportion of the Population Aged 20–59 years (%) |
| --- | --- |
| Tobacco Smoking (Daily) | 25.7 |
| Physical Inactivity | 55.5 |
| Overweight (BMI ≥ 25.0) | 47.5 |
| Less than Recommended Consumption of Fruits and Vegetables | 64.7 |
| High Blood Pressure | 8.3 |
| Diabetes* | 2.7 |

Source: Statistics Canada, Canadian Community Health Survey. www.cvdinfobase. ca/cvdbook.

* For the purposes of this report diabetes is listed as a major risk factor.

## Physical Inactivity

Most Canadians get too little physical activity. As reported by the Canadian Fitness and Lifestyle Research Institute, 56 percent of Canadians (aged 20 and older) are inactive.[21] People who are not even somewhat physically active face a much greater risk of fatal heart attack than those who engage in some form of exercise or activity. Women who are active have lower coronary heart disease rates than those who are inactive. According to a recent study, even walking for a minimum of half an hour a day reduces women's risk of coronary heart disease.[22] However, in men, more rigorous exercise produced greater protection against heart disease. Those who ran for an hour or more per week reduced their risk of heart disease by 42 percent, compared with an 18 percent reduction for those who walked briskly for a half-hour per day or more. With walking, pace, not duration, was linked with lower danger of heart disease.[23]

## Tobacco Smoke

The two most important preventable risk factors for respiratory disease are tobacco smoke and exposure to second-hand smoke. The slightly less than five million Canadians who smoke cigarettes increase their risk of developing lung cancer, chronic obstructive pulmonary disease (COPD), and asthma. The major cause of preventable death in Canada is tobacco use.[24] Smokers who have heart attacks are more likely to die from them than are nonsmokers. Smoking is the major risk factor for *peripheral vascular disease,* in which the vessels that carry blood to the leg and arm muscles become hardened and clogged.

Both active and passive smoking accelerate the process by which arteries become clogged and increase the risk of heart attacks and strokes. Health Canada estimates that approximately 45 000 people die each year from smoking-related causes.[25] It is estimated that exposure to second-hand smoke causes over 1000 deaths per year in Canada. Overall, nonsmokers exposed to secondhand smoke are at a 25 percent higher relative risk of developing coronary heart disease than nonsmokers not exposed to secondhand tobacco smoke.

Cigarette smoking and secondhand smoke can damage the heart in several ways:

- The nicotine may repeatedly overstimulate the heart.
- Carbon monoxide may take the place of some of the oxygen in the blood, which reduces the oxygen supply to the heart muscle.
- Tars and other smoke residues may damage the lining of the coronary arteries, making it easier for cholesterol to build up and narrow the passageways.

- Smoking increases blood clotting, leading to a higher incidence of clotting in the coronary arteries and subsequent heart attack. Clotting in the peripheral arteries is also increased, which can cause leg pain with walking and, ultimately, stroke.
- Even ex-smokers may have irreversible damage to their arteries.

## High Blood Pressure (Hypertension)

Since 2005, May 17 has been declared World Hypertension Day (WHD) by the World Hypertension League.[26] In Canada, the Canadian Hypertension Society has joined forces to support this initiative. Why would we need to improve awareness of hypertension in Canada? High blood pressure is a major risk factor for both stroke and coronary heart disease, and it increases cardiovascular risk by two to three times.[27] There are approximately five million Canadians living with high blood pressure—40 percent of them not even aware of their condition.[28]

Blood pressure is a result of the contractions of the heart muscle, which pumps blood through your body, and the resistance of the walls of the vessels through which the blood flows. Each time your heart beats, your blood pressure goes up and down within a certain range. It's highest when the heart contracts; this is called *systolic blood pressure.* It's lowest between contractions; this is called *diastolic blood pressure.* A blood pressure reading consists of the systolic measurement "over" the diastolic measurement, recorded in millimetres of mercury (mmHg) by a sphygmomanometer.

High blood pressure, or **hypertension,** occurs when the artery walls become constricted so that the force exerted as the blood flows through them is greater than it should be. Physicians see blood pressure as a continuum: the higher the reading, the greater the risk of stroke and heart disease.

As a result of the increased work in pumping blood, the heart muscle of a person with hypertension can become stiffer. This stiffness increases resistance to filling up with blood between beats, which can cause shortness of breath with exertion. Hypertension accelerates the development of plaque build-up within the arteries. When combined with obesity, smoking, high cholesterol levels, or diabetes, hypertension increases the risks of cardiovascular problems several times. However, you can control high blood pressure through diet, exercise, and medication (if necessary).

## Blood Fats

**Cholesterol** is a fatty substance found in certain foods and also manufactured by the body. The measurement of cholesterol in the blood is one of the most reliable indicators of the formation of plaque, the sludge-like substance that builds up on the inner walls of arteries. You can lower blood cholesterol levels by cutting back on foods high in saturated fats and exercising more, thereby reducing the risk of a heart attack. Several studies have shown that for every 1 percent drop in blood cholesterol, there is a 2 percent decrease in the likelihood of a heart attack.[29]

**Lipoproteins** are compounds in the blood that are made up of proteins and fat. The different types are classified by their size or density. The heaviest are *high-density lipoproteins,* or HDLs, which have the highest portion of protein. These "good guys" pick up excess cholesterol in the blood and carry it back to the liver for removal from the body. A HDL level of higher than 1.0 mmol/L for men and 1.3 mmol/L for women substantially decreases the risk of heart disease (cholesterol levels are measured in millimole of cholesterol per litre of blood). *Low-density lipoproteins,* or LDLs, and very low-density lipoproteins (VLDLs) carry more cholesterol than HDLs and deposit it on the walls of arteries—they're the "bad guys." The higher your LDL cholesterol, the greater your risk for heart disease. The recommended level of LDLs is less than 3.5 mmol/L[30] (see Table 10-3 to interpret your cholesterol level).

The body contains another type of fat called **triglyceride.** It is the most common form of fat found within our body. Triglycerides do not adhere to the walls of our blood vessels. They are more like thick cream that flows through our blood after meals. They have been linked to an increased risk of coronary artery disease, especially in women, since they increase the tendency of the blood to clot.[31] Triglyceride levels tend to be highest in those whose diets are high in calories, sugar, alcohol, and refined starches. High levels of these fats may increase the risk of obesity, and cutting back on these foods can reduce high triglyceride levels. The recommended level of triglycerides is less than 1.7 mmol/L.

While some studies show that people with high triglyceride levels do not show signs of plaque build-up in their blood, many people who have heart disease also have high triglyceride levels. Presently, the exact relationship is not clear.[32]

## Metabolic Syndrome

**Metabolic syndrome,** also known as Syndrome X or insulin-resistant syndrome, is a cluster of medical abnormalities that increases the risk of heart disease and diabetes. Genetics, lack of exercise, and overeating are its probable causes. According to the National Institutes of Health, three or more of the following symptoms indicate metabolic syndrome:

✓ Waist measurement of more than 102 centimetres (40.2 inches for Caucasian men) or 90 centimetres (35.4 inches for Asian men) and more than

88 centimetres (34.6 inches) for Caucasian women or 80 centimetres (31.5 inches) for Asian women (in one recent study, waist circumference proved the best indicator of increased heart risk).[33]

✓ Levels of triglycerides of more than 1.7 mmol/L.

✓ Levels of high-density lipoprotein—"good" cholesterol—of lower than 1.0 mmol/L in men or 1.3 mmol/L in women.

✓ Blood pressure of 130 mm Hg systole over 85 mm Hg diastole (130/85) or higher.

✓ Fasting blood sugar of 5.6 mmol/L or higher.[34]

## Diabetes Mellitus

**Diabetes mellitus,** a disorder of the endocrine system, increases the likelihood of hypertension and atherosclerosis, thereby increasing the risk of heart attack and stroke.[35] Even before developing diabetes, individuals at high risk for this disease—those who are overweight, have a family history of the disease, have mildly elevated blood pressure and blood sugar levels, and above-ideal levels of harmful blood cholesterol—may already be at increased risk of heart disease. Up to one-half of diabetics also have hypertension, another risk factor. Cardiovascular disease is the most prevalent complication of diabetes mellitus.[36] More than 80 percent of people with diabetes die from some form of heart or blood vessel disease.[37] (More information on diabetes is presented later in the chapter.)

## Weight

According to the Canadian Diabetes Association, if you are between the ages of 18 and 64 and are overweight—that is, if you have a body mass index (BMI) of 25.0–29.9 (excess weight) or a BMI greater than 30.0 (obesity), you are at risk of developing high blood pressure and diabetes. The greater the BMI, the greater the risk of heart disease and stroke.[38] Weight loss significantly reduces high blood pressure, another risk factor for heart disease.

There is also cause for alarm about the growing obesity epidemic among Canadian children. Young people who are obese over a long period of time are more likely to become overweight adults, putting them at risk for heart disease, juvenile diabetes, and adult-onset diabetes. A landmark study on overweight and obese children in China[39] (some as young as nine years old) found that the carotid arteries—arteries that feed blood to the brain—were thickening and that large blood vessels in their arms were not functioning properly. The results matched those of adults who had been smoking for more than 10 years. Dr. Ruth Collins-Nakai, a Canadian pediatric cardiologist, suggests that the situation in Canada would be similar. The good news is that dietary changes and increased physical activity can reverse the trend.

## Psychosocial Factors

Various psychological and social influences may affect vulnerability to heart disease. Anger and hostility, depression and anxiety, stress levels, work characteristics, and social supports are all factors that may act alone or combine and exert different effects at different ages and stages of life.

New research is linking emotional health to heart health. Emerging studies on depression and heart disease suggest that the two are linked. Dr. Brian Baker from the Heart and Stroke Foundation tells us that heart-disease patients are more likely to become depressed. This has been known for a long time.[40] However, some research suggests that depression might actually trigger heart disease. A large study done on postmenopausal women found that women who become depressed are 50 percent more likely to develop heart disease.[41]

Stress levels of college and university students have also been studied. Results from a survey, conducted nationally among 597 university students under the age of 30, where the relationship between study habits, exam-related stress, and coping mechanisms was measured, revealed that 40 percent of the students experienced high levels of stress. The main causes of stress were having too many exams to study for (20 percent), pressure to do well in school (19 percent), and balancing study time with other responsibilities (18 percent). High stress levels were the most common in Saskatchewan and Manitoba (52 percent) and Ontario (47 percent). They were the lowest in Quebec (27 percent). If you are a student experiencing stress, learning how to balance study time with non-study activities can help lower your risk of cardiovascular disease.[42]

Job stress also can be hard on the heart, particularly for employees who have little control over their work. A lack of social supports also seems to increase risk, possibly because intimate, caring relationships may buffer the effect of other stressors in life.

## Risk Factors You Can't Control

### Heredity

Anyone whose parents, siblings, or other close relatives suffered heart attacks before age 50 is at increased risk of developing heart disease. Certain risk factors, such as abnormally high blood levels of lipids, can be passed down from generation to generation. All is not lost, however. You may not be able to rewrite your family history, but you can lower your inherited risks. Your behaviour, including the decisions you make about the foods you eat or the decision not to smoke, do make a difference. As an added preventive step, some cardiologists are prescribing a small daily dose of aspirin to individuals with a history of coronary artery disease who are at risk of clots forming that could block blood supplies to the heart, brain, and other organs (daily aspirin is not advised for individuals who are not at risk because of their age or health history).

### Race and Ethnicity

As reported in *The Growing Burden of Heart Disease and Stroke in Canada, 2003*, Aboriginal peoples, South Asians, and Eastern Europeans are particularly vulnerable to heart disease. Aboriginal adults 20 years of age and older were more likely to be overweight and to smoke compared to the Canadian population as a whole. Some studies have also found that Aboriginal peoples have a higher incidence of diabetes. All of these factors are risk conditions for heart disease.[43]

Research also shows that new immigrants develop increased rates of cardiovascular disease as they begin to adopt unhealthy lifestyle behaviours that are sometimes the norm among Canadians. Further research needs to be done to determine whether people with special genetic predispositions to heart disease have a greater chance of developing high blood pressure, heart disease, and stroke.[44]

### Age and Gender

Eighty percent of Canadians aged 20–59 have at least one risk factor for heart disease or stroke. These include daily smoking, physical inactivity, being overweight, self-reported high blood pressure, and self-reported diabetes.[45] By the age of 70, one in five women and one in four men have been told by a physician that they have heart problems.[46]

More men (of all ages) than women die of heart disease and stroke, but the male to female ratio decreases from 5 to 1 among those 40–49 years of age to 1.2 to 1 among those aged 90 years and older.[47] While more men than women die from coronary heart disease and heart attack, more women than men die from congestive heart failure. Heart disease and stroke combined are the leading cause of hospitalization for women (excluding childbirth and pregnancy).[48]

Seven times as many women die every year from these two diseases than die from breast cancer, making heart disease and stroke a major cause of death for women. The Canadian Heart and Stroke Foundation's *Heart Smart™ Women: A Guide to Living with and Preventing Heart Disease and Stroke* is designed to teach women about how heart disease and stroke can affect their lives and what they can do to reduce risk factors for these conditions. The guide can be accessed at www.heartandstroke.com/site/c.ikIQLcMWJtE/b.4356323/k.D18E/HeartSmart8482_Women_A_guide_to_living_with_and_preventing_heart_disease_and_stroke.htm.

The gender issues with regard to risk factors begin early. Young women between 12 and 19 years of age are

1.5 times more likely to be physically inactive than young men. Researchers have also long believed that postmenopausal hormone replacement therapy (HRT) protected women from heart disease. However, recent studies have shown this not to be true. A major long-term study, the Women's Health Initiative, has shown that women on HRT actually have an increased risk of heart attack and stroke.[49] The Canadian Heart and Stroke Foundation recommends that women do not use hormone replacement therapy solely for the purpose of preventing heart disease or stroke and that women discuss the risks of HRT with their physician.

## Male Pattern Baldness

**Male pattern baldness** (the loss of hair at the vertex, or top, of the head) is associated with an increased risk of heart attack in men under age 55. A study of 1437 men showed a "modest" increased risk for those men who had lost hair at the top of their heads but not for those with receding hairlines. Scientists speculate that men with male pattern baldness who lose their hair quickly may metabolize male sex hormones differently than others, thereby increasing the likelihood of heart disease.[50] Health experts advise bald men to follow basic guidelines, such as not smoking and controlling their cholesterol levels, to lower any possible risk.

## Your Lipoprotein Profile

Medical science has changed the way it views and targets the blood fats that endanger the healthy heart. In the past, the focus was primarily on total cholesterol in the blood.

The higher this number was, the greater the risk of heart disease. New guidelines and recommendations now call for more comprehensive testing, called a *lipoprotein profile*.

This blood test, which should be performed after a 9- to 12-hour fast, provides readings of:

- ✔ Total cholesterol
- ✔ LDL (bad) cholesterol, the main culprit in the build-up of plaque within the arteries
- ✔ HDL (good) cholesterol, which helps prevent cholesterol build-up
- ✔ Triglycerides, which are blood fats released into the bloodstream after a meal

## What Is a Healthy Cholesterol Reading?

The answer to this question has become more complex. In general, a total cholesterol reading of less than 5.2 mmol/L is considered healthy. However, one single cholesterol count no longer applies to everyone (see Table 10-3).

The greatest threat to your heart's health is LDL cholesterol. The degree of danger of a higher reading depends not just on the number itself, but on whether or not you have other risk factors for heart disease. These include age (over 45 in men, over 55 in women), smoking, high blood pressure, high blood sugar, diabetes, abdominal obesity, and a family history of heart disease. Depending on your individual risk, your doctor may recommend lifestyle changes or medications that lower cholesterol.

An optimal LDL reading is less than 3.5 mmol/L. HDL, good cholesterol, also is important, particularly in women. A HDL reading of higher than 1.0 mmol/L for men and 1.3 mmol/L for women is recommended.

### ▼ Table 10-3 Target Cholesterol Ranges

| Type of Lipid | Total Cholesterol | LDL Cholesterol | HDL Cholesterol | Total Cholesterol/ HDL-Cholesterol Ratio | Triglycerides |
|---|---|---|---|---|---|
| Target Level | Less than 5.2 mmol/L | Less than 3.5 mmol/L | Higher than 1.0 mmol/L for men and 1.3 mmol/L for women | Less than 5.0 mmol/L | Less than 1.7 mmol/L |

Your doctor will help establish a target level for you based on your personal risk factors, taking into account your age, total cholesterol level, smoking status, HDL-C level, and systolic blood pressure.

A lipoprotein profile also measures triglycerides, the free-floating molecules that transport fats in the bloodstream. Ideally, this should be less than 1.7 mmol/L.

## Lowering Cholesterol

Depending on your lipoprotein profile and an assessment of other risk factors, your physician may recommend that you take steps to lower your LDL cholesterol. For some people, therapeutic life changes can make a difference. Lowering your fat intake, especially saturated fat, is a "heart-smart" thing to do.[51] Simply eating more often may have an effect on cholesterol. According to several small studies, "grazers" who eat small meals six or more times a day tend to have lower cholesterol levels than "gorgers" who eat three times a day.[52] There is also growing evidence that increasing the amount of fibre you eat is beneficial for lowering cholesterol levels.

Drug therapy is also another option, but this is only recommended when a high cholesterol level does not respond to dietary intervention. Bile acid sequestrants, fibric acids, and statins are categories of cholesterol-lowering drugs that your doctor can prescribe. Each of them has advantages and disadvantages. Sometimes combined drug therapy is suggested.[53]

## The Silent Killers

The two most common forms of cardiovascular disease in this country are high blood pressure (hypertension) and coronary artery disease, the gradual narrowing of the blood vessels of the heart. Often these two problems go together.

## High Blood Pressure

Hypertension forces the heart to pump harder than is healthy. Because the heart must force blood into arteries that are offering increased resistance to blood flow, the left side of the heart often becomes enlarged. The term *essential hypertension* indicates that the cause is unknown, as is usually the case. Occasionally, abnormalities of the kidneys or the blood vessels feeding them or certain substances in the bloodstream are identified as the culprits. Whatever its cause, hypertension is dangerous because excessive pressure can wear out arteries, leading to serious cardiovascular diseases, vision problems, and kidney disease (see Figure 10-3).

Physicians urge all adults to have their blood pressure checked at least once a year. A blood pressure reading that's slightly above normal isn't necessarily proof of a blood pressure problem. Due to nervousness, blood pressure may shoot up when anxious individuals enter a medical office,

causing what's known as *white coat hypertension*. Other factors, such as warm weather or variations in how health-care practitioners do the test, also can cause elevated readings.

## ???? What Is a Healthy Blood Pressure?

Ideal blood pressure is 120/80 mm Hg (120 systolic pressure, 80 diastolic pressure). Hypertension is diagnosed when blood pressure rises above 140/90 mm Hg (see Table 10-4). In the past, physicians relied mainly on the diastolic reading—the second and lower of the two blood pressure numbers—in diagnosing hypertension. In young people, diastolic pressure, a reflection of the constriction of the small blood vessels, continues to be a good indicator of cardiovascular risk. However, a rise in systolic blood pressure—the first and higher of the numbers in a blood pressure reading—also can be dangerous.

Systolic hypertension, a reading of 140 mm Hg or higher, reflects stiffening or hardening of the large arteries. Systolic blood pressure typically rises with age and poses the greatest risk for those middle-aged and older.[54] However, the ideal time to start caring about blood pressure is in your twenties and thirties. In a young person, even mild hypertension can cause organs such as the heart, brain, and kidneys to start to deteriorate. By age 50 or 60, the damage may be irreversible.

### Know Your Numbers

"Even if you think you're fine and you have no history of heart or artery disease, get your blood pressure checked, know your numbers, and, if necessary, get your systolic blood pressure down below 125," says Dr. Dagenais, a Heart and Stroke Foundation researcher.[55]

In a study that followed more than 10 000 healthy men for 25 years, those with high blood pressure in young adulthood were at higher risk for eventually dying from heart disease.[56] Men and women are equally likely to develop hypertension, but in women, blood pressure tends to rise around the time of menopause. For individuals who smoke, are overweight, don't exercise, or have high cholesterol levels, hypertension multiplies the risk of heart disease and stroke. At ultra-high risk are people with diabetes or kidney disease.[57]

### Preventing Hypertension

Prevention pays off when it comes to high blood pressure. The most effective preventive measures involve lifestyle changes. The best approach for individuals who are overweight and who have high normal blood pressure values is weight loss. Exercise may be effective in lowering mildly elevated blood pressure.

**Eye damage**
Prolonged high blood pressure can damage delicate blood vessels on the retina, the layer of cells at the back of the eye. If the damage, known as retinopathy, remains untreated, it can lead to blindness.

**Stroke**
High blood pressure can damage vessels that supply blood to the brain, eventually causing them to rupture or clog. The interruption in blood flow to the brain is known as a stroke.

**Heart attack**
High blood pressure makes the heart work harder to pump sufficient blood through narrowed arterioles (small blood vessels). This extra effort can enlarge and weaken the heart, leading to heart failure. High blood pressure also damages the coronary arteries that supply blood to the heart, sometimes leading to blockages that can cause a heart attack.

**Damage to artery walls**
Artery walls are normally smooth, allowing blood to flow easily. Over time, high blood pressure can wear rough spots in artery walls. Fatty deposits can collect in the rough spots, clogging arteries and raising the risk of a heart attack or stroke.

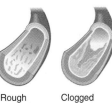

Rough
artery walls

Clogged
artery

**Kidney failure**
Prolonged high blood pressure can damage blood vessels in the kidney, where wastes are filtered from the bloodstream. In severe cases, this damage can lead to kidney failure and even death.

▲ **Figure 10-3** Consequences of High Blood Pressure
If left untreated, elevated blood pressure can damage blood vessels in several areas of the body and lead to serious health problems.

Source: Hespenheide Design

### ▼ Table 10-4 What the Blood Pressure Numbers Mean

Blood pressure on arteries, measured in millimetres of mercury, has two components. The harder it is for blood to flow, the higher both readings are.

| Rating | First Number: Systolic Pressure When Heart Beats | Second Number: Diastolic Pressure Between Heartbeats |
|---|---|---|
| High | 140 and up | 90 and up |
| High Normal | 130–139 | 85–89 |
| Normal | Less than 130 | Less than 85 |
| Optimal | Less than 120 | Less than 80 |

Source: Heart and Stroke Foundation of Canada. © Reproduced with the permission of the Heart and Stroke Foundation of Canada, 2008. www.heartandstroke.ca.

Restriction of sodium intake also helps. Salt is sodium chloride, and it is the major source of sodium in our diets. However, experts at Dietitians of Canada suggest that individuals should limit their sodium intake to no more than 2300 milligrams per day (about 5 millilitres).[58] Canadians are encouraged to limit their salt intake. Dr. George Fodor, a Heart and Stroke Foundation of Canada spokesperson, and Carol Dombrow, a registered dietitian, suggest that although the body requires about 5 millilitres of salt each day to function, most Canadians eat an average of 15 millilitres of salt each day. Much of the salt consumed in our diet comes from hidden salt added in the processing of many foods. Approximately 35 percent of Canadians are salt-sensitive. This means that excess dietary salt has the ability to raise their blood pressure, which in turn can increase their risk of heart disease.[59]

Healthy eating is also a key factor, and foods that are rich in potassium, such as dried and fresh fruit and vegetables, appear to help maintain the normal function of the heart and lower blood pressure.[60, 61] Adults should consume at least 4.7 grams of potassium per day. Presently, Canadian men consume between 3.2 and 3.4 grams, and women eat 2.4 to 2.6 grams. Once again, fruits and vegetables are recommended since they are both low in sodium and high in potassium. Foods with the highest amount of potassium per calorie are spinach, cantaloupe, almonds, brussel sprouts, mushrooms, bananas, oranges, grapefruits, and potatoes.

## Treating Hypertension

For some people, particularly those with mild hypertension, lifestyle changes alone can bring blood pressure down. For other people, diet and exercise are not enough. Medications called beta-blockers and diuretics are recommended as the first-line treatment for hypertension, but newer drugs such as angiotensin-converting enzyme (ACE) inhibitors and calcium channel blockers are becoming increasingly popular. No single drug works well for everyone, so physicians have to rely on clinical judgment and trial and error to find the best possible medication for an individual patient.[62]

## Coronary Artery Disease

The general term for any impairment of blood flow through the blood vessels, often referred to as "hardening of the arteries," is **arteriosclerosis.** The most common form is **atherosclerosis,** a disease of the lining of the arteries in which **plaque**—deposits of fat, fibrin (a clotting material), cholesterol, other cell parts, and calcium—narrows the artery channels (see following photos).

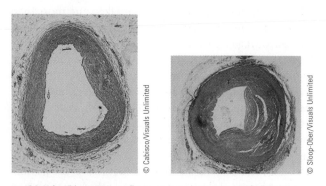

© Cabisco/Visuals Unlimited

© Sloop-Ober/Visuals Unlimited

▲ (a) A healthy coronary artery. (b) An artery partially blocked by the build-up of atherosclerotic plaque.

## What Happens During a Heart Attack?

Each year in Canada, there are over 70 000 heart attacks, and 19 000 Canadians die from them.[63] The medical name for a heart attack, or coronary, is **myocardial infarction (MI).** The *myocardium* is the cardiac muscle layer of the wall of the heart. It receives its blood supply and thus its oxygen and other nutrients from the coronary arteries. If a coronary artery is blocked by a clot or plaque or by a spasm, the myocardial cells do not get sufficient oxygen, and the portion of the myocardium deprived of its blood supply begins to die (see Figure 10-4). Although such an attack may seem sudden, usually it has been building up for years, particularly if the person has ignored risk factors and early warning signs.

Individuals should seek immediate medical care if they experience the following symptoms:

✔ A tight ache, heavy, squeezing pain, or discomfort in the centre of the chest, which may last for 30 minutes or more and is not relieved by rest
✔ Chest pain that radiates to the shoulder, arm, neck, back, or jaw
✔ Anxiety
✔ Sweating or cold, clammy skin
✔ Nausea and vomiting
✔ Shortness of breath
✔ Dizziness, fainting, or loss of consciousness

The two hours immediately following the onset of such symptoms are the most crucial. About 40 percent of those who suffer a MI die within this time. According to the Heart and Stroke Foundation of Canada, Canadians, on average, wait almost five hours before deciding to get help. This greatly reduces the chance of surviving a heart attack. Over 80 percent of heart attack patients admitted to hospital survive. In recent years, the death rate among patients hospitalized for a heart attack has dropped from 13.4 to 11.1 percent.[64]

There are gender differences to note, however. Women wait hours longer after a heart attack before going to the hospital, then are treated less aggressively than men. This delay, which allows further damage to the oxygen-starved heart, results partly because women tend to experience less painful heart attack symptoms. Sometimes they feel only pressure or a burning feeling, not crushing pain. Younger female victims are more likely than men to have other health problems, such as diabetes, high blood pressure, and heart failure.[65]

Clot-dissolving drugs called thrombolytic agents are the treatment of choice for acute myocardial infarction in most clinical settings. Administered through a *catheter* (flexible tube) threaded through the arteries to the site of the blockage (the more effective method of delivery) or

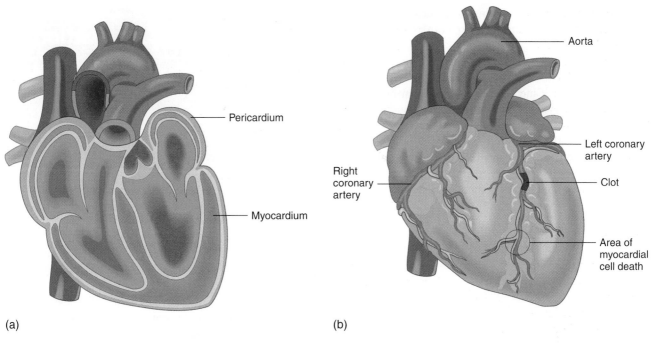

(a)

(b)

▲ **Figure 10-4** The Making of a Heart Attack.
(a) The bulk of the heart is composed mainly of the myocardium, the muscle layer that contracts. (b) A clot in one of the arteries that feeds into the myocardium can cut off the blood supply to part of the myocardium, causing cells in that area to die. This is called a myocardial infarction, or heart attack.

Source: Hespenheide Design

injected intravenously (the faster, cheaper method of delivery), these agents can save lives and dissolve clots but don't remove the underlying atherosclerotic plaque.

Patients receiving such therapy may require further procedures, such as bypass surgery or **angioplasty,** which can reduce their risk of another heart attack or death. In a coronary bypass, an artery from the patient's leg or chest wall is grafted onto a coronary artery to detour blood around the blocked area.

## Stroke

When the blood supply to a portion of the brain is blocked, a cerebrovascular accident, or **stroke,** occurs. The result is a sudden loss of brain function.[66] In Canada, there are more than 50 000 strokes each year. About 14 000 people die from stroke each year—it is the third leading cause of death in our country. Presently about 300 000 Canadians live with the effects of stroke. The financial burden of stroke is high—it costs the Canadian economy about $2.7 billion per year.[67]

Yet strokes can be prevented, and key risk factors can be modified through either lifestyle changes or drugs. The most important steps are treating hypertension, not

smoking, managing diabetes, lowering cholesterol, and taking aspirin.

## ???? What Causes a Stroke?

There are two types of stroke: *ischemic stroke,* which is the result of a blockage that disrupts blood flow to the brain, and *hemorrhagic stroke,* which occurs when a blood vessel ruptures.[68] About 80 percent of strokes are ischemic,[69] and one of the most common causes of ischemic stroke is the blockage of a brain artery by a thrombus, or blood clot—a *cerebral thrombosis.* Clots generally form around deposits sticking out from the arterial wall. Sometimes a wandering blood clot (embolus), carried in the bloodstream, becomes wedged in one of the cerebral arteries. This is called a *cerebral embolism,* and it can completely plug up a cerebral artery.

About 20 percent of strokes are hemorrhagic.[70] In hemorrhagic stroke, a diseased artery in the brain floods the surrounding tissue with blood. The cells nourished by the artery are deprived of blood and can't function, and the blood from the artery forms a clot that may interfere with brain function. This is most likely to occur if the patient suffers from a combination of hypertension and atherosclerosis. Hemorrhage (bleeding) may also be caused by a head injury or by the bursting of an aneurysm, a blood-filled pouch that balloons out from a weak spot in the wall of an artery.

Brain tissue, like heart muscle, begins to die if deprived of oxygen, which may then cause difficulty speaking and walking and loss of memory. These effects may be slight or severe, temporary or permanent, depending on how widespread the damage is and whether other areas of the brain can take over the function of the damaged area. About 30 percent of stroke survivors develop dementia, a disorder that robs a person of memory and other intellectual abilities.

The following symptoms should alert you to the possibility that you or someone with you has suffered a stroke:

✔ Sudden weakness or loss of strength
✔ Numbness of face, arm, or leg
✔ Loss of speech, or difficulty speaking or understanding speech
✔ Dimness or loss of vision, particularly double vision in one eye
✔ Unexplained dizziness
✔ Change in personality
✔ Change in pattern of headaches

## Risk Factors for Strokes

In Canada about 15 000 people every year have a transient ischemic attack (TIA). This is also known as a mini-stroke.[71] It is a short-term lack of blood supply to the brain. Most TIAs last from 30 seconds to 10 minutes, but they can last up to 24 hours. Minor damage to the brain often goes unnoticed because healthy brain cells that are left carry out the normal brain functions.[72] People who've experienced TIAs are at the highest risk for stroke. Other risk factors, like those for heart disease, include some that can't be changed (such as gender and race) and some that can be controlled.[73]

✔ **Gender.** The lifetime risk of having an acute stroke is higher in men, but a greater percentage of women than men die from stroke.[74] Women are also at increased risk at times of marked hormonal changes, particularly pregnancy and childbirth. Past studies have shown an association between oral contraceptive use and stroke, particularly in women over age 35 who smoke. The newer low-dose oral contraceptives have not shown an increased stroke risk among women aged 18 to 44. In general, the risk factors and the effects of stroke are the same for both men and women, but there are some differences in the recovery and rehabilitation stages. Women appear to recover better from language loss after a stroke compared to men. This is because women tend to use larger portions of both sides of their brain for language than men do. Hospital stay tends to be longer for women than men. This might have to do with the lack of a caregiver or helper at home.

## Strategies for Prevention

### How to Prevent a Stroke

▲ Quit smoking. Smokers have twice the risk of stroke that nonsmokers have. When they quit, their risk drops 50 percent in two years. Five years after quitting, their risk is nearly the same as nonsmokers.

▲ Keep blood pressure under control. Treating hypertension with medication can lead to a 40 percent reduction in fatal and nonfatal strokes.

▲ Eat a low-saturated-fat, low-cholesterol diet. This will reduce your risk of fatty build-up in blood vessels. Be sure to include fruits and vegetables in your diet.

▲ Avoid obesity. Extra weight burdens the blood vessels as well as the heart.

▲ Exercise. Moderate amounts of exercise improve circulation and may help dissolve deposits in the blood vessels that can lead to stroke.

▲ Get enough Vitamin $B_{12}$—2.4 mg/day. Dr. David Spence, the head of the Stroke Prevention and Atherosclerosis Centre in London, Ontario, indicates that preliminary evidence links $B_{12}$ to stroke reduction.[75]

✔ **Age.** A person's risk of stroke more than doubles every decade after age 55.
✔ **Hypertension.** Detection and treatment of high blood pressure are the best means of stroke prevention.
✔ **High red blood cell count.** A moderate to marked increase in the number of a person's red blood cells increases the risk of stroke.
✔ **Heart disease.** Heart problems can interfere with the flow of blood to the brain; clots that form in the heart can travel to the brain, where they may clog an artery.
✔ **Blood fats.** Although the standard advice from cardiologists is to lower harmful LDL levels, what may be more important for stroke risk is a drop in the levels of protective HDL.
✔ **Diabetes mellitus.** Diabetics have a higher incidence of stroke than nondiabetics.

## Understanding Cancer

The uncontrolled growth and spread of abnormal cells causes cancer. Normal cells follow the code of instructions embedded in DNA (the body's genetic material); cancer cells do not. Think of the DNA within the nucleus of a cell as a computer program that controls the cell's functioning, including its ability to grow and reproduce itself. If this program or its operation is altered, the cell goes out of control. The nucleus no longer regulates growth. The abnormal cell divides to create other abnormal cells, which again divide, eventually forming **neoplasms** (new formations), or tumours.

Tumours can be either *benign* (slightly abnormal, not considered life-threatening) or *malignant* (cancerous). The only way to determine whether a tumour is benign is by microscopic examination of its cells. Cancer cells have larger nuclei than the cells in benign tumours, they vary more in shape and size, and they divide more often.

At one time cancer was thought to be a single disease that attacked different parts of the body. Now scientists believe that cancer comes in countless forms, each with a genetically determined molecular "fingerprint" that indicates how deadly it is. With this understanding, doctors can identify how aggressively a tumour should be treated.

Without treatment, cancer cells continue to grow, crowding out and replacing healthy cells. This process is called **infiltration,** or invasion. Cancer cells may also **metastasize,** or spread to other parts of the body via the bloodstream or lymphatic system (see Figure 10-5). For many cancers, as many as 60 percent of patients may have metastases (which may be too small to be felt or seen without a microscope) at the time of diagnosis.

Although all cancers have similar characteristics, each is distinct. Some cancers are relatively simple to cure, whereas others are more threatening and mysterious. The earlier any cancer is found, the easier it is to treat and the better the patient's chances of survival.

Cancers are classified according to the type of cell and the organ in which they originate, such as the following:

- ✔ *Carcinoma,* the most common kind, which starts in the epithelium, the layers of cells that cover the body's surface or line internal organs and glands.
- ✔ *Sarcoma,* which forms in the supporting or connective tissues of the body: bones, muscles, blood vessels.
- ✔ *Leukemia,* which begins in the blood-forming tissues (bone marrow, lymph nodes, and the spleen).
- ✔ *Lymphoma,* which arises in the cells of the lymph system, the network that filters out impurities.

## Who Is at Risk for Developing Cancer?

According to the 2008 Canadian Cancer Statistics document, there will be an estimated 166 400 new cases of cancer and 73 800 deaths from cancer in 2008. Three types of cancer account for the majority of new cases—prostate, lung, and colorectal cancer in men and breast, lung, and colorectal in women.[76] Lung cancer remains the leading cause of cancer death for both men and women, and colorectal cancer is the second-leading cause of death from cancer.[77]

There are many risk factors that we cannot change, such as age and our genetic inheritance. However, as with cardiovascular disease, there are some risk factors that we can change. Tobacco use, unhealthy diet, physical inactivity, excess body weight, alcohol consumption, overexposure to the sun, and exposure to environmental and workplace carcinogens raise our risk of developing cancer.[78]

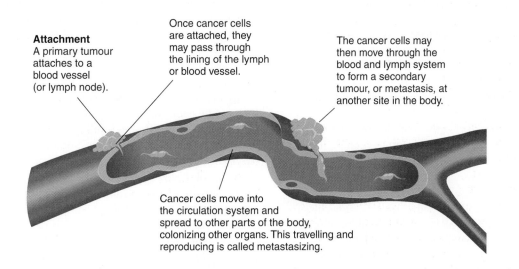

**Attachment**
A primary tumour attaches to a blood vessel (or lymph node).

Once cancer cells are attached, they may pass through the lining of the lymph or blood vessel.

The cancer cells may then move through the blood and lymph system to form a secondary tumour, or metastasis, at another site in the body.

Cancer cells move into the circulation system and spread to other parts of the body, colonizing other organs. This travelling and reproducing is called metastasizing.

▲ **Figure 10-5** Metastasis, or Spread of Cancer
Cancer cells can travel through the blood vessels to spread to other organs or through the lymphatic system to form secondary tumours.

Source: Hespenheide Design

## Emily Young—Finding Yourself in the Unexpected

Cancer among children is rare, but Emily Young was diagnosed with the disease early in life. Fortunately, she has survived, grown up, and is determined to find a way to share her story so that she might inspire others to have hope in difficult times.

They say that mothers have intuition when it comes to their children, and in Emily's case that was true for her mother. Emily's mother felt that something was not quite right with her three-year-old daughter, although a number of physicians and medical experts told her that Emily just had a low immune system. A full diagnosis of Acute Lymphatic Leukemia (ALL) took almost two years.

On Emily's first day of kindergarten, she had to leave school and go to the local hospital to begin cancer treatment. This visit would prove to be challenging. The hospital was not set up to treat young people for cancer. The doctors and nurses did not even have the supplies they needed. Emily remembers that they were out of what she calls "sticky covers" that are used to cover a special anesthetic cream that numbs the skin before the spinal tap needle is put in the spine. She laughed as she told me they had to be creative and use plastic wrap instead.

Her cancer treatments would continue in Vancouver at BC Children's Hospital. Ferry trips every other weekend were expensive and exhausting. Grandparents and friends helped when they could. Chemotherapy treatments continued until Emily was nine.

As we pause during the interview, Emily takes a breath. She is remembering another young girl who she met at a cancer support group. This girl would become Emily's very best friend. Unfortunately, that friendship would be cut short. Emily, at the age of nine, would be told she had a clean bill of health. Her friend, told she had a relapse, would return to the hospital for further treatment and die due to a medical mistake. She is still not comfortable talking about this. She still misses her friend. She is one of three of the ten young people in that support group who are still alive.

Emily Young, riding with the Tour de Rock Cops for Cancer fundraiser, Victoria, British Columbia.

©Times Colonist, Victoria, B.C.

Throughout Emily's cancer treatment and after she was in remission, she faced other challenges, too. The school system was not set up to support children going through extensive therapy. She missed field trips and spelling bees, tests, and, as she says, "even the basics." This gap in her education is something she must still deal with today.

Between ages 11 and 16, Emily did find some comfort and fun at *Camp Good Times* and *Camp Ogo Pogo,* camps designed for children who have or have had cancer. She has also taken a leader in training program so she can assist at the camp. It was at this camp she began to realize that her story could impact people in a positive way. Her story might give people hope.

The sharing of her story would not happen until she was in grade 12. For the most part, Emily did not talk about her experience with cancer. She had other things to think about and other things to do, so she didn't tell her friends or teachers. It was as Emily says "something I lived through, but didn't live with." Outside of high school, Emily was involved with a program called Cops For Cancer Tour de Rock. In four regions of British Columbia, during September and October of each year, members of law enforcement agencies participate in official team cycling tours in support of children with cancer. On Vancouver Island, the Tour de Rock covers more than 1000 kilometres over the course of fourteen days and nights.

The law enforcement members of the Tour de Rock often ride in honour of young people who have had cancer. It would be at a school assembly, when Emily was in grade 11, that one of these riders, visiting the high school to promote the Tour de Rock, would tell the entire school that she was riding on behalf of Emily. It was "my coming out so to speak—the entire school body ended up finding out that I had cancer as a child."

Emily finished grade 12 and started university. She was healthy, happy, and "on my path." Then, in January 2007, there came a knock on the door. A police officer came to invite Emily to ride in the tenth Anniversary for the Vancouver Island Cops for Cancer Tour de Rock. Emily tells me that she had always had this idea in the back of her mind. She had always wondered how she might "give back—or pay it forward." She had often thought about the doctors and nurses who had supported her during her treatments—all the people who worked so hard to save the lives of children they didn't even know with no guarantee that their help would keep these children alive. She had thought about being a participant in the ride.

When first asked to ride in the tour, she did say to herself, "You have got to be kidding me! 1000 kilometres down Vancouver Island! I think my dad said it best, 'Emily, you are good at shopping, you are good at reading, and you don't ride a bike.'" But, for some unexplainable reason, Emily said yes and started training. It was hard. There were distance, speed, and hill training sessions, three times a week. So many emotions surfaced when she trained. There were times she thought she would quit. But after the media launch, she knew she would make a full commitment.

On September 20, 2007, after six months and 4200 kilometres of training, Emily began the tour. Unfortunately, things did not go as planned. Having ridden 223 kilometres into the ride she lost all feeling in her left leg, from her knee to her toes. She couldn't walk. She was in agony. Within 20 minutes, her knee was swollen to the size of her torso. It turned black. Doctors said it was an injury or trauma, but Emily had not fallen or been hit.

She continued to ride to the next town, but after eight days on the tour, five of them riding, she was sent home. Some specialists suggested that her cancer had come back. Other doctors told her it was an irregular inflammation caused by some asymptomatic event and suggested that her leg might have to be cut to release the pressure. For eight months she was not able to participate in physical activity. A full year later, the bruising and pain are still there—with no explanation.

She says she has mixed emotions about not finishing the tour and having to deal with another setback. "I kind of feel, well the best way to put it is through failing so to speak, I have succeeded. I had and have so many people supporting me. The really cool thing is that I raised 150 000 dollars for cancer research." She says that the tour was a pivotal moment, a time to reflect on what happened to her as a young girl and a way for her to start to understand how that experience has impacted her. "When you are a kid and dealing with cancer, a teddy bear or a lollipop is going to make you feel better. When you are twenty and you are told that your cancer might have come back, that doesn't work."

Life is still challenging, but Emily is thankful, too. As she says, "I have not come through this with bells on my toes. Some people say that the juice is worth the squeeze, and in my case, the juice was worth the squeeze, but my juice is not always sweet. Not finishing the tour was hard. However, I think if I had not been injured on the tour I might not have grown so much. As crazy at it sounds, I am thankful for that." Her short-term goal is to complete her university degree. Her long-term goal is to finish the Tour with the team in 2010. She wants to begin her ride from the point she stopped. She wants to make it across the finish line. She wants to raise more money for the Tour de Rock—"because I have to finish."

Asked if she has advice for other students, she says, "We all heal in different ways. Things don't always finish the way you want them to. It is in the unexpected that you find something different, something challenging, you find yourself. If things always turned out the way you think they should, you would never find yourself, you would not have your own story."

## Heredity

The most likely sites for inherited cancers to develop are the breast, brain, blood, muscles, bones, and adrenal glands. The telltale signs of inherited cancers include:

✓ **Early development.** Genetic forms of certain diseases strike earlier than non-inherited cancers. For example, the average age of women diagnosed with breast cancer is 62. But if breast cancer is inherited, the average age at diagnosis is 44, an 18-year difference.

✓ **Family history.** Anyone with a close relative (mother, father, sibling, child) with cancer has about three times the usual chance of getting the same type of cancer.

✓ **Multiple targets.** The same type of hereditary cancer often strikes more than once—in both breasts or both kidneys, for instance, or in two separate parts of the same organ.

✓ **Unusual gender pattern.** Genes may be responsible for cancers that generally don't strike a certain gender—for example, breast cancer in a man.

✓ **Cancer family syndrome.** Some families with unusually large numbers of relatives affected by cancer seem clearly cancer-prone. For instance, in Lynch syndrome (a form of colon cancer), more than 20 percent of the family members in at least two generations develop cancer of both the colon and the endometrium.

Women who have a first-degree (mother, sister, or daughter) family history of breast cancer have about a two-fold increased risk of developing breast cancer compared with women who do not have a family history of the disease. This means that they are about twice as likely to develop breast cancer.

In hereditary cancers, such as retinoblastoma (an eye cancer that strikes young children) or certain colon cancers, a specific cancer-causing gene is passed down from generation to generation. The odds of any child with one affected parent inheriting this gene and developing the cancer are 50–50. Tracing cancers through a family tree is one simple way of checking your own risk.

## Viruses

Researchers have long known that viruses can cause tumours in animals, but only recently have they shown a connection between several different viruses and cancer in humans. Viruses have been implicated in certain leukemias (cancers of the blood system) and lymphomas (cancers of the lymphatic system), cancers of the nose and pharynx, liver cancer, and cervical cancer. Human immunodeficiency virus (HIV) can lead to certain lymphomas and leukemias and to a type of cancer called Kaposi's sarcoma. Human papillomavirus (HPV) has been linked to an increased risk of cervical cancer and cancer of the penis.[79]

## How Can I Reduce My Cancer Risk?

Environmental factors may cause between 80 and 90 percent of cancers. At least in theory, these cancers can be prevented by avoiding cancer-causing substances or using substances that protect against cancer-causing factors. How do you start protecting yourself? Simple changes in lifestyle—smart eating, not smoking, protecting yourself from the sun, exercising regularly—are essential.

### Cancer-Smart Nutrition

Diets high in antioxidant-rich fruits and vegetables have long been linked with lower rates of oesophageal, lung, colon, and stomach cancer. It appears that antioxidants—substances that prevent the damaging effects of oxidation in cells—can block genetic damage induced by free radicals that could lead to some cancers. However, scientific studies have not proven conclusively that any specific antioxidant, particularly in supplement form, can prevent cancer.

Researchers are continuing to investigate a variety of antioxidants that have shown promise as cancer-fighters. The mineral selenium, which promotes antioxidant activity, may protect against prostate cancer and possibly also lower the risk of cancer of the lung, colon, and esophagus. Diets rich in Vitamin C, Vitamin D, and folate also may have some specific benefits against breast cancer.

An awareness campaign by the Canadian Cancer Society encourages us to follow the *Eating Well With Canada's Food Guide* and to increase the number of

▲ Eating 5 to 10 servings of fruits and vegetables a day can help reduce your cancer risk.

© 2000 PhotoDisc, Inc.

servings of vegetables and fruit per day we eat to reduce our risk of cancer, heart disease, and stroke.[80]

A number of recent studies show that women tend to be the primary meal preparers in Canadian families and so have a direct influence on what type of meals they serve. Time is a large constraint to healthy eating. Many women do not have or take the time to plan, purchase, and prepare healthy foods for themselves and their families. Cost and difficulty catering to family needs were also challenges mentioned.[81]

As well, many people are not aware of the health benefits of eating a variety of fruits and vegetables as recommended by Health Canada and the Canadian Cancer Society.[82] Lack of basic cooking skills and the ready option of fast-food restaurants are also cited as reasons why consumption of fruits and vegetables are low among many Canadian families. As we face the growing research that suggests Canada is heading toward a cancer crisis, we must figure out ways to make healthy eating realistic and manageable. As a student, you face many pressures—studying, working, tight budgets, stress, residence cafeteria food choices, or lack of cooking facilities.

The good news is that healthy eating does make a difference. Attempting to make small changes in our nutrition habits is the best place to start.

## Tobacco Smoke

Cigarette smoking is the single most devastating and preventable cause of cancer deaths in Canada. It causes about 30 percent of cancers in Canada and more than 85 percent of lung cancers. Lung cancer is the leading type of cancer death for both men and women. In 2008, an estimated 459 Canadians were diagnosed with lung cancer every week. Approximately 20 200 people died of the disease in 2008.[83]

Cigarettes cause most cases of lung cancer and increase the risk of cancer of the mouth, pharynx, larynx, esophagus, pancreas, and bladder. Pipes, cigars, and smokeless tobacco also increase the danger of cancers of the mouth and throat. Unfortunately, secondhand tobacco smoke can also increase the risk of cancer even among those who've never smoked.

## Possible Carcinogens

Although it may not be possible to avoid all possible **carcinogens** (cancer-causing chemicals), you can take steps to minimize your danger. Many chemicals used in industry, including nickel, chromate, asbestos, and vinyl chloride, are carcinogens; employees as well as people living near a factory that creates smoke, dust, or gases are at risk. If your job involves their use, follow safety precautions at work. If you are concerned about possible hazards in your community, check with local environmental-protection officials.

Women and men who frequently dye their hair, particularly with very dark shades of permanent colouring, may be at increased risk for leukemia (cancer of blood-forming cells), non-Hodgkin's lymphoma (cancer of the lymph system), multiple myeloma (cancer of the bone marrow), and, in women, ovarian cancer. Lighter shades and less permanent tints do not seem to be a danger.

## Early Detection

Cancers that can be detected by screening account for approximately half of all new cancer cases. Screening examinations, conducted regularly by a health-care professional, can lead to early diagnosis of cancers of the breast, colon, rectum, cervix, prostate, testicles, and oral cavity and can improve the odds of successful treatment. Self-examinations for cancers of the breast, testicles, and skin may also result in detection of tumours at earlier stages. The five-year relative survival rate for all these cancers is about 81 percent. If we all participated in regular cancer screenings, this rate could increase to more than 95 percent.[84]

## Common Types of Cancer

Cancer refers to a group of more than a hundred diseases characterized by abnormal cell growth. Table 10-5 shows estimated new cases and deaths for cancer sites by sex in Canada. The most common are discussed in the following sections.

## Skin Cancer

Skin cancer is the most common cancer in Canada. It accounts for about one-third of all new diagnosed cancers. Thankfully, it ranks much lower as a cause of death.[85] Sunlight is the primary culprit. Once scientists thought exposure to the B range of ultraviolet light (UVB), the wavelength of light responsible for sunburn, posed the greatest danger. However, longer-wavelength UVA, which penetrates deeper into the skin, also plays a major role in skin cancers.[86] An estimated 80 percent of total lifetime sun exposure occurs during childhood, so sun protection is especially important in youngsters. Tanning salons and sunlamps also increase the risk of skin cancer because they produce ultraviolet radiation. A half-hour dose of radiation from a sunlamp can be equivalent to the amount you would get from an entire day in the sun.

Recently, there have been reports on the benefits of unprotected sun exposure for the production of Vitamin D—a vitamin the skin naturally produces when exposed to

▼ **Table 10-5 Estimated New Cases and Deaths for Cancers by Sex, Canada, 2008**

| | New Cases 2008 Estimates | | | Deaths 2008 Estimates | | |
|---|---|---|---|---|---|---|
| | **Total** | **M** | **F** | **Total** | **M** | **F** |
| **All Cancers** | **166 400** | **87 000** | **79 400** | **73 800** | **38 800** | **35 000** |
| Prostate[1] | 24 700 | 24 700 | – | 4 300 | 4 300 | – |
| Lung* | 23 900 | 12 600 | 11 300 | 20 200 | 11 000 | 9 200 |
| Breast | 22 600 | 170 | 22 400 | 5 400 | 50 | 5 300 |
| Colorectal | 21 500 | 11 800 | 9 700 | 8 900 | 4 800 | 4 100 |
| Non-Hodgkin Lymphoma | 7 000 | 3 800 | 3 200 | 3 100 | 1 700 | 1 400 |
| Bladder[2] | 6 700 | 5 100 | 1 700 | 1 800 | 1 250 | 530 |
| Melanoma | 4 600 | 2 500 | 2 100 | 910 | 560 | 350 |
| Leukemia* | 4 500 | 2 600 | 1 850 | 2 400 | 1 400 | 1 000 |
| Kidney* | 4 400 | 2 700 | 1 750 | 1 600 | 1 000 | 600 |
| Thyroid | 4 300 | 890 | 3 400 | 180 | 65 | 110 |
| Body of Uterus | 4 200 | – | 4 200 | 790 | – | 790 |
| Pancreas | 3 800 | 1 800 | 1 950 | 3 700 | 1 800 | 1 950 |
| Oral | 3 400 | 2 300 | 1 100 | 1 150 | 760 | 380 |
| Stomach | 2 900 | 1 850 | 1 000 | 1 850 | 1 150 | 720 |
| Brain | 2 600 | 1 450 | 1 100 | 1 750 | 1 000 | 740 |
| Ovary | 2 500 | – | 2 500 | 1 700 | – | 1 700 |
| Multiple Myeloma* | 2 100 | 1 150 | 960 | 1 350 | 730 | 630 |
| Esophagus | 1 600 | 1 200 | 410 | 1 750 | 1 300 | 430 |
| Liver | 1 550 | 1 200 | 380 | 680 | 520 | 150 |
| Cervix | 1 300 | – | 1 300 | 380 | – | 380 |
| Larynx | 1 200 | 1 000 | 220 | 530 | 440 | 90 |
| Hodgkin Lymphoma | 890 | 480 | 410 | 110 | 60 | 50 |
| Testis | 890 | 890 | – | 30 | 30 | – |
| Non-melanoma Skin | 73 000 | 40 000 | 33 000 | 260 | 160 | 100 |
| All Other Cancers | 13 500 | 7 100 | 6 400 | 9 300 | 4 900 | 4 400 |

Source: Chronic Disease Surveillance Division, CCDPC. Public Health Agency of Canada, page 12. Available at www.cancer.ca/Canada-wide/Publications/Publications%20on%20cancer%20statistics/~/media/CCS/Canada%20wide/Files%20List/English%20files%20heading/pdf%20not%20in%20publications%20section/Canadian%20Cancer%20Society%20Statistics%20PDF%202008_614137951.ashx. Reproduced with the permission of the Minister of Public Works and Government Services Canada, 2008.

– Not applicable

* Caution is needed if the 2008 estimates are compared to previously published estimates as definitions for these cancers have changed.

[1] Prostate cancer estimates are higher than in previous years' publications because most provinces have opted to use projections based on modelling rather than averaging.

[2] The substantial increase in incidence of bladder cancer as compared with previous years reflects the decision to include in situ carcinomas (excluding Ontario) as of the 2006 edition of *Canadian Cancer Statistics*. See Table A3 for in situ bladder cancer in Ontario.

Note: "All Cancers" excludes the estimated new cases of non-melanoma skin cancer (basal and squamous) but includes the estimated 260 deaths with underlying cause of other malignant neoplasms of skin (ICD-10 code C44). Total of rounded numbers may not equal rounded total number. Please refer to *Appendix II: Methods* for further details.

solar UVB rays. This message contradicts the health message of protecting our skin from the sun to reduce the risk of skin cancer. Research does suggest that adequate levels of Vitamin D may protect against some types of cancer, but the Canadian Cancer Society's position is that it is still unclear about what amount of sun exposure or dietary supplementation is required to reach adequate levels of Vitamin D.[87]

The most common skin cancers are *basal cell* (involving the base of the epidermis, the top level of the skin) and *squamous cell* (involving cells in the epidermis). Watch for skin lesions known as actinic keratoses (AKs), rough red or brown scaly patches that develop in the upper layer of the skin, usually on the face, lower lip, bald scalp, neck, and back of the hands and forearms. Forty percent of squamous cell carcinomas, the second leading cause of skin cancer deaths, begin as AKs. Treatments include surgical removal; cryosurgery (freezing the skin); electrodesiccation (heat generated by an electric current); topical chemotherapy; and removal with lasers, chemical peels, or dermabrasion.

Smoking and exposure to certain hydrocarbons in asphalt, coal tar, and pitch may increase the risk of squamous cell skin cancer. Other risk factors include occupational exposure to carcinogens and inherited skin disorders, such as xeroderma pigmentosum and familial atypical multiple-mole melanoma.

Malignant *melanoma,* the deadliest type of skin cancer, continues to claim lives. There has been a 41 percent increase in the death rate in men since 1988. The melanoma death rate for women has risen by 23 percent.[88] This increase in risk is due mostly to overexposure to UV radiation.

Melanoma occurs more often among people over 40 years old but is increasing in younger people, particularly those who had severe sunburns in childhood.[89]

Individuals with any of the following characteristics are at increased risk:

- Fair skin, light eyes, or fair hair
- A tendency to develop freckles and to burn instead of tan
- A history of childhood sunburn or intermittent, intense sun exposure
- A personal or family history of melanoma
- A large number of *nevi,* or moles (200 or more, or 50 or more if under age 20) or dysplastic (atypical) moles[90]

© chris fotoman Smith/Alamy

▲ The "healthy" glow of tanned skin may be the precursor to a severe, even fatal, case of skin cancer.

## Detection

The most common predictor for melanoma is a change in an existing mole or development of a new and changing pigmented mole. The most important early indicators are change in colour, an increase in diameter, and changes in the borders of a mole (see Figure 10-6). An increase in height signals a corresponding growth in depth under the skin. Itching in a new or long-standing mole also should not be ignored.[91]

## Strategies for Prevention

### Seven Warning Signs of Cancer

If you note any of the following seven warning signs, immediately schedule an appointment with your doctor:

- ▲ Change in bowel or bladder habits
- ▲ A sore that doesn't heal
- ▲ Unusual bleeding or discharge
- ▲ Thickening or lump in the breast, testis, or elsewhere
- ▲ Indigestion or difficulty swallowing
- ▲ Obvious change in a wart or mole
- ▲ Nagging cough or hoarseness

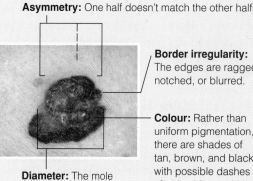

**Asymmetry:** One half doesn't match the other half

**Border irregularity:** The edges are ragged, notched, or blurred.

**Colour:** Rather than uniform pigmentation, there are shades of tan, brown, and black, with possible dashes of red, white, and blue.

**Diameter:** The mole is larger than 6 mm (about the size of a pencil eraser). (The melanoma shown here is magnified about 20 times its actual size.)

© James Stevenson/SPL/Custom Medical Stock

▲ **Figure 10-6** ABCD: The Warning Signs of Melanoma
An estimated 95 percent of cases of melanoma arise from an existing mole. A normal mole is usually round or oval, less than 6 millimetres (about 1/4 inch) in diameter, and evenly coloured (black, brown, or tan). Seek prompt evaluation of any moles that change in ways shown in the photo.

## Treatment

If caught early, melanoma is highly curable, usually with surgery alone. Once it has spread, chemotherapy with a single drug or a combination can temporarily shrink tumours in some people. However, the five-year survival rate for metastatic melanoma is less than 10 percent.

## Breast Cancer

According to Dr. Paul Goss, the ExCel Research study chair, "Breast cancer is a major public health issue. Every 30 seconds somewhere in the world a woman is diagnosed with this disease."[92] In Canada, breast cancer is the most commonly diagnosed cancer in Canadian women and the second most common cause of cancer death in women. Women have a one in nine chance of developing breast cancer in their lifetime.[93]

Risk factors include:

✔ **Age.** Breast cancer can occur in women of any age, but each woman's risk increases as she ages.
✔ **Family history.** Having a first-degree relative—mother, sister, or daughter—with breast cancer does increase risk, and if the relative developed breast cancer before menopause, the cancer is more likely to be hereditary.
✔ **Age at menarche.** Women who had their first period before age 12 are at greater risk than women who began menstruating later. The reason is that the more menstrual cycles a woman has, the longer her exposure to estrogen, a hormone known to increase breast cancer danger. For similar reasons, childless women, who menstruate continuously for several decades, are also at greater risk.
✔ **Age at birth of first child.** An early pregnancy—in a woman's teens or twenties—changes the actual maturation of breast cells and decreases risk. But if a woman has her first child in her forties, precancerous cells may actually flourish with the high hormone levels of the pregnancy.
✔ **Breast biopsies.** Even if laboratory analysis finds no precancerous abnormalities, women who require such tests are more likely to develop breast cancer. Fibrocystic breast disease, a term often used for "lumpy" breasts, is not a risk factor.
✔ **Estrogen.** The role of estrogen replacement as a cancer risk factor remains controversial. Some studies have documented an increase in certain types of breast cancer in women who have used hormone replacement therapy (HRT) for more than five years.

Current research that looks at preventive strategies as a way of lowering risk factors has shown that postmenopausal women who were active throughout their entire lives reduce their risk of breast cancer by 42 percent and that women who became active only after menopause had a similarly decreased risk.[94]

## Detection

The Canadian Cancer Society suggests that a combination of three screening techniques offers women the best defence against breast cancer. "Recent research findings about the effectiveness of breast screening or **mammography** have been sending mixed messages to Canadian women," Dr. Barb Whylie, Director, Cancer Control Policy, Canadian Cancer Society, says. "I empathize with women who are trying to figure out the best way to protect themselves against breast cancer in light of these new research findings. We are continuing to recommend three breast-screening techniques. The important factor is the combination of these three techniques—we believe this offers women the best defence against breast cancer."[95]

Based on its recent evaluation of the new evidence, the Canadian Cancer Society recommends combining:

✔ *Mammography* every two years for women between the ages of 50 and 69 (see Figure 10-7).
✔ *Clinical breast examination* by a trained health-care professional at least every two years for all women.
✔ *Regular breast self-examination (BSE).* Women should report any changes to their doctor.

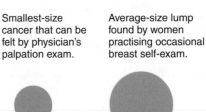

Cancer calcifications of this size and smaller can be seen on mammograms.

Average-size lump found by mammogram.

Average-size lump found by women practising frequent breast self-exam.

Smallest-size cancer that can be felt by physician's palpation exam.

Average-size lump found by women practising occasional breast self-exam.

▲ **Figure 10-7** Cancer Sizes Found by Breast Cancer Detection Methods

## Treatment

Breast cancer can be treated with surgery, radiation, and drugs (chemotherapy and hormonal therapy). Doctors may use one of these options or a combination, depending on the type and location of the cancer and whether the disease has spread.

▲ A clinical breast examination by a trained health-care professional is recommended for all women at least every two years.

Most women undergo some type of surgery. **Lumpectomy** or breast-conserving surgery removes only the cancerous tissue and a surrounding margin of normal tissue. A modified radical **mastectomy** includes the entire breast and some of the underarm lymph nodes. Radical mastectomy, in which the breast, lymph nodes, and chest wall muscles under the breast are removed, is rarely performed today because modified radical mastectomy has proven just as effective. Removing underarm lymph nodes is important to determine if the cancer has spread, but a new method, sentinel node biopsy, allows physicians to pinpoint the first lymph node into which a tumour drains (the sentinel node) and remove only the nodes most likely to contain cancer cells.

Radiation therapy is treatment with high-energy rays or particles to destroy cancer. In almost all cases, lumpectomy is followed by six to seven weeks of radiation. Chemotherapy is used to reach cancer cells that may have spread beyond the breast—in many cases even if no cancer is detected in the lymph nodes after surgery.

In March 2005, a major clinical trial looking at new ways to prevent breast cancer was launched. The study is testing the drug *exemestane*—a member of a class of drugs called aromatase inhibitors. Exemestane suppresses estrogen production, which has been found to develop some types of breast cancer. Forty-five thousand postmenopausal women from Canada, the United States, and Spain will be followed over a five-year period. An evaluation of the impact of physical activity on reducing breast cancer will also be made. Exemestane was approved by Health Canada in 2000 for the treatment of advanced breast cancer in postmenopausal women whose tumours had stopped responding to *tamoxifen*, another drug used in breast cancer therapy.[96]

## Cervical Cancer

Cervical cancer starts in the cells of the cervix—the lower portion of a woman's uterus. The most common type of cervical cancer (squamous cell cancer) starts in the cells that line the surface of the cervix.[97]

The primary risk factor for cervical cancer is infection with certain types of the human papillomavirus (HPV), discussed in Chapter 9. However, not every HPV infection becomes cervical cancer, and while HPV infection is very common, cervical cancer is not. Other risk factors for cervical cancer include early age of first intercourse, multiple sex partners, genital herpes, and significant exposure to secondhand smoke.

Regular Pap tests are an excellent way to find cervical cancer at an early stage when it can be treated successfully.

## Ovarian Cancer

Ovarian cancer is the leading cause of death from gynecological cancers. Risk factors include a family history of ovarian cancer; personal history of breast cancer; obesity; infertility (because the abnormality that interferes with conception may also play a role in cancer development); and low levels of transferase, an enzyme involved in the metabolism of dairy foods. Often women develop no obvious symptoms until the advanced stages, although they may experience painless swelling of the abdomen, irregular bleeding, lower abdominal pain, digestive and urinary abnormalities, fatigue, backache, bloating, and weight gain.

## Colon and Rectal Cancer

Colorectal cancer is the second most common cancer for both men and women.[98] Most colorectal cancer starts in the cells that line the inside of the colon or the rectum. There is no single cause of colorectal cancer, but some factors do appear to increase the risk of developing it. They include age (especially those over 50), polyps (small growths on the inner wall of the colon and rectum), a family history, diet, obesity, physical inactivity, heavy alcohol consumption, smoking, and living with inflammatory bowel disease.

Early signs of colorectal cancer are bleeding from the rectum, blood in the stool, or a change in bowel habits. The simplest test for this common cancer, the fecal occult blood test, detects blood in a person's stool. Treatment may involve surgery, radiation therapy, or chemotherapy.

## Prostate Cancer

Prostate cancer is the most commonly diagnosed cancer in Canadian men. It is the third most common cause of cancer death in men, although the death rates are falling.[99] The risk of prostate cancer increases with age, family history, exposure to the heavy metal cadmium, high number of sexual partners, and history of frequent sexually transmitted infections. An inherited predisposition may account for 5 to 10 percent of cases. A purported link between vasectomy and prostate cancer has been disproven.[100]

The development of a simple screening test that measures levels of a protein called prostate-specific antigen (PSA) in the blood has revolutionized the diagnosis of prostate cancer. However, the prostate screening test has been called controversial by the Canadian Cancer Society because they have found insufficient evidence that PSA screening will reduce the number of prostate cancer deaths. In addition, because the PSA test does not discriminate between cancers that require treatment and those that do not, individuals may undergo unnecessary treatment that carries the risk of severe side effects such as impotence, urinary incontinence, and death. New research is expected to become available in the near future and will hopefully shed more light on this method of prostate cancer screening.[101]

## Testicular Cancer

Testicular cancer occurs mostly among young men between the ages of 18 and 35, who are not normally at risk of cancer. Testicular cancer starts in the cells of the testicle. At highest risk are men with an undescended testicle (a condition that is almost always corrected in childhood to prevent this danger). To detect possibly cancerous growths, men should perform monthly testicular self-exams, as shown in Figure 10-8.

Although college- and university-age men are among those at highest risk of testicular cancer, three in four do not know how to perform a testicular self-examination. Only 8 to 14 percent examine their testicles regularly.[102]

Often the first sign of this cancer is a slight enlargement of one testicle. There also may be a change in the way it feels when touched. Sometimes men with testicular cancer report a dull ache in the lower abdomen or groin, along with a sense of heaviness or sluggishness. Lumps on the testicles also may indicate cancer.

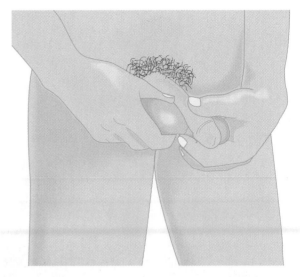

▲ **Figure 10-8** Testicular Self-Exam
The best time to examine your testicles is after a hot bath or shower, when the scrotum is most relaxed. Place your index and middle fingers under each testicle and the thumb on top, and roll the testicle between the thumb and fingers. If you feel a small, hard, usually painless lump or swelling, or anything unusual, consult a urologist.

A man who notices any abnormality should consult a physician. If a lump is indeed present, a surgical biopsy is necessary to find out if it is cancerous. If the biopsy is positive, a series of tests generally is needed to determine whether the disease has spread.

Treatment for testicular cancer generally involves surgical removal of the diseased testis, sometimes along with radiation therapy, chemotherapy, and the removal of nearby lymph nodes. The remaining testicle is capable of maintaining a man's sexual potency and fertility. Only in rare cases is removal of both testicles necessary. Testosterone injections following such surgery can maintain potency. The chance for a cure is very high if testicular cancer is spotted early.

## Diabetes Mellitus

More than two million Canadians have diabetes mellitus, a disease in which the body doesn't produce or respond properly to insulin, a hormone essential for daily life. This number is expected to increase dramatically as the population ages.[103]

In those who have diabetes, the pancreas, which produces insulin (the hormone that regulates carbohydrate and fat metabolism) doesn't function as it should. When the pancreas either stops producing insulin (Type 1 or *insulin-dependent diabetes*) or doesn't produce sufficient insulin to meet the body's needs or does not properly use the insulin it does make (Type 2 or *non-insulin-dependent diabetes*), almost every body system can be damaged. Gestational diabetes, a third type of diabetes, is a temporary condition that occurs during pregnancy. It affects approximately 3.5 percent of all pregnancies and involves an increased risk of developing diabetes for both mother and child.

## Who Is at Risk for Developing Diabetes?

New clinical practice guidelines launched by the Canadian Diabetes Association in September 2008 suggested that six million more Canadians are now at risk for Type 2 diabetes. The new guidelines describe these "at-risk" individuals as having **prediabetes** or impaired glucose intolerance (IGT), meaning that blood glucose levels are near but not quite reaching the level that defines a diabetes diagnosis. The new clinical guidelines emphasize the importance of early identification of risk factors in the prediabetes stage in order to prevent the onset of diabetes and the serious health complications that accompany the disease.[104]

Other factors for developing diabetes include being a member of a high-risk ethnic group (Aboriginal, Hispanic, Asian, South Asian, or African descent) and being overweight—especially if you carry that weight around your middle.[105] Eighty to 90 percent of Type 2 diabetes cases are attributable to overweight and obesity.[106]

Children are now at an increased risk for developing diabetes, too. Although Type 2 diabetes was once a disease occurring almost exclusively in adults, it now appearing in increasing rates in children.[107] This could be in part due to the fact that being overweight is now one of the most common medical conditions of childhood. About 95 percent of children with Type 2 diabetes are overweight at diagnosis.[108] Of special concern are First Nations communities, in which Type 2 diabetes is being diagnosed in Canadian First Nations children as young as eight years of age, and rates appear to be increasing rapidly.[109]

Uncontrolled glucose levels slowly damage blood vessels throughout the body, so individuals who become diabetic early in life may face challenging complications even before they reach middle age. Diabetes is the number-one cause of blindness, non-traumatic amputations, and kidney failure. Diabetes also increases by two or three times the risk of heart attack or stroke.[110]

A lack of physical activity greatly increases the risk for developing Type 2 diabetes. Television watching is strongly associated with weight and obesity, a risk factor for diabetes in both children and adults. In a 10-year study of 1058 individuals with Type 2 diabetes, watching television for 2 to 10 hours a week increased the risk of diabetes by 66 percent; 21 to 40 hours per week more than doubled the risk; and more than 40 hours a week nearly tripled the risk.[111]

Those at highest risk include relatives of diabetics (whose risk is two and a half times that of others), obese persons (85 percent of diabetics are or were obese), older persons (four out of five diabetics are over age 45), and mothers of large babies (an indication of maternal prediabetes). A child of two parents with Type 2 diabetes faces an 80 percent likelihood of also becoming diabetic.

In Canada, a new partnership has developed between the Canadian Diabetes Association and the University of British Columbia (UBC), where scientists at the Centre for Research in Childhood Diabetes (CRCD) hope to become world leaders in childhood diabetes research.[112]

The early signs of diabetes are frequent urination, excessive thirst, a craving for sweets and starches, and weakness. Diagnosis is based on tests of the sugar level in the blood. Researchers are working to develop a test that would help identify telltale antibodies in the blood; this could indicate that pancreas cells are being destroyed years before the first signs of diabetes.

## Dangers of Diabetes

Before the development of insulin injections, diabetes was a fatal illness. Today, diabetics can have normal lifespans. However, both types of diabetes can lead to devastating complications, including an increased risk of heart attack or stroke, kidney failure, blindness, and loss of circulation to the extremities.

Diabetic women who become pregnant face higher risks of miscarriage and babies with serious birth defects; however, precise control of blood sugar levels before conception and in early pregnancy can lower the likelihood of these problems. The development of diabetes during pregnancy, called *gestational diabetes,* may pose potentially serious health threats to mother and child years later. Women who develop gestational diabetes are more than three times as likely to develop Type 2 diabetes if they have a second pregnancy; their infants may be at increased risk of cardiovascular disease later in life.

Managing this disease is also a tremendous challenge. Data from the Diabetes In Canada Evaluation (DICE), the largest diabetes study of its kind in Canada, shows that one in two people with Type 2 diabetes does not have their blood sugar under control. As well, the majority of people who have diabetes are also dealing with serious health conditions such as heart disease, stroke, and kidney and eye disease.[113]

## Diabetes and Ethnic Minorities

Researchers now believe that the interaction of environmental factors and genes varies among different racial and ethnic groups. Of great concern is the number of Aboriginal people living with diabetes. Information from the *Pathway to Wellness, A Handbook for People Living with Diabetes,* published by the National Aboriginal Diabetes Association, states that diabetes rates are very high among First Nations people—at least three to five times that of the national population. Research from an Aboriginal peoples survey completed by Health Canada showed that 6.5 percent of First Nations people over the age of 15 have been diagnosed with Type 2 diabetes and the numbers are growing. Rates in First Nations communities are also above the national average: 8.4 percent of people on reserves have diabetes, while approximately 5.5 percent of Métis people have diabetes.[114]

Much work is being done through agencies such as the National Aboriginal Diabetes Association (NADA) to promote healthy living and assist Aboriginal people dealing with this disease.

## Treatment

There is no cure for diabetes at this time. The best treatment option is to keep blood sugar levels as stable as possible to prevent complications such as kidney damage. Home glucose monitoring allows diabetics to check their blood sugar levels as many times a day as necessary and to adjust their diet or insulin doses as appropriate.

Those with Type 1 diabetes require daily doses of insulin via injections, an insulin infusion pump, or oral medication. Those with Type 2 diabetes can control their disease through a well-balanced diet, exercise, and weight management. However, insulin therapy may be needed to keep blood glucose levels near normal or normal, thereby reducing the risk of damage to the eyes, nerves, and kidneys.

New clinical data from a study called Treating to New Targets (TNT) shows that intensive cholesterol-lowering to targets below what the medical profession is currently recommending significantly reduces the risk of heart attack and stroke for people with diabetes and heart disease.[115]

Medical advances hold out bright hopes for diabetics. Laser surgery, for instance, is saving eyesight. Bypass operations are helping restore blood flow to the heart and feet. Dialysis machines and kidney and pancreas transplants save many lives. Researchers are exploring various approaches to prevention, including early low-dose insulin therapy, oral insulin to correct immune intolerance, and immunosuppressive drugs. Still on the horizon is the promise of a true cure through transplanting insulin-producing cells from healthy pancreases. In preliminary trials, this procedure has helped patients become insulin-independent.[116]

In the words of Dr. Stewart Harris, Chair of the Expert Guidelines Committee and associate professor and McWhinney Chair for Family Medicine Studies at the University of Western Ontario, "We now have solid clinical evidence that it is possible to prevent one of the most common and costly chronic diseases affecting Canadians. Type 2 diabetes and its related complications can be prevented by lifestyle modifications—moderate weight loss and regular exercise—and in some people by the appropriate use of drugs. But diabetes must be prevented *sooner,* and diagnosed *earlier.* And once diagnosed, all types of diabetes must then be managed *much more aggressively.*"[117]

## The X & Y Files

## Gender Differences In Disease

Disease doesn't discriminate. In general, men and women are vulnerable to the same illnesses, but there are differences in the diseases that strike each gender. Women are more prone to arthritis, osteoporosis, and joint problems, while men are more likely felled by heart attacks and cancer.

Half of all men, compared to a third of women, develop cancer. Smoking, which for many years was much more prevalent among men, accounts for some of this difference. As more women became smokers in the last 30 years, lung cancer rates in women have doubled.

In some cancers, estrogen may somehow protect against distant metastases. This protection may be why women have a 12 percent lower death rate from cancer of the stomach and lung than men and a 33 percent greater chance of surviving malignant melanoma.

Some diseases, such as diabetes, afflict more women than men and pose a graver threat to their health. While more men develop ulcers and hernias, women are three to four times more likely to get gallbladder disease. Irritable bowel syndrome (IBS), one of the most common digestive disorders, causes such varied symptoms in the genders that some gastroenterologists think of it as a completely different disease in men and women. IBS affects women three times as often as men.

## CHAPTER 10
### Making This Chapter Work for You

1. The heart
   a. has four chambers, which are responsible for pumping blood into the veins for circulation through the body.
   b. pumps blood first to the lungs where it picks up oxygen and discards carbon dioxide.
   c. beats about 10 000 times and pumps about 300 litres of blood per day.
   d. has specialized cells that generate electrical signals to control the amount of blood that circulates through the body.

2. Risk factors for heart disease that cannot be controlled include
   a. male pattern baldness.
   b. diabetes mellitus.
   c. sedentary lifestyle.
   d. blood fat cells.

3. Your lipoprotein profile
   a. provides a breakdown of the different types and levels of blood fats circulating in your body.
   b. is best obtained at a health fair where the results are uniformly accurate.
   c. will give a total cholesterol level, which is the amount of triglycerides and LDL cholesterol levels added together.
   d. should be evaluated after eating a full meal.

4. Hypertension
   a. is diagnosed when blood pressure is consistently less than 130/85 mm Hg.
   b. may be treated with dietary changes, which include eating low-fat foods and avoiding sodium.
   c. can cause fatty deposits to collect on the artery walls.
   d. usually does not respond to medication, especially in severe cases.

5. A heart attack
   a. occurs when the myocardium receives an excessive amount of blood from the coronary arteries.
   b. is typically suffered by individuals who have irregular episodes of atherosclerosis.
   c. can be treated successfully up to four hours after the event.
   d. occurs when the myocardial cells are deprived of oxygen-carrying blood, causing them to die.

6. You can protect yourself from certain types of cancer by
   a. eating a diet rich in antioxidants.
   b. avoiding people who have had cancer.
   c. wearing sunscreen with a SPF of less than 15.
   d. using condoms during sexual intercourse.

7. Which of the following statements about skin cancer is true?
   a. Individuals with a large number of moles are at decreased risk for melanoma.
   b. The most serious type of skin cancer is squamous cell carcinoma.
   c. The safest way to get a tan and avoid skin cancer is to use tanning salons and sunlamps instead of sunbathing in direct sunlight.
   d. Individuals with a history of childhood sunburn are at increased risk for melanoma.

8. A woman's risk of developing breast cancer increases if
   a. she began menstruating before 12 years of age.
   b. she had her first child when in her teens or twenties.
   c. her husband's mother had breast cancer.
   d. she has fibrocystic breast disease.

9. Prostate cancer
   a. occurs mostly among men between the ages of 18 and 35.
   b. has been linked to having a vasectomy.
   c. is the most commonly diagnosed cancer in Canadian men.
   d. risk does not increase with age.

10. Which of the following statements about diabetes mellitus is *false*?
    a. The two types of diabetes are insulin-dependent and non-insulin-dependent.
    b. The incidence of diabetes has decreased in the last decade, especially among Canadian women and children.
    c. Individuals with diabetes must measure the levels of glucose in their blood to ensure that it does not rise to unsafe levels.
    d. Untreated or uncontrolled diabetes can lead to coma and eventual death.

Answers to these questions can be found on page 450.

## Self Responsibility

*It's not that some people have willpower and some don't. It's that some people are ready to change and others are not.*

**James Gordon, M.D.**

As you have discovered throughout this chapter, lowering your risk of major diseases takes knowledge, commitment, time, and energy. Where are you on the continuum of Prochaska's Stages of Change model when it comes to self-care and self-responsibility? What risk factors can you change with regard to heart disease, cancer, and diabetes? How can you move forward on a healthy living plan?

## Social Responsibility

*So many people spend their health gaining wealth, and then have to spend their wealth to regain their health.*

**A.J. Reb**

Many non-profit organizations have opportunities for volunteer work: arranging conference setup, canvassing for fundraising, participating in education fairs, and organizing fundraising events such as the CIBC Run for the Cure. Consider giving of your time for a health cause.

## Critical Thinking

1. Have you had a lipoprotein profile lately? Do you think it's necessary for you to obtain one? If your reading was or is borderline or high, what lifestyle changes could you make to help control your cholesterol level?

2. Do you have family members who have had cancer? Were these individuals at risk for cancer because of specific environmental factors, such as long-term exposure to tobacco smoke? If no particular cause was identified, what other factors could have triggered their diseases? Are you concerned that you might have inherited a genetic predisposition to any particular type of cancer because of your family history?

3. A friend of yours, Karen, discovered a small lump in her breast during a routine self-examination. When she mentions it, you ask if she has seen a doctor. She tells you that she hasn't had time to schedule an appointment; besides, she says she's not sure it's really the kind of lump one has to worry about. What advice would you give her?

CENGAGENOW™

If your textbook package includes CengageNOW™, go to http://west.cengagenow.com/ilrn/ to link to CengageNOW™ for Health, your online study tool. First take the **Pre-test** for this chapter to get your personalized **Study Plan,** which will identify topics you need to review and direct you to the appropriate resources. Then take the **Post-test** to determine what concepts you have mastered and what you still need work on.

## SITES & BYTES

### Canadian Cancer Society
www.cancer.ca

You will find comprehensive information about different kinds of cancer: statistics, early detection, prevention, treatment options, alternative treatments, and coping strategies for families.

### Canadian Diabetes Association
www.diabetes.ca

Here you will find the latest information on both Type 1 and Type 2 diabetes mellitus, including suggestions regarding diet and exercise. The online bookstore features meal planning guides, cookbooks, and self-care guides.

### Heart and Stroke Foundation of Canada
www.heartandstroke.com

This comprehensive site features a searchable database of all major cardiovascular diseases, plus information on healthy lifestyles and current research. You can find out about your own personal risk profile by completing the Heart & Stroke Risk Assessment™. This profile will provide a free, confidential, customized action plan for healthy living.

### The Lung Association of Canada
www.lung.ca

At this site you can access information and programs that are conducted at the national, provincial, and municipal levels. Current research and general information about respiratory health is abundant.

### National Aboriginal Diabetes Association
www.nada.ca

At this site you will find general information about diabetes, the *Pathway to Wellness—A Handbook for People Living with Diabetes* and the *Pathway to Wellness—A Handbook for Community Health Workers*, as well as a resource directory.

Please note that links are subject to change. If you find a broken link, use a search engine such as www.google.ca and search for the website by typing in keywords.

### InfoTrac® College Edition Activity
Hippisley-Cox, J., et al. (2002, September 21). Married couples' risk of same disease: Cross sectional study. *British Medical Journal, 325*(7365), 636.

1. Married partners of people with which types of chronic diseases are at increased risk of developing the same disease themselves?

2. What factors could explain this finding?

3. According to this study, there was a lack of adequate evidence for spouse concordance for which types of chronic diseases?

You can find additional readings relating to major diseases with InfoTrac® College Edition, an online library of more than 5000 journals and publications. Follow the instructions for accessing InfoTrac® College Edition that were packaged with your textbook; then search for articles using a keyword search.

For additional links and resources, visit our text-specific website at www.health.nelson.com.

## Key Terms

The terms listed here are used within the chapter on the page indicated. Definitions of the terms are in the Glossary at the end of the book.

| | | | |
|---|---|---|---|
| **angioplasty** 255 | **diabetes mellitus** 249 | **mammography** 264 | **prediabetes** 267 |
| **aorta** 244 | **diastole** 244 | **mastectomy** 265 | **stroke** 255 |
| **arteriosclerosis** 254 | **hypertension** 248 | **metabolic syndrome** 249 | **systole** 244 |
| **atherosclerosis** 254 | **infiltration** 257 | **metastasize** 257 | **triglyceride** 249 |
| **atrium** 244 | **lipoproteins** 249 | **myocardial infarction** | **ventricles** 244 |
| **capillaries** 244 | **lumpectomy** 265 | **(MI)** 254 | |
| **carcinogens** 261 | **male pattern** | **neoplasms** 257 | |
| **cholesterol** 248 | **baldness** 251 | **plaque** 254 | |

# References

1. Heart and Stroke Foundation. (2008). Home. News. Heart Disease. Available at www.heartandstroke.com/site/c.ikIQLcMWJtE/b.3483991/k.34A8/Statistics.htm.

2. Beaglehole, R. (2001). Global cardiovascular disease prevention: Time to get serious. *Lancet, 358,* 661.

3. Edwards, T. (2001). Lifestyle influences and coronary artery disease prevention. *Physician Assistant, 25*(8), 19.

4. The Healthy Heart Kit. (2003, December 29). Public Health Agency of Canada. Health Canada and Heart and Stroke Foundation of Canada. Available at www.phac-aspc.gc.ca/ccdpc-cpcmc/hhk-tcs/index.html.

5. Craig, C.L., & Cameron, C. (2004). Increasing physical activity: Assessing trends from 1998–2003. Ottawa, ON: *Canadian Fitness and Lifestyle Research Institute.* Available at www.cflri.ca/cflri/cflri.html.

6. Public Health Agency of Canada. (2003, October 8). Physical activity unit: How do I know I am doing enough physical activity to stay healthy? Available at www.phac-aspc.gc.ca/pau-uap/paguide/activity_enough.html.

7. Heart and Stroke Foundation of Canada. (n.d.). Family eating. Available at www.heartandstroke.com/atf/cf/%7B99452D8B-E7F1-4BD6-A57D-B136CE6C95BF%7D/FamilyEating.pdf.

8. Heart and Stroke Foundation of Canada. (n.d.). Dietary fat and cholesterol: Simple steps to making healthy choices. Available at www.heartandstroke.com/atf/cf/%7B99452D8B-E7F1-4BD6-A57D-B136CE6C95BF%7D/fat_chol.pdf.

9. Rolnick, A. (2008, March). Heart and Stroke Foundation of Canada. The skinny on fats. Available at www.heartandstroke.com/site/c.ikIQLcMWJtE/b.3909077/k.C5AB/The_skinny_on_fats.htm.

10. Heart and Stroke Foundation of Canada. (2007, June 20). Home. News. Press Releases. An important step closer to removing trans fats in foods in Canada. Available at www.heartandstroke.com/site/apps/nlnet/content2.aspx?c=ikIQLcMWJtE&b=3485819&ct=4512773.

11. Lunn, L., & Buttriss, J.L. (2008). Incorporating omega-3 in the food chain—why, where and how? *Nutrition Bulletin, 33*(3), 250–56.

12. Hu, F., & Willet, W.C. (2002). Optimal diets for prevention of coronary heart disease. *Journal of the American Medical Association, 288,* 2569–78.

13. Flax facts. (2002, May). *University of California at Berkeley Wellness Letter, 18*(8), 1–2.

14. Ibid.

15. Statistics Canada. (2002, October 3). Moderate alcohol consumption and heart disease. *The Daily.* Available at www.statcan.ca/Daily/English/021003/d021003a.htm.

16. American Heart Association. (2001, October 8). A few minutes of risk assessment could mean more of life. News release. October 8, 2001.

17. Heart and Stroke Foundation of Canada. (2003). The growing burden of heart disease and stroke in Canada, 2003. Chapter 1—Risk factors. Available at www.cvdinfobase.ca/cvdbook/CVD_En03.pdf.

18. Green, J.S., Grant, M., Hill, K.L., Brizzolra, J., & Belmont, B. (2003). Heart disease risk perception in college men and women. *Journal of American College Health, 15*(5), 207–11.

19. Spencer, L. (2002). Results of a heart disease risk-factor screening among traditional college students. *Journal of American College Health, 50*(6), 291.

20. Heart and Stroke Foundation of Canada. (2003). The growing burden of heart disease and stroke in Canada, 2003. Chapter 1—Risk factors. Available at www.cvdinfobase.ca/cvdbook/CVD_En03.pdf.

21. Canadian Fitness and Lifestyle Research Institute (2005). 2005 Physical activity and sport monitor. Ottawa, ON: Author. Available at www.cflri.ca/eng/statistics/surveys/pam2005.php.

22. Weemering, M.L. (2002). Physical activity and coronary heart disease in women: Is "No pain, no gain" passé? *Association of Perioperative Registered Nurses Journal, 76*(2), 331.

23. Tanasescu, M., et al. (2002). Exercise type and intensity in relation to coronary heart disease in men. *Journal of the American Medical Association, 288*(16), 1994.

24. Public Health Agency of Canada. (2007). Life and breath: Respiratory disease in Canada. (Chapter 2) Tobacco Use. Minister of Health. Available at www.phac-aspc.gc.ca/publicat/2007/lbrdc-vsmrc/pdf/PHAC-Respiratory-WEB-eng.pdf.

25. Health Canada Online. (2007, November 26). Healthy Living. Tobacco. Framework convention on tobacco control. Available at www.hc-sc.gc.ca/hl-vs/tobac-tabac/about-apropos/int/framework-cadre-eng.php.

26. Institute of Circulatory and Respiratory Health. (2007, February 20). World hypertension day. Available at www.cihr-irsc.gc.ca/e/33446.html.

27. Heart and Stroke Foundation of Canada. (2003). The growing burden of heart disease and stroke in Canada, 2003. Chapter 1—Risk factors. Available at www.cvdinfobase.ca/cvdbook/CVD_En03.pdf.

28. Heart and Stroke Foundation of Canada. (2005, May 10). 5 million Canadians affected—Minister Dosanjh attends blood pressure clinic event to mark world hypertension day. Press release. Available at www.cihr-irsc.gc.ca/e/28015.html.

29. National Cholesterol Education Program Expert Panel on Detection, Evaluation, and Treatment of High Blood Cholesterol in Adults. (2002). Prevalence of metabolic syndrome based on results of NHANES III. *Nutrition Research Newsletter, 21*(2), 7.

30. Heart and Stroke Foundation of Canada. (2001, September 22). Home. Health Information. Heart Disease. What is blood cholesterol. Available at www.heartandstroke.com/site/c.ikIQLcMWJtE/b.3484027/k.5C04/High_blood_cholesterol.htm.

31. Ibid.

32. Ibid.

33. Siani, A., et al. (2002). The relationship of waist circumference to blood pressure: The Olivetti heart study. *American Journal of Hypertension, 15*(9), 780.

34. Ruth MacManus refutes the myth of "borderline" diabetes. (n.d.). In Diabetes Dialogue. (1996, Spring). Canadian Diabetes Association. Available at www.diabetes.ca/Section_About/borderline.asp.

35. Canadian Diabetes Association. (2005–2008). About Diabetes. What is diabetes? Available at www.diabetes.ca/about-diabetes/what/facts.

36. Mooradian, A.D. (2003, January 13). Cardiovascular disease in type 2 diabetes mellitus. Current management guidelines. Review article. *Archives of Internal Medicine, 163.* Available at www.archinternmed.com.

37. Canadian Diabetes Association. (2005–2008). About Diabetes. What is diabetes? Available at www.diabetes.ca/about-diabetes/what/facts.

38. Ibid.

39. Woo, K.S., et al. (2004). Effects of diet and exercise on obesity-related vascular dysfunction in children. *Circulation, 109,* 1981–86.

40. Pratt, L.A., et al. (1996). Depression, psychotropic medication and risk of myocardial infarction. Prospective data from the Baltimore ECA follow-up. *Circulation, 94*(12), 3123.

41. Wassertheir-Smoller, S., Shumaker, S., Ockene, J., et al. (2004). Depression and cardiovascular sequelae in postmenopausal women: The women's health initiative. *Archives of Internal Medicine, 164,* 289–98.

42. Ipsos-Reid and Kumon Math and Reading Centre. (2005, April 12). Canadian university students on study habits and exam-related stress. Available at www.ipsos.ca.

43. Heart and Stroke Foundation of Canada. (2003). The growing burden of heart disease and stroke in Canada, 2003. Chapter 1—Risk factors. Available at www.cvdinfobase.ca/cvdbook/CVD_En03.pdf.

44. Ibid.

45. Heart and Stroke Foundation of Canada. (n.d.). Taking Control. Lowering your risk of heart disease and stroke. Available at www.heartandstroke.com/atf/cf/%7B99452D8B-E7F1-4BD6-A57D-B136CE6C95BF%7D/TAKING_CONTROL_ENG_FEB08.PDF.

46. Ibid.

47. Heart and Stroke Foundation of Canada. (2008, February 4). Press release. Think heart disease is a man's disease? Think again. Available at www.heartandstroke.com/site/apps/nlnet/content2.aspx?c=ikIQLcMWJtE&b=3485819&ct=5012433.

48. Heart and Stroke Foundation of Canada. (n.d.). Health Information. Heart Disease. Prevention of Risk Factors. Women's unique risk factors. Available at www.heartandstroke.com/site/c.ikIQLcMWJtE/b.3484041/k.86DC/Womens_unique_risk_factors.htm.

49. Writing Group for the Women's Health Initiative Investigators. (2002). Risks and benefits of estrogen plus progestin healthy post-menopausal women: Principal results from the women's health initiative randomized controlled trial. *Journal of the American Medical Association, 288,* 321.

50. Lotufo, P., et al. (2000). Male pattern baldness and coronary heart disease. *Journal of the American Medical Association, 160*(2).

51. Heart and Stroke Foundation of Canada. (n.d.). What is blood cholesterol? www.heartandstroke.com/site/c.ikIQLcMWJtE/b.3484161/k.5B14/High_blood_cholesterol.htm.

52. Heartbeats: Graze your way to lower cholesterol. (2002). *Harvard Heart Letter, 12*(9).

53. Heart and Stroke Foundation. Living with cholesterol. Available at www.heartandstroke.com/atf/cf/%7B99452D8B-E7F1-4BD6-A57D-B136CE6C95BF%7D/Living_with_Cholesterol_ENG.pdf.

54. Baker, C., et al. (2001). Hypertension. *Heart, 86*(3), 251.

55. Heart and Stroke Foundation of Canada. (2008, May 1). Stroke prevention and risk factors. High blood pressure. Available at www.heartandstroke.bc.ca/site/c.kpIPKXOyFmG/b.3644599/k.2C53/High_blood_pressure_hypertension.htm.

56. Miura, K., & Daviglus, M. (2001). Relationship of blood pressure to 25-year mortality due to coronary heart disease, cardiovascular diseases, and all causes in young adult men. *Archives of Internal Medicine, 161*(12), 1501.

57. Hales, D. (2000, June 25). The stealth killer. *Parade.*

58. Dietitians of Canada. (2008). What is the difference between different kinds of salt? What should I use if I'm trying to lower my blood pressure? Available at www.dietitians.ca/resources/resourcesearch.asp?fn=view&contentid=11277.

59. Heart and Stroke Foundation of Canada. (2008). Health Information. Healthly Living. Healthy Eating. Salt. Available at www.heartandstroke.bc.ca/site/c.kpIPKXOyFmG/b.B663/Salt.htm.

60. American Heart Association. (2005, September 20). The importance of potassium. Available at www.americanheart.org.

61. Whelton, P.K., et al. (1997). Effects of oral potassium on blood pressure. Meta-analysis of randomized controlled clinical trials. *Journal of the American Medical Association, 277*(2). Available at http://jama.ama-assn.org/cgi/content/abstract/277/20/1624.

62. Malik, I., et al. (2002). Easier to take a pill than change the lifestyle, but not as effective as the combination. *Heart, 87*(5), 494.

63. Heart and Stroke Foundation of Canada. (2001, September 22). Health Information. Statistics. Heart Disease. Available at www.heartandstroke.com/site/c.ikIQLcMWJtE/b.3483991/k.34A8/Statistics.htm.

64. Canadian Institute for Health Information (2006, June 7). Heart attack survival rates improve—Stroke death rates remain the same.

Available at www.cihi.ca/cihiweb/dispPage.jsp?cw_page=media_07jun2006_e.

65. Legato, M. (2000). Gender and the heart: Sex-specific differences in normal anatomy and physiology. *Journal of Gender-Specific Medicine, 3*(7).

66. Heart and Stroke Foundation of Canada. (2002, June 1). News. Statistics. Stroke. Available at www.heartandstroke.com/site/c.ikIQLcMWJtE/b.3483991/k.34A8/Statistics.htm.

67. Ibid.

68. Ibid.

69. Ibid.

70. Ibid.

71. Heart and Stroke Foundation of Canada. (2008). Health Information. Stroke. What is Stroke? Stroke: Transient Ischemic Attacks. Available at www.heartandstroke.com/site/c.ikIQLcMWJtE/b.3484151.

72. Heart and Stroke Foundation of Canada. (2006, June). Health Information. Stroke. Other Information for Stroke. Mini Strokes: What you need to know. Understanding TIA—An interactive patient workbook. Available at www.heartandstroke.com/site/c.ikIQLcMWJtE/b.3882225/k.50DC/Mini_strokes_What_you_need_to_know.htm.

73. Chatfield, J. (2001). American Heart Association scientific statement on the primary prevention of ischemic stroke. *American Family Physician, 64*(3), 513.

74. Heart and Stroke Foundation of Canada. (2008). Health Information. Stroke. Stroke Prevention and Risk Factors. Available at www.heartandstroke.com/site/c.ikIQLcMWJtE/b.3483939/k.4D69/Stroke_prevention_and_risk_factors.htm.

75. Ibid.

76. Canadian Cancer Society/National Cancer Institute of Canada. (2008). Canadian cancer statistics 200. Available at http://ncic.cancer.ca/Cancer%20control/Canadian%20Cancer%20Statistics.aspx?sc_lang=en.

77. Ibid.

78. Ibid.

79. Zenilman, J. (2001). Chlamydia and cervical cancer. *Journal of the American Medical Association, 285*(1).

80. Canadian Cancer Society. (2008, June 26). Make healthy eating choices. Available at www.cancer.ca/Canada-wide/Prevention/Eat%20well/Make%20healthy%20eating%20choices.aspx?sc_lang=en.

81. Ibid.

82. Ibid.

83. Canadian Cancer Society/National Cancer Institute of Canada. (2008). Canadian Cancer Statistics 2008. Available at http://ncic.cancer.ca/Cancer%20control/Canadian%20Cancer%20Statistics.aspx?sc_lang=en.

84. Zoorob, R., et al. (2001). Cancer screening guidelines. *American Family Physician, 63*(6), 1101.

85. Canadian Cancer Society. (2005, April 12). Media backgrounder: Prevention. Available at www.cancer.ca/ccs/internet/mediareleaselist/0,3208,3172_343093094_399105192_langId-en,00.html.

86. Goldstein, B., & Goldstein, A. (2001). Diagnosis and management of malignant melanoma. *American Family Physician, 63*(7), 1101.

87. Canadian Cancer Society. (2008, July 29). Prevention. Use sun sense. Available at www.cancer.ca/Canada-wide/Prevention/Use%20SunSense.aspx?sc_lang=en.

88. Canadian Cancer Society. (2003, May 26). Media backgrounder: Malignant melanoma in Canada. Available at www.cancer.ca/ccs/internet/mediareleaselist/0,3208,3172_210504884_56668171_langId-en,00.html.

89. Skin cancer: Shedding light on melanoma. (2001). *Harvard Women's Health Watch, 9*(1).

90. Ibid.

91. Goldstein, B., & Goldstein, A. (2001). Diagnosis and management of malignant melanoma. *American Family Physician, 63*(7), 1101.

92. Canadian Cancer Society. (2008, August 17). Breast cancer stats. Available at www.cancer.ca/Canada-wide/About%20cancer/Cancer%20statistics/Stats%20at%20a%20glance/Breast%20cancer.aspx.

93. Ibid.

94. Ibid.

95. Canadian Cancer Society. (2008, September 11). Early detection and screening for breast cancer. Available at www.cancer.ca/Canada-wide/About%20cancer/Types%20of%20cancer/Early%20detection%20and%20screening%20for%20breast%20cancer.aspx.

96. Canadian Cancer Society. (2005, March 30). Landmark breast cancer prevention study launches in Canada and the United States. Media release. Available at www.cancer.ca/ccs/internet/mediareleaselist/0,3208,3172_343093094_390690360_langId-en,00.html.

97. Canadian Cancer Society. (2008, September 11). What is cervical cancer? Available at www.cancer.ca/Canada-wide/About%20cancer/Types%20of%20cancer/What%20is%20cervical%20cancer.aspx.

98. Canadian Cancer Society. (2008, August 17). Media backgrounder: Colorectal cancer statistics. Media release. Available at www.cancer.ca/Canada-wide/About%20cancer/Cancer%20statistics/Stats%20at%20a%20glance/Colorectal%20cancer.aspx.

99. Canadian Cancer Society. (2004, September 16). Media backgrounder: Prostate cancer. Media release. Available at www.cancer.ca/ccs/internet/mediareleaselist/0,3208,3172_210504871_272426109_langId-en,00.html.

100. Strayer, S. (2002). Vasectomy not a risk factor for prostate cancer. *Journal of Family Practice, 51*(9), 791.

101. Canadian Cancer Society (2006, 11 April). Media backgrounder: Canadian Cancer Statistics 2006—Screening: Insufficient evidence for prostate, lung and ovarian cancers. Available at www.cancer.ca/Canada-wide/About%20us/Media%20centre/CW-Media%20releases/CW-2006/Media%20backgrounder%20Canadian%20Cancer%20Statistics%202006%20-%20Screening%20Insufficient%20evidence%20for%20prostate%20%20lung%20and%20ovarian%20cancers.aspx.

102. Courtenay, W. (2000). Behavioral factors associated with disease, injury, and death among men: Evidence and implications for prevention. *Journal of Men's Studies, 9*(1), 81.

103. Canadian Diabetes Association. (2005, February 23). Seriousness of diabetes recognized in budget. Canadian Diabetes Association welcomes new funding for diabetes prevention and management. *Reaching Out* (Spring 2005). Available at www.diabetes.ca/files/CDA-NE-Ontario-Newsletter.pdf.

104. Canadian Diabetes Association. (2008, September 18). More Canadians than ever before now at risk. News release. Available at www.diabetes.ca/get-involved/news/more-canadians-than-ever-before-now-at-risk.

105. Canadian Diabetes Association. (n.d.). Diabetes facts. Available at www.diabetes.ca/about-diabetes/what/facts.

106. Lau, D. (2007). Evidence-based Canadian obesity clinical practice guidelines: Relevance to diabetes management. *Canadian Journal of Diabetes, 31*(2), 148–52. Available at www.diabetes.ca/Files/D-Lau-May2007.pdf.

107. Canadian Diabetes Association. (n.d.). Children and type 2 diabetes. Available at www.diabetes.ca/about-diabetes/youth/type2.

108. Lau, D. (2007). Evidence-based Canadian obesity clinical practice guidelines: Relevance to diabetes management. *Canadian Journal of Diabetes, 31*(2), 148–52. Available at www.diabetes.ca/Files/D-Lau-May2007.pdf.

109. Ibid.

110. Sherwin, Robert. Personal interview.

111. Hu, F., et al. (2001). Diet, lifestyle, and the risk of type 2 diabetes mellitus in women. *New England Journal of Medicine, 345*(11), 790.

112. Canadian Diabetes Association. (2005, April 20). Canadian Diabetes Association, UBC partner on funding for childhood diabetes research. News release. Available at www.medicalnewstoday.com/articles/23378.php.

113. Canadian Diabetes Association. (2005, September 20). Canadian diabetes study: A wake-up call. News Release. Available at www.gsk.ca/english/docs-pdf/20050920.pdf.

114. National Aboriginal Diabetes Association. (n.d.). Pathway to wellness: A handbook for people living with diabetes. Available at www.nada.ca/resources/resources_pathways.php.

115. Canadian Diabetes Association. (2005, June 20). Canadians with diabetes and heart disease benefit from intensive cholesterol-lowering. News Release. Available at www.medicalnewstoday.com/articles/26420.php.

116. Hales, D. (2001, February 4). Should you be tested for diabetes? *Parade.*

117. Smiley, T. (2005). The community pharmacist's role in the management of Type 2 diabetes. Canadian Pharmacists Association. Available at www.cpha.learning.mediresource.com/homestudy/courses/CPhA05_diabetes05_w.pdf.

# CHAPTER
# 11

# Drug Use, Misuse, and Abuse

After studying the material in this chapter, you will be able to:

- **Describe** the factors affecting individuals' responses to drugs.
- **Give examples** of appropriate and inappropriate use of over-the-counter and prescription medications.
- **Discuss** the factors affecting drug dependence.
- **Describe** the methods of use and the effects of common drugs of abuse.
- **Describe** the treatment methods available for drug dependence.

P eople who try illegal drugs don't think they'll ever lose control. But with continued use, drugs produce changes in an individual's body, mind, and behaviour. In time, a person's need for a drug can outweigh everything else, including the values, people, and relationships he or she once held dearest.

Substance use, misuse, and abuse have long been important public-health concerns in Canada. According to a study done by Tjepkema, published in 2004, an estimated 3.1 million people—13 percent of the population—reported they had used illicit drugs in the past year, and 194 000 people (0.8 percent) reported they were dependent on illicit drugs.[1] The challenges of drug use and abuse are many—injection drug use and HIV/AIDS, drug labs and grow operations, street use of prescription drugs, methamphetamine abuse, and social problems.

This chapter provides information on the nature and effects of drugs, the impact of drugs on individuals and society, and the drugs Canadians most commonly use, misuse, and abuse. It also includes a section on treating drug dependence and abuse with options for individual programs and information about how some communities in Canada are finding ways to address this important health issue.

**???? FREQUENTLY ASKED QUESTIONS**

**FAQ: What should I know about buying over-the-counter drugs? p. 279**

**FAQ: What causes drug dependence and abuse? p. 283**

**FAQ: How common is drug use on campus? p. 285**

# Understanding Drugs and Their Effects

A **drug** is any substance that is taken to change the way you feel and function.[2] In some circumstances, taking a drug can help the body heal or relieve physical and mental distress. In other circumstances, taking a drug can distort reality, undermine well-being, and threaten survival. No drug is completely safe; all drugs have multiple effects that vary greatly in different people at different times. Knowing how drugs affect the brain, body, and behaviour is crucial to understanding their impact and making responsible decisions about their use.

**Drug misuse** is the taking of a drug for a purpose or by a person other than that for which it was medically intended. Borrowing a friend's prescription for penicillin when your throat feels scratchy is an example of drug misuse. It can also mean inadvertently not complying with prescription medication instructions.[3] The World Health Organization defines **drug abuse** as excessive drug use that is inconsistent with accepted medical practice. Taking prescription painkillers to get high is an example of drug abuse.

Risks are involved with all forms of drug use. Even medications that help cure illnesses or soothe symptoms have side effects and can be misused. Some substances that millions of people use every day, such as caffeine, pose some health risks. Others—like the most commonly used drugs in our society, alcohol and tobacco—can lead to potentially life-threatening problems. With some illicit drugs, any form of use can be dangerous.

Many factors determine the effects a drug has on an individual. These include how the drug enters the body, the dosage, the drug action, and the presence of other drugs in the body—as well as the physical and psychological make-up of the person taking the drug and the setting in which the drug is used.

## Routes of Administration

Drugs can enter the body in a number of ways (see Figure 11-1). The most common way of taking a drug is by swallowing a tablet, capsule, or liquid. However, drugs taken orally don't reach the bloodstream as quickly as drugs introduced into the body by other means. A drug taken orally may not have any effect for 30 minutes or more.

Drugs can enter the body through the lungs either by inhaling smoke—for example, from marijuana—or by inhaling gases, aerosol sprays, or fumes from solvents or other compounds that evaporate quickly.

Drugs can also be injected with a syringe subcutaneously (beneath the skin), intramuscularly (into muscle tissue, which is richly supplied with blood vessels), or intravenously (directly into a vein). **Intravenous (IV)** injection gets the drug into the bloodstream immediately (within

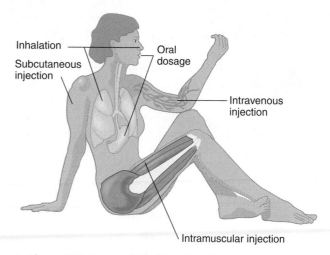

▲ **Figure 11-1** Routes of Administration of Drugs.

Source: Hespenheide Design

seconds in most cases); **intramuscular** injection, moderately quickly (within a few minutes); and **subcutaneous** injection, more slowly (within 10 minutes).

Injection can be extremely dangerous because many diseases, including hepatitis and infection with human immune deficiency virus (HIV), can be transmitted by sharing contaminated needles. Injection-drug users who are HIV-positive are the chief source of transmission of HIV among heterosexuals.

## Dosage and Toxicity

The effects of any drug depend on the amount an individual takes. Increasing the dose usually intensifies the effects produced by smaller doses. Also, the kind of effect may change at different dose levels. For example, low doses of barbiturates may relieve anxiety, while higher doses can induce sleep, loss of sensation, and even coma and death.

The dosage level at which a drug becomes poisonous to the body, causing either temporary or permanent damage, is called its **toxicity.** In most cases, drugs are eventually broken down in the liver by special body chemicals called *detoxification enzymes.*

## Individual Differences

Each person responds differently to different drugs, depending on circumstances or setting. The enzymes in the body reduce the levels of drugs in the bloodstream; because there can be 80 variants of each enzyme, every person's body may react differently.

Often drugs intensify the emotional state of a person. If you're feeling depressed, a drug may make you feel more depressed. A generalized physical problem, such as having the flu, may make your body more vulnerable to the effects of a drug. Genetic differences among individuals may account for varying reactions.

Personality and psychological attitude also play a role in drug effects, so that one person may have a frighteningly bad trip on the same dosage of a drug on which another person has a positive experience. To a certain extent, this depends on each user's *mind-set*—his or her expectations or preconceptions about using the drug.

## Medications

Many of the medications and pharmaceutical products available in this country do indeed relieve symptoms and help cure various illnesses. However, improper use of medications leads to hospitalizations and added health-care costs for Canadians. Because drugs are powerful, it's important to know how to use them appropriately.

### What Should I Know about Buying Over-the-Counter Drugs?

More than half a million health products are readily available without a doctor's prescription. This doesn't mean that they're necessarily safe or effective. Indeed, many widely used **over-the-counter (OTC) drugs** pose unsuspected hazards.

Among the most potentially dangerous is aspirin, the "wonder drug" in practically everyone's home pharmacy. When taken by someone who's been drinking (often to prevent or relieve hangover symptoms), aspirin increases blood-alcohol concentrations. Along with other nonsteroidal anti-inflammatory drugs, such as ibuprofen (brand names include Advil® and Nuprin®), aspirin can damage the lining of the stomach and lead to ulcers in those who take large daily doses for arthritis or other problems. Kidney problems have also been traced to some pain relievers, including acetaminophen (Tylenol®). Some health products that aren't even considered true drugs can also cause problems. Many Canadians take food supplements, even though the Health Products and Food Branch of Health Canada[4] has never approved their use for any medical disorder.

A growing number of drugs that once were available only with a doctor's prescription can now be bought over the counter. These include Monistat®, which combats vaginal yeast infections, and nicotine replacement patches and gum to aid smokers trying to quit. For consumers, the advantages of this greater availability include lower prices and fewer visits to the doctor. The disadvantages, however, are the risks of misdiagnosing a problem and misusing or overusing medications.

Like other drugs, OTC medications can be used improperly, often simply because of a lack of education about proper use. Among those most often misused are the following:

✔ **Nasal sprays.** Nasal sprays relieve congestion by shrinking blood vessels in the nose. If they are used too often or for too many days in a row, however, the blood vessels widen instead of contracting, and the surrounding tissues become swollen, causing more congestion. The result can be complete loss of smell.

✔ **Laxatives.** Brands that contain phenolphthalein irritate the lining of the intestines and cause muscles to contract or tighten, often making constipation worse rather than better. A high-fibre diet and more exercise are safer and more effective remedies for constipation.

✔ **Eye drops.** Eye drops make the blood vessels of the eye contract. With overuse (several times a day for several weeks), the blood vessels expand, making the eye look redder than before.

✔ **Sleep aids.** Although over-the-counter sleeping pills are widely used, there has been little research on their use and possible risks.

✔ **Cough syrup.** Chugging cough syrup is a growing problem, in part because young people think of dextromethorphan (DXM), a common ingredient in cough medicine, as a "poor man's version" of the popular drug ecstasy.[5]

## Prescription Drugs

Medications are a big business in this country. Presently, there are no accurate statistics on the number of people in Canada who engage in the non-medical use of prescription drugs or who experience dependence on prescription drugs. However, by analyzing distribution and sales statistics and year-to-year trends in prescription practices, sources tell us that Canadians reported the fourth-highest per capita use of prescription narcotics in the world and the second-highest use of sedative-hypnotics and that Canada was among the top 15 countries in the use of prescription amphetamines.[6]

College and university students, like other consumers, often take medicines without discussing them with their physician. Both doctors and patients make mistakes when it comes to prescription drugs. The most frequent mistakes doctors make are overdosing or underdosing, omitting information from prescriptions, ordering the wrong dosage form (a pill instead of a liquid, for example), and not recognizing a patient's allergy to a drug.

## Nonadherence

Many prescribed medications aren't taken the way they should be; millions simply aren't taken at all. Many people have trouble understanding dosage information or can't read standard labels. The dangers of nonadherence (not properly taking prescription drugs) include recurrent infections, serious medical complications, and emergency hospital treatment. The drugs most likely to be taken incorrectly are those that treat problems with no obvious symptoms (such as high blood pressure), require complex dosage schedules, treat psychiatric disorders, or have unpleasant side effects.

Some people skip prescribed doses or stop taking medications because they fear that any drug can cause tolerance and eventual dependence. Others fail to let doctors know about side effects, such as stomach irritation.

## Physical Side Effects

Most medications, taken correctly, cause only minor complications. However, no drug is entirely without side effects for all individuals taking it. Serious complications that may occur include heart failure, heart attack, seizures, kidney and liver failure, severe blood disorders, birth defects, blindness, memory problems, and allergic reactions.

Allergic reactions to drugs are common. The drugs that most often provoke allergic responses are penicillin and other antibiotics (drugs used to treat infection). Aspirin, sulpha drugs, barbiturates, anticonvulsants, insulin, and local anesthetics can also provoke allergic responses. Allergic reactions range from mild rashes or hives to anaphylaxis—a life-threatening constriction of the airways and sudden drop of blood pressure that causes rapid pulse, weakness, paleness, confusion, nausea, vomiting, unconsciousness, and collapse. This extreme response, which is rare, requires immediate treatment with an injection of epinephrine (adrenaline) to open the airways and blood vessels.

## Psychological Side Effects

Dozens of drugs—over-the-counter and prescription—can cause changes in the way people think, feel, and behave. Unfortunately, neither patients nor their physicians usually connect such symptoms with medications. Doctors may not even mention potential mental and emotional problems because they don't want to scare patients away from what otherwise may be a very effective treatment.

Among the medications most likely to cause psychiatric side effects are drugs for high blood pressure, heart disease, asthma, epilepsy, arthritis, Parkinson's disease, anxiety, insomnia, and depression. Some drugs—such as the powerful hormones called *corticosteroids,* used for asthma, autoimmune diseases, and cancer—can cause different psychiatric symptoms, depending on dosage and other factors. Other drugs, such as ulcer medications, can cause delirium and disorientation, especially when given in high doses or to elderly patients. More subtle problems, such as forgetfulness or irritability, are common reactions to many drugs that are likely to be ignored or dismissed. The older you are, the sicker you are, and the more medications you're taking, the greater your risk of developing some psychiatric side effects. Even medications that don't usually cause problems, such as antibiotics, can cause psychiatric side effects in some individuals.

Any medication that slows down bodily systems, as many high blood pressure and cardiac drugs do, can cause depressive symptoms. Estrogen in birth control pills can cause mood changes. As many as 15 percent of women using oral contraceptives have reported feeling depressed or moody. For many people, switching to another medication quickly lifts a drug-induced depression.

All drugs that stimulate or speed up the central nervous system can cause agitation and anxiety—including the almost 200 allergy, cold, and congestion remedies containing pseudoephedrine hydrochloride (Sudafed®). Other common culprits in inducing anxiety are caffeine and theophylline, a chemical relative of caffeine found in many medications for asthma and other respiratory problems. These drugs act like mild amphetamines in the body, making people feel hyperactive and restless.

## Drug Interactions

OTC and prescription drugs can interact in a variety of ways. For example, mixing some cold medications with tranquilizers can cause drowsiness and coordination problems, thus making driving dangerous. Moreover, what you eat or drink can impair or completely wipe out the effectiveness of drugs or lead to unexpected effects on the body. For instance, aspirin takes five to ten times as long to be absorbed when taken with food or shortly after a meal than when taken on an empty stomach. If tetracyclines encounter calcium in the stomach, they bind together and cancel each other out.

To avoid potentially dangerous interactions, check the label(s) for any instructions on how or when to take a medication, such as "with a meal." If the directions say that you should take a drug on an empty stomach, take it at least one hour before eating or two or three hours after eating. Don't drink a hot beverage with a medication; the temperature may interfere with the effectiveness of the drug. Don't open, crush, or dissolve tablets or capsules without checking first with your physician or pharmacist.

Whenever you take a drug, be especially careful of your intake of alcohol, which can change the rate of metabolism and the effects of many different drugs. Because it dilates the blood vessels, alcohol can add to the dizziness sometimes caused by drugs for high blood pressure, angina, or depression. Also, its irritating effects on the stomach can worsen stomach upset from aspirin, ibuprofen, and other anti-inflammatory drugs.

## Caffeine Use and Misuse

Caffeine, which has been drunk, chewed, and swallowed since the Stone Age, is the most widely used **psychotropic** (mind-affecting) drug in the world. Coffee has exploded into a multi-billion-dollar worldwide fascination, spawning a massive global industry employing over 20 million people and ranking, as a commodity, second in terms of dollars traded worldwide after petroleum.[7]

Although there is no human requirement for caffeine in our diet, findings from the Canadian Coffee Drinking Study[8] show that 81 percent of Canadians drink coffee occasionally and that 63 percent of those over the age of 18 drink coffee on a daily basis. Coffee is the number-one beverage choice of Canadian adults. We drink an average of 2.6 cups of coffee per day. Men and women are equally likely to be coffee consumers, although men appear to drink slightly more coffee than women.

Coffee contains 100–150 milligrams of caffeine per cup; tea, 40–100 milligrams; cola, and about 45 milligrams. Most medications that contain caffeine are one-third to one-half the strength of a cup of coffee. However, some, such as Excedrin®, are very high in caffeine (see Table 11-1). Health Canada recommends consuming no more than 400 milligrams of caffeine a day. Popular 568-millilitre jumbo cups of coffee served at many coffee shops deliver this dose in a single serving.[9]

The effects of caffeine vary. As a **stimulant,** it relieves drowsiness, helps in the performance of repetitive tasks, and improves the capacity for work. Some athletes feel that caffeine gives them an extra boost that allows them to go farther and longer in endurance events. Consumption of high doses of caffeine can lead to dependence, anxiety, insomnia, rapid breathing, upset stomach and bowels, and dizziness.

In a study of college men and women who normally consumed fewer than three caffeinated beverages per day, caffeine boosted anxiety but did not significantly affect performance on various low-intensity tasks, except for hand-eye coordination, which improved.[10]

Although there is no conclusive proof that caffeine causes birth defects, it does cross the placenta into the tissues of a growing fetus. Because of an increased risk of miscarriage, Health Canada has recommended that pregnant women avoid or restrict their caffeine intake. Some fertility specialists also have urged couples trying to conceive to

| ▼ Table 11-1 Caffeine Counts | |
| --- | --- |
| **Substance (typical serving)** | **Caffeine (milligrams)** |
| Coffee (brewed), one 227 ml cup | 135 |
| Espresso, one 56 ml cup | 100 |
| Instant coffee, one 227 ml cup | 95 |
| Red Bull, 250 ml can | 80 |
| Excedrin, two pills | 130 |
| No Doz, one pill | 200 |
| Coca-Cola Classic, 355 ml | 34.5 |
| Diet Coke, 355 ml | 46.5 |
| Tea, one 227 ml cup | 50 |
| Dark chocolate, 28 ml | 20 |
| Milk chocolate, 28 ml | 6 |
| Cocoa, 142 ml | 4 |
| Decaffeinated coffee, 227 ml cup | 5 |

© Corbis

▲ Coffee and work often go hand in hand, but too much caffeine can lead to dependence, anxiety, and other problems.

reduce caffeine intake to increase their chance of success. Women who are heavy caffeine users tend to have shorter menstrual cycles than nonusers. A Health Canada study also suggests coffee consumption increases the risk of bladder cancer in men. Men who drank four cups of coffee or more daily were almost twice as likely to get bladder cancer as members of a control group who did not drink coffee. Bladder cancer is the fourth most common cancer in Canadian men.[11] However, other studies have not shown a coffee–cancer link—possibly because of the numerous compounding lifestyle factors of study participants.

## Substance Use and Disorders

People have been using **psychoactive** (mood-altering) chemicals for centuries. Citizens of ancient Mesopotamia and Egypt used opium. More than 3000 years ago, Hindus included cannabis in religious ceremonies. For centuries the Inca in South America have chewed the leaves of the coca bush. Although drugs existed in most ancient societies, their use was usually limited to small groups. Today millions of people regularly turn to drugs to pick them up, bring them down, alter perceptions, or ease psychological pain.

Both men and women are vulnerable to substance-use disorders, although they tend to have different patterns of drug use (see The X & Y Files: "Men, Women, and Drugs"). The 1960s ushered in an explosive increase in drug use and in the number of drug users in our society. Marijuana use soared in the 1960s and 1970s; cocaine, in the 1980s. In 1986, crack—a cheap, smokeable form of cocaine—hit the streets, and the number of regular cocaine users zoomed. Club drugs, such as ecstasy (MDMA) and methamphetamine (crystal meth), are now the drug of choice among young people.

In a study of 7800 Canadian undergraduate students from 16 universities, approximately 47.5 percent reported the use of an illicit drug during their life and 29.6 percent reported use in the past twelve months, with 18.7 percent since the beginning of their academic year. This study showed that the rates were similar to non-university peers.[12]

The word **addiction,** as used by the general population, refers to the compulsive use of a substance, loss of control, negative consequences, and denial. Mental health professionals describe drug-related problems in terms of *dependence* and *abuse.*

### Dependence

Individuals may develop **psychological dependence** and feel a strong craving for a drug because it produces pleasurable feelings or relieves stress and anxiety. **Physical dependence** occurs when a person develops *tolerance* to the effects of a drug and needs larger and larger doses to achieve intoxication or another desired effect. Individuals who are physically dependent and have a high tolerance to a drug may take amounts many times those that would produce intoxication or an overdose in someone who was not a regular user.

Men and women with a substance-dependence disorder may use a drug to avoid or relieve withdrawal symptoms, or they may consume larger amounts of a drug or use it over a longer period than they'd originally intended. They may repeatedly try to cut down or control drug use without success; spend a great deal of time obtaining or using drugs or recovering from their effects; give up or reduce important social, occupational, or recreational activities because of their drug use; or continue to use a drug despite knowledge that the drug is likely to cause or worsen a persistent or recurring physical or psychological problem.

Specific symptoms of dependence vary with particular drugs. Some drugs, such as marijuana, hallucinogens, and phencyclidine, do not cause withdrawal symptoms. The degree of dependence also varies. In mild cases, a person may function normally most of the time. In severe cases, the person's entire life may revolve around obtaining, using, and recuperating from the effects of a drug.

Individuals with drug dependence become intoxicated or high on a regular basis—whether every day, every weekend, or several binges a year. They may try repeatedly to stop using a drug and yet fail, even though they realize their drug use is interfering with their health, family life, relationships, and work.

### Abuse

Some drug users do not develop the symptoms of tolerance and withdrawal that characterize dependence, yet they use drugs in ways that clearly have a harmful effect on them. These individuals are diagnosed as having a *psychoactive substance-abuse disorder.* They continue to use drugs despite their awareness of persistent or repeated social, occupational, psychological, or physical problems related to drug use, or they use drugs in dangerous ways or situations (before driving, for instance).

### Intoxication and Withdrawal

**Intoxication** refers to maladaptive behavioural, psychological, and physiologic changes that occur as a result of substance use. **Withdrawal** is the development of symptoms that cause significant psychological and physical distress when an individual reduces or stops drug use. (Intoxication and withdrawal from specific drugs are discussed later in this chapter.)

### Polyabuse

Most users prefer a certain type of drug but also use several others; this behaviour is called **polyabuse.** The average user who enters treatment is on five different drugs. The more drugs anyone uses, the greater the chance of side effects, complications, and possibly life-threatening interactions.

## The X&Y Files

# Men, Women, and Drugs

Beginning at a very early age, males and females show different patterns in drug use. Among 12-year-olds who have been offered drugs, boys are more likely to have received those offers from other males or their parents. Girls are most likely to have been offered drugs by a female friend or family member. Boys are more likely to receive offers in a public setting, such as on the street or in a park, and the offers typically emphasize "benefits," such as improved status or self-image. Girls are more likely to receive a straightforward, "Do you want some?" offer or one that minimizes the risks of drug use. For girls, these offers are usually made in a private setting, such as a friend's home.

Later in life, men generally encounter more opportunities to use drugs than women, but given an opportunity to use drugs for the first time, both genders are equally likely to do so and to progress from initial use to dependence. However, men are more likely than women to use illicit drugs. Based on data from the 2002 *Community Health Survey: Mental Health and Well-Being*, 16 percent of men and 9 percent of women had used illicit drugs in the past year. For more than half of the men (55 percent), use had been at least monthly compared with 38 percent of the women. Daily users represented 10 percent and 7 percent of the two groups, respectively.[14, 15]

Vulnerability to some drugs varies with gender. Both are equally likely to become addicted to or dependent on cocaine, heroin, hallucinogens, tobacco, and inhalants. Women are more likely than men to become addicted to or dependent on sedatives and drugs designed to treat anxiety or sleeplessness and less likely than men to abuse alcohol and marijuana.

Males and females may differ in their biological responses to drugs. Women may be more sensitive than men to the cardiovascular effects of cocaine. In human studies, women and men given equal doses of cocaine experienced the same cardiovascular response, despite the fact that blood concentrations of cocaine did not rise as high in women as in men. Male and female long-term cocaine users showed similar impairment in tests of concentration, memory, and academic achievement following sustained abstinence, even though women in the study had substantially greater exposure to cocaine. Female cocaine users also were less likely than men to exhibit abnormalities of blood flow in the brain's frontal lobes. These findings suggest a gender-related mechanism that may protect women from some of the damage cocaine inflicts on the brain. However, women are more vulnerable to poor nutrition and below-average weight, depression, physical abuse, and, if pregnant, preterm labour or early delivery.

Women are nearly twice as likely as men to become infected with HIV by sharing needles with other injection-drug users and by engaging in unprotected sex.

There are also differences between men and women who seek treatment for drug abuse. Women in treatment programs are less likely than men to have graduated from high school and to be employed and are more likely than men to have other health problems, to have sought previous drug treatment, to have attempted suicide, and to have suffered sexual abuse or other physical abuse. Traditional drug-treatment programs, created for men, have proven to be less effective for women than programs that provide more comprehensive services, including child care, assertiveness training, and parenting training.

## Coexisting Conditions

Mental disorders and substance-abuse disorders have a great deal of overlap. "A little more than a third of those with a psychiatric disorder also have a chemical dependency problem, and a little more than a third of those with a chemical dependency problem have a psychiatric disorder," notes psychiatrist Richard Frances.[13] Individuals with such *dual diagnoses* require careful evaluation and appropriate treatment for the complete range of complex and chronic difficulties they face.

 ## What Causes Drug Dependence and Abuse?

No one fully understands why some people develop drug dependence or abuse disorders, whereas others, who may experiment briefly with drugs, do not. Inherited body chemistry, genetic factors, and sensitivity to drugs may make some individuals more susceptible. These disorders may stem from many complex causes.

## Biology of Dependence

Some scientists now view drug dependence as a brain disease triggered by frequent use of drugs that change the biochemistry and anatomy of neurons and alter the way they work.[16] A major breakthrough in understanding dependence has been the discovery that certain mood-altering substances and experiences—a puff of marijuana, a slug of whiskey, a snort of cocaine, a big win at blackjack—trigger a rise in a brain chemical called *dopamine*, which is associated with feelings of satisfaction and euphoria. This brain chemical or neurotransmitter, one of the crucial messengers that links nerve cells in the brain, rises during any pleasurable experience, whether it be a loving hug or a taste of chocolate.

Addictive drugs have such a powerful impact on dopamine and its receptors (its connecting cells) that they change the pathways within the brain's pleasure centres. Various psychoactive chemicals create a craving for more of the same. According to this hypothesis, addicts do not specifically yearn for heroin, cocaine, or nicotine but for the rush of dopamine that these drugs produce. Other brain chemicals, including glutamate, GABA (gamma-aminobutyric acid), and possibly norepinephrine, may also be involved. Some individuals who are born with low levels of dopamine may be particularly susceptible to addiction.

## Other Routes of Addiction

Scientists believe certain individuals are at greater risk of drug dependence because of psychological factors, including difficulty controlling impulses, a lack of values that might constrain drug use (whether based in religion, family, or society), low self-esteem, feelings of powerlessness, and depression. The one psychological trait most often linked with drug use is denial. Young people in particular are absolutely convinced that they will never lose control or suffer in any way as a result of drug use.

Many diagnosed drug users have at least one mental disorder, particularly depression or anxiety. Disorders that emerge in adolescence, such as bipolar disorder, may increase the risk of substance abuse. Many people with psychiatric disorders abuse drugs. Individuals may self-administer drugs to treat psychiatric symptoms; for example, they may take sedating drugs to suppress a panic attack.

Individuals who are isolated from friends and family or who live in communities where drugs are widely used have higher rates of drug abuse. Young people from lower socioeconomic backgrounds are more likely to use drugs than their more affluent peers, possibly because of economic disadvantage; family instability; a lack of realistic, rewarding alternatives and role models; and increased hopelessness.

### Strategies for Prevention

#### Saying No to Drugs

If people offer you a drug, here are some ways to say no:

▲ Let them know you're not interested. Change the subject. If the pressure seems threatening, just walk away.

▲ Have something else to do: "No, I'm going for a walk now."

▲ Be prepared for different types of pressure—teasing, persuasion, coercion.

▲ Keep it simple. "No, thanks," "No," or "No way" all get the point across.

▲ Make friends with people who won't offer you drugs.

Those whose companions are substance abusers are far more likely to use drugs. Peer pressure to use drugs can be a powerful factor for adolescents and young adults. The likelihood of drug abuse is also related to family instability, parental rejection, and divorce.

When researchers followed families for a decade and a half and interviewed both children and their mothers, they found that youngsters who felt attached to their parents and showed greater responsibility and less rebelliousness were less likely to use drugs. Their attitudes and behaviours insulated them from socializing with drug-using peers, resulting in less drug use in their early and late twenties.[17] Clear rules and expectations from parents also can go a long way toward preventing or delaying alcohol and marijuana use in children, even if there is tension in the parent–child relationship.[18]

Parents' own attitudes and drug-use history can also affect their children's likelihood of drugs. In one study, parents who perceived little risk associated with marijuana use had children with similar attitudes, and the children of parents who had used marijuana were about three times more likely to try the drug than children whose parents had never used the drug.[19]

Drugs such as crack cocaine that produce an intense, brief high lead to dependence more quickly than slower-acting agents such as cocaine powder. Drugs that cause uncomfortable withdrawal symptoms, such as barbiturates, may lead to continued use to avoid such discomfort.

Drug use involves certain behaviours, situations, and settings that users may, in time, associate with getting high. Even after long periods of abstinence, some former drug users find that they crave drugs when they return to a site of drug use or meet people with whom they used drugs. Former cocaine users report that the sight of white powder alone can serve as a cue that triggers a craving.

Most individuals who use drugs first try them as adolescents. Teens are likely to begin experimenting with tobacco, beer, wine, or hard liquor and then smoke marijuana or sniff inhalants. Teens who smoke cigarettes are more likely to use drugs and to drink heavily than nonsmoking youths. Some then go on to try sedative-hypnotics, stimulants, and hallucinogens. A much smaller percentage of teens try the opioids. Over time, some individuals give up certain drugs, such as hallucinogens, and return to old favourites, such as alcohol and marijuana. A smaller number continues using several drugs.

## The Toll of Drugs

Drugs affect a person's physical, psychological, and social health. The effects of drugs can be *acute* (resulting from a single dose or series of doses) or *chronic* (resulting from long-term use). Acute effects vary with different drugs. Stimulants may trigger unpredictable rage; an overdose of heroin may lead to respiratory depression, a breathing impairment that can be fatal.

Over time, chronic drug users may feel fatigued, cough constantly, lose weight, become malnourished, and ache from head to toe. They may suffer blackouts, flashbacks, and episodes of increasingly bizarre behaviour, often triggered by escalating paranoia. Their risk of overdose rises steadily, and they must live with constant stress: the fear of getting busted for possession or of losing a job if they test positive for drugs, the worry of getting enough money for their next fix, and the dangers of associating with dealers and other users.

Information from the Canadian Addiction Survey[20] shows that reported drug-related harm involves friendships and social life (14.8 percent); physical health (20.3 percent); home life or marriage (11.4 percent); work, studies, or employment opportunities (13.4 percent); and financial position (12 percent). There were no differences between youth 15 to 19 years of age and those 20 to 24 years of age in terms of lifetime-reported harms.[21]

The toll of drug use can be especially great on the young because it disrupts many critical developmental tasks of adolescence and young adulthood. Early use of drugs can lead to drug-related crime; poor achievement in high school, college, or university; and job instability.

## ????  How Common Is Drug Use on Campus?

Alcohol is the number-one drug of abuse on college and university campuses. Marijuana remains the most commonly used illegal drug. However, there is a large gap between actual drug use on campus and how prevalent students believe drug use to be. When researchers compared students' self-reports of frequency of drug use with what students perceived to be the frequency of drug use by "the average student," they found that students greatly overestimate the use of a variety of drugs.[22]

According to the 2004 Canadian Campus Survey (respondents were from across Canada and were on average 22 years old), 32.1 percent of students at universities had used marijuana in the past 12 months, and 8.7 percent had used other illicit drugs.[23]

Various factors influence which students use drugs, including the following:

✔ **Perception of risk.** Students seem most likely to try substances they perceive as being safe or low risk. Of these, the top three are caffeine, alcohol, and tobacco; marijuana is listed fourth in terms of perceived safety.

✔ **Alcohol use.** Individuals often engage in more than one risk behaviour, and researchers have documented correlations among smoking, drinking, and drug use. Among college and university students, those who report binge drinking are much more likely than other students to report current or past use of marijuana, cocaine, or other illegal drugs.[24]

✔ **Environment.** As with alcohol use, students are influenced by their friends, their residence, the general public's attitude toward drug use, and even the Internet. Increasingly, college health officials are realizing that they must change the environment to promote healthier lifestyle choices. One successful innovation is substance-free dorms.[25] The University of Victoria in British Columbia now offers students the option of living on "substance-free" floors that promote arts and culture, healthy living, diversity, academic focus, and the inclusion of graduate students.[26]

## Drugs and Driving

One important impact of drugs is their effect on driving ability. Often, drivers using alcohol also test positive for other drugs. Different drugs affect driving ability in different ways. Here are the facts from the Canadian Centre on Substance Abuse:

✔ Alcohol affects perception, coordination, and judgment, and increases the sedative effects of tranquilizers and barbiturates.

✔ Marijuana affects a wide range of driving skills—including the ability to track (stay in the lane) through curves, brake quickly, and maintain speed and a safe distance between cars. It also slows thinking and reflexes. Normal driving skills remain impaired for four to six hours after smoking a single joint. There is an elevated risk of traffic collisions among heavy cannabis users.[27]

✔ Sedatives, hypnotics, and anti-anxiety agents slow reaction time and interfere with hand-eye coordination and judgment. The greatest impairment is in the first hour after taking the drug. The effects depend on the particular drug.

✔ Amphetamines, after repeated use, impair coordination. They can also make a driver more edgy and less coordinated, and thus more likely to be involved in an accident.

✔ Hallucinogens distort judgment and reality and cause confusion and panic, thus making driving extremely dangerous.

## Common Drugs of Abuse

The psychoactive substances most often associated with both abuse and dependence include alcohol (discussed in Chapter 12), amphetamines, cannabis (marijuana), cocaine, club drugs, hallucinogens, inhalants, opioids, phencyclidine (PCP), and sedative-hypnotic drugs. Table 11-2 groups the common drugs of abuse by their effect on the mind; Table 11-3 shows the mean age of substance abuse by age and sex, lifetime users aged 15–24, in Canada, in 2004.

## Amphetamines

**Amphetamines,** stimulants that were once widely prescribed for weight control because they suppress appetite, have emerged as a global danger. They trigger the release of epinephrine (adrenaline), which stimulates the central nervous system. Amphetamines are sold under a variety of names: amphetamine (brand name: Benzedrine®; street name: bennies), dextroamphetamine (Dexedrine®, dex), methamphetamine (Methedrine®, meth, speed), and Desoxyn® (copilots). Related *uppers* include the prescription drugs methylphenidate (Ritalin®), pemoline (Cylert®), and phenmetrazine (Preludin®). Amphetamines are available in tablet or capsule form. Abusers may grind and sniff the capsules or make a solution and inject the drug.

Methamphetamine (MA), also known as **crystal meth**, is a white, odourless, bitter-tasting crystalline powder that readily dissolves in water or alcohol. It can be snorted, swallowed, or injected.[28] *Ice* (or crank, crystal, glass, or tina) is a smokeable form of methamphetamine. This drug is very popular among young people across Canada, and its potential to harm users is greater than ever.[29] Because of the significant health, social, and economic harm caused by this drug[30] for young people, their families, law enforcement officers, and our environment, stiff new penalties for possession,

trafficking, importation, exportation, and production of methamphetamine were announced in August 2005.

Methamphetamine was moved to Schedule 1 of the Controlled Drugs and Substances Act, which allows for the highest maximum penalties.[31] This is just one of a number of strategies (education, laws for illegal possession of chemicals for purposes of producing this drug, and rehabilitation) being taken to deal with the devastation methamphetamine is having on communities everywhere.[32]

"Meth" is made by heating chemical ingredients together and includes these not-so-appealing ingredients: [33]

✔ Red phosphorus—used to make safety matches, fireworks, and pesticides

✔ Hydrochloric acid—used to treat industrial waste

✔ Anhydrous ammonia—a source of fertilizer for farm crops

### How Users Feel

Amphetamines produce an initial intense, pleasurable rush that lasts for a few minutes. This rush is then followed by a prolonged physical and psychological high, a state of hyper-alertness and energy that can last from 4 to 12 hours. Higher doses make users feel *wired:* talkative, excited, restless, and irritable.

Adverse effects include confusion, rambling or incoherent speech, anxiety, mood swings, headache, and palpitations. Individuals may become paranoid; be convinced they are having profound thoughts; feel increased sexual interest; and experience unusual perceptions, such as ringing in the ears, a sensation of insects crawling on their skin, or hearing their name called. Methamphetamine produces exceptionally long-lasting toxic effects, including psychosis, violence, seizures, and cardiovascular abnormalities. Brain-imaging studies show changes in heavy users' brains that may affect learning and memory.[34]

### Risks

Dependence on amphetamines can develop with episodic or daily use. Users typically take amphetamines in large doses to prevent crashing. Bingeing—taking high doses over a period of several days—can lead to an extremely intense and unpleasant crash characterized by a craving for the drug, shakiness, irritability, anxiety, and depression. Two or more days are required for recuperation. Other risks include increased heart rate, dilated pupils, elevated blood pressure, perspiration or chills and nausea or vomiting, impaired breathing, chest pain, heart arrhythmia; confusion, seizures, impaired movements or muscle tone; or even coma.

### Withdrawal

Amphetamine withdrawal usually persists for more than 24 hours after cessation of prolonged, heavy use. Its characteristic features include fatigue, disturbing dreams, much

## ▼ Table 11-2 Drug Categories and Descriptions

| Type of Drug | Drug Name | Common Name | Description | How It's Used | Related Paraphernalia | Signs and Symptoms of Use |
|---|---|---|---|---|---|---|
| **Cannabis** | **Marijuana** | Pot, grass, reefer, weed, Colombian hash, sinsemilla, joint, blunts, Acapulco gold, Thai sticks, skunk, 420 | Like dried oregano or tea leaves, from a pale green to a brown colour | Usually smoked in hand-rolled cigarettes, pipes, or thin cigars or ingested | Rolling papers, pipes, bongs, baggies, roach clips | Sweet burnt odour, neglect of appearance, loss of motivation, slow reactions, red eyes, memory lapses |
| | **Hash** | Hash, resin, brown, boom, chronic gangster, hemp | Substance varying from soft to very hard in consistency; light brown to black in colour | Smoked or ingested | Pipes, bong pipes, safety pins, hot knives | Loss in inhibitions, relaxation, reduction of anxiety, hilarity, fatigue, drowsiness |
| | **Hash Oil** | Oil, honey oil, liquid hash | Thick liquid substance; yellow, orange-yellow, dark brown, or black in colour | Smoked | Spoons, hash pipe | Odour, red eyes, pasty mouth, slurred speech, slowed mental reactions, increased appetite |
| **Depressants** (Depress the nervous system) | **Alcohol** | Booze, hooch, juice, brew, alcopops (hard lemonade or fruit juices) | Clear or amber-coloured liquid; sweet, fruit-flavoured malt-based drinks | Swallowed in liquid form | Flask, bottles, cans, use of food colour to disguise it; colourful and innocent-looking labels | Impaired judgment, poor muscle coordination, lowered inhibitions |
| | **Barbiturates** Amyl®, Seconal®, Nembutal®, Butisol®, Tuinal® Phenobarbital® | Barbs, downers, yellows, yellow jackets, reds, red birds, phennies, tooies, red devils, blue devils | Variety of tablets, capsules, powder | Swallowed in pill form or injected | Syringe, needles | Drowsiness, confusion, impaired judgment, slurred speech, needle marks, staggering gait |
| | **Tranquilizers/ Benzodiazepines** Ativan®, Halcion®, Valium®, Librium®, Miltown®, Xanax® | Vs, blues, downers, candy, sleeping pills | Variety of tablets | Swallowed in pill form or injected | Syringe, pill bottles, needles | Drowsiness, faulty judgment, disorientation |
| | GHB (gamma-hydroxybutyrate) | Georgia home boy, grievous bodily harm, liquid ecstasy, G | Clear liquid, tablet, capsule | Swallowed, dissolved in drinks | Drinks, pop cans | Can relax or sedate, drowsiness, nausea, vomiting, headache, loss of consciousness, loss of reflexes, seizures, coma, death |
| | Rohypnol® | Roofies, roche, love drug, forget-me pill | Tablet | Dissolved in drinks, swallowed | Drinks, pop cans | Amnesia, decreased blood pressure, urinary retention, sedative effect |

*continued*

▼ **Table 11-2 Drug Categories and Descriptions (continued)**

| Type of Drug | Drug Name | Common Name | Description | How It's Used | Related Paraphernalia | Signs and Symptoms of Use |
|---|---|---|---|---|---|---|
| **Opioids and Morphine Derivatives** | **Heroin** | Brown sugar, dope, H, horse, junk, skag, skunk, smack, white horse, point | White or brown powders, tablets, capsules, liquid | Injected, smoked, snorted; may be blended with marijuana | Syringes, spoon, lighter, needles, medicine dropper | Lethargy, loss of skin colour, track marks, constricted pupils, decreased coordination |
| | **Morphine** (Roxanol, Duramorph) | M, Miss Emma, monkey, white stuff | Oral solutions, immediate and sustained-release tables and capsules, suppositories, and injectable preparations | Swallowed, injected, inhaled, smoked | Hypodermic needles, small cotton balls, spoons or bottle caps, tie-offs, razor blades, straws, pipes | Reduces gut motility, faintness, bradychardia, palpitations, flushing, dry mouth, visual distortions |
| | **Oxycodone HCL, Percocet** | | White, odourless, crystalline power, or pink oval tablet, blue round tablet, peach oval tablet, yellow capsule-shaped tablet | Chewed and swallowed, crushed and snorted, crushed, dissolved in water and then injected | Spoons, needles, water | Respiratory depression, apnea, respiratory arrest, shock, lightheadedness, dizziness, nausea, drowsiness, vomiting |
| **Stimulants** (Stimulate the nervous system) | **Amphetamines, Biphetamine, Dexedrine** | Speed, uppers, bennies, dexies, meth, crank, black beauties, white crosses, LA Turnaround, hearts, truck drivers | Variety of tablets, capsules, and crystal-like rock salt | Swallowed in pill or capsule form, smoked, or injected | Syringe, needles | Excess activity, irritability, nervousness, mood swings, needle marks, dilated pupils, talkativeness then depression |
| | **MDMA (Methylenedioxy-Methamphetamine)** | Adam, clarity, Ecstasy, Eve, lover's speed, peace, STP, X, XTC, beans, disco biscuits, smarties, scoobies, peanut, dove | Tablets, imprinted logos | Usually swallowed in tablet form, or crushed and sniffed | Razor blade, straws, glass surface | Increased alertness, excitation, insomnia, loss of appetite, panic attacks, respiratory failure |
| | **Methamphetamine, Desoxyn** | Chalk, crank, crystal, fire, glass, go fast, ice, meth, speed, P | White, odourless, bitter tasting crystalline powder, fine transparent shiny crystals, or tablets with various logos and colours | Snorted, injected, or smoked | Needles, pipes | Impaired memory and learning, hyperthermia, cardiac toxicity, renal failure, liver toxicity |
| | **Cocaine** | Coke, snow, toot, white lady, blow, bump, flake, rock | White odourless powder | Usually inhaled; can be injected, swallowed, or smoked | Razor blade, straws, glass surfaces | Restlessness, dilated pupils, oily skin, talkativeness; euphoric short-term high, followed by depression |

▼ **Table 11-2 Drug Categories and Descriptions (continued)**

| Type of Drug | Drug Name | Common Name | Description | How It's Used | Related Paraphernalia | Signs and Symptoms of Use |
|---|---|---|---|---|---|---|
| | Tobacco/Nicotine | Smokes, butts, cigs, cancer sticks, snuff, dip, chew, plug | Dried brown organic material, bidis flavoured with mint or chocolate; smokeless is moist | Burned and inhaled as cigarettes, pipes, cigars, cigarillos; chewed; or inhaled through the nose as snuff | Rolling papers, pipes, spit cups, cigar cutters, lighters, matches | Shortness of breath, respiratory illnesses; oral, lung, and other cancers |
| Hallucinogens (Alter perceptions of reality) | PCP (phencyclidine) | Angel dust, killer weed, supergrass, hog, peace pill, boat, Crazy Eddie, mess | White powder or tablet | Usually smoked, can be inhaled (snorted), injected, or swallowed in tablets | Tinfoil | Slurred speech, blurred vision, lack of coordination, confusion, agitation, violence, unpredictability, "bad trips" |
| | LSD (lysergic acid diethylamide) | Acid, cubes, blotter, boomers, microdot, yellow sunshines, purple haze, white lightning | Odourless, colourless, tasteless powder | Absorbed orally in blotter paper, liquid, or tablets | Blotter papers, tinfoil | Dilated pupils, illusions, hallucinations, disorientation, mood swings, nausea, flashbacks |
| | Mescaline | Mesc, buttons, cactus, caps, peyote | Capsules, tablets, tops of cactus, dried roots | Smoked, chewed, or brewed as tea | Water, pots | Anxiety, racing heart, dizziness, diarrhea, vomiting, headache |
| | Psilocybin | Magic mushrooms, purple passion, shrooms, mush, Fly agaric, liberties | Dry, fibrous substance of varying colours | Ingestion, eaten raw or brewed as a tea | Water, pots | Fear, paranoia, distortion of colour, sound, and objects, speed up or slow down time |
| Inhalants (Substances abused by sniffing) | Solvents, aerosols | Airplane glue, gasoline, dry cleaning solution, correction fluid | Chemicals that produce mind-altering vapours | Inhaled or sniffed, often with the use of paper or plastic bags | Cleaning rags, empty spray cans, tubes of glue, baggies | Poor motor coordination; bad breath; impaired vision, memory, and thoughts; violent behaviour |
| | Nitrates amyl & butyl | Poppers, locker room, rush, snappers | Clear yellowish liquid | Inhaled or sniffed from gauze or single-dose glass vials | Cloth-covered bulb that pops when broken, small bottles | Slowed thought, headache |
| | Nitrous oxide | Laughing gas, whippets | Colourless gas with sweet taste and smell | Inhaled or sniffed by mask or cone | Aerosol cans such as whipped cream, small canisters | Light-headed, loss of motor control |

Sources: From "A Parent's Guide for the Prevention of Alcohol, Tobacco and Other Drug Use." Copyright © 2000 Lowe Family Foundation, Inc., Revised 2001. (Lowe Family Foundation, 3339 Stuyvesant Pl. NW, Washington DC, 20015, 202–362-4883.); National Institute on Drug Abuse (NIDA Home, Drugs of Abuse/Related Topics, Commonly Abused Drugs, Available at www.drugabuse.gov/DrugsPages/DrugsofAbuse.html; Royal Canadian Mounted Police Home, Safe Home Safe Communities, Drug Situation in Canada, Report 2006, Available at www.rcmp-grc.gc.ca/drugs/drugs_2006_e.htm.

▼ **Table 11-3 Illicit Drug Use, Lifetime and Past-Year, Canadians, Aged 15–24, 2004**

| Drug | Total | Males | Females |
|------|-------|-------|---------|
| Cannabis | N = 1177<br>M = 15.6<br>[15.34-15.78] | N = 615<br>M = 15.6<br>[15.28-15.95] | N = 562<br>M = 15.5<br>[15.21-15.77] |
| Cocaine | N = 254<br>M = 18.1<br>[17.51-18.62] | N = 140<br>M = 18.2<br>[17.54-18.96] | N = 114<br>M = 17.8<br>[16.91-18.69] |
| Speed | N = 151<br>M = 17.7<br>[17.13-18.33] | N = 86<br>M = 17.8<br>[17.13-18.43] | N = 65<br>M = 17.7<br>[16.52-18.83] |
| Hallucinogens | N = 332<br>M = 17.1<br>[16.46-17.64] | N = 203<br>M = 17.4<br>[16.65-18.17] | N = 129<br>M = 16.4<br>[15.49-17.35] |
| Ecstasy | N = 243<br>M = 18.4<br>[17.69-19.17] | N = 128<br>M = 18.3<br>[17.2-18.9] | N = 115<br>M = 18.6<br>[17.05-20.10] |

Source: Flight, J. (Research Analyst). (2007). *Canadian addiction survey (CAS)*. A national survey of Canadians' use of alcohol and other drugs. Substance use by Canadian youth. Cat. No. H128-1/07-499E. HC Pub. 4964. Available at www.hc-sc.gc.ca/hl-vs/pubs/adp-apd/cas-etc/youth-jeunes/index-eng.php. Reproduced with the permission of the Minister of Public Works and Government Services Canada, 2009.

Note: None of the differences between males and females is statistically significant.
N = sample size
M = mean

more or less than usual sleep, increased appetite, and speeding up or slowing down of physical movements. Those who are unable to sleep despite their exhaustion often take sedative-hypnotics to help them rest and may then become dependent on them as well as amphetamines. Symptoms usually reach a peak in two to four days, although depression and irritability may persist for months. Suicide is a major risk.

Experts say that crystal meth is one of the most addictive and hardest to treat street drugs there is. Some addiction counsellors suggest that the relapse rate is 92 percent. Tragic stories are becoming public across Canada as this drug takes over the lives of young people everywhere. In Kamloops, British Columbia, there is a special program called The Meth Kickers Progra m, offered at The Phoenix Centre, an addictions treatment facility. The Canadian Broadcasting Corporation produced a special documentary on crystal meth. You can view the documentary online by accessing the CBC—Fifth Estate website at www.cbc.ca/fifth/darkcrystal/addiction.html. The powerful stories illustrate this major problem in cities large and small.

## Cannabis

**Marijuana** (pot) and **hashish** (hash)—the most widely used illegal drugs—are derived from the cannabis plant. The major psychoactive ingredient in both is *THC (delta-9-tetrahydrocannabinol)*. Research from the 2007 Canadian Addiction Survey (CAS), *A national survey of Canadians' use of alcohol and other drugs, Substance use by Canadian youth,* indicates that 61.4 percent of youth have used

cannabis in their lifetime, and 37.0 percent have used it at least once in the past 12 months. After age 24, the reported lifetime use of cannabis declines across age groups reaching a reported rate of 3.1 percent among those aged 75 or older. Males were more likely than females to have used cannabis in their lifetime (64.7 percent versus 58.0 percent) and in the past year (41.4 percent versus 32.3 percent). Youth from Quebec had a higher prevalence of lifetime and current cannabis use than the national average. Young people from the Atlantic region had a significantly lower prevalence of lifetime use.[35]

THC triggers a series of reactions in the brain that ultimately lead to the high that users experience when they smoke marijuana. Heredity influences an individual's response to marijuana—research suggests that there may be a genetic basis for an individual's response to THC.

Different types of marijuana have different percentages of THC. Because of careful cultivation, the strength of today's marijuana is much greater than that used in the 1970s; the physical and mental effects are therefore greater. Usually, marijuana is smoked in a joint (hand-rolled cigarette) or pipe; it may also be eaten as an ingredient in other foods (as when baked in brownies), though with a less predictable effect. The circumstances in which marijuana is smoked, the communal aspects of its use, and the user's experience all can affect the way a marijuana-induced high feels.[36]

Some individuals have used marijuana to deal with certain medical and health conditions. In 2001, Health Canada developed a framework—the Marijuana Medical Access Regulations (MMAR)—to allow people with serious medical conditions to possess or cultivate marijuana for medical purposes. An application for authorization to possess this drug must be completed. The support of a doctor is also necessary. These regulations have been put in place because marijuana is still not approved as a therapeutic drug in Canada. Health Canada is currently doing some research to determine the benefits and risks of this drug.[37]

In Canada, a proposed Cannabis Reform Bill has been introduced whereby alternative penalties for possession of 15 grams or less of marijuana or one gram or less of cannabis resin would be adopted. Tickets or fines would apply instead of criminal charges being laid. New offences providing tougher penalties for illegal growers would also be adopted.[38] This Bill has yet to pass in Parliament.

## How Users Feel

In low to moderate doses, marijuana typically creates a mild sense of euphoria, a sense of slowed time, a dreamy sort of self-absorption, and some impairment in thinking and communicating. Users report heightened sensations of colour, sound, and other stimuli; relaxation; and increased confidence. The sense of being *stoned* peaks within half an hour and usually lasts about three hours. Even when alterations in perception seem slight, as noted earlier, it is not safe to drive a car for as long as four to six hours after smoking marijuana.[39] Some users experience acute paranoia or anxiety, which may be accompanied by a panicky fear of losing control. They may believe that their companions are ridiculing or threatening them and experience a panic attack, a state of intense terror.

The immediate physical effects of marijuana include increased pulse rate, bloodshot eyes, dry mouth and throat, slowed reaction times, impaired motor skills, increased appetite, and diminished short-term memory (see Figure 11-2). The drug remains in the body's fat cells 50 hours or more after use, so people may experience psychoactive effects for

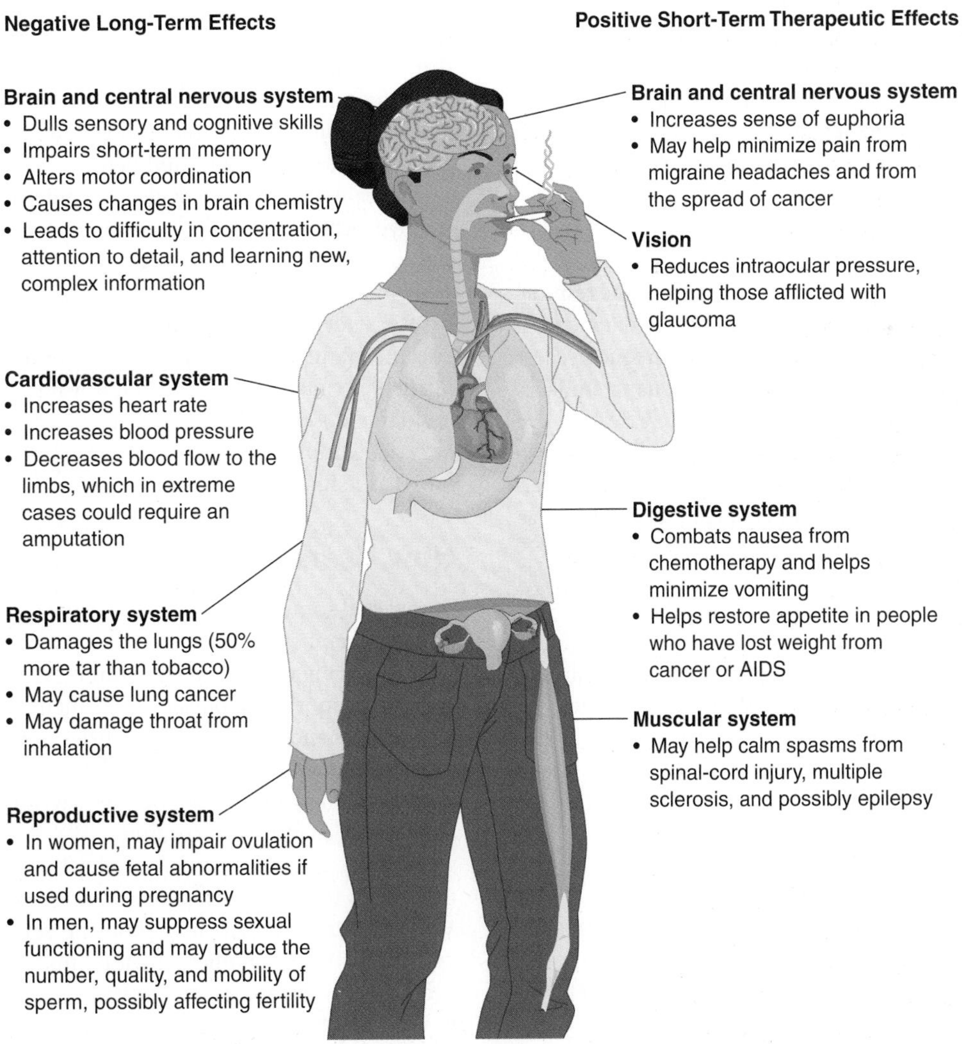

**Negative Long-Term Effects**

**Brain and central nervous system**
- Dulls sensory and cognitive skills
- Impairs short-term memory
- Alters motor coordination
- Causes changes in brain chemistry
- Leads to difficulty in concentration, attention to detail, and learning new, complex information

**Cardiovascular system**
- Increases heart rate
- Increases blood pressure
- Decreases blood flow to the limbs, which in extreme cases could require an amputation

**Respiratory system**
- Damages the lungs (50% more tar than tobacco)
- May cause lung cancer
- May damage throat from inhalation

**Reproductive system**
- In women, may impair ovulation and cause fetal abnormalities if used during pregnancy
- In men, may suppress sexual functioning and may reduce the number, quality, and mobility of sperm, possibly affecting fertility

**Positive Short-Term Therapeutic Effects**

**Brain and central nervous system**
- Increases sense of euphoria
- May help minimize pain from migraine headaches and from the spread of cancer

**Vision**
- Reduces intraocular pressure, helping those afflicted with glaucoma

**Digestive system**
- Combats nausea from chemotherapy and helps minimize vomiting
- Helps restore appetite in people who have lost weight from cancer or AIDS

**Muscular system**
- May help calm spasms from spinal-cord injury, multiple sclerosis, and possibly epilepsy

▲ **Figure 11-2** Some Effects of Marijuana on the Body
Some negative long-term effects and positive short-term therapeutic effects of marijuana use.

several days after use. Drug tests may produce positive results for days or weeks after last use.

## Risks

Marijuana produces a range of effects in different bodily systems, such as diminished immune responses and impaired fertility in men. Other risks include damage to the brain, lungs, and heart and to babies born to mothers who use marijuana during pregnancy or while nursing.

## Brain

THC produces changes in the brain that affect learning, memory, and the way the brain integrates sensory experiences with emotions and motivations. Short-term effects include problems with memory and learning; distorted perceptions; difficulty thinking and problem-solving; loss of coordination; increased anxiety; and panic attacks. Long-term use produces changes in the brain similar to those seen with other major drugs of abuse.[40]

According to a study of college students, heavy users who smoked marijuana almost every day showed significant difficulty sustaining attention, shifting attention to meet the demands of changes in the environment, and registering, processing, and using information.[41]

## Lungs

Regular marijuana smokers have many of the same respiratory problems as tobacco smokers, including daily cough and phlegm, chronic bronchitis, and more frequent chest colds. The amount of tar inhaled by marijuana smokers and the level of carbon monoxide absorbed are three to five times greater than among tobacco smokers. Chronic use can lead to bronchitis, emphysema, and lung cancer. Smoking a single joint can be as damaging to the lungs as smoking five tobacco cigarettes.

## Heart

Otherwise healthy people have suffered heart attacks shortly after smoking marijuana. According to recent estimates, the risk of heart attack triples within an hour of smoking pot.[42] Smoking marijuana while shooting cocaine can potentially cause deadly increases in heart rate and blood pressure.[43]

## Pregnancy

Babies born to mothers who use marijuana during pregnancy are smaller than those born to mothers who did not use the drug, and the babies are more likely to develop health problems.[44] A nursing mother who uses marijuana passes some of the THC to the baby in her breast milk. This may impair the infant's motor development (control of muscle movement).

## Withdrawal

Marijuana users can develop a compulsive, often uncontrollable craving for the drug. Stopping after long-term marijuana use can produce *marijuana withdrawal syndrome,* which is characterized by insomnia, restlessness, loss of appetite, and irritability.

## Cocaine

**Cocaine** (coke, snow, lady) is a white crystalline powder extracted from the leaves of the South American coca plant. Usually mixed with various sugars and local anesthetics such as lidocaine and procaine, cocaine powder is generally inhaled. When sniffed or snorted, cocaine anesthetizes the nerve endings in the nose and relaxes the lung's bronchial muscles.

Cocaine can be dissolved in water and injected intravenously. The drug is rapidly metabolized by the liver, so the high is relatively brief, typically lasting only about 20 minutes. This means that users will commonly inject the drug repeatedly, increasing the risk of infection and damage to their veins. Many intravenous cocaine users prefer the practice of *speedballing,* the intravenous administration of a combination of cocaine and heroin.

Cocaine alkaloid, or *freebase,* is obtained by removing the hydrochloride salt from cocaine powder. *Freebasing* is smoking the fumes of the alkaloid form of cocaine. *Crack,* pharmacologically identical to freebase, is a cheap, easy-to-use, widely available, smokeable, and potent form of cocaine named for the popping sound it makes when burned. Because it is absorbed rapidly into the bloodstream and large doses reach the brain very quickly, it is particularly dangerous. However, its low price and easy availability have made it a common drug of abuse.

## How Users Feel

A powerful stimulant to the central nervous system, cocaine targets several chemical sites in the brain, producing feelings of soaring well-being and boundless energy. Users feel they have enormous physical and mental ability, yet are also restless and anxious. After a brief period of euphoria, users slump into a depression. They often go on cocaine binges, lasting from a few hours to several days, and consume large quantities of cocaine.

With crack, dependence develops quickly. As soon as crack users come down from one high, they want more crack. Whereas heroin addicts may shoot up several times a day, crack addicts need another hit within minutes. Thus, a crack habit can quickly become more expensive than heroin addiction. Some addicts have $1000-a-day habits. Police have traced many brutal crimes and murders to young crack addicts, who often are extremely paranoid and dangerous. Smoking crack doused with liquid PCP, a practice known as *space-basing*, has especially frightening effects on behaviour.

With continuing use, cocaine users experience less pleasure and more unpleasant effects. Eventually they may reach a point at which they no longer experience euphoric effects and crave the drug simply to alleviate their persistent hunger for it.

## Risks

Cocaine dependence is an easy habit to acquire. With repeated use, the brain becomes tolerant of the drug's stimulant effects, and users must take more of it to get high. Those who smoke or inject cocaine can develop dependence within weeks. Those who sniff cocaine may not become dependent on the drug for months or years.

The physical effects of acute cocaine intoxication include dilated pupils, elevated or lowered blood pressure, perspiration or chills, nausea or vomiting, speeding up or slowing down of physical activity, muscular weakness, impaired breathing, chest pain, and impaired movements or muscle tone. Prolonged cocaine snorting can result in ulceration of the mucous membrane of the nose and damage to the nasal septum (the membrane between the nostrils) severe enough to cause it to collapse. Men who use cocaine regularly have problems maintaining erections and ejaculating. They also tend to have low sperm counts, less active sperm, and more abnormal sperm than nonusers. Both

male and female chronic cocaine users tend to lose interest in sex and have difficulty reaching orgasm.

Cocaine use can cause blood vessels in the brain to clamp shut and can trigger a stroke, bleeding in the brain, and potentially fatal brain seizures. Cocaine users can also develop psychiatric or neurological complications (see Figure 11-3). Repeated or high doses of cocaine can lead to impaired judgment, hyperactivity, non-stop babbling, feelings of suspicion and paranoia, and violent behaviour. The brain never learns to tolerate cocaine's negative effects; users may become incoherent and paranoid and may experience unusual sensations, such as ringing in their ears, feeling insects crawling on the skin, or hearing their name called.

Cocaine can damage the liver and cause lung damage in freebasers. Smoking crack causes bronchitis as well as lung damage and may promote the transmission of HIV through burned and bleeding lips. Some smokers have died of respiratory complications, such as pulmonary edema (the build-up of fluid in the lungs).

Cocaine causes the heart rate to speed up and blood pressure to rise suddenly. Its use is associated with many cardiac complications, including arrhythmia (disruption of heart rhythm), angina (chest pain), and acute myocardial infarction (heart attack). These cardiac complications can lead to sudden death.[45] The most common ways of dying from cocaine use are persistent seizures that result in respiratory collapse, cardiac arrest from arrhythmias, myocardial infarction, and intracranial hemorrhage or stroke. Cocaine-induced elevations in blood pressure can lead to kidney failure.

Cocaine users who inject the drug and share needles put themselves at risk for another potentially lethal problem: HIV infection. Other complications of injecting cocaine include skin infections, hepatitis, inflammation of the arteries, and infection of the lining of the heart.

The combination of alcohol and cocaine is particularly lethal. When people mix cocaine and alcohol, they compound the danger each drug poses. The liver combines the two agents and manufactures cocaethylene, which intensifies cocaine's euphoric effects, while possibly increasing the risk of sudden death.[46]

Cocaine is dangerous for pregnant women and their babies, causing miscarriages, developmental disorders, and life-threatening complications during birth. Infants born to cocaine and crack users can suffer withdrawal and may have major complications or permanent disabilities. Cocaine babies have higher-than-normal rates of respiratory and kidney troubles, visual problems, and developmental retardation, and they may be at greater risk of sudden infant death syndrome.

## Withdrawal

When addicted individuals stop using cocaine, they often become depressed. Other symptoms of cocaine withdrawal include fatigue, vivid and disturbing dreams, excessive or too little sleep, irritability, increased appetite, and physical slowing

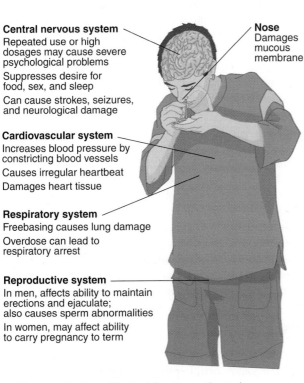

**Central nervous system**
Repeated use or high dosages may cause severe psychological problems
Suppresses desire for food, sex, and sleep
Can cause strokes, seizures, and neurological damage

**Cardiovascular system**
Increases blood pressure by constricting blood vessels
Causes irregular heartbeat
Damages heart tissue

**Respiratory system**
Freebasing causes lung damage
Overdose can lead to respiratory arrest

**Reproductive system**
In men, affects ability to maintain erections and ejaculate; also causes sperm abnormalities
In women, may affect ability to carry pregnancy to term

**Nose**
Damages mucous membrane

▲ **Figure 11-3** Some Effects of Cocaine on the Body

down or speeding up. This initial crash may last one to three days after cutting down or stopping the heavy use of cocaine. Some individuals become violent, paranoid, and suicidal.

Symptoms usually reach a peak in two to four days, although depression, anxiety, irritability, lack of pleasure in usual activities, and low-level cravings may continue for weeks. As memories of the crash fade, the desire for cocaine intensifies. For many weeks after stopping, individuals may feel an intense craving for the drug. Experimental medical approaches for treating cocaine dependence include antidepressant drugs, anticonvulsant drugs, and the naturally occurring amino acids tryptophan and tyrosine. Recent research has found that, depending on personal characteristics such as abstract reasoning ability and religious motivation, some cocaine abusers fare better with cognitive-behavioural therapy, while others do better with 12-step programs.[47]

## Club Drugs

**Club drugs** include MDMA (ecstasy), gamma hydroxybutyrate (GHB), flunitrazepam (Rohypnol®), LSD and amphetamines, and methamphetamine (see Table 11-2). Their primary users are teens and young adults at nightclubs, bars, and raves or trance events, night-long dances often held in warehouses. They try these low-cost drugs to increase their stamina and experience a high that supposedly deepens the rave or trance experience.

Some club drugs, although illegal in Canada, are sold elsewhere in the world as legitimate drugs. Two examples are

**gamma hydroxybutyrate (GHB)**, a depressant with potential benefits for people with narcolepsy, and Rohypnol®, used as a tranquilizer. GHB is usually found in liquid form. Rohypnol® comes in a small pill or white tablet form. Both are colourless, odourless, and have no taste when mixed with a drink.

Although users may think of club drugs as harmless and fun, they can produce a range of unwanted effects, sometimes even causing death. GHB can cause dizziness, nausea, vomiting, seizures, unconsciousness, coma, and memory loss. Rohypnol® causes sedation, loss of inhibitions, blackouts, and amnesia. Sexual violence is often linked with the use of these drugs. When used with alcohol, these drugs can be even more harmful because they involve the same brain mechanism. Some people have been known to have extreme, even fatal, reactions the first time they use club drugs. Club drugs found in party settings are often adulterated or impure and thus even more dangerous.[48]

## Ecstasy

**Ecstasy** is the most common street name for methylenedioxymethamphetamine (MDMA), a synthetic compound with both stimulant and mildly hallucinogenic properties. Ecstasy use has been increasing substantially, particularly among young people. Although it can be smoked, inhaled (snorted), or injected, ecstasy is almost always taken as a pill or tablet. Its effects begin in 45 minutes and last for two to four hours.

A study done in Montreal, Quebec, including 210 participants recruited from three large-scale events (3000 to 10 000 people), determined that MDMA was the third most commonly used drug for use in the preceding 30 days, with 40 percent reporting MDMA use during this period. They also reported a 75.2 percent MDMA lifetime use. The findings of this study were consistent with research findings in rave samples surveyed in Australia.[49]

### How It Feels

MDMA belongs to a family of drugs called *enactogens,* which literally means "touching within." As a mood elevator, it produces a relaxed, euphoric state but does not produce hallucinations. Users of ecstasy often say they feel at peace with themselves and at ease and empathic with others. Like hallucinogenic drugs, MDMA can enhance sensory experience, but it rarely causes visual distortions, sudden mood changes, or psychotic reactions. Regular users may experience depression and anxiety the week after taking MDMA.

### Risks

Ecstasy poses risks similar to those of cocaine and amphetamines. These include psychological difficulties (confusion, depression, sleep problems, drug craving, severe

▲ Club drugs, made in a laboratory and sold on the street, aren't subject to quality controls and don't always contain what the buyer expects.

© Tekimage/SPL/Photo Researchers, Inc.

anxiety, and paranoia) and physical symptoms (muscle tension, involuntary teeth clenching, nausea, blurred vision, rapid eye movement, faintness, chills, sweating, and increases in heart rate and blood pressure that pose a special risk for people with circulatory or heart disease).[50]

Continued use of ecstasy can lead to psychological dependence because users seek to recreate the exhilarating high and avoid the plunge into unhappiness and emptiness that comes after use. Because ecstasy is *neurotoxic* (damaging to brain cells), it depletes the brain of serotonin, a messenger chemical involved with mood, sleep, and appetite, and can lead to depression, anxiety, and impaired thinking and memory.[51]

According to brain-imaging studies, ecstasy alters neuronal function in a brain structure called the hippocampus, which helps create short-term memory[52] (see Figure 11-4). Regular ecstasy use affects memory, learning, and general intelligence.

MDMA can produce nausea, vomiting, and dizziness. When combined with extended physical exertion such as dancing, club drugs can lead to hyperthermia (severe overheating), severe dehydration, serious increases in blood pressure, stroke, and heart attack. Individuals with high blood pressure, heart trouble, or liver or kidney disease are in the greatest danger.[53]

MDMA has been implicated in some cases of acute hepatitis, which can lead to liver failure. Another danger comes from the practice of taking Prozac®, a drug that modulates the mood-altering brain chemical serotonin, before ecstasy. This can cause jaw clenching, nausea, tremors, and, in extreme cases, potentially fatal elevations in body temperature.

Although not a sexual stimulant (if anything, MDMA has the opposite effect), ecstasy fosters strong feelings of intimacy that may lead to risky sexual behaviour. The psychological effects of ecstasy become less intriguing with repeated use, and the physical side effects become more uncomfortable. Ecstasy poses risks to a developing fetus, including a greater likelihood of heart and skeletal abnormalities and long-term learning and memory impairments in children born to women who used MDMA during pregnancy.[54]

## Hallucinogens

The drugs known as **hallucinogens** produce vivid and unusual changes in thought, feeling, and perception. The most widely used is *LSD (lysergic acid diethylamide* or *acid)*, which was initially developed as a tool to explore mental illness. It became popular in the 1960s and resurfaced among teenagers in the 1990s. LSD is taken orally, either blotted onto pieces of paper that are held in the mouth or chewed along with another substance, such as a sugar cube. Much less commonly used is *peyote*, whose active ingredient is *mescaline*.

### How Users Feel

LSD produces hallucinations, including bright colours and altered perceptions of reality. Effects from a single dose begin within 30 to 60 minutes and last 10 to 12 hours. During this time, there are slight increases in body temperature, heart rate, and blood pressure. Sweating, chills, and goose pimples may appear. Some users develop headache and nausea.

Mescaline produces vivid hallucinations—including brightly coloured lights, animals, and geometric designs—within 30 to 90 minutes of consumption. These effects may persist for 12 hours.

The effects of hallucinogens depend greatly on the dose, the individual's expectations and personality, and the setting for drug use. Many users report religious or mystical imagery and thoughts; some feel they are experiencing profound insights. Usually the user realizes that perceptual changes are caused by the hallucinogen, but some become convinced that they have lost their minds. Drugs sold as hallucinogens are frequently mixed with other drugs, such

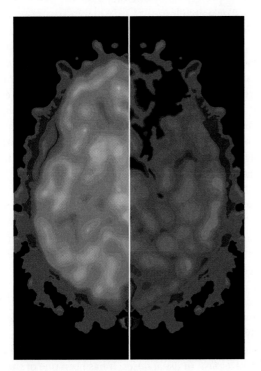

▲ **Figure 11-4** Effects of Ecstasy on the Brain
These brain scans show the sharp difference in human brain function for an individual who has never used drugs (left) and one who used the club drug ecstasy many times but had not used any drugs for at least three weeks before the scan (right). In the left scan, the bright reddish colour shows active serotonin sites in the brain. Serotonin is a critical neurochemical that regulates mood, emotion, learning, memory, sleep, and pain. In the right scan, the dark sections indicate areas where serotonin is not present even after three weeks without any drugs.

Source: National Institute on Drug Abuse, www.clubdrugs.org. Courtesy of U.S. Department of Health & Human Services.

as PCP and amphetamines, combinations that can produce unexpected and frightening effects.

## Risks

Physical symptoms include dilated pupils, rapid heart rate, sweating, heart palpitations, blurring of vision, tremors, and poor coordination. These effects may last 8 to 12 hours. Hallucinogen intoxication also produces changes in emotions and mood, such as anxiety, depression, fear of losing one's mind, and impaired judgment.

LSD can trigger irrational acts. LSD users have injured or killed themselves by jumping out of windows, swimming out to sea, or throwing themselves in front of cars. Some individuals may experience *flashbacks* (re-experiencing symptoms felt while intoxicated), which include geometric hallucinations, flashes of colour, halos around objects, and other perceptual changes.

## Inhalants

**Inhalants** or **deleriants** are chemicals that produce vapours with psychoactive effects. The most commonly abused inhalants are solvents, aerosols, model-airplane glue, cleaning fluids, and petroleum products such as kerosene and butane. Some anesthetics and nitrous oxide (laughing gas) are also abused. The use of inhalants is on the rise in Canada—especially among young Inuit and Aboriginal people in isolated communities[55] where up to 60 percent of youth report inhalant use.[56]

### How Users Feel

Inhalants very rapidly reach the lungs, bloodstream, and other parts of the body. Intoxication often occurs within five minutes and can last more than an hour. Inhalants interfere with thinking and impulse control, so users may act in dangerous or destructive ways.

Often there are visible external signs of use: a rash around the nose and mouth; breath odours; residue on face, hands, and clothing; redness, swelling, and tearing of the eyes; and irritation of throat, lungs, and nose that leads to coughing and gagging. Nausea and headache also may occur.

### Risks

Regular use of inhalants leads to tolerance, so the sniffer needs more and more to attain the desired effects. Younger children who use inhalants several times a week may develop dependence. Chronic users experience a range of mental health problems, from mild impairment to severe dementia.

Although some young people believe inhalants are safe, this is far from true. Users risk the loss of motor skills, seizures, diarrhea, anxiety, and even death from a single use. Inhalation of butane from cigarette lighters displaces oxygen in the lungs, causing suffocation. Users also can suffocate while covering their heads with a plastic bag to inhale the substance or from inhaling vomit into their lungs while high.

In Canada, treatment centres have been established in a number of provinces through the Native Youth Solvent Abuse program (NYSA). Research continues about the type of treatment program that best helps youth who abuse solvents.

## Opioids

The **opioids** include *opium* and its derivatives (*heroin, morphine, codeine*). The opioids come from a resin taken from the seedpod of the Asian poppy. **Nonopioids**, such as *meperidine* (Demerol®), *methadone,* and *propoxyphene* (Darvon®), are chemically synthesized. A common prescribed semi-synthetic opioid is oxycondone hydrochloride (OxyContin®). Whether natural or synthetic, taken illegally or prescribed by doctors, these drugs are powerful *narcotics,* or painkillers.

*Heroin* (also known as horse, junk, smack, or downtown), the most widely abused opioid, is illegal in Canada. In other nations, it is used as a potent painkiller for conditions such as terminal cancer. Heroin users typically inject the drug into their veins. However, individuals who experiment with recreational drugs often prefer *skin-popping* (subcutaneous injection) rather than *mainlining* (intravenous injection); they also may snort heroin as a powder or dissolve it and inhale the vapours. Regardless of the method of administration, tolerance can develop rapidly.

*Morphine,* used as a painkiller and anesthetic, acts primarily on the central nervous system, eyes, and digestive tract. By producing mental clouding, drowsiness, and euphoria, it does not decrease the physical sensation of pain as much as it alters a person's awareness of the pain; in effect, he or she no longer cares about it.

*Codeine,* a weaker painkiller than morphine, is an ingredient in liquid products prescribed for relieving coughs and in tablet and injectable form for relieving pain. The synthetic narcotic *propoxyphene* (Darvon®), a somewhat less potent painkiller than codeine, is no more effective than aspirin in usual doses. It has been one of the most widely prescribed drugs for headaches, dental pain, and menstrual cramps. At higher doses, Darvon® produces a euphoric high, which may lead to misuse.

In the past decade, concern about the drug OxyContin® has increased. Since its introduction in 1995, it has become a popular prescription medication used to control moderate to severe pain and chronic pain related to cancer and other terminal conditions. In Canada, there were approximately 822 000 prescriptions written for OxyContin® in 2004.[57] Used to gain euphoric effects, it induces a high similar to heroin, is highly addictive, and produces side effects, such as confusion, altered mental state, vomiting, nausea, and even death.

Research on the widespread use of this drug has begun by the government of Newfoundland and Labrador. Data indicate that the quantity of OxyContin® tables prescribed and dispensed increased by 200 percent from 2000 to 2003. Research shows that this growth is also similar in other provinces.[58]

The illicit use of OxyContin® by young people has also grown, especially in Atlantic Canada. Concern about this phenomenon sparked an investigation in Atlantic Canada in 2004, finding that the source of non-medicinal-use OxyContin® originated from a small number of physicians who were prescribing controlled substances excessively, that diversion of the drug for non-medical purposes was widespread, and that there was a growing number of adolescents abusing OxyContin®.[59]

## How Users Feel

All opioids relax the user. When injected, they can produce an immediate *rush* (high) that lasts 10 to 30 minutes. For two to six hours thereafter, users may feel indifferent, lethargic, and drowsy; they may slur their words and have problems paying attention, remembering, and going about their normal routine. Some people experience very unpleasant feelings, such as anxiety and fear. Other effects include a sensation of warmth or heaviness, dry mouth, facial flushing, and nausea and vomiting (particularly in first-time users).

## Risks

Addiction is common. Almost all regular users of opioids rapidly develop drug dependence, which can lead to lethargy, weight loss, loss of sex drive, and the continual effort to avoid withdrawal symptoms through repeated drug administration. In addition, they experience anxiety, insomnia, restlessness, and craving for the drug. Users continue taking opioids as much to avoid the discomfort of withdrawal, a classic sign of opioid addiction, as to experience pleasure.

Opioid intoxication is characterized by changes in mood and behaviour, such as initial euphoria followed by apathy or discontent and impaired judgment. Opioid poisoning or overdose causes shock, coma, and depressed respiration and can be fatal. Emergency medical treatment is critical.

Over time, users who inject opioids may develop infections of the heart lining and valves, skin abscesses, and lung congestion. Infections from unsterile solutions, syringes, and shared needles can lead to hepatitis, tetanus, liver disease, and HIV transmission. Depression is common and may be both an antecedent and a risk factor for needle-sharing.

## Withdrawal

If a regular user stops taking an opioid, withdrawal begins within 6 to 12 hours. The intensity of the symptoms depends on the degree of the addiction; they may grow stronger for 24 to 72 hours and gradually subside over a period of 7 to 14 days, though some symptoms, such as insomnia, may persist for several months. Irritability, nausea or vomiting, muscle aches, runny nose or eyes, dilated pupils, sweating, diarrhea, and fever are other symptoms.

Treatment studies for OxyContin® are just beginning. The Canadian Centre for Substance Abuse (CCSA) indicates that presently the best practice includes a period of detoxification followed by behaviour-oriented therapies. An exploration of options specific to young people continues.

## Methadone Maintenance

Opioid dependence is a very difficult addiction to overcome. Studies demonstrate that only 10 to 30 percent of heroin users are able to maintain abstinence. This fact contributed to the development of a unique, yet still controversial, treatment for opioid dependence: the use of methadone, a long-acting opioid that users can substitute for heroin or other opioids.[60]

Methadone is used in two basic ways to treat opioid dependence: as an opioid substitute for detoxification, usually with a gradual tapering of methadone over a period of 21 to 180 days, and as a maintenance treatment. Methadone maintenance has been criticized by some as nothing more than being an illegal opioid, such as heroin, although research has documented several positive benefits including decreased use of illicit opioids; decreased criminal behaviour; decreased risk of contracting HIV infection; and improvements in physical health, employment, and other lifestyle factors.

## Phencyclidine (PCP)

**PCP** (**phencyclidine** or Sernyl®; angel dust, peace pill, lovely, and green) is an illicit drug manufactured as a tablet, capsule, liquid, flake, spray, or crystal-like white powder that can be swallowed, smoked, sniffed, or injected. Sometimes, it is sprinkled on crack, marijuana, tobacco, or parsley, and smoked. A fine-powdered form of PCP can be snorted or injected. Once, PCP was thought to have medicinal value as an anesthetic, but its side effects, including delirium and hallucinations, make it unacceptable for medical use.

## How Users Feel

The effects of PCP are utterly unpredictable. It may trigger violent behaviour or irreversible psychosis the first time it is used, or the twentieth time, or never. In low doses, PCP produces changes—from hallucinations or euphoria to feelings of emptiness or numbness—similar to those produced by other psychoactive drugs. Higher doses may produce a stupor that lasts several days, increased heart rate and blood pressure, flushing, sweating, dizziness, and numbness.

The behavioural changes associated with PCP intoxication include belligerence, aggressiveness, impulsiveness, unpredictability, agitation, poor judgment, and impaired functioning at work or in social situations. The physical symptoms of PCP intoxication include involuntary eye movements, increased blood pressure or heart rate, numbness or diminished responsiveness to pain, impaired coordination and speech, muscle rigidity, seizures, and a painful sensitivity to sound.

## Sedative-Hypnotic Drugs

**Sedative-hypnotics,** also known as anxiolytic or anti-anxiety drugs, depress the central nervous system, reduce activity, and induce relaxation, drowsiness, or sleep. They include the benzodiazepines and the barbiturates.

The **benzodiazepines**—the most widely used drugs in this category—are commonly prescribed for tension, muscular strain, sleep problems, anxiety, panic attacks, anesthesia, and in the treatment of alcohol withdrawal. They include such drugs as *chlordiazepoxide* (Librium®), *diazepam* (Valium®), *oxazepam* (Serax®), *lorazepam* (Ativan®), *flurazepam* (Dalmane®), and *alprazolam* (Xanax®). They differ widely in their mechanism of action, absorption rate, and metabolism, but all produce similar intoxication and withdrawal symptoms.

Benzodiazepine sleeping pills have largely replaced the **barbiturates,** which were used medically in the past for inducing relaxation and sleep, relieving tension, and treating epileptic seizures. These drugs are usually taken by mouth in tablet, capsule, or liquid form. When used as a general anesthetic, they are administered intravenously. Barbiturates such as *pentobarbital* (Nembutal®, yellow jackets), *secobarbital* (Seconal®, reds), and *thiopental* (Pentothal®) are short-acting and rapidly absorbed into the brain. The longer-acting barbiturates, such as *amobarbital* (Amytal®, blues, downers) and *phenobarbital* (Luminal®, phennies), are usually taken orally and absorbed slowly into the bloodstream, take a while to reach the brain, and have an effect for several days.

### How Users Feel

Low doses of these drugs may reduce or relieve tension, but increasing doses can cause a loosening of sexual or aggressive inhibitions. Individuals using this class of drugs may experience rapid mood changes, impaired judgment, and impaired social or occupational functioning. High doses produce slurred speech, drowsiness, and stupor.

### Risks

All sedative-hypnotic drugs can produce physical and psychological dependence within two to four weeks. A complication specific to sedatives is *cross-tolerance* (cross-addiction), which occurs when users develop tolerance for one sedative or become dependent on it and develop tolerance for other sedatives as well.

Taken in combination with alcohol, these drugs have a synergistic effect that can be dangerous or even lethal. Alcohol in combination with sedative-hypnotics leads to respiratory depression and may result in respiratory arrest and death.

### Withdrawal

Withdrawal from sedative-hypnotic drugs may range from relatively mild discomfort to a severe syndrome with grand mal seizures, depending on the degree of dependence. Withdrawal symptoms include malaise or weakness, sweating, rapid pulse, coarse tremors (of the hands, tongue, or eyelids), insomnia, nausea or vomiting, temporary hallucinations or illusions, physical restlessness, anxiety or irritability, and grand mal seizures. Withdrawal may begin within two to three days after stopping drug use, and symptoms may persist for many weeks. Regular users of any of these drugs should not try to quit suddenly, as they run the risk of seizures, coma, and death.

## Anabolic Steroids

**Anabolic steroids** are a synthetic artificial version of the male sex hormone testosterone. This hormone is responsible for the growth of bones and muscles. Steroids are controlled substances, legally available by prescription in Canada. They are sometimes used to treat specific medical conditions. Unfortunately, the illegal use of steroids has become widespread across Canada. According to the 2004 Canadian Addiction Survey, about 1 percent of Canadian males ages 15 and over report using steroids at least once.[61] Some people use steroids to improve athletic performance, while others use them to change their physical appearance.

### How Users Feel

Many young people believe that the use of steroids will help them feel more confident, that by having a well-developed body they will gain respect and admiration from their peers. Unfortunately, people who use steroids often experience both negative physical and psychological side effects. Physically, users can expect to have persistent headaches, nosebleeds, and stomach aches. Severe acne and hair loss are other side effects. Psychologically, users often experience increased aggressiveness and bursts of anger, known as "roid rage."[62]

## Risks

There are many serious health risks associated with the use of steroids. For males, shrunken testes and lowered sperm count, which may lead to sterility and impotence, is a risk. For females, irregular periods are common. Other risks include damage and tumour growth in the liver and kidneys, high blood pressure, and increased cholesterol levels that may lead to heart disease. Steroids can prevent bones from growing and also causes premature fusion of the long bones. This can result in stunted growth. Mood swings sometimes cause aggressive and violent behaviour. Using steroids can also be life-threatening. Sharing needles to inject steroids can result in Hepatitis B and C and HIV infection.

The use of steroids is also a risk for athletes, since it is a violation of the Sport Federation and International Olympic Committee anti-doping rules. A first offence results in a two-year ban from the sport and a lifetime ban from government funding. A second offence results in a lifetime ban from the sport. Both bans result in a loss of any record or medal obtained while using steroids.[63]

## Withdrawal

As with many other drugs, withdrawal can be difficult. You can't stop using steroids and keep the muscle mass and weight gain. Fatigue and depression are common. As well, the effects of steroids may be permanent in both males and females.

## Treating Drug Dependence and Abuse

The most difficult step for a drug user is to admit that he or she *is* in fact an addict. If drug abusers are not forced to deal with their problem through some unexpected trauma, such as being fired or going bankrupt, those who care—family, friends, co-workers, doctors—may have to confront them and insist that they do something about their addiction. Often this *intervention* can be the turning point for addicts and their families.

A personal treatment plan may consist of individual psychotherapy, marital and family therapy, medication, and behaviour therapy. Once an individual has made the decision to seek help for substance abuse, the first step usually is

detoxification, which involves clearing the drug from the body. An exception is methadone maintenance, discussed earlier in this chapter, which does not rely on complete detoxification.

Controlled and supervised withdrawal within a medical or psychiatric hospital may be recommended if an individual has not been able to stop using drugs as an outpatient or in a residential treatment program. Detoxification is most likely to be complicated in a polysubstance abuser, who may require close monitoring and treatment of potentially fatal withdrawal symptoms.

Medications are used in detoxification to alleviate withdrawal symptoms and prevent medical and psychiatric complications.[64] Once withdrawal is complete, these medications are discontinued, so the individual is in a drug-free state. However, individuals with mental disorders may require appropriate psychiatric medication to manage their symptoms and reduce the risk of relapse.

The aim of chemical dependence treatment is to help individuals establish and maintain their recovery from alcohol and drugs of abuse. Recovery is a dynamic process of personal growth and healing in which the drug user makes the transition from a lifestyle of active substance use to a drug-free lifestyle.

Whatever their setting, chemical-dependence treatment programs initially involve some period of intensive treatment followed by one or two years of continuing aftercare.

Therapy groups provide an opportunity for individuals who have often been isolated by their drug use to participate in normal social settings. Small groups with other former drug users can be especially valuable because they all share the experience of drug use. A professional therapist assists the group members during the group session. After their discharge from inpatient treatment, individuals who became involved in self-help groups are less likely to use drugs, cope better with stress, and develop richer friendship networks.

## 12-Step Programs

Since its founding in 1935, Alcoholics Anonymous (AA)—the oldest, largest, and most successful self-help program in the world—has spawned a worldwide movement. Check out the website at www.aa.org.

As many as 200 different recovery programs are based on the spiritual **12-step program** of AA. Participation in 12-step programs for drug abusers, such as Substance Anonymous, Narcotics Anonymous, and Cocaine Anonymous, is of fundamental importance in promoting and maintaining long-term abstinence.

The basic precept of 12-step programs is that members have been powerless when it comes to controlling their addictive behaviour on their own. These programs don't

## Human Potential

### Ashlie—The Other Side Of Drug Addiction

We often hear about people who struggle with drug addiction. Their stories are often very poignant. However, there is another side of drug addiction too—the stories from family members and friends. This story is about one young woman's attempt to watch, assist, and learn from her sister's drug addiction.

Ashlie's story begins when she was in grade 5. She lived with her mother, grandmother, and her older sister. The two girls were involved in numerous sporting activities, horseback riding being one of them. While she and her sister were both very competitive children, often comparing their successes to each other, she lived in a typical middle-class family dealing with typical sister rivalry. A change in their relationship would occur when Ashlie's sister entered middle school. Ashlie's sister began skipping classes and pulling back from the many individual and family activities that had been the norm for them. Family life became a little more difficult.

To deal with the changes that were occurring, Ashlie became even more competitive, working hard in school to "get on the straight A wall," doing even better in sports, and attempting to be the "good girl" in the family. It became important for Ashlie to "go in the opposite direction than my sister. I couldn't do the things she was doing because I could see how it was hurting my mom and my grandma." The changes in Ashlie's sister's behaviour continued, and over the years regular drug use would become an issue that the entire family had to face. This impacted Ashlie greatly. "When a family member is in trouble, it is important to reach out to them, to support them, to assist in any way you can. That is what good families do." That is what happened in Ashlie's family. The focus on Ashlie's sister became all-consuming. From day to day, everyone had to deal with the uncertainty that comes with someone using drugs. Would Ashlie's sister come home? If so, would she be all right? Would she ask for more money? Would she be angry or sad? Would she continue to use drugs, or would she recognize that her drug use was

Ashlie, on a road trip through the Canadian Rocky Mountains.

© Courtesy of Ashlie Ferguson.

destroying not only her personal life, but also an entire family's life? What could anyone do? What should everyone do?

When you speak with Ashlie, you sense that she is wise beyond her years. Even as a high school student, she spent many hours trying to figure things out, making suggestions to her mother and grandmother as to how to deal with her sister. She was convinced that giving her sister money to buy drugs was not the answer. She wanted them to set some boundaries. She didn't want the police coming to their home. She wanted them to take action—something they could not seem to do. She has recently talked to her grandmother about her requests made so long ago and has discovered that although her requests were reasonable, even necessary, it was so very difficult to take charge and to do what might have been best for the whole family. As her grandmother said, "What if your sister calls in the night and needs picking up or needs money and we don't go to her? What if that one time will make a difference—that 1 percent chance that she is reaching out to us? What if it is that one time she might not make it if we don't go? What if she dies?"

Ashlie found ways to escape. She started hiding her feelings. She kept things "very light." She got involved "in a million things" to keep busy. She says she can't think of any time that she has felt such a deep level of anger. She started to question whether or not she was a happy person or if she was depressed. She recalls a specific time in grade 12 when she "crashed." She got a bad mark on an exam and "left the class bawling." She had a breakdown. During a visit with a counsellor, she "unloaded all this stuff." She realizes now that she is a "bundler. I bundle things up, and they accumulate. Eventually, I can't keep adding on to my bundle. The weight is just too heavy."

She knew she had to leave her mother's home to survive, but she didn't understand why she was the one who had to go. After all, she was doing all the right things—getting good marks in school, participating in activities, and helping her mother and grandmother as much as she could. She ventured to her dad's side of the family but did not find the solace or support she really needed to deal with the emotional upheaval in which she found herself. She lived with an aunt for a time. She still feels like "kind of an island. I don't really fit in anywhere. Maybe that was a coping thing, but I think I'd rather be by myself than live in a situation where there is so much uncertainty, so little grounding, and no anchor."

Another turning point for Ashlie was when she found out her sister was pregnant. She was worried for the baby. It was one thing for her sister to abuse her own body. It was another to bear witness of self-infliction to infliction of another life. She was moved deeply—knowing that this child might have to start her life without the best chance possible—that the child could be born incapacitated in some way. Ashlie believes that this is "crossing the line, it is unethical."

What was even more difficult for Ashlie to understand was the hopefulness that her sister's pregnancy seemed to have on the rest of her family. The pregnancy, as it turned out, would not be the thing that saved her sister, although there was talk of a house with a white picket fence, a SUV, and a dog. The second chance has still not materialized.

Ashlie's grandmother is now raising Ashlie's niece. Ashlie's sister is still a drug user.

Ashlie still feels responsible in many ways. She senses that she will need to become a surrogate mother for her niece. Sometimes she feels resentful about this, but most of the time she is fine. She is trying to figure out how she might support her niece once she graduates from university. She says, "Who isn't living a double life? We all feel alone at times, but we are all unified at the same time. We all know so little about the people we meet. What people see from the outside is just a little glance. What I have to deal with is like, yet unlike what other people have to deal with. Everyone has their story."

Her advice to others who face similar challenges is this: First of all, know that lifestyle choices you make do impact others, even though you might think they only impact you. Be responsible for your own actions. Know that your life story will change and will keep on changing. The fact that at times your situation might be all encompassing doesn't mean that there is nothing else. Give the rest of "you" a chance, too. The family or relationship issues are only a fraction of who you are. You are an individual, too. You are still your own person, and you have control over what you want to achieve and who you want to be. Know, also, that challenges we face do make us stronger, wiser, and help us push past obstacles that sometimes seem impossible to deal with. Also, there is "no perfect." It takes awhile to learn that, especially when you are entrapped. Finally, know that everyone's grass is not greener than yours—people you know and admire may be going through the same thing. I often look at other people and wish "I could be that cool." It took my roommate to help me understand that I am that person to other people, too—I am cool, too, and I have a lot to offer and a lot to give.

recruit members. The desire to stop must come from the individual, who contacts a local AA group.

Meetings of various 12-step programs are held daily in almost every city in Canada. (Some chapters, whose members often include the disabled or those in remote areas, meet via Internet chat rooms or electronic bulletin boards.) There are no dues or fees for membership. Many individuals belong to several programs because they have several problems, such as alcoholism, substance abuse, and

pathological gambling. All have only one requirement for membership: a desire to stop an addictive behaviour.

## Relapse Prevention

The most common clinical course for substance abuse disorders involves a pattern of multiple relapses over the course of a lifespan. When relapses do occur, they should be viewed as neither a mark of defeat nor evidence of moral weakness. While painful, they do not erase the progress that has been achieved and ultimately may strengthen self-understanding. They can serve as reminders of potential pitfalls to avoid in the future. Therapists emphasize that every lapse does not have to lead to a full-blown relapse. Users can turn to the skills acquired in treatment—calling people for support or going to meetings—to avoid a major relapse.

One key to preventing relapse is learning to avoid obvious cues and associations that can set off intense cravings. This means staying away from the people and places linked with past drug use. The theory behind this approach, which is called *extinction* of conditioned behaviour, is that with repeated exposure—for example, to videotapes of dealers selling crack cocaine—the arousal and craving will diminish. While this technique by itself cannot ward off relapses, it does seem to enhance the overall effectiveness of other therapies.

## Four Pillars Drug Strategy— City of Vancouver

Many political groups and a variety of agencies across Canada are attempting to find ways to address substance abuse in their communities. One such example is the city of Vancouver, which has adopted an approach called the Four Pillars Drug Strategy—originally begun in both Switzerland and Germany in the 1990s. The aim of this strategy is to reduce drug-related harm in Vancouver, B.C. The four pillars of the city's drug policy are:[65]

✔ *Harm reduction*—reducing the spread of deadly communicable diseases, preventing drug overdose deaths, increasing substance users' contact with health-care services and drug treatment programs, and reducing consumption of drugs in the street.
✔ *Prevention*—using a variety of strategies to educate people about substance misuse, the negative health impacts and legal risks associated with drug use, and to encourage people to make healthy choices.
✔ *Treatment*—offering individuals access to services such as counselling, methadone programs, daytime and residential treatment, housing support, and medical care.
✔ *Enforcement*—targeting organized crime, drug dealing, drug houses, and problem businesses and improving coordination with health services and other drug-treatment agencies.

Adopted as policy in May 2001, this program is a cooperative project that relies on coordination between a number of agencies that include federal, provincial, and municipal governments; health groups; non-profit organizations and advocacy groups; and the Vancouver Police Department. The program is being reviewed by federal, provincial, and municipal governments. There is no long-term funding for this project in place at this time. Research has shown that similar approaches have resulted in a dramatic reduction in drug use in communities.[66] You can access up-to-date information on this strategy by visiting the city of Vancouver website at http://vancouver.ca/fourpillars/index.htm.

## All Nations' Healing Hospital— Fort Qu' Appelle, Saskatchewan

In June 2004, the All Nations' Healing Hospital was opened in Fort Qu' Appelle, Saskatchewan. The facility, located on First Nations' land, operates as an independent, non-profit corporation affiliated with the Regina Qu' Appelle Regional Health Authority. Traditional First Nations' values and concepts are integrated with health-care services. In addition to medical services, community-oriented and integrated mental-health therapy services are offered—with a culturally sensitive approach. These include addiction and support services where there is a recognition of the relationship between mind, body, spirit, and community healing.[67]

## NAOMI Project

The NAOMI Project (North American Opiate Medication Initiative) is a Canadian study currently being conducted in two cities, Montreal and Vancouver.[68] This study will allow researchers to measure the impact of two types of intervention—the conventional oral methadone therapy and the use of injectable heroin treatment on illicit drug consumption, participation in criminal activity, health status, and biopsychosocial dimensions of the participant's lives.[69]

## Health Canada

In 2005, Health Canada contributed more than $71 million between 2005 and 2008 for national, regional, and community initiatives that address substance abuse in Canada. These funds were directed through the Drug Strategy Community Initiatives Fund and the Alcohol and Drug Treatment and Rehabilitation Program, funding initiatives such as the Addiction by Prescription Project, headed up by the East Prince Women's Information Centre in Prince Edward Island; the Crystal Meth Informational Video

## Strategies for Prevention

### Relapse-Prevention Planning

The following steps, from Terence Gorski and Merlene Miller's *Staying Sober: A Guide for Relapse Prevention*, can lower the likelihood of relapses:

▲ *Stabilization and self-assessment.* Get control of yourself. Find out what's going on in your head, heart, and life.

▲ *Education.* Learn about relapse and what to do to prevent it.

▲ *Warning sign identification and management.* Make a list of your personal relapse warning signs. Learn how to interrupt them before you lose control.

▲ *Inventory training.* Learn how to become consciously aware of warning signs as they develop.

▲ *Review of the recovery program.* Make sure your recovery program is able to help you manage your warning signs of relapse.

▲ *Involvement of significant others.* Teach them how to help you avoid relapses.

Project, through the Regina Treaty/Status Indian Services, Inc.; and the Engaging Problematic Substance Users—Taking Health to the Streets—Nurses Teaching Nurses, through the British Columbia Centre for Disease Control. Since 2008, the Drug Strategy Community Initiatives Fund continues to support health promotion and prevention projects that aim to help youth become and stay drug-free.[70] In 2008, the Canadian government announced the provision of $111 million in financial support over five years to provincial and territorial governments to support drug-treatment services for youth.[71] Health Canada also invested $10 million in the Canadian Centre on Substance Abuse, helping fund programs to reduce illicit drug use among Canadian youth between the ages of 10 and 24, focusing on risk and protective factors before drug use begins.[72]

To learn more about Canada's approach to dealing with the problems of drug abuse, visit the National Anti-Drug Strategy webpage at www.nationalantidrugstrategy.gc.ca/nads-sna.html.

CHAPTER 11

**Making This Chapter Work for You**

1. Which of the following statements about drugs is *false*?
   a. Toxicity is the dosage level of a prescription.
   b. Drugs can be injected into the body intravenously, intramuscularly, or subcutaneously.
   c. Drug misuse is the taking of a drug for a purpose other than that for which it was medically intended.
   d. An individual's response to a drug can be affected by the setting in which the drug is used.

2. To help ensure that an over-the-counter or prescription drug is safe and effective,
   a. take smaller dosages than indicated in the instructions.
   b. test your response to the drug by borrowing a similar medication from a friend.
   c. ask your doctor or pharmacist about possible interactions with other medications.
   d. buy all of your medications online.

3. Which of the following drugs does not cause withdrawal symptoms?
   a. caffeine
   b. marijuana
   c. heroin
   d. aspirin

4. Individuals with substance-use disorders
   a. are usually not physically dependent on their drug of choice.
   b. have a compulsion to use one or more addictive substances.
   c. require less and less of the preferred drug to achieve the desired effect.
   d. suffer withdrawal symptoms when they use the drug regularly.

5. Amphetamine is very similar to which of the following in its effects on the central nervous system?
   a. marijuana
   b. heroin
   c. cocaine
   d. alcohol

6. Which of the following statements about marijuana is *false*?
   a. People who have used marijuana may experience psychoactive effects for several days after use.
   b. Marijuana has shown some effectiveness in treating chemotherapy-related nausea.
   c. Unlike long-term use of alcohol, regular use of marijuana does not have any long-lasting health consequences.
   d. Depending on the amount of marijuana used, its effects can range from a mild sense of euphoria to extreme panic.

7. Cocaine dependence can result in all of the following *except*
   a. stroke.
   b. paranoia and violent behaviour.
   c. heart failure.
   d. enhanced sexual performance.

8. Which of the following statements about club drugs is true?
   a. Club drugs can produce many unwanted effects, including hallucinations and paranoia.
   b. Most club drugs do not pose the same health dangers as "hard" drugs such as heroin.
   c. MDMA is the street name for ecstasy.
   d. When combined with extended physical exertion, club drugs can lead to hypothermia (lowered body temperature).

9. The opioids
   a. are not addictive if used in a prescription form such as codeine or Demerol®.
   b. produce an immediate but short-lasting high and a feeling of euphoria.
   c. include morphine, which is typically used for cough suppression.
   d. are illegal in Canada, but are allowed in other countries to help control severe pain.

10. Which of the following statements about drug dependence treatment is *false*?
    a. Chemical-dependence treatment programs usually involve medications to alleviate withdrawal symptoms.
    b. Detoxification is usually the first step in a drug treatment program.
    c. Relapses are not uncommon for a person who has undergone drug treatment.
    d. The 12-step recovery program modelled after Alcoholics Anonymous has been shown to be ineffective with individuals with drug dependence disorders.

Answers to these questions can be found on page 450.

## Self Responsibility

*Courage is not the lack of fear. It is acting in spite of it.*

**Mark Twain**

Saying no, listening to stop, and learning to say yes to healthy lifestyle choices takes courage. If you find yourself moving toward choices that include drug abuse, reflect on the reasons why you are willing to put your body, mind, and spirit at risk. Use Prochaska's Stages of Change model to determine what preparations you can make to change this way of thinking. What would an action plan look like that would move

## Social Responsibility

*The only society that works today is also one founded on mutual respect, on a recognition that we have responsibility collectively and individually, to help each other on the basis of each other's equal worth. A selfish society is a contradiction in terms.*

**Tony Blair**

you away from destructive lifestyle habits to habits that could enhance your well-being? What encouragement do you need to help you move into maintenance of a healthy and well life?

Careers in social work, youth programming, addictions counselling, and government can be both rewarding and meaningful. Many agencies offer cooperative education or internship opportunities.

## Critical Thinking

1. Some people in Canada argue that marijuana should be a legal drug such as alcohol and tobacco. What is your opinion on this issue? Defend your position.

2. Suppose a close friend is using crystal meth. You fear that she is developing a substance-abuse disorder. What can you do to help her realize the dangers of her behaviour? What resources are available at your school or in your community to help her deal with both her drug problem and her financial needs?

If your textbook package includes CengageNOW™, go to http://west.cengagenow.com/ilrn/ to link to CengageNOW™ for Health, your online study tool. First take the **Pre-test** for this chapter to get your personalized **Study Plan,** which will identify topics you need to review and direct you to the appropriate resources. Then take the **Post-test** to determine what concepts you have mastered and what you still need work on.

## SITES & BYTES

### Canadian Centre on Substance Abuse (CCSA)
**www.ccsa.ca**

You can access the Canadian Addiction Survey (CAS)—a national survey of Canadians' use of alcohol and other drugs at this site.

### Health Canada
**www.hc-sc.gc.ca**

Numerous reports, fact sheets, and current news releases about Canada's Drug Strategy are available at this site.

### Canadian Centre for Ethics in Sport
**www.cces.ca**

If you are an athlete, coach, or educator, this site will provide you with the latest information on the Canadian anti-doping program.

### United Native Friendship Centre
**www.unfc.org**

The goal of this agency is to assist Aboriginal people in addressing alcohol and drug issues. Information about education and prevention programs, treatment programs, and counselling is available at this site.

Please note that links are subject to change. If you find a broken link, use a search engine such as www.google.ca and search for the website by typing in keywords.

### InfoTrac® College Edition Activity
Campus Health Cover Story (2008). Students in need, schools at the ready: Substance abuse, depression and eating disorders are ever-present problems on college and university campuses. But higher ed leaders are on the case. *University Business, 11*(7), 35–45.

1. Describe one campus drug reduction strategy that was discussed in the article.

2. Describe one individual drug reduction strategy that was discussed in this article.

3. After reading through the descriptions of the many challenges new students face when they attend a college or university discussed in this article, what

*continued*

strategies would you put in place on your campus that might keep students safe? What other alternative activities might students be encouraged to become involved in, rather than drug use?

You can find additional readings related to drug abuse with InfoTrac® College Edition, an online library of

more than 5000 journals and publications. Follow the instructions for accessing InfoTrac® that were packaged with your textbook; then search for articles using a keyword search.

For additional links and resources, visit our text-specific website at www.health.nelson.com.

## Key Terms

The terms listed here are used within the chapter on the page indicated. Definitions of terms are in the Glossary at the end of the book.

addiction 282
amphetamines 286
anabolic steroids 298
barbiturates 298
benzodiazepines 298
club drugs 294
cocaine 292
crystal meth 286
deleriants 296
drug 278

drug abuse 278
drug misuse 278
ecstasy (MDMA) 294
gamma hydroxybutyrate (GHB) 294
hallucinogens 295
hashish 290
inhalants 296
intramuscular 278

intravenous (IV) 278
marijuana 290
nonopioids 296
opioids 296
over-the-counter (OTC) drug 279
PCP (phencyclidine) 297
physical dependence 282
polyabuse 282
psychoactive 282

psychological dependence 282
psychotropic 281
sedative-hypnotics 298
stimulant 281
subcutaneous 278
toxicity 278
12-step program 299
withdrawal 282

## References

1. Tjepkema, M. (2004). Alcohol and illicit drug dependence. *Supplement to Health Reports, 15.* Statistics Canada, Catalogue 82-003. Available at www.statcan.ca/english/freepub/82-003-SIE/2004000/pdf/82-003-SIE20040007447.pdf.
2. Canada's Drug Strategy Division. (2000). Straight facts about drugs and drug abuse. Health Canada. Available at www.hc-sc.gc.ca/hl-vs/pubs/adp-apd/straight_facts-faits_mefaits/index-eng.php.
3. Ibid.
4. Health Products and Food Branch. (2007, October 31) About us. Health Canada. Available at www.hc-sc.gc.ca/ahc-asc/branch-dirgen/hpfb-dgpsa.
5. A cough syrup ingredient is a popular drug. (2000). *Pediatrics, 106*(5), 1125.
6. Canadian Centre on Substance Abuse. (2005). *Substance abuse in Canada: Current challenges and choices.* Ottawa, ON: Author. Available at www.ccsa.ca/2005%20CCSA%20Documents/ccsa-004032-2005.pdf.
7. Equator Coffee. (n.d.). About coffee: Industry overview. Available at www.equator.ca/aboutcoffee/industry.asp.
8. Coffee Association of Canada. (n.d.). Highlights 2003 Canadian coffee drinking study. Available at www.coffeeassoc.com/coffeeincanada.htm.
9. CTV.ca. (2004, May 18). Many Canadians jolted by high caffeine levels. Available at www.ctv.ca/servlet/ArticleNews/story/CTVNews/1084908682911_80317882.
10. Scott, W.H., Jr., et al. (2002). Effects of caffeine on performance of low intensity tasks. *Perceptual and Motor Skills, 94*(2), 52.
11. Canadian Cancer Society/National Cancer Institute of Canada (2008). Canadian cancer statistics 2008. Available at www.cancer.ca/Canada-wide/About%20cancer/Cancer%20statistics/Canadian%20Cancer%20Statistics.aspx.
12. Adlaf, E.M., Begin, P., & Sawka, E. (eds.). (2005). *Canadian addiction survey (CAS): A national survey of Canadians' use of alcohol and other drugs: Prevalence of use and related harms: Detailed report.* Ottawa, ON: Canadian Centre on Substance Abuse. Available at www.ccsa.ca/Eng/Priorities/Research/CanadianAddiction/Pages/default.aspx.
13. Frances, Richard. Personal interview.
14. Tjepkema, M. (2004). Alcohol and illicit drug dependence. *Supplement to Health Reports, 15.* Statistics Canada, Catalogue 82-003. Available at www.statcan.ca/english/freepub/82-003-SIE/2004000/pdf/82-003-SIE20040007447.pdf.
15. Adlaf, E.M., Gliksman, L., Demers, A., & Newton-Taylor, B. (2003, March 1). Illicit drug use among Canadian university undergraduates. *Canadian Journal of Nursing Research, 35*(1), 24–43.
16. Report makes case for addiction as chronic disease. (2000). *Alcoholism & Drug Abuse Weekly, 12*(43), 3.
17. Brook, J., et al. (2000). Longitudinally foretelling drug use in the late twenties: Adolescent personality and social-environment antecedents. *Journal of Genetic Psychology, 161*(1), 37.

18. Parental ground rules work in prevention. (2000). *Alcoholism & Drug Abuse Weekly, 12*(30), 7.

19. Parental attitudes, history affect children's drug use. (2001, August 20). *Alcoholism & Drug Abuse Weekly, 13*(32), 7.

20. Flight, J. (Research Analyst). (2007). *Canadian addiction survey (CAS). A national survey of Canadians' use of alcohol and other drugs. Substance use by Canadian youth.* Cat. No. H128-1/07-499E. HC Pub. 4946. Available at www.hc-sc.gc.ca/hl-vs/pubs/adp-apd/cas-etc/youth-jeunes/index-eng.php.

21. Ibid.

22. Bon, R., et al. (2001). Normative perceptions in relation to substance use and HIV-risky sexual behaviors of college students. *Journal of Psychology, 135*(2), 165.

23. Adlaf, M.A., Demers, A. & Glikman, L. (2005). Canadian campus survey 2004. Toronto, Centre for Addiction and Mental Health. Available at www.camh.net/Research/Areas_of_research/Population_Life_Course_Studies/CCS_2004_report.pdf.

24. Jones, S., et al. (2001). Binge drinking among undergraduate college students in the United States: Implications for other substance use. *Journal of American College Health, 50*(1), 33.

25. Wechsler, H., et al. (2001). Drinking levels, alcohol problems and second-hand effects in substance-free college residences: Results of a national study. *Journal of Studies on Alcohol, 62*(1), 23.

26. Poliquin, J. (2004). New residences welcome students home. *The Ring, 30*(8). Available at http://ring.uvic.ca/04sep09/news/residences.html.

27. Canadian Centre on Substance Abuse (CCSA). (2003). Cannabis & driving: FAQs. Available at http://www.ccsa.ca/2003%20and%20earlier%20CCSA%20Documents/ccsa-008429-2003.pdf.

28. Volkow, N., et al. (2001, March). Higher cortical and lower subcortical metabolism in detoxified methamphetamine abusers. *American Journal of Psychiatry, 158*, 383.

29. Canadian AIDS Society. (2004, May 20). Fact sheet: Crystal meth and HIV. Available at www.cdnaids.ca/web/backgrnd.nsf/cl/cas-bg-0087.

30. Ibid.

31. Health Canada. (2007, January 11). Publication of the Order Amending Schedules I and III to the Controlled Drugs and Substances Act (Methamphetamine). Available at www.hc-sc.gc.ca/dhp-mps/substancontrol/pol/reg-docs/gazette2/methamphetamine-eng.php.

32. Ibid.

33. Canadian Centre on Substance Abuse. (2005, August). Methamphetamine fact sheet. Available at www.ccsa.ca/2005 CCSA Documents/ccsa-011134-2005.pdf.

34. Volkow, N., et al. (2001, March). Higher cortical and lower subcortical metabolism in detoxified methamphetamine abusers. *American Journal of Psychiatry, 158*, 383.

35. Flight, J. (Research Analyst). (2007). *Canadian addiction survey (CAS). A national survey of Canadians' use of alcohol and other drugs. Substance use by Canadian youth.* Cat. No. H128-1/07-499E. HC Pub. 4946. Available at www.hc-sc.gc.ca/hl-vs/pubs/adp-apd/cas-etc/youth-jeunes/index-eng.php.

36. Centre for Addiction and Mental Health. (2008). About marijuana. Available at www.camh.net/About_Addiction_Mental_Health/Drug_and_Addiction_Information/about_marijuana.html.

37. Health Canada. (2007, May 23). About medical marijuana. Available at www.hc-sc.gc.ca/dhp-mps/marihuana/about-apropos/index-eng.php.

38. Department of Justice. (2004, November). Cannabis reform bill. Available at www.justice.gc.ca/eng/news-nouv/nr-cp/2004/doc_31276.html.

39. Mann, R.E., Brands, B., MacDonald, S., & Stoduto, G. (2003). Impacts of cannabis on driving: An analysis of current evidence with an emphasis on Canadian data. Prepared for Road Safety and Motor Vehicle Regulation Directorate. Transport Canada: Ottawa, Ontario. Available at www.tc.gc.ca/roadsafety/tp/tp14179/menu.htm.

40. National Institute on Drug Abuse. (n.d.). Available at www.nida.nih.gov.

41. Ibid.

42. Mittleman, M. (2001). Triggering myocardial infarction by marijuana. *Journal of the American Medical Association, 286*(6), 655.

43. Marijuana may boost heart attack risk. (2001). *Alcoholism & Drug Abuse Weekly, 13*(37), 7.

44. Walling, A. (2001). Marijuana use during pregnancy. *American Family Physician, 63*(12), 2463.

45. Swift, P., & Singer, D. (2001). Cocaine use and acute left ventricular dysfunction. *Lancet, 357*, 1586.

46. National Institute on Drug Abuse. (n.d.). Available at www.nida.nih.gov.

47. Shine, B. (2000, March). Some cocaine abusers fare better with cognitive-behavioral therapy, others with 12-Step programs. *National Institute on Drug Abuse, NIDA Notes, 15*(1).

48. Strote, J., et al. (2002). Increasing MDMA use among college students: Results of a national survey. *Journal of Adolescent Health, 30*(1), 64.

49. Gross, S.R., Barrett, S.P., Shestowsky, J.S., & Pihl, R.O. (2002). Ecstasy and drug consumption patterns: A Canadian rave population study. *Canadian Journal of Psychiatry, 47*(6), 546–51.

50. National Institute on Drug Abuse. (n.d.). Available at www.nida.nih.gov.

51. Ecstasy. (2002). *Psychiatric Services, 53*(6), 667.

52. Long-term ecstasy use impairs memory. (2001). *Science News, 159*(18), 280.

53. From MDMA to ecstasy. (2001). Brown University Digest of Addiction Theory and Application, 20(6), 4.

54. Can ecstasy's effects be passed on to offspring? (2001). *Brown University Child and Adolescent Behavior Letter, 17*(8), 1.

55. Weir, E. (2001). Inhalant use and addiction in Canada. *Canadian Medical Association Journal, 164*(3). Available at www.cmaj.ca.

56. Canadian Centre on Substance Abuse. (2004, November 23). Youth residential solvent treatment program design: An examination of the role of program length and length of client stay. Introduction, conclusions and recommendations. Available at www.ccsa.ca/2003%20and%20earlier%20CCSA%20Documents/extl-003881-2003.pdf.

57. Canadian Centre on Substance Abuse. (2006). OxyContin® (ocydondone hydrochloride). Fact sheet. Available at www.ccsa.ca/2006%20CCSA%20Documents/ccsa-003642-2006.pdf.

58. Health and Community Services. (2004, January 30). OxyContin task force interim report. Government of Newfoundland & Labrador. Available at www.health.gov.nl.ca/health/publications/oxycontininterim/default.htm.

59. Canadian Centre on Substance Abuse. (2006). OxyContin® (ocydondone hydrochloride). Fact sheet. Available at www.ccsa.ca/2006%20CCSA%20Documents/ccsa-003642-2006.pdf.

60. Standcliff, S., et al. (2001). Methadone maintenance. *American Family Physician, 63*(12), 2335.

61. Adlaf, E.M., Begin, P., & Sawka, E. (eds.). (2005). *Canadian addiction survey (CAS): A national survey of Canadians' use of alcohol and other drugs: Prevalence of use and related harms: Detailed report.* Ottawa, ON: Canadian Centre on Substance Abuse. Available at www.ccsa.ca/Eng/Priorities/Research/CanadianAddiction/Pages/default.aspx.

62. Western Health Watch. (1996). Roid rage. University of Western Ontario. Available at www.shs.uwo.ca/publications/fitness/steroids.htm.

63. Addictions Foundation of Manitoba. (2005). Fast facts on anabolic steroids. Available at www.afm.mb.ca/maaw/Resource_Kit/FastFacts/2005%20PDF/2.5.13%20Kit%202005%20Section%20Drugs%20Sports%20rev%202.pdf.

64. Sloves, H. (2000). Drug treatment for drug addiction: Surmounting the barriers. *Behavioural Health Management, 20*(4), 42.

65. City of Vancouver. (2005, June 15). City of Vancouver four pillars drug strategy. Available at http://vancouver.ca/fourpillars/index.htm.

66. City of Vancouver. (2004, July 1). History of the four pillars in Vancouver. Available at http://vancouver.ca/fourpillars/fs_fourpillars.htm.

67. Important event celebrating new Fort Qu'Appelle hospital—June 12, 2004. (2004, June 12). Sask-Has. Government of Saskatchewan. Available at www.gov.sk.ca/news?newsId=90894f30-be3a-41e0-896a-5543dd94e3bf.

68. North American Opiate Medication Initiative. (2008). North American opiate medication initiative (NAOMI) Status Report, March 2008. Available at www.naomistudy.ca/pdfs/March2008NAOMIUpdate.pdf.

69. CIHR. (2005, June 6). The NAOMI project: Montreal components of the Canadian study using medically prescribed injection heroin to be conducted by the CHUM. Press release. Available at www.cihr-irsc.gc.ca/e/28330.html.

70. Health Canada (2008). The Drug Strategy Community Initiatives fund—At a glance. Available at www.hc-sc.gc.ca/hl-vs/drug-drogues/dscif-ficsa/index-eng.php.

71. Government of Canada (2008, April 28). Drug Treatment Funding Program. News backgrounder. Available at www.nationalantidrugstrategy.gc.ca/back-fich/doc2008_04_28.html.

72. Health Canada (2008, January 30). Government of Canada invests $10 million in Canadian Centre on Substance Abuse. News Release. Available at www.hc-sc.gc.ca/ahc-asc/media/nr-cp/_2008/2008_15-eng.php.

## CHAPTER 199

# Alcohol and Tobacco Use, Misuse, and Abuse

© Scott Leman/Shutterstock.

Alcohol and tobacco are the most widely used mind-altering substances in the world. The use of alcohol and tobacco on college and university campuses is no exception. Although some new studies reveal that many university students are making healthy choices about alcohol,[1, 2] an increasing number engage in the dangerous practice of binge drinking. In a random sample of 7800 Canadian students from 16 universities, 62.7 percent reported consuming five or more drinks on a single occasion at least once during the fall semester. Some 34.8 percent of students reported consuming eight or more drinks. On average, drinkers reported having five or more drinks almost five times during the fall semester and having eight or more drinks almost twice during the same period.[3]

Tobacco use is also a health issue among young Canadians, although the smoking rate among youth aged 15 to 19 years, at 15 percent, or 331 000 teens, remained unchanged between 2006 and 2007. The smoking rate of young adult smokers aged 20 to 24 dropped slightly. It was 25 percent, about 575 000, in 2007, compared to 27 percent in 2006. Data collected for the 2007 Canadian Tobacco Use Monitoring Survey (CTUMS) showed that 19.1 percent or about 5.2 million people of the Canadian population aged 15 years and older were current smokers.[4]

Although some individuals view smoking and drinking as recreational activities, the more individuals smoke and drink, the less likely they are to eat a nutritious diet and follow a healthy

**After studying the material in this chapter, you will be able to:**

- **Describe** the effects of alcohol on the body, behaviour, and thought.
- **Define** alcohol abuse, dependence, and alcoholism, and **list** their symptoms.
- **List** the negative consequences to individuals and to our society from alcohol abuse.
- **List** the health effects of smoking tobacco or using smokeless tobacco.
- **Describe** the social impact of tobacco use.
- **List** the health effects of environmental tobacco smoke.

lifestyle. This chapter provides information that can help you understand, avoid, and change behaviours that could have an impact on your health, happiness, and life.

# Alcohol and Its Effects

Pure alcohol is a colourless liquid obtained through the fermentation of a liquid containing sugar. **Ethyl alcohol,** or *ethanol,* is the type of alcohol in alcoholic beverages. Another type—methyl or wood alcohol—is a poison that should never be drunk. Any liquid containing 0.5 to 80 percent ethyl alcohol by volume is an alcoholic beverage. However, different drinks contain different amounts of alcohol.

One drink can be any of the following:

✔ One bottle or can, 340 millilitres (12 ounces), of beer, which is 5 percent alcohol.
✔ One glass, 113 millilitres (4 ounces), of table wine, such as burgundy, which is 12 percent alcohol.
✔ One small glass, 71 millilitres (2 1/2 ounces), of fortified wine, which is 20 percent alcohol.
✔ One shot, 28 millilitres (one ounce), of distilled spirits (such as whiskey, vodka, or rum), which is 50 percent alcohol.

All of these drinks contain close to the same amount of alcohol. With distilled spirits (such as bourbon, scotch, vodka, gin, and rum), alcohol content is expressed in terms of **proof,** a number that is *twice* the percentage of alcohol: 100-proof bourbon is 50 percent alcohol; 80-proof gin is 40 percent alcohol.

But the words *bottle* and *glass* can be deceiving in this context. Drinking a 454-millilitre (16-ounce) bottle of malt liquor, which is 6.4 percent alcohol, is not the same as drinking a 340-millilitre (12-ounce) glass of 3.2 percent beer. Two bottles of high-alcohol wines packaged to resemble much less powerful wine coolers can lead to alcohol poisoning, especially in those who weigh less than 68 kilograms (150 pounds). This is one reason alcoholic drinks are a serious danger for young people.

## How Much Alcohol Can I Drink?

The best way to figure how much you can drink safely is to determine the amount of alcohol in your blood at any given time, or your **blood-alcohol concentration (BAC).** BAC is expressed in terms of the percentage of alcohol in the blood and is often measured from breath or urine samples. Food, kind and quantity of beverage, weight, sex, and rate of elimination determine BAC after the consumption of alcohol.

Law-enforcement officers use BAC to determine whether a driver is legally drunk. There are two levels of government that deal with impaired driving in Canada. The federal Criminal Code of Canada, section 253(b), puts the BAC limit at 0.08. At a provincial level, there are nine provinces that impose administrative licence suspensions on drivers whose BAC is under .08. Drivers lose their licence for 4 to 24 hours.[5] A full report by the Canada Safety Council on Canada's Blood Alcohol Laws can be accessed at www.safety-council.org/info/traffic/impaired/BAC-research.pdf.

A BAC of 0.05 percent indicates approximately 5 parts alcohol to 10 000 parts other blood components. Most people reach a 0.05 level after consuming one or two drinks and experience all the positive sensations of drinking—relaxation and euphoria—without feeling intoxicated. If they continue to drink past the 0.05 percent BAC level, they gradually lose control of speech, balance, and emotions (see Table 12-1). At a BAC of 0.2 percent, they may pass out. At a BAC of 0.3 percent, they could lapse into a coma; at 0.4 percent, they could die.

For some people, even very low blood alcohol concentrations can cause a headache, upset stomach, or dizziness. These reactions often are inborn. People who have suffered brain damage, often as a result of head trauma or encephalitis, may lose all tolerance for alcohol, either temporarily or permanently, and behave abnormally after drinking small amounts. The elderly, as well as those who are unusually fatigued or have a debilitating physical illness, may also have a low tolerance for alcohol and respond inappropriately to a small amount.

## How Much Alcohol Is Too Much?

According to Canadian guidelines for low-risk drinking, weekly alcohol intake should not exceed 14 standard drinks for males and 9 drinks for females. Daily consumption should not exceed two drinks among males or females.[6] Your own limit may well be less, depending on your gender, size, and weight. Some people—such as women who are pregnant or trying to conceive; individuals with problems, such as ulcers, that might be aggravated by alcohol; those taking medications such as sleeping pills or antidepressants; and those driving or operating any motorized equipment—shouldn't drink at all.

The dangers of alcohol increase along with the amount you drink. Heavy drinking, as defined in the *2007 Canadian Addiction Survey (CAS),*[7] means having five drinks or more at one sitting for men and four or more drinks at one

▼ **Table 12-1 Dose-Specific Effects of Alcohol Intoxication**

| BAC | Dose-Specific Effects of Alcohol Intoxication* |
|---|---|
| 0.02–0.03 | No loss of coordination, slight euphoria, and loss of shyness. Depressant effects are not apparent. |
| 0.04–0.06 | Feeling of well-being, relaxation, lower inhibitions, sensation of warmth. Euphoria. Some minor impairment of reasoning and memory, lowering of caution. **Driving skills may be impaired at this level of intoxication.** |
| 0.07–0.09 | Slight impairment of balance, speech, vision, reaction time, and hearing. Euphoria. Judgment and self-control are reduced and caution, reason, and memory are impaired. **Driving skills are always impaired at this level of intoxication. It is illegal to operate a motor vehicle in Manitoba at this level of intoxication.** |
| 0.10–0.125 | Significant impairment of motor coordination and loss of good judgment. Speech may be slurred; balance, vision, reaction time, and hearing will be impaired. Euphoria. |
| 0.13–0.15 | Gross-motor impairment and lack of physical control. Blurred vision and major loss of balance. Euphoria is reduced, and dysphoria is beginning to appear. |
| 0.16–0.20 | Dysphoria (anxiety, restlessness) predominates; nausea may appear. |
| 0.25 | Needs assistance in walking; total mental confusion. Dysphoria with nausea and some vomiting. |
| 0.30 | Loss of consciousness. |
| 0.4 and up | Onset of coma, possible death due to respiratory arrest.** |

Source: Adapted from Bailey, William J., *Drug Use in American Society*, 3rd ed., (Minneapolis: Burgess, 1933); The University of Manitoba Security Services, University of Manitoba Alcohol Education Program. Dose-Specific Effects of Alcohol Intoxication. Available at http://umanitoba.ca/campus/security/safety/alcohol.html. Copyright © 2005 University of Manitoba.

\* The effects of alcohol intoxication vary from person to person and are influenced by such factors as weight, age, and sex.
\*\* Death can occur at lower blood alcohol levels in some individuals.

sitting for women. Heavy drinking destroys the liver, weakens the heart, elevates blood pressure, damages the brain, and increases the risk of cancer. Individuals who drink heavily have a higher mortality rate than those who have two or fewer drinks a day. However, the boundary between safe and dangerous drinking isn't the same for everyone. For some people, the upper limit of safety is zero: once they start, they can't stop.

## Intoxication

If you drink too much, the immediate consequence is that you get drunk—or, more precisely, intoxicated. **Intoxication** is defined as an "abnormal state that is essentially a poisoning."[8] Alcohol intoxication, which can range from mild inebriation to loss of consciousness, is characterized by at least one of the following signs: slurred speech, poor coordination, unsteady gait, abnormal eye movements, impaired attention or memory, stupor, or coma. Medical risks of intoxication include falls, hypothermia in cold climates, and increased risk of infections because of suppressed immune function.

Time and a protective environment are the recommended treatments for alcohol intoxication. Anyone who passes out after drinking heavily should be monitored regularly to ensure that vomiting (the result of excess alcohol irritating the stomach) doesn't block the breathing airway. Always make sure that an unconscious drinker is lying on his or her side, with the head lower than the body. Intoxicated drinkers can slip into shock, a potentially life-threatening condition characterized by a weak pulse, irregular breathing, and skin-colour changes. This is an emergency, and professional medical care should be sought immediately.

## Impact of Alcohol

Unlike drugs in tablet form or food, alcohol is directly and quickly absorbed into the bloodstream through the stomach walls and upper intestine. The alcohol in a typical drink reaches the bloodstream in 15 minutes and rises to its peak concentration in about an hour. The bloodstream carries the alcohol to the liver, heart, and brain.

Alcohol is a *diuretic*, a drug that speeds up the elimination of fluid from the body. Most of the alcohol you drink can leave your body only after it has been metabolized by the liver, which converts about 95 percent of the alcohol to carbon dioxide and water. The other 5 percent is excreted unchanged, mainly through urination, respiration, and perspiration. Alcohol lowers body temperature, so you should never drink to get or stay warm.

Alcohol affects the major organ systems of the body and is a known risk factor for several cancers such as those of the mouth, larynx, esophagus, and liver.[9] New studies have recently identified alcohol consumption as a risk factor for breast cancer, too.[10]

Then there is the other side of the story—a growing body of research that suggests that moderate consumption of alcohol can have positive effects. Benefits include prevention or reduction of health problems such as diabetes, stress, depression, hypertension, and senility.[11] However, not all researchers are convinced that drinking alcohol supports healthy living. Some say that moderate drinkers may participate in regular physical activity, make healthy food choices, and see their physicians for regular checkups, which might account for their overall health status. There is also a concern that researchers have used selected populations such as older adults where the benefits become much stronger.[12] The risks of alcohol consumption can outweigh the benefits, especially for young people. Pregnant women should not drink, and people who do not drink should not necessarily be encouraged to start.

## Digestive System

Alcohol reaches the stomach first, where it is partially broken down. The remaining alcohol is absorbed easily through the stomach tissue into the bloodstream. In the stomach, alcohol triggers the secretion of acids, which irritate the stomach lining. Excessive drinking at one sitting may result in nausea; chronic drinking may result in peptic ulcers (breaks in the stomach lining) and bleeding from the stomach lining.

The alcohol in the bloodstream eventually reaches the liver. The liver, which bears the major responsibility of fat metabolism in the body, converts this alcohol to fat. After a few weeks of four or five drinks a day, liver cells start to accumulate fat. Alcohol also stimulates liver cells to attract white blood cells, which normally travel throughout the bloodstream engulfing harmful substances and wastes. If white blood cells begin to invade body tissue, such as the liver, they can cause irreversible damage.

## Cardiovascular System

Alcohol gets mixed reviews regarding its effects on the cardiovascular system. People who drink moderate amounts of alcohol have lower mortality rates after a heart attack, as well as a lower risk of heart attack, compared to abstainers and heavy drinkers.[13] It also appears that both beer and distilled spirits improve health and longevity similarly to red wine consumption.[14] Moderate drinkers also have less build-up of cholesterol in their arteries and are less likely to die of heart disease than heavy drinkers or teetotallers. It is important to remember that heart health can be improved through regular physical activity, lowering stress levels, and healthy eating.

Heavier drinking triggers the release of harmful oxygen molecules called free radicals, which can increase the risk of heart disease, stroke, and cirrhosis of the liver. Alcohol can weaken the heart muscle, causing a disorder called *cardiomyopathy*. The combined use of alcohol and other drugs, including tobacco and cocaine, greatly increases the likelihood of damage to the heart.

## Immune System

Chronic alcohol use can inhibit the production of both white blood cells, which fight off infections, and red blood cells, which carry oxygen to all the organs and tissues of the body. Alcohol may increase the risk of HIV infection by altering the judgment of users so that they more readily engage in activities, such as unsafe sexual practices, that put them in danger. If you drink when you have a cold or the flu, alcohol interferes with the body's ability to recover. It also increases the chance of bacterial pneumonia in flu sufferers.

## Brain and Behaviour

At first, when you drink, you feel "up." In low dosages, alcohol affects the regions of the brain that inhibit or control behaviour, so you might feel more relaxed. However, you also experience losses of concentration, memory, judgment, and fine motor control, and you have mood swings and emotional outbursts. Moderate and heavy drinkers show signs of impaired intelligence, slowed-down reflexes, and difficulty remembering. Research has shown that heavy drinking also depletes the brain's supplies of crucial chemicals, including dopamine, gamma aminobutyric acid, opioid peptides, and serotonin, that are responsible for our feelings of pleasure and well-being. At the same time, alcohol promotes the release of stress chemicals, such as corticotropin releasing factor (CRF), that create tension and depression.

Heavy alcohol use may pose special dangers to the brains of drinkers at both ends of the age spectrum. Adolescents who drink regularly show impairments in their neurological and cognitive functioning.[15] Elderly people who drink heavily appear to have more brain shrinkage, or atrophy, than those who drink lightly or not at all.

Because alcohol is a central nervous system depressant, it slows down the activity of the neurons in the brain, gradually dulling the responses of the brain and nervous system. One or two drinks act as a tranquilizer or relaxant. Additional drinks result in a progressive reduction in central nervous system activity, leading to sleep, general anaesthesia, coma, and even death. Moderate amounts of alcohol can have disturbing effects on perception and judgment, including the following:

✔ **Impaired perceptions.** You're less able to adjust your eyes to bright lights because glare bothers you more. Although you can still hear sounds, you can't distinguish between them or accurately determine their source.

✔ **Dulled smell and taste.** Alcohol itself may cause some vitamin deficiencies, and the poor eating habits of heavy drinkers result in further nutrition problems.

✔ **Diminished sensation.** On a freezing winter night, you may walk outside without a coat and not feel the cold.

✔ **Altered sense of space.** You may not realize, for instance, that you have been in one place for several hours.

✔ **Impaired motor skills.** Writing, typing, driving, and other tasks involving your muscles are impaired. Drinking large amounts of alcohol impairs reaction time, speed, accuracy, and consistency, as well as judgment.

✔ **Impaired sexual performance**. While drinking may increase your interest in sex, it may also impair sexual response, especially a man's ability to achieve or maintain an erection.

## Increased Risk of Harm and Dying

Although most people do not have problems with alcohol and do not suffer from harm when they drink, findings from the 2007 *Canadian Addiction Survey* show that people who do use alcohol are at an increased risk of harm—either to themselves or from drinking by others[16] (see Table 12-2 and Table 12-3). Almost 21 percent (1 in 5) of former and current youth drinkers reported that their drinking had caused harm to themselves and to others at some time in the past year prior to the survey, and 28.8 percent of the respondents to the survey reported that they had been harmed at least once in the past year because of someone else's drinking.[17]

Alcohol also kills. In 2005, it was estimated that 3226 individuals were killed in motor vehicle crashes in Canada. Mothers Against Drunk Driving Canada (MADD of Canada) estimated that, at a minimum, 1210 of these fatalities involved impaired driving.[18] According to data released by the Canadian Institute for Health Information (CIHI), the highest proportion of people (27 percent) who were admitted to a specialized trauma hospital in 2002–03 due to alcohol-related injuries were youth between the ages of 10 and 24. They were followed by people aged 25 to 29 years of age (22 percent). Most of the collisions resulting in major trauma occurred on weekends (77 percent) and at night (72 percent). The most likely month for injuries to occur was June.[19]

Alcohol also plays a role in homicides and suicides and is the leading cause of cirrhosis of the liver, a chronic disease that causes extensive scarring and irreversible damage. Older drinkers over age 50 face the greatest danger of premature death from cirrhosis of the liver, hepatitis, and other alcohol-linked illnesses.

Mortality rates increase with the amount of alcohol consumed. The mortality rate for alcoholics is two and a half times higher than for nonalcoholics of the same age.

## Interaction with Other Drugs

Alcohol can interact with other drugs—prescription and nonprescription, legal and illegal. Of the 100 most frequently prescribed drugs, more than half contain at least one ingredient that interacts adversely with alcohol. Because alcohol and other psychoactive drugs may work on the same areas of the brain, their combination can produce an effect much greater

▼ **Table 12-2 Percentages of Past-year Drinkers Reporting Various Types of Harm from One's Own Alcohol Use in the Past Year, Canada, Aged 15–24[1], 1989, 1994, and 2004**

| Was there ever a time in your life when you felt your alcohol use had a harmful effect on the following? If yes, was this during the past 12 months? | NADS 1989 % [CI] | CADS 1994 % [CI] | CAS 2004 % [CI] |
|---|---|---|---|
| Friendships and social life | 8.8 [7.1–11.0] | 6.3 [5.0–7.9] | 7.6 [5.7–10.2] |
| Physical health | 10.7 [8.7–13.0] | 10.8 [9.1–12.8] | 12.0 [9.4–15.1] |
| Home life or marriage | 4.5 [3.3–6.1] | (1) [2.0–4.3] | 2.9 |
| Work, studies, or employment opportunities | 4.8 [3.5–6.5] | 4.2 [3.1–5.7] | 4.8 [3.3–7.1] |
| Financial position | 8.7 [6.9–10.7] | 11.7 [9.7–13.6] | 8.7 [6.5–11.5] |

Source: From Flight, J. (Research Analyst). (2007). *Canadian Addiction Survey (CAS). A national survey of Canadians' use of alcohol and other drugs. Substance use by Canadian youth.* Cat. No. H128-1/07-499E. HC Pub. 4946. Available at www.hc-sc.gc.ca/hl-vs/pubs/adp-apd/cas-etc/youth-jeunes/index-eng.php, page 106 (Table 8.4). Reproduced with the permission of the Minister of Public Works and Government Services Canada, 2008.

Notes: CI = confidence interval
[1] Question asked separately in the CADS: Home life and spouse/partner.

▼ **Table 12-3 Percentage Reporting Various Harms from Other People's Drinking in the Past Year, Canada, Aged 15–24 and 18–24[1], 1989, 1994, and 2004**

| Have you ever been or have you ever had the following due to someone else's drinking? | NADS 1989 % [CI] | CADS 1994 % [CI] | CAS 2004 % [CI] |
|---|---|---|---|
| Insulted or humiliated | 37.8 [34.8–40.9] | 35.2 [32.6–38.0] | 36.1 [31.9–40.5] |
| Arguments/quarrels | 32.4 [29.5–35.4] | 28.2 [25.7–30.8] | 31.9 [27.9–36.2] |
| Family problems or marriage difficulties | 11.6 [9.7–13.7] | 7.8* [6.5–9.4] | 13.9* [11.2–17.2] |
| Passenger with a drunk driver | 23.1 [20.5–25.9] | 19.7 [17.6–22.0] | 32.5* [26.6–39.1] |
| Pushed or shoved | (2) | 30.5 [28.0–32.2] | 32.7 [228.6–37.0] |
| Hit/Assaulted | 17.5 [15.4–20.0] | 11.0 [9.3–13.0] | 10.1 [7.9–12.9] |

Source: From Flight, J. (Research Analyst). (2007). *Canadian Addiction Survey (CAS). A national survey of Canadians' use of alcohol and other drugs. Substance use by Canadian youth.* Cat. No. H128-1/07-499E. HC Pub. 4946. Available at www.hc-sc.gc.ca/hl-vs/pubs/adp-apd/cas-etc/youth-jeunes/index-eng.php, page 107 (Table 8.5). Reproduced with the permission of the Minister of Public Works and Government Services Canada, 2008.

Notes: CI = confidence interval
* Significantly different from CAS.
[1] In NADS and CADS, question asked of those 15 years or older; in CAS, question asked of those 17 years or older.
[2] Not asked in HADS (pushed/shoved and hit/assaulted were combined).

▼ **Table 12-4 Alcohol and Drug Reactions**

| Drug | Possible Effects of Interaction |
|---|---|
| Analgesics (painkillers); Narcotic (codeine, Demerol®, Percodan®) | Increase in central nervous system depression, possibly leading to respiratory failure and death |
| Nonnarcotic (Aspirin®, Tylenol®) | Irritation of stomach resulting in bleeding and increased susceptibility to liver damage |
| Antabuse | Nausea, vomiting, headache, high blood pressure, and erratic heartbeat |
| Anti-anxiety drugs (Valium®, Librium) | Increase in central nervous system depression; decreased alertness; and impaired judgment |
| Antidepressants | Increase in central nervous system depression; certain antidepressants in combination with red wine could cause a sudden increase in blood pressure |
| Antihistamines (Actifed®, Dimetapp® and other cold medications) | Increase in drowsiness; driving more dangerous |
| Antibiotics | Nausea, vomiting, headache; some medications rendered less effective |
| Central nervous system stimulants (caffeine, Dexedrine®, Ritalin®) | Stimulant effects of these drugs may reverse depressant effect of alcohol but do not decrease its intoxicating effects |
| Diuretics (Diuril®, Lasix®) | Reduction in blood pressure resulting in dizziness upon rising |
| Sedatives (Dalmane®, Nembutal, Quaalude) | Increase in central nervous system depression, possibly leading to coma, respiratory failure, and death |

than that expected of either drug by itself. The consequences of this synergistic interaction can be fatal (see Table 12-4). Alcohol is particularly dangerous when combined with depressants and anti-anxiety medications.

Aspirin, long used to prevent or counter alcohol's effects, may actually enhance its impact by significantly lowering the body's ability to break down alcohol in the stomach, resulting in a higher BAC. This increase could make a difference in impairment for individuals driving cars or operating machinery.

If you want to drink while taking medication, be sure you read the warnings on non-prescription drug labels or prescription-drug containers; ask your doctor about possible alcohol–drug interactions; and check with your pharmacist if you have any questions about your medications, especially over-the-counter (OTC) products.

## Drinking in Canada

Information gathered by the Canadian Centre on Substance Abuse and reported in the *2007 Canadian Addiction Survey*[20] indicates that alcohol is the substance most commonly used by Canadian youth, with 90.8 percent of youth having used alcohol in their lifetime and 82.9 percent having used alcohol in the past 12 months. Of the 82 percent of youth who consumed alcohol over the past year, over one-third (36.9 percent) reported doing so at least once a week, and 33.7 percent reported consuming five or more drinks per typical drinking occasion. However, the most common drinking pattern among youth is light infrequent drinking at 38.7 percent.

A new finding in the 2007 Canadian Addiction Survey was that there were no sex differences in the prevalence of lifetime or current use among youth aged 15 to 24. This is different from adults where males report more alcohol use that females (81.8 percent versus 76.1 percent, respectively). However, males were more likely than females to consume alcohol one to three times a week and four or more times a week over the past year. Youth who started drinking at a younger age were also more likely to consume alcohol four or more times per week when compared with those who started drinking at a later age.[21]

## Why People Drink

The most common reason people drink alcohol is to relax. Because it depresses the central nervous system, alcohol can make people feel less tense. Other motivations for drinking include the celebration of important occasions, friendship, lowering inhibitions, self-medication, and role modelling. Some of our most admired celebrities appear regularly in commercials for alcohol. This can be a powerful form of advertising—an encouragement to drink.

Canadian undergraduate students report similar reasons for drinking, although social reasons appear to be their primary motivation. These include aesthetic reasons—to enjoy the taste or to enhance a meal, to celebrate, and to be sociable or polite. Other reasons are to get drunk, to feel good, to relax, and to comply with others.[22]

## How Common Is Drinking on College and University Campuses?

Drinking has long been part of the college and university experience. As can be expected, undergraduates display diverse drinking patterns. Light infrequent drinking (less than five drinks on the days they drink and weekly drinking) were reported by 38.7 percent of students. Light frequent drinking was reported by 16.1 percent. Heavy infrequent drinking was reported by 13.3 percent of youth. Abstainers were 9.3 percent, and former drinkers were 8.1 percent.[23]

Of concern is the one-third (33.7 percent) of students who reported heavy drinking patterns indicated by the usual consumption of five or more drinks per typical drinking day. This level of consumption is linked to an increased risk of alcohol-related problems.[24]

For the majority of students, alcohol usually does not interfere with school and work responsibilities. The Canadian Centre for Social Norms Research studied the perceptions and beliefs of university students across the country to gain a greater understanding of the behaviours of students and alcohol use. This 2005 study concluded that:[25]

- ✔ The majority of students (63 percent) drink twice per month or less.
- ✔ When students do drink, most (64 percent) consume one to four drinks at parties or bars.
- ✔ Most students overestimate both the quantity and frequency of drinking by their peers.
  - Eighty percent of students believe that their peers typically drink once per week or more often. One-third believe that their fellow students drink at least three times per week.
  - Sixty-seven percent of students believe that their peers consume five or more drinks per occasion. One-quarter believe the average consumption is seven or more drinks.
- ✔ Ninety-three percent thought they should not drink to levels that interfered with academics or other responsibilities.

At the University of Alberta, 70 percent of students drink alcohol twice a month or less, whereas 78 percent thought that their peers drink once a week or more often. When students do drink, only 60 percent drink one to three drinks. Some don't drink at all.[26]

However, alcohol use can become problematic and even tragic. A single episode, combined with poor judgment or bad luck, can lead to life-altering and sometimes life-threatening consequences.[27] To educate students about the risks of alcohol consumption, some colleges and universities are now offering alcohol-education programs such as alcohol-awareness weeks, special lifestyle-orientation sessions, formally structured peer-helper programs, and campus-wide alcohol policies.[28] Other alcohol prevention programs include alcohol-free events; expanding hours for access to student centres, gyms, and fitness centres; substance-free residence options; limiting alcohol availability; and banning or restricting alcohol advertising on campus.

## Rachael Willier—A New Life—A Second Chance

Sometimes life is difficult. Sometimes life presents challenges that seem insurmountable. Yet, Rachael Willier found a way to move forward in her life in a positive way. This is her story in her own words.

When I was a child, I had a pretty good life for the most part. I spent most of my days in the woods with my best friend (my dog) catching snakes and salamanders. I lived in the country with my mother, my new stepdad, and my new little brother. Things were fine until I realized that the new man in our lives, my new stepfather, was both verbally and physically abusive to both my mother and me. Being so young it was hard for me to handle, so I blocked most of it out, spending much of my time in the woods to distract myself from what was going on at home.

It was easy enough to keep myself occupied with my dog by my side when we lived close to the woods. Then we moved into the city. Shortly after our move, our dog got hit and killed by a car. My best friend of six years and my distraction from all that was wrong in life was gone. I was forced to face all that was going on in my home. I would have to come home each day to face my stepfather who had alcohol problems.

I was also just beginning junior high. Feeling alone and confused, it didn't take me long to discover cigarettes and alcohol, and then marijuana. The marijuana made everything seem not so bad.

Over the next year, I spent a lot of time drinking and smoking marijuana. I was still attending school but found that certain subjects like math were a bit of a struggle. On one of my trips to Halifax one summer day, someone offered me some acid. I was 13, going on 14. Acid was better and lasted longer than marijuana and alcohol. When I was on acid, nothing mattered, nothing existed but the world I created for myself. Everything was good and happy and trippy and fun. From there, it all went downhill. I needed drugs, all drugs, any drugs. I ate every kind of drug I could get my hands on, from acid to ecstasy, to pcp, and everything in between.

After a while of coming home high, treating my little brother poorly and skipping school, my mother decided she would give me a choice; because she cared for me, she wanted me to

Rachael Willier, a recipient of a 2007 Canada Post Aboriginal Education Incentive Award.

© Courtesy of Caitlin Johnson

straighten up. If I was not willing to do so, she wanted me to leave. After not much thought, at the age of 15, I left my mother's house and found home on the streets of Halifax.

I tried to go to school that year, but it was too frustrating. After being on the streets for awhile, I moved to a relative's home in Calgary, Alberta. Unfortunately, there were more of the same problems.

I decided then that I was hopeless. I was destined to be an alcoholic and drug addict. I spent the next few years trying to keep up with my addictions. I hitchhiked around the country, sleeping in old abandoned buildings, cemeteries, and people's couches. I did my best to be drunk or high the whole time.

One day when I was 16 years old, a friend and I were free climbing a cliff when I fell almost 300 feet down. I ended up in the hospital. I had 58 stitches in my face and several fractures and dislocations, and there was a chance I would suffer from minor brain damage for the rest of my life.

After my fall, I decided to make one more attempt to clean up and get my life back on track. Also, about a year after my fall, I discovered that I had a math learning disability. My mother agreed to let me come home. I was about 17 years old when she had two guests from a program called Leave Out ViolencE (L.O.V.E.). They invited me to participate in the program with the promise of free chocolate milk and endless food twice a week! I would also have the opportunity to learn more about photography and write articles for publication in the program's national paper.

During the program, I slowly began to replace drugs with photography. I began writing when I was feeling angry or frustrated. These things also helped me to remember all the other things I had forgotten about—things that are normal to your average child like riding a bike or swimming. I started walking a lot and skateboarding. I was quickly put into the next phase of the program where I learned social skills that did not involve finding, preparing, or doing drugs. I was slowly regaining hope.

With time to reflect about my life, I also remembered that I really liked cars and fixing things. I decided that I wanted to become a mechanic. In order to do that, I would need to go back to school and get my high school credits. In order to do that, I would have to get off the drugs, so that is where I began.

With the help of many community members and my mother, in 2006 at the age of 20, I enrolled in the Adult Learning Program at NSCC where I could get my high school credits. Shortly after beginning the ALP, I was accepted into the mechanics program for the following year, providing I was willing to complete each high school credit required.

I am now a high school and college graduate. I completed each credit required in the ALP with marks for each in the 80s, including math. I have been off chemicals for nearly five years, marijuana for more than four, and alcohol for over two years. I spend my free time helping people in my community who are going through the things that I have been through and intend to continue to do so wherever my life takes me. I have regained hope in myself and in my dreams, and I'm looking forward to a clean and happy future.

I have become very close with my mother over the past few years, too. She is a huge support in every journey I take, and I visit her as often as possible. My little brother has also become one of my best friends. I now have a little sister as well. I do all that I can to make sure my brother and sister know about the world and their choices so that they can make the best ones. My father and I are still not in contact, but I did find a valuable friendship in his other children as well.

I am so grateful for all the people who have helped me in getting where I am today. I am thankful that I have a second chance.

We congratulate Rachael as a recipient of a 2007 Canada Post Aboriginal Education Incentive Award. As part of a nationwide scholarship program and commitment to furthering individual potential, Canada Post offers this award that celebrates the motivation and determination of Aboriginal people who have courageously conquered personal, economic, or social adversity in the pursuit of learning. Award criteria can be found on the Canada Post website at www.canadapost.ca.

## Binge Drinking

**Binge drinking**—defined as the consumption of five or more alcoholic drinks in a row by men and four or more by women—is the leading cause of preventable death among undergraduates and the most serious threat to their intellectual, physical, and psychological development.

Glicksman et al.[29] report that heavy or binge drinking among Canadian undergraduates is common. The groups that reported the highest rates of binge drinking were male, students living in residence, students with low academic orientation, and those with what he describes as a high recreational orientation. In recent years, several students have died after consuming numerous drinks in a short period of time, while others have sustained serious injuries or caused others to be injured.

Why do students binge? Some educators view bingeing as a product of the college or university environment.[30]

More students binge drink at the beginning of the school year and then cut back as the semester progresses and academic demands increase. Binge drinking also peaks following exam times, during athletic home-game weekends, and during reading break. Many new students engage in binge drinking for the first time very soon after they arrive on campus. Binges become less common in their subsequent years at school. Real life, one educator notes, is "a strong disincentive" to this type of drinking.[31]

Surveys consistently show that students who engage in binge drinking, particularly those who do so more than once a week, experience a far higher rate of problems than other students. Frequent binge drinkers are likely to miss classes, vandalize property, and drive after drinking. Frequent binge drinkers are also more likely to experience five or more different alcohol-related problems and to use other substances, including nicotine and drugs.[32]

## The X&Y Files

# Alcohol, Tobacco, and Gender

In the past, far more men than women drank. Today, both genders are likely to consume alcohol. However, there are well-documented differences in how often and how much men and women drink. In general, men drank more frequently, consumed a larger quantity of alcohol per drinking occasion, and report more problems related to drinking.

Women are at greater risk of organ damage from heavy alcohol use and have higher rates of liver cirrhosis. One reason is that females do not respond to long-term heavy use of alcohol with the same protective physiological mechanisms as men. Drinking the same amount of alcohol causes more damage to the female liver. Women drinkers also are at greater risk of heart disease, osteoporosis, and breast cancer.

In recent years, researchers have been comparing and contrasting the reasons why men and women drink. Undergraduate women and men are equally likely to drink for stress-related reasons; both perceive alcohol as a means of tension relaxation. Some psychologists theorize that men engage in *confirmatory drinking*—that is, they drink to reinforce the image of masculinity associated with alcohol consumption. Both genders may engage in *compensatory drinking*, consuming alcohol to heighten their sense of masculinity or femininity.

Male and females smokers share certain characteristics: Most start smoking as teenagers; the lower their educational level, the more likely they are to smoke. But there are gender differences in tobacco use. In the last decade, smoking rates among adult women stopped their previous decline and have risen sharply among teenage girls. Men of all ages are more likely than women to use other forms of tobacco, such as cigars and chewing tobacco.

The genders smoke for different reasons. Men smoke to decrease boredom and fatigue and to increase arousal and concentration. Women smoke to control their weight and to decrease stress, anger, and other negative feelings.

Women tend to be less successful than men in quitting smoking. Possible reasons include gender differences in the effectiveness of therapies, a greater fear of weight gain among women, the inability to take certain anti-smoking drugs while pregnant, and the menstrual cycle's effect on withdrawal symptoms. Women drop out at higher rates from traditional stop-smoking programs and are less responsive to nicotine-replacement therapies. The approaches that work best for them combine medication and behavioural treatments, including support groups.

Students on campuses with many binge drinkers report higher rates of secondhand problems caused by others' alcohol use, compared with students on campuses with lower rates of binge drinking. These problems include loss of sleep, interruption of studies, assaults, vandalism, and unwanted sexual advances.[33]

## The Toll of Drinking for College and University Students

Results from the *Canadian Campus Survey* show that university students report a number of consequences of drinking: having a hangover, regretting their actions, memory loss, missing classes, having unplanned sexual relations and unsafe sex, and drinking and driving.[34] According to the Commission on Substance Abuse at Colleges and Universities in the United States, alcohol is involved in two-thirds of college student suicides, 9 of 10 rapes, and 95 percent of violent crimes on campus.[35]

## Aboriginal Communities

Alcohol abuse is a leading self-reported threat to the health and quality of life for many Aboriginal people. The misuse of alcohol has been traced to stresses related to acculturation, poverty, racial discrimination, and powerlessness. Certainly not all Aboriginal people drink, and not all who drink do so to excess. But experts in alcohol treatment are increasingly recognizing racial and ethnic differences in risk factors for drinking problems, patterns of drinking, and most effective types of treatment.

Within the First Nations and Inuit Health Department of Health Canada, the National Native Alcohol and Drug Abuse Program (NNADAP)[36] supports First Nations and Inuit people with prevention activities such as school programs, intervention activities such as native spiritual and cultural programs, and aftercare activities such as sharing circles and support groups.

Support also comes from First Nations people themselves. Just one example is the Circle of All Nations Program developed by William Commanda, an Aboriginal North American Chief, who lives on the Maniwaki Reserve.[37]

# Women and Alcohol—Special Considerations

Problems directly related to a woman's alcohol use range from the consequences of risky sexual behaviour after alcohol consumption, to severe physiological problems related to fertility and pregnancy. Because they have a far smaller quantity of a protective enzyme in the stomach to break down alcohol before it is absorbed into the bloodstream, women absorb about 30 percent more alcohol into their bloodstream than men. The alcohol travels through the blood to the brain, so women become intoxicated much more quickly. Because there's more alcohol in the bloodstream to break down, the liver may also be adversely affected. In alcoholic women, the stomach seems to completely stop digesting alcohol, which may explain why women alcoholics are more likely to suffer liver damage than men.

Alcohol brings many other health dangers to women:

✔ **Gynecologic problems.** Moderate to heavy drinking may contribute to infertility, menstrual problems, sexual dysfunction, and premenstrual syndrome.

✔ **Pregnancy and fetal alcohol syndrome.** According to the Public Health Agency of Canada's National Advisory Committee on Fetal Alcohol Spectrum Disorder, abstinence from alcohol should be recommended to all women during pregnancy. Women who are planning to become pregnant are also encouraged to abstain.[38] Drinking during pregnancy puts the fetus at risk for effects related to prenatal alcohol exposure. Alcohol is oxidized more slowly in the fetus because the liver is underdeveloped, which can result in a cluster of physical and mental defects called **fetal alcohol syndrome (FAS):** small head, abnormal facial features, jitters, poor muscle tone, sleep disorders, sluggish motor development, failure to thrive, short stature, delayed speech, mental retardation, and hyperactivity. As a result of their mother's alcohol consumption, many more babies suffer **fetal alcohol effects (FAE):** low birth weight, irritability as newborns, and permanent mental impairment.

✔ **Breast cancer.** Numerous studies have suggested an increased risk of breast cancer among women who drink, and many physicians feel that those at high risk for breast cancer should stop, or at least reduce, their consumption of alcohol.

✔ **Osteoporosis.** As women age, their risk of osteoporosis, a condition characterized by calcium loss and bone thinning, increases. Alcohol can block the absorption of many nutrients, including calcium, and heavy drinking may worsen the deterioration of bone tissue.

✔ **Heart disease.** Women who are very heavy drinkers are more at risk of developing irreversible heart disease than men who drink even more.

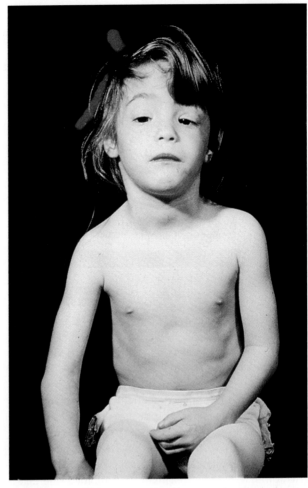

▲ A child with fetal alcohol syndrome (FAS) has distinctive facial characteristics that vary with the severity of the disease, including droopy eyelids, a thin upper lip, and a wide space between the nose and upper lip.

© K.L. Jones/LLRResearch

Women who abuse alcohol also face a special burden: intense social disapproval. Many become cross-addicted to prescription medicines, or they develop eating disorders or sexual dysfunctions. Also, women are more likely to blame their symptoms on depression or anxiety, whereas men attribute them directly to alcohol. As a result, women often obtain treatment later in the course of their illness, at a point when their problems are more severe.

# Drinking and Driving

Impaired driving is no longer the leading criminal cause of death in Canada, but it remains a leading cause. According to the Canada Safety Council, most Canadians consider drinking and driving to be unacceptable. Yet, drinking and driving is still causing tragic accidents. Because of the efforts of MADD Canada,[39] SADD (Students Against Destructive Decisions), and other lobbying groups,

## Strategies for Prevention

### How to Prevent Drunk Driving

- ▲ When going out in a group, always designate one person who won't drink at all to serve as the driver.
- ▲ Never get behind the wheel if you've had more than two drinks within two hours, especially if you haven't eaten.
- ▲ Never let intoxicated friends drive home. Call a taxi, drive them yourself, or arrange for them to spend the night in a safe place.

provincial and federal governments are cracking down on drivers who drink.

To keep drunk drivers off the road, many cities have set up checkpoints to stop cars and inspect drivers for intoxication. Two National Safe Driving Weeks— May 21–27 and December 1–7—remind Canadians of the hazards of driving under the influence of alcohol. Key campaign messages are that it is unsafe to operate any vehicle after drinking and that if you have been drinking, you should use a designated driver, call a family member or friend who has not been drinking and ask for a ride, take a cab, or stay where you are overnight.[40]

## Alcohol-Related Problems

By the simplest definition, problem drinking is the use of alcohol in any way that creates difficulties, potential difficulties, or health risks for an individual. Like alcoholics, problem drinkers are individuals whose lives are in some way impaired by their drinking. The only difference is one of degree. Alcohol becomes a problem and a person becomes an alcoholic when the drinker can't "take it or leave it." He or she spends more and more time anticipating the next drink, planning when and where to get it, buying and hiding alcohol, and covering up secret drinking.

**Alcohol abuse** involves continued use of alcohol despite awareness of social, occupational, psychological, or physical problems related to drinking or drinking in dangerous ways or situations (before driving, for instance). A diagnosis of alcohol abuse is based on one or more of the following occurring at any time during a 12-month period:

- ✔ A failure to fulfill major role obligations at work, school, or home (such as missing work or school).

- ✔ The use of alcohol in situations in which it is physically hazardous (such as before driving).
- ✔ Alcohol-related legal problems (such as drunk-driving convictions).
- ✔ Continued alcohol use despite persistent or recurring social or interpersonal problems caused or exacerbated by alcohol (such as fighting while drunk).

**Alcohol dependence** is a separate disorder in which individuals develop a strong craving for alcohol because it produces pleasurable feelings or relieves stress or anxiety. Over time, they experience physiological changes that lead to *tolerance* of its effects; this means that they must consume larger and larger amounts to achieve intoxication. If they abruptly stop drinking, they suffer *withdrawal,* a state of acute physical and psychological discomfort. A diagnosis of alcohol dependence is based on three or more of the following symptoms occurring during any 12-month period:

- ✔ Tolerance, as defined by either a need for markedly increased amounts of alcohol to achieve intoxication or desired effect or a markedly diminished effect with continued drinking of the same amount of alcohol as in the past.
- ✔ Withdrawal, including at least two of the following symptoms: sweating, rapid pulse, or other signs of autonomic hyperactivity; increased hand tremor; insomnia; nausea or vomiting; temporary hallucinations or illusions; physical agitation or restlessness; anxiety; or grand mal seizures.
- ✔ Drinking to avoid or relieve the symptoms of withdrawal.
- ✔ Consuming larger amounts of alcohol or drinking over a longer period than was intended.
- ✔ Persistent desire or unsuccessful efforts to cut down or control drinking.
- ✔ A great deal of time spent in activities necessary to obtain alcohol, drink it, or recover from its effects.
- ✔ Important social, occupational, or recreational activities given up or reduced because of alcohol use.
- ✔ Continued alcohol use despite knowledge that alcohol is likely to cause or exacerbate a persistent or recurring physical or psychological problem.

**Alcoholism** is a primary, chronic disease in which genetic, psychosocial, and environmental factors influence its development and manifestations. The disease is often progressive and fatal. Its characteristics include an inability to control drinking, a preoccupation with alcohol, continued use of alcohol despite adverse consequences, and distorted thinking, most notably denial. Like other diseases, alcoholism is not simply a matter of insufficient willpower, but a complex problem that causes many symptoms, can have serious consequences, and yet can improve with treatment.

▲ Alcohol dependence may spring from the perception that alcohol relieves stress and anxiety or creates a pleasant feeling. Chronic drinking—especially daytime drinking and drinking alone—can be a sign of serious problems, even though the drinker may otherwise appear to be in control.

## What Causes Alcohol Dependence and Abuse?

Although the exact causes of alcohol dependence and alcohol abuse are not known, certain factors—including biochemical imbalances in the brain, heredity, cultural acceptability, and stress—all seem to play a role. They include the following:

✔ **Genetics.** Scientists who are working toward mapping the genes responsible for addictive disorders have not yet been able to identify conclusively a specific gene that puts people at risk for alcoholism. However, epidemiological studies have shown evidence of heredity's role. Studies of twins suggest that heredity accounts for two-thirds of the risk of becoming alcoholic in both men and women. An identical twin of an alcoholic is twice as likely as a fraternal twin to have an alcohol-related disorder. The incidence of alcoholism is four times higher among the sons of Caucasian alcoholic fathers, regardless of whether they grow up with their biological or adoptive parents.

✔ **Stress and traumatic experiences.** Many people start drinking heavily as a way of coping with psychological problems. Alcohol often is linked with depressive and anxiety disorders. Men and women with these problems may start drinking in an attempt to alleviate their anxiety or depression.

✔ **Parental alcoholism.** According to researchers, alcoholism is four to five times more common among the children of alcoholics, who may be influenced by the behaviour they see in their parents.

✔ **Drug abuse.** Alcoholism is associated with the abuse of other psychoactive drugs, including marijuana, cocaine, heroin, amphetamines, and various anti-anxiety medications. Adults under age 30 and adolescents are most likely to use alcohol plus several drugs of abuse. Middle-aged men and women are more likely to combine alcohol with benzodiazepines, such as anti-anxiety medications or sleeping pills, which may be prescribed for them by a physician.

Whatever the reason they start, some people keep drinking out of habit. Once they develop physical tolerance and dependence, they may not be able to stop drinking on their own.

## Medical Complications of Alcohol Abuse and Dependence

Excessive alcohol use adversely affects virtually every organ system in the body, including the brain, digestive tract, heart, muscles, blood, and hormones. In addition, because alcohol interacts with many drugs, it can increase the risk of potentially lethal overdoses and harmful interactions. Among the major risks and complications are:

✔ **Liver disease.** Because the liver is the organ that breaks down and metabolizes alcohol, it is especially vulnerable to its effects. Chronic heavy drinking can lead to alcoholic hepatitis (inflammation and destruction of liver cells) and, in people who continue drinking beyond this stage, cirrhosis (irreversible scarring and destruction of liver cells). The liver eventually may fail completely, resulting in coma and death.

✔ **Cardiovascular disease.** Heavy drinking can weaken the heart muscle (causing cardiomyopathy), elevate blood pressure, and increase the risk of stroke. The combined use of alcohol and tobacco greatly increases the likelihood of damage to the heart.

✔ **Cancer.** Alcohol use may contribute to cancer of the liver, stomach, and colon, as well as malignant melanoma, a deadly form of skin cancer. Alcohol, in combination with tobacco use, also increases the risk of cancer of the mouth, tongue, larynx, and esophagus. Several major studies have implicated alcohol as a possible risk factor in breast cancer, particularly in young women.

✔ **Brain damage.** Chronic brain damage resulting from alcohol consumption is second only to Alzheimer's disease as a cause of cognitive deterioration in adults. Long-term heavy drinkers may suffer memory loss and be unable to think abstractly, recall names of common objects, and follow simple instructions.

✔ **Vitamin deficiencies.** Alcoholism is associated with vitamin deficiencies, especially of thiamin ($B_1$), which

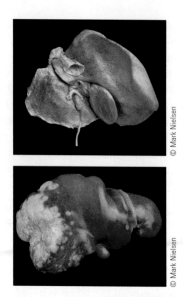

© Mark Nielsen

© Mark Nielsen

▲ A normal liver (top) compared to one with cirrhosis.

may be responsible for certain diseases of the neurological, digestive, muscular, and cardiovascular systems. Lack of thiamin may result in Wernicke-Korsakoff syndrome, which is characterized by disorientation, memory failure, hallucinations, and jerky eye movements and can be disabling enough to require lifelong custodial care.

✔ **Digestive problems.** Alcohol triggers the secretion of acids in the stomach that irritate the mucous lining and cause gastritis. Chronic drinking may result in peptic ulcers (breaks in the stomach lining) and bleeding from the stomach lining.

✔ **Reproductive and sexual dysfunction.** Alcohol interferes with male sexual function and fertility through direct effects on testosterone and the testicles. Damage to the nerves in the penis by heavy drinking can lead to impotence. In women who drink heavily, a drop in female hormone production may cause menstrual irregularity and infertility.

✔ **Fetal alcohol syndrome.** Because no one knows how much alcohol—if any—is safe during pregnancy, Canada's National Advisory Committee on Fetal Alcohol Spectrum Disorder recommends that pregnant women not drink at all. Women who do drink should practise effective contraception.

✔ **Accidents and injuries.** Alcohol contributes to deaths caused by car accidents, burns, falls, and choking.

✔ **Higher mortality.** Injury is the leading alcohol-related cause of death, chiefly in car accidents involving a drunk driver. Digestive disease, most notably cirrhosis of the liver, is second. Alcohol is a factor in suicides, too. Alcoholics who attempt suicide may have other risk factors, including major depression, poor social support, serious medical illness, and unemployment.

✔ **Withdrawal dangers.** Withdrawal can be life-threatening when accompanied by medical problems, such as grand mal seizures, pneumonia, liver failure, or gastrointestinal bleeding.

## Alcoholism Treatments

Today, individuals whose drinking could be hazardous to their health may choose from a variety of approaches. Treatment that works well for one person may not work for another. As research into the outcomes of alcohol treatments has grown, more attempts have been made to match individuals to approaches tailored to their needs and more likely to help them overcome their alcohol problems.

In a study of 222 men and women who had seriously abused alcohol, those who remained sober for more than a decade credited a variety of approaches, including Alcoholics Anonymous, individual psychotherapy, and other groups such as Women for Sobriety. There is no one sure path to sobriety—a wide variety of treatments may offer help and hope to those with alcohol-related problems.[41] Recent studies done on campus-based initiatives show that the most successful approaches include a commitment from the institution to address the issue of student drinking; the provision of funds for preventive and recovery programs; accessible community services that can provide support for students; encouraging municipal, provincial, and federal governments to take action; and involving students themselves in designing student-centred alcohol awareness and recovery programs.[42]

## Tobacco and Its Effects

Tobacco, a herb that can be smoked or chewed, directly affects the brain. While its primary active ingredient is nicotine, tobacco smoke contains almost 400 other compounds and chemicals, including gases, liquids, particles, tar, carbon monoxide, cadmium, pyridine, nitrogen dioxide, ammonia, benzene, phenol, acrolein, hydrogen cyanide, formaldehyde, and hydrogen sulfide.

### How Nicotine Works

A colourless, oily compound, **nicotine** is poisonous in concentrated amounts. If you inhale while smoking, 90 percent of the nicotine in the smoke is absorbed into your body. Even if you draw smoke only into your mouth and not into your lungs, you still absorb 25 to 30 percent of the nicotine. Nicotine is a dangerous, addictive drug that is regulated in Canada (see Figure 12-1).

Nicotine stimulates the cerebral cortex, the outer layer of the brain that controls complex behaviour and mental activity, and enhances mood and alertness. Investigators have shown

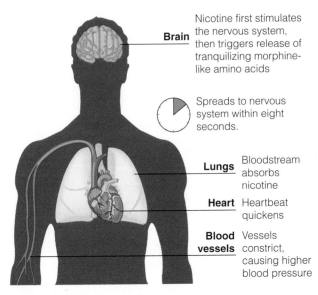

Nicotine first stimulates the nervous system, then triggers release of tranquilizing morphine-like amino acids

**Brain**

Spreads to nervous system within eight seconds.

**Lungs** Bloodstream absorbs nicotine

**Heart** Heartbeat quickens

**Blood vessels** Vessels constrict, causing higher blood pressure

▲ **Figure 12-1** The Immediate Effects of Nicotine on The Body
The primary active ingredient in tobacco is nicotine, a fast-acting and potent drug.

Sources: American Cancer Society, National Cancer Institute.

that nicotine may enhance smokers' performance on some tasks but leaves other mental skills unchanged. Nicotine also acts as a sedative. How often you smoke and how you smoke determine nicotine's effect on you. If you're a regular smoker, nicotine will generally stimulate you at first, then tranquilize you. Shallow puffs tend to increase alertness because low doses of nicotine facilitate the release of the neurotransmitter *acetylcholine,* which makes the smoker feel alert. Deep drags, on the other hand, relax the smoker because high doses of nicotine block the flow of acetylcholine.

Nicotine stimulates the adrenal glands to produce adrenaline, a hormone that increases blood pressure, speeds up the heart rate by 15 to 20 beats a minute, and constricts blood vessels (especially in the skin). Nicotine also inhibits the formation of urine, dampens hunger, irritates the membranes in the mouth and throat, and dulls the taste buds so foods don't taste as good as they would otherwise. Nicotine is a major contributor to heart and respiratory diseases.

## Tar and Carbon Monoxide

As it burns, tobacco produces **tar,** a thick, sticky dark fluid made up of several hundred different chemicals—many of them poisonous, some of them *carcinogenic* (enhancing the growth of cancerous cells). As you inhale tobacco smoke, tar and other particles settle in the forks of the branch-like bronchial tubes in your lungs, where precancerous changes are apt to occur. In addition, tar and smoke damage the mucus and the cilia in the bronchial tubes, which normally remove irritating foreign materials from your lungs.

Smoke from cigarettes, cigars, and pipes also contains **carbon monoxide,** the deadly gas that comes out of the

exhaust pipes of cars, in levels 400 times those considered safe in industry. Carbon monoxide interferes with the ability of the hemoglobin in the blood to carry oxygen, impairs normal functioning of the nervous system, and is at least partly responsible for the increased risk of heart attacks and strokes in smokers.

## Health Effects of Cigarette Smoking

Figure 12-2 shows a summary of the physiological effects of tobacco and the other chemicals in tobacco smoke. If you're a smoker who inhales deeply and started smoking before the age of 15, you're trading a minute of future life for every minute you now spend smoking. On average, smokers die nearly seven years earlier than nonsmokers.[43] Smoking not only eventually kills, it also ages you: Smokers get more wrinkles than nonsmokers.

But the effects of smoking are far more than skin-deep. A cigarette smoker is 10 times more likely to develop lung cancer than a nonsmoker and 20 times more likely to have a heart attack. Those who smoke two or more packs a day are 15 to 25 times more likely to die of lung cancer than nonsmokers.

### Heart Disease and Stroke

Although a great deal of publicity has been given to the link between cigarettes and lung cancer, heart attack is actually the leading cause of deaths for smokers. Smoking doubles the risk of heart disease, and smokers who suffer heart attacks have only a 50 percent chance of recovering. Smokers have a 70 percent higher death rate from heart disease than nonsmokers, and those who smoke heavily have a 200 percent higher death rate.

Smoking is more dangerous than the two most notorious risk factors for heart disease: high blood pressure and high cholesterol. If smoking is combined with one of these, the chances of heart attack are four times greater. Women who smoke and use oral contraceptives have a ten times higher risk of suffering heart attacks than women who do neither.

Smoking also causes a condition called *cardiomyopathy,* which weakens the heart's ability to pump blood. Although researchers don't know precisely how smoking poisons the heart muscle, they speculate that either nicotine or carbon monoxide has a direct toxic effect. Other coronary diseases may be associated with smoking. *Aortic aneurysm* is a bulge in the aorta (the large artery attached to the heart) caused by a weakening of its walls. *Pulmonary heart disease* is a heart disorder caused by changes in blood vessels in the lungs.

Even people who have smoked for decades can reduce their risk of heart attack if they quit smoking. However,

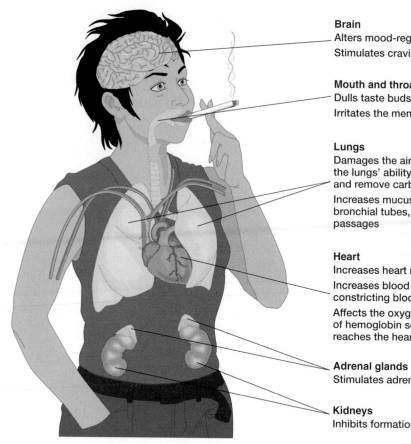

**Brain**
Alters mood-regulating chemicals
Stimulates cravings for more nicotine

**Mouth and throat**
Dulls taste buds
Irritates the membranes

**Lungs**
Damages the air sacs, which affects the lungs' ability to bring in oxygen and remove carbon dioxide

Increases mucus secretion in the bronchial tubes, which narrows air passages

**Heart**
Increases heart rate
Increases blood pressure by constricting blood vessels
Affects the oxygen-carrying ability of hemoglobin so less oxygen reaches the heart

**Adrenal glands**
Stimulates adrenaline production

**Kidneys**
Inhibits formation of urine

▲ **Figure 12-2** Some Effects of Smoking on the Body

recent studies indicate some irreversible damage to blood vessels. Progression of atherosclerosis (hardening of the arteries) among former smokers continues at a faster pace than among those who never smoked.

In addition to contributing to heart attacks, cigarette smoking increases the risk of stroke two to three times in men and women, even after other risk factors are taken into account. According to one study of middle-aged men, giving up smoking leads to a considerable decrease in the risk of stroke within five years of quitting, particularly in smokers of fewer than 20 cigarettes a day. Those with hypertension show the greatest benefit. The risk for heavy smokers declines but never reverts back to that of men who never smoked.

## Cancer

The more people smoke, the longer they smoke, and the earlier they start smoking, the more likely they are to develop lung cancer. Smokers of two or more packs a day have lung cancer mortality rates 15 to 25 times greater than nonsmokers. If smokers stop smoking before cancer has started, their lung tissue tends to repair itself, even if there

were already precancerous changes. Former smokers who haven't smoked for 15 or more years have lung cancer mortality rates only somewhat above those for nonsmokers.

Chemicals in cigarette smoke and other environmental pollutants switch on a particular gene in the lung cells of some individuals. This gene produces an enzyme that helps manufacture powerful carcinogens, which set the stage for cancer. The gene seems more likely to be activated in some people than others, and people with this gene are at much higher risk of developing lung cancer. However, smokers without the gene still remain at risk because other chemicals and genes also may be involved in the development of lung cancer.

Smokers who are depressed are more likely to get cancer than non-depressed smokers. Although researchers don't know exactly how smoking and depression may work together to increase the risk of cancer, one possibility is that stress and depression cause biological changes that lower immunity, such as a decline in natural killer cells that fight off tumours.

Despite some advances in treating lung cancer, fewer than 10 percent survive for five years after diagnosis. This is one of the lowest survival rates of any type of cancer. If the cancer has spread from the lungs to other parts of the body, only 1 percent survive for five years after diagnosis.

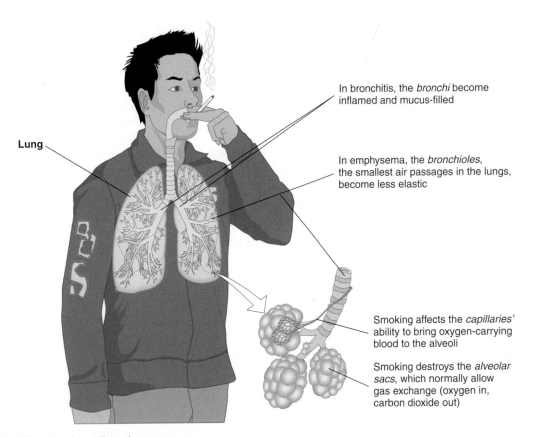

In bronchitis, the *bronchi* become inflamed and mucus-filled

In emphysema, the *bronchioles*, the smallest air passages in the lungs, become less elastic

Lung

Smoking affects the *capillaries'* ability to bring oxygen-carrying blood to the alveoli

Smoking destroys the *alveolar sacs*, which normally allow gas exchange (oxygen in, carbon dioxide out)

▲ **Figure 12-3** How Smoking Affects the Lungs

## Respiratory Diseases

Smoking quickly impairs the respiratory system. Even some teenage smokers show signs of respiratory difficulty—breathlessness, chronic cough, excess phlegm production—when compared with nonsmokers of the same age. Cigarette smokers are up to 18 times more likely than nonsmokers to die of non-cancerous diseases of the lungs.

Cigarette smoking is the major cause of chronic obstructive pulmonary disease (COPD), which includes emphysema and chronic bronchitis. COPD is characterized by progressive limitation of the flow of air into and out of the lungs. In emphysema, the limitation of air flow is the result of disease changes in the lung tissue, affecting the bronchioles (the smallest air passages) and the walls of the alveoli (the tiny air sacs of the lung), as shown in Figure 12-3. Eventually, many of the air sacs are destroyed, and the lungs become much less able to bring in oxygen and remove carbon dioxide. As a result, the heart has to work harder to deliver oxygen to all organs of the body.

In chronic bronchitis, the bronchial tubes in the lungs become inflamed, thickening the walls of the bronchi, and the production of mucus increases. The result is a narrowing of the air passages. Smoking is more dangerous than any form of air pollution, but exposure to both air pollution and cigarettes is particularly harmful. Although each may cause bronchitis, together they have a synergistic effect—that is, their combined impact exceeds the sum of their separate effects.

## Other Smoking-Related Problems

Smokers are more likely than nonsmokers to develop gum disease, and they lose significantly more teeth. Smoking may also contribute to the loss of teeth and teeth-supporting bone, even in individuals with good oral hygiene.

Cigarette smoking is associated with stomach and duodenal ulcers; mouth, throat, and other types of cancer; and cirrhosis of the liver. Smoking may worsen the symptoms or complications of allergies, diabetes, hypertension, peptic ulcers, and disorders of the lungs or blood vessels. Some men who smoke 10 cigarettes or more a day may experience sexual impotence. Cigarette smokers also tend to miss work one-third more often than nonsmokers, primarily because of respiratory illnesses. In addition, each year cigarette-ignited fires claim thousands of lives.

Cigarette smoking may also increase the likelihood of anxiety, panic attacks, and social phobias. The exact mechanism is unknown, but one theory is that nicotine may have anxiety-generating effects that act on the nervous system.[44]

## Financial Cost of Smoking

Economically, smoking costs Canada over $17 billion annually. Direct health-care costs from tobacco use are $4.4 billion. The total cost of cigarette smoking to Canadian society includes greater work absenteeism, higher insurance premiums, increased disability payments, and the training costs to replace employees who die prematurely from smoking. In the course of a lifetime, the average smoker can expect to spend tens of thousands of dollars on cigarettes—but that's only the beginning. The potential costs for medical services that might be needed for smoking-related diseases is even higher. But the greatest toll—the pain and suffering of cancer and cardiac disease victims and their loved ones—obviously cannot be measured in dollars and cents.

## Why Do People Start Smoking?

Most people are aware that an enormous health risk is associated with smoking, but many don't know exactly what that risk is or how it might affect them. The two main factors linked with the onset of a smoking habit are age and education. Other factors associated with the reasons for smoking are also discussed in the following sections.

## Genetics

Researchers speculate that genes may account for about 50 percent of smoking behaviour, with environment playing an equally important role. Studies have shown that identical twins, who have the same genes, are more likely to have matching smoking profiles than fraternal twins. If one identical twin is a heavy smoker, the other is also likely to be; if one smokes only occasionally, so does the other.

This suggests that some individuals do have a strong genetic predisposition toward tobacco use. However, when smoking is strongly discouraged, they do not express that genetic tendency. On the other hand, if smoking is socially acceptable, the genetic tendency to smoke emerges.

## Parental Role Models

Children who start smoking are 50 percent more likely than youngsters who don't smoke to have at least one smoker in their family. A mother who smokes seems a particularly strong influence on making smoking seem acceptable. The majority of youngsters who smoke say that their parents also smoke and are aware of their own tobacco use.

## Adolescent Experimentation and Rebellion

Young people who are trying out various behaviours may take up smoking because they're curious or because they want to defy adults. Others simply want to appear grown-up or "cool." Teenagers often misjudge the addictive power of cigarettes. Many, sure that they'll be able to quit any time they want, figure that smoking for a year or two won't hurt them. But when they try to quit, they can't. Like older smokers, most young people who smoke have tried to quit at least once.

## Limited Education

People who have graduated from college or university are much less likely to smoke than high school graduates; those with fewer than 12 years of education are most likely to smoke.

## Weight Control

Smokers burn up an extra 100 calories a day—probably because nicotine increases metabolic rate. Once they start smoking, many individuals say they cannot quit because they fear they'll gain weight. Smoking can also suppress appetite. Women who stop smoking gain an average of 3.7 kilograms (8 pounds), while men put on an average of 2.7 kilograms (6 pounds). The reasons for this weight gain

### Strategies for Prevention

#### Why Not to Light Up

Before you start smoking—before you ever face the challenge of quitting—think of what you have to gain by *not* smoking:

▲ A significantly reduced risk of cancer of the lungs, larynx, mouth, esophagus, pancreas, and bladder

▲ Half the risk of heart disease that smokers face

▲ A lower risk of stroke, chronic obstructive pulmonary disease (COPD), influenza, ulcers, and pneumonia

▲ A lower risk of having a low birth weight baby

▲ A longer lifespan

▲ Potential savings of tens of thousands of dollars that you would otherwise spend on tobacco products and medical care include nicotine's effects on metabolism as well as emotional and behavioural factors, such as the habit of frequently putting something into one's mouth. Yet as a health risk, smoking a pack and a half to two packs a day is a greater danger than carrying 27 kilograms (60 pounds) of extra weight.

Weight gain can be counteracted by aerobic exercise and limiting alcohol and foods high in sugar and fat.

## Aggressive Marketing

The Canadian tobacco industry spends about $20 million a year on marketing and sponsorship.[45] Most television and radio tobacco advertising ceased in the early 1970s, lifestyle product advertising in magazines and newspapers is prohibited, and the Canadian Tobacco Act banned the promotion of tobacco company sponsorships in 2003.[46] However, Canadians are exposed to crossover marketing from the United States—especially in magazine advertising.[47] Tobacco companies use very sophisticated methods to market their product. Full-page ad campaigns are only one way to sell cigarettes. Tobacco product placement is another—a familiar name or logo being used by or placed behind actors in movies, music videos, and television shows. Tobacco products are glamorized. Experts generally conclude that tobacco advertising attempts to reassure us that smoking is okay and not a threat to our health.[48]

The largest Canadian tobacco company, Imperial Tobacco, made about $900 million in operating earnings in 2000. It is owned by British American Tobacco in the United Kingdom. Outside of the United States, British American tobacco sells the most cigarettes worldwide.[49] Even though scientists have proven that smoking is dangerous to our health and cigarette production and sales in Canada have dropped over the past two decades (see Figure 12-4 and Figure 12-5), cigarette companies are now focusing their marketing efforts in third-world countries where the regulations are not as stringent.

## Stress

In studies that have analyzed the impact of life stressors, depression, emotional support, marital status, and income, researchers have concluded that an individual with a high stress level is approximately 15 times more likely to be a smoker than a person with low stress. About half of smokers identify workplace stress as a key factor in their smoking behaviour.

## Addiction

According to recent research, the first symptoms of nicotine addiction can begin within a few days of starting to smoke and after just a few cigarettes, particularly in teenagers.[50] The findings, based on a study of almost 700 adolescents, challenges the conventional belief that nicotine dependence is a gradual process that takes hold after prolonged daily smoking.

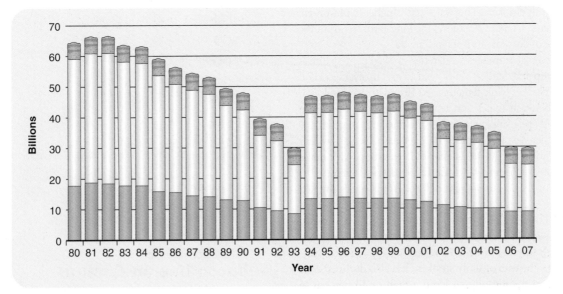

▲ **Figure 12-4** Cigarette Sales in Canada 1980–2007

Source: The Tobacco Industry. Cigarette and fine cut sales in Canada 1980–2007. Health Canada, 2008. Available at www.hc-sc.gc.ca/hl-vs/tobac-tabac/research-recherche/indust/_sales-ventes/canada-eng.php#cig. Reproduced with the permission of the Minister of Public Works and Government Services Canada, 2008.

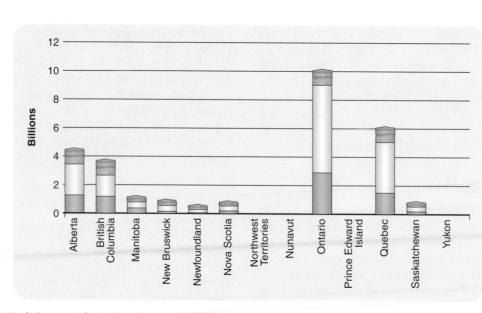

▲ **Figure 12-5** Total Cigarette Sales in Canada 2007 by Province

Source: The Tobacco Industry. Cigarette and fine cut sales in Canada 1980–2007. Health Canada, 2008. Available at www.hc-sc.gc.ca/hl-vs/tobac-tabac/research-recherche/indust/_sales-ventes/canada-eng.php#cig. Reproduced with the permission of the Minister of Public Works and Government Services Canada, 2008.

# Smoking in Canada

Tobacco use remains the most serious and widespread addictive behaviour in the world and the major cause of preventable deaths in our society. According to the latest results from the Canadian Tobacco Use Monitoring Survey (CTUMS), for data collected for 2007, just over five million people, representing 19 percent of the population aged 15 years and older, were currently smokers. Seventy-six percent reported smoking daily. Approximately 20 percent of men aged 15 and older were currently smokers. This was slightly higher than women, at 18 percent.[51] Table 12-5 shows the long-term trends in the prevalence of current smokers in Canada.

The average number of cigarettes smoked per day differs by age group and gender. Males aged 15 and up averaged 17.0 cigarettes per day, while females aged 15 and up averaged 13.7. The gap between males and females is closer in the 15- to 19-year-old age group, with males smoking an average of 12.9 cigarettes per day and females 10.5 per day. The gap widens slightly among the 20- to 24-year-old age group, with males smoking an average of 14.7 cigarettes per day and females 10.8 per day. For the 25- to 34-year-old age group, males smoked on average 14.7 cigarettes per day and females 11.1.[52]

The good news is that Canada ranked 14th lowest among 19 OECD (Organization for Economic Co-operation and Development) countries reporting on tobacco consumption. The rate of daily smokers has also declined over the past two decades, down from a high of 33 percent in 1981. Unfortunately, smokers in Canada tend to smoke, on average, slightly more cigarettes per day than smokers in other OECD countries.[53]

## ▼ Table 12-5  Smoking Prevalence, Canada, 1999–2007

The table below shows the long-term trends in the prevalence of current smokers in Canada for the following three age groups: aged 15+, youth aged 15–19, and young adults aged 20–24.

| Both Sexes | Total | 15–19 yrs | 20–24 yrs |
|---|---|---|---|
| 1999 (%) | 25 | 28 | 35 |
| 2000 (%) | 24 | 25 | 32 |
| 2001 (%) | 22 | 22.5* | 32 |
| 2002 (%) | 21 | 22 | 31 |
| 2003 (%) | 21 | 18 | 30 |
| 2004 (%) | 20 | 18 | 28 |
| 2005 (%) | 19 | 18 | 26 |
| 2006 (%) | 19 | 15 | 27 |
| 2007 (%) | 19 | 15 | 25 |

Source: Canadian Tobacco Use Monitoring Survey (CTUMS) 2007. Health Canada. Healthy Living. Tobacco. Research. Tobacco Use Statistics. Results highlights. Available at www.hc-sc.gc.ca/hl-vs/tobac-tabac/research-recherche/stat/ctums-esutc_2007-eng.php. Reproduced with the permission of the Minister of Public Works and Government Services Canada, 2008.

\* Note that this number should not be rounded up to 23%.

## Tobacco Use on Campus

Today's students use a broad range of tobacco products: cigarettes, cigars, pipes, and smokeless tobacco. Tobacco use is higher among students who use alcohol or marijuana, and students who use tobacco are more likely to smoke marijuana, binge drink, have more sexual partners, have lower grades, rate parties as important, and spend more time socializing with friends. They are less likely than nonusers to rate athletics or religion as important. Cigarette smoking among students declined between 1998 and 2004, from 17 percent to 13 percent.

First-year students who did not smoke regularly in high school and who live in smoke-free residences are 40 percent less likely to smoke than those in unrestricted housing, according to a study of the smoking behaviour of 4495 students at 101 schools.[54] Despite concern about student smoking, many colleges and universities do not offer smoking-cessation programs to students who want to quit. Those that do primarily refer students to campus support groups or community-based programs.

Students smoke for a number of reasons, including having the option to smoke, no parental rules to follow or defiance of parental norms, fears of weight gain, inability to manage stress, denial of nicotine addiction, and drinking behaviour.[55]

Working toward campus-wide nonsmoking policies and tobacco/smoke-free environments will take effort from both administration and students. Some ideas that are being implemented in colleges and universities across Canada include the following:

✔ Prohibition of campus-controlled advertising, sales, or free sampling of tobacco products and of sponsorship of campus events by tobacco-promoting organizations.

✔ Prohibition of smoking in all public areas, including classrooms, auditoriums, laboratories, libraries, gymnasiums, meeting rooms, stadiums, buses, vans, private offices, and dining facilities.

✔ Prohibition of smoking in residences.

✔ Prevention and education initiatives directed against tobacco use.

▲ Smoking often goes hand in hand with drinking.

✔ Programs that include practical steps to quit tobacco use.

## Smoking and Aboriginal People

Cigarette smoking is a major cause of disease and death in all population groups; however, the smoking rates in First Nations and Inuit communities are more than double the rate in the overall population of Canada. This has resulted in a serious and growing health concern. At one time, tobacco was used in ceremonies and prayer by First Nations Peoples. It was also used as a purifying agent and had deep spiritual meanings. Tobacco was highly valued and considered to be a sacred substance.

According to information from the First Nations and Inuit Tobacco Control Strategy (FNITC), the use of commercial tobacco products does not support the medicinal, ceremonial, and sacred use of tobacco in First Nations cultures.[56] Unfortunately, cigarette smoking and the chewing of smokeless tobacco is sometimes defended on the grounds of the traditional use of tobacco. However, the teachings of many Elders suggest that there is a critical difference between traditional and non-traditional tobacco practices.

The FNITC strategy has been developed to include core values that respect North America's First Nations and Inuit cultures, responsibility of community members who are encouraged to practise lifestyles free of tobacco misuse, and holisim—or holistic beliefs—that imply all members of the community have a role to play in promoting health as a priority.[57]

## Smoking and Women

Approximately 18 percent of females aged 15 and up currently smoke. Smoking rates among females aged 15 to 19 are 15.2 percent and 22.6 percent for females aged 20 to 24. Nineteen percent of females between 25 and 34 years of age are currently smokers, compared to 13.5 percent of females aged 55 and over.[58] Globally, smoking prevalence among women varies from as low as 7 percent in developing countries to 24 percent in developed countries.[59]

Women with less than a high school education are three times more likely to smoke than those with a college diploma or university degree.[60] As discussed in The X & Y Files: "Alcohol, Tobacco, and Gender," women smoke for different reasons and in different ways than men. They also suffer unique consequences.

If a woman smokes, her annual risk of dying more than doubles after age 45 compared with a woman who has never smoked. Women who smoke face an increased risk of lung cancer and cancer of the pharynx and bladder. Smoking may also increase the risk of liver, colon, cervical, kidney, and pancreatic cancer. Links to other health risks include depression, stroke, bleeding in the brain, diseases of the blood vessels, and respiratory diseases such as chronic obstructive pulmonary disease.

The risk of heart attack in women who smoke 25 or more cigarettes a day is more than 500 percent greater than the risk in women who don't smoke. Even smoking just one to four cigarettes a day doubles the risk. Women who smoke low-nicotine cigarettes are four times more likely to have a first heart attack than women who don't smoke—the same risk as for those who smoke high-nicotine cigarettes.

Women who smoke also are more likely to develop osteoporosis, a bone-weakening disease. They tend to be thin, which is a risk factor for osteoporosis, and they enter menopause earlier, thus extending the period of jeopardy from estrogen loss.

Smoking directly affects women's reproductive organs and processes. Women who smoke are less fertile and experience menopause one or two years earlier than women who don't smoke. Smoking also greatly increases the possible risks associated with taking oral contraceptives. Older women who smoke are weaker, have poorer balance, and are at greater risk of physical disability than nonsmokers.

Women who smoke during pregnancy increase their risk of miscarriage and pregnancy complications, including bleeding, premature delivery, and birth defects such as cleft lip or palate. Women who smoke are twice as likely to have an ectopic pregnancy (in which a fertilized egg develops in the fallopian tube rather than in the uterus) and to have babies of low birth weight as those who have never smoked. However, women who stop smoking before pregnancy reduce their risk of having a low birth weight baby to that of women who don't smoke. Even those who quit three or four months into the pregnancy have babies with higher birth weights than those who continue smoking throughout pregnancy.

## Other Forms of Tobacco

Cigars, pipes, and smokeless and chewing tobacco all put the user at risk of cancer of the lip, tongue, mouth, and throat, as well as other diseases and ailments.

### Cigars

After cigarettes, cigars are the tobacco product most widely used by college and university students. Most cigar use is occasional; fewer than 1 percent of current cigar users on campus smoked daily.[61] Cigar smoking is as dangerous even though smokers do not inhale. Cigars are known to cause cancer of the lung and the digestive tract. The risk of death related to cigars approaches that of cigarettes as the number of cigars smoked and the amount of cigar smoke inhaled increases. Cigar smoking can lead to nicotine addiction, even if the smoke is not inhaled. The nicotine in the smoke from a single cigar can vary from an amount roughly equivalent to that in a single cigarette to that in a pack or more of cigarettes.

### Pipes

Many cigarette smokers switch to pipes to reduce their risk of health problems. But former cigarette smokers may continue to inhale, even though pipe smoke is more irritating to the respiratory system than cigarette smoke. People who have only smoked pipes and who do not inhale are much less likely to develop lung and heart disease than cigarette smokers. However, they are as likely as cigarette smokers to develop—and die of—cancer of the mouth, larynx, throat, and esophagus.

### Smokeless Tobacco

The consumption of smokeless tobacco products is rising, particularly among young males. These substances include snuff, finely ground tobacco that can be sniffed or placed inside the cheek and sucked, and chewing tobacco, tobacco leaves mixed with flavouring agents such as molasses. With both, nicotine is absorbed through the mucous membranes of the nose or mouth.

Many young people who use smokeless tobacco are emulating professional baseball players who keep wads of tobacco jammed in their cheeks. These users often lack awareness of its dangers.[62] Smokeless tobacco can cause cancer and non-cancerous oral conditions and lead to nicotine addiction and dependence. Smokeless tobacco users are more likely than nonusers to become cigarette smokers. Powerful carcinogens in smokeless tobacco include nitrosamines, polycyclic aromatic hydrocarbons, and radiation-emitting polonium. Its use can lead to the development of white patches on the mucous membranes of the mouth, particularly on the site where the tobacco is placed. Most lesions of the mouth lining that result from the use of smokeless tobacco dissipate six weeks after the use of the tobacco products is stopped. However, when first found, about 5 percent of these lesions are cancerous or exhibit changes that progress to cancer within ten years if not properly treated. Cancers of the lip, pharynx, larynx, and esophagus have all been linked to smokeless tobacco.

In recent years, there has been a decline in chewing tobacco, but an increase in the use of moist snuff, a product that is higher in nicotine and potential cancer-causing chemicals. The use of snuff increases the likelihood of oral cancer by more than four times. Other effects include bad breath, discoloured or missing teeth, cavities, gum disease, and nicotine addiction.

## Secondhand Tobacco Smoke

Maybe you don't smoke—never have, never will. That doesn't mean you don't have to worry about the dangers of smoking, especially if you live or work with people who smoke. **Secondhand cigarette smoke,** or environmental tobacco smoke, is the most hazardous form of indoor air pollution and ranks behind cigarette smoking and alcohol as the third-leading preventable cause of death.

On average, a smoker inhales what is known as **mainstream smoke** eight or nine times with each cigarette, for a total of about 24 seconds. However, the cigarette burns for about 12 minutes, and everyone in the room (including the smoker) breathes in what is known as **sidestream smoke.**

According to the Lung Association of Canada, incomplete combustion from the lower temperatures of a smouldering cigarette makes sidestream smoke dirtier and chemically different from mainstream smoke. It has twice as much tar and nicotine, five times as much carbon monoxide, and 50 times as much ammonia. Because the particles in sidestream smoke are small, this mixture of irritating gases and carcinogenic tar reaches deeper into the lungs.[63]

### ???? What Are the Risks of Secondhand Smoke?

Even a little secondhand smoke is dangerous.[64] According to Health Canada, exposure to secondhand smoke causes over 1000 deaths per year.[65] In a 10-year Harvard University study that tracked 10 000 healthy women who never smoked, regular exposure to other people's smoke at home or work almost doubled the risk of heart disease. As a cancer-causing agent, secondhand smoke may be more than a hundred times more hazardous than outdoor pollutants regulated by federal law.

Approximately 80 percent of exposure to secondhand smoke occurs in the workplace. Lobbying by nonsmokers and health advocates assisted in the adoption of the 1989 Non-Smoker's Health Act. Smoking is now prohibited in federal and federally regulated workplaces, on interprovincial transit, and on airplanes. Most provinces have also enacted laws and bylaws that address the issue of secondhand smoke in public places. Unfortunately, there is not yet a consistent level of protection from one area to another within provinces or from one province to another.[66]

Public-opinion polls show that many Canadians believe secondhand smoke is a health hazard. For example, 83 percent of Saskatchewan residents support the ban on smoking in public places, while 86 percent of New Brunswick residents and 82 percent of Manitoba residents support the legislative ban on smoking in public and workplaces in those provinces.[67]

The hospitality sector, with over one million workers, is one of the most significant areas where workplace exposure to secondhand smoke is an issue. Some workplaces have designated smoking areas, but in some cases, the ventilation system for these spaces are not separate from the system serving the rest of the building. This means that all workers and patrons are exposed to the tasteless, odourless chemicals that remain in the air even after visible smoke has dissipated. Smokers also jeopardize nonsmokers by increasing the danger of fire.

One of the main arguments put forth by groups and individuals opposed to smoke-free legislation is that businesses, especially bars and restaurants, will lose revenue. However, many studies have shown that smoke-free legislation has no long-term negative impact on restaurant, bar, hotel, and tourism receipts.[68] Another argument by the smoking lobby groups is that banning smoking on the job might impair rather than enhance productivity because employees would take more frequent breaks to go to lounges where smoking is permitted—or else would suffer the negative effects of nicotine withdrawal.

Children are also regularly exposed to secondhand smoke. They are more than 50 percent more likely to suffer damage to their lungs and have breathing problems such as asthma. They are also much more likely to be at risk of brain tumours. Much of their exposure comes from living with smoking parents or guardians. Over one million children age 18 years old and under are exposed regularly to secondhand smoke every year.[69]

In 2008, Ontario passed a ban on smoking while driving with children under 16. However, there is concern about how fines of $250.00 per offence will be enforced. Other provinces that have introduced legislation to change the Motor Vehicle Act give police the power to issue tickets to anyone caught smoking in a vehicle with anyone under the age of 16 include British Columbia, Nova Scotia, Prince Edward Island, and the Yukon Territory.

## Politics of Tobacco

More than three decades after government health authorities began to warn of the dangers of cigarette smoking, tobacco remains a politically hot topic. In the United States, after many years of difficult negotiations, the tobacco

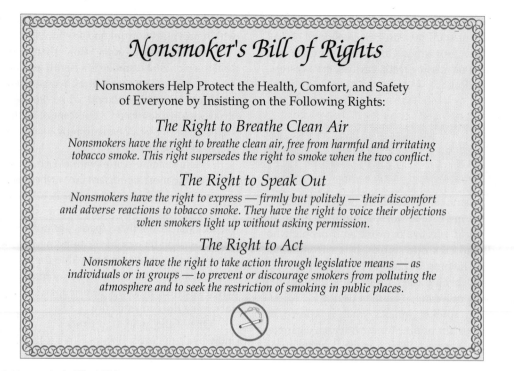

▲ **Figure 12-6** Nonsmoker's Bill of Rights

industry and the attorneys general from nearly 40 states reached a historic settlement. Major tobacco companies have agreed to pay more than $200 billion to settle smoking-related lawsuits filed by 46 states, to finance anti-smoking campaigns, to restrict marketing, to permit federal regulation of tobacco, and to pay fines if tobacco use by minors does not decline.

In Canada, federal politicians are working closely with politicians in other countries to support the Framework Convention on Tobacco Control (FCTC)—the first ever global public-health treaty.[70] This treaty was signed on July 15, 2003, at the United Nations, by Canada and other member countries of the World Health Organization who have committed to protect present and future generations from the health and economic consequences of tobacco consumption and exposure to tobacco smoke. The FCTC was adopted by member countries of the WHO at the World Health Assembly on May 21, 2003. Negotiations took almost three years. Canada played a key role in the development of the FCTC. Closer to home, we are guided by our national Federal Tobacco Control Strategy, which includes a combination of tobacco-control efforts in protection, prevention, and cessation and harm-reduction initiatives.

An example of a combined effort being put in place with regard to tobacco-control strategies is the province of Saskatchewan. From work started by a small committed group of nonsmoking advocates to mayors and councillors, the Minister of Health, and the MLA, all public places in Saskatchewan became smoke free as of January 1, 2005.[71] Nonsmokers' Bills of Rights are also being developed in many communities across Canada (see Figure 12-6).

## Quitting

Most people who eventually quit on their own have already tried other methods. In recent studies, some people who tried to quit smoking reported a small improvement in withdrawal symptoms over two weeks, but then their symptoms levelled off and persisted. Others found that their symptoms intensified rather than lessened over time. For reasons scientists cannot yet explain, former smokers who start smoking again put their lungs at even greater jeopardy than smokers who never quit.[72]

According to therapists, quitting usually isn't a one-time event but a dynamic process that may take several years and four to ten attempts. The good news is that half of individuals who ever smoked have managed to quit. Thanks to new products and programs, it may be easier now than ever before to become an ex-smoker.

### Quitting on Your Own

More than 90 percent of former smokers quit on their own—by throwing away all their cigarettes, by gradually cutting down, or by first switching to a less potent brand. One characteristic of successful quitters is that they see themselves as active participants in health maintenance and take personal responsibility for their own health. Often they experiment with a variety of strategies, such as learning relaxation techniques. In women, exercise has proven especially effective for quitting and avoiding weight gain. Making a home a smoke-free zone also increases a smoker's likelihood of successfully quitting.

## Stop-Smoking Groups

Joining a support group doubles your chances of quitting for good. Instructors explain the risks of smoking, encourage individuals to think about why they smoke, and suggest ways of unlearning their smoking habit. A quitting day is set for the third or fourth session.

Stop-smoking classes are sometimes available through student health services on many college and university campuses, as well as through public-health departments. Many businesses sponsor smoking-cessation programs for employees, available through Employee Assistance Programs (EAPs). Motivation may be even higher in these programs than in programs outside the workplace because of the social support.

Some smoking-cessation programs rely primarily on **aversion therapy,** which provides a negative experience every time a smoker has a cigarette. This may involve taking drugs that make tobacco smoke taste unpleasant, having smoke blown at you, or rapid smoking (the inhaling of smoke every six seconds until you're dizzy or nauseated).

## Nicotine-Replacement Therapy

This approach uses a variety of products that supply low doses of nicotine in a way that allows smokers to taper off gradually over a period of months. Nicotine-replacement therapies include products such as gum and patches. They are not effective as long-term approaches, according to a recent study;[73] however, these products may help smokers quit, especially when combined with a support group or counselling.

Because nicotine is a powerful, addictive substance, using nicotine replacements for a prolonged period is not advised. Pregnant women and individuals with heart disease shouldn't use them at all.

Nicotine-replacement therapies don't affect the psychological dependence that makes quitting smoking so hard. That's why the key to long-term success in quitting smoking is getting support.

### Nicotine Gum

Nicotine gum, sold as Nicorette®, contains a nicotine resin that's gradually released as the gum is chewed. Absorbed through the mucous membrane of the mouth, the nicotine doesn't produce the same rush as a deeply inhaled drag on a cigarette. However, the gum maintains enough nicotine in the blood to diminish withdrawal symptoms.

Its side effects include mild indigestion, sore jaws, nausea, heartburn, and stomachache. Also, because Nicorette® is heavier than regular chewing gum, it may loosen fillings or cause problems with dentures. Drinking coffee or other beverages may block absorption of the nicotine in the gum; individuals trying to quit smoking shouldn't ingest any substance immediately before or while chewing nicotine gum.

Most people use nicotine gum as a temporary crutch and gradually taper off until they can stop chewing it relatively painlessly. However, 5 to 10 percent of users transfer their dependence from cigarettes to the gum. When they stop using Nicorette®, they experience withdrawal symptoms, although the symptoms tend to be milder than those prompted by quitting cigarettes.

### Nicotine Patches

Nicotine transdermal-delivery system products, or patches, provide nicotine, their only active ingredient, via a patch attached to the skin by an adhesive. Like nicotine gum, the

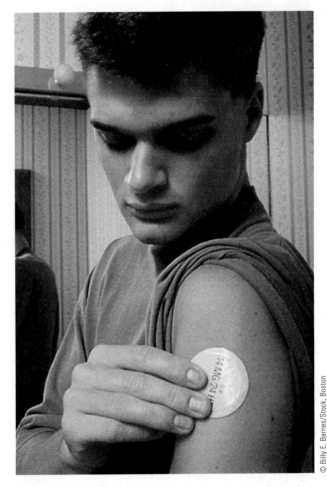

▲ A nicotine patch releases nicotine transdermally (through the skin) in measured amounts, which are gradually decreased over time.

© Billy E. Barnes/Stock, Boston

nicotine patch minimizes withdrawal symptoms, such as intense craving for cigarettes. Nicotine patches are replaced daily during therapy programs that run between 6 and 16 weeks. There is no evidence that continuing their use for more than eight weeks provides added benefit.

Some patches deliver nicotine around the clock and others for just 16 hours (during waking hours). Those most likely to benefit from nicotine-patch therapy are people who smoke more than a pack a day, are highly motivated to quit, and participate in counselling programs. While using the patch, 37 to 77 percent of people are able to abstain from smoking. When combined with counselling, the patch can be about twice as effective as a placebo, enabling 26 percent of smokers to abstain for six months.

Patch wearers who smoke or use more than one patch at a time can experience a nicotine overdose; some users have even suffered heart attacks. Occasional side effects include redness, itching, or swelling at the site of the patch application; insomnia; dry mouth; and nervousness.

CHAPTER

**12**

**Making This Chapter Work for You**

1. Which of the following statements about the effects of alcohol on the body systems is true?
   a. In most individuals, alcohol sharpens the responses of the brain and nervous system, enhancing sensation and perception.
   b. Alcohol speeds up the elimination of fluid from the body.
   c. French researchers have found that drinking red wine with meals may have a positive effect on the digestive system.
   d. The leading alcohol-related cause of death is liver damage.

2. Which of the following statements about drinking on college and university campuses is true?
   a. The percentage of students who frequently binge drink has increased.
   b. The number of women who binge drink has decreased.
   c. Because of peer pressure, students tend to drink less alcohol when they live in residences.
   d. Students who live in substance-free dormitories tend to binge drink when alcohol is available.

3. Which of the following statements about fetal alcohol syndrome is true?
   a. Women who plan to get pregnant can drink in moderation.
   b. Alcohol is oxidized more slowly in the fetus because the liver is underdeveloped.
   c. Drinking during pregnancy will not affect the fetus because it is protected by the placenta.
   d. It is difficult to distinguish a baby with FAS.

4. Women who have drinking problems
   a. often have suffered from fetal alcohol syndrome as a result of their mother's alcohol consumption.
   b. are less likely to have an alcoholic parent than men with drinking problems.
   c. are at higher risk for osteoporosis than women who are not heavy drinkers.
   d. are less likely to suffer liver damage than men.

5. Which of the following statements about alcohol abuse and dependence is *false*?
   a. Alcohol dependence involves a persistent craving for and an increased tolerance to alcohol.
   b. An individual may have a genetic predisposition for developing alcoholism.
   c. Alcoholics often abuse other psychoactive drugs.
   d. Alcohol abuse and alcohol dependence are different names for the same problem.

6. Which of the following statements about tobacco and its components is true?
   a. Nicotine settles in the lungs, eventually causing precancerous changes.
   b. Tobacco stimulates the kidneys to form urine.
   c. Carbon monoxide contained in tobacco smoke impairs oxygen transport in the body.
   d. Tar is the addictive substance in tobacco.

7. Cigarette smokers
   a. are more likely to die of lung cancer than heart disease.
   b. usually develop lung problems after years of tobacco use.
   c. have two to three times the risk of suffering a stroke than nonsmokers.
   d. may completely reverse the damage to their blood vessels if they quit smoking.

8. Tobacco use on college and university campuses
   a. is most often in the form of smokeless tobacco products used by students to avoid detection.
   b. is more prevalent among those students who also use marijuana, binge drink, and spend more time socializing with friends.
   c. has decreased in the past 10 years because almost all schools have adopted a no-smoking policy on their premises.
   d. is considered a minor problem by most student health centre directors, since less than a third of students smoke.

9. Secondhand tobacco smoke is
   a. the smoke inhaled by a smoker.
   b. more hazardous than outdoor pollution as a cancer-causing agent.
   c. less hazardous than mainstream smoke.
   d. less likely to cause serious health problems in children than in adults.

10. Quitting smoking
    a. usually results in minor withdrawal symptoms.
    b. will do little to reverse the damage to the lungs and other parts of the body.
    c. can be aided by joining a support group.
    d. is best done by cutting down on the number of cigarettes you smoke over a period of months.

Answers to these questions can be found on page 450.

## Self Responsibility

*It makes absolutely no sense to put something in your mouth and set it on fire.*

**George Sheehan**

Sometimes it is hard to let go of a lifestyle habit that has become comfortable, even though it might not be a healthy habit. If you are someone who has been thinking about making some changes with regard to alcohol consumption or tobacco use, you are already in the contemplation stage of Prochaska's Stages of Change model. Ask yourself what next steps would move you into preparation and action. What would maintenance look and feel like to you? Can you visualize yourself at the termination stage where a healthy

## Social Responsibility

*We cannot live only for ourselves. A thousand fibres connect us with our fellow men.*

**Herman Melville**

lifestyle habit becomes the habit of choice for you? Start slowly, embrace change, and move along the continuum of the change model toward healthy living.

Healthy lifestyle habits make a difference not only to personal health and wellness, but also to global health and wellness. Connect with campus initiatives that support healthy living options. Educate other students about responsible alcohol consumption. Work toward a smoke-free campus.

## Critical Thinking

1. Driving home from a night out partying, 20-year-old Rick has had too much to drink. As he crosses the dividing line on the two-lane road, the driver of an oncoming car—a young mother with two young children in the backseat—swerves to avoid an accident. She hits a concrete wall and dies instantly, but her children survive. Rick has no record of drunk driving. Should he go to prison? Is he guilty of manslaughter? How would you feel if you were the victim's husband or if you were Rick's friend?

2. Have you ever been around people who have been intoxicated when you have been sober? What did you think of their behaviour? Were they fun to be around? Was the experience not particularly enjoyable, boring, or difficult in some way? Have you ever been intoxicated? How do you behave when you are drunk? Do you find the experience enjoyable? What do the people around you think of your actions when you are drunk?

3. Has smoking become unpopular among your friends or family? What social activities continue to be associated with smoking? Can you think of any situation in which smoking might be frowned upon?

4. How would you motivate someone you care about to stop smoking? What reasons would you give for them to stop? Describe your strategy.

CENGAGENOW™

If your textbook package includes CengageNOW™, go to http://west.cengagenow.com/ilrn/ to link to CengageNOW™ for Health, your online study tool. First take the **Pre-test** for this chapter to get your personalized **Study Plan,** which will identify topics you need to review and direct you to the appropriate resources. Then take the **Post-test** to determine what concepts you have mastered and what you still need work on.

# SITES & BYTES

## Canadian Centre on Substance Abuse
www.ccsa.ca

At this site you can access current and comprehensive reports such as the *Canadian Addiction Survey* (CAS) (2007) and *Substance Abuse in Canada: Current Challenges and Choices* (2005). These detailed reports provide us with information on Canadians' use of alcohol and other drugs.

## Canadian Safety Council
www.safety-council.org

The Canada Safety Council is a national, non-government, charitable organization dedicated to safety. The mission of this organization is to lead in the national effort to reduce preventable deaths and injuries. This is an excellent site for information about traffic safety and Canada's blood alcohol laws. Current research and reports are available.

## Clean Air Coalition of BC
www.cleanaircoalitionbc.com

A joint venture between the BC Lung Association and Heart and Stroke Foundation of BC & Yukon. Their goal: a smoke-free B.C. Check out this site to find out how you might join the coalition for a smoke-free campus.

## Health Canada Tobacco Control Program
www.gosmokefree.ca

A national one-stop shop for information about tobacco—facts, industry news, research, our Federal Tobacco Control Strategy, and ideas and resources on how to make your workplace and home smoke-free.

## Ontario Tobacco Research Unit
www.otru.org

The Ontario Tobacco Research Unit is the research component of the Ontario Tobacco Strategy. Led by a multidisciplinary team, this research unit carries out research and evaluation and explores data sources and questions about tobacco use in Canada.

Please note that links are subject to change. If you find a broken link, use a search engine such as www.google.ca and search for the website by typing in keywords.

## InfoTrac® College Edition Activity
Fletcher, P.C., & Camblin, A. (2008). Preliminary examination of first year female university students: Smoking practices and beliefs in a city with no-smoking legislation. (Report). *College Student Journal, 42*(4), 1145–51.

1. Discuss the most frequently reported reason for beginning smoking by students in this study.

2. As a health-care educator or active living advocate, how might you design a smoking awareness program for young people that would address the number-one reason why students in this study began smoking.

3. Describe the smoking policies on your college or university campus. How are students, faculty, and staff moving toward a smoke-free campus?

You can find additional readings relating to alcohol and tobacco use with InfoTrac® College Edition, an online library of more than 5000 journals and publications. Follow the instructions for accessing InfoTrac® that were packaged with your textbook; then search for articles using a keyword search.

For additional links and resources, visit our text-specific website at www.health.nelson.com.

## Key Terms

The terms listed here are used within the chapter on the page indicated. Definitions of terms are in the Glossary at the end of the book.

# References

1. Chapelsky, M. (2004, November 3). Students drink less than you think. Student view. *Express News* (University of Alberta). Available at www.expressnews.ualberta.ca/article.cfm?id=6176.

2. Farquharson, V. (2005, August 25). Drinking outside the box. A U.S. journalist finds McGill students have a mature attitude toward booze. *McGill Reporter, 38.* Available at www.mcgill.ca/reporter/38/01/drinking.

3. Gliksman, L., Adlaf, E.M., Demers, A., & Newton-Taylor, B. (2003). Heavy drinking on Canadian campuses. *Canadian Journal of Public Health, 94*(1), 13–36.

4. Health Canada. (August 26, 2008). Canadian Tobacco Monitoring Survey (CTUMS) 2007. Summary of annual results for 2007. Available at www.hc-sc.gc.ca/hl-vs/tobac-tabac/research-recherche/stat/_ctums-esutc_2007/ann_summary-sommaire-eng.php.

5. Paciocco, D.M. (2002). Canada's blood alcohol laws—An international perspective. Ottawa, ON: Canada Safety Council. Available at www.safety-council.org/info/traffic/impaired/BAC-execsum.html.

6. Adlaf, E.M., Begin, P., & Sawka, E. (eds.). (2005). *Canadian addiction survey (CAS): A national survey of Canadians' use of alcohol and other drugs: Prevalence of use and related harms: Detailed report.* Ottawa, ON: Canadian Centre on Substance Abuse. Available at www.ccsa.ca/Eng/Priorities/Research/CanadianAddiction/Pages/default.aspx.

7. Flight, J. (Research Analyst). (2007). *Canadian addiction survey (CAS). A national survey of Canadians' use of alcohol and other drugs. Substance use by Canadian youth.* Cat. No. H128-1/07-499E. HC Pub. 4946. Available at www.hc-sc.gc.ca/hl-vs/pubs/adp-apd/cas-etc/youth-jeunes/index-eng.php.

8. Merriman-Webster Online Dictionary. (n.d.). Available at www.m-w.com.

9. Aronson, K. (2003, April 29). Commentary. Alcohol: A recently identified risk factor for breast cancer. *Canadian Medical Association Journal, 168*(9).

10. Ibid.

11. Hanson, D.J. (n.d.). Benefits of moderate drinking result from alcohol itself. Sociology Department, State University of New York. Available at www2.potsdam.edu/hansondj/Controversies/1088441583.html.

12. Harrison, P. (1997, November 17). Royal College debates whether MDs should promote moderate consumption of alcohol. *Canadian Medical Association Journal, 159*(10).

13. Mukamal, K., et al. (2001). Prior alcohol consumption and mortality following acute myocardial infarction. *Journal of the American Medical Association, 285,* 1965.

14. Hanson, D.J. (n.d.). Benefits of moderate drinking result from alcohol itself. Sociology Department, State University of New York. Available at www2.potsdam.edu/hansondj/Controversies/1088441583.html.

15. Mukamal, K., et al. (2001). Prior alcohol consumption and mortality following acute myocardial infarction. *Journal of the American Medical Association, 285,* 1965.

16. Flight, J. (Research Analyst). (2007). *Canadian addiction survey (CAS). A national survey of Canadians' use of alcohol and other drugs. Substance use by Canadian youth.* Cat. No. H128-1/07-499E. HC Pub. 4946. Available at www.hc-sc.gc.ca/hl-vs/pubs/adp-apd/cas-etc/youth-jeunes/index-eng.php.

17. Ibid.

18. MADD Canada. (n.d.). The magnitude of the alcohol/drug-related crash problem in Canada. Available at www.madd.ca/english/research/magnitudememo.html.

19. Canadian Institute for Health Information. (2005, June 22). More than half of all alcohol-related severe injuries due to motor vehicle collisions. Available at http://secure.cihi.ca/cihiweb/dispPage.jsp?cw_page=media_22jun2005_e.

20. Flight, J. (Research Analyst). (2007). *Canadian addiction survey (CAS). A national survey of Canadians' use of alcohol and other drugs. Substance use by Canadian youth.* Cat. No. H128-1/07-499E. HC Pub. 4946. Available at www.hc-sc.gc.ca/hl-vs/pubs/adp-apd/cas-etc/youth-jeunes/index-eng.php.

21. Ibid.

22. Kairouz, S., Gliksman, L., Demers, A., & Adlaf, E.M. (2002). For all these reasons, I do... drink: A multilevel analysis of contextual reasons for drinking among Canadian undergraduates. *Journal of Studies on Alcohol, 63,* 600–8.

23. Flight, J. (Research Analyst). (2007). *Canadian addiction survey (CAS). A national survey of Canadians' use of alcohol and other drugs. Substance use by Canadian youth.* Cat. No. H128-1/07-499E. HC Pub. 4946. Available at www.hc-sc.gc.ca/hl-vs/pubs/adp-apd/cas-etc/youth-jeunes/index-eng.php.

24. Ibid.

25. Perkins, H.W., Hains, M.P., & Rice, R. (2005). Misperceiving the college drinking norm and related problems: A nationwide study of exposure to prevention information, perceived norms and student alcohol misuse. *Journal of Studies on Alcohol, 66,* 470–78.

26. Chapelsky, M. (2005). Students drink less than you think. *Express News.* University of Alberta. Available at www.expressnews.ualberta.ca/article.cfm?id=6176.

27. Schulenberg, J., & Maggs, J. (2002). A developmental perspective on alcohol use and heavy drinking during adolescence and the transition to young adulthood. *Journal of Studies on Alcohol, 63*(2), 54.

28. Dejong, W., & Langford, L.M. (2002). A typology for campus-based alcohol prevention: Moving toward environmental management strategies. (Panel 2: Prevention and treatment of college alcohol problems.) *Journal of Studies on Alcohol, 63*(2), 140–48.

29. Adlaf, E.M., Demers, A., & Gliksman, L. (eds.). (2005). *Canadian campus survey 2004.* Toronto: Centre for Addiction and Mental Health. Available at www.camh.net/Research/Areas_of_research/Population_Life_Course_Studies/CCS_2004_report.

30. Hildebran, K., & Johnson, D. (2001). Comparison of patterns of alcohol use between high school and college athletes and nonathletes. *Research Quarterly for Exercise and Sport, 72*(1), A–30.

31. Brower, A. (2002). Are college students alcoholics? *Journal of American College Health, 50*(5), 253.

32. Jones, S., et al. (2001). Binge drinking among undergraduate college students in the United States: Implications for other substance use. *Journal of American College Health, 50*(1), 33.

33. Wechsler, H., et al. (2001). Drinking levels, alcohol problems, and second-hand effects in substance-free college residences: Results of a national study. *Journal of Studies on Alcohol, 62*(1), 23.

34. Adlaf, E.M., Demers, A., & Gliksman, L. (eds.). (2005). *Canadian campus survey 2004.* Toronto: Centre for Addiction and Mental Health. Available at www.camh.net/Research/Areas_of_research/Population_Life_Course_Studies/CCS_2004_report.

35. Jones, S., et al. (2001). Binge drinking among undergraduate college students in the United States: Implications for other substance use. *Journal of American College Health, 50*(1), 33.

36. First Nations and Inuit Health. (2005, April 8). National native alcohol and drug abuse program. Health Canada. Available at www.hc-sc.gc.ca/fnih-spni/substan/ads/nnadap-pnlaada_e.html.

37. Heald, H.F. (2004/2005, December/January). Still learning from mother earth: William Commanda, an Aboriginal North American chief, survived cancer and alcoholism to pioneer the idea of a "circle of nations." Available at www.forachange.co.uk/index.php?se=William%20Commanda&stoid=488.

38. Chudley, A.E., Conry, J., Cook, J.L., Loock, C., Rosales, T., & LeBlanc, N. (2005, March). Fetal alcohol spectrum disorder: Canadian guidelines for diagnosis. *Canadian Medical Association Journal, 172*(5 supplement). Available at www.cmaj.ca/cgi/content/full/172/5_suppl/S1.

39. MADD Canada. (n.d.). Available at www.madd.ca.

40. Canada Safety Council. (2006). Traffic safety: Activities and highlights—2004. Available at www.safety-council.org/CSC/AR.html.

41. Fletcher, A. (2001). *Sober for good.* New York: Houghton Mifflin.

42. Dejong, W., & Langford, L.M. (2002). A typology for campus-based alcohol prevention: Moving toward environmental management strategies. (Panel 2: Prevention and treatment of college alcohol problems.) *Journal of Studies on Alcohol, 63*(2), 140–48.

43. Reducing tobacco use: The quest to quit. (2001, March–April). *Facts of Life: Issue Briefing for Health Reporters, 6*(3).

44. Johnson, J., et al. (2000). Association between cigarette smoking and anxiety disorders during adolescence and early adulthood. *Journal of the American Medical Association, 284*(18), 2348.

45. Ling, P.M., & Glantz, A. (2002). Using tobacco-industry marketing research to design more effective tobacco control campaigns. *JAMA, 287*(22), 2983–89.

46. Ibid.

47. Health Canada. (2008, January 10). The industry: Tobacco marketing makes us sick. Available at www.hc-sc.gc.ca/hl-vs/tobac-tabac/youth-jeunes/scoop-primeur/indust-eng.php.

48. Ibid.

49. Ling, P.A., & Glantz, A. (2002). Why and how the tobacco industry sells cigarettes to young adults: Evidence from industry documents. *American Journal of Public Health, 202*(926), 908–16.

50. DiFranza, J. (2000). Initial symptoms of nicotine dependence in adolescents. *Tobacco Control, 9.*

51. Health Canada. (2008). Canadian tobacco use monitoring survey (CTUMS) 2007. Supplementary tables, CTUMS 2007. Available at www.hc-sc.gc.ca/hl-vs/tobac-tabac/research-recherche/stat/ctums-esutc/index_e.

52. Health Canada. (2008, August 26). Canadian tobacco use monitoring survey (CTUMS) 2007. Supplementary tables, CTUMS, 2007: Table 1. Smoking status and average number of cigarettes smoked per day, by age group and sex, age 15+ years, Canada 2007. Available at www.hc-sc.gc.ca/hl-vs/tobac-tabac/research-recherche/stat/_ctums-esutc_2007/ann-table1-eng.php.

53. Canadian Institute for Health Information. (2005, June 9). Less than one-fifth of adult Canadians smoke—The lowest rate among OECD countries. Available at http://secure.cihi.ca/cihiweb/dispPage.jsp?cw_page=media_09jun2005_e.

54. Wechsler, H., et al. (2001). College smoking policies and smoking cessation programs: Results of a survey of college health center directors. *Journal of American College Health, 49*(5).

55. Ramsay, J., & Hoffman, A. (2004). Smoking cessation and relapse prevention among undergraduate students: A pilot demonstration project. *Journal of American College Health, 53*(1), 11–16.

56. First Nations and Inuit Health. (2005, April 12). First Nations and Inuit tobacco control strategy program framework. Health Canada. Available at www.hc-sc.gc.ca/fniah-spnia/substan/tobac-tabac/commun/index-eng.php.

57. Ibid.

58. Health Canada. (2008, August 26). Canadian tobacco use monitoring survey (CTUMS) 2007. Supplementary tables, CTUMS, 2007: Table 1. Smoking status and average number of cigarettes smoked per day, by age group and sex, age 15+ years, Canada 2007. Available at www.hc-sc.gc.ca/hl-vs/tobac-tabac/research-recherche/stat/_ctums-esutc_2007/ann-table1-eng.php.

59. Report: Tobacco-related deaths increase among women. (2001, April 2). *Alcoholism & Drug Abuse Weekly, 13*(14), 5.

60. *Women and smoking: A report of the surgeon general—2001.* (2001). Washington, DC: U.S. Department of Health and Human Services.

61. Rigotti, N.A., et al. (2002). Tobacco use by Massachusetts public college students: Long-term effect of the Massachusetts tobacco control program. *Tobacco Control, 11*(2), ii20.

62. Goebal, L., et al. (2000, December). Young users of smokeless tobacco lack awareness of its dangers. *Nicotine & Tobacco Research.*

63. The Canadian Lung Association. (n.d.). Smoking bans. Available at www.lung.ca/ca/articles/smokingbans.html.

64. Glantz, S., & Parmley, W. (2001, September). Even a little second-hand smoke is dangerous. *Journal of American Medical Association, 91*(9), 1416.

65. Health Canada. (2002). The facts: Second-hand smoke in the workplace. News release. Available at www.hc-sc.gc.ca/hl-vs/tobac-tabac/second/do-faire/threat-menace-eng.php.

66. Ibid.

67. Ibid.

68. Health Canada. (n.d.). The facts about tobacco: Second-hand smoke. Available at www.hc-sc.gc.ca/hl-vs/pubs/tobac-tabac/sfpp-fslp/sfpp-fslp3-eng.php.

69. Ibid.

70. Health Canada. (2003, July 15). Canada signs framework convention on tobacco control. News release. Available at www.hc-sc.gc.ca/english/media/releases/2003/2003_56.htm.

71. Lung Association of Saskatchewan. (2004). Smoke free dining in Saskatoon—January 2004. Available at www.sk.lung.ca/content.cfm?edit_realword=smokefreestoon.

72. Study shows dangers of resuming smoking. (2001, October 22). *Alcoholism & Drug Abuse Weekly, 13*(40), 8.

73. Pierce, J., & Gilpin, E. (2002). Impact of over-the-counter sales on effectiveness of pharmaceutical aids for smoking cessation. *Journal of the American Medical Association, 288*(10), 1260.

# Traditional and Complementary Health-Care Approaches

You have more health-care options than previous generations could have imagined. Canadians have access to more health-care services and health practitioners, undergo more surgery, take more prescription drugs, and spend more time in hospitals today than they have in past decades. Not surprisingly, our medical costs are increasing. According to the 2007 Canadian Institute of Health Information (CIHI) *Health Care in Canada* report, overall spending on health care in 2006 reached an estimated $148 billion—an average of $4458 per person.[1] The combined public and private health-care bill grew by over 300 percent in the last 23 years.

Canadians are also accessing complementary and alternative health care (CAHC), also known as complementary and alternative medicine (CAM). This term includes a broad range of healing philosophies, approaches, and therapies not traditionally taught in medical schools or provided in hospitals.[2] Esmail,[3] reports that in 2006, 74 percent had used at least one alternative therapy some time in their lives.

College and university health has been defined as "the caring intersection between health and education."[4] As a college or university student, you are concerned with and responsible for both. This chapter will help prepare you for making informed health-care choices. As Dr. Donald Ardell states, "All dimensions of high level wellness are equally important, but self-responsibility seems more equal than all the rest."[5]

**After studying the material in this chapter, you will be able to:**

- **Discuss** strategies for self-care.
- **List** ways of evaluating health news and online medical advice.
- **List** your rights as a medical consumer.
- **Describe** the different types of complementary and alternative therapies and **explain** what research has shown about their effectiveness.
- **Explain** what managed care is.

**??? FREQUENTLY ASKED QUESTIONS**

**FAQ: How can I evaluate online health advice? p. 344**

**FAQ: What are federal, provincial, and territorial health-care responsibilities? p. 347**

**FAQ: Is complementary and alternative health care safe and effective? p. 352**

# Becoming a Knowledgeable Health-Care Consumer

Knowing how to spot health problems, how to evaluate health news, what to expect from health-care professionals, and where to turn for appropriate treatment can ensure you receive the best possible care—when you need it.

## Self-Care

Most people do treat themselves. You probably self-prescribe aspirin or acetaminophen for a headache, chicken soup or orange juice for a cold, or a weekend trip to unwind from stress. At the very least, you should know what your **vital signs** are and how they compare against normal readings. Vital signs include your temperature, your blood pressure, your pulse, and your respiration rate.

Once, a thermometer was the only self-testing equipment found in most Canadian homes. Now there are numerous home tests available to help consumers monitor everything from pregnancy to blood pressure levels. The new tests are generally as accurate as those administered by a professional. You should always follow directions precisely, and if your concerns persist, see your doctor.

## How Can I Evaluate Online Health Advice?

The Internet has changed the way people obtain information. According to Underhill and McKeown, about 16.8 million Canadians aged 18 or older used the Internet for personal non-business reasons during 2005. Data from the 2005 Canadian Internet Use Survey showed that an estimated 8.7 million (35 percent) were classified as "health users," accessing online health information.[6] (See Table 13-1.)

✔ Health users were more likely to access the Internet daily.
✔ Health users spent at least five hours a week online.
✔ B.C. residents are the Canadians most likely to look for online health information. Residents of Ontario and Alberta are close behind.
✔ Women were twice as likely as men to seek health information online.
✔ Health users were most likely to search for information on a specific disease.
✔ Half of health users reported searching for information on lifestyle, diet, nutrition and exercise, medications, and alternative therapies.[7]

The Internet permits ease of access to cutting-edge medical knowledge and bridges the communication gap created by high-tech medicine. However, it also has serious drawbacks. According to a recent analysis, simple queries for terms such as *obesity* or *depression* often lead to irrelevant sites, relevant sites with incomplete information, or sites that are difficult for most consumers to understand.[8] Even when information is technically precise, people may not know how to interpret it properly.

The sale of Internet prescriptions has become a controversial issue in Canada and the United States.[9] The concerns are about public safety. Many physicians do not examine patients before they write prescriptions for those who are purchasing drugs on the Internet. Another concern is rooted in protecting the pharmaceutical industry's profitability. A large proportion of Internet prescription

▼ Table 13-1 Internet Health Users, by Age, Sex, and Type of Search, Household, Population Aged 18 or Older, Canada Excluding Territories, 2005

| Type of Search | 18 to 44 | | 45 or older | |
| --- | --- | --- | --- | --- |
| | Men | Women | Men | Women |
| | % | | % | |
| Lifestyle | 52 | 53 | 44 | 48 |
| Specific diseases | 49 | 55* | 59 | 66* |
| Specific symptoms | 48 | 49 | 43 | 43 |
| Drugs or medications | 34 | 41* | 44 | 48 |
| Health-care system | 22 | 20 | 19 | 15* |
| Alternative therapy | 19 | 26* | 23 | 27 |
| Surgeries | 15 | 16 | 18 | 17 |

Source: 2005 Canadian Internet Use Survey. Underhill, C., & McKeown, L. (2008, February). Getting a second opinion: Health information and the Internet. Statistics Canada. Health Reports. Catalogue no. 82-003-X. Available at www.statcan.ca/english/freepub/82-003-XIE/2008001/article/10515-en.pdf, page 3.

* Significantly different from estimate for men in same age group (p < 0.05)

sales are to customers in the United States, with estimates of upward of U.S. $1 billion in sales per year.

The Canadian Medical Protective Association (CMPA) has warned their members not to prescribe or co-sign prescriptions for Americans seeking prescription drugs, either on the Internet or in person. The Alberta College of Pharmacists is working on a new standard of practice and a code of ethics that would apply to all pharmacies, including those operating over the Internet.[10] However, presently there are more questions than answers in how to deal with the blend of technology and medicine.

Other "cyberdocs" offer "virtual house calls" with board-certified physicians who engage in private chat sessions on minor illnesses and prescribe medicine. In the future, video-conferencing may allow doctors to examine patients in cyberspace. However, there are no professional standards for doctors on the Internet, and experts advise caution. The doctor who treats your allergies may be an urologist or pathologist who is not up to date on new therapies or is unaware of potential side effects.

Health Canada is attempting to play a role in electronic health (e-health) issues. Health experts recognize that information and communications technology might help to overcome the challenges of delivering health care in Canada. Collection, management, and use of patient health information; convenient access to health education; and increased communication among health-care providers are all positive benefits of an e-health or tele-health system. However, ethical considerations and evaluation of the effectiveness of such a system need to be addressed to protect both medical professionals and the general public.[11]

Here are some specific guidelines for evaluating online health sites:[12]

✔ **Check the creator.** Websites are produced by health agencies, health-support groups, school health programs, health-product advertisers, health educators, health-education organizations, and provincial and federal governments. Read site headers and footers carefully to distinguish biased commercial advertisements from unbiased sites created by scientists and health agencies.

✔ **Look for possible bias.** Websites may be attempting to provide healthful information to consumers, but they also may be attempting to sell a product. Many sites are merely disguised advertisements.

✔ **Check the date.** If you are looking for the most recent research, check the date the page was created and last updated as well as the links. Several non-working links signal that the site isn't carefully maintained.

✔ **Check the references.** As with other health-education materials, Web documents should provide the reader with references. Unreferenced suggestions may be unwarranted, scientifically unsound, and possibly unsafe.

✔ **Consider the author.** Is he or she recognized in the field of health education or otherwise qualified to publish a health-information Web document? Does the author list his or her occupation, experience, and education?

# Evaluating Health News

Cure! Breakthrough! Medical miracle! These words make catchy headlines. Remember that although medical breakthroughs and cures do occur, most scientific progress is made one small step at a time.

Medical opinions invariably change over time, sometimes going from one extreme to another. For instance, several decades ago the treatment of choice for breast cancer was radical mastectomy—removal of the woman's breast, lymph nodes, and chest wall. Since then, much less extensive surgery (lumpectomy), coupled with chemotherapy or radiation, or both, has proven equally effective. Once individuals who had suffered heart attacks were advised to limit all physical activity. Today, a progressive exercise program is a standard component of rehabilitation.

Health researchers are struggling to find better ways of assessing what they know and need to know in order to offer more complete and balanced information to consumers. However, sometimes the only certainty is uncertainty. Try to gather as much background information and as many opinions as you can. Weigh them carefully—ideally with a trusted physician—and make the decision that seems best for you.

When reading a newspaper or magazine article, listening to a radio or television report about a medical advance, or searching the Internet, look for answers to the following questions:

✔ Who are the scientists involved? Are they recognized, legitimate health professionals? What are their credentials? Are they affiliated with respected medical or scientific institutions? Be wary of individuals whose degrees or affiliations are from institutions you've never heard of, and be sure that the person's educational background is in a discipline related to the area of research reported.

✔ Where did the scientists report their findings? The best research is published in peer-reviewed professional journals. One example is the *New England Journal of Medicine*. Research developments also may be reported at meetings of professional societies.[13]

✔ Is the information based on personal observations? Does the report include testimonials from cured patients or satisfied customers? If the answer to either question is yes, be wary.[14]

✔ Does the article, report, or advertisement include words like *amazing, secret,* or *quick*? Does it claim to be something the public has never seen or been offered before? Such sensationalized language is often a tip-off to a dubious treatment.

✔ Is someone trying to sell you something? Manufacturers who cite studies to sell a product have been known to embellish the truth.

✔ Does the information defy all common sense? Be skeptical. If something sounds too good to be true, it probably is.

## Quackery

Every year thousands of Canadians search for medical miracles that never happen. Millions of dollars are spent on medical **quackery,** unproven health products and services. Those who lose only money are the lucky ones. Many also waste precious time, during which their conditions worsen. Some suffer needless pain, along with crushed expectations. Far too many risk their lives on a false hope—and lose.

Watch out for marketing techniques such as *bait and switch,* where retailers advertise a product at a low price to lure you into their store, but are sold out when you arrive. Attempts are then made to persuade you to purchase a higher-quality product at a higher price. The *brand-loyalty approach* is also used to sell health products. A retailer or advertiser might try to convince you that a specific brand name means quality, but they do not tell you that in many cases the active ingredients of the product are the same as those in lower-priced products. *Product misrepresentation* is yet another approach used. If the sales pitch says that 9 out of 10 doctors endorse a certain product, be sure to ask questions such as: Which doctors? What are their credentials? Were they paid to endorse the product? It is also important to check out the legitimacy of health food or lifestyle stores. Where one health store might have reputable and qualified personnel, others might not.

In the fitness and health industry, there is a direct emphasis on physical appearance and sales pitches that attempt to make you believe that getting or staying fit is easy—no effort is needed to lose weight, become muscular, look great. Noted personalities are used to endorse products that they may not even use. Before and after pictures are also used to encourage you to buy the product. Computer technology is often the reason why the model looks terrific in the after picture. Multi-level marketing of nutrition supplements or health products is also a problem in Canada. Many fitness facilities hire people with no knowledge of medicine or health to sell, on commission, products such as nutrition supplements.

## Your Medical Rights

Certain rights in health care are recognized in Canada. Canadians have access to their own medical records and the right to have those records kept private. Privacy is becoming an issue as patient's records are now being computerized

## Strategies for Prevention

### Protecting Yourself Against Quackery

▲ Arm yourself with up-to-date information about your condition or disease from reputable organizations, such as the Canadian Institute for Health Information (CIHI).

▲ Ask for a written explanation of what a treatment does and why it works, evidence supporting all claims (not just testimonials), and published reports of the studies that have been done, including specifics on numbers treated, doses, and side effects.

▲ Be skeptical of self-styled "holistic practitioners," treatments supported by crusading groups, and endorsements from self-proclaimed experts or authorities.

▲ Don't quickly part with your money. Be especially careful because provincial medical plans and employee insurance companies won't reimburse for unproven therapies.

▲ Don't discontinue your current treatment without your physician's approval. Many physicians encourage supportive therapies—such as relaxation exercises, meditation, or visualization—as a supplement to standard treatments.

and stored in large databases. You have the right to receive treatment that is provided with a reasonable degree of care.[15] As a consumer, you have basic rights to help ensure that you know about any potential dangers, receive competent diagnosis and treatment, and retain control and dignity in your interactions with health-care professionals. You can designate someone else to make decisions about your care if and when you cannot.

Some hospitals in Canada have a patient advocate or representative. These individuals can help you communicate with physicians, make any special arrangements, and get answers to questions or complaints.

Canadians also have the right to give consent to donate an organ while alive or have organs removed in the event of an accident, injury, or illness that leaves them brain dead. However, you cannot agree to donate a body part for money or other compensation.

## Your Right to Information

By law, you have the right to give your informed consent for hospitalization, surgery, and other major treatments.

**Informed consent** is a right, not a privilege. Use this right to its fullest. Ask questions. Seek other opinions. Make sure that your expectations are realistic and that you understand the potential risks, as well as the possible benefits, of a prospective treatment. Informed consent is also required for research studies. You have the right to know whether a procedure is experimental.

# Canada's Health-Care System

In the past, when people were sick, they went to their family physician and paid in cash. Today, health care involves many more people, places, and processes. As a college or university student, you can turn to student health services if you get sick. There, a medical doctor may evaluate your symptoms and provide basic care, or you may rely on a primary-care physician in your hometown to perform regular checkups or manage a chronic condition. If you're injured in an accident, you probably will be treated at the nearest emergency room. If you become seriously ill and require highly specialized care, you may have to go to a hospital to receive treatment.

## A Brief History of Our Health-Care System

"The practice of medicine and the range and nature of treatment options has changed significantly since Medicare was introduced 40 years ago," said Roy Romanow, in his *2002 Final Report of the Commission on the Future of Health Care in Canada*.[16] What you might know and understand as health care today did look very different in the past.

The person credited with establishing Canada's health-care system is Tommy Douglas, the late premier of Saskatchewan. In 1948, his governing party, the Co-operative Commonwealth Federation (CCF), introduced a universal hospital insurance plan for the residents of the province. In 1957, his government introduced an insurance scheme for physician services.[17] Then, in 1964, the federal government, under the Hospital Insurance and Diagnostic Services Act (HIDSA), agreed to reimburse provinces for a portion of the costs of providing insurance to their residents. By 1972, all of the provinces had joined the plan, creating a nationwide Medicare program for hospital and physician services.[18]

In 1985, the Medical Care Act and the HIDSA were replaced by the Canada Health Act (CHA). The act is based on five principles: public administration, universality, accessibility, portability, and comprehensiveness.[19] These principles have become the conditions that provinces must abide by to receive federal transfer funds that support the national health insurance plan. The 13 interlocking provincial and territorial health insurance plans share common features and basic standards of coverage which ensure that all residents of Canada have reasonable access to medically necessary hospital and physician services on a prepaid basis and on uniform terms and conditions.[20] Residence in a province or territory is the basic requirement for insured health-care coverage. Each province determines minimum residence requirements.

We appear to be at a crossroads with regard to our Medicare system. Health-care costs are prohibitive, waiting lists are long, and there is a physician shortage in our country. More and more people are advocating a move toward private health care or public–private health-care partnerships. In April 2001, the prime minister established the Commission on the Future of Health Care in Canada and appointed Roy J. Romanow as the commissioner. Mr. Romanow's mandate was to review Medicare, engage Canadians in a national dialogue on its future, and make recommendations to enhance our health system's quality and sustainability. His assessment was that while Medicare is as sustainable as Canadians want it to be, we need to take steps toward transforming it into a truly national, more comprehensive, responsive, and accountable health-care system.[21]

The 47 recommendations in the report that outline actions in 10 critical areas are being reviewed. Currently, although health care is a highly political issue, movement on the recommendations has been slow.[22]

## What Are Federal, Provincial, and Territorial Health-Care Responsibilities?

The federal government is responsible for:[23]

✔ Setting and administering national principles or standards for the health-care system through the Canada Health Act.

✔ Assisting in the financing of provincial health-care services through fiscal transfers.

✔ Delivering direct health services to specific groups, including veterans, Native Canadians living on reserves, military personnel, inmates of federal penitentiaries, and the Royal Canadian Mounted Police.

✔ Fulfilling other health-related functions, such as health protection, disease prevention, and health promotion.

The provincial and territorial governments are responsible for:

✔ Managing and delivering health-care services.

✔ Planning, financing, and evaluating the provision of hospital care.

✔ Physician and allied health-care services.
✔ Managing some aspects of prescription care and public health.

We are fortunate to have one of the best medical systems in the world, and support for our public health-care system is still strong. In a 2003 Statistics Canada survey, 85 percent of Canadians were either very or somewhat satisfied with the medical care they had received within the last year.[24] Just across the border, in the United States, as many as 33 million Americans lack health insurance. Many others are underinsured. Nearly one in three young adults between ages 18 and 24 has no health insurance—the highest proportion of any age group.

## Canada's Health-Care Providers

According to the Canadian Institute for Health Information report—*Health Care in Canada 2007*—about 1.5 million people across the country work in health care. In 2005, there were two physicians for every 1000 people in Canada. As well, there was a decrease in the number of physicians leaving Canada and an increase in the number returning.[25] Registered nurses (RNs), licensed practical nurses (LPNs), and registered psychiatric nurses (RPNs) accounted for just under 50 percent of all health-care workers.[26] Licensed nurse practitioners are also working in various parts of Canada. They are registered nurses with additional education in health assessment, diagnosis, and management of illness and injury.[27]

The skills needed by health-care professionals working in Canada vary, and the scope of practice of health-care providers is changing. A number of younger doctors are seeing fewer patients than doctors their age did 10 years ago,[28] and there has been a decrease in the number of family doctors performing surgeries, delivering babies, and providing care to patients in a hospital setting, although more are doing mental-health counselling in their practices.[29] There are also many new initiatives in Canada to recruit and train nurses, since many RNs are leaving the workforce by age 55 instead of 65.

However, men and women are still entering medical schools, and many nursing programs have waiting lists for prospective students. According to the National Physician Survey, 2004, 79 percent of all physicians and other specialists stated that intellectual stimulation and challenge were factors leading to their career choice.[30]

Canada has many universities and colleges that train physicians. If you are interested in becoming a doctor, you can find out more about medical schools in Canada by accessing a directory of schools for careers in the medical and health-care service—www.canadian-universities.net/Schools/Medical-Schools.html. The Canadian Nurses Association provides information about nursing schools in Canada. Go to www.cna-aiic.ca/CNA/nursing/becoming/students/nursing_programs/default_e.aspx.

To become a doctor, you must earn an undergraduate degree and then attend medical school. Students in their final year of studies in medicine must take examinations set by the Medical Council of Canada before they can be licensed to practice. Medical students can decide if they would like to work as a general practitioner (GP) or a specialist. A GP has general knowledge in all health and medical areas. He or she will direct patients to specialists if more care is needed. Further specialist studies in various fields such as family medicine, internal medicine, and general surgery can be taken at a postgraduate level. Nurses must take academic courses, too. Nine university schools of nursing have accelerated programs that allow students to complete a Bachelor of Science in Nursing (BScN) in two or three years.[31] Many community and university colleges offer nursing-diploma programs.

Some other types of doctors include:

✔ *Gynecologists*—who deal with the care of women during pregnancy, childbirth, and recovery. They also diagnose and treat disorders that affect the female reproductive organs.
✔ *Dermatologists*—who specialize in skin physiology and pathology and diagnose and treat skin diseases.
✔ *Family practitioners*—who help diagnose long-term health issues that are passed on through generations.
✔ *Orthopedic doctors*—who deal with the prevention and correction of injuries or disorders of the skeletal system and muscles, joints, and ligaments.
✔ *Urologists*—who specialize in the diagnosis and treatment of diseases of the urinary tract and urogenital system.
✔ *Pediatricians*—who specialize in the care of infants and children.
✔ *Endocrinologists*—who study the glands and hormones and their related disorders, such as diabetes.
✔ *Oncologists*—who deal with the diagnosis, treatment, and prevention of tumours.

This list is by no means complete. A more comprehensive list is available at www.bookofdoctors.com.

Nurses can work in hospital settings, care homes, schools, and community-outreach programs. Nurse specialities include cardiovascular, critical care, emergency, gerontology, hospice palliative care, occupational health, and psychiatric and mental health nursing. More information about nursing careers is available through the Canadian Nurses Association at www.cna-aiic.ca.

Careers in the health-care field also include those in allied sectors. Dietitians, nutritionists, medical laboratory technicians, dentists, health-information educators, addiction counsellors, and pharmacists are just some examples. Working with an allied health professional may support personal health care. Temple[32] reports that many physicians in Canada have a weak knowledge of nutrition. So visiting a registered dietitian for sound advice on healthy eating might be beneficial.

# Complementary and Alternative Health Care (CAHC)

The last decade has seen an increase in the use of a broad range of therapies sometimes called complementary, alternative, unconventional, or holistic. Alternative treatments are typically given outside the mainstream medical system, and many have not been corroborated by clinical trials.[33]

The medical research community uses the term **complementary and alternative health care (CAHC)** to apply to all health-care approaches, practices, and treatments not widely taught in medical schools and not generally used in hospitals. They include many healing philosophies, approaches, and therapies, including preventive techniques designed to delay or prevent serious health problems before they start and **holistic** methods that focus on the whole person and the physical, mental, emotional, and spiritual aspects of well-being (see Table 13-2). Some examples are nutritional therapies, herbal and botanical therapies, physical therapies, body/energy or life-force therapies, mind-body practices, and complementary and alternative health systems such as traditional Chinese medicine, Ayurvedic medicine, First Nations healing traditions, naturopathic medicine, and environmental medicine.[34]

Fees for treatment vary from one health practice to another and from one province or territory to another. As a general rule, Canadians are expected to cover a large part of the cost of CAHC services. In some provinces, depending on the service, individuals must pay the entire cost of the treatment.[35]

▼ **Table 13-2 Use of Alternative Medicine or Therapies for Wellness in the Past 12 Months in Canada, by Therapy, 1997 and 2006**

|  | 1997 | 2006 |
| --- | --- | --- |
| Yoga | 86% | 92% |
| Aromatherapy | 66% | 87% |
| Prayer/spiritual practice | 83% | 85% |
| Special diet programs | 77% | 83% |
| Lifestyle diet | 87% | 83% |
| Relaxation techniques | 84% | 81% |
| Naturopathy | 69% | 81% |
| Massage | 66% | 72% |
| High dose/mega vitamins | 83% | 71% |
| Herbal therapies | 72% | 70% |
| Self-help group | 74% | 67% |
| Chelation | 100% | 65% |
| Biofeedback | 100% | 64% |
| Energy healing | 64% | 63% |
| Osteopathy | 100% | 61% |
| Homeopathy | 57% | 58% |
| Imagery techniques | 86% | 56% |
| Spiritual or religious healing by others | 59% | 56% |
| Chiropractor care | 46% | 55% |
| Acupuncture | 32% | 48% |
| Hypnosis | 78% | 45% |
| Folk remedies | 54% | 43% |

Base: Used therapy in past 12 months

Source: Esmail, N. (2008). Complementary and alternative medicine in Canada: Trends in use and public attitudes 1997–2006. Fraser Institute, *Public Policy Sources, 87*(May 2007), 3–53. Available at www.fraserinstitute.org/commerce.web/product_files/ComplementaryAlternativeMedicine.pdf, page 21.

## Why People Use Complementary and Alternative Therapies

Many Canadians try complementary and alternative health care for a variety of reasons. Most people who use CAHC say that it fits with their values and beliefs about life and health. They may have concerns about side effects from conventional medical treatments and drug therapies, or they may have had a disappointing experience with mainstream medicine.[36]

They often believe that body, mind, and spirit are all involved in health. According to several surveys, people believe that most physicians don't provide enough information on nutrition and exercise and ignore the social and spiritual aspects of care.[37]

Most Canadians who do try CAHC do so as a complementary health practice. They rarely abandon all conventional health care. People also tend to use complementary and alternative health-care practices for chronic conditions as well as potentially terminal illnesses such as HIV and cancer. They do not tend to use these treatments to treat conditions or injuries that require urgent care.[38]

The number of people who use CAHC varies by province, territory, and region. According to the Fraser Institute report, British Columbians use alternative medicine the most with 10.9 visits per year on average compared to 9.9 in Ontario, 8.8 in Alberta, 6.1 in Quebec, 5.5 in Saskatchewan and Manitoba, and 5.4 in Atlantic Canada.[39] Increased levels of income and education resulted in more use of alternative therapies.

## Julia Pritchard—A Young Woman's Dream of Medical School

Our human potential story for this chapter is about a young woman who grew up "wanting to be a doctor." Her story is one of commitment, tenacity, and belief in herself. It is also a story about a young woman who wants to make a difference.

Getting into medical school is not an easy task. In addition to excellent undergraduate marks, selection committees are looking for students who can take on leadership roles within our health-care system. In Julia's story, we see how she put the pieces of the "application puzzle" together and gained one of the revered places at the University of British Columbia's medical school. Her story also highlights her belief that career choice is not made from one conscious decision, but a lifetime of experiences that shape the idea of how we hope our lives to be.

When asked about her teenage years, Julia talks about her life as an elite competitive gymnast. "Gymnastics taught me self-discipline and self-motivation from a young age," says Julia. In a sport that can be very demanding both physically and emotionally, Julia soon learned that success was measured by setting well-defined short- and long-term goals, time management, and organizational skills. Little did she know that she was developing essential skills that would be vital in her path toward medical school.

Participation in a grade 10 Trek outdoor education program was another important experience for Julia. The focus on adventure, environmental education, and character development helped Julia grow from a shy young woman to someone who took on leadership roles. As Julia reflects on her participation in this program she says, "It is clear that teamwork is essential in today's multidisciplinary nature of medicine, and as a graduate of the Trek program, I gained enough self-confidence to both lead groups and also be effective in group decision-making."

However, it was Julia's volunteer work at *Camp Goodtimes,* a summer camp for children with cancer, that helped her discover her true inspiration

Julia Pritchard enjoying a family getaway on Galiano Island with her dog Samson.

for medicine. "Until this point, I had the ambition to become a physician, but I couldn't pinpoint why I had made that career goal. Working so closely with these children and their families and experiencing their strength and courage, I was transformed." She also learned that you get back what you give.

Work as a volunteer support worker with the Victoria Women's Sexual Assault Centre, as a scientist at the BC Cancer Research Centre, and as a research assistant at the Healthy Heart Society of British Columbia have challenged Julia's scientific thinking, problem-solving, and troubleshooting skills. Julia believes that, as a physician, these skills are essential in providing a treatment plan that balances the need to cure disease with any physical, emotional, or cultural limitations of the patient. This work has also introduced Julia to the Aboriginal culture's holistic approach to health care and helped her gain a broader understanding of the World Health Organization's definition of health as "a state of complete physical, mental, and social well-being and not merely the absence of disease or infirmity."

Taken together, all of these achievements and experiences have provided Julia with an excellent footprint on which to become a skilled and ethical physician. To quote from Julia's application to medical schools: "I believe I am prepared, through my academic progress; I am a participant, shown through my volunteerism and advocacy activities; and I am professional, shown by my work ethic and drive toward lifelong learning. I am ready to become a physician."

Julia recognizes that her journey has only just started with her acceptance to the Vancouver Fraser Medical Program at the UBC. She knows that her early experiences have helped her to get into medical school, but she also believes that they will assist her to become a self-motivated, lifelong learner who will emerge as a skilled, yet self reflective, physician. Her advice to other students who may be considering a career as a medical professional: "Set goals, work hard, ask for help when needed, and

understand that we all have special gifts and skills to share with others. We can all make a difference in this world, and we can do this by trusting in our own abilities and reaching out with care and compassion."

As Julia's instructor in a course titled "Human Wellness and Potential" and the Canadian author of this textbook, I am honoured that Julia was willing to share her story of success. I look forward to Julia's graduation from medical school and know that we will be in good hands as she begins her career as a physician. All the best, Julia.

## The X&Y Files

## Men and Women as Health-Care Consumers

The genders differ significantly in the way they use health-care services. Women see more doctors than men, take more prescription drugs, are hospitalized more, and control the spending of three of every four health-care dollars.

Many experts believe that the need for birth control and reproductive health services gets women into the habit of making regular visits to health-care professionals, primarily gynecologists. There are no comparable specialists for men, who tend to visit urologists (specialists in male reproductive organs) only when they develop problems. Men also are conditioned to take a stoic, tough-it-out attitude to early symptoms of a disease.

Men feel they are not allowed to manifest illness unless it's overt, says family practitioner Martin Miner, who has conducted research on men and health care. One reason men die earlier than women is because of the length of time they wait to go for treatment.

The genders also differ in the symptoms and syndromes they develop. For instance, men are more

prone to back problems, muscle sprains and strains, allergies, insomnia, and digestive problems. Men develop heart disease about a decade earlier in life than women. More men develop ulcers and hernias; women are more likely to get gallbladder disease and irritable bowel syndrome. An estimated 3 to 6 percent of men suffer from migraines, compared with 15 to 17 percent of women. Yet women and men spend similar proportions of their lifetimes—about 81 percent—free of disability.

The genders also differ in access to health services. Women and men are about equally likely to use complementary and alternative medicine—but different types. Men outnumber women in use of chiropractic services and acupuncture, while women are more likely to try herbal medicine, mind-body remedies, folk remedies, movement and exercise techniques, and prayer or spiritual practices. Both sexes turn to alternative treatments for the same reason: a desire for greater control over their health.

## Doctors and CAHC

**Integrative medicine,** which combines selected elements of both conventional and alternative medicine in a comprehensive approach to diagnosis and treatment, is gaining greater acceptance within the medical community.[40] More

medical schools are teaching courses in CAHC, and some physicians say they've recommended alternative therapies to their patients at least once in the preceding year.[41]

Many doctors are calling upon their colleagues not to dismiss or embrace CAHC but to consider each approach thoroughly and evaluate its potential to benefit patients.

In a survey of physicians, most—60 percent more women than men—wanted to learn more about CAHC. The most common reasons were "to dissuade patient if alternative method is unsafe and/or ineffective" and "to recommend method to patient if safe and effective." The physicians who felt "very positive" or "somewhat positive" about CAHC therapies were more interested in education but no more comfortable in discussing CAHC with patients.[42]

The World Health Organization has released a global plan to address the safety of traditional and complementary medicines. The strategy aims to help countries regulate such medicines and to make them safer and more accessible to their populations.[43]

Fundamental to integrative care is the necessity of establishing links between the two types of health-care options and enhancing communication between patients, doctors, complementary health-care providers, and government agencies that oversee health care in Canada. Consumers have been bridging this gap and appear to have been the driving force behind the current move toward integrative health care.[44]

## Is Complementary and Alternative Health Care Safe and Effective?

Safety and effectiveness have specific meanings in health care. Health practices are usually considered safe if the benefits outweigh the risks. By scientifically studying a practice, under controlled conditions, researchers can determine whether a practice is harmful. Health practices are considered to be effective if they are helpful when used or experienced in a research study, under usual conditions.[45]

Scientifically studying the safety and effectiveness of complementary and alternative health practices is relatively new. Much of the information about CAHC has been based upon opinion—anecdotal evidence and folklore, not controlled studies. The research that has been done has focused on medicinal herbs, chiropractic, homeopathy, and acupuncture.[46]

The Canadian Complementary Medical Association (CCMA) is a non-profit medical society dedicated to the educational and political support of physicians interested in and practising complementary medicine. This association is encouraging scientific research and development of sound, innovative therapies and preventive medical measures. It is also promoting continuing medical education among physicians in a diverse spectrum of complementary medical therapies and is attempting to increase public knowledge and understanding of CAHC through educational programs.[47] As studies are conducted, some alternative therapies are gaining acceptance, while others have shown little or no demonstrable benefits.[48]

Many people have criticized health-care providers for giving alternative therapies a "free ride" by not demanding the same proof and regulation required of traditional treatments.[49] In Canada, training standards have been set by a governing organization for a particular health practice. Among these licensed therapies, training standards are not necessarily "standard." They may vary widely from province to province or territory. For example, chiropractors must be registered or licensed, and the Council of Chiropractic Education of Canada supervises chiropractic education in Canada. Homeopaths are not regulated in Canada, although the Canadian Association of Homeopathic Physicians requires training and a clinical internship.[50]

If you decide to seek complementary and alternative health care, ask yourself the following questions:

✔ Is it safe? The fact that a treatment does not require hospitalization or surgery does not guarantee it is safe.
✔ Is it effective? Research the type of therapy you are considering. Know the risks.
✔ Is the practitioner qualified? Find out what licences are necessary for the practitioner to practise. What is his or her educational background?
✔ What has been the experience of other people who have been cared for by the practitioner you are considering?
✔ What are the costs? Many CAHC services are not covered fully by provincial medical plans. Find out if your extended health benefits cover any of the charges.

## Natural Health Products

In response to growing concerns about the regulatory environment for Natural Health Products (NHPs), a term used to describe a variety of products such as herbal medicines, homeopathic remedies, and nutritional supplements, Health Canada developed a regulatory framework that came into effect January 1, 2004. The Natural Health Products Directorate (NHPD) now oversees regulations for all NHPs sold in Canada. A two-year transition period for site licensing and a six-year transition period for product licensing is allowing the industry to gradually adjust to these new requirements.[51]

All NHPs sold in Canada now require pre-market assessment and authorization of their safety and effectiveness. A listing of each product's medicinal and non-medicinal ingredients must also appear on product labels. Although the regulations for these products are not embraced fully by all alternative health-care practitioners and NHP manufacturers, it is hoped that they will allow for industry innovation in bringing new products to the market while ensuring that Canadians have access to NHPs that are safe, effective, and of high quality.[52]

## Alternative Health-Care Programs and Services

### Aboriginal Healing

Many Aboriginal health-care providers experience and understand the gaps in the current health-care system for Aboriginal people. These gaps include access and appropriateness of services. Aboriginal healing is a way of integrating health services available through our Canadian health system and using a uniquely Aboriginal perspective that incorporates the four aspects of health—spiritual, emotional, intellectual, and physical. Healing circles, sweat lodges, traditional medicine, and the use of medicine wheels and healing ceremonies are some of the approaches that are being used to support the health and wellness of Aboriginal people. One example is the Turtle Island Native Network, which has a special focus on healing and wellness. You can access this site at www.turtleisland.org/healing/healing-wellness.htm.

### Acupuncture

An ancient Chinese form of medicine, **acupuncture** is based on the philosophy that a cycle of energy circulating through the body controls health. Pain and disease are the result of a disturbance in the energy flow, which can be corrected by inserting long, thin needles at specific points along longitudinal lines, or *meridians,* throughout the body. Each point controls a different corresponding part of the body. Once inserted, the needles are rotated gently back and forth or charged with a small electric current for a short time. Western scientists aren't sure exactly how acupuncture works, but some believe that the needles alter the functioning of the nervous system.

There are two main approaches to training in Canada within this field. Acupuncture training can be part of a degree in Traditional Chinese Medicine (TCM) or taught as a stand-alone practice. Medical acupuncture training is geared toward licensed health professionals, such as doctors, physiotherapists, dentists, naturopaths, and chiropractors.[53]

A NIH consensus development panel that evaluated current research into acupuncture concluded that there is "clear evidence" that acupuncture can control nausea and vomiting in patients after surgery or while undergoing chemotherapy and relieve postoperative dental pain.[54] Ongoing studies are evaluating the efficacy of acupuncture for chronic headaches and migraines.

In *acupressure,* the therapist uses his or her finger and thumb to stimulate certain points, relieve pain, and relax muscles. **Reflexology** is based on the theory that massaging certain points on the foot or hand relieves stress or pain in

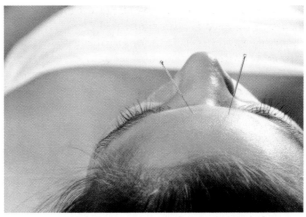

▲ The ancient Chinese practice of acupuncture produces healing through the insertion and manipulation of needles at specific points throughout the body. The procedure is not painful.

corresponding parts of the body.[55] These methods seem most effective in easing chronic pain, arthritis, and withdrawal from nicotine, alcohol, or drugs.

### Ayurveda

**Ayurveda** is a traditional form of medical treatment in India, where it has evolved over thousands of years. Its basic premise is that illness stems from incorrect mental attitudes, diet, and posture. Practitioners use a discipline of exercise, meditation, herbal medication, and proper nutrition. In India, students enter Bachelors of Ayurvedic Medicine and Surgery programs after high school graduation. In North America, portions of this program of study are taught in general-interest courses and programs for health professionals.

### Biofeedback

**Biofeedback** uses machines that measure temperature or skin responses and then relays this information to the subject. People can learn to control usually involuntary functions, such as circulation to the hands and feet, tension in the jaws, and heartbeat rates. Biofeedback has been used to treat dozens of ailments, including asthma, epilepsy, pain, and Reynaud's disease (a condition in which the fingers become painful and white when exposed to cold). Some extended health-benefit plans now cover biofeedback treatments.

### Chiropractic

**Chiropractic** is a treatment method based on the theory that many human diseases are caused by misalignment of the bones (subluxation). Each provincial chiropractic

© Terry Walsh/Shutterstock.

© iStockphoto.com/Hector Joseph Lumang

▲ A chiropractor can help relieve shoulder and back pain; herbal medicines are a popular form of alternative medicine.

regulatory body has the authority to grant a licence to practise chiropractic. Registered or licensed chiropractors, or D.C.s (Doctor of Chiropractic), must complete a four- to five-year course of full-time study.[56] Research in the last 10 years has demonstrated its efficacy for acute lower back pain. Research is also being conducted on other potential benefits, including headaches and arthritis, but findings are inconclusive at this time. Some medical professionals do not recommend using chiropractic for any condition not clearly related to disorders of the back or neck.[57]

## Herbs, Botanical Medicines, and Dietary Supplements

Herbs, **botanical medicines**, and dietary supplements are the most popular form of complementary and alternative health care in North America. In 2002, two out of three Canadians said they had used a natural health product in the past month. That same year, Canadians spent about $1.8 billion on herbs and supplements.[58] Natural health-care products are used to treat both internal and external conditions. They can be taken by mouth or applied to the body. They are sold in many different forms—raw herbs and teas, salves and creams, liquid extracts, and tablets or capsules.

Natural health-care products are not necessarily safe just because they are from natural sources. Some may cause side effects or allergic reactions. Others may be harmful to people with certain health conditions, such as pregnancy or heart disease. They may also interact with other medications, even non-prescription drugs such as aspirin (see Table 13-3). One example is St. John's wort, which affects the action of drugs such as the anti-clotting agent warfarin (Coumadin). When taken with dextromethorphan, an ingredient in cough syrup, St. John's wort can cause

serotonin syndrome, a potentially fatal condition characterized by rapid pulse, high fever, and convulsions. Another example is the amphetamine-like herb called *ephedra,* or Ma huang, sold as an energy booster and weight-loss aid. It can cause dangerous rises in blood pressure and speed up the heart rate. More than 800 injuries and 17 deaths have been linked to this herb.[59] It is important to tell your doctor about any natural health products you are taking—especially when he or she may be prescribing medications.

## Homeopathy

**Homeopathy** is based on three fundamental principles: "like cures like"; treatment must always be individualized and holistic; and less is more—the idea that increasing dilution (and lowering the dosage) can increase efficacy.[60] Doses of animal, vegetable, or mineral substances are administered as serially diluted solutions. The more diluted the solution, the stronger it is thought to be—the opposite of the way we usually think about the strength of pharmaceutical drugs. Homeopathic remedies may be given directly as drops, or the diluted solution may be sprayed onto granules or powder. Remedies taken in solid forms are held in the mouth until they dissolve—they are not to be swallowed.

## Massage Therapy

**Massage therapy** is a general term for a number of techniques that involve manipulation of the muscles and connective tissues. Massage is used to relieve muscle tension and stress, improve flexibility, and enhance a patient's sense of well-being. Different types of massage vary with approaches that range from the very light touches used in lymphatic drainage massage to deep tissue manipulation. Examples are Swedish massage, Ayurvedic massage, Thai massage, and Shiatsu massage.

Provincial governing bodies called "Colleges" set training requirements for the profession in B.C., Ontario, and Newfoundland and Labrador. In the other provinces and territories, massage therapy is overseen by professional associations. The Canadian Massage Therapist Alliance is urging all provincial and territorial governments to regulate the profession of massage therapy.[61]

## Naturopathy

**Naturopathy** or naturopathic medicine is a comprehensive, holistic health system that incorporates therapies from traditional Chinese medicine, Ayurveda, homeopathy, and Western herbalism, as well as nutritional approaches, body therapies, and other healing practices. This system also

## ▼ Table 13-3 Some Popular Herbal Remedies

| Herb | Used For | Does It Work? | Warning |
|------|----------|---------------|---------|
| Acidophilus | Diarrhea, digestive problems, upset stomach, or yeast infections caused by use of antibiotics | Acidophilus, either in live lactobacillus acidophilus cultures in yogurt or in capsules, can restore the body's normal bacterial balance. | Refrigerate to preserve potency. |
| Aloe vera | Sunburn, cuts, burns, eczema, psoriasis | In studies on both humans and animals, aloe vera applied directly to the skin has been shown to speed healing and have antibacterial, anti-inflammatory, and mild anesthetic effects. | Refrigerate gel to extend its shelf life. |
| Chamomile | Relaxation, better sleep, stomachaches, menstrual cramps | Laboratory and animal studies indicate that chamomile's active compounds have properties that combat inflammation, bacterial infection, and spasms. | People allergic to plants in the daisy family, such as ragweed, may have an allergic reaction. |
| Echinacea | Colds and flu | Inconsistent findings, although one study found that flu sufferers who used Echinacea extract recovered more quickly than others. | Use for more than eight weeks at a time may lessen its effectiveness and suppress immunity. Should not be taken by pregnant women and those with diabetes, tuberculosis, or autoimmune disorders. |
| Garlic | Fighting infection, preventing heart disease and cancer, stimulating the immune system | Extensive laboratory and animal studies and a review of clinical trials have shown that the active ingredient in garlic has anti-infective and anti-tumour properties and lowers cholesterol. | Check with your doctor if you take blood-thinning medication, including aspirin or ibuprofen, because garlic also is an anticoagulant. |
| Ginkgo biloba | Improving memory, cognition, and circulation | There is some evidence that ginkgo biloba can help stabilize mental deterioration in patients with early Alzheimer's disease or stroke-related dementia. One study found that healthy seniors who took ginkgo performed mental tasks better. | Do not take with aspirin because of the risk of excessive bleeding. Should not be used during pregnancy. Side effects include upset stomach, headache, and an allergic skin reaction. |
| Ginseng | Improving mental and physical energy and stamina | Small studies have shown that ginseng can help improve mental performance and respiratory function during exercise. | If used for more than two weeks, ginseng can cause nervousness and heart palpitations, especially in those with high blood pressure. |
| Goldenseal | Colds, allergies, upper respiratory tract infections | Little research has been done, but some laboratory and animal studies suggest that one of goldenseal's components may have some antibiotic and antihistamine effects. | Goldsenseal should not be used instead of traditional antibiotics or for more than ten days at a time. Long-term use may interfere with the normal bacterial balance in the digestive system. |
| St. John's wort | Anxiety and depression | Older studies showing benefits had serious flaws. Recent, more rigorous research has shown that St. John's wort is not effective against major depression. | Side effects include stomach pain, bloating, constipation, nausea, fatigue, dry mouth. St. John's wort should never be taken in combination with prescription antidepressants. |

emphasizes natural remedies, such as sun, water, heat, and air, as treatments for disease. Naturopathic doctors take health histories and perform physical examinations using standard diagnostic instruments and laboratory tests. Lifestyle information is also often requested.[62]

Naturopathic doctors (N.D.s) must complete pre-admission requirements that include three years of pre-medical studies at an accredited university in Canada. Then they must complete four years of professional training at a recognized college of naturopathic medicine.

## Physiotherapy

**Physiotherapy** is sometimes considered a complementary or alternative health-care profession. Due to its popularity in Canada, it is now seen by some medical professionals as being part of the primary health-care system. Physiotherapists, also known as physical therapists, are educated and trained to assess, restore, and maintain physical function. They can assess the strength and endurance of muscles. They can also assess the impact of an injury or a physical disability on physical function. They provide treatment with modalities such as ultrasound and assist in program planning and exercise rehabilitation to restore movement and reduce pain.[63]

The minimum entry-level educational qualification to practise physiotherapy in Canada is a Baccalaureate-level degree. Many programs also offer post-graduate programs in physiotherapy, rehabilitation, or related disciplines at the Master's or Doctoral level. They are affiliated with the Accreditation Council of Canadian Physiotherapy Academic Programs (ACCPAP).[64] Some physiotherapists take advanced training in specific areas such as orthopedics and sports physiotherapy.

If you are interested in finding out about other alternative therapies such as Alexander technique, aromatherapy, reiki, therapeutic touch, and visualization, you can access the Public Health Agency of Canada at www.phac-aspc.gc.ca/chn-rcs/cah-acps-eng.php?rd=complement_eng.

**CHAPTER 13 Making This Chapter Work for You**

1. Which of the following statements is *false*?
   a. Home health tests are available for pregnancy.
   b. Vital signs include temperature, blood pressure, pulse, and cholesterol level.
   c. Health expenditures in Canada are expected to continue to rise in the next five years.
   d. Most students have received some type of health information from their college or university.

2. Which of the following statements about health information on the Internet is true?
   a. Chat rooms are the most reliable source of accurate medical information.
   b. Physicians who have websites must adhere to a strict set of standards set by the Canadian Medical Association.
   c. Government-sponsored sites such as that of Health Canada and the Canadian Health Network are reliable sources of accurate health-care information.
   d. The Internet is a safe and cost-effective source of prescription drugs.

3. Patients have all the rights below *except* which of the following?
   a. access to their medical records
   b. medical care that meets accepted standards of quality
   c. to donate a body part for compensation
   d. to leave the hospital against their physician's advice

4. Informed consent means
   a. the patient has informed the doctor of his or her symptoms and has consented to treatment.
   b. the physician has informed the patient about the treatment to be given and has consented to administer the treatment.
   c. the patient has informed the doctor of his or her symptoms, and the doctor has consented to administer treatment.
   d. the physician has informed the patient about the treatment to be given, and the patient has consented to the treatment.

5. People use complementary and alternative therapies
   a. to spend less money on health care.
   b. to take an active role in their own treatment.
   c. to show their disdain for the medical establishment.
   d. to take more prescription drugs.

6. Examples of complementary and alternative therapies include all of the following *except*
   a. psychiatry.
   b. acupuncture.
   c. chiropractic.
   d. homeopathy.

7. Herbal remedies that appear to have positive health effects include
   a. ayurveda for controlling asthma.
   b. acidophilus for improving memory.
   c. aloe vera for diabetes.
   d. garlic for preventing infection and tumour growth.

8. Which statement is *false*?
   a. Acupuncture has been shown to control nausea in patients after surgery.
   b. Reflexologists massage points on the foot or hand to relieve stress or pain in corresponding parts of the body.
   c. People can learn to control involuntary functions through biofeedback.
   d. Naturopathy is based on the premise that "like cures like."

9. Which statement is true regarding health care in Canada?
   a. Medicare was designed after a private-care system.
   b. Provincial residency is not a requirement for Medicare.
   c. Canadians have reasonable access to medically necessary hospital and physician services on a prepaid basis.
   d. Canadians have a fee-for-service medical system.

10. Physiotherapists provide all services listed below *except*
   a. assess muscular strength.
   b. prescribe medication.
   c. assist in exercise rehabilitation.
   d. assess the physical limitations of an injury.

Answers to these questions can be found on page 450.

## Self Responsibility

*The first wealth is health.*

**Emerson**

Sometimes the pressures of studying and working prevent students from assessing their health and accessing health care. Have you been ignoring some signs and symptoms of health-related issues? If so, how can you move from contemplation to preparation to action?

## Social Responsibility

*The patient should be made to understand that he or she must take charge of his [or her] own life. Don't take your body to the doctor as if he [or she] were a repair shop.*

**Quentin Regestein**

Taking responsibility for our own health is an important step toward living life to its fullest.

Taking care of yourself allows you to then take care of others when they need it. Try to think of self-care as a path to personal potential.

## Critical Thinking

1. Have you used any complementary or alternative approaches to health care? If so, were you satisfied with the results? How did your experience with the CAHC practitioner compare with your most recent experience with a traditional medical practitioner?

2. Jocelyn has been experiencing a great deal of fatigue and frequent headaches for the past couple of months. She doesn't have a family doctor and doesn't want to spend the time trying to find one. So she did some research on the Internet about ways to relieve her symptoms and was considering taking a couple of herbal supplements that were touted as potential treatments. If she asked you for your advice, what would you tell her? Do you think self-care is appropriate in this situation?

If your textbook package includes CengageNOW™, go to http://west.cengagenow.com/ilrn/ to link to CengageNOW™ for Health, your online study tool. First take the **Pre-test** for this chapter to get your personalized **Study Plan,** which will identify topics you need to review and direct you to the appropriate resources. Then take the **Post-test** to determine what concepts you have mastered and what you still need work on.

## SITES & BYTES

### Aboriginal Healing Foundation
**www.ahf.ca**

The site has articles, educational material, stories, and links to other agencies and organizations that promote awareness of healing issues.

### Building on Values: The Future of Health Care in Canada—Final Report November 2002
**www.cbc.ca/healthcare/final_report.pdf**

A comprehensive report on Canada's health care system by Roy J. Romanow, Commissioner. Forty-seven recommendations provide a roadmap for reforming and renewing our health-care system.

### Canadian Institute for Health Information (CIHI)
**www.cihi.ca**

This site offers current health research, quick statistics, client services, information about health standards, and an annual report titled *Health Care in Canada.*

### Complementary and alternative medicine in Canada: Trends in use and public attitudes 1997–2006 (Fraser Institute, *Public Policy Sources,* 87[May 2007], 3–53)
**www.fraserinstitute.org/commerce.web/ product_files/ComplementaryAlternativeMedicine.pdf**

A current and comprehensive report on complementary and alternative medicine in Canada.

Please note that links are subject to change. If you find a broken link, use a search engine such as www.google.ca and search for the website by typing in keywords.

**InfoTrac® College Edition Activity**   Caulfield, T.A., & Feasby, C. (2001). Potions, promises and paradoxes: Complementary medicine and alternative medicine and malpractice law in Canada. *Health Law Journal,* Annual, 183–203.

1. How do the authors define complementary and alternative medicine in this article?

2. What do the authors say about the legal obligations of physicians who provide information or treatment of complementary and alternative medicine?

3. Why do you think there is so much public interest in complementary and alternative medicine?

You can find additional readings relating to traditional and complementary health care with InfoTrac® College Edition, an online library of more than 5000 journals and publications. Follow the instructions for accessing InfoTrac® that were packaged with your textbook; then search for articles using a keyword search.

For additional links and resources, visit our text-specific website at www.health.nelson.com.

## Key Terms

The terms listed here are used within the chapter on the page indicated. Definitions of the terms are in the Glossary at the end of this book.

acupuncture 353
Ayurveda 353
biofeedback 353
botanical medicines 354
chiropractic 353

complementary and
   alternative health care
   (CAHC) 349
holistic 349
homeopathy 354

informed consent 347
integrative medicine 351
massage therapy 354
naturopathy 354
physiotherapy 356

quackery 346
reflexology 353
vital signs 344

## References

1. Canadian Institute for Health Information. Health care in Canada 2007. Ottawa: CIHI 2007. Available at http://secure.cihi.ca/cihiweb/products/hcic2007_e.pdf.
2. Public Health Agency of Canada. (2003, March 21). Publications. Perspectives on complementary and alternative health care. Available at www.phac-aspc.gc.ca/publicat/pcahc-pacps/pdf/comp_define.pdf.
3. Esmail, N. (2007, May). Complementary and alternative medicine in Canada: Trends in use and public attitudes 1997–2006. Fraser Institute, *Public Policy Sources, 87,* 3–53. Available at www.fraserinstitute.org/commerce.web/product_files/ComplementaryAlternativeMedicine.pdf.
4. Swinford, P. (2002). Advancing the health of students: A rationale for college health programs. *Journal of American College Health, 50*(6), 261.
5. Ardell, D. (1977). *High level wellness: An alternative to doctors, drugs and disease,* tenth edition. Berkeley, CA: Ten Speed Press, p. 94.
6. Underhill, C., & McKeown, L. (2008, February). Getting a second opinion: Health information and the Internet. Statistics Canada. Health Reports. Catalogue no. 82-003-X. Available at www.statcan.ca/english/freepub/82-003-XIE/2008001/article/10515-en.pdf.
7. Ibid.
8. Good health is hard to find on the Internet. (2001). *Medicine & Health, 55*(21), 5.
9. Morgan, S., & Hurley, J. (2004). Internet pharmacy: Prices on the up-and-up. Analysis. *Canadian Medical Association Journal, 170*(6), 945.
10. Gregoire, L. (2003). Alberta MDs warned not to co-sign American prescriptions. *Canadian Medical Association Journal, 168*(7), 886.
11. Ibid.
12. British Columbia Medical Association. (n.d.). Finding health information on the web (brochure). Available at www.bcma.org/files/web_info.pdf.
13. Wilson, P. (2002). How to find the good and avoid the bad or ugly: A short guide to tolls for rating quality of health information on the Internet. Education and debate. *British Medical Journal, 324,* 598–602.
14. Gagliardi, A., & Jadad, A.R. (2002). Examination of instruments used to rate quality of health information on the Internet: Chronicle of a voyage with an unclear destination. *British Medical Journal, 324,* 569–73.
15. Flood, C., & Epps, T. (2001, October 9). Can a patient's bill of rights address concerns about waiting lists? A draft working paper. Health Law Group, Faculty of Law, University of Toronto.
16. Romanow, R.J. (2002). Building on values: The future of health care in Canada—Final report. Commission on the Future of Health Care in Canada. National Library of Canada. Available at www.cbc.ca/healthcare/final_report.pdf.

17. Canadian Medicine: Doctors and Discoveries. (n.d.). Part III The Nature of Health Care Delivery. Thomas C. Douglas: The father of Canadian health care. Available at www.mta.ca/about_canada/study_guide/doctors/index.html.
18. Health Canada. (2008, February 6). Canada Health Act Annual Report 2006–2007. Canada Health Act overview. Chapter 1. Available at www.hc-sc.gc.ca/hcs-sss/pubs/cha-lcs/2006-cha-lcs-ar-ra/chap_1-eng.php.
19. Ibid.
20. Ibid.
21. Romanow, R.J. (2002). Building on values: The future of health care in Canada—Final report. Commission on the Future of Health Care in Canada. National Library of Canada. Available at www.cbc.ca/healthcare/final_report.pdf.
22. Ibid.
23. Health Canada. (2008, February 6). Canada Health Act Annual Report 2006–2007. Canada Health Act overview. Chapter 1. Available at www.hc-sc.gc.ca/hcs-sss/pubs/cha-lcs/2006-cha-lcs-ar-ra/chap_1-eng.php.
24. Canadian Institute for Health Information. (2007). *Health care in Canada 2007.* Ottawa: CIHI. Available at http://secure.cihi.ca/cihiweb/dispPage.jsp?cw_page=AR_43_E.
25. Canadian Institute for Health Information. (2008, October 16). Number of physicians who moved abroad or returned from abroad 1969–2006. Available at http://secure.cihi.ca/cihiweb/en/smdb_2006_fig8_e.html.
26. Canadian Institute for Health Information. (2008, October 16). Quick Stats. Health human resources—Physicians and nurses. Available at http://secure.cihi.ca/cihiweb/dispPage.jsp?cw_page=statistics_results_topic_physicians_e&cw_topic=Health%20Human%20Resources&cw_subtopic=Physicians.
27. Canadian Nurses Association. (2005, July 2). Nurse practitioners a viable solution to health care access. News release. Available at www.cna-nurses.ca/CNA/nursing/statistics/default_e.aspx.
28. Watson, D.E., et al. (2004). Family physician workloads and access to care in Winnipeg: 1991–2001. *Canadian Medical Association Journal, 171*(4), pp. 339–42.
29. Canadian Institute for Health Information. (2004). *The evolving role of Canada's family physicians: 1992–2001.* Ottawa, ON: Author.
30. National physician survey, 2004. (2007, July 5). College of Family Physicians of Canada (CFPC), Canadian Medical Association (CMA), Royal College of Physicians and Surgeons of Canada (RCPSC). Available at www.cfpc.ca/English/cfpc/research/janus%20project/nps/default.asp?s=1.
31. Canadian Institute for Health Information. (2007). *Health care in Canada 2007.* Ottawa: CIHI. Available at http://secure.cihi.ca/cihiweb/dispPage.jsp?cw_page=AR_43_E.

32. Temple, N.J. (1999). Survey of nutrition knowledge of Canadian physicians. *Journal of the American College of Nutrition, 18,* 26–29.

33. Public Health Agency of Canada. (2008, April 1). Complementary and alternative health. Available at www.phac-aspc.gc.ca/chn-rcs/cah-acps-eng.php?rd=complement_eng.

34. Ibid.

35. Esmail, N. (2007, May). Complementary and alternative medicine in Canada: Trends in use and public attitudes 1997–2006. Fraser Institute, *Public Policy Sources, 87,* 3–53. Available at www.fraserinstitute.org/commerce.web/product_files/ComplementaryAlternativeMedicine.pdf.

36. Ibid.

37. Vernarec, E. (2002). Why do patients turn to CAM? *RN, 65*(5), 25.

38. British Columbia Health Guide. (2007, October 1). Complementary medicine. www.bchealthguide.org/kbase/topic/special/aa63785/sec1.htm.

39. Esmail, N. (2007, May). Complementary and alternative medicine in Canada: Trends in use and public attitudes 1997–2006. Fraser Institute, *Public Policy Sources, 87,* 3–53. Available at www.fraserinstitute.org/commerce.web/product_files/ComplementaryAlternativeMedicine.pdf.

40. Rees, L., & Weil, A. (2001). Integrated medicine imbues orthodox medicine with the values of complementary medicine. *British Medical Journal, 322*(7279), 119.

41. Berman, B. (2001). Complementary medicine and medical education: Teaching complementary medicine offers a way of making teaching more holistic. *British Medical Journal, 33*(7279), 121.

42. Winslow, L.C., & Shapiro, H. (2002). Physicians want education about complementary and alternative medicine to enhance communication with their patients. *Archives of Internal Medicine, 162*(10), 1176.

43. WHO considers traditional and complementary medicine. (2002). *British Medical Journal, 324*(7348), 1234.

44. Natural health products and complementary and alternative health care. (2004, July 20). Applied research and analysis directorate (ARAD). *Health Policy Research Bulletin, 1*(7), 6.

45. Esmail, N. (2007, May). Complementary and alternative medicine in Canada: Trends in use and public attitudes 1997–2006. Fraser Institute, *Public Policy Sources, 87,* 3–53. Available at www.fraserinstitute.org/commerce.web/product_files/ComplementaryAlternativeMedicine.pdf.

46. Ibid.

47. The Canadian Complementary Medical Association (CCMA). (n.d.). About the CCMA. Available at www.ccmadoctors.ca/about_the_ccma.htm.

48. Jonas, W. (2002, September). Policy, the public, and priorities in alternative medicine research. *Annals of the American Academy of Political and Social Science, 29.*

49. Nahin, R., & Straus, S. (2001). Research into complementary and alternative medicine: Problems and potential. *British Medical Journal, 33*(7279), 161.

50. Park, J. (2005, March). Use of alternative health care. Statistics Canada. *Health Reports, 16*(2), 39–42.

51. Natural health products and complementary and alternative health care. (2004, July 20). Applied research and analysis directorate (ARAD). *Health Policy Research Bulletin, 1*(7).

52. Ibid.

53. Alternative Medicine Examiners Council of Canada. (AMECC). (n.d.). Complementary and alternative medicine education. Available at www.cpmdq.com/htm/govcandiencouncil.htm.

54. Cummings. M. (2001). Commentary: Controls for acupuncture—Can we finally see the light? *British Medical Journal, 322*(7302), 1578.

55. Reflexology Association of Canada. (n.d.). Available at www.reflexologycanada.ca.

56. Canadian Chiropractic Association. (2008). Home. Chiropractic education. Available at www.ccachiro.org/Client/cca/cca.nsf/web/Chiropractic%20Education?OpenDocument.

57. Canadian Chiropractic Association. (2008). Home. Facts and FAQ's. Chiropractic treatment and patient safety. Available at www.ccachiro.org.

58. Public Health Agency of Canada. (2006, December 15). Healthy Living. Safe use of natural health products. Available at www.hc-sc.gc.ca/hl-vs/iyh-vsv/med/nat-prod-eng.php.

59. Haller, C., & Benowitz, N. (2000). Adverse cardiovascular and central nervous system events associated with dietary supplements containing ephedra alkaloids. *New England Journal of Medicine, 343*(25), 1833.

60. Homeopathy Council of Canada. (2008). What is homeopathy? Canadian Academy of Homeopathy. Available at http://hmcc.ca/AboutHomeopathy.php.

61. Canadian Massage Therapist Alliance (CMTA). (2004). Frequently asked questions. Available at www.cmta.ca.

62. Canadian Association of Naturopathic Doctors. (n.d.). Questions and answers about naturopathic medicine. Available at www.naturopathicassoc.ca.

63. Physiotherapy Foundation of Canada. (n.d.). What is physiotherapy? Available at www.physiotherapyfoundation.ca/english.php.

64. Canadian Physiotherapy Association. (n.d.). Physiotherapy as a career. Available at www.physiotherapy.ca/public.asp?WCE=C=11|K=222416|RefreshS=Container|RefreshT=222416|A=Body.

© Gorilla/Shutterstock

Accidents, injuries, assaults, and crimes may seem like things that happen only to other people, only in other places. But no one is immune from danger, even college and university students. Common injuries for students include those that are alcohol-related, traffic accidents, and physical and sexual assaults.[1]

Recognizing the threat of intentional and unintentional injury is the first step to ensuring your personal safety. You may think that the risk of something bad happening is simply a matter of chance, of being in the wrong place at the wrong time. That's not always the case. Certain behaviours, such as using alcohol or drugs and not buckling your seat belt, greatly increase the risk of harm. Ultimately, you have more control over your safety than anyone or anything else in your life.

This chapter is a primer in self-protection. Included are recommendations for common sense safety on the road, at home, and outdoors. This chapter also explores other serious threats to personal safety in our society, such as sexual victimization and violence on college and university campuses. Living life to the fullest means taking some risks; however, we can all take steps to stay safe and prevent injuries.

**After studying the material in this chapter, you will be able to:**

- **List** and **explain** factors that increase the likelihood of an accident.
- **Describe** safety procedures for road, residential, and outdoor safety.
- **Define** sexual victimization, sexual harassment, and sexual coercion.
- **Describe** recommended actions for preventing rape.

**???? FREQUENTLY ASKED QUESTIONS**

**FAQ: What is sexual harassment? p. 374**

**FAQ: How can I prevent date rape? p. 376**

# Unintentional Injury: Why Accidents Happen

Unintentional injuries are a serious public-health concern in Canada. The economic burden of unintentional and intentional injuries combined is estimated to be greater than $12.7 billion per year or 8 percent of the total direct and indirect costs of illness—ranking fourth after cardiovascular disease, musculoskeletal conditions, and cancer.[2] Unintentional injuries alone cost Canadians more than $ 8.7 billion annually.[3] Many nonfatal injuries result in disabilities and physical impairments such as blindness, spinal cord injury, and brain injury.

Falls account for more than 40 percent of the total amount and motor vehicle crashes, 20 percent. The remaining 40 percent of total costs are attributed to drowning, poisoning, fires, and a range of other injuries.[4] Accidents, especially motor vehicle crashes, kill more college- and university-age men and women than all other causes combined; the greatest number of lives lost to accidents is among those 25 years of age (see Figure 14-1).

Many factors influence an individual's risk of accident or injury, including age, alcohol and drug use, stress, and thrill-seeking.

## Age

Injuries (not including adverse events in medical care) are the leading cause of death for Canadians between the ages of one and 44 and the fourth-leading cause of death for all Canadians.[5] Unintentional injuries accounted for almost 70 percent of injury-related deaths among children and youth. The other group most affected is seniors. The most common cause of injury among seniors is falls.

## Alcohol and Drugs

Although there has been a downward trend of rates of impaired-driving incidents over the past 20 years, alcohol is still a contributing factor in road fatalities (see Figure 14-2). According to a 2005 national survey on drinking and driving, 15 percent of Canadian drivers reported driving a vehicle within two hours of consuming alcohol in the past 30 days. There were also 1.5 million drivers who reported driving when they thought they were impaired, and 16 percent reported that they did this four or more times.[6] Impaired drivers continue to account for 29 percent of all driver fatalities.[7] Transport Canada and the Canadian Council of Motor Transport Administrators are working to make Canada's roads safer. The Strategy to Reduce Impaired Driving Task Force (STRID 2010) is targeting intervention efforts at four specific groups: hardcore drinking drivers, new or young drivers, social drinkers, and first-time convicted drivers.[8]

A recent study of full-time college students revealed that 20 percent of students drove after drinking some amount of alcohol, 10 percent drove after drinking five or more drinks, and 23 percent rode with a driver who was high or drunk.[9] Students who attended schools with more restrictions on underage drinking and that devoted more resources to enforcing drunk-driving laws reported less drinking and driving.[10]

A growing movement of young people—MADD Youth in Canada[11] and the Canadian Youth Against Impaired Driving (CYAID)[12]—are doing a lot to educate students

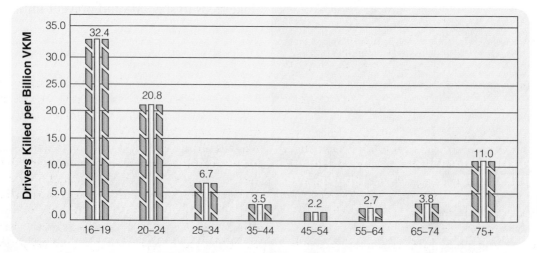

▲ **Figure 14-1** Young Drivers Aged 16–19 Years Have Much Higher Fatality Rates than the General Driving Population

Source: *Road safety vision 2010.* 2005 Annual Report. Canadian Council of Motor Transport Administrators. Transport Canada. p.23. Available at www.tc.gc.ca/roadsafety/vision/2005/pdf/rsv2005se.pdf. Transport Canada, 2005. Reproduced with the permission of the Minister of Public Works and Government Services Canada, 2008.

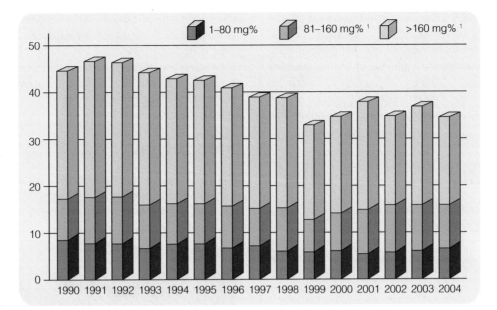

▲ **Figure 14-2** Percentage of Fatally Injured Drivers Tested and Found to Have Been Drinking

Source: Traffic Injury Research Foundation. Transport Canada. Traffic Collision Statistics. Collision Statistics 2005. October 12, 2007. Available at www.tc.gc.ca/ roadsafety/tp/tp3322/2005/page6.htm. Reproduced with the permission of the Minister of Public Works and Government Services Canada, 2008.

*BAC: Blood Alcohol Concentration.
mg%: Weight of alcohol in the bloodstream stated as milligrams in 100 millilitres of blood.
[1] Prior to 2001 BAC categories were reported as 81–150 mg% and >150 mg%.
Note: 2005 data were not available at the time of publication.

about the consequences of drinking and driving. MADD Youth, working with Mothers Against Drunk Driving (MADD), has grown to become a dominant peer-to-peer youth education and prevention organization. Provincial agencies, such as the Insurance Corporation of British Columbia (ICBC), are also targeting high school, college, and university students with programs such as Road Sense. A speakers bureau and resource package support this educational program, which also includes student visits to local morgues and demonstrations and videos of vehicle crashes.[13] Other provinces have similar programs.

Other studies done on college and university students show that accidents and falls are common for intoxicated students. Head injuries and broken bones are commonly reported. Alcohol poisoning is another serious health concern, with sometimes fatal consequences.[14]

Much less is known about the impact of drugs and traffic accidents because of the difficulty of measuring the presence and amount of drugs in drivers. There is evidence that a moderate or high dose of psychoactive drugs impairs driver performance.[15] Some studies have reported that the largest degree of impairment is observed with tasks involving attention, tracking, and psychomotor skills. Other studies show that drug use is often combined with alcohol use, thus adding to the effects. These effects can be equivalent to adding the effects of the two substances together, or can be multiplicative, in which the effects of

the drugs taken together are greater than the addition of the effects of the two substances.

The Criminal Code of Canada (section 253a) permits police to lay a charge of impaired driving if they believe a person's ability to operate a vehicle is impaired by "alcohol or a drug." In some provinces, police officers are being trained as drug-recognition experts.[16] The healthy choice is to not drink or do drugs and drive. Being responsible can lower the risk of unintentional injury.

## Stress

Demanding schedules have led to changes in lifestyle. More and more college and university students are attempting to balance studying and part- or full-time work. If you are stressed out or sleep-deprived, you pose a risk to yourself and to others.[17] Paying less attention to what we're doing can result in an increase in accidents. The 2003 findings of the Canada Safety Council and the Steel Alliance driving survey showed that the number of drivers who admit to at least one act of aggressive driving over the past year rose from 84 percent in 1999 to 88 percent in 2003. Passing on the right-hand side of the road, speeding, passing cars under risky conditions, and showing visible anger toward other drivers were some examples cited. Stress was the main reason given.[18] As well, over half the drivers surveyed drove while tired during the year, including one in 10 who admitted to falling asleep behind the wheel, and 97 percent of drivers in the 18- to 49-year-old age group admitted to multitasking (drinking coffee, putting on music, reaching for objects in the car, talking on cell phones) while driving. If you find yourself having a series of small mishaps or near misses, do something to lower your stress level, rather than waiting for something more harmful to happen.

## Thrill-Seeking

To some people, activities that others might find terrifying—such as skydiving or parachute jumping—are stimulating. These thrill seekers may have lower-than-normal levels of the brain chemicals that regulate excitement. Because the stress of potentially hazardous sports may increase the levels of these chemicals, they feel pleasantly aroused rather than scared. However, these activities can result in numerous injuries. Adventure racing is an extreme sport that is becoming popular. The world's top expedition racers run, bike, hike, and paddle for sometimes five or six days almost non-stop. Even marathoners and triathletes often push their bodies to a level that takes a significant toll. Structural damage to joints, bones, and muscles can occur. Lack of sleep, poor nutrition, and dehydration can cause the body's metabolic systems to overheat, and damage to the kidneys and heart can be the result.[19]

In some cases, taking risks can enhance personal well-being. Preparation, planning, and having an understanding of inherent risks can help to prevent unintentional injuries.

## Safety on the Road

Since 1984, fatalities resulting from traffic collisions in Canada have decreased, and serious injuries have declined. However, deaths and injuries resulting from traffic collisions continue to be the major transportation-safety problem in Canada. In 2004, 2725 road users were killed in traffic collisions, and over 212 000 were injured. More than 18 000 of the injury victims suffered serious injuries and required hospital care for 24 hours.[20] Traffic collisions cause more than 90 percent of all transportation-related fatalities. The societal costs of traffic collisions are enormous. Information from Transport Canada's 2005 Annual Report, *Road Safety Vision 2010,* estimates that economic losses are in the billions of dollars.

Responsibility for road safety is shared between our federal and provincial/territorial levels of government. The federal government, through Transport Canada, develops motor vehicle safety regulations and is responsible for the

Criminal Code of Canada. The provincial and territorial governments have direct jurisdiction over driver and vehicle licensing. Municipalities are becoming involved in road safety too, through police services and injury prevention efforts.[21] But road safety also needs Canadians to adopt safe driving habits.

## Safe Driving

Basic precautions can greatly increase your odds of reaching a destination alive, without injuring yourself or others.

Vehicles equipped with seat belts, air bags, padded dashboards, safety glass windows, a steel frame, and

## Strategies for Prevention

### How to Drive Safely

▲ Don't drive while under the influence of alcohol or other drugs, including medications that may impair your reflexes, cause drowsiness, or affect your judgment.

▲ Never get into a car if you suspect the driver may be intoxicated or affected by a drug.

▲ Be alert and anticipate possible hazards. Don't let yourself be distracted by conversations, passenger directions, arguments, food or drink, or scenic views. If you become exhausted, pull over and rest.

▲ Don't get too comfortable. Alertness matters. Use the rearview mirror often. Use the turn signals when changing lanes or making a turn.

▲ If you are transporting small children, make sure they are in safety or booster seats or buckled up. Children under 12 years of age are not permitted in the front seat of a car that has an airbag.

▲ Drive more slowly if weather conditions are bad. Make sure that your car has the proper equipment, such as chains or snow tires, and that you know how to respond in case of a skid.

▲ Properly maintain your car, replacing windshield wipers, tires, and brakes when necessary. Keep flares and a fire extinguisher in your car for use in emergencies.

▲ To avoid a head-on collision, generally veer to the right—onto a shoulder, lawn, or open space. Steer your way to safety; avoid hitting the brakes hard once you leave the pavement. If you have to hit something stationary, look for a soft target.

side-impact beams all help protect against injury or death. The size and weight of a vehicle also matter.

## Seat Belts

In Canada, the latest seat belt surveys (2004 for rural and 2005 for urban) showed that in rural areas, 86.9 percent of Canadians buckled up, while 91.1 percent in urban areas did so, too. Some gender disparities were evident with 4.1 percent less males than females using seat belts and 5.0 percent lower for drivers aged 25 or younger when compared with drivers of other ages.[22]

One of the targets of *Road Safety Vision 2010* is increasing seat belt use. National collision data reveal that approximately 40 percent of all fatally injured occupants and almost 20 percent of those seriously injured were not wearing seat belts at the time of the collision.[23] Transport Canada is currently evaluating possible ignition interlock approaches to promote seat belt use. One idea being tested is that of requiring a time delay before unbelted drivers would be able to put their vehicle into gear.[24]

When lap-shoulder belts are used properly, they reduce the risk of fatal injury to front-seat passengers by 45 percent and the risk of moderate-to-critical injury by 50 percent. The risk of death or severe injury increases nearly fivefold for front-seat passengers when back-seat passengers are not wearing seat belts. In a collision, unbelted back-seat passengers may be thrown forward, pushing the front-seat passengers into the dashboard and the windshield.[25]

## Air Bags

Air bags supplement the protection provided by using seat belts. They are connected to sensors that detect sudden deceleration. When activated, the sensors send an electrical signal that ignites a chemical propellant. When ignited, the propellant produces nitrogen gas, which inflates the air bag. This process occurs in less than 1/20th of a second. Most air bags have internal tether straps that shape the fabric and limit the movement of the bag. Vents in the rear allow the bag to deflate slowly to cushion the passenger's head as it moves forward into the bag.[26]

In low- to moderate-speed collisions, your seat belt is usually sufficient to prevent serious injury. However, in high-speed crashes, your seat belt may not be able to prevent your head (if you are the driver) from striking the steering wheel or your passenger's head from hitting the dashboard.[27] Front air bags are designed to protect the head and upper body in frontal crashes. They are not designed to open in rear-end collisions, side impacts, or rollovers. You should adjust the vehicle's front seats as far to the rear as possible to give the air bags as much room as possible in which to inflate.

Although air bags have been found to save lives, Transport Canada has been receiving complaints from the public about injuries caused by air bags that inflate in low-speed collisions and about incidents in which air bags did not open when they were supposed to open. Air bags sometimes cause injuries because they must inflate very quickly with great force. Most of the injuries incurred are minor—bruises and abrasions—but some are more serious, such as broken arms. There have been some cases when the head or chest was against the module when the air bag opened and fatal injuries occurred.[28]

Children or people of small stature are vulnerable. Children under age 12 should be seated in the back of vehicles that have air bags installed. You should also never install a rear-facing infant car seat in a seat equipped with an air bag. If it were to deploy, the infant car seat would be propelled into the back of the seat.

Air-bag systems of the future are already being developed. Known as "smart" air bags, some will possess two levels of activation. One will be appropriate for occupants who are using their seat belts; the other will work for an unbelted occupant. New air-bag systems might also have proximity sensors that will gauge how close you are to the air-bag module. They will be equipped with a warning system that will signal when someone is too close. Some vehicles already have a manual cutoff switch that allows an occupant to switch off the passenger-side air bag when an infant-restraint system is being used.[29]

## Cellular Phones

Many of the 15 million wireless phones in Canada are used in motor vehicles. They can be of great benefit if you need to call for help or report an accident. Canadians use cell phones to call 911 over six million times annually. The use of cell phones has also proven to reduce stress levels of drivers because they can call employers, friends, or family if they are late for appointments or dinner.

Unfortunately, cell phones have also been cited as a major contributing factor to motor vehicle accidents. When cell phones are being used, the driver's attention is diverted from the road to the phone or the person on the phone.[30]

One study done by the Ergonomics Division of the Road Safety Directorate found that drivers who used cell phones spent more time looking straight ahead, which narrowed their visual inspection area; spent less time focusing on the instruments and rearview, right, and left mirrors; and had more episodes of hard braking.[31] A 2008 meta-analysis of the effects of cell phones on driver performance found an increase of 0.25s reaction time (RT) for both handheld and hands-free phones. The researchers also suggest that the observed performance decrements most likely underestimate the true behaviour of drivers using cell phones in their own vehicles. One other important finding was that the drivers using either type of phone do not compensate while driving by giving greater headway or reducing speed.[32]

Another study done on college students revealed some disturbing statistics. The students reported that 21 percent of the accidents or near accidents that they had experienced involved at least one driver using a cell phone. The most frequently cited reason for the accident or near accident was the driver's talking while driving (TWD), rather than their attempt to dial or answer. Contrary to the researchers' expectations, more of the students who experienced accidents were using hands-free models. Female students were more likely than male students to use a cell phone while driving.[33]

Some provinces are looking into banning the use of cell phones while driving. Currently, Newfoundland and Labrador, Quebec, and Nova Scotia have banned the use of handheld cell phones while driving, and Ontario is debating it. With the new generation of cell phones now available, drivers are not only talking, but attempting to read e-mails, send text messages, and access the Internet, thus prompting policymakers to consider new legislation.

If you drive with a cellular phone, avoid unnecessary calls and make driving your top priority. Here are some basic safety tips from the Canada Safety Council:[34]

✔ Keep your eyes on the road. Keep your hands on the wheel.

✔ Program frequently called numbers and your local emergency number into the speed-dial feature of your phone for easy, one-touch dialling. When available, use auto answer or voice-activated dialling.

✔ Never dial while driving. Stop. Pull off the road, or have your passenger dial for you.

✔ Take a message. You can always retrieve your messages when you have an opportunity to pull over.

✔ Know when to stop talking. Keep conversations brief. If the topic is stressful or emotional or if the driving becomes hazardous, end your call and continue when you're not in the traffic.

✔ Don't take notes while driving.

## Safe Cycling

Cycling is popular with Canadians of all ages. It is good for your heart, improves your balance and coordination, helps with weight control, and helps the environment. But there are some inherent risks in riding a bicycle. In 2004, there were 56 bicycle fatalities, with 36 percent being individuals 19 and under and 64 percent over 19.[35] Most injuries suffered by bicyclists are fractures, dislocations, and other non-life-threatening injuries. Head injuries are the most dangerous, accounting for an estimated two-thirds of cyclist fatalities. Even a mild head injury can have serious

long-term consequences. The good news is that they can be largely prevented by wearing a helmet. While children, by law, must wear bicycle helmets in most provinces, laws for adults are not consistent across the country.

A 2002 Canada Safety council survey found that although 97 percent of Canadians realized helmets prevented serious injury, over half of Canadian adults who ride bicycles don't wear helmets.[36] Topping the list of reasons why they didn't: they just don't bother (14 percent), they didn't like the appearance (14 percent), they weren't "cool" (13 percent), they were uncomfortable (11 percent), and they were inconvenient or cumbersome (10 percent).[37]

British Columbia was the first province to mandate bicycle helmets in 1996. Alberta, Ontario, New Brunswick, and Nova Scotia now all have legislation mandating the use of helmets.[38] Having a law in place is only part of the solution. Helmets worn too far back and straps that are too loose or not clipped at all do not prevent head injuries.

About 90 percent of cycling fatalities are caused by cyclists being struck by motor vehicles. Alcohol use is another factor. A Traffic Injury Research Foundation study found that 25 percent of cyclist fatalities involved cyclists who had been drinking.[39]

If you are going to ride a bicycle for sport or commuting, use road smarts:

✔ Obey the rules of the road. A bicycle is classified as a vehicle.

✔ Equip your bike with a horn and lights—front and back. Wear reflective gear and a CSA-approved helmet.

✔ Ride defensively. Anticipate the actions of other road users. Watch for car doors, debris, grates, or holes in the road.

✔ Fit your bike correctly. You should be able to straddle it comfortably with both feet on the ground.

✔ Keep it well maintained—chain clean and oiled, brakes adjusted, gears in working order, tires in good condition.

✔ When using a scooter, skateboard, or in-line skates, wear a helmet, too.

## Safety at Home

Injuries can occur at home, too. Falls are the most common injury requiring medical attention and the sixth-leading cause of death in Canada.[40] They result from poor footgear, poor lighting, slippery or uneven walkways, broken stairs or handrails, or objects left where people walk. Poison also poses a great threat. Adults may be poisoned by mistakenly taking someone else's prescription drugs or taking medicines in the dark and swallowing the wrong one.

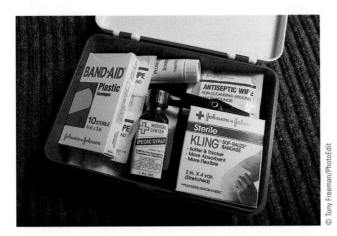

▲ Your home first-aid kit should include (at minimum) bandages, sterile gauze pads, adhesive tape, scissors, cotton, antibiotic ointment, a needle, safety pins, calamine lotion, syrup of ipecac to induce vomiting, and a thermometer.

Fires cause many home injuries and result from three ingredients—fuel, a heat source, and oxygen. Paper, wood, flammable liquids such as oils, gasoline, some paints, and burning cigarettes are often the cause of fires—even in resident housing at colleges and universities. In a national survey, 67 percent of colleges had at least one dorm without a sprinkler system.[41] If a fire does start, you might have only two to five minutes to get out of a building alive. Whether you live in a house, an apartment, or in residence, a fire-escape plan can save time and lives. If a fire breaks out, get out as quickly as possible, but don't run. If you're on an upper floor and your escape routes are blocked, open a window (top and bottom, if possible) and wait or signal from the window for help. Never try to use an elevator in a fire. Make sure everyone is familiar with these escape routes. Designate an area outside where all dorm residents, roommates, or family members should meet after escaping from a fire.

Think about purchasing an emergency first-aid kit to have in your room, apartment, or house. Consider investing in extra bottled water, candles and matches or a lighter, flashlight and batteries, and personal supplies to have handy as part of your emergency survival kit. Check out your campus security division to find out more about emergency preparedness or contact your provincial or territorial emergency management organization.

## Recreational Safety

According to the Canada Safety Council, every year Canadians are injured during recreational activities such as hiking, skiing, snowboarding, off-roading, or boating.[42] Many of the victims suffer from head injuries requiring emergency room or hospital treatment. Environmental concerns such as heat and cold also need to be considered to keep outdoor enthusiasts safe.

## Sport and Recreational Activities

Canada's parks, forests, and wilderness areas are well used by hikers, campers, backpackers, climbers, canoeists, ATV riders, and others who seek adventure or just want to enjoy nature. Canada Safety Council president Emile Theirien says that "no one ever expects to get lost or injured when they first set out, but the unpredictable can and does happen."[43] If you are going to participate in an outdoor or sports field trip, think ahead: What conditions might you face? Find out about the area you plan to explore. Bring a good map and check the weather forecast. Tell other people about your plans—are you going surfing, skiing, or hiking in the mountains? What is your intended route and timetable? Go with others and stay with your group. Wear proper clothes, footwear, and sport-activity protection such as helmets, pads, and mouth guards. Invest in a wilderness survival kit that you can take along. Use common sense and take precautions. Manage your risks.

Skiing and snowboarding are popular sports for college and university students. Serious head injuries account for less than 3 percent of total injuries among skiers and snowboarders, yet they are the leading cause of death. Injuries can have lifelong consequences. While the number of snowboarding injuries has not surpassed those related to skiing, boarding injuries are usually more severe. Eighty-eight percent of people injured while snowboarding in 2000 were between the ages of 10 and 19, and 80 percent of them were male. Half of the injuries were fractures, of which over 40 percent were to the arm. Wear protective equipment, including a helmet specifically designed for skiing and snowboarding.[44]

A report released in January 2003 by the Canadian Institute for Health Information (CIHI) revealed that snowmobiling leads to more serious injuries than any other sport. The problem is thrill seekers who speed, ride after drinking—often at night—and misuse the equipment, zooming across roads, thin ice, or rough terrain. According to the Canada Safety Council, most snowmobile deaths and injuries can be prevented.[45] ATV-related activities are now the third most common cause of severe injuries next to cycling and snowmobiling.[46]

Boating is the number-one cause of drowning in Canada.[47] Wear a lifejacket or a Personal Flotation Device (PFD) if you boat. A lifejacket is designed to turn the wearer's body face up. A PFD is designed to keep a conscious person's head out of water in calm conditions and assist them in rough water. The new PFDs offer comfort, style, and flexibility and come in a wide range of models and sizes. There are also PFDs with hypothermia protection—a valuable feature in some of our cold Canadian waters.[48]

There are new rules for personal watercraft use. Since September 15, 2002, all operators of personal watercrafts (PWC) must have proof of competency. All operators born after April 1, 1983 must have proof of competency onboard the craft. Proof of competency includes a pleasure craft operator card, or proof of having taking a boating-safety course prior to April 1, 1999, or a completed rental boat safety checklist. Accredited courses and tests are available. Experienced boaters can take the test without completing the course. A new Safe Boating Guide manual is available from Transport Canada.[49]

## Handling Heat

Two common heat-related maladies are **heat cramps** and **heat stress.** Heat cramps are caused by hard work and heavy sweating in the heat. Heat stress may occur simultaneously or afterward, as the blood vessels try to keep body temperature down. **Heat exhaustion,** a third such malady, is the result of prolonged sweating with inadequate fluid replacement (see Table 14-1).

The first step in treating these conditions is to stop exercising, move to a cool place, and drink plenty of water. Don't resume work or activity until all the symptoms have disappeared; see a doctor if you're suffering from heat exhaustion. **Heat stroke** is a life-threatening medical emergency caused by the breakdown of the body's mechanism for cooling itself. The treatment is to cool the body down:

move to a cooler environment, sponge down with cool water, and apply ice to the back of the neck, armpits, and groin. Immersion in cold water could cause shock. Get medical help immediately.

Being safe in the sun is also important. Incidents of skin cancer in Canada have risen, and dermatologists encourage all Canadians to use sunscreen.[50] The problem of overexposure to UV rays is also an indoor issue. A study done on college students found that despite their awareness of the risks associated with ultraviolet light exposure, many students used tanning beds to get a so-called "healthy tan." Forty-seven percent had used a tanning lamp or bed in the past year. Ninety-two percent of the current users said that they used tanning lamps because they "enjoyed a tanned appearance." The authors of the study also noted that students with a positive family history of skin cancer were 1.5 times more likely to use tanning lamps than those without family history. They went on to suggest that awareness of the dangers does not always alter our behaviour when we are faced with pressures to conform and "look good."[51]

## Coping with Cold

The tips of the toes, fingers, ears, nose, chin, and cheeks are most vulnerable to exposure from high wind speeds and low temperatures, which can result in **frostnip.** Because frostnip is painless, you may not even be aware of it occurring. Watch for a sudden blanching or lightening of your skin. The best early treatment is warming the area by firm, steady pressure with a warm hand; blowing on it with hot breath; holding it against your body; or immersing it in warm (not hot) water. As the skin thaws, it becomes red and starts to tingle. Be careful to protect it from further damage. Don't rub the skin vigorously or with snow, since you could damage the tissue.

More severe is **frostbite,** which can be either superficial or deep. *Superficial frostbite,* the freezing of the skin and tissues just below the skin, is characterized by a waxy look and firmness of the skin, although the tissue below is soft. Initial treatment should be to slowly re-warm the area. As the area thaws, it will be numb and turn bluish or purple, and blisters may form. Cover the area with a dry, sterile dressing, and protect the skin from further exposure to cold. See a doctor for further treatment. **Deep frostbite,** the freezing of skin, muscle, and even bone, requires medical treatment. It usually involves the tissues of the hands and feet, which appear pale and feel frozen. Keep the victim dry and as warm as possible on the way to a medical facility. Cover the frostbitten area with a dry, sterile dressing.[52]

The gradual cooling of the centre of the body may occur at temperatures above, as well as below, freezing—usually in wet, windy weather. When body temperature

| ▼ **Table 14-1 Heat Dangers** | | |
|---|---|---|
| **Illness** | **Symptoms** | **Treatment** |
| Heat cramps | Muscle twitching or cramping; muscle spasms in arms, legs, and abdomen | Stop exercising; cool off; drink water. |
| Heat stress | Fatigue, pale skin, blurred vision, dizziness, low blood pressure | Stop exercising; cool off; drink water. |
| Heat exhaustion | Excessive thirst, fatigue, lack of coordination, increased sweating, elevated body temperature | Stop exercising; cool off; drink water. See a doctor. |
| Heat stroke | Lack of perspiration, high body temperature (over 40.5°C [105°F]), dry skin, rapid breathing, coma, seizures, high pulse | Cool the body; sponge down with cool water; apply ice to the back of the neck, armpits, and groin. Get immediate medical help. |

## Stephen Canning—Mountains Melting

To take risks in life is living. All of us take risks in different ways. Stephen Canning, a writer, photographer, student, and young mountaineer, took risks every time he climbed a mountain. But it was with excitement, courage, and character that he kept climbing. He was also one of those charismatic people who seemed to inspire all who came within his orbit.

Our human potential story for this chapter is a short piece of writing by Stephen—a piece called *Death*. It was found on his computer, the summer of 2004, after he lost his life on Mount Logan, the highest peak in Canada and the second highest peak in North America. His words remind us that it is important to live life to the fullest, while at the same time accept the inherent risks of living a full life. His spirit lives on through his writing, his amazing photographs, and his family and friends, who have created a Stephen Canning Memorial Scholarship at the University of Victoria. You can read more about Stephen and view some of his photography at www. speakwell.com/well/2004winter/canning.php.

### Death

When I die, I want people to say that I inspired them. I don't care so much that they say I was a good man or a kind man or a happy man or a great man. I want them to say that they lived their life a little bit differently because of me. That they saw the world filled with a bit more adventure. That they were a little bit less afraid to do something that they truly wanted.

That seems to be the only theme running through everything I do. Writing is obviously about inspiration. Guiding; ditto. Environmental sciences, again, are really about finding enough evidence that you can convince people to live a little differently.

If even one person stands up at my funeral and says that I inspired them, that will be enough. The world will know that I died happily.

Chances are, I'll probably go in an avalanche or a climbing accident or something like that and people will say, "at least he died doing something he loved." What hogwash. It doesn't matter how you die. It's

Stephen Canning, writer, photographer, student, mountaineer.

how you lived up to that point that mattered. Rather than spending most of my time trying to avoid the inevitable: death, I hope to have lived with it firmly in my view.

All of these activities: climbing and skiing and base jumping and whatever else it is that we do. We don't do these things merely for the physical sensation of doing them. We do them because they let us glimpse death. They let us live with death constantly in our lives. It is always peaking over the horizon. When a climber dies, they are perhaps one of the few lucky people who manage death acceptingly. They've looked at death before, shook hands, sat down for a cup of tea. Most people spend their lives ignoring death, pretending it doesn't exist, denying it to the end.

Once you have accepted death, your passing should not be tragic. It should be an inevitable

*continued*

reality. It is the final chapter, which was written before the first.

To live without a fear of death makes you capable of great things. You worry less about what people think of you. You worry less about money. You worry less about failure. You are able to put yourself more fully into everything that you do.

This is the inspiration that I want to have given to people. To let them live with a bit less fear. To push them a little bit closer to the eternal.

A Stephen Canning Memorial Scholarship has been established in his honour. You can contact the University of Victoria by phone: 250.721.7624 or e-mail: devdonor@uvic.ca.

falls below 35°C (95°F), the body is incapable of re-warming itself because of the breakdown of the internal system that regulates its temperature. This state is known as **hypothermia.** The first sign of hypothermia is severe shivering. Then the victim becomes uncoordinated, drowsy, listless, confused, and is unable to speak properly. Symptoms become more severe as body temperature continues to drop, and coma or death can result.[53]

Hypothermia requires emergency medical treatment. Try to prevent any further heat loss: move the victim to a warm place, cover him or her with blankets, remove wet clothing, and replace it with dry garments. If the victim is conscious, administer warm liquids, not alcohol.

## Intentional Injury: Living in a Dangerous World

The World Health Organization (WHO) defines violence as "the intentional use of physical force or power, threatened or actual, against oneself, another person, or a group or community, that either results in, or has a high likelihood of resulting in, injury, death, psychological harm, mal-adjusted development, or deprivation."[54] In the first comprehensive review of the global impact of violence, WHO estimated that violence claimed more than 1.6 million lives in 2000.[55] Nearly half of these deaths were suicides, almost a third were homicides, and about a fifth were casualties of armed conflict. Men accounted for three-quarters of all victims of homicide, with the highest rates among those between the ages of 15 and 29.[56]

## Violence in Canada

According to the Crime Statistics in Canada 2007 report, our national crime rate declined for a third consecutive year (see Figure 14-3). This drop was linked mainly to decreases in counterfeiting and high volume property offences such as theft $5000 and under, break-ins, common

assault, and motor vehicle thefts.[57] This is the lowest level of crime reported in 30 years. Crime rates fell in all provinces and territories except Newfoundland and Labrador, the Yukon, and the Northwest Territories.

Crimes that did increase in 2007 were drug offences, up by 4 percent, with cannabis possession accounting for most of this increase, and impaired driving, which rose 3 percent, which followed two consecutive annual decreases.[58]

## Hate Crimes

Recent years have seen the emergence of violent crimes motivated by hatred of a particular person's (or group of persons') race, religion, sexual orientation, or political values. Overall, over one-half of the hate crimes were motivated by race or ethnicity (57 percent). The second most common hate motivation was about religion (43 percent).

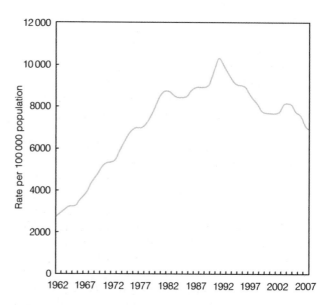

▲ **Figure 14-3** Crime Rate 1962–2007

Source: Statistics Canada. *The Daily.* Crime Statistics 2007. (July 17 2008). Available at www.statcan.ca/Daily/English/080717/d080717b.htm.

## The X & Y Files

## Which Gender Is at Greater Risk?

Just like illness, injury doesn't discriminate against either gender. Both men and women can find themselves in harm's way—but for different reasons. Here are some gender differences in vulnerability with statistics taken from the "Family Violence in Canada: A Statistical Profile" 2008 report.[61]

- Men are more likely to die of an occupational injury than women.
- Males are most often the victims and the perpetrators of homicides in Canada.
- Boys and men are more likely to be perpetrators of interpersonal violence, including homicide, physical assault, sexual assault, domestic abuse, and hate-related crimes. Men are more likely than women to be assaulted as an adult.

- Males are more likely to be harassed by an acquaintance. Women are more likely to be harassed by their spouse or partner.
- Females continue to be the most likely victims of police-reported spousal violence, accounting for 83 percent of victims compared to 17 percent males. This holds true for every province and territory across Canada.
- Female victims of spousal violence are more than twice as likely to be injured as male victims.
- Women are three times more likely to fear for their lives than men and twice as likely to be targets of more than 10 violent episodes.

Sexual orientation was the motivation in about one-tenth of the incidents.[59] Blacks and South Asians were among those most frequently targeted in hate crimes motivated by race or ethnicity. The majority of incidents motivated by religion involved anti-Semitism followed by those targeting Muslims.[60]

The most common types of hate-crime violations include mischief or vandalism, assault, uttering threats, and hate propaganda. One-quarter of hate crimes were motivated by religion and 1 in 10 by sexual orientation.[62] Often the violent hate crime involves the threat of force. Physical force using weapons such as knives and pellet guns is common. Many injuries sustained during a hate crime are deemed to be minor, but about 7 percent of victims suffer major injuries—sometimes death. In almost half of all hate crimes, the perpetrator was a stranger.

Many administrators at Canadian colleges and universities are denouncing hate crime and doing more to educate faculty, staff, and students about this issue. One example is Toronto's Ryerson University, where the university, the Canadian Arab Federation, and the Canadian Jewish Congress Ontario Region joined together to educate students about the hate graffiti and flyers found in the multi-faith prayer rooms on campus and other locations on campus in the summer of 2004. The flyers included threats of violence against Arabs and Muslims. Ryerson President Claude Lajeuness said, "This is clearly an attempt to provoke ill will within Ryerson University. Our faculty, staff and students are working together to ensure that the

## Strategies for Change

### Coping with the Threat of Violence and Terrorism

Uncertainty can be the most difficult aspect of living in a dangerous world. While you cannot eliminate risk, the following strategies can help you deal with it:

▲ Act despite fear. Take that first step even if you are anxious, trusting that the second will be easier.

▲ Adjust your attitude. The way you appraise a situation—as a threat that endangers your life or as a challenge that can be overcome—has a tremendous impact on your psychological and physical responses.

▲ Draw on your spiritual beliefs. Faith and values provide a bridge over the unknown.

▲ Dare to hope. This may be the most life-affirming coping strategy of all.

atmosphere of respect and cooperation that has been our hallmark, and which we value so highly, is not diminished."[63] In a healthy community differences are celebrated, not feared.

## Crime on Campus

Because of concerns about safety on college and university campuses, more schools are taking tougher stands on student behaviour. Many have established codes of conduct barring the use of alcohol and drugs in residences, fighting, and sexual harassment. Many also have instituted policies requiring suspension or expulsion for students who violate this code.

As a preventive measure, proactive steps are being put in place. Public safety initiatives include safe-walk programs, campus security patrols, outdoor emergency phones, and increased numbers of security guards. Sexual-assault services provide counselling, crisis intervention, and educational programs. Students are urged to walk in groups and lock their doors and windows. Student and parent orientations often include mandatory sessions on campus safety and sexual assault.

Property crimes such as burglary and theft are the most common. However, students today must also cope with the dangers of alcohol, drugs, fire, and even gambling. Here's how to keep yourself safe:[64]

- ✔ Visit your campus security division and access safety brochures. Learn about safety on the campus.
- ✔ Drink responsibly. Stay away from drinking games and contests.
- ✔ Be aware of who is serving you drinks. Don't accept any drinks from strangers.
- ✔ Be especially vigilant about date-rape drugs. Don't leave your drink where someone can slip a drug into it.
- ✔ Take advantage of your campus's safe-walk services.
- ✔ Lock up your valuables. If you cycle, keep your bike locked up.
- ✔ Don't give out your dorm, apartment, or house key to anyone. Don't let strangers into your dorm or apartment.
- ✔ Take all fire alarms seriously.
- ✔ Stay away from Internet gambling sites. Avoid any type of illegal gambling.

Most student crime is committed by students themselves. The more aware you are that crime is a possibility on campus, the better prepared you will be to prevent crime in the first place or deal with crime should it happen to you.

## Sexual Victimization and Violence

Sexual victimization refers to any situation in which a person is deprived of free choice and forced to comply with sexual acts. This is not only a woman's issue—men are also victimized. In recent years, researchers have come to view acts of sexual victimization along a continuum, ranging from street hassling, stalking, and obscene telephone calls to rape, battering, and incest.

## ???? What Is Sexual Harassment?

All forms of sexual harassment or unwanted sexual attention—from the display of pornographic photos to the use of sexual obscenities to a demand for sex by anyone in a position of power or authority—are illegal.

## Sexual Harassment on Campus

Sexual harassment can undermine a student's well-being and academic performance. Its effects include diminished ambition and self-confidence, reduced ability to concentrate, sleeplessness, depression, physical aches, and numerous other ailments. Students can experience sexual harassment from their professors or staff that work on campus. To combat hostile or offensive sexual environments, many colleges and universities have set up committees to handle student complaints and to take action should sexual harassment occur. Universities also are discouraging and, in some cases, restricting consensual relationships between teachers and students, especially any dating of students by their academic professors or advisers. Although such relationships may seem consensual, in reality they may not be because of the power faculty members have to determine students' grades and futures.

If you encounter sexual harassment as a student or an employee on campus, report it to your department chair, dean, or administrator. If you don't receive an adequate response to your complaint, talk with the campus counsellors, who can help you deal with the emotional issues that you might be faced with and assist you in reporting this crime. Sexual-harassment guidelines prevent any discrimination against you in terms of grades or the loss of a job or scholarship if you report harassment.

## Sexual Victimization of Students

As our society has become more aware of issues such as sexual harassment and coercion, there has been growing recognition that college and university campuses are not ivory towers isolated from these dangers.

According to reports from the Canadian Federation of Students:[65]

- ✔ 20 percent of female students said they had unwanted sexual intercourse because they were overwhelmed by a man's continued arguments and pressure.

✔ 6.6 percent of female students said that they had unwanted sexual intercourse because a man threatened or used some degree of force.

✔ 13 percent of female students said that when they were drunk or high, a man attempted unwanted sexual intercourse.

Rape statistics from an organization called Women Against Violence Against Women (WAVAW) state that there were 546 000 sexual assaults in Canada in 2004. Approximately three-quarters of the assaults involved unwanted sexual touching. One-quarter were classified as sexual attacks that involved force or attempted force. Girls and young women between the ages of 15 and 24 are the most likely victims, and between 1999 and 2004, there does not appear to have been a reduction in rates of sexual assault in Canada.[66]

In another study where researchers examined the prevalence and sexual assault of 3642 female university students from six universities across Ontario, 24 percent of female students reported being physically assaulted, and 15 percent reported being sexually assaulted the previous year. Of those experiencing assault, 40 percent had been the victim of two or more types of assaults.[67]

Sexual assault can take place in intimate relationships and between dating partners, friends, acquaintances, or strangers. Rapes committed by acquaintances of the victim are the most common forms of sexual assault, closely followed by sexual assaults by dating or other relationships partners.

## Sexual Coercion and Rape

At a bar on a weekend night, a group of intoxicated young men grab a woman and squeeze her breasts as she struggles to get free. At a party, a man offers his date drugs and alcohol in the hope of lowering her resistance to sex. Although some people don't realize it, such actions are forms of **sexual coercion** (forced sexual activity), which is very common on and off college and university campuses.

Sexual coercion can take many forms, including exerting peer pressure, taking advantage of one's desire for popularity, threatening an end to a relationship, getting someone intoxicated, stimulating a partner against his or her wishes, or insinuating an obligation based on the time or money one has expended. Men may feel that they need to live up to the sexual stereotype of taking advantage of every opportunity for sex. Women are far more likely than men to encounter physical force.

**Rape** refers to sexual intercourse with an unconsenting partner under actual or threatened force. *Statutory rape* refers to sexual intercourse between an adult and a partner under the age of 16. On May 1, 2008, the Tackling Violent Crime Act raised the legal age of consent in Canada, from

14 to 16 years of age, the first time this age has been raised since 1892. There is a "close-in-age exception" included in the new law, whereby 14 and 15 year olds can have sex with someone less than five years older than themselves. Our new law is now in line with laws in Britain, Australia, and many jurisdictions in the United States. In *acquaintance rape*, or *date rape*, the victim knows the rapist. In *stranger rape*, the rapist is an unknown assailant. Both stranger and acquaintance rapes are serious crimes that can have a devastating impact on their victims.

A national survey done in Canada found that half of all Canadian women have experienced at least one incident of sexual or physical violence. Statistics also show that one in four Canadian women will be sexually assaulted during her lifetime.[68]

The motives of rapists vary. Those who attack strangers often have problems establishing intimate relationships, have poor self-esteem, feel inadequate, and may have been sexually abused as children. Some rapists report a long history of fantasizing about rape and violence, generally while masturbating. Others commit rape out of anger that they can't express toward a wife or girlfriend. The more sexually aggressive men have been, the more likely they are to see such aggression and violence as normal and to believe rape myths, such as that it's impossible to rape a woman who doesn't really want sex. Sexually violent and degrading photographs, films, books, magazines, and videos may contribute to some rapists' aggressive behaviours. Hardcore pornography depicting violent rape has been strongly associated with judging oneself capable of sexual coercion and aggression and with engaging in such acts.

Alcohol and drugs also play a major role. Many rapists drink prior to an assault, and alcohol may interfere with a victim's ability to avoid danger or resist attack.

For many years, the victims of rape were blamed for doing something to bring on the attack. Researchers have since shown that women are raped because they encounter sexually aggressive men, not because they look or act a certain way. Although no woman is immune to attack, many rape victims are children or adolescents. Women who were sexually abused or raped as children are at greater risk than others. Scientists are exploring the reasons for this greater vulnerability.

Women who successfully escape rape attempts do so by resisting verbally and physically, usually by yelling and fleeing. Women who use forceful verbal or physical resistance (screaming, hitting, kicking, biting, and running) are more likely to avoid rape than women who try pleading, crying, or offering no resistance.

## Acquaintance or Date Rape

Most rapes are committed by someone who is known to the victim. Both women and men report having been forced into sexual activity by someone they know. Many college and university students are in the age group most likely to face this threat: women aged 16 to 25 and men under 25.

Women who describe incidents of sexual coercion that meet the legal definition of rape often don't label it as such. They may have a preconceived notion that true rape consists of a blitz-like attack by a stranger, or they may blame themselves for getting into a situation in which they couldn't escape. They may feel some genuine concern for others who would be devastated if they knew the truth (for example, if the rapist were the brother of a good friend or the son of a neighbour).

The same factors that lead to other forms of sexual victimization can set the stage for date rape. Socialization into an aggressive role, acceptance of rape myths, and a view that force is justified in certain situations increase the likelihood of a man's committing date rape. Some men also believe that when a woman is silent or acts in a passive way that a woman might want to be touched or have sex.[69]

Other factors can also play a role:

✔ **Personality and early sexual experiences.** Certain factors may predispose individuals to sexual aggression, including first sexual experience at a very young age, earlier and more frequent than usual childhood sexual experiences (both forced and voluntary), hostility toward women, irresponsibility, lack of social consciousness, and a need for dominance over sexual partners.

✔ **Situational variables (what happens during the date).** Men who initiate a date, pay all expenses, and provide transportation are more likely to be sexually aggressive, perhaps because they feel they are in a power position.

✔ **Acceptance of sexual coercion.** Some social groups, such as athletic teams, may encourage the use of alcohol; reinforce stereotypes about masculinity; and emphasize violence, force, and competition. The group's shared values, including an acceptance of sexual coercion, may keep individuals from questioning their behaviour.

✔ **Drinking.** Alcohol use is one of the strongest predictors of acquaintance rape. Men who've been drinking may not react to subtle signals, may misinterpret a woman's behaviour as a come-on, and may feel more sexually aroused. At the same time, drinking may impair a woman's ability to effectively communicate her wishes and to cope with a man's aggressiveness.

✔ **Date-rape drugs.** Drugs such as Rohypnol (roofie, La Rocha, rope, Mexican Valium, Rib Roche, R-2), a tranquilizer used overseas, and gamma hydroxybutyrate (GHB), a depressant with potential benefits for people with narcolepsy, have been implicated in cases of acquaintance or date rape. Since both are odourless, colourless, and tasteless, victims have no way of knowing whether their drink has been tampered with. The subsequent loss of memory leaves victims with no explanation for where they've been or what has happened.

Rohypnol can cause impaired motor skills and judgment, lack of inhibitions, dizziness, confusion, lethargy, very low blood pressure, coma, and death. Deaths also have been attributed to GHB overdoses.

✔ **Gender differences in interpreting sexual cues.** In research comparing college men and women, the men typically overestimated the woman's sexual availability and interest, seeing friendliness, revealing clothing, and attractiveness as deliberately seductive. In one study of date rape, the men reported feeling "led on," in part because their female partners seemed to be dressed more suggestively than usual.

## How Can I Prevent Date Rape?

For men:

✔ Remember that it's okay to not "score" on a date.
✔ Don't assume that a sexy dress or casual flirting is an invitation to sex.
✔ Be aware of your partner's actions. If she pulls away or tries to get up, understand that she's sending you a message—one you should acknowledge and respect.
✔ Restrict drinking, drug use, or other behaviours (such as hanging out with a group known to be sexually aggressive in certain situations) that could affect your judgment and ability to act responsibly.
✔ Think of the way you'd want your sister or a close woman friend to be treated by her date. Behave in the same manner.

For women:

✔ Back away from a man who pressures you into other activities you don't want to engage in on a date, such as chugging beer or drag racing with his friends.
✔ Avoid misleading messages and behaviour that may be interpreted as sexual teasing.
✔ Despite your clearly stated intentions, if your date behaves in a sexually coercive manner, use a strategy of escalating forcefulness—direct refusal, vehement verbal refusal.
✔ Avoid using alcohol or other drugs when you definitely do not wish to be sexually intimate with your date.

It has been over a decade since Parliament rewrote the Criminal Code (1999) to make it clear that voluntary consent is a prerequisite to any sexual activity. Unfortunately, old myths and stereotypes continue to surface in Canada's courtrooms and in the minds of some Canadians. No

Means No campaigns, on many campuses across the country, continue to raise the issue of violence against women. Change of attitudes, behaviours, and beliefs that allow and sometimes encourage violence at the individual, community, and societal level must be embraced.[70]

## Male Rape

No one knows how common male rape is because men are less likely to report such assaults than women. In a recent survey in England, nearly 3 percent of men reported non-consensual sexual experiences as adults. Other researchers estimate that the victims in about 10 percent of acquaintance-rape cases are men. These hidden victims often keep silent because of embarrassment, shame, or humiliation, as well as their own feelings and fears about homosexuality and conforming to conventional sex roles.

Although many people think men who rape other men are always homosexuals, most male rapists consider themselves to be heterosexual. Young boys aren't the only victims. The average age of the male rape victims is 24. Rape is a serious problem in prison, where men may experience brutal assaults by men who usually resume sexual relations with women once they're released.

## Impact of Rape

Rape-related injuries include unexplained vaginal discharge, bleeding, infections, multiple bruises, and fractured ribs. Victims of sexual violence often develop chronic symptoms, such as headaches, backaches, high blood pressure, sleep disorders, pelvic pain, and fertility problems. But sexual violence has both a physical and a psychological impact. The psychological scars of a sexual assault take a long time to heal. Therapists have linked sexual victimization with hopelessness, low self-esteem, high levels of self-criticism, and self-defeating relationships. An estimated 30 to 50 percent of women develop post-traumatic stress disorder following a rape. Many do not seek counselling until a year or more after an attack, when their symptoms have become chronic or intensified.[71]

Acquaintance rape may cause fewer physical injuries but greater psychological torment. Often too ashamed to tell anyone what happened, victims may suffer alone, without skilled therapists or sympathetic friends to reassure them. Women raped by acquaintances blame themselves more, see themselves less positively, question their judgment, have greater difficulty trusting others, and have higher levels of psychological distress. Nightmares, anxiety, and flashbacks are common. The women may avoid others, become less capable of protecting themselves, and continue to be haunted by sexual violence for years. A therapist can help these victims begin the slow process of healing.

## What to Do in Case of Rape

If a woman has been raped, she will have to decide whether to report the attack to the police. Even an unsuccessful rape attempt should be reported because the information a woman may provide about the attack—the assaulter's physical characteristics, voice, clothes, car, even an unusual smell—may prevent another woman from being raped.

Only a small percentage of college and university women who are raped report their assault to police; many don't even tell a close friend or relative about the assault. Women who are raped should call a friend or a rape-crisis centre. A rape victim should not bathe or change her clothes before calling the police. Semen, hair, and material under her fingernails or on her apparel all may be useful in identifying the man who raped her.

A rape victim who chooses to go to a doctor or hospital should remember that she may not necessarily have to talk to police. A doctor can collect the necessary evidence, which will then be available if she later decides to report the rape to police. All rape victims should talk with a doctor or health-care worker about testing and treatment for sexually transmitted infections and post-intercourse conception.

Many rape victims find it very helpful to contact a rape-crisis centre, where qualified staff members assist in

▲ Counselling from a trained professional can help ease the trauma suffered by a rape victim.

dealing with the trauma. These individuals can also put victims in touch with other survivors of rape and support groups. Many colleges and universities have such programs. It is important to remember that the victim hasn't committed a crime.

## Halting Sexual Violence: Prevention Efforts

Sexual violence has its roots in social attitudes and beliefs that demean women and condone aggression. According to international research, much sexual violence takes place within families, marriage, and dating relationships. In many settings, rape is a culturally approved strategy to control and discipline women. In these places, laws and policies to improve women's status are critical to ending sexual coercion.

All men and women should recognize misleading rape myths and develop effective ways of communicating to avoid misinterpretation of sexual cues. Students should

also know to whom they can turn to learn more about and seek help for sexual victimization: counsellors, campus police, deans of student affairs, and campus chaplains.

A non-profit agency, the Centre for Children and Families in the Justice System, one of many such agencies in Canada, supports victims of violence. If you are planning a career in the human service area, you might want to check out their website—www.lfcc.on.ca/index.htm. Many comprehensive handbooks, manuals, publications, and reports, such as *Helping an Abused Woman: 101 Things to Say and Do* (2008), *Little Eyes, Little Ears: How Violence Against a Mother Shapes Children as They Grow* (2007), *Woman Abuse Affects our Children: An Educator's Guide* (2007), and *When Teens Hurt Teens: Helping the Victims of Youth-on-Youth Criminal Violence* (2006), are all available online.

First Nations groups are moving forward on family-violence programs. One such program is administered by the Saskatchewan Justice Victims Services Branch. It is called the Circle Project Association Inc., and it supports at-risk Aboriginal families that are dealing with family violence as well as non-Aboriginal people who need assistance.[72]

**CHAPTER 14**

**Making This Chapter Work for You**

1. You can help keep yourself safe by doing all of the following *except*
   a. using seat belts when driving or a passenger.
   b. wearing pyjamas made of nonflammable materials.
   c. removing or fixing loose carpets.
   d. hiking without an emergency plan.

2. Which of the following factors affects an individual's risk of accident or injury?
   a. hunger level
   b. stress level
   c. amount of automobile insurance coverage
   d. knowledge of CPR

3. Safe-driving tips include all of the following *except*
   a. avoid driving at night for the first year after getting a licence.
   b. make sure your car has snow tires or chains before driving in hazardous snowy conditions.
   c. if riding with an intoxicated driver, keep talking to him so that he doesn't fall asleep at the wheel.
   d. don't let packages or people obstruct the rear or side windows.

4. Which of the following statements about home safety is true?
   a. Falls pose the greatest threat of injury in the home, followed by poison.
   b. The three ingredients of fire are fuel, a heat source, and oxygen.
   c. The risk of falls is lowest in the elderly.
   d. When using cleaning products, make sure that windows are tightly closed.

5. Which of the following statements about recreational safety hazards is true?
   a. Hypothermia is a life-threatening medical emergency caused by the inability of the body to cool itself.
   b. The most common heat-related conditions are heat stroke and heat exhaustion.
   c. Most drownings occur at organized facilities.
   d. Frostbite usually affects the tissues of the hands and feet.

6. Which of the following statements about hate crimes is *false*?
   a. Over half of all hate crimes are motivated by race or ethnicity.
   b. Often the violent hate crime involves the threat of force.
   c. Hate-crime victims sustain only minor injuries.
   d. The most common types of hate-crime violations include mischief or vandalism, assault, uttering threats, and hate propaganda.

7. Which statement about violence on college and university campuses is *false*?
   a. Property crimes account for most crimes on campus.
   b. On college and university campuses, crimes are most often committed by outside community members.
   c. Students must now also cope with the dangers of alcohol, drugs, fire, and even gambling.
   d. Crime statistics for colleges and universities are posted on the Internet.

8. Sexual victimization
   a. includes sexual harassment, sexual coercion, and rape.
   b. is gender-specific, affecting women who are violated emotionally or physically by men.
   c. is rare in academic environments such as college campuses.
   d. most commonly takes the form of physical assault and stalking.

9. Which of the following statements about rape is true?
   a. When a person is sexually attacked by a stranger, it is referred to as rape. When a person is sexually attacked by an acquaintance, it is referred to as sexual coercion.
   b. Statutory rape is defined as sexual intercourse initiated by a woman under the age of consent.
   c. Men who rape other men usually consider themselves heterosexuals.
   d. Women who flirt and dress provocatively are typically more willing to participate in aggressive sex than women who dress conservatively and do not flirt.

10. Ways to protect or prevent rape include:
    a. using alcohol and drugs only in familiar surroundings.
    b. not drinking or taking date-rape drugs.
    c. avoid angering a sexually aggressive person by becoming passive and quiet.
    d. not discussing your sexual limits on a first or second date because just talking about sex will encourage your date to think you are interested in a sexual relationship.

Answers to these questions can be found on page 450.

## Self Responsibility

*I want to LIVE my life. For me that means taking chances. I will not let fear stop me from doing things that I really want to do.*

**Ray Greenlaw**

Taking good care in risky situations is possible if you recognize potential risks and prepare for them. There is a balance to living with purpose and living recklessly. What stage of change are you in when it comes to safety on the road, safety at home or work, recreational safety,

## Social Responsibility

*Relationships are all there is. Everything in the universe only exists because it is in relationship to everything else. Nothing exists in isolation. We have to stop pretending we are individuals that can go it alone.*

**Margaret Wheatley**

and safety within your relationships? How can you stay safe—yet challenge yourself to reach your goals and visions? How do you treat others when in a relationship? Take good care of others—take good care of yourself. Respect others—respect yourself.

## Critical Thinking

1. Can you name two risk factors in your daily life that might increase the likelihood of accidental injury? What actions have you taken to keep yourself safe?

2. A friend of yours, Eric, frequently makes crude or derogatory comments about women. What might you say to him?

3. At one university, women raped by acquaintances or dates scrawled the names of their assailants on the walls of women's restrooms on campus. Several young men whose names appeared on the list objected, protesting that they were innocent and were being unfairly accused. Do you think it violates the rights of men? How do you feel about naming women who've been raped in news reports?

## CENGAGENOW™

If your textbook package includes CengageNOW™, go to http://west.cengagenow.com/ilrn/ to link to CengageNOW™ for Health, your online study tool. First take the **Pre-test** for this chapter to get your personalized **Study Plan,** which will identify topics you need to review and direct you to the appropriate resources. Then take the **Post-test** to determine what concepts you have mastered and what you still need work on.

## SITES & BYTES

### National Aboriginal Circle Against Family Violence
**www.nacafv.ca**

This site provides you with information about culturally appropriate programs and services that address family violence. Publications, reports, and newsletters are available.

### Canada Safety Council
**www.safety-council.org**

At this site you can find safety education information which can help you avoid injury. Information on safety legislation and links to public safety awareness campaigns are also available.

Please note that links are subject to change. If you find a broken link, use a search engine such as www.google.ca and search for the website by typing in keywords.

**InfoTrac® College Edition Activity** Docheff, D., Gawlak, R., Van Houten, A., Moore, M., Morehart, C., Terry, C., Murphy, M., Presley, C.L., Crawford, Sc. A.G.M., & Soukup, G.J. (2008). Should any form of extreme sport or extreme dance be included in the curriculum. *The Journal of Physical Education, Recreation & Dance, 79*(2), 9–11.

1. Discuss the main themes presented in this qualitative interview study by the college professors and students about the inclusion of extreme sports in a college or university curriculum.

2. Share with your classmates, your opinion of the inclusion of extreme sports in a physical education, recreation, or kinesiology college curriculum.

3. As a health, wellness, or recreation professional, how might you introduce a program of extreme sports into personal training sessions or youth or adult recreation settings? Or would you? Why or why not?

You can find additional readings relating to injury and violence with InfoTrac® College Edition, an online library of more than 5000 journals and publications. Follow the instructions for accessing InfoTrac® that were packaged with your textbook; then search for articles using a keyword search.

For additional links and resources, visit our text-specific website at www.health.nelson.com.

## Key Terms

The terms listed here are used within the chapter on the page indicated. Definitions of terms are in the Glossary at the end of the book.

**deep frostbite** 370
**frostbite** 370
**frostnip** 370

**heat cramps** 370
**heat exhaustion** 370
**heat stress** 370

**heat stroke** 370
**hypothermia** 372
**rape** 375

**sexual coercion** 375

## References

1. Keeling, R. (2002, September). Risks to students' lives: Setting priorities. *Journal of American College Health, 51*(2), 53.
2. Public Health Agency of Canada. (2006, April 24). Injury Prevention. Facts on injury. Available at www.phac-aspc.gc.ca/injury-bles/facts-eng.php.
3. Ibid.
4. Ibid.
5. Ibid.
6. Canada Safety Council. (2005, December). Information. Traffic Safety. Impaired Driving. Drunk driving progress and problems. Available at www.safety-council.org/info/traffic/impaired/progress.html.
7. Transport Canada. (2005, March 9). Road Safety. Smashed: Impaired driving in Canada: Progress…but the journey continues. TP1535E. Available at www.tc.gc.ca/roadsafety/tp/tp1535/progress.htm.
8. Canadian Council of Motor Transport Administrators. (2005). *Road safety vision 2010.* 2005 annual report. Transport Canada. Available at www.tc.gc.ca/roadsafety/vision/2005/pdf/rsv2005se.pdf.
9. Weschler, H., et al. (2005). Drinking and driving among college students: The influence of alcohol-control policies. *American Journal of Preventive Medicine, 25*(3), 212–18.
10. Ibid.
11. MADD Youth in Canada. (n.d.). Mad youth in Canada. Let's keep each other alive. Available at www.madd.ca/english/youth/index.html.
12. Canadian Youth Against Impaired Driving. (n.d.). SADD Alberta. Conferences. Available at www.saddalberta.com/?q=node/14.
13. Insurance Corporation of British Columbia. (n.d.). Geared 2 Youth. Road safety events and activities. Available at www.icbc.com/youth/activities.asp.
14. Fitzgerald, N. (2002). Safety on campus. *Careers & Colleges, 22*(18), 18.
15. Mann, R.E., Brands, B., Macdonald, S., & Stoduto, G. (2003, May). Impacts of cannabis on driving: An analysis of current evidence with an emphasis on Canadian data. Executive summary. Transport Canada. Available at www.tc.gc.ca/roadsafety/tp/tp14179/menu.htm.
16. Ibid.
17. Canada Safety Council. (n.d.). Balance of priorities a must for safety. Available at www.safety-council.org/info/OSH/worklife.html.
18. Canadian Safety Council. (2003, May 16). Traffic congestion steams Canadian drivers. Available at www.safety-council.org/info/traffic/aggression.html.
19. Park, A. (2005). Can you push yourself too hard? You bet! Just ask the athletes who run the world's most brutal races. (Getting fit/Extreme sports). *Time, 165*(23), 69.
20. Canadian Council of Motor Transport Administrators. (2005). *Road safety vision 2010.* 2005 annual report. Transport Canada. Available at www.tc.gc.ca/roadsafety/vision/2005/pdf/rsv2005se.pdf.
21. Ibid.
22. Ibid.
23. Ibid.
24. Ibid.
25. Stephenson, J. (2002). Backseat seat belts. *Journal of the American Medical Association, 287*(6), 706.
26. Transport Canada. (2005, November 16). Safety issues for Canadians: Air bags (revised). TP 2436 Road safety leaflet CL 9601 (E). Available at www.tc.gc.ca/roadsafety/absg/airboce.htm.
27. Ibid.
28. Ibid.
29. Ibid.

30. Transport Canada. (2007, October 12). Road Safety. Cell phones and driving: Questions and answers. Available at www.tc.gc.ca/road-safety/tp2436/rs200106/q-a.htm.

31. Harbluk, J.L., & Noy, Y.I. (2002). The impact of cognitive distraction on driver visual behaviour and vehicle control. Transport Canada. Minister of Public Works and Government Services, represented by the Minister of Transport. Available at www.tc.gc.ca/roadsafety/tp/tp13889/menu.htm.

32. Caird, J.K., Willness, C.R., Steel, P., & Scialfa, C. (2008). A meta-analysis of the effects of cell phones on driver performance. *Accident Analysis & Prevention, 40*(4), 1282–93.

33. Seo, D.C., & Torabi, M.R. (2004). The impact of in-vehicle cell-phone use on accidents or near-accidents among college students. *Journal of American College Health, 53*(3), 101–8.

34. Canada Safety Council. (2005, May). Safe driving—It's your call. Available at www.safety-council.org/info/traffic/cellular.html.

35. Canada Safety Council. (2006, May). Safe cycling is not just for kids. Available at www.safety-council.org/info/sport/adultbike.html.

36. Canada Safety Council. (2005). Helmets: Attitudes and actions. Survey finds most kids wear helmets, most adults don't. Available at www.safety-council.org/info/sport/helmets.html.

37. Ibid.

38. Ibid.

39. Canada Safety Council. (2006, May). Safe cycling is not just for kids. Available at www.safety-council.org/info/sport/adultbike.html.

40. Government of British Columbia. (2007, December 17). Population Health and Wellness Ministry of Health Services. Preventing injuries. Available at www.health.gov.bc.ca/prevent/preventing_injuries.html.

41. Fitzgerald, N. (2002). Safety on campus: Most schools are safe havens for learning. But dangers—crime, alcohol abuse, hazards—do exist. Knowing the realities can help you protect yourself. *Careers & Colleges, 22*(4), 18–21.

42. Canada Safety Council. (2004). Information. Safety in the great outdoors. Available at www.safety-council.org/info/sport/wild.html.

43. Ibid.

44. Canada Safety Council. (2006, March). Helmets for skiers and boarders. Available at www.safety-council.org/info/sport/snowboard.html.

45. Canada Safety Council. (2004, February). Training.Booze, reckless-ness blamed for snowmobile crashes. Available at www.safety-council.org/training/snow/snowmo.htm.

46. Ibid.

47. Canada Safety Council. (2005). Information. Pleasure boaters and PFDs. Available at www.safety-council.org/info/sport/PFDs.html.

48. Ibid.

49. Transport Canada. (2008, June 20). Office of Boating Safety. The safe boating guide. Available at www.tc.gc.ca/marinesafety/tp/tp511/menu.htm.

50. Canadian Dermatology Association. (2008, August 08). Sun screen FAQs. Sun awareness program. Available at www.dermatology.ca/sap/safety_resources/sunscreen_faqs/index.html.

51. Larkin, M. (2002). US university students ignore tanning lamp risk. *Lancet, 360,* 1226.

52. Canada Safety Council. (2005). Information. Occupational Health and Safety. Cold facts. Available at www.safety-council.org/info/OSH/coldfact.htm.

53. Ibid.

54. Heath, I. (2002). Treating violence as a public health problem: The approach has advantages but diminishes the human rights perspec-tive. *British Medical Journal, 325*(7367), 726.

55. Krug, E., et al. (2002). The world report on violence and health. *Lancet, 360,* 1083.

56. Mayor, S. (2002). WHO report shows public health impact of violence. *British Medical Journal, 325*(7367), 731.

57. Dauvergne, M. (2007). Crime statistics in Canada, 2007. *Juristat. Canadian Centre for Justice Statistics.* Statistics Canada – Catalogue no. 85-002-X, 28 (7). Available at www.statcan.ca/english/freepub/85-002-XIE/85-002-XIE2008007.pdf.

58. Ibid.

59. Statistics Canada. (2008, June 9). Study: hate motivated crime. *The Daily.* Available at www.statcan.ca/Daily/English/080609/d080609a.htm.

60. Ibid.

61. Family violence in Canada: A statistical profile. 2008. Lucie Ogrodnik (ed.). *Canadian Centre for Justice Statistics.* Statistics Canada – Catalogue no. 85-224-X. Available at www.statcan.ca/english/freepub/85-224-XIE/85-224-XIE2008000.pdf.

62. Ibid.

63. Ryerson University. (2008). Crime prevention. Security and Emergency Services. Discrimination and Harassment Prevention Services. Available at www.ryerson.ca/security/prevention/harassment_prevention.html.

64. Fitzgerald, N. (2002). Safety on campus: Most schools are safe havens for learning. But dangers—crime, alcohol use, hazards—do exist. Knowing the realities can help you protect yourself. *Careers & Colleges, 22*(4), 18–21.

65. Canadian Federation of Students. (n.d.). Quick Navigation. Date rape: No means no. Available at www.cfs-fcee.ca/nomeansno/index_e.html.

66. Women Against Violence Against Women (WAVAW). (2005). Statistics. Available at www.wavaw.ca/index.cfm?page_id=22.

67. Newton-Taylor, B., DeWit, D., & Gliksman, L. (1998). Prevalence and factors associated with physical and sexual assault of female university students in Ontario. *Health Care for Women International, 19*(2), 155–64.

68. Women Against Violence Against Women (WAVAW). (2005). Statistics. Available at www.wavaw.ca/index.cfm?page_id=22.

69. Women Against Violence Against Women (WAVAW). (2005). Rape myths. Available at www.wavaw.ca/index.cfm?page_id=21.

70. Canadian Federation of Students. (n.d.). Quick Navigation. Date rape: No means no. Available at www.cfs-fcee.ca/nomeansno/index_e.html.

71. Hensley, L.G. (2002). Treatment of survivors of rape: Issues and interventions. *Journal of Mental Health Counselling, 24*(4), 330–47.

72. Saskatchewan Justice Victims Services. (n.d.). Aboriginal family violence programs administered by Saskatchewan Justice Victims Services Branch: Circle Project Association, Inc. Government of Saskatchewan. Available at www.justice.gov.sk.ca/Aboriginal-Family-Violence-Programs.

# CHAPTER 15

# A Lifetime of Health

Too young to worry about getting old? Think again. Whether you're in your teens, twenties, thirties, or older, you can take steps that will add healthy, active, productive years to your life.

**Aging**—the characteristic pattern of normal life changes that occurs as humans, plants, and animals grow older—remains inevitable. However, at any age, at any stage of life, and at any level of fitness, you can do a great deal to influence the impact that the passage of time has on you. More and more Canadians are extending not just their lifespan, but also their *health span*—their years of health and vitality. You can do the same. This chapter provides a preview of the changes age brings, the steps you can take to age healthfully and move through midlife, and the ways you can make the most of all the years of your life.

# Living in an Aging Society

Seniors are a growing population group in Canada. According to the 2006 census, one in seven Canadians is a senior. Low fertility rate and increasing life expectancy are the main reasons for the aging of the Canadian population. Between 1981 and 2006, the number of seniors increased from 2.4 million to 4.3 million.[1] The proportion of seniors in Canada in 2006 was 13.7 percent.[2] The rapid growth in the senior population is expected to continue well into the future—especially those individuals aged 55 to 64 or the "young seniors" who are nearing retirement. There were nearly 3.7 million in this age group which was an increase of 28.1 percent from 2001.[3] See Figure 15-1 for the percentage of seniors in each Canadian province and territory.

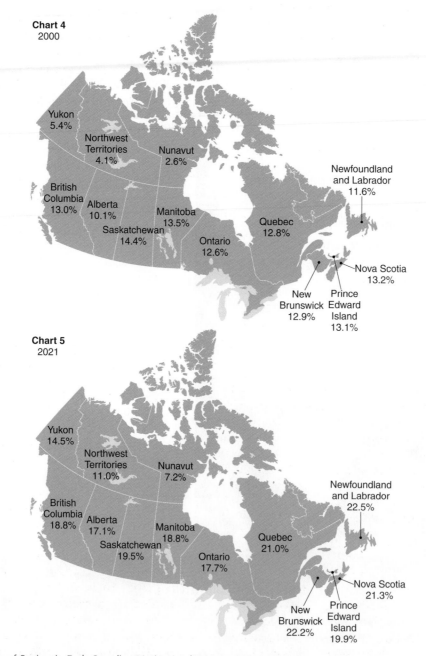

**Chart 4**
2000

Yukon 5.4%
Northwest Territories 4.1%
Nunavut 2.6%
Newfoundland and Labrador 11.6%
British Columbia 13.0%
Alberta 10.1%
Saskatchewan 14.4%
Manitoba 13.5%
Ontario 12.6%
Quebec 12.8%
New Brunswick 12.9%
Prince Edward Island 13.1%
Nova Scotia 13.2%

**Chart 5**
2021

Yukon 14.5%
Northwest Territories 11.0%
Nunavut 7.2%
Newfoundland and Labrador 22.5%
British Columbia 18.8%
Alberta 17.1%
Saskatchewan 19.5%
Manitoba 18.8%
Ontario 17.7%
Quebec 21.0%
New Brunswick 22.2%
Prince Edward Island 19.9%
Nova Scotia 21.3%

▲ **Figure 15-1** Percentage of Seniors in Each Canadian Province and Territory, 2000 and 2041
The senior's population is expected to reach 6.7 million in 2020 and 9.2 million in 2041.

Source: Canada's Aging Population. Division of Aging Seniors, Public Health Agency of Canada, 2002. Available at www.phac-aspc.gc.ca/seniors-aines/pubs/fed_paper/pdfs/fedpager_e.pdf. Reproduced with the permission of the Minister of Public Works and Government Services Canada, 2008.

Seniors live in all provinces and territories, but the highest number of seniors live in Saskatchewan; 15.4 percent of Saskatchewan's population is seniors. This is well above the national average. East of Ontario the population tends to be older, while the west boasts a younger population, particularly in Alberta, with just 10.7 percent of the population being seniors. The three territories have the youngest population where only 1 person in 20 was aged 65 or over on average.[4]

When we look at the population based on census metropolitan area (CMA), the senior population in Calgary, Alberta, was 9.4 percent as compared to 19.0 percent in Kelowna, British Columbia. Peterborough, Ontario, followed Kelowna as the second oldest CMA, then Victoria, British Columbia. In mid-size urban centres, Parksville, British Columbia, and Elliot Lake, Ontario, were the "oldest" in Canada. The 2006 census shows that about one in three people in these communities were 65 years or older.[5]

Women form the majority of the Canadian seniors' population—about two-thirds of the senior population. This is due in part to the higher life expectancy of women, which is 82.5 years compared to 77.7 years for men.[6] Aboriginal seniors make up a relatively small proportion of Canada's Aboriginal population. However, they are living longer, and their population is growing significantly. In 2001, 39 000 Aboriginal seniors represented 4 percent of the total Aboriginal population. This percentage is expected to rise to 6.5 percent by 2017.[7] War-service veterans who served in the First and Second World Wars or the Korean conflict make up a significant segment of our senior population. In Canada, approximately one in five male seniors has served in wartime.

It is estimated that just over one in four Canadian seniors was born outside Canada. Many of them immigrated to Canada when they were children or young adults. Most seniors can speak one or both of Canada's official languages, although there are older adults who are unable to speak either English or French. More females than males are unable to converse in either of our official languages.

Throughout your life, you will confront a variety of issues related not just to your age, but also to that of the aging Canadian population. These include:

✔ **Retirement costs.** Unless changes are made to decrease the demand on the Old Age Security program (OAS) and the Canada/Quebec pension plans (CPP/QPP), taxes on workers may be increased.

✔ **Health costs.** Some experts argue that health costs will soar because people over age 65 use more health services and require more medical care than those who are younger. However, others contend that nations with a large elderly population do not necessarily spend more of their national wealth on health care.

✔ **Grey-power politics.** Senior citizens go to the polls in larger numbers than younger voters. With such voting power, programs for the elderly may make up a larger share of future federal budgets.

## Successful Aging

The life expectancy of Canadian seniors has risen substantially over the course of the last century. Canadians are not only living longer, but also are staying healthy and independent longer. Thirty seven percent of seniors aged 65 to 74 report that their health is good, while 40 percent report that their health is very good or excellent. Those seniors 75 years or older indicate that 36 percent believe their health to be good and 32 percent believe their health to be very good or excellent.[8] Among the factors contributing to a longer health span are improved medical care, diet, exercise, and public-health advances.

Genes, as studies of identical twins have revealed, influence only about 30 percent of the rate and ways in which we age. "The rest is up to us," says Michael Roizen, M.D., author of *RealAge*, who notes that it's possible to become healthier, fitter, and biologically younger with time. "With relatively simple changes, someone whose chronological age is 69 can have a physiological age of 45. And the most amazing thing is that it's never too late to live younger."[9]

### Fit for Life

At one time, medical experts thought that aging meant weakness, frailty, and declining strength. Now we know better: no one is ever too old to get in shape. Rather than telling seniors to take it easy, the Active Living Coalition for Older Adults encourages them to engage in the full range of physical activities, including aerobic conditioning.[10] As much as 50 percent of the physiological declines commonly attributed to aging are due to sedentary living and can be dramatically reversed.

Proactive health-promoting behaviours, such as exercising and not smoking, contribute to a high quality of life, even when begun late in life.[11] People who are not physically fit are more likely to die younger than those who are, even if they are physically healthy.[12] In addition to physical activity, social interactions, such as entertaining friends and getting involved with religious activities, lead to greater life satisfaction as people get older.[13]

Exercise is so effective in preserving well-being that gerontologists describe it as "the closest thing to an anti-aging pill." It slows many changes associated with advancing age, such as loss of lean muscle tissue, increase in body fat, and decreased work capacity. It lowers the risk of heart disease and stroke in the elderly—and greatly improves

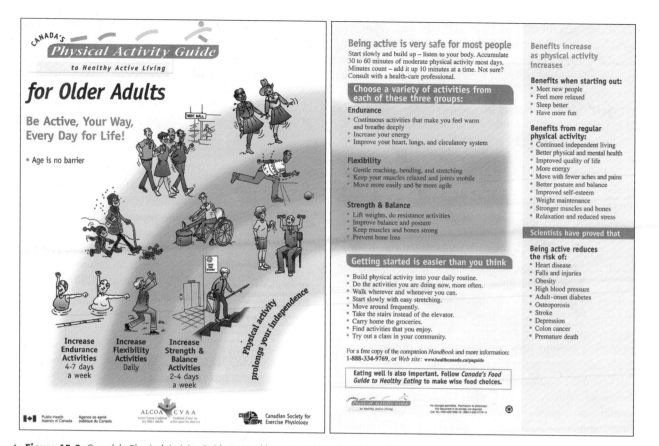

▲ **Figure 15-2** Canada's Physical Activity Guide to Healthy Active Living for Older Adults. Be Active, Your Way, Every Day for Life!

Source: Canada's Physical Activity Guide to Healthy Active Living for Older Adults. Public Health Agency of Canada. Health Canada. Available at www.phac-aspc.gc.ca/pau-uap/paguide/older/index.html. Reproduced with the permission of the Minister of Public Works and Government Services Canada, 2008.

general health. Male and female runners over age 50 have much lower rates of disability and much lower health-care expenses than less active seniors. Even less intense activities, such as gardening, dancing, and brisk walking, can delay chronic disability.[14] Walking has proven helpful in delaying cognitive decline in older women.[15]

*Canada's Physical Activity Guide to Healthy Active Living for Older Adults* promotes physical activity—every day for life (see Figure 15-2). Endurance, flexibility, strength, and balance exercises are recommended. Starting slowly is the key—especially if you have not been active for awhile. Thirty to 60 minutes of physical activity most days is ideal. The benefits of regular physical activity are many:[16]

✔ Greater ability to live independently
✔ Better physical and mental health
✔ Better posture and balance
✔ Lower risk of dying from coronary heart disease and of developing high blood pressure, colon cancer, and diabetes
✔ Reduced blood pressure in some people with hypertension
✔ Fewer symptoms of anxiety and depression

Despite these potential benefits, 60 percent of older adults in Canada are inactive.[17] Yet even sedentary individuals in their eighties and nineties can participate in an exercise program—and gain significant benefits. Results from a number of studies being conducted at the Canadian Centre for Activity and Aging, which is affiliated with the Faculties of Health Sciences and Medicine and Dentistry at the University of Western Ontario, have shown that regular physical exercise can help keep older adults functioning and mobile.[18]

## ??? Does Body Composition Change with Age?

Both weight and body-fat percentage typically increase in adulthood. Starting in their twenties, many men and women put on an average of 0.45 kilograms (1 pound) of weight a year. By age 65, they have gained about 18 kilograms (40 pounds). Because activity levels decline with age, the average individual also loses 0.22 kilograms (0.5 pounds) of lean body mass a year. The result is a change in body composition over time: a 9-kilogram (20-pound) loss of lean tissue and an 18-kilogram (40-pound) gain in body fat.

Body composition can affect how well older individuals function. Researchers have documented that physical activity—both aerobic workouts and resistance exercise—can increase and maintain lean body tissue.

## The Aging Brain

Scientists used to think that the aging brain, once worn out, could never be fixed. Now they know that the brain can and does repair itself. When neurons (brain cells) die, the surrounding cells develop "fingers" to fill the gaps and establish new connections, or synapses, between surviving neurons. Although self-repair occurs more quickly in young brains, the process continues in older brains. Even victims of Alzheimer's disease, the most devastating form of senility, have enough healthy cells in the diseased brain to re-grow synapses. Scientists hope to develop drugs that someday may help the brain repair itself.

Mental ability does not decline along with physical vigour. Researchers have been able to reverse the supposedly normal intellectual declines of 60- to 80-year-olds by tutoring them in problem-solving. Reaction time, intellectual speed and efficiency, nonverbal intelligence, and maximum work rate for short periods may diminish by age 75. However, understanding, vocabulary, ability to remember key information, and verbal intelligence remain about the same.

### Thinking Young

The healthiest seniors are actively engaged in life, resilient, optimistic, productive, and socially involved, observes John Rowe, M.D., of the MacArthur Foundation Research Network on Successful Aging.[19] While seniors are not immune to life's slings and arrows, successful "agers" bounce back after a setback and have a can-do attitude about the challenges they face. They also tend to be lifelong learners who may take up entirely new hobbies late in life—pursuits that stimulate production of more connections between neurons and that may slow aging within the brain.

Just as with muscles, the best advice for keeping your brain healthy as you age is "use it or lose it." Some memory loss among healthy older people is normal, but this is reversible with training in simple methods, such as word associations, that improve recall.

### Memory

Some memory skills, particularly the ability to retrieve names and quickly process information, inevitably diminish over time. What normal changes should you expect? Here is a preview:

✔ **Recalling information takes longer.** As individuals reach their mid- to late sixties, the brain slows down, but usually just by a matter of milliseconds. As long as they're not rushed, older adults eventually adapt and perform just as well as younger ones.

✔ **Distractions become more disruptive.** Many college and university students can study and listen to the stereo at the same time. Thirty-something moms can soothe the baby, field questions about homework, and put together a dinner all at once. But as individuals pass age 50, they find it much more difficult to divide their attention or to remember details of a story after having switched their attention to something else.

✔ **"Accessing" names gets harder.** The ability to remember names, especially those you don't use frequently, diminishes by as much as 50 percent between ages 25 and 65. Preventive strategies can help, such as repeating a person's name when introduced, writing down the name as soon as possible, and making obvious associations with the name.

✔ **Learning new information is harder.** The quality of memory doesn't change, just the speed at which we receive, absorb, and react to information. Strategies like taking notes or outlining material become critical for older students, especially when learning new skills. However, adding to existing knowledge remains as easy as ever.

✔ **Wisdom matters.** In any memory test involving knowledge of the world, vocabulary, or judgment, older people outperform their younger counterparts.

## Moving Through Midlife

Although men don't experience the dramatic midlife hormonal changes that women do, their primary sex hormone, testosterone, gradually declines by 30 to 40 percent between ages 48 and 70. This change, sometimes called *andropause*, may cause decreased muscle mass, greater body fat, loss of bone density, flagging energy, lowered fertility, and impaired virility. Some researchers are experimenting with testosterone supplements, but their safety and efficacy are not yet known.

The major changes that occur during a woman's middle years are more evident than those in men. Women enter into **perimenopause,** the period from a woman's first irregular cycles to menopause, the end of menstruation.

### Perimenopause

The average onset for perimenopause is 45 years, but it can start anytime between the ages of 39 and 51. The average time frame for perimenopause is about five years, but this stage has a range of two to eight years.[20] During this time, the egg cells, or oocytes, in a woman's ovaries start to *senesce* or die off at a faster rate. Eventually, the number of egg cells drops to a tiny fraction of the estimated two million packed

## Norman Jack MacKenzie— A Visionary and Lifelong Educator

Our human potential story for this chapter celebrates the achievements of Jack MacKenzie, someone who has spent a lifetime helping others and who is an example of living life to the fullest even though his official retirement date was 21 years ago. At 81 years of age, Jack continues to volunteer and educate others about the benefits of active living, something he has been doing all his life.

Jack grew up in Manitoba, in a town called Neepawa. Both of his parents were teachers, and eventually he would follow in their footsteps. After graduating from high school, he went to the University of Manitoba, where he obtained a BSc and a diploma in Education. He would go on to obtain a MA from the University of Toronto in Political Economy, a Bachelor in Health and Physical Education, and a MA in Physical/Outdoor Education from Michigan State University.

Jack first taught in Swan River, Manitoba, and then became the Supervisor of Physical Education for the Brandon, Manitoba schools. He then moved to Saskatchewan to lead the Physical Education Department at the Regina Public School Board. Jack always believed that health, recreation, and "quality" physical education were important elements in a healthy, active lifestyle. He truly believed that the education system could and should play a major role in encouraging children to live active, healthy lives. His role expanded to develop and include the outdoor-education programs when he became the Coordinator of Fitness and Community Resources in 1964. Over the years, he worked as a supervisor, vice-principal, and program coordinator.

After-school programs are common now, but Jack was the first person in Regina to implement "out-of-school" programs that involved taking children to local facilities for physical education as an integral part of the school curriculum. Skating, swimming, cross-country skiing, canoeing, and curling are all examples of programs in which the children participated.

Jack MacKenzie, teacher, volunteer, and outdoor educator in front of the Jack MacKenzie Elementary School in Regina, Saskatchewan, which was named in his honour.

© Larry Easton

Between 1968 and 1969, Jack travelled the world to look at physical education, health, and outdoor education programs. He was most impressed with a program in France that balanced the school day between physical education, academics, and the arts. When he returned to Regina, he created and implemented a similar program that was supported by teachers, the administration, and parents. This program was featured by the Canadian Broadcasting Corporation and in a national magazine, which together generated hundreds of enthusiastic letters from people all over Canada and abroad.

Jack continued to provide outstanding leadership for 31 years, tirelessly promoting and implementing physical-education programs, especially for young people. The respect he gained from colleagues and students resulted in many, many awards and include the first Bernadine M. Melanson Memorial Award from the Saskatchewan Outdoor Education Association in 1978, the Award of Merit from the Saskatchewan Physical Education Association in 1979, the R. Tait McKenzie Award of Honour from CAHPERD in 1988, and, possibly the ultimate tribute for an educator, a school in Regina named in his honour in 2000—the Jack MacKenzie Elementary School.

Jack has also been inducted as a Fellow into the North American Society for Health, Physical Education, Recreation, Sport and Dance Professionals in 2000. He officially retired in June 1987.

Jack was, and continues to be, an outdoor enthusiast. He is the cofounder of Saskairie, a non-profit outdoor-education centre located on the edge of Moose Mountain Provincial Park. You can still find Jack out on the land chopping wood and cleaning the bunkhouses of this centre, which has been used by children and community groups since 1972. He has served his community well—as a volunteer for a multitude of organizations including the Saskatchewan Camping Association, the Saskatchewan Outdoor Education Association, the Regina Natural History Society, and the Saskatchewan Physical Education Association.

Jack has also shared his knowledge of physical education and outdoor education through public speaking and consulting. He has hosted a number of documentaries for the Discovery Channel, where he takes viewers down a river on canoeing adventures against the background of the Canadian Shield. A special video, *What the Eyes Don't See,* highlights a canoe trip with a friend, Ted Ohlsen, who is blind. Hugh Reoch, a retired school principal, recalls fondly the mentorship Jack provided him over the years and the impact these videos had on him:

"Your mentorship has led to having uncounted numbers of enjoyable hours canoeing in the Qu'Appelle lakes and in the north, including your beloved Churchill River country. The videos are used as teaching tools for the young and old so that they may appreciate the vastness, diversity and beauty of our country."

Of Jack MacKenzie's vision, Joe Milligan, a recreation consultant in Saskatchewan says: "He is living proof of the positive effect one person can have when they have the vision and the tenacity to make it a reality. Jack's unselfish commitment to quality physical recreation and a positive healthy lifestyle will continue to be an inspiration to educators and recreation professionals for many generations to come."

Jack was featured in a 2006 calendar of Outstanding Bachelors of Saskatchewan, put out by the magazine *Prairies North,* having been nominated by the staff, parents, and hundreds of students from the school named after him. Jack's legacies are far-reaching, and we have only shared just a few special stories here.

We leave you with some thoughts from Jack with regard to education: "The future of our planet depends on the young people of today, and the nature and quality of their education—for which we have responsibility. That education will be determined by those ideals and goals we deem to be important and relevant; they represent a crucial investment for the 21st century. And what is becoming increasingly apparent are those values and behaviours that will lead to the survival and well-being of our planet and ourselves."

---

into her ovaries at birth. Trying to coax some of the remaining oocytes to ripen, the pituitary gland churns out extra follicle-stimulating hormone (FSH). This surge is the earliest harbinger of menopause, occurring 6 to 10 years before a woman's final periods. Eventually the other menstrual messenger, luteinizing hormone (LH), also increases, but at a slower rate.

These hormonal shifts can trigger an array of symptoms. The most common are night sweats (a *subdromal hot flash,* in medical terms), which can be just intense enough to disrupt sleep. About 10 to 20 percent of perimenopausal women also experience daytime hot flashes, a symptom that becomes more prevalent with the more drastic and enduring hormonal changes of menopause itself.[21]

## Menopause

**Menopause,** defined as the complete cessation of menstrual periods for 12 consecutive months, generally arrives at age 51 or 52. About 10 to 15 percent of women breeze through this transition with only trivial symptoms. Another 10 to 15 percent are virtually disabled. The majority fall somewhere in between these extremes. Women who undergo surgical or medical menopause (the result of removal of their ovaries or chemotherapy) often experience abrupt symptoms, including flushing, sweating, sleeplessness, early morning awakenings, involuntary urination, changes in libido, mood swings, perception of memory loss, and changes in cognitive function.

Dwindling levels of estrogen subtly affect many aspects of a woman's health, from her mouth (where dryness, unusual tastes, burning, and gum problems can develop) to her skin (which may become drier, itchier, and overly sensitive to touch). The drop in estrogen levels also may cause hot flashes (bursts of perspiration that last from a few seconds to 15 minutes), which often happen at night, disturbing sleep and causing fatigue. With less estrogen to block them, a woman's androgens, or male hormones, may have a greater impact, causing acne, hair loss, and, according to some anecdotal reports, surges in sexual appetite. Other women, however, report a drop in sexual desire.

At the same time, a woman's clitoris, vulva, and vaginal lining begin to shrivel, sometimes resulting in pain or bleeding during intercourse. Since the thinner genital tissues are less effective in keeping out bacteria and other pathogens, urinary tract infections may become more common. Some women develop breast or ovarian cysts, which usually go away on their own. Eventually, a woman's ovaries don't respond at all to her pituitary hormones. After the last ovulatory cycle, progesterone is no longer secreted, and estrogen levels decrease rapidly.

Women experiencing menopause face risks of various diseases, including heart disease, stroke, and breast cancer.[22] Because estrogen or progestin may play a role in these risks, for many years **hormone replacement therapy (HRT)** was routinely prescribed to ease short-term symptoms of menopause, such as hot flashes, improve a woman's quality of life, and reduce long-term health risks.[23] However, recent research has challenged this practice.[24]

In 1991, the U.S. National Institutes of Health (NIH) launched a major study called the Women's Health Initiative (WHI). This was a set of studies involving healthy postmenopausal women that was carried out in 40 U.S. centres. The study included a clinical trial to evaluate the risks and benefits of two types of HRT (estrogen and progestin), which were administered in pill form. The researchers were looking for how this type of treatment affected women's health. In July 2002, after an average of 5.2 years of follow-up with the participants, the NIH prematurely ended the combined HRT component of this trial. It was found that there were more risks than benefits among the women using the combined HRT compared to the women in the placebo group. Specifically, the researchers found that there were more cases of coronary heart disease, strokes, blood clots, invasive breast cancer, and dementia. Although the actual numbers of cases in the test group of participants appeared to be low, they were very significant given that millions of women were (and still are) taking combined HRT. It is now deemed to be a public-health issue.[25]

The NIH made a decision to stop a second study in 2004 where women who had hysterectomies were taking estrogen only. It was found that estrogen alone appeared to increase the risk of stroke and blood clots, although it did decrease the risk of breast cancer compared to women who were given a placebo.

The HRT story continues. At the First Global Summit on Menopausal-Related issues, held in Zurich in March 2008, a report that had been released to the World Congress on Menopause was discussed. Experts attending the summit now suggest that HRT is safe for women entering menopause who are healthy. The researchers concluded that the women in the Women's Health Initiative study had a larger number of people with higher risk factors than normal and that the average age of the study participants was 10 years older than the age most women begin taking HRT. The conclusions shared at this summit suggest that HRT does not increase the risk of chronic heart disease in healthy women who are between the ages of 50 to 59, that the slightly increased risk of breast cancer is minimal compared to other risk factors, that HRT does not impair mental processes in healthy women in this age group, and that it might delay cognitive dysfunction as well. The expert's recommendation is that women consult with their doctor in order to decide if HRT is an appropriate plan of action for menopause.[26]

In Canada, the Society of Obstetricians and Gynecologists of Canada advise that combined HRT continue to be used to treat moderate to severe menopausal symptoms, but that the lowest effective dosage be used for short-term use. The society also asked doctors not to prescribe HRT to prevent heart disease or dementia.[27]

Because of the findings, many other medical groups have revised their guidelines for HRT. The North American Menopause Society recommends against the use of HRT for preventing heart disease in both healthy women and those who already have heart problems. Although this society considers HRT an acceptable treatment for menopausal symptoms, they advise caution regarding its prolonged use.

There are alternatives, both in terms of medication and lifestyle changes, to HRT. Testosterone creams, used in the vagina, can help with dryness and irritation. Many postmenopausal women relieve symptoms and lower their risk of future health problems by exercising—which can lower the risk of heart disease—and strengthening bones by eating calcium-rich foods and supplements.

Some women have reported relief from hot flashes, fatigue, depression, and other menopausal symptoms with vitamins and herbal therapies. Some of these herbs have undergone clinical trials. For the safest use of herbs, consult your doctor or a qualified alternative practitioner, such as a naturopathic doctor or traditional Chinese medicine practitioner. Purchase herbs that have been standardized—look for a Drug Information Number (DIN) or General Public (GP) number, which shows that Health Canada has reviewed and approved the product's information, labelling, and instructions for use.

## Sexuality and Aging

Health and sexuality interact in various ways as we age. A study based on 3005 participants, published in the *New England Journal of Medicine* in 2007, found that older adults between 57 and 85 remain sexually active. Fifty-eight percent of sexually active respondents in the youngest age group—between 57 and 64—reported engaging in oral sex within the past 12 months, as did 31 percent in the oldest age group. Fifty-four percent of sexually active

© iStockphoto.com/Wouter van Caspel

▲ For older couples, sexual desire and pleasure can be enhanced by years of intimacy and affection.

participants in the study between the ages of 75 and 85 reported having sex once a week or more.

The study also showed that when sexual activity declined, it had much to do with poor physical health than lack of desire.[28] The most commonly reported reason for sexual inactivity among individuals with a partner was the male partner's physical health. Women who had diabetes were less likely to be sexually active than women who did not, and men with this disease often suffered erectile difficulties. Dr. Lindau, one of the researchers of this study, suggests that doctors should be aware of the connection between sexual activity and health because older adult men and women might stop taking prescribed medication for other health issues if it negatively affects their sex life. According to the research findings, only 38 percent of men and 22 percent of women had discussed sex with their doctors since the age of fifty.[29]

Aging does cause some changes in sexual response. Women produce less vaginal lubrication. An older man needs more time to achieve an erection or orgasm and to attain another erection after ejaculating. Both men and women experience fewer contractions during orgasm. However, none of these changes reduces sexual pleasure or desire.

## Do Nutritional Needs Change over Time?

Many elderly people who live independently do not get adequate amounts of one or more essential nutrients. Among the nutrients often lacking in older adults are folate, Vitamin D, calcium, Vitamin E, magnesium, Vitamins $B_6$ and $B_{12}$, Vitamin C, and zinc.

The reasons are many: limited income, difficulty getting to stores, chronic illness, medications that interfere with the metabolism of nutrients, problems chewing or digesting, poor appetite, inactivity, illness, depression, and lack of sunshine in some parts of Canada.

Nutritionists urge the elderly, as they do all Canadians, to concentrate on eating healthful foods; many also recommend daily nutritional supplements, which may provide the added benefit of improving cognitive function in healthy people over 65. In a study of 86 older people living independently who took either a supplement or a placebo, those taking the supplement showed significant improvements in short-term memory, problem-solving ability, abstract thinking, and attention.[30]

In Canada, many seniors are widowed. Among widowed seniors, eating disorders are considered to be one of the most troubling problems related to bereavement. A disruption of normal patterns of eating, meal skipping, less dietary variety, and reduced home food preparation often result in poor health.[31]

## The Challenges of Age

Aging brains and bodies become vulnerable to diseases such as Alzheimer's and osteoporosis. Other common life problems, such as depression, substance misuse, and safe driving, become more challenging as we age.

### Alzheimer's Disease

**Dementia** is a syndrome that consists of a number of symptoms such as loss of memory, judgment and reasoning, and changes in mood and behaviour. **Alzheimer's disease** is the most common form of dementia. It is estimated that 420 600 people 65 years and older have Alzheimer's and related dementias, and 280 000 have Alzheimer's disease. The number of people in Canada with dementia is expected to grow to over 75 million by 2031.[32]

The features of Alzheimer's is a gradual onset and progressive deterioration of brain cells and mental capacity. At first, the symptoms resemble ordinary memory lapses. Eventually, people with Alzheimer's lose their ability to learn and remember anything new, the names of their family and friends, and their way around. People with Alzheimer's often begin avoiding social contact, become upset at otherwise trivial events, and end up having trouble dressing or feeding themselves because they are unable to remember how to function. Once their brains lose the capacity to regulate elementary body functions, people with Alzheimer's die of malnutrition, dehydration, infection, or heart failure. The average interval between early symptoms and death is 7 to 10 years, although it can last between 2 and 20 years.

Women are more likely to develop Alzheimer's than men. By age 85, as many as 28 to 30 percent of women suffer from Alzheimer's, and women with this form of dementia perform significantly worse than men in various visual, spatial, and memory tests.

Even though medical science cannot restore a brain that is in the process of being destroyed by an organic brain disease such as Alzheimer's, medications can control difficult behavioural symptoms and enhance or partially restore cognitive ability. Often physicians find other medical or psychiatric problems, such as depression, in these patients; recognizing and treating these conditions can have a dramatic impact.

## Osteoporosis

Another age-related disease is **osteoporosis,** a condition in which losses in bone density become so severe that a bone will break after even slight trauma or injury (see Figure 15-3). The Osteoporosis Society of Canada states that 1.4 million Canadians suffer from osteoporosis and that women develop osteoporosis four times more often than men. The cost of treating this disease and the fractures it causes is estimated to be $1.3 billion in Canada.[33] Women have smaller skeletons and are more vulnerable than men; in extreme cases, their spines may become so fragile that just bending causes severe pain.

Osteoporosis doesn't begin in old age. In fact, the best time for preventive action is early in life. Increased calcium intake, Vitamin D, and regular physical activity, particularly during childhood and the growth spurt of adolescence, can produce a heavier, denser skeleton and reduce the risk of the complications of bone loss later in life.

Various factors can increase a woman's risk of developing osteoporosis, including family history (a mother, grandmother, or sister with osteoporosis, fractures, height loss, or humped shoulders); petite body structure; white or Asian background; menopause before age 40; smoking; heavy alcohol consumption; loss of ovarian function through chemotherapy, radiation, or hysterectomy; low calcium intake; and a sedentary lifestyle.

In the past, doctors often prescribed hormone replacement therapy to protect aging bones; this is no longer the recommended practice.[34] Alternatives include raloxifene (Evista®), bisphosphonates (Didrocal®, Fosamax®, and Actonel®) that slow the breakdown of bone and may even increase bone density, and calcitonin, a naturally occurring hormone that increases bone mass in the spine. Other possible therapies are sodium fluoride, parathyroid hormone (PTH), and some forms of Vitamin D.

The first evidence-based clinical practice guidelines for osteoporosis in the world were published in the November 12, 2002, *Canadian Medical Association Journal* (CMAJ). These guidelines focus on prevention, diagnosis, and treatment. They include recommendations on bone mineral density testing (BMD), fracture risks, nutrition,

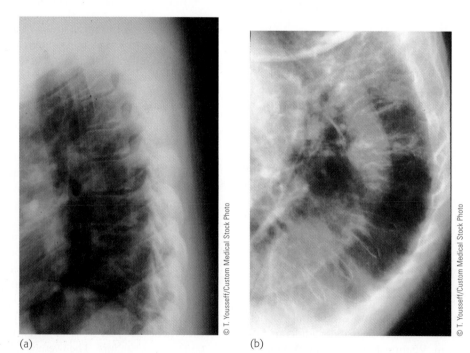

(a)                    (b)

© T. Yousseff/Custom Medical Stock Photo

▲ **Figure 15-3** The Effect of Osteoporosis on the Back
(a) A healthy spine: the bony segments (vertebrae) are square with no loss of height. (b) An osteoporotic spine: The curvature is due to compression fractures that occur because the bones are weakened through loss of mineral density.

## Strategies for Prevention

### Lowering Your Risk of Osteoporosis

Regardless of your age and gender, you can prevent future bone problems by taking some protective steps now. The most important guidelines are as follows:

▲ Get adequate calcium. Aim for 1200 milligrams a day.

▲ Exercise regularly. Both aerobic exercise and weight training can help preserve bone density.

▲ Drink alcohol only moderately. More than two or three alcoholic beverages a day impairs intestinal calcium absorption.

▲ Don't smoke. Smokers tend to be thin (a risk factor for osteoporosis) and enter menopause earlier, thus extending the period of jeopardy from estrogen loss.

▲ Let the sunshine in (but don't forget your sunscreen). Vitamin D, a vitamin produced in the skin in reaction to sunlight, boosts calcium absorption.

physical activity, and treatment options.[35] Updates to this document were published in 2004.[36]

## Substance Misuse and Abuse

Misuse and abuse of prescription and over-the-counter medications occur frequently among the elderly. This may be in part because the great majority of seniors use prescription or over-the-counter medication. Many seniors tend to have more than one health problem and receive multiple prescriptions. Sometimes they combine prescription drugs with over-the-counter products or with natural remedies. The drugs may interact and cause a confusing array of symptoms and reactions.

The most commonly misused drugs are sleeping pills, tranquilizers, pain medications, and laxatives. Sometimes a person innocently uses more than the prescribed dose or simultaneously takes several prescriptions of the same drug. Some older people are aware of their over-reliance on drugs but don't like how they feel when they don't take the pills.

Problems remembering, concentrating, and thinking are the most common psychological side effects of drugs in the elderly. As people age, their bodies take longer to

metabolize drugs, so medications like sleeping pills build up in the body. In some provinces, education programs such as the Safe Meds for Seniors Program are offered by pharmacists. Funded by the Government of Ontario, these seminars cover a variety of important topics with regard to medication use. Donnie Edwards, the Interim CEO of the OPA says, "Almost 50 percent of all medication used by seniors may be used inappropriately. Medication-related problems result in 25 percent of hospital admissions of patients over 50 years of age. By educating our seniors on medication therapy, we can improve health care outcomes, reduce hospital visits, and help control health care costs."[37]

A study released in September 2007 by the Canadian Institute for Health Information (CIHI) indicates that the proportion of seniors taking potentially harmful prescribed medication drugs decreased from more than one in three seniors (34 percent) in 2000–01 to just over one in four seniors (27 percent) in 2005–06. The study examined medications on public drug program claims in Alberta, Saskatchewan, Manitoba, and New Brunswick on the Beers list—an internationally recognized list of medications identified as potentially inappropriate for seniors. The study also showed that the use of the antidepressant, amitriptyline, which carries high potential health risks, had increased over the five years. The top five Beers list drugs most prescribed were hormone replacement drugs; amitriptyline; digoxin, a treatment for heart conditions; oxybutynin, a treatment for incontinence; and temazepam, a treatment for sleep disorders.[38]

In some older adults, alcohol can make mental confusion and memory problems worse. Community surveys suggest people older than 65 consume less alcohol and have fewer alcohol-related problems than younger drinkers; however, surveys conducted in health-care settings have found increasing prevalence of alcoholism among older adults. In addition to the direct risks of alcohol, older individuals face related dangers when they drink, including falls, fractures, accidents, medication interactions, depression, and cognitive changes.[39]

### ??? Is It Ever Too Late to Quit Smoking?

Despite the well-documented benefits of quitting, many seniors still smoke. According to the 2006 Canadian Tobacco Use Monitoring Survey (CTUMS), 11.5 percent of Canadians 55 or over are current smokers, with 9.5 percent being daily smokers.[40] Some research suggests that older smokers are more likely to be "hardcore" smokers—heavy smokers who expect never to quit smoking. Older smokers are also less likely to accept the health risks that are associated with smoking. The largest amount of smoking-related health-care costs in Canada is spent on hospital care, with higher costs attributable to older smokers. The mortality rate among current smokers who are over the age of 65 is twice that of people who have never smoked.

Cigarette smoking is the principle cause of **chronic obstructive pulmonary disease (COPD),** a lung disorder that causes airways to become partially obstructed. The two main forms of this disease are chronic bronchitis, an inflammation of the airways in the lungs, and emphysema, which damages and destroys lung tissue.[41] COPD often affects people over 60. The treatments include bronchodilators, inhaled steroids, antibiotics, vaccines, and supplemental oxygen.[42]

The sooner a smoker stops using tobacco, the greater the health benefits. The MacArthur Foundation Study shows that while risks of smoking persist into old age, so do the benefits of quitting smoking—at any age.[43] A person who smokes more than 20 cigarettes a day and quits at age 65 increases life expectancy by two or three years. When older people stop tobacco use, their circulation and lung function increase, they suffer less cardiovascular illness, and their quality of life improves.[44]

## Depression

Depression is a serious problem among the elderly. In the over-65 age group, at least one million seniors are living with a mental illness.[45] As many as 20 percent of seniors suffer mild to severe depression, ranging from 5 to 10 percent of seniors living in the community and 30 to 40 percent of seniors in long-term care facilities.[46] Depression can be hard to recognize, especially among older adults. It is often confused with aging itself. As well, many seniors hold negative attitudes about depression. This stops some of them from seeking help. It is estimated that seniors are among the most undertreated populations for mental health, with depression in more than one-third of people aged 65 or over going undetected.[47]

Older people face many challenges, including declining health, social isolation, and physical limitations. Deteriorating health can change a planned, happy retirement into one that includes fear, confusion, and chronic pain. Caring for loved ones also takes a toll. As many as 20 percent of people 65 years of age and older spend their days caring for their spouses, partners, or friends who need assistance bathing, dressing, eating, and toileting.[48] Losing a loved one affects mental well-being, too. About one-third of Canadian seniors are coping with the loss of their life partners, as well as the gradual loss of their friends and relatives. Wade and Pevalin,[49] in a study on marital transitions and mental health, found that those who experience the loss of a spouse go through an adjustment phase prior to and after the death. There were significantly higher proportions of people with poor mental health during this time compared to people who remain married.

However, depressed older adults are as likely to benefit from medication as younger individuals. More than 70 percent of the depressed elderly improve dramatically with treatment. There is a downside to the medical approach to treatment though. According to reports from the National Advisory Council on Aging, up to 50 percent of all prescriptions are not taken correctly, and up to 20 percent of all hospital admissions are due to adverse reactions to medications or not following prescription-drug instructions.[50] Some of the widely prescribed medications for seniors are known to be addictive and cause side effects. Benzodiazepine medications, which include Ativan®, Valium®, Serax®, and Xanax®, commonly prescribed for treating acute anxiety and insomnia, are only meant for short-term use. In many cases, use of these drugs becomes prolonged and side effects from their use include increased fatigue, impaired performance, and decreased ability to learn new things.

Since loneliness and loss are often important contributing factors to depression, psychiatrists often combine counselling, such as psychotherapy, with medication. Maintaining positive relationships with family and friends, seeking opportunities to express feelings, pursing activities that are enjoyable, and participating in regular physical activity can also help.

## Driving Risks

Half of Canadians 65 years and older who live in private households drive a motor vehicle. Drivers over 80 years of age are the fastest-growing segment of the driving population.[51] While age alone is not an indicator of impairment, age-related changes can affect driving ability. Over the years, road fatalities have dropped significantly in most age groups; however, this is not the case for people over 65.[52] The most common contributing factors in accidents involving older drivers include pulling out from the side of the road or changing lanes without looking, careless backing up, inaccurate turning, failure to yield the right of way, and difficulty reading traffic signs. Unlike younger drivers, older drivers' accidents seldom involve high speeds. Rather, problem driving in older adults involves visual, cognitive, and motor skills, which may decline with aging.

Medications are a factor when driving—especially for older adults. Drugs that combat anxiety and insomnia can make a person drowsy. Antihistamines can affect concentration. Combining over-the-counter and prescription drugs can be very dangerous. Table 15-1 shows some of the potential side effects medications can have.

▼ **Table 15-1 Medication Effects for the Older Driver**

| Medical Condition | Type of Medication | Potential Effects |
| --- | --- | --- |
| Anxiety | Sedatives | Drowsiness, staggering, blurred vision |
| Arthritis and rheumatism | Analgesics (pain relievers) | Drowsiness, inability to concentrate, ringing in ears |
| Common cold | Antihistamines, antitussives (cough suppressants) | Drowsiness, blurred vision, dizziness |
| Fatigue | Stimulants | Overexcitability, false sense of alertness, dizziness |
| Heart arrhythmia | Antiarrhythmics | Blurred vision, dizziness |
| Hypertension | Antihypertensives (blood pressure drugs) | Drowsiness, blurred vision, dizziness |

Source: From Drugs and the Older Driver. Information. Available at www.safetycouncil.org/info/seniors/medicati.htm. © 2005 Canada Safety Council.

## Death and Dying

According to mortality data from Statistics Canada, life expectancy for males and females combined is 80.2 years. Men can expect to live 77.8 years, and women can expect to live 82.6 years.[53] (See The X & Y Files: "Why Do Women Live Longer Than Men?".) Among older Canadians, cancer and heart disease are the top killers.

### Defining Death

In our society, death isn't a part of everyday life, as it once was. The definition of death has become more complex. Death has been broken down into the following categories:

✔ **Functional death.** The end of all vital functions, such as heartbeat and respiration.
✔ **Cellular death.** The gradual death of body cells after the heart stops beating. If placed in a tissue culture or, as is the case with various organs, transplanted to another body, some cells can remain alive indefinitely.
✔ **Cardiac death.** The moment when the heart stops beating.
✔ **Brain death.** The end of all brain activity, indicated by an absence of electrical activity (confirmed by an electroencephalogram, or EEG) and a lack of reflexes. The destruction of a person's brain means that his or her personality no longer exists; the lower brain centres controlling respiration and circulation no longer function.

✔ **Spiritual death.** The moment when the soul, as defined by many religions, leaves the body.

### Denying Death

Most of us don't quite believe that we're going to die. A reasonable amount of denial helps us focus on the day-to-day realities of living. However, excessive denial can be life-threatening. One important factor in denial is the nature of the threat. It's easy to believe that death is at hand when someone's pointing a gun at you; it's much harder to think that cigarette smoking might cause your death 20 or 30 years down the road. Elisabeth Kübler-Ross, a psychiatrist who has extensively studied the process of dying, describes the downside of denying death in *Death: The Final Stage of Growth:*

> It is the denial of death that is partially responsible for people living empty, purposeless lives; for when you live as if you'll live forever, it becomes too easy to postpone the things you know that you must do. You live your life in preparation for tomorrow or in the remembrance of yesterday—and meanwhile, each today is lost. In contrast, when you fully understand that each day you awaken could be the last you have, you take the time that day to grow, to become more of who you really are, to reach out to other human beings.[54]

### Emotional Responses to Dying

Elisabeth Kübler-Ross has identified five typical stages of reaction that a person goes through when facing death (see Figure 15-4).

1. *Denial ("No, not me").* At first knowledge that death is coming, a terminally ill patient rejects the news. The denial overcomes the initial shock and allows the person to begin to gather together his or her resources. Denial, at this point, is a healthy defence mechanism. It can become distressful, however, if it's reinforced by the relatives and friends of the dying patient.
2. *Anger ("Why me?").* In the second stage, the dying person begins to feel resentment and rage regarding imminent death. The anger may be directed at God

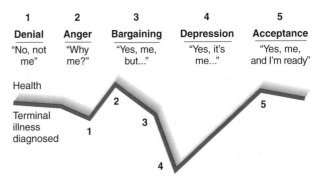

▲ **Figure 15-4** Kübler-Ross's Five Stages of Adjustment to Death.

## The X & Y Files

# Why Do Women Live Longer Than Men?

The gender gap in longevity has been shrinking since 1990; however, women still outlive men. Life expectancy at the age of 65 improved for men in Canada in 2004. It rose by 0.4 years to 77.8 years. Senior women saw a gain of 0.2 years to 82.6 years. The gap in female-male life expectancy in 2004 was the smallest in the past 25 years. The gender difference in mortality rates emerges from the moment of conception. Baby girls are less likely to die in the womb or after delivery than baby boys. Once past age 30, women consistently outnumber and outlive men.

Why do men die sooner? The female edge may begin at conception with the extra X chromosome, which provides a backup for defects on the X gene and a double dose of the genetic factors that regulate the immune system. In addition, the female hormone estrogen bolsters immunity and protects heart, bone, brain, and blood vessels.

In some cancers, estrogen may somehow protect against distant metastases. In contrast, testosterone may dampen the immune response in males—possibly to prevent attacks on sperm cells that might otherwise be mistaken as alien invaders. When the testes are removed from mice and guinea pigs, their immune systems become more active. In men, lessened immunity may lower resistance to cancer as well as infectious disease. Half of all men—compared with a third of women—develop cancer. Smoking, which for a long time was much more prevalent among men, accounts for some of this difference.

Testosterone also has been implicated in men's risk of heart disease and stroke. Originally designed to equip men with an instantaneous burst of power—essential for survival in Stone Age times—this potent male hormone may surge so intensely that it wreaks havoc throughout the cardiovascular system.

Males also die more often as a result of intentional and unintentional injury. Overall, men are three times more likely than women to die in accidents, mainly in cars and on the job. Men also are four times more likely to die violently. Nine in 10 murderers and 8 in 10 murder victims are men.

---

or at the patient's family and caregivers, who can do little but try to endure any expressions of anger, provide comfort, and help the patient on to the next stage.

3. *Bargaining ("Yes, me, but…")*. In this stage, a patient may try to bargain, usually with God, for a way to reverse, or at least postpone, dying. The patient may promise, in exchange for recovery, to do good works or to see family members more often. Alternatively, the patient may say, "Let me live long enough to see my grandchild born" or "to see the spring again."

4. *Depression ("Yes, it's me")*. In the fourth stage, the patient gradually realizes the full consequences of his or her condition. This may begin as grieving for health that has been lost and then become anticipatory grieving for the loss that is to come of friends, loved ones, and life itself. This stage is perhaps the most difficult: The dying person should not be left alone during this period. Neither should loved ones try to cheer up the patient, who must be allowed to grieve.

5. *Acceptance ("Yes, me, and I'm ready")*. In this last stage, the person has accepted the reality of death: The moment looms as neither frightening nor painful, neither sad nor happy—only inevitable. The person who waits for the end of life may ask to see fewer visitors, to separate from other people, or perhaps to turn to just one person for support.

Several stages may occur at the same time, and some may happen out of sequence. Each stage may take days or only hours or minutes. Throughout, denial may come back to assert itself unexpectedly, and hope for a medical breakthrough or a miraculous recovery is forever present.

Some experts dispute Kübler-Ross's basic five-stage theory as too simplistic and argue that not all people go through such well-defined stages in the dying process. The way a person faces death is often a mirror of the way he or she has faced other major stresses in life: Those who have had the most trouble adjusting to other crises will have the most trouble adjusting to the news of their impending death.

An individual's will to live can postpone death for a while. The prospect of an upcoming birthday postpones death in women but hastens it in men. The will to live typically fluctuates in terminal patients, varying along with depression, anxiety, shortness of breath, and a sense of well-being.[55]

You can assure that your wishes are heeded by several means, including advance directives, living wills, and holographic wills.

## What Are Advance Directives?

**Advance directives** are used to specify the kind of medical treatment individuals want in case of a medical crisis. These documents indicate a person's preferences. Hospitals and other institutions often make decisions on an individual's behalf, particularly if family members are not available or if they disagree. Advance directives also help physicians, who often do not feel comfortable making these kinds of decisions about life-extending treatments for their terminally ill patients.[56]

A *health-care proxy* is an advance directive that gives someone else the power to make decisions on your behalf. People typically name a relative or close friend as their agent. You need to let family, friends, and your primary physician know about the type of care you would or wouldn't want to receive in various circumstances, such as an accident that results in an irreversible coma.

You can also sign an advance directive specifying that you want to be allowed to die naturally—a **do-not-resuscitate (DNR)** directive indicates that you do not want to be resuscitated in case your heart stops beating.

## What Is a Living Will?

A **living will** isn't just for people who don't want to be kept alive by artificial means. Individuals can also use these advance directives to indicate that they want all possible medical treatments and technology used to prolong their lives. Some provinces recognize living wills as legally binding, and a growing number of health-care professionals and facilities offer patients help in drafting living wills. Give copies to anyone who might have input in decisions on your behalf. You should also give copies to your physician.

### Wills

Perhaps you think that only wealthy or older people need to write wills. However, if you're married, have children, or own property, you should prepare a will. There are three types of wills: formal, notarial, and holographic. A formal will is a typed document, prepared by a lawyer or a notary, and signed by you in front of at least two witnesses who cannot be a beneficiary or your spouse. A notarial will is similar to the formal will but only used in Quebec. It is prepared by a notary and signed before the notary and a witness. A **holographic will** is prepared in

▲ Humanitarian caregiving for both critically ill patients and their loved ones can help to take some of the fear out of death.

## Preparing for Death

Throughout this book we have stressed the ways in which you can determine how well and how long you live. You can also make decisions about the end of your life, particularly its impact on other people. To clarify your thinking on this difficult subject, ask yourself the following questions:

- ✔ Would I prefer to receive or refuse any specific treatments if I were unconscious or incapable of voicing my opinion?
- ✔ Would I like my bodily systems to be kept functioning by extraordinary life-sustaining measures, even though my natural systems had failed? If I could not survive without mechanical assistance, would I want to be kept alive or resuscitated if my heart were to stop?
- ✔ Would I like the province to decide how to distribute my property, or would I rather name the recipients of my estate?
- ✔ Would I like to decide how to handle my funeral arrangements?

your handwriting and signed by you, with no witness necessary. Experts advise against this type of will because it is often subject to misinterpretation and challenge, and it is not recognized in all provinces. It is important that you specify who you wish to raise your children and who should have your property. If you die *intestate* (without a will), the province will make these decisions for you. Even a modest estate can be tied up in court for a long period of time, depriving family members of money when they need it most.

## Suicide

Suicide among the elderly is a danger that often goes unnoticed. Elderly men are at a far greater risk of attempting suicide than women, with almost five times as many senior men committing suicide. Of all groups in Canada, men over the age of 85 have the highest rate of completed suicides. Men over 70 are also hospitalized at higher rates than women for attempted suicide.[57]

One of the main factors leading to suicide is illness, especially terminal illness. A great deal of debate centres on quality of life, yet there is no reliable or consistent way to measure this. Patients who are dying may feel they have some quality of life, even when others do not recognize it, or their evaluations of the quality of their lives may fluctuate. Dying patients who say their lives are not worth living may be suffering from depression; hopelessness is one of its characteristic symptoms.[58]

### "Rational" Suicide

An elderly widow suffering from advanced cancer takes a lethal overdose of sleeping pills. A woman in her fifties, diagnosed with Alzheimer's disease, asks a doctor to help her end her life. Are these suicides "rational" because these individuals used logical reasoning in deciding to end their lives?

The question is intensely controversial. Advocates of the right to self-deliverance argue that individuals in great pain or faced with the prospect of a debilitating, hopeless battle against an incurable disease can and should be able to decide to end their lives. As legislatures and the legal system tackle the thorny issue of an individual's right to die, mental health professionals worry that suicidal wishes, even in those with fatal diseases, often stem from undiagnosed depression.

A number of studies have indicated that most patients with painful, progressive, or terminal illnesses do not want to kill themselves. The percentage of those who report thinking about suicide ranges from 5 to 20 percent, and most of these have major depression. Many mental health professionals argue that what makes patients with severe illnesses suicidal is depression, not their physical condition.

Because depression may indeed warp the ability to make a rational decision about suicide, mental health professionals urge physicians and family members to make sure individuals with chronic or fatal illnesses are evaluated for depression and treated with medication, psychotherapy, or both.

## Grief

The death of a loved one may be the single most upsetting and feared event in a person's life. Losing a parent in childhood can have a lasting impact. A study that followed 100 orphans found that as young adults they suffered significantly higher depressive symptoms.[59] When both parents die, individuals may feel like orphaned children. They mourn not just for the father and mother who are gone, but also for their lost role of being someone's child.

The death of a family member produces a wide range of reactions, including anxiety, guilt, anger, and financial concern. Many may see the death of an old person as less tragic than the death of a child or young person. A sudden death can be more of a shock than one following a long illness. A suicide can be particularly devastating. The death of a child can be even more traumatic.

Grieving may continue for many years. Eventually, parents may be able to resolve their grief and accept the death as "God's will" or as "something that happens." Others deal with their grief by keeping busy or by substituting other problems or situations to take their minds off their loss. Yet many parents who lose a child continue to grieve for many years. Although the pain of their loss diminishes with time, they view it as part of themselves and describe an emptiness inside—even though most have rich, meaningful, and happy daily lives.

The loss of a mate can also have a profound impact, although men's and women's responses to the death may depend on how their spouses died. Men whose wives die suddenly face a greater risk of dying themselves than those whose wives die after a long illness. Women whose husbands die after a long illness face greater risk of dying than other widows. The reason may be that men whose wives were chronically ill learned how to cope with the loss of their nurturers, while women who spend a long time caring for an ill husband may be at greater risk because of the combined burdens of caregiving and loss of financial support.

Bereavement is not a rare occurrence on college and university campuses, but it is largely an ignored problem. Counsellors have called upon universities to help students who have lost a loved one through initiatives such as training students to provide peer support and raising consciousness about bereavement.[60]

## Grief's Effect on Health

Men and women who lose partners, parents, or children endure so much stress that they are at increased risk of serious physical and mental illness and even of premature death. Studies of the health effects of grief have found the following:

✓ Grief produces changes in the respiratory, hormonal, and central nervous systems and may affect functions of the heart, blood, and immune systems.

✓ Grieving adults may experience mood swings between sadness and anger, guilt and anxiety. They may feel physically sick, lose their appetite, sleep poorly, or fear that they're going crazy because they "see" the deceased person in different places.

✓ Friendships and remarriage offer the greatest protection against health problems.

✓ Some widows may have increased rates of depression, suicide, and death from cirrhosis of the liver. The greatest risk factors are poor previous mental and physical health and a lack of social support.

✓ Grieving parents, partners, and adult children are at increased risk of serious physical and mental illness, suicide, and premature death.

## Methods of Mourning

Grief is a psychological necessity, not self-indulgence. Psychotherapists refer to grief as work, and it is—slow, tedious, and painful. Yet only by working through grief—dealing with feelings of anger and despair, and adjusting emotionally and intellectually to the loss—can bereaved individuals make their way back to the living world of hope and love.

Some widows and widowers move through the grieving process without experiencing extreme distress. Others stop somewhere in the midst of normal grieving and continue to pine for the deceased, become overly reliant on others, or show signs of denial, avoidance, or anxiety.

## How Can You Help Survivors of a Loss?

Although we grieve for the dead, the living are the ones who need our help. Bereavement is such an intense state that survivors may be too numb or too stunned to ask for help. Family and friends must take the initiative and spend time with those who are mourning the loss of a loved one, even if that means sitting together silently. Offer empathy and support, and let the grieving person know with verbal and nonverbal expressions that you care and wish to help. Simply being there is enough to let your friend know you care.

Giving help over the first few days is important, but grieving people continue to need support for many months. The first anniversary of a death or the first holiday spent alone can be particularly difficult.

Most bereaved people don't need professional psychological counselling. In most instances, sharing their feelings with friends is all that's needed. However, you should urge a friend or relative to seek help if he or she shows no sign of grieving or exhibits as much distress a year after the loss as during the first months. Therapy and medication can be enormously helpful—and potentially life-saving.

**CHAPTER 15**

**Making This Chapter Work for You**

1. Factors that contribute to a long life and successful aging include all of the following *except*
   a. healthy weight.
   b. moderate smoking.
   c. regular exercise.
   d. social involvement.

2. Physically fit people over age 60
   a. have a lower risk of dying from chronic heart disease.
   b. can regain the fitness level of a 25-year-old.
   c. show no difference in levels of anxiety and depression.
   d. have higher body-fat percentages.

3. Which statement about the aging brain is *false*?
   a. When brain cells die, surrounding cells can fill the gaps to maintain cognitive function.
   b. Remembering names and recalling information may take longer.
   c. "Use it or lose it."
   d. Mental and physical ability both decline with age.

4. Which statement about aging is *false*?
   a. People over age 70 who take vitamin supplements showed improvement in short-term memory and problem-solving ability.
   b. Fitness and frequency of sexual activity are linked.
   c. Hormone replacement therapy reduces the risk of heart disease in menopausal women.
   d. Seniors who take up new hobbies late in life may slow aging within the brain.

5. Which statement about age-related problems is correct?
   a. Osteoporosis affects only women.
   b. Alzheimer's disease is a form of dementia.
   c. Depression is no more prevalent in the older population.
   d. Drug interactions do not occur in the elderly.

6. When should concern change to intervention?
   a. Uncle Charlie is 85 and continues to drive himself to the grocery store and to the senior centre during the daytime.
   b. Nana takes pills at breakfast, lunch, and dinner, but sometimes mixes them up.
   c. Mom's hot flashes have become a family joke.
   d. Your older brother can never remember where he put his car keys.

7. According to Elisabeth Kübler-Ross, an individual facing death goes through all of the following emotional stages *except*
   a. bargaining.
   b. acceptance.
   c. denial.
   d. repression.

8. The gender gap related to longevity
   a. is due to deficiencies in the Y chromosome.
   b. results from the presence of a mutant gene.
   c. may be due to the X chromosome and its hormonal influences on the immune system.
   d. is about 13 years in Canada.

9. An advance directive
   a. indicates who should have your property in the event that you die.
   b. may authorize which individuals may not participate in your health care if you are unable to care for yourself.
   c. can specify your desires related to the use of medical treatments and technology to prolong your life.
   d. should specify which physician you designate to be your health-care proxy.

10. You can best help a friend who is bereaved by
    a. encouraging him to have a few drinks to forget his pain.
    b. simply spending time with her.
    c. avoiding talking about his loss because it is awkward.
    d. reminding her about all she still has in her life.

Answers to these questions can be found on page 450.

## Self Responsibility

*Our care should not be to have lived long as to have lived enough.*

**Seneca**

Presently, you may be in the pre-contemplation or contemplation stage of preparing for older adulthood. That is the case for many college and university students, but preparation can begin at any time. Choices you make today will affect you as you age. Visualize yourself as an older adult. What activities

## Social Responsibility

*What we have done for ourselves alone dies with us; what we have done for others and the world remains and is immortal.*

**Albert Pike**

do you hope to be doing? How can lifestyle choices you make now support your vision of older adulthood? Many older adults living in assisted living or care homes would welcome a visit from a college or university student. Consider volunteering once or on a regular basis.

## Critical Thinking

1. How are your parents or other mentors staying fit and alert as they age? Do you think you might use similar strategies?

2. Have your living parents and grandparents written advanced directives or a living will? Have you discussed with them their preferences regarding treatment in the event of a medical crisis? If you haven't had this discussion with your family, how can you begin the process of helping your parents or grandparents communicate their wishes?

3. Many people are chronically unconscious, kept alive by artificial respirators and feeding tubes. If you were in an accident that left you in a vegetative state, would you want doctors to do everything possible to fight for your life, or would you want to have the right to decide when to end your life?

CENGAGENOW™

If your textbook package includes CengageNOW™, go to http://west.cengagenow.com/ilrn/ to link to CengageNOW™ for Health, your online study tool. First take the **Pre-test** for this chapter to get your personalized **Study Plan,** which will identify topics you need to review and direct you to the appropriate resources. Then take the **Post-test** to determine what concepts you have mastered and what you still need work on.

## SITES & BYTES

### Active Living Coalition for Older Adults
**www.alcoa.ca**

This agency is a partnership of organizations and individuals who are interested in the field of aging. Reports, fact sheets, and information on how older adults can maintain their well-being and independence through healthy living are available at this site.

### National Seniors Council
**www.seniorscouncil.gc.ca/en/home.shtml**

Reporting to a variety of federal government agencies, the National Seniors Council advises on quality of life and health and well-being issues of seniors. You can find reports and research at this site.

### Osteoporosis Canada
**www.osteoporosis.ca**

Free publications, educational programs, medically accurate information for people dealing with osteoporosis and health-care workers, and current up-to-date research are available at this site.

Please note that links are subject to change. If you find a broken link, use a search engine such as www.google.ca and search for the website by typing in keywords.

**InfoTrac® College Edition Activity** Payn, T., Pfeiffer, K.A., Hutto, B., Vena, J.E., LaMonte, M.J., Blair, S.N., & Hooker, S.P. (2008, June). Daily steps in midlife and older adults: Relationship with demographic, self-rated heatlh, and self-reported physical activity (Epidemiology) (Report). *Research Quarterly for Exercise and Sport, 79*(1), 128(5).

1. List the three purposes of this study.
2. Describe the study protocol that the researchers used to evaluate the experimental pedometer intervention.
3. Discuss the unexpected findings of this study and describe what implications this finding has on the use of pedometers as an interactive intervention with midlife and older adults.

You can find additional readings relating to aging and death with InfoTrac® College Edition, an online library of more than 5000 journals and publications. Follow the instructions for accessing InfoTrac® that were packaged with your textbook; then search for articles using a keyword search.

For additional links and resources, visit our text-specific website at www.health.nelson.com.

## Key Terms

The terms listed here are used within the chapter on the page indicated. Definitions of the terms are in the Glossary at the end of the book.

| | | | |
|---|---|---|---|
| **advance directives** 399 | **chronic obstructive** | **do-not-resuscitate** | **living will** 399 |
| **aging** 385 | **pulmonary disease** | **(DNR)** 399 | **menopause** 391 |
| **Alzheimer's disease** 393 | **(COPD)** 396 | **holographic will** 399 | **osteoporosis** 394 |
| | **dementia** 393 | **hormone replacement** | **perimenopause** 389 |
| | | **therapy (HRT)** 392 | |

## References

1. Statistics Canada. (2007, July 17). *The Daily.* 2006 Census. Age and sex. Available at www.statcan.ca/Daily/English/070717/d070717a.htm.
2. Ibid.
3. Ibid.
4. Ibid.
5. Ibid.
6. Statistics Canada. (2007, February 27). *The Daily.* A portrait of seniors. 2006. Available at www.statcan.ca/Daily/English/070227/d070227b.htm.
7. Ibid.
8. Ibid.
9. Roizen, Michael. Personal interview.
10. Active Living Coalition for Older Adults. (2008, May/June). Celebrating active healthy lives. Vol. 2. No. 2. Available at www.alcoa.ca/e/newsletters/2008_05_may_jun.pdf.
11. Kahana, E., et al. (2002). Long-term impact of preventive proactivity on quality of life of the old-old. *Psychosomatic Medicine, 64,* 392.

12. Myers, J., et al. (2002). Exercise capacity and mortality among men referred for exercise testing. *New England Journal of Medicine, 346*, 793.

13. Gibson, H. (2002, January 29). *UF study: Healthy aging depends on social as well as physical activity.* University of Florida News Office.

14. Andrews, G. (2001). Care of older people: Promoting health and function in an aging population. *British Medical Journal, 322*(7288), 728.

15. Tabbarah, M., et al. (2002). The relationship between cognitive and physical performance. *Journals of Gerontology,* Series A, *57*(4), 228.

16. Public Health Agency of Canada. (n.d.). Canada's physical activity guide to healthy active living for older adults. Health Canada. Available at www.phac-aspc.gc.ca/pau-uap/paguide/older/index.html.

17. Public Health Agency of Canada. (n.d.). Why should I be active? Guide for older adults. Available at www.phac-aspc.gc.ca/pau-uap/paguide/older/why.html.

18. Canadian Centre for Activity and Aging. (2005, Spring). *Canadian Centre for Activity and Aging Newsletter,* (10). Available at www.alcoa.ca/research_u_docs/2005_04apr_en_tips.pdf.

19. Rowe, John. Personal interview.

20. Canadian consensus on menopause and osteoporosis. (2002). 2002 update. Society of Obstetricians and Gynaecologists of Canada. Available at www.sogc.org/guidelines/pdf/osteomeno.pdf.

21. CEMCOR. Centre for Menstrual Cycle and Ovulation Research. (n.d.). Could I be in perimenopause? Available at www.cemcor.ubc.ca/ask/onset_of_perimenopause.

22. U.S. Preventive Services Task Force. (2002). *Hormone replacement therapy for primary prevention of chronic conditions.* Rockville, MD: Agency for Healthcare Research and Quality.

23. Hlatky, M., et al. (2002). Quality of life and depressive symptoms in postmenopausal women after receiving hormone therapy: Results from the heart and estrogen/progestin replacement study (HERS) trial. *Journal of the American Medical Association, 287*(5), 591.

24. Nelson, H., et al. (2002). Postmenopausal hormone replacement therapy scientific review. *Journal of the American Medical Association, 288*(7), 872. 24.

25. The Canadian Women's Health Network. (n.d.). HTR in the news. The Women's Health initiative at a glance. Available at www.cwhn.ca/resources/menopause/hrt-glance.html.

26. CBC News. (2008, May 20). Home. Health. In depth health. Hormone replacement therapy: FAQ. Available at www.cbc.ca/health/story/2008/05/20/f-health-hrt.html.

27. Ibid.

28. Lindau, S.T., Schumm, L.P., Laumann, E.O., Levinson, W., O'Muircheartaigh, Colm. A., Waite, L.J. (2007). A student of sexuality and health among older adults in the United States. *New England Journal of Medicine, 357*(8), 762–74.

29. Ibid.

30. Sato, R., et al. (2000, October 15). A prospective study of vitamin C and cognitive function in older adults. *Gerontologist,* p. 218.

31. Active Living Coalition for Older Adults. (2003, December). Research Update. Issue 6. Healthy eating and regular physical activity: A winning combination for older adults. Available at www.alcoa.ca/research_u_docs/2003_12dec_en_update.pdf.

32. Alzheimer Society of Canada. (2005, March). Common Questions. Available at www.alzheimer.ca/english/misc/faqs.htm.

33. Osteoporosis Canada. (2007). About Osteoporosis. What is Osteoporosis. Available at www.osteoporosis.ca/english/about%20osteoporosis/what-is/default.asp?s=1.

34. Osteoporosis Canada. (2008). About Osteoporosis. Drug treatments. Available at www.osteoporosis.ca/english/about%20osteoporosis/drug%20treatments/default.asp?s=1.

35. Brown, J.P., Josse, R.G., and the Scientific Advisory Council of the Osteoporosis Society of Canada. (2002). 2002 clinical practice guidelines for the diagnosis and management of osteoporosis of Canada. *Canadian Medical Association Journal, 167*(10 suppl.).

36. Brown, J.P., & Josse, R.G. (2004). 2002 clinical practice guidelines for the diagnosis and management of osteoporosis of Canada. Published November 12, 2002. Revised August 26, 2004. *Canadian Medical Association Journal, 167*(10 suppl), S1–S34. Available at www.cmaj.ca/cgi/data/167/10_suppl/s1/DC1/1.

37. Ontario Pharmacists' Association. (n.d.). Home. Programs. Safe meds program. Available at www.opatoday.com/SSMUP.asp

38. Canadian Institute for Health Information. (2007, September 13). News. Decrease in seniors taking potentially harmful drugs between 2000 and 2006. Available at http://secure.cihi.ca/cihiweb/dispPage.jsp?cw_page=media_13sep2007_e.

39. Thomas, V., & Rockwood, K. (2001). Alcohol abuse, cognitive impairment, and mortality among older people. *Journal of the American Geriatrics Society, 49*(4), 415.

40. Health Canada. (2007, December 12). Healthy Living. Tobacco use statistics. Canadian Tobacco Use Monitoring Survey. CTUMS, Annual 2006. Available at www.hc-sc.gc.ca/hl-vs/tobac-tabac/research-recherche/stat/_ctums-esutc_2006/ann-table1eng.php.

41. The Lung Association (Canada). (2008, July 3). Home. Lung Diseases. COPD. Available at www.lung.ca/diseases-maladies/copd-mpoc_e.php.

42. Ibid.

43. Rowe, John. Personal interview.

44. The Lung Association (Canada). (2008, July 3). Home. Lung Diseases. COPD. Treatment. Available at www.lung.ca/diseases-maladies/copd-mpoc_e.php.

45. Canadian Coalition for Senior's Mental Health. (May 2004). Position paper: Mental health and the home care sector. Available at www.ccsmh.ca/en/advocacy/election.cfm.

46. Here to Help. (2006). Publications. Fact Sheets. Senior's mental health and addictions issues. Available at www.heretohelp.bc.ca/publications/factsheets/seniors.

47. Ibid.

48. Ibid.

49. Wade, T.J., & Pevalin, D.J. (2004, June). Marital transitions and mental health. *Journal of Health and Social Behaviour, 45*, 155–70.

50. Here to Help. (2006). Senior's mental health and addictions issues. Available at www.heretohelp.bc.ca/publications/factsheets/seniors.

51. Canada Safety Council. (2004). Safety and the aging driver. Available at www.safety-council.org/info/seniors/safedriv.html.

52. Canada Safety Council. (2004). Safety tips for the older driver. Available at www.safety-council.org/info/seniors/driving.htm.

53. Statistics Canada. (2006, December 20). *The Daily.* Deaths. 2004. Available at www.statcan.ca/Daily/English/061220/d061220b.htm.

54. Kübler-Ross, E. (1975). *Death: The final stage of growth.* Englewood Cliffs, NJ: Prentice Hall.

55. Carpenter, E. (2001, October 15). The end of life odyssey. *Gerontologist,* p. 51.

56. Landers, S. (2002, September 2). Decisions on end-of-life care shouldn't be left to the end. *American Medical News.*

57. Here to Help. (2006). Senior's mental health and addictions issues. Available at www.heretohelp.bc.ca/publications/factsheets/seniors.

58. Farsides, B., & Dunlop, R. (2001). Measuring quality of life: Is there such a thing as a life not worth living? *British Medical Journal, 322*(7300), 1481.

59. Ifeagwazi, C., et al. (2001). The influence of early parents' death on manifestations of depressive symptoms among young adults. *Omega—Journal of Death and Dying, 42*(2), 151.

60. Balk, D. (2001, January). College student bereavement, scholarship, and the university. *Death Studies, 25*(1), 67.

# Working Toward a Healthy Environment

Ours is a planet in peril. A recent report of the Intergovernmental Panel on Climate Change documents increasing dangers to the planet Earth and its inhabitants. Sea levels are rising. Forests are being destroyed. Droughts in Asia and Africa have become more frequent and more intense. Despite some recent improvements, millions of people are dying every year from the effects of climate change.[1]

Environmental concerns may seem so enormous that nothing any individual can do will have an effect. This is not the case. All of us, as citizens of the world, can help find solutions to the challenges confronting our planet. The first step is realizing that we have a personal responsibility for safeguarding the health of our environment and, thereby, our own well-being. We cannot be "well" in an "unwell" world.

This chapter introduces you to some international experts who encourage all of us to stand up, take notice, and put an action plan into place with regard to current environmental issues. It also explores the complex interrelationships between our world and our well-being. It discusses major threats to the environment—including atmospheric changes; air, water, and noise pollution; chemical risks; and radiation—and provides specific guidance on what you can do about them.

**After studying the material in this chapter, you will be able to:**

- **Define** important environmental terms.
- **Describe** a number of national, provincial, and campus environmental initiatives.
- **List** the major types of outdoor and indoor pollution.
- **List** and **describe** actions that individuals can take to protect the environment.

**??? FREQUENTLY ASKED QUESTIONS**

**FAQ: What is climate change? p. 410**

**FAQ: What can I do to protect the planet? p. 412**

**FAQ: What health risks are caused by pesticides? p. 421**

## Environmental Awareness

Planet Earth—once taken for granted as a ball of rock and water that has existed for our use for all time—now is seen as a single, fragile **ecosystem** (a community of organisms that share a physical and chemical environment). An ecosystem approach recognizes the interrelationships between land, air, water, wildlife, human beings, and activities.[2] According to many environmental experts, we have to take responsibility for our environment and to embrace these interrelationships because there is no other option. This responsibility includes being more aware of the environmental costs of technological advances. While technology continues to raise the standard of living in industrialized countries, it often does so at a terrible environmental cost.

The dangers of technological developments became evident in the post-World War II era when we had to deal with toxic radioactive wastes because of atomic-weapons technology, the devastation of nature due to the indiscriminate use of pesticides and herbicides, and the heavy pollution of our air and water with petroleum by-products. We began to realize that we were changing our world as we knew it. We also heard from First Nations people and a group of distinguished scientists, philosophers, and citizens, whose writings and research have called on us to pay attention to our environment. Some of those who are looking to the future are featured following.

### First Nations Environmental Network

The First Nations Environmental Network (FNEN) is a circle of First Nations peoples who came together in the 1980s because of environmental concerns such as clear-cutting, herbicides, dams, and oil and gas exploration.[3] Many First Nations communities were being affected by degrading environmental practices, so there was a need to take action to ensure a sustainable future.

The mission of FNEN is to protect and restore the harmony of all life through traditional values, following the path of the ancestors. FNEN is committed to connecting indigenous peoples to the wider national and international community.

Their outreach is inspired by the traditional teachings of the braid, which weaves together the past, the present, and the future[4] and seeks to balance three aspects:

- ✔ *Mind*—where environmental awareness of Mother Earth is expressed through education.
- ✔ *Body*—where efforts are expressed through grassroots activism.
- ✔ *Spirit*—where ceremonies, spiritual gatherings, healing circles, and individual work help to strengthen the connection to the powers of Mother Earth, Sky, and All Relations.

There have been many positive changes in Canada because of the actions of the members of the FNEN. Some examples include opposition to nuclear waste dumping in Saskatchewan adjacent to or on Native reserves; support for Bear Watch efforts to stop trophy hunting and poaching of black bears and grizzly bears for body parts; stopping destructive logging practices in many provinces; and efforts to stop low-level military flights to protect traditional lands.[5]

Embracing traditional indigenous knowledge into environmental management seems fitting as we all move forward on planning for our future. Our economy and our very survival depend on respecting Mother Earth, Sky, and All Relations.[6, 7]

### Rachel Carson

Rachel Carson, the author of one of the twentieth century's most important books, *Silent Spring* (1962),[8] alerted us to the consequences of attempting to control nature with the use of poisonous chemicals to kill insects. The 40th anniversary edition of her book was published in 2002.

Sometimes called the mother of the environmental movement,[9] Carson challenged the practices of agricultural scientists and the U.S. government and called for new policies to protect human health and our environment.[10] Although she was attacked by individuals in the chemical industry and accused of being an alarmist, her research and writing helped to awaken public concern. This resulted in a government report that called for more research into the potential health hazards of pesticide use and urged care in the use of chemicals in homes and in industry.

### Al Gore

Al Gore, former vice president of the United States, is an environmental activist and author who suggests that the climate change issue is one of the most important moral issues of our time. In 1992, he wrote a bestseller titled *Earth in the Balance: Ecology and the Human Spirit*.[11] The book explained the dire consequences of global warming, while presenting a range of options we could adopt to deal with our environmental problems.

In 2006, Gore wrote a new book titled *An Inconvenient Truth: The Planetary Emergency of Global Warming and What We Can Do about It*.[12] This book struck an accord with a worldwide audience. The information presented in this book reminds us that it is vital we recognize the crisis we are facing. Gore warns that we have a moral imperative to act. The documentary that followed the publication of the book and became one of the top documentaries in history won an Academy Award for Documentary Feature. Gore has also founded and chairs *The Alliance for Climate Protection*,[13] a non-profit, nonpartisan organization that is building a movement to encourage the political will to solve our climate crisis. The *WE Campaign*, a project of the Alliance, encourages Americans to work toward repowering the United States with 100 percent of its electricity from clean energy sources within ten years. This initiative has also moved to other countries around the world.

In 2007, Gore was awarded a Nobel Peace Prize, shared with the Intergovernmental Panel on Climate Change and given for efforts to build up and disseminate greater knowledge about human-made climate change. He also assisted in the organization of Live Earth benefit concerts in both 2007 and 2008. In his latest book, *The Assault on Reason*,[14] Gore argues that some politicians are ignoring scientific evidence that tells us we have a planetary emergency. He encourages all of us to be proactive when it comes to the climate change crisis—even when the changes may be "inconvenient."

## David Suzuki

Dr. David Suzuki, an internationally renowned Canadian scientist, academic, broadcaster, writer, and founder and Chair of the David Suzuki Foundation, has also explored the connectedness of all things. His foundation, started in 1990, focuses on four program areas: forests and wild lands, oceans and sustainable fishing, climate change and clean energy, and the web of life and sustainable living.

Considered to be one of North America's leading environmentalists, Suzuki has worked to find ways for society to live in balance with our natural world. He was the first person in Canada to own a car with a hybrid engine, which runs on electricity and conventional fuel. In addition to conducting important research, writing, and public speaking, Suzuki continues to encourage individual action to change the world.[15] He lists six priorities: (1) stop global warming, (2) take the nature challenge (see page 415), (3) go carbon neutral, (4) protect our oceans, (5) read the Suzuki newsletter, and (6) go pesticide-free.[16]

## Roberta Bondar

Another Canadian environmental ally is astronaut Roberta Bondar,[17] who was part of the flight crew on the space shuttle *Discovery*, which launched on January 22, 1992. She

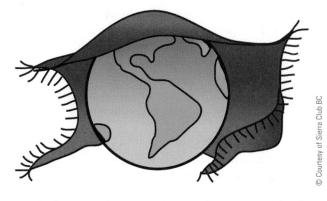

was the first Canadian woman to travel in space. Her books, *Passionate Vision: Discovering Canada's National Parks* and *Touching the Earth*, are visual and written accounts of the beauty of our Earth. She encourages us to change the way we think about our relationship with our planet. She suggests that every generation has a common goal—to be healthy and happy:

> After observing the planet for eight days from space, I have a deeper interest and respect for the forces that shape our world. Each particle of soil, each plant and animal is special. I also marvel at the creativity and ingenuity of our own species, but at the same time, I wonder why we all cannot see that we create our future each day, and that our local actions affect the global community, today as well as for generations to come. From the distance of space flight, it's easy to believe that we can live in harmony with one another and the environment. . . . We must not thrust upon children the responsibility of saving the environment. We are all involved.[18]

## Andrew Weaver

We are fortunate to have in our midst yet another Canadian who is also calling for action. Dr. Andrew Weaver, a world-class climatologist, researcher, and educator, works closely with other scientists in the Canadian Centre for Climate Modelling and Analysis,[19] a division of Environment Canada,[20] which is housed at the University of Victoria. He, along with other colleagues, has developed an Earth system climate model that is now used by scientists around the world to study climate change. "The evidence keeps mounting that most climate warming observed over the last 50 years is due to human activities," he says. "This is acknowledged by the world's leading scientists and sends a strong signal to governments that informed policy is urgently needed to determine a course of action for the future."[21]

Weaver, a lead author on the United Nations Intergovernmental Panel on Climate Change, the organization that received, along with Al Gore, the 2007 Nobel Peace Prize, is also the author of a book titled *Keeping Our Cool: Canada in a Warming World*.[22] Weaver shares with us his opinion that the climate change we are starting to experience will now be larger and faster than it has been at any time in the last 10 000 years. The emphasis on climate change in Canada is especially insightful. This book is a must-read if you want to understand more fully the impact of greenhouse gas emissions and what we must do to stabilize our climate. On a hopeful note, Weaver also offers solutions for a sustainable future.

## Our Planet, Our Health

Our environment affects our well-being both directly and indirectly. Changes in temperature and rainfall patterns disturb ecological processes in ways that can be hazardous to our health. The environment may account for 25 to 40 percent of diseases worldwide. Depletion of the ozone layer has already been implicated in the increase in skin cancers and cataracts. As well, global warming might lead to changes in one-third to one-half of the world's vegetation types and to the extinction of many plant and animal species.

 ## What Is Climate Change?

**Climate change** is any long-term significant change in the "average weather" that a given region experiences. The change can include variations within the Earth's atmosphere and variations in solar radiation, the Earth's orbit, and greenhouse gas concentrations (see Figure 16-1). According to NASA's Goddard Institute for Space Studies, the Earth's average surface temperature has risen by an estimated 0.8 degrees Celsius (or 1.4 degree Fahrenheit) since the last century.[23]

No one can predict exactly what the effects of a continuing temperature rise will be, but some experts have predicted severe drought and a rise in ocean levels of 0.6 metres (2 feet) to 6 metres (20 feet)—conditions that will affect everyone on Earth. Polar bears and indigenous peoples living in the Arctic are already suffering from sea-ice loss, and it has been suggested that the region might have an ice-free summer by 2040.[24] According to the Arctic Climate Impact Assessment Report, with data collected and compiled between 2000 and 2004, average temperatures in western Canada and eastern Russia have risen at twice the global average.[25]

Why is our planet getting warmer? Scientists and policymakers have been heatedly debating this question for years. Global warming may have many causes, including natural processes such as volcanic activity, solar radiation, and human activities, that have resulted in atmospheric changes (see Figure 16-2). Some scientists argue that the mean surface temperatures of the last 100 years are not unusual, but the extremely rapid warming in the last 15 years cannot be explained by natural forces alone.[26]

A warmer world is expected to produce more severe flooding in some places and more severe droughts in others, jeopardizing natural resources and the safety of our water

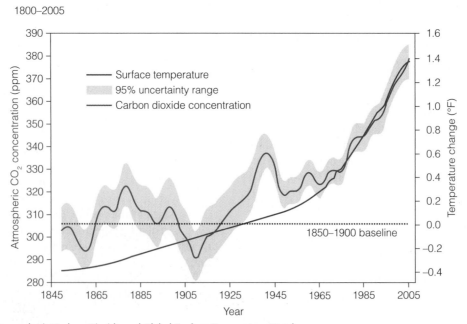

▲ **Figure 16-1** Atmospheric Carbon Dioxide and Global Surface Temperature Trends

Source: Pew Centre on Global Climate Change. Available at www.pewclimate.org. Home. Inside Global Warming Basics. Facts and Figures. Observed temperatures and greenhouse gas trends. – From Figure 2B. Atmospheric GHG Concentrations & Global Surface Temperature Trends. The Last 150 years. www.pewclimate.org/global-warming-basics/facts_and_figures/temp_ghg_trends.

supply. Warmer weather—a consequence of changes in atmospheric gases and climate—worsens urban–industrial air pollution and, if the air also is moist, increases concentrations of allergenic pollens and fungal spores. These are truly problems without borders—climate change is now a reality in Canada.

So what are we doing about these issues on a global scale? In 1997, in Kyoto, Japan, an international treaty called the Kyoto Protocol was negotiated by a number of nations. In 2001, 165 countries signed onto the treaty. Kyoto commits some 40 industrialized nations to limit carbon emissions or reduce them to levels below those of 1990. On February 16, 2005, the Kyoto Protocol officially came into force—a historic milestone, according to environmental experts.[27] It is the first, and only, binding international agreement that sets targets to reduce greenhouse gas emissions that cause climate change. There were 141 countries that ratified it, including every major industrialized country except the United States, Australia, and Monaco. Monaco ratified the accord in February 2006.

This treaty requires countries to move to more responsible ways of producing and using energy. Under Kyoto, the target to reduce greenhouse gas emissions, between 2008 and 2012, is different for each country. For the European Union, the target is 8 percent from their 1990 levels. For Japan, it is 7 percent; for Canada, it is 6 percent.

Developing countries such as India and China do not have to commit to reducing their greenhouse gas emissions in the first phase. This is because their per-capita emissions are much lower than those of developed countries. However, in the second phase of compulsory emission reductions, which will be negotiated in this next decade, the developing nations will be expected to come on board.[28]

Although Canada was a signatory to the United Nations Framework Convention on Climate Change (UNFCCC) and was required to report on their climate change status, a change of government and commitment to the Kyoto Accord occurred in October 2006 when then–Prime Minister Harper's Conservative government introduced Canada's Clean Air Act and subsequent eco-ACTION plan. It appears that Harper ignored the legally binding Kyoto targets with this made-in-Canada environmental initiative. However, if Canada does not meet its Kyoto targets by 2012, it will be required to make up the difference during the second phase of the accord as well as endure penalties. At the time of writing this chapter, Canadians are in a wait-and-see position with the government of the day with regard to the "politics of climate change."[29]

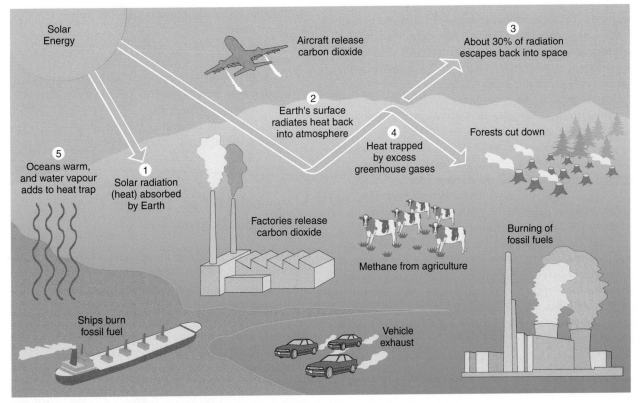

▲ **Figure 16-2** Why the World Is Heating Up
The build-up of carbon dioxide and other greenhouse gases in the atmosphere could result in the greatest climate change in human history. A combination of factors, including the burning of fossil fuels and deforestation, is causing the atmosphere to retain heat. Scientists estimate that the world will become hotter within 100 years—the hottest it's been in two million years.

The Intergovernmental Panel on Climate Change (IPCC), established in 1988, continues to work on this complex issue, too.[30] Established by the World Meteorological Association (WMO) and the United Nations Environment Programme (UNEP), this panel assesses the latest scientific, technical, and socioeconomic information about climate change and shares this information with policymakers and any interested parties around the world. Hundreds of scientists contribute to the IPCC. The *Climate Change 2007: Synthesis Report,* approved in November 2007, provides an integrated view of climate change.[31]

Information from Canada's 2006 Greenhouse Gas Inventory shows that greenhouse gas emissions in Canada totalled 721 megatonnes of carbon dioxide equivalent.[32] Much of the emissions are from wasteful energy use. This was a decrease of 1.9 percent from 2005 levels and 2.8 percent from 2003 levels.

However, this reduction does not meet our Kyoto commitment. The reductions came from changes in electricity and heat generation—reduced coal and increased hydro and nuclear generation—lower emissions from fossil fuel production, and reduced demand for heating fuels because of the warmer winters during 2004–06. The greatest increases in GHGs were from light-duty gasoline trucks, an increase of electricity and heat generation, and heavy-duty diesel vehicles.

Canada's emissions are about 2 percent of total global emissions. This comes from a country with about 0.5 percent of the world's population. The average Canadian produces four times the global average level of emissions—23.6 tonnes per person, per year[33] (see Figure 16-3). Supporting the Kyoto Accord is only the first step to a healthier environment. Leadership is needed to develop new, clean, energy-efficient technologies right here in our own country. Developing countries need assistance to take a greener path, too.

The Canadian plan to meet our country's targets includes mandatory cut-backs in emissions for large factories and power plants; updated standards for more energy-efficient buildings, homes, vehicles, and appliances; financial incentives for smaller businesses to cut emissions; and tax breaks or financial support for public transit and alternative fuels. There are concerns from industry lobby groups that Kyoto will cost Canada jobs and hurt our economy. There are also experts who suggest that Kyoto will not only help our environment, but also create more jobs in alternative energy activities and produce net cost savings for Canadian consumers through energy savings and a chance to market new processes and technologies in a global market.[34]

## Pollution

Any change in the air, water, or soil that could reduce its ability to support life is a form of **pollution.** Natural events, such as smoke from fires triggered by lightning, can cause pollution. The effects of pollution depend on the concentration (amount per unit of air, water, or soil) of the **pollutant,** how long it remains in the environment, and its chemical nature. An *acute effect* is a severe, immediate reaction, usually after a single, large exposure. For example, pesticide poisoning can cause nausea and dizziness, even death. A *chronic effect* may take years to develop or may be a recurrent or continuous reaction, usually after repeated exposures. The development of cancer after repeated exposure to a pollutant such as asbestos is an example of a chronic effect.

Environmental agents that trigger changes, or **mutations,** in the genetic material (the DNA) of living cells are called **mutagens.** The changes that result can lead to the development of cancer. A substance or agent that causes cancer is a *carcinogen:* all carcinogens are mutagens; most mutagens are carcinogens. Furthermore, when a mutagen affects an egg or a sperm cell, its effects can be passed on to future generations. Mutagens that can cross the placenta of a pregnant woman and cause a spontaneous abortion or birth defects in the fetus are called **teratogens.**

Among the health problems that have been linked with pollution are the following:

- Headaches and dizziness
- Eye irritation and impaired vision
- Nasal discharge
- Cough, shortness of breath, and sore throat
- Constricted airways
- Constriction of blood vessels and increased risk of heart disease
- Chest pains and aggravation of the symptoms of colds, pneumonia, bronchial asthma, emphysema, chronic bronchitis, lung cancer, and other respiratory problems
- Birth defects and reproductive problems
- Nausea, vomiting, and stomach cancer

## What Can I Do to Protect the Planet?

The choices we make and the actions we take can improve the health of our Earth. Being environmentally aware and putting plans into action does not mean that we have to sacrifice every comfort or spend great amounts of money. However, for almost everyone, there's plenty of room for improvement. If enough people make small individual changes, they can have an enormous impact.

You can start with the 4 R's—Reduce, Reuse, Recycle, and Recover. One basic environmental action is to **reduce:** buying products packaged in recycled materials or purchasing products that have a lesser amount of packaging. Packaging makes up about half our garbage by volume, one-third by weight. Consider how you're going to dispose

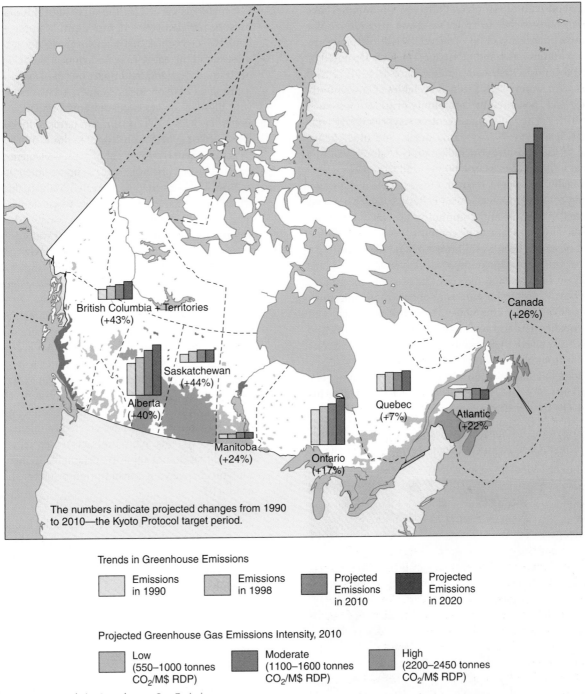

▲ **Figure 16-3** Trends in Greenhouse Gas Emissions

Source: *The Atlas of Canada*. Trends in Greenhouse Gas Emissions 1998–2010. Natural Resources Canada. Home. Explore our maps. Accessed October 4, 2008.
Available at http://atlas.nrcan.gc.ca/site/english/maps/climatechange/atmospherestress/trendsgreenhousegasemission. Reproduced with the permission of Natural Resources Canada 2008, courtesy of the Atlas of Canada.

of a product and the packaging materials before purchasing it. For example, you might bring your own cloth grocery bags to the store. Some municipalities are moving toward banning single-use plastic bags entirely. Other communities are now using recyclable bags made partially of cornstarch or selling reusable cloth bags.

What you cannot reduce, try to **reuse.** When possible, repair items instead of purchasing new ones. Use jars, tins,

and plastic containers to store household and food items. If you cannot reuse, **recycle,** at home, at work, and at school. Recycling—collecting, reprocessing, marketing, and using materials once considered trash—has become a necessity for several reasons: we've run out of space for all the garbage we produce; waste sites are often health and safety hazards; recycling is cheaper than landfill storage or incineration (a major source of air pollution); and recycling helps save energy and natural resources. Different communities take different approaches to recycling. Many provide regular curbside blue box pickup of recyclables. Most programs pick up bottles, cans, and newspapers—either separated or mixed together. Other communities have drop-off centres where consumers can leave recyclables. Conveniently located and sponsored by community organizations (such as charities or schools), these centres accept beverage containers, newspapers, cardboard, metals, and other items. Some recycling centres, including grocery stores, will buy back aluminum cans, plastic bottles, and tetra packs.

Finally, you might **recover.** One example is the refurbishing of old computers, called E-Recycle, which are then donated to schools and community groups.[35] Parts can also be salvaged. Hazardous computer parts are then disposed of safely. "Tech trash" buried in landfills is creating a new hazard because trace amounts of potentially hazardous agents, such as lead and mercury, can leak into the ground and water.[36] Another option is to donate to organizations such as Habitat for Humanity. Their ReStores accept and resell quality new and used building materials to generate funds to support their building programs and keep our landfills from overflowing.[37]

Some students have found the use of Barry Commoner's Four Laws of Ecology helpful. They are outlined in his book, *The Closing Circle: Nature, Man, and Technology.*[38]

1. *Everything Is Connected to Everything Else.* Our environment is a closed ecosystem, powered by the sun.

▲ Recycling is an easy way to help save energy and conserve resources.

The materials needed for the survival of this planet must be recycled over and over again. Natural ecosystems are so complex that many of us do not see or understand the entire range of connections. We must begin to understand the impact our personal and collective lives have on such a system. Ask yourself how your lifestyle choices affect our environment.

2. *Everything Must Go Somewhere.* In terms of the second law of ecology, there is no "away" to throw things. In nature, there is no concept of waste—elements excreted by one organism serve as nourishment for another. Human beings have created "industrialization," which in turn has fostered a society where items are designed to be disposable—to throw "away." Ask yourself the following: Where does your waste go? And what impact does that waste have on the ecosystem? Our garbage will accumulate and pollute landfill sites for decades and—if science proves correct—centuries to come.

3. *Nature Knows Best.* In nature, for every organic compound produced by a living thing, there is an enzyme somewhere in the ecosystem that is capable of breaking it down. This is essential to the harmony of the ecosystem. Unfortunately, technology has been responsible for the creation of substances that cannot be broken down. In some cases, these non-biodegradable products have created problems in diverse ecosystems. What products or services do you use that do not support sustainable living? How can you change your consumption or use of these products?

4. *There Is No Such Thing as a Free Lunch.* For every technological gain there is an ecological price tag. Sometimes, this price tag can be delayed for a time; however, we eventually pay the price. Air pollution, water pollution, and land pollution, which has poisoned the food we grow and eat, are examples of costs we have incurred for modern living. Unfortunately, when clean-up costs become monumental, environmental initiatives are often stalled. What are you doing to clean up after yourself?

Try calculating your ecological footprint using any of the following tools.

✔ **www.myfootprint.org/en**
✔ **www.edf.org/papercalculator**
✔ **www.ecoaction.gc.ca/tools-outils-eng.cfm** (appliance use, commuting, fuel consumption, home heating, idling, water use)

If you are concerned about our environment and want to make a difference, you might want to try the David Suzuki Foundation's Nature Challenge.[39] We are encouraged by Suzuki to pick at least three of the ten most effective

Courtesy of Sierra Club BC

▲ The Sierra Club BC works to protect and preserve British Columbia's natural wilderness and wildlife. Check for local, provincial, or national groups or agencies you can work with.

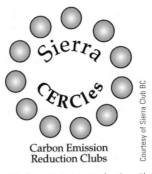

Carbon Emission Reduction Clubs

Courtesy of Sierra Club BC

▲ Sierra CERCles (Carbon Emission Reduction Clubs) are small, socially connected groups of people who find ways to reduce carbon footprints.

ways we can help conserve nature and improve our quality of life. They are:

1. Reduce home energy use by 10 percent.
2. Choose an energy-efficient home and appliances.
3. Don't use pesticides.
4. Eat meat-free meals one day a week.
5. Buy locally grown and produced food.
6. Choose a fuel-efficient vehicle.
7. Walk, bike, carpool, or take transit.
8. Choose a home close to work or school.
9. Support alternative transportation.
10. Learn more and share with others.

If you are a student, it might be difficult to put into practice all of these suggestions, but by starting small—even choosing to change one thing, you will be making a difference. Linking up with community groups might be one way to start your own lifestyle changes.

One such group is the Sierra Club BC.[40] Since 1969, this organization has been working to protect and preserve British Columbia's natural wilderness and wildlife. It also wants to ensure that B.C. is a global leader when tackling climate change. From an award-winning Environmental Education program, reaching 10 000 school children across B.C. each year, to monitoring provincial forestry policy, to tracking provincial commitments to reduce greenhouse gas emissions, members of this organization are making a difference. Under their Community Conversations Program, the Sierra Club offers several outreach programs. Two of these programs are Sierra Club HouseCooling Parties and Sierra CERCles.

Sierra Club HouseCooling Parties are the first step in the Sierra CERCles (Carbon Emission Reduction Clubs)

program. A small group of five to ten people get together for a social evening with a purpose—to share questions, hopes, and reactions to climate change as it relates to their homes, families, and friends. Inspiration and peer support can then lead to a personal and professional commitment to change one small thing at a time to reduce climate impact.

Sierra CERCles generally grow out of HouseCooling Parties. Through Sierra CERCles, citizens from across British Columbia are engaged in training workshops that teach how to host small gatherings of neighbours, family, friends, or co-workers. The objective of the Sierra CERCles project is to seed climate change conversations inspiring action and commitment from participants. CERCles are supported by a team of staff and volunteers at Sierra Club BC. Easy to use tools and action-oriented resources are available to help everyone learn and do more about climate change.

## The Greening of College and University Campuses

There is a new movement at colleges and universities—campus environmental sustainability. From hiring sustainability coordinators, building LEED (Leadership and Energy in Environmental Design)[41] buildings, switching energy sources, providing subsidized access to public transit to educating the campus population, environmental activism is evident from administration, faculty, staff, and students who are attempting to "green" their campuses. Some students are basing their decisions on what institute to attend on how sustainable an institution is.[42]

Other students are forming environmental organizations. Common Energy [43] is one example. This non-profit organization began at the University of Victoria in November 2006. Founded by a group of students, Common Energy became a network of students, staff, faculty, and community partners that focused on moving the university "beyond climate-neutral"—where it does more to solve the problems of climate change that it does to cause them. The main focus of Common Energy is on how individuals can help "middle-sized" (universities and municipalities) institutions take effective action on climate change. The university was chosen first because of its special nature—the production of knowledge. The members of Common Energy have produced a guide on how to go beyond climate-neutral. A Common Energy group has now been established at the University of British Columbia, too. They have also helped to found the BC Campus Climate Network, which links climate change groups across the province.

In an article by David Suzuki titled "Environmentalism and the Responsibility of Academia," he calls on academe to:

> educate people about the reality of the biosphere within which we live and derive a living. We have to show them that we remain animals, as dependent on the quality of air, water, soil and energy and on biodiversity, as any other species. We have to make science an integral part of the way we plan and strategize into the future. And we have to openly acknowledge the strengths and weaknesses of both the scientific enterprise and the economic system that shapes so much of our lives.[44]

As college and university students, you have the opportunity to make changes at your academic institution. Become more educated about climate change issues, find out what environmental initiatives are in place, volunteer, become an advocate or activist, and make a difference. Table 16-1 will provide you with some ideas of green and sustainability initiatives in a sample of Canadian universities across Canada.

▼ **Table 16-1 Calling All Campuses—Environmental Initiatives**

Examples of green and sustainability initiatives in a sample of Canadian universities and university colleges

| University | Who's Who, What's What | Web link |
| --- | --- | --- |
| **Alberta** | | |
| University of Alberta | ECOS—Environmental Coordination Office of Students | www.su.ualberta.ca/services_and_businesses/services/ecopage |
| University of Calgary | The Students' Union and Office of Sustainability—the Green Cafe | www.ucalgary.ca/sustainability/studentforum2008 |
| University of Lethbridge | Sustainability Management | www.uleth.ca/sustainability/index.cfm |
| **British Columbia** | | |
| Royal Roads University | Sustainability Initiatives | www.royalroads.ca/about-rru/governance/sustainability |
| Simon Fraser University | Centre for Sustainable Community Development | www.sfu.ca/cscd |
| University of British Columbia | UBC Student Environment Centre (SEC) | www.ams.ubc.ca/student_life/resource_groups/sec |
| University of Northern British Columbia | Canada's Green University: Living It | www.unbc.ca/green/living.html |
| University of Victoria | Common Energy UVic | www.uvic.commonenergy.org |
| Vancouver Island University | Campus Sustainability Committee | www.viu.ca/sustainability/CSC.asp |
| **Manitoba** | | |
| University of Manitoba | Office of Sustainability: Greenie Awards | www.umanitoba.ca/campus/physical_plant/sustainability/yourpart/430.htm |
| University of Winnipeg | Campus Sustainability Office | www.uwinnipeg.ca/index/sus-index |
| **New Brunswick** | | |
| Mount Allison University | Environment MTA | www.mta.ca/environment |
| University of New Brunswick | UNB's Students' Environmental Society | http://thegreenpages.ca/portal/nb/2008/01/unb_students_environmental_soc.html |
| **Newfoundland** | | |
| Memorial University | Sustainability @ Memorial | www.mun.ca/facman/Sustainability |
| **Nova Scotia** | | |
| Acadia University | The Sustainability Office | http://www.acadiau.ca/sustain/main/index.htm |
| Dalhousie University | Sustainability at Dalhousie | http://sustainability.dal.ca/index.php |

▼ **Table 16-1 Calling All Campuses—Environmental Initiatives (continued)**

| University | Who's Who, What's What | Web link |
|---|---|---|
| **Ontario** | | |
| Brock University | Brock Dining Services: Sustainability | www.brocku.ca/foodservices/sustainablitiy%20.php |
| Carleton University | Carleton Sustainable Campus Network | www.carleton.ca/cscn/home.html |
| Queen's University | STRIVE: Students Taking Responsible Initiatives for a Viable Environment | www.myams.org/sustainability/strive |
| Ryerson University | Sustainability Initiatives | www.ryerson.ca/about/vpadministration/sustainability_initiatives |
| University of Ottawa | Sustainable Development Office | www.sustainable.uottawa.ca |
| University of Toronto | Sustainability Office: University of Toronto Scarborough | www.utsc.utoronto.ca/~sustain |
| University of Waterloo | UW Food Services: Sustainability and Environmental Initiatives | www.foodservices.uwaterloo.ca/sustainability |
| York University | York University Climate Change Research | www.yorku.ca/mediar/archive/Release.asp?Release=1517 |
| **Prince Edward Island** | | |
| University of PEI | Office of Sustainability | www.upei.ca/environment/campus_sustainability |
| **Quebec** | | |
| Concordia University | Sustainable Concordia | http://sustainable.concordia.ca |
| McGill University | Rethink McGill | http://www.mcgill.ca/rethink |
| **Saskatchewan** | | |
| University of Regina | The Sustainable Campus Advisory Group (SCAG) | http://uregina.ca/piwowarj/SustainableCampus/campusfacultystaff-SCAG1.htm |
| University of Saskatchewan | University of Saskatchewan Sustainability Online | http://facilities.usask.ca/sustainability |

## Clearing the Air

Air pollution of any sort can cause numerous ill effects. As pollutants destroy the hair-like cilia that remove irritants from the lungs, individuals may suffer chronic bronchitis, characterized by excessive mucus flow and continuous coughing. Air pollution can be as harmful to breathing capacity as smoking. Residents of polluted cities are exposed to some of the same toxic gases, such as nitrogen oxide and **carbon monoxide,** found in cigarettes. Emphysema may develop or worsen, as pollutants constrict the bronchial tubes and destroy the air sacs in the lungs, making breathing more difficult. A Health Canada study done on eight Canadian cities (Quebec City, Montreal, Ottawa, Toronto, Hamilton, Windsor, Calgary, and Vancouver) determined that 5900 deaths per year could be attributed to air pollution.[45]

In addition to respiratory diseases, air pollution also contributes to heart disease, cancer, and weakened immunity. For the elderly and people with asthma or heart disease, polluted air can be life-threatening. Even healthy individuals can be affected, particularly if they exercise outdoors during high-pollution periods. Carbon monoxide has been shown to impair joggers' exercise performance.

Toxic substances in polluted air can enter the human body in three ways: through the skin, through the digestive system, and through the lungs. The combined interaction of two or more hazards can produce an effect greater than that of either one alone. Pollutants can affect an organ or organ system directly or indirectly.

## Smog

A combination of smoke and fog, **smog** is made up of chemical vapours from auto exhaust, industrial and commercial pollutants (volatile organic compounds, carbon monoxide, nitrogen oxides, sulphur oxides, particulates), and ozone. The most obvious sources of these pollutants are motor vehicles, industrial factories, electric utility plants, and wood-burning stoves. These chemicals react with sunlight, especially during high-pressure systems and periods of low wind speeds, to form smog.

Sulphur dioxide smog (grey-air smog) is produced by burning oil of high sulphur content. Some larger Canadian cities are now dealing with grey-air smog. Like cigarette smoke, grey-air smog affects the cilia in the respiratory passages; the lungs are unable to expel particulates, such as

# Strategies for Change

## Doing Your Part for Cleaner Air

▲ Drive a car that gets high gas mileage and produces low emissions. Keep your speed at or below the speed limit.

▲ Keep your tires inflated and your engine tuned. Seventy percent of cars and light trucks in Canada have at least one tire that is overinflated or underinflated. Maintaining the correct tire pressure could reduce your GHGs by at least one-eighth of a tonne each year. Recycle old batteries and tires. (Most stores that sell new ones will take back old ones.)

▲ Turn off your engine if you're going to be stopped for more than a minute. If you avoid idling for just three minutes each day of the year, $CO_2$ emissions could be reduced by 1.4 million tonnes annually. We could save 630 million litres of fuel—equivalent to taking 320 000 cars off the road for an entire year.[46]

▲ Collect all fluids that you drain from your car (motor oil, antifreeze) and recycle or properly dispose of them.

soot, ash, and dust, which remain and irritate the tissues. This condition is hazardous to people with chronic respiratory problems.[47]

Photochemical smog (brown-air smog) is also found in large traffic centres. This type of smog results principally from nitric oxide in car exhaust reacting with oxygen in the air and forming nitrogen dioxide, which produces a brownish haze and, when exposed to sunlight, other pollutants.

One of these, *ozone*, the most widespread pollutant, can impair the body's immune system and cause long-term lung damage. (Ozone in the upper atmosphere protects us by repelling harmful ultraviolet radiation from the sun, but ozone in the lower atmosphere is a harmful component of air pollution.) Automobiles also produce carbon monoxide, a colourless and odourless gas that diminishes the ability of red blood cells to carry oxygen. The resulting oxygen deficiency can affect breathing, hearing, and vision.

## Indoor Pollutants

Because people in industrialized nations spend more than 90 percent of their time inside buildings, the quality of the air they breathe can have an even greater impact on their well-being than outdoor pollution. The most hazardous form of indoor air pollution is cigarette smoke—we discussed this in Chapter 12. Table 16-2 lists some other common indoor pollutants and describes the potential health risks.

▼ **Table 16-2 Common Indoor Pollutants**

| Indoor Pollutant | Description | Health Risks |
|---|---|---|
| Formaldehyde | Comes from the materials buildings are made of and the appliances inside them. Examples include carpet backing, furniture, foam insulation, plywood, and particle board. | Can cause nausea, dizziness, headaches, heart palpitations, stinging eyes, burning lungs; shown to cause cancer in animals. |
| Asbestos | Mineral used for building insulation. Consumer products containing asbestos are now banned under the Hazardous Products Act.[48] | Linked to lung and gastrointestinal cancer among asbestos workers and families. |
| Lead | In many homes painted with lead-based paint (prior to 1960). Also in air and water. New regulations have been set for lead content in paint and surface coating material and children's jewellery.[49] The lead content limit has been reduced from 5000 mg/kg to 600 mg/kg. | High risk to fetus and children under seven years of age. In children, lead can kill brain cells and cause poor concentration, reduced short-term memory, slower reaction time, and learning disabilities. In adults, exposure to low levels can cause headaches, high blood pressure, irritability, tremors, and insomnia. Exposure to high levels can cause anemia, stomach pain, vomiting, diarrhea, and constipation. Long-term exposure can impair fertility, damage kidneys and the central nervous system, and result in stillbirths or miscarriage. |

▼ **Table 16-2 Common Indoor Pollutants (continued)**

| Indoor Pollutant | Description | Health Risks |
|---|---|---|
| **Mercury** | A metal found in paint, enamels, varnishes, and lacquers. A new mercury content limit of 10mg/g for all surface materials has been set by Health Canada.[50] | Health effects on children can include a decrease in intelligence, delay in walking and talking, lack of coordination, blindness, and seizures. |
| **Carbon monoxide (CO) and nitrogen dioxide (NO$_2$)** | A tasteless, odourless, colourless, and non-irritating gas produced by the incomplete combustion of fuel in space heaters, furnaces, water heaters, and engines. NO$_2$ gas comes from natural gas or propane stoves. Canada's National Ambient Air Quality Objectives (NAAQOs) prescribe targets for air quality.[51] | Can be deadly. Reduces the delivery of oxygen to the blood. Effects include headaches, nausea, vomiting, fatigue, and dizziness. NO$_2$ can lead to respiratory illness. |

## Protecting Your Hearing

Data from a British Columbia Workers' Compensation Board study showed that many young adults entering the workforce already had a hearing loss due to overexposure to noise. Impaired hearing is increasing—especially among young people. Hearing loss can have an impact on speech, language, and literacy as well as social development.[52]

Loudness, or the intensity of a sound, is measured in **decibels (dB).** A whisper is 20 decibels; a conversation in a living room is about 50 decibels. On this scale, 50 is not 2 1/2 times louder than 20, but 1000 times louder: each 10 dB rise in the scale represents a tenfold increase in the intensity of the sound. Very loud but short bursts of sounds (such as gunshots and fireworks) and quieter but longer-lasting sounds (such as power tools) can induce hearing loss.

Sounds under 70 dB don't seem harmful. However, prolonged exposure to any sound over 85 dB (the equivalent of a power mower or food blender) or brief exposure to louder sounds can harm hearing. The noise level at rock concerts can reach 110–140 dB, about as loud as an air-raid siren. Portable CD players and personal listening devices such as iPods can generate potentially harmful sound levels of up to 115 dB. Cars with extremely loud music systems can produce an ear-splitting 145 dB—louder than a jet engine or thunderclap (see Figure 16-4).

Most hearing loss occurs on the job. The people at highest risk are firefighters, police, military personnel, construction and factory workers, musicians, farmers, and truck drivers. Other sources of danger include live or recorded high-volume music, recreational vehicles, airplanes, lawn-care equipment, woodworking tools, some appliances, and chain saws. Even low-level office noise can undermine well-being and increase health risks.[53]

Noise-induced hearing loss is 100 percent preventable; it is also, unfortunately, irreversible. Hearing aids are the only treatment, but they do not correct the problem. They just amplify sound to compensate for hearing loss.

Noise can harm more than our ears: High-volume sound has been linked to high blood pressure and other stress-related problems that can lead to heart disease, insomnia, anxiety, headaches, colitis, and ulcers. Noise frays the nerves; people tend to be more anxious, irritable, and angry when their ears are constantly barraged with sound.

## The Quality of Our Drinking Water

In Chapter 9, there was a discussion of water quality in Canada, so we will not look at this issue further here. For further information, you may want to access the Canadian Drinking Water Quality Guidelines, developed by Health Canada, which have made Canadians more aware of the importance of safe drinking water. These guidelines have been established for all public and private drinking-water supplies.[54]

We will, however, mention briefly the environmental impact of bottled water. Any water sold in sealed containers is considered to be bottled water. It can be spring water, mineral water, or water from a variety of water sources that may have been treated to make it fit for human consumption.[55] The popularity of bottled water has risen dramatically in the past decade, in part because some people think bottled water is safer than tap water. Is this true?

Although bottled water is usually disinfected to remove harmful organisms, many studies have shown that bacteria are found in most bottled waters. Other studies have shown that the levels of bacteria increase quickly to maximum levels after six weeks at room temperature. Since ultraviolet light destroys harmful organisms, this regrowth of harmless flora is not seen as a health hazard. Refrigeration is recommended after you open your bottled water, however.[56]

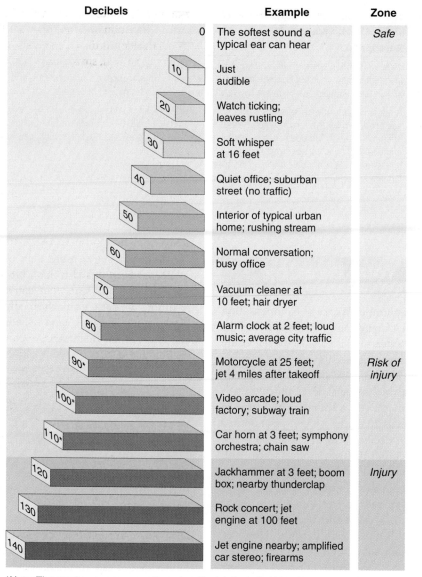

| Decibels | Example | Zone |
|---|---|---|
| 0 | The softest sound a typical ear can hear | *Safe* |
| 10 | Just audible | |
| 20 | Watch ticking; leaves rustling | |
| 30 | Soft whisper at 16 feet | |
| 40 | Quiet office; suburban street (no traffic) | |
| 50 | Interior of typical urban home; rushing stream | |
| 60 | Normal conversation; busy office | |
| 70 | Vacuum cleaner at 10 feet; hair dryer | |
| 80 | Alarm clock at 2 feet; loud music; average city traffic | |
| 90* | Motorcycle at 25 feet; jet 4 miles after takeoff | *Risk of injury* |
| 100* | Video arcade; loud factory; subway train | |
| 110* | Car horn at 3 feet; symphony orchestra; chain saw | |
| 120 | Jackhammer at 3 feet; boom box; nearby thunderclap | *Injury* |
| 130 | Rock concert; jet engine at 100 feet | |
| 140 | Jet engine nearby; amplified car stereo; firearms | |

*Note: The maximum exposure allowed on the job by federal law in hours per day is 90 decibels, 8 hours; 100 decibels, 2 hours; 110 decibels, 1/2 hour.

▲ **Figure 16-4** Loud and Louder
The human ear perceives a 10-decibel increase as a doubling of loudness. Thus, the 100 decibels of a subway train sound much more than twice as loud as the 50 decibels of a rushing stream.

How does bottled water link to environmental concerns? In a number of communities in Canada where large bottled-water manufacturing plants are located, citizens are concerned about the large quantities of water being removed from local water sources. Bottlers are not required to pay for the water that they take. Environmental assessments of the impact that this industry has on our local ecosystems are not being done in most cases.[57]

Ontario has recently put in place a moratorium on new and expanded permits to "harvest" water while new policies for consumption can be developed.[58] Another concern is the fact that plastic bottles are environmentally unfriendly. The World Wildlife Fund estimates that around 1.5 million tonnes of plastic are used globally each year in water bottles. The production and distribution of the bottles burns fossil fuels and results in the release of thousands of tonnes of harmful emissions.[59]

Many of these water bottles—9 out of 10—end up in the garbage instead of being recycled. It is estimated that they can take up to 1000 years to biodegrade. If they are incinerated, toxic chlorine is released into the air. If they are left in a landfill, they can contaminate groundwater.

According to the Climate Action Network, supplying Americans with water bottles for one year consumes more than 1.5 million barrels of oil, which is enough to generate electricity for more than 250 000 homes, or fuel 100,000 cars for a year.[60] This is just one more example of the cause-and-effect relationship between nature and our technological society.

In Canada, there is a gathering revolt, too. Students at colleges and universities across Canada are encouraging 'bottled water-free zones' and supporting the purchase of reusable coffee mugs and water bottles. The United Church of Canada is also doing their part by asking its members to ban bottled water at meetings, events, and services. We must continue to raise questions about the cost of bottled water on our environment and our health.[61]

## Fluoride

In Canada, most of us are exposed to fluorides on a daily basis—through trace amounts found in our food and the fluoride added to drinking water supplies to prevent tooth decay. Fluorides are chemical compounds that have been shown to protect tooth enamel against the acids that cause tooth decay. About 40 percent of Canadians receive fluoridated water.[62]

The risks of using fluoride appear to be very small; however, if children under the age of six ingest high levels of fluorides during the period of tooth formation, they can develop a condition known as dental fluorosis, a condition that causes white or brown stains to appear on the teeth. It does not affect the function of the teeth, just the appearance. Health Canada has set labelling requirements for dental products such as toothpaste that contain fluoride since many young children tend to swallow these products.[63]

Excessive fluoride can increase bone loss and fractures in premenopausal and postmenopausal women. Health professionals advise consumers to use only small amounts of fluoridated toothpaste, rinse thoroughly after brushing, and use fluoride supplements only when the home water supply is known to be deficient.

## Chlorine

Chlorine is a disinfectant added to our drinking water to reduce or eliminate microorganisms such as bacteria and viruses. Chlorine is the most commonly used drinking-water disinfectant. Current research suggests that the health risks of drinking water treated with chlorine are much less than the risks from trihalomethanes (THRs), a common by-product of chlorine when it reacts with organic matter present in water supplies.[64] However, many Canadians are becoming concerned about chlorinated water supplies and

a number of cities are now using ozone to disinfect their water. Ozonation does not produce THMs. When ozone is used as the main disinfectant, small amounts of chlorine must still be used, since ozone breaks down quickly.

## Chemical Risks

Pesticides are toxic. If you or your family use pesticides in or around your home, safe handling and proper application procedures must be followed. Before purchasing or using pesticide products, check out possible alternatives that might be available to you. Insecticidal soaps, boric acid, and pyrethrum have low toxicity to humans and can be effective.

Purchase only domestic-class products bearing a PCP registration number. Commercial or industrial class products are intended for use only by licensed applicators. People and pets should leave the area you are treating.

You should wear protective clothing such as rubber gloves, long-sleeved shirts, coveralls, and goggles. Do not use a pesticide indoors that is intended for outdoor use. Don't smoke, drink, or eat while applying pesticides. After use, make sure you wash your face and hands with soapy water. Clean your clothing before re-using it. Wash this clothing separately from your other clothing items.

### What Health Risks Are Caused by Pesticides?

Although some research suggests that pest-control products can be used without posing a significant risk to our health or our environment, other studies indicate that exposure to pesticides may pose a risk to pregnant women and their fetuses. Exposure to toxic chemicals causes about 3 percent of developmental defects.[65] Other studies have shown a link to chronic diseases related to past exposure to toxic substances, including lung cancer, bladder cancer, leukemia, lymphoma, chronic bronchitis, and disorders of the nervous system. **Endocrine disruptors,** chemicals that act on or interfere with human hormones, particularly estrogen, may pose a different threat. Scientists are investigating their impact on fertility, falling sperm counts, and cancers of the reproductive organs.

**Chlorinated hydrocarbons** include several high-risk substances—such as DDT, kepone, and chlordane—that may cause cancer, birth defects, neurological disorders, and damage to wildlife and the environment. They are extremely resistant to breakdown.[66]

DDT, a synthetic chlorinated insecticide, kills insects by attacking biochemical processes in their nervous systems. Although it was seen as a technological triumph of

## Human Potential

## Naomi Devine—Working for Climate Change

Our human potential story for this chapter is about a young woman who is facing the challenge of climate with perseverance and commitment. I asked Naomi to share her thoughts on the work she does on behalf of our environment. Get ready to be inspired.

Climate change is the defining issue of my generation. This seems daunting—but what generational challenge hasn't been that way? To be more specific, we need to be climate-neutral in my lifetime. Mountains are difficult to climb, but many of us find the resolve within ourselves to do what needs to be done. Climate change is our collective mountain challenge.

I often refer to myself as a child of the "David Suzuki" generation. I was always aware of damage

Naomi Devine, Cofounder of Common Energy, Sustainability Program Assistant University of Victoria.

being done to the natural world. My favourite place as a youngster was a small river running through a park. Having a natural affinity for water, I wanted to play in this river. Unfortunately, I was too young to understand how the three letters "PCBs" were ruining my daily adventure. I do remember that it made me upset that I couldn't play in an area I loved so much.

My grandfather set the stage for finding solutions. He talked about getting power from the sun so we could take our house off the grid. I'm sad to say that the solar dream I had as a child has not come true.

I enrolled at the University of Victoria to complete a degree in Environmental Studies and Political Science. At UVic, I also got involved in groups on and off of the campus. I became a director of the UVic Sustainability Project and started the Victoria Chapter of the BC Sustainable Energy Association (BCSEA). I wanted to work on how we handle the design of our energy system. Climate change is a very large symptom of poor energy system design.

In 2006, I was chosen to be a member of the Canadian Youth Delegation to the United Nations Framework Convention on Climate Change Conference in Nairobi, Kenya. I wanted to see how our government would negotiate on our behalf in the international climate talks. What I found shocked and embarrassed me—Canada was de facto pulling out of Kyoto, and doing its best to stall the consensus-based negotiations. Witnessing this first-hand motivated me further to action. I promised myself that I would not allow this type of non-action to continue—that I would find a way to hold politicians and organizations accountable for their actions (or non-action) on the climate file.

Upon my return, a group of friends and I founded an organization called Common Energy, at UVic. We wanted a different approach to climate change. We created a goal—to have UVic move "beyond climate-neutral"—where its collective actions did more to solve the problems of climate change than it did to cause them. The university is the site of knowledge production in society. We felt it should have a role in helping meet the challenges presented by climate change. This network of over

100 students, staff, faculty, and community members began researching and writing a report on how the university could move beyond climate-neutral. We focused on six key areas—energy, food, transportation, civic engagement and governance, buildings, infrastructure and ecology, and business and the economy. A final report on institutional action on climate change was published a year and a half later. It was the first of its kind.

Another chapter of Common Energy was then organized at the University of British Columbia. We also helped form the BC Campus Climate Network, which has launched a provincial "goBeyond" project to help other students do something similar on their campuses. The success of this initiative has been amazing.

From my work with Common Energy, I was asked to sit on the British Columbia's Climate Action Team with the request to provide expert advice to the premier on how B.C. could meet its newly legislated greenhouse gas emissions targets—33 percent below 2007 levels by 2020. B.C. was the first jurisdiction in North America to legislate hard targets on GHG emission reductions. I worked with 29 well-respected climate scientists, economists, and business and non-governmental organization leaders. Our recommendations are now before the public for comment.

There is still work to be done; however, I feel that Common Energy has served as a successful model of collaboration on a complex issue. We were able to take people from a variety of backgrounds (from climate experts like Dr. Andrew Weaver to concerned citizens who wanted to act) and give them a way to take meaningful action on this issue. Learning to work together effectively is sometimes a large challenge; however, the payoff is producing solutions that have the greatest effect with the deepest support. We need to reproduce this model of working together over and over so that we meet the challenge of climbing our generation's mountain, and solving the climate crisis.

---

the 1940s and was used widely until the 1960s, DDT proved to be a persistent pesticide, a toxin that remains in the environment for as long as 15 years before degrading. When sprayed to kill insect pests, it also killed the natural predators of that pest. The peak year for use in the United States was 1959, when nearly 80 million pounds were applied. From then, usage declined steadily to about 13 million pounds in 1971, most of it applied to cotton.

DDT has also been found in humans and appears to be a risk factor for breast cancer in women. Because of the work of Rachel Carson and others, DDT use was restricted in 1969 and banned in the United States in 1972.[67] However, it is still manufactured in the United States and sold in developing nations. It now contaminates products such as coffee, tea, and bananas, which are then sold back to consumers in Canada and the United States.

**Organic phosphates,** including chemicals such as malathion, break down more rapidly than the chlorinated hydrocarbons. Most are highly toxic, causing cramps, confusion, diarrhea, vomiting, headaches, and breathing difficulties. Higher levels in the blood can lead to convulsions, paralysis, coma, and death.

▲ Pesticides protect crops from harmful insects, plants, and fungi, but may endanger human health.

© Alistair Scott/Shutterstock

## Invisible Dangers

Among the unseen threats to health are various forms of *radiation,* energy radiated in the form of waves or particles.

### Electromagnetic Fields

Electricity plays a central role in our society today. We use it to light our homes, prepare our food, run our computers, and operate numerous household appliances such as televisions, radios, and **video display terminals (VDTs).** Any electrically charged conductor generates two kinds of invisible fields: electric and magnetic. Together they're called **electromagnetic fields (EMFs).** Every time you use electrical appliances such as a microwave oven, you are exposed to EMFs or **microwaves.** For years, these fields were considered harmless. However, studies have revealed some health risks.

Laboratory research on animals has shown that alternating current, which changes strength and direction 60 times a second (and electrifies most of North America), emits EMFs that may interfere with the normal functioning of human cell membranes, which have their own electromagnetic fields. The result may be mood disorders, changes in circadian rhythms (our inner sense of time), miscarriage, developmental problems, or cancer. Researchers have documented an increase in breast-cancer deaths in women who worked as electrical engineers, as electricians, or in other high-exposure jobs and a link between EMF exposure and an increased risk of leukemia and possibly brain cancer.

Scientists at Health Canada are aware of these studies, but they have determined that the evidence is not strong enough to conclude that EMFs definitely cause cancer and suggest that more studies are needed.[68] See Table 16-3 for a description of some common invisible dangers.

## ▼ Table 16-3 Invisible Dangers

| Invisible Dangers | Possible Health Risks |
| --- | --- |
| **Video Display Terminals**—computer monitors | VDTs have been blamed for increases in reproductive problems, miscarriages, low birth weights, and cataracts, yet research by Health Canada has shown that leakage is well below present standards for safe occupational exposure.[69] |
| **Microwaves**—extremely high-frequency electromagnetic waves; a form of radiofrequency electromagnetic energy | According to Health Canada, if the door on a microwave oven has a proper seal and there is no build-up of food or dirt around the seal, then there is no evidence that the microwave radiation emitted from the oven will pose a health risk.[70] There are concerns that the chemicals in plastic wrap or containers that are used in microwaves can cause cancer in mice. Consumers should also be cautious about plastic-encased heat receptors included in convenience food. |
| **Cellular Phones**—The number of cell phones in Canada has risen from 100,000 in 1987 to more than 15 million in 2005. | Researchers have documented changes in biological tissue exposed to radio frequency (RF) electromagnetic energy generated by cell phones.[71] Concern has grown about possible links to slow-growing tumours and brain cancer. No long-term studies have been conducted, however, and so one cannot rule out the dangers of cancers and cardiac and neurological impacts. |

# Other Environmental Issues

## Irradiated Foods

The use of radiation on food, from either radioactive substances or devices that produce X-rays, is known as **irradiation.** It doesn't make the food radioactive; its primary benefit is to prolong the food's useful life. Irradiation can kill microorganisms that might grow in food; the sterilized food can then be stored for years in sealed containers at room temperature without spoiling.

Nutritional studies have shown no significant decreases in the quality of the foods, but high-dose treatments may cause vitamin losses similar to those that occur during canning. It's also possible that the ionizing effect of radiation creates new compounds in foods that may be mutagenic or carcinogenic.

Irradiated foods are believed to be safe to eat. In Canada, several federal agencies are involved in regulating aspects of the food-irradiation process, two of which include the Health Products and Food Branch of Health Canada and the Canadian Food Inspection Agency (CFIA).[72]

## Multiple Chemical Sensitivity

The proliferation of chemicals in modern society has led to an entirely new disease, **multiple chemical sensitivity (MCS),** also called environmentally triggered illness, universal allergy, or chemical AIDS. There is no agreed-upon definition for the condition, no medical test that can diagnose it, and no proven treatment. Symptoms can include chest pain, depression, difficulty remembering, dizziness, fatigue, headache, inability to concentrate, nausea, and aches and pains in muscles and joints. Medical professionals have become convinced that MCS is a real and serious health problem that requires investigation.

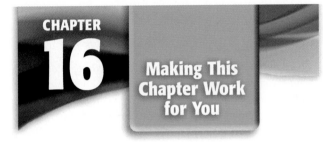

## CHAPTER 16

### Making This Chapter Work for You

1. Threats to the environment include
   a. an open ecosystem.
   b. depletion of the oxygen layer.
   c. ecological processes.
   d. global warming.

2. Mutagens
   a. are caused by birth defects.
   b. result in changes to the DNA of body cells.
   c. are agents that trigger changes in the DNA of body cells.
   d. are caused by repeated exposure to pollutants.

3. Which of the following statements about global warming is true?
   a. Global warming is not an environmental issue in our society.
   b. Global warming may result in severe drought and a rise in ocean levels.
   c. Increasing tree cover and agricultural lands will contribute to global warming.
   d. Increasing carbon dioxide production will slow the progress of global warming.

4. One of the most important things you can do to help protect the environment is
   a. recycle paper, bottles, cans, and unwanted food.
   b. use as much water as possible to help lower the ocean water levels.
   c. avoid energy-depleting fluorescent bulbs.
   d. use plastic storage containers and plastic wrap to save trees from being cut down.

5. Which of the following statements about air pollution is *false*?
   a. Late-model automobiles emit much less pollution per kilometre than cars that were new in 1970.
   b. The three types of smog include sulphur dioxide smog, produced by burning oil; photochemical smog, resulting from car exhaust; and carbon monoxide smog, caused by fossil fuels.
   c. Ozone in the upper atmosphere protects us from harmful ultraviolet radiation from the sun, but in the lower atmosphere, it is a harmful air pollutant.
   d. Air pollution can cause the same types of respiratory health problems as smoking.

6. Indoor pollutants include
   a. lead, which is often found in paint and can result in nervous system damage in adults and impaired fertility and kidney damage in children.
   b. radon, which is found in building materials and can cause heart disease.
   c. asbestos, which may be found in building insulation and can cause lung disease.
   d. carbon monoxide, which can be produced by furnaces and engines and can result in chronic illnesses such as emphysema.

7. You can protect your hearing by
   a. avoiding prolonged exposure to sounds under 70 decibels.
   b. using foam earplugs when operating noisy tools or attending rock concerts.
   c. limiting noise exposure to short bursts of loud sounds such as fireworks.
   d. drinking alcohol in noisy environments to mute the sounds.

8. Which of the following statements about drinking water safety is true?
   a. Drinking water safety has been significantly increased in those communities that add chlorine to the water.
   b. The use of fluoride is the most commonly used drinking-water disinfectant.
   c. Bottled water is completely free of chemical contaminants.
   d. Well water is always safe.

9. Which of the following statements about electromagnetic fields is true?
   a. Overwhelming evidence indicates a strong link between electromagnetic fields around power lines and cancer and other diseases.
   b. The electromagnetic fields emitted by electric blankets are probably less dangerous than those from hair dryers.
   c. The amount of radiation from video display terminals exceeds present standards for safe occupational exposure.
   d. Electrical engineers and electricians who have high exposure to EMFs may be at greater risk for developing leukemia.

10. Which statement about radiation usage is *false*?
    a. Chemicals in plastic wrap may leak into foods heated in microwave ovens.
    b. Radiofrequency signals from cell phones cause brain cancer.
    c. Irradiation can be used to kill microorganisms in food.
    d. Irradiation can delay the ripening of fruits.

Answers to these questions can be found on page 450.

## Self Responsibility

*Environmental problems affect the water we drink, the air we breathe, and the food we eat. You can start solving the world's problems in your own back yard.*

**David Suzuki**

If you refer to Prochaska's Stages of Change model, where are you on the continuum? Are you in the pre-contemplation stage—not really aware of the impact you are having on the environment? Are you

## Social Responsibility

*I used to think that my job didn't have anything to do with the environment. Then I realized that my job, as well as everyone else's job, impacts the environment in some way. And now advocating for sustainability has become my number 1 responsibility.*

**Ray Anderson**

contemplating making some changes in how you live to lighten your environmental footprint? What could you do today that would make a difference?

## Critical Thinking

1. How do you contribute to environmental pollution? How might you change your habits to protect the environment?

2. An excerpt from a recent newspaper article states: "Children living near a local refinery suffer from a high rate of asthma and allergies, and an environmental group says the plant may be to blame." The refinery has met all the local air-quality standards, employs hundreds in the community, and pays taxes, which support police, fire, and social services. If you were a city council member, how would you balance health and environmental concerns with the need for industry in your community?

3. In one poll, people given a choice between a high standard of living (but with hazardous air and water pollution and the depletion of natural resources) and a lower standard of living (but with clean air and drinking water), would prefer clean air and drinking water and a lower standard of living. What about you? Do you think most people are willing to change their lifestyles to preserve the environment?

CENGAGENOW™

If your textbook package includes CengageNOW™, go to http://west.cengagenow.com/ilrn/ to link to CengageNOW™ for Health, your online study tool. First take the **Pre-test** for this chapter to get your personalized **Study Plan,** which will identify topics you need to review and direct you to the appropriate resources. Then take the **Post-test** to determine what concepts you have mastered and what you still need work on.

## SITES & BYTES

### The David Suzuki Foundation
www.davidsuzuki.org

Find information on climate change, forests and wild lands, oceans and fishing, and sustainability. Sign up for the Nature Challenge or access numerous current environmental reports.

### Earth Day Network
www.earthday.net

Access this site and click on Your Ecological Footprint and fill out a quiz that estimates how much productive land and water you need to support what you use and what you discard. You can compare your ecological footprint to other people around the world.

### Environment Canada
www.ec.gc.ca

This site helps connect Canadians, exchange information, and share knowledge for environmental decision-making.

### First Nations Environmental Network
www.fnen.org

This site has information about First Nations' environmental issues as well as reports and articles on global issues.

### BookLounge.ca
www.booklounge.ca/multimedia/turnerchris/index.html

An interview with Chris Turner, the author of *The Geography of Hope: A Tour of the World We Need* (Toronto: Random House, 2007). Listen to Chris share his globetrotting adventure where he discovered individuals and communities showing us how to live sustainably.

### Global Footprint Network
www.footprintnetwork.org/index.php

Global Footprint Network serves as the steward of the National Footprint Accounts, the calculation system that measures the ecological resource use and resource capacity of nations over time. The network currently includes 75 partner organizations on five continents.

Please note that links are subject to change. If you find a broken link, use a search engine such as www.google.ca and search for the website by typing in keywords.

### InfoTrac® College Edition Activity
Peterson, J. (2008, June 20). A green curriculum involves everyone on campus. *The Chronicle of Higher Education*, 54(41).

1. Describe how the carbon budget on college and university campuses has tipped farther out of balance in this past decade.

2. Discuss four "green" initiatives adopted at Oberlin College that have helped move this academic institution toward environmental sustainability.

3. Describe how Oberlin students are being educated about sustainability and climate change issues through coursework.

You can find additional readings relating to safeguarding the environment with InfoTrac® College Edition, an online library of more than 5000 journals and publications. Follow the instructions for accessing InfoTrac® that were packaged with your textbook; then search for articles using a keyword search.

For additional links and resources visit our text-specific website at www.health.nelson.com.

## Key Terms

The terms listed here are used within the chapter on the page indicated. Definitions of terms are in the Glossary at the end of the book.

# References

1. IPCC. (2007). Climate change 2007: Synthesis report. Contribution of working groups I, II and III to the Fourth Assessment Report of the Intergovernmental Panel on Climate Change [Core Writing Team, Pachauri, R.K. and Reisinger, A. (eds).]. Geneva, Switzerland: IPCC. Available at www.ipcc.ch/pdf/assessment-report/ar4/syr/ar4_syr_spm.pdf.

2. Environment Canada. (2008, August 21). Ecosystem initiatives. Available at www.ec.gc.ca/ecosyst/backgrounder.html.

3. First Nations Environmental Network. (2008, October 6). Our vision. Available at www.fnen.org/?q=node/22.

4. First Nations Environmental Network. (2008, October 1). Our goals. Available at www.fnen.org/?q=node/23.

5. First Nations Environmental Network. (2008, October 2). History and profile. Available at www.fnen.org/?q=node/25.

6. Duerden, F., Kuhn, R.G., & Black, S. (1996). An evaluation of the effectiveness of First Nations participation in the development of land-use plans in the Yukon. *The Canadian Journal of Native Studies*, 16(1), 105–24.

7. Borrows, J. (1997). Living between water and rocks: First Nations, environmental planning and democracy. *University of Toronto Law Journal*, 47(4), 417–69.

8. Carson, R. (1962). *Silent spring*. Boston: Houghton Mifflin.

9. Rachel Carson. (2008, September 19). Women in history, living vignettes of notable women from U.S. history. Available at www.lkwdpl.org/wihohio/cars-rac.htm.

10. Lear, L. (2008, September 15). Biography. *Rachel Louise Carson*. Available at www.rachelcarson.org.

11. Gore, A. (1992). *Earth in the balance: Ecology and the human spirit*. Boston: Houghton Mifflin.

12. Gore, A. (2006). *An inconvenient truth: The planetary emergency of global warming and what we can do about it*. Emmaus, PA: Rodale.

13. Al Gore. (2008, September 12). Official website. Available at www.algore.com.

14. Gore, A. (2007). *The assault on reason*. New York: Penguin Press.

15. Suzuki, D. (2003). *The David Suzuki reader: A lifetime of ideas from a leading activist and thinker*. Vancouver: Greystone Books.

16. Suzuki, D. (2008, August 29). David Suzuki Foundation website. Available at www.davidsuzuki.org.

17. Bondar, R. (2008, August 21). Official website. Available at www.robertabondar.com.

18. Bondar, R. (1994). *Touching the earth*. Toronto: Key Porter Books, p. 87.

19. Environment Canada. (2008, August 29). Canadian Centre for Climate Modelling and Analysis. Introduction. Available at www.cccma.ec.gc.ca/eng_index.shtml.

20. Environment Canada. (2008, August 29). Overview. Brochure. The Canadian Centre for Climate Modelling and Analysis. Available at www.cccma.ec.gc.ca/20051116_brochure_e_pgs.pdf.

21. McCallum, S. (2008, August 28). Back to the future. University of Victoria. Knowledge. Personal interview with Dr. Andrew Weaver. Available at http://communications.uvic.ca/edge/weaver.html.

22. Weaver, A. (2008). *Keeping our cool: Canada in a warming world*. Toronto: Penguin Group.

23. National Geographic.com. (2007, June 14). Global warming fast facts. Available at http://news.nationalgeographic.com/news/2004/12/1206_041206_global_warming.html.

24. Ibid.

25. Ibid.

26. Weaver, A., et al. (2000). The causes of 20th century warming. *Science, 290*(5499), 2081.

27. David Suzuki Foundation. (n.d.). Kyoto protocol. Available at www.davidsuzuki.org/Climate_Change/Kyoto.

28. David Suzuki Foundation. (n.d.). Kyoto protocol: Frequently asked questions. Available at www.davidsuzuki.org/Climate_Change/Kyoto/FAQs.asp.

29. Draper, D., & Reed., M.G. (2009). *Our environment: A Canadian perspective* (4th ed.). Toronto: Nelson Education.

30. Intergovernmental Panel on Climate Change. (n.d.). Home. www.ipcc.ch.

31. IPCC. (2007). *Climate change 2007: Synthesis report. Contribution of working groups I, II and III to the Fourth Assessment Report of the Intergovernmental Panel on Climate Change* [Core Writing Team, Pachauri, R.K. and Reisinger, A. (eds.)]. Geneva, Switzerland: IPCC. Available at www.ipcc.ch/pdf/assessment-report/ar4/syr/ar4_syr_spm.pdf.

32. Environment Canada. (2008, October 6). GHG Home. Canada's 2006 Greenhouse Gas Inventory: A summary of trends. Information on greenhouse gas sources and sinks. Available at http://www.ec.gc.ca/pdb/ghg/inventory_report/2006/som-sum_eng.cfm#s2.

33. David Suzuki Foundation. (n.d.). Kyoto protocol: Frequently asked questions. Available at www.davidsuzuki.org/Climate_Change/Kyoto/FAQs.asp.

34. Ibid.

35. Environment Canada. (2008, September 17). Home, What You Can Do. At Home. Beyond paper and plastic recycling. Available at www.ec.gc.ca/education/default.asp?lang=En&n=12762D1C-1.

36. Environment Canada. (2003, June 26). EnviroZine. Mounting concerns over electronic waste. Available at www.ec.gc.ca/EnviroZine/english/issues/33/feature1_e.cfm.

37. Habitat for Humanity. (n.d.). ReStores. http://habitat.ca/findarestorep1380.php.

38. Commoner, B. (1971). *The closing circle: Nature, man and technology*. New York: Knopf.

39. David Suzuki Foundation. (n.d.). The nature challenge: Ten simple things you can do to protect nature. Available at www.davidsuzuki.org/WOL/Challenge.

40. Sierra Club BC. (n.d.) Home. Available at www.sierraclub.bc.ca.

41. Canada Green Building Council. (n.d.). Leed Canada. Available at www.cagbc.org/leed/what/index.php.

42. Greene, H., & Greene, M. (2008). Sustainable admissions: How prospective student are tracking down institutions' environmental records and using them in the college decision-making process. *University Business, 11*(7), 57–58.

43. Common Energy. (2008, September 22). Available at http://uvic.commonenergy.org/wiki/Welcome_to_uvic.commonenergy.org.

44. Suzuki, D. (2008). Environmentalism and the responsibility of academe. *Academic Matters: The Journal of Higher Education,* May June, p. 8.

45. Health Canada. (2008, February 7). Air Quality and Health. Health risks. Available at www.hc-sc.gc.ca/ewh-semt/pubs/contaminants/air_quality-eng.php.

46. National Resources Canada. (2008, July 23). Office of Energy Efficiency. Emission impacts resulting from idling. Available at www.oee.nrcan.gc.ca/transportation/idling/impact.cfm?attr=8.

47. Health Canada. (2006, December 14). Healthy Living. It's Your Health. Smog and your health. Available at www.hc-sc.gc.ca/hl-vs/iyh-vsv/environ/smog-eng.php.

48. Health Canada. (2008, January 15). Healthy Living. It's Your Health. Health risks of asbestos. Health Canada. Available at www.hc-sc.gc.ca/hl-vs/iyh-vsv/environ/asbestos-amiante-eng.php.

49. Health Canada. (2008, August 9). Healthy Living. It's Your Health. Effects of lead on human health. Available at: www.hc-sc.gc.ca/hl-vs/iyh-vsv/environ/lead-plomb-eng.php.

50. Health Canada. (2006, December 14). Healthy Living. It's Your Health. Mercury and human health. Available at www.hc-sc.gc.ca/hl-vs/iyh-vsv/environ/merc-eng.php.

51. Health Canada. (2007, December 9). Environmental and Workplace Health. National ambient air quality objectives for carbon monoxide – Executive summary. Available at www.hc-sc.gc.ca/ewh-semt/pubs/air/naaqo-onqaa/carbon-monoxyde-carbone/index-eng.php.

52. Health Canada. (2006, December 12). Healthy Living. It's Your Health. Hearing loss and leisure noise. Available at www.hc-sc.gc.ca/hl-vs/iyh-vsv/environ/leisure-loisirs-eng.php.

53. Ibid.

54. Health Canada. (2008, August 28). Environment and Workplace Health. Water Quality. Canadian drinking water guidelines. Available at www.hc-sc.gc.ca/ewh-semt/water-eau/drink-potab/guide.

55. Health Canada. (2002, August 27). Food and Nutrition. Making it clear: Renewing the federal regulations on bottled water: A discussion paper. Available at www.hc-sc.gc.ca/fn-an/consultation/init/bottle_water-eau_embouteillee_tc-tm-eng.php.

56. Health Canada. (2007, August 7). Questions and answers on bottled water. Available at www.hc-sc.gc.ca/fn-an/securit/facts-faits/faqs_bottle_water-eau_embouteillee-eng.php.

57. Canadian Environmental Law Association. (2004, April 11). Bottled water FAQs. Available at www.cela.ca/faq/water.shtml.

58. Ibid.

59. Knopper, M. (2008, May/June). Emagazine.com Cover Story. Bottled water backlash. Available at www.emagazine.com/view/?4186&src=.

60. Ibid.

61. Ibid.

62. Health Canada. (2008, July 31). Healthy Living. It's Your Health. Fluoride and human health. Available at www.hc-sc.gc.ca/hl-vs/iyh-vsv/environ/fluor-eng.php.

63. Ibid.

64. Health Canada. (2006, December 14). Healthy Living. It's Your Health. Drinking water chlorination. Available at www.hc-sc.gc.ca/hl-vs/iyh-vsv/environ/chlor-eng.php.

65. Health Canada. Pest Management Regulatory Agency. (2004, June 16). Pesticide use in and around the home. Health Canada. Available at www.pmraarla.gc.ca/english/consum/pesticidehome-e.html.

66. Health Canada. (2008, February 7). Environmental and Workplace Health. Pesticides and health. Available at www.hc-sc.gc.ca/ewh-semt/pubs/contaminants/pesticides-eng.php.

67. US Environmental Protection Agency. (1972, December 31). DDT ban takes effect. Available at www.epa.gov/history/topics/ddt/01.htm.

68. Health Canada. (2004, April 29). Healthy Living. It's Your Health. Electric and magnetic fields at extremely low frequencies. Available at www.hc-sc.gc.ca/hl-vs/iyh-vsv/environ/magnet-eng.php.

69. Health Canada. (2006, December 19). Healthy Living. It's Your Health. Safety of exposure to electric and magnetic fields from computer monitors and other video display terminals. Available at www.hc-sc.gc.ca/hl-vs/iyh-vsv/prod/monit-eng.php.

70. Health Canada. (2006, December 19). Healthy Living. It's Your Health. Radiation safety of microwave ovens. Available at www.hc-sc.gc.ca/hl-vs/iyh-vsv/prod/micro-eng.php.

71. Health Canada. (2006, December 19). Healthy Living. It's Your Health. Safety and safe use of cellular phones. Available at www.hc-sc.gc.ca/hl-vs/iyh-vsv/prod/cell-eng.php.

72. Health Canada. (2002, November 25). Food and Nutrition. Food Safety. Food irradiation. Available at www.hc-sc.gc.ca/fn-an/securit/irridation.

# The Spirit of Health and Wellness

Spirituality can be a challenging topic to discuss. However, it is an important topic and as Riyad Ahmed Shahjahan says, spirituality "cannot be left on the margins" and should be part of our discussions in academic institutions.[1] Current research shows that an interest in the spiritual dimension of health and wellness is growing among college and university students.[2, 3]

Spirituality means different things to different people. For some, it is an organized faith or formal religion based on a connection with an all-powerful being or God. For others, spirituality is not confined to one set of doctrines or experiences. It is a discovery of our self—about finding our unique abilities so that we can serve humanity and leave legacies.

This chapter presents various definitions of spirituality. Reflect upon them and ask yourself:

✔ How does the spiritual dimension of wellness connect to the other dimensions of wellness within your life—social, occupational, physical, intellectual, and emotional? Or does it?
✔ How can an understanding of spirituality support your own health and wellness?
✔ Are there ways you can become spiritually well just as you can become physically well?

Also included are brief descriptions of the major religions of the world and an overview of current research on the connection between spirituality and overall health. The chapter concludes with a section on how the spirit of health and wellness invites possibilities for human potential.

**After studying the material in this chapter, you will be able to:**

- **Discuss** different definitions of spirituality.
- **Discuss** why spirituality is important.
- **List** and **describe** some of the major religions of the world.
- **Describe** ways in which spirituality can enhance your health, wellness, and personal potential.

# Spirituality

## ??? What Is Spirituality?

If you look up the word **spirituality** in Webster's dictionary, you will find that it can be a sacred matter of things of an ecclesiastical nature. It can also be something highly valued or important.[4] Dr. John Travis suggests that spirituality is a connection with everything in creation—an animating force, the principle of unification, shared consciousness.[5] Erriker and Erriker might agree, since they view spirituality as belonging in society.[6] For others, the understanding of spirituality is built upon the idea that there is a higher intelligence, a fundamental or creative power—a universal energy or source. Many words such as God, Spirit, Higher Power, the Light, Higher Self, Cosmic Intelligence, or Christ Consciousness have been used to describe this source. Scherurs supports this way of thinking—that spirituality is a personal relationship with a transcendent Being.[7] Other definitions include:

✔ A movement toward living an authentic life, embracing a more authentic self.[8]
✔ A search for the sacred or divine through any life experience or route.[9]
✔ A growth process that leads to the realization of the ultimate purpose and meaning of life.[10]
✔ A belief in unseen powers in all natural phenomena and that all things are dependent on one another.[11]
✔ The development of a deep appreciation for the depth and expanse of life and natural forces that exist in the universe.[12]

As you can see by the many definitions of spirituality, it is difficult to consistently and clearly define the term. This has presented a problem for some researchers who are studying in this area. The validity of their research is sometimes in question, since it is hard to measure the relationship between spirituality, religion, and health[13] when a common definition seems to be out of reach. Estanek[14] suggests that it might even be unwise to try to agree on one definition of spirituality and that we try instead to recognize the complexity of the term. However, Ingersoll and Bauer discovered that although it is a challenge to define the term, many researchers do agree on common elements within the dimension of spiritual wellness. These elements include "hope, meaning, purpose in life, connectedness, honesty, compassion, forgiveness, rituals, recognition of what is held to be sacred, and transcendent beliefs and experiences that may include a sense of a higher power"[15] (see Figure 17-1).

The term **religion** is often used to refer to a somewhat different definition than spirituality. Sometimes described as "a specific system of belief about deity, often involving rituals, a code of ethics, and a philosophy of life,"[16] it usually represents a special doctrine or group of people.[17]

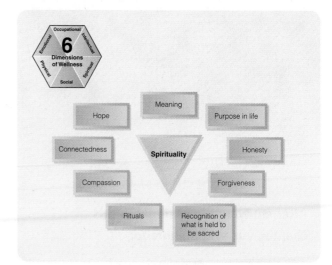

▲ **Figure 17-1** Elements of the Spiritual-Wellness Dimension

Sources: Adapted and integrated from: Banks, R. (1980); Chandler, Holden, & Kolander (1992); Hinterkopf (1998); and Ingersoll (1994, 1998) as reported in Ingersoll, R.E., & Bauer, A.L. (2004). An Integral Approach to Spiritual Wellness in School Counseling Settings. *Professional School Counseling*, 7(5), 301–8. 6 Dimensions of Wellness Model from Hettler, B., M.D. 1976, 1979; National Wellness Institute, 1993. Available at www.nationalwellness.org.

Whether or not you follow the teachings of a formal religion or believe that spirituality is about finding personal meaning, spirituality is about feeling more complete and fulfilled as a human being. To embrace the "spirit" part of our being, we must be open to the idea that while a healthy and well life can include getting a good education, a decent career, and making money, it can also mean making a difference and connecting with our inner self, nature, or a higher being. As described in Chapter 1, spiritually well individuals learn how to experience love, joy, peace, and fulfillment.

## Body, Mind, and Spirit

We often talk about health and wellness as a connection of our body, mind, and spirit. Academic writing and research about this connection is evident in the early 1900s, in the writings of Starbuck,[18] who wrote about the psychology of religion, and James,[19] who wrote a series of lectures titled *The Varieties of Religious Experience*. Between the 1920s and 1960s, a number of psychologists began to understand this connection, too. Jung[20] wrote about the role of spirituality and psychological health, and Frankl[21] developed a counselling approach called Logotherapy, which included the spiritual nature of life and mental health and therapy through meaning. Seeman et al. suggest that in the past few decades "there has been a resurgence of interest" in investigating the potential impact that religion and spirituality might have on health outcomes.[22] Norman Cousins' books *Anatomy of An Illness*[23] and *Head First: The Biology of Hope*

▲ Practising yoga harmonizes the body, mind, and spirit.

iofoto/Shutterstock

and the Healing Power of the Human Spirit,[24] which both emphasize spiritual factors in a recovery process from a serious illness, are two examples.

There has also been a move in some academic institutions to integrate body, mind, and spiritual wellness into curriculum to educate students about holistic living in an attempt to foster healthy campus communities.[25, 26] While studies in spirituality have been traditionally found in departments of psychology, human and social development, medicine, nursing, social work, and religious or First Nations studies,[27] they are now being offered in departments of kinesiology, physical education, and recreation and health education. This is a positive shift as more and more studies are beginning to show a relationship between spirituality, health beliefs, and health behaviours in college and university students. One example is research conducted by Nagel and Sgoutas-Emch, which found that younger, healthier individuals with higher spirituality scores are more active.[28] The body, mind, and spirit of health and wellness are inseparable. The key to discovering our own spirituality is to understand that our spirit connects us to our body, our mind, and with others in the sharing of our human experience. When you take positive steps to brighten your spirit, strengthen your body, or improve your mind, you can expect gains in your total well-being.

## The Importance of Spirituality

Although reports on attendance at religious services show a decline in Canada—32 percent of Canadians attend about once a month—53 percent of adult Canadians participate in religious activities once a month on their own. Activities include personal prayer, meditation, and reading of sacred texts.[29] Another interesting finding is that about 21 percent of Canadian adults (one in five), who infrequently engage in or never attend religious services do engage in some type of personal religious practice on their own. Almost half of Canadian adults (44 percent) believe that religious or spiritual connections are a very important part of their life.[30]

Findings reported in the *2005 General Social Survey* (GSS) indicate that older Canadians are much more likely than younger people to attend religious services on a regular basis (see Figure 17-2). Of Canadians 65 years and older, 37 percent attended a religious service at least once a week compared to 16 percent of young people ages 15 to 24 and 25 to 44.[31]

Yet, while many college and university students might not be attending formal religious services, they are searching for spiritual well-being. According to an American survey, which reflects responses from 3680 undergraduates attending 46 colleges, 77 percent of respondents said they prayed, 78 percent said they discussed religion or spirituality with their friends, and 73 percent said their spiritual or religious beliefs have helped them develop their identities.[32] Another study, which examined the association between spirituality and perceived wellness among college students, found that life purpose, optimism, and a sense of coherence were positively linked to overall health and wellness.[33]

Kuh and Gonyea analyzed data from a National Survey on Student Engagement (NSSE) in 2004 to determine how students who participated in spiritual activities spent their time on campus compared to students who did not. They learned that (1) students who engage in spirituality enhancing practices appear to participate more in a variety of campus activities, (2) that students who view the campus culture or climate outside of class time as supportive of their social and non-academic needs report a deepened sense of spirituality, and (3) students who attend faith-based academic institutions engage more in spiritual worship more frequently than students in non-faith based institutions, but appear to have fewer serious conversations with students whose beliefs about religion, politics, and personal life differ from their own.[34]

Another study by Muller and Dennis, designed to determine whether life-change was related to spirituality in college students found that those college students who reported experiencing higher levels of both positive and negative life-change, scored lower on spirituality, yet had a higher desire to find spirituality, even when their motivation to do so was low.[35] Based on their findings, these authors suggest that health educators at colleges and universities might consider creating learning environments where self-reflection about life meaning and purpose and spirituality could be explored. An ongoing project in California at UCLA's Higher Education Research Institute supports this finding. Comparing student's interest in

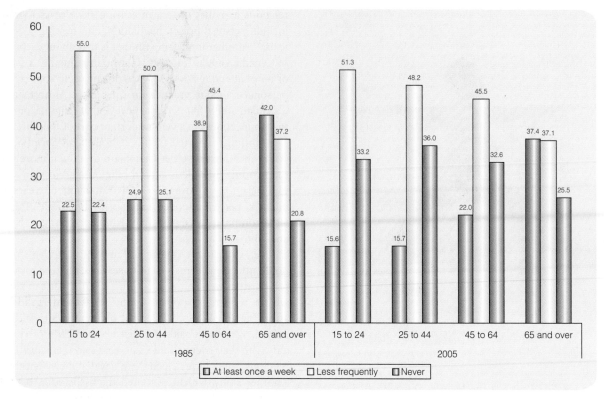

▲ **Figure 17-2** Frequency of Religious Attendance, by Age, 1985 to 2005

Source: Statistics Canada, *General Social Survey,* 1985 to 2005. Lindsay, Colin. (June 2008). Canadians attend weekly religious services less than 20 years ago. Component of Statistics Canada Catalogue no. 89-630-X. Matter of Fact, No. 3. Available at www.statcan.ca/english/freepub/89-630-XIE/2008001/article/10650-en.htm.

spiritual matters over a three-year period, more than 50 percent of students believed that developing a meaningful philosophy of life and integrating spirituality into their lives was essential or very important in 2007, compared to 40 percent in 2004.

Due in part to the findings of studies such as these, there has been an increase in the use of spiritual health models in a variety of courses at colleges and universities.[36] In addition to courses and religious and spiritual campus initiatives, a new, first of its kind, Religion in Canada Institute (RCI) has been established at Trinity Western University. Researchers, faculty, and students associated with RCI will engage in religious research and scholarly networking in Canada. Topics of investigation already include religion and ethnicity, culture and conflict, spirituality and health, religion and globalization, and faith-based social services, to name just a few.[37]

What courses, programs, and services does your university offer to support your spiritual well-being?

Spirituality is also important in the health-care field. There is some evidence that suggests there is a relationship between spirituality, religious involvement, and better health outcomes. Of course, that does not mean if you are

a spiritual or religious person, you will not get sick or that illness is due to a lack of faith or spiritual connection.

It does appear, however, that people who belong to religious communities or congregations, attend religious services, or report that they have strong spiritual beliefs live longer than those who don't.[38] Seeman et al. have reviewed scientific studies that attempted to measure the physiological benefits of Judeo-Christian religious practices to blood pressure and immune function.[39] Although they found that some studies suffered from methodological problems, overall, there was reasonable evidence to support that greater religious involvement appeared to lower blood pressure and lower the prevalence of hypertension. They say that stronger research methodology and experimental design must be developed for future studies, but they also suggest that scientific research has the potential to provide us with important insights into the spirituality, religiosity, and health connection.[40] Cancer patients have reported that their religious or spiritual beliefs help them cope with the disease and improve their quality of life.[41] As well, research has shown faith to be a method individuals recovering from serious mental illness rely on to gain more control in their lives.[42]

Current research about spirituality and the health of college and university students is also showing that (1) students who report themselves as being healthy appear to be linking a spiritual dimension into their definition of individual health and wellness, (2) that there appears to be a positive relationship between increased participation in physical activity and self-reported levels of spirituality, and (3) students who have reported a higher level of life satisfaction with a self-reported level of spirituality might be integrating a spiritual dimension with an emotional dimension of health.[43]

As our understanding of the complex relationships between health and healing grows, we might all begin to learn about supporting a healing process that integrates medicine, spirituality, and religion.

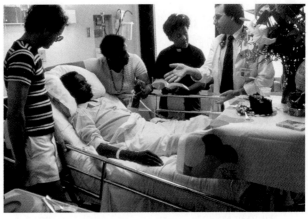

▲ Integrating medicine, spirituality, and religion can help in the process of healing.

## Embracing Spirituality

You may wonder, as you read this chapter, how you might "fit" spirituality into your life while you are attempting to stay physically active, eat in a healthy way, keep up with your school work, and have a social life, too. Do you really need to embrace spirituality to be well? Just like physical activity and nutrition programs change over time, or the demands of school work ebb and flow, so does the spiritual dimension of your life. People working in the spiritual health and wellness area suggest that when we are ready to learn more about and embrace spirituality, we will find the time. Their suggestion is be open to the concept of spirituality and find comfortable ways to support your spiritual dimension.

### How Do I Begin Learning about My Spiritual Dimension?

How do you gain a greater understanding of your own spirituality? You can start by asking yourself these questions:

- ✔ What is my understanding of spirituality?
- ✔ What am I passionate about? What are my strengths?
- ✔ What type of work and personal experiences make me feel good about myself—make me feel healthy and well?

Just as you prepare to begin a fitness program or organize your work space to study for an exam, you can prepare for your spiritual journey by starting somewhere, taking small steps, and moving forward.

### Connectedness to Oneself

Many people are very busy with day-to-day tasks or dealing with problems that come their way and don't feel the need to spend time reflecting about spirituality or connecting with their inner selves. Yet there is a growing body of research that tells us that setting aside some time to question who we are and what we want to accomplish can bring a richness to our life and be healthy for us.[44]

Sometimes a focus on the spiritual-wellness dimension by college and university students is neglected. Developing a personal adult identity when you are at college or university is difficult enough. Developing your spiritual self can be even more difficult, some might say even risky. Spirituality might seem to be a lofty goal, one that is difficult to achieve. You might also have feelings of anxiety about the concept of spirituality or God or are beginning to question the doctrine of a familiar religion. Yet it is the questioning and the searching that helps us discover our spiritual selves. There is no "one way" to become a spiritual person.

Listen to your intuition or hunches. Begin to notice which situations or events test your abilities and challenge your way of thinking. As you engage in reflective practice, you may start to notice that there are times you feel uncertain and experience chaos within. At other times you might experience sensations of peacefulness, a clear mind, and a feeling of centeredness.

### Connectedness to Others

As spiritual growth takes place, many people come to believe that all human beings are connected to one another. This oneness is what some people call God. Others call it universal energy. When you come to this understanding of connectedness, you are presented with alternatives to the way you plan and live your life. You begin to believe that one person can make a difference and that person might be you.

Some psychologists refer to connectedness as our **conscience.** When you listen to your conscience, you see yourself as someone who is part of a bigger world and know

## Human Potential

### Erin van Wiltenburg—See Them Run—A Story of Courage and Conviction

Sometimes we are fortunate to be inspired by individuals who seem to have found their calling, who live life with meaning and purpose. In this final Human Potential story, you will meet a young woman named Erin van Wiltenburg, a 21-year-old University of Victoria student, who is one of those remarkable individuals. Coupled with her strong faith, her passion for social justice issues, and known for her ability to make seemingly ludicrous ideas become a reality, Erin's life motto is this: "Life is not a journey to the grave with the intention of arriving safe and pretty, but rather arriving, skidding in broadside, thoroughly out of breath, and proclaiming loudly, 'WOW! What a ride!'"

In 2005, Erin, just 19 at the time, found herself frustrated with the seemingly futile direction of her elite-level triathlon career. Inspired by a local newspaper article written about disabled children living in an orphanage in Maralal, Kenya, Erin decided to try to find purpose for her life by developing a summer integration sports program for these children. Raising funds to allow her to travel to Africa was just the first step in what would be a poignant time of personal transformation. Working for three months in the rural orphanage in the Samburu district with abandoned disabled kids would instill a spiritual passion within her that is still driving her today.

The work at the orphanage was very challenging, yet when asked about the young people she met, Erin speaks with passion and love. She tells of a girl named Nasusui. "I met Nasusui in Kenya at the orphanage and discovered that she had been burned alive, starved, and abused due to a birth defect. From ages 8 to 11, she was kept in solitary confinement where she was sexually abused by a family friend. No one in the village aided her because she was disabled. It wasn't until a humanitarian aid worker intervened that she was brought to safety to the orphanage I was working at.

"I remember Nasusui telling me her story as a 12-year-old. The injustice brought tears to my eyes,

Patrick Donker, Erin van Wiltenburg, and Reuben Jentink. See Them Run marathon fundraiser in Africa.

© Courtesy of Erin van Wiltenburg

and grabbing my hand, she asked: 'Erin, why are you crying?' I told her I was sorry. In her broken English she, in a quiet, confident voice, said: 'I am blessed Erin because God has brought me here.'"

Erin, like Nasusui, believes that everything in life happens for a reason: "I think God's definition of success and failure is very different than our human terms. We, as humans, are so entrenched in a society that values material worth, self-promotion, and ease that we have lost the sense that there is a spiritual world woven into our daily existence. And if we could acknowledge and have faith in the divine pattern and design, we would find that God in fact weaves life's circumstances in awe-inspiring ways and shapes us into remarkable people. That doesn't mean it's always easy, but it is always worth it."

Erin has learned to have faith in, what she calls, "the divine agenda." Through integrating spiritual values into her own daily existence, Erin lives to help others. She devotes her life to spiritual issues and is determined to advocate for human dignity across the globe. In 2006, Erin began a project called the "100 Item Challenge," in which she lived with only one hundred things. Trying to link the gap between western consumption and third-world poverty, Erin challenges people to redefine the word "need." Erin's presentations to groups of college and university students are life-changing. One student's comments illustrate Erin's impact: "*I was truly touched by today's presentation. It was amazing to see the dedication and selflessness that Erin has. What she is doing deserves the utmost respect from all of us. To give your time, self, and money so readily to help others is not something we see every day, especially in young people. Erin has inspired me to step out of my routine everyday life, to help out those in both my own community and our global society."*

In 2008, Erin made another commitment to the children of Africa. She decided to raise money for African education by running across the African continent. Completing a gruelling 4200 kilometres on foot across Namibia, Zambia, and Tanzania, Erin, along with friends Reuben Jentink and Patrick Donker, and supported by her sister and brother-in-law, Anna van Wiltenburg and Drew Beiderwieden, as well as an African guide Dawid Passon, ran 5 to 6 marathons a week for four months to raise awareness and make a difference for African children. Erin also credits other family, friends, community members, and numerous agencies in helping her realize her dream. To share in Erin's adventure, go to www.see-them-run.com.

"Spirituality has taught me to love myself. And once you love yourself, it is really easy to love other people. It's easy to take risks for other people when you believe you're not in control of the end result. Sometimes you don't end up where you anticipated, but you always end up a better person."

---

that what you do has an impact on others. When we don't hear or listen to our conscience our ego takes over. **Ego** is our self-centeredness. Ego is important, of course. Taking care of yourself is a necessary part of taking care of others. We have said many times throughout this textbook that if you are not healthy and well, it is difficult to fulfill dreams and visions. However, when ego becomes the centre of your life, selfishness and materialism can become the focus of living. Ego without conscience allows us to behave in ways that are not healthy and well. It allows us to believe that we can abuse our bodies, our souls, and the world at large without consequences. Ego can keep us from discovering our human potential.

There are many examples of people making a difference by connecting with one another. All of the Human Potential stories included in this textbook are examples of individuals attempting to reach out to others. Take a moment to think about people you know in your own community, in your province, or in Canada who are making a difference by connecting with others. How do these individuals inspire you? If you are already reaching out and connecting with others how can you begin to share with others how these experiences are meaningful to you? Can you prepare a presentation for a student group? Can you organize a workshop on spirituality and community connection?

Collective problems must be solved by us—collectively. The spiritual dimension can be a vehicle for making our contributions to the world. You can think of it as re-purposing your skills. When people get together to do good work, hope is renewed, and visions move to action. In a study investigating relational spirituality, Faver found that social caregiving renewed and refreshed people. The

## Strategies for Change

### Your Spiritual Journey

- ▲ Redefine success—include living well and doing what you like to do as part of that success.
- ▲ Work on becoming a better person. Judge less, love more, practice forgiveness, demonstrate kindness, and honour others.
- ▲ Look at the world around you with optimism.
- ▲ Spend time each day alone in receptive silence.
- ▲ Believe the best about you.

sense of relatedness to their work or cause became a source of energy and vitality. Some participants in her study said the consistent presence of supportive co-workers, friends, and fellow parishioners was a powerful sustaining life force.[45]

## Transcendence

In many articles and books about spirituality, the term transcendence appears. **Transcendence** can be defined as extending notably beyond ordinary limits.[46] It has also been described as being in harmony with what we do not necessarily understand, what seems distant from us, but what seems mysteriously linked to us.

At some time or another, most of us have experienced moments of transcendence. These moments are different, memorable times when you experience joy, togetherness, and great satisfaction. These moments leave us changed, sometimes for a brief time and sometimes forever. Roberta Bondar, the first Canadian female astronaut to travel in space had these words to say upon her return to earth from her space flight aboard the space shuttle *Discovery*:

> I feel the joy inside my entire body as I gently right myself in preparation for the last dive down through the access port between the mid-deck and flight deck.... The image of the bright blue atmosphere as a rainbow between the black universe and the sliding sheets of Earth's landscape stays with me as I complete my tasks. It seems to promise a pot of gold at its end, the likes of which I have never known. I promise myself that I will have adventure, love and fun each day of my life. I will always think of Earth as never before, cherishing the sense of awe that this flight has inspired within me. I cannot imagine what new dimensions of thought will surround my life's work, because of this moment in time.[47]

These moments open us up to possibilities. They help us create new options. They show us glimpses of the connection to all things. Participants in Faver's study reported having the feeling that at certain times they felt they were in exactly the right place and doing what they were uniquely suited to do. One participant suggested that there is a moment in which we wake up and know that what we are doing is making a difference.[48] Understanding just what it is that we are meant to do—even for a time—can support the emotional and mental dimensions of health and wellness.

Becoming spiritually well is a personal process. Some people start with themselves while others reach beyond themselves to assist people in need or to work for a cause. Still others find their spiritual connection within nature.

## The Spirit of Nature

Humans are one part of the natural world. The forces of nature are another. Connecting with nature helps us to understand our place in it. Many people are discovering that an attachment to the land and nature contributes to their health and wellness. For centuries, throughout the world, plants have contributed to healing.[49] Plants have also been used in spiritual ceremonies, sometimes for health purposes. In some healing traditions, certain animals are perceived to have qualities that can assist humans through times of crisis. There is even research that suggests we can recover from stress more effectively if we visit a natural setting instead of staying in an urban area.[50]

## Healing and Nature

In Chapter 16, "Working Toward a Healthy Environment," we discussed a number of serious environmental issues that are changing the landscape of our country—of our world. Many of those issues are "people-made." If nature can heal, and the scientific evidence seems to support this concept, we must heed the cries from environmentalists, scientists, teachers, and Canadians across the country that "something must be done." Perhaps what is missing in our environmental planning processes is the spiritual dimension. This quotation from David Suzuki seems all the more meaningful when you think about your own spiritual connection to nature:

> The way we see the world shapes the way we treat it. If a mountain is a deity, not a pile of ore; if a river is one of the veins of the land, not potential irrigation water; if a forest is a sacred grove, not timber; if other species are our biological kin, not resources; or if the planet is our mother, not an opportunity— then we will treat each one with greater respect. That is the challenge, to look at the world from a different perspective.[51]

How do we educate ourselves and others about the importance of nature and the human spirit? We can start by rephrasing our questions about nature. Herb Hammond and Stephanie Judy, ecosystem consultants, suggest that people who are sensitive to nature's spirit ask questions differently. Some examples include:

✔ Not, "How can we cover our tracks?"
   But, "How can we leave no tracks?"
✔ Not, "How much can we take?"
   But, "What must we leave?"
✔ Not, "How can we improve on nature?"
   But, "How can we plan with nature?"[52]

With a sense of spiritual connection to nature, we move from managing our environment to caring for our environment. When we care for our environment, it is easier to care for ourselves and each other and stay well.

## First Nations' Spirituality

First Nations peoples across Canada have various spiritual beliefs, sacred items, and ceremonies. While there are differences among tribal groups, there is a common belief that native spiritual life is a connectedness of all natural things. A moving and profound description of this connectedness is told in *The Story of the Sacred Tree*.[53] First, the Creator planted a Sacred Tree under which the people could gather. Under this tree people would find "healing, power, wisdom and security."[54] The roots spread into Mother Earth, and the branches reached upward to Father Sky. The fruits of the tree were the good things that the Creator gave to the people—"teachings that show the path to love, compassion, generosity, patience, wisdom, justice, courage, respect, humility and many other wonderful gifts."[55]

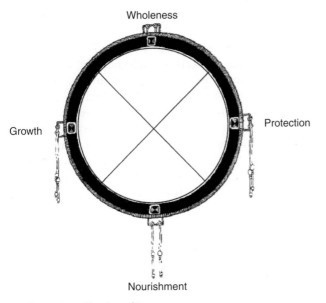

Wholeness

Growth

Protection

Nourishment

▲ **Figure 17-3** The Sacred Tree

Source: Four Worlds International Institute for Human and Community Development. Lethbridge, Alberta. Available at www.4worlds.org.

Figure 17-3 shows the Four Great Meanings of the Sacred Tree. Placed within the ancient symbol of the Medicine Wheel, the four great meanings are protection, nourishment, growth, and wholeness. The following brief description does not tell the whole story. For that you are encouraged to read this book, available from the Four Worlds International Institute at www.4worlds.org.

✔ *Protection*—The Sacred Tree is symbolic of a gathering place for different tribes and peoples of the world. It provides a place of protection, peace, contemplation, and centring. It "gives rise to a vision, not of what we are, but of what we can become."[56]

✔ *Nourishment*—The Sacred Tree is symbolic of the nourishment we need to live and sustain growth. Eating the fruit of the tree represents the interaction of the human, physical, and spiritual aspects of our lives. The leaves, which fall to the ground, represent the passing of the generations and the spiritual teachings that are left behind. The wisdom of the past nourishes the present and the future.[57]

✔ *Growth*—The Sacred Tree is symbolic of pursuing life experiences and respecting our inner spiritual growth. This includes growing in the qualities of the four directions—physically, mentally, emotionally, and spiritually. It also represents the cycles of time and life, the changing seasons and our lifelong relationship to creation.[58]

✔ *Wholeness*—The Sacred Tree is symbolic of the Great Spirit as the centre pole of creation. It is here we can balance and begin to understand ourselves as human beings. The roots, which are unseen, represent the invisible aspects of our being, while the parts of the Sacred Tree that are above ground are the visible aspects of ourselves. Understanding and balancing of all of our parts provides the nurturing environment for further growth and wholeness.[59]

The authors of this book conclude with the thought that gaining an understanding of the Sacred Tree is an eternal journey. By reflecting and acting upon the teachings of the Sacred Tree, we can bring a renewal to the life of humanity.[60]

## Religions of the World

### What Are the Major Classical World Religions?

There are many different religions of the world. Major classical world religions number 12: Baha'i, Buddism, Christianity, Confucianism, Hinduism, Islam, Jainism, Judaism, Shinto, Sikhism, Taoism, and Zoroastrianism.[61] Functionally oriented religions include some of the preceding religions plus the orthodox Eastern Church, Protestantism, and Catholicism.[62] Alternative religions include Agnostics, Atheists, Humanists, and New Age, while others find faith in cosmology and ecology. First Nations spirituality might also be considered by some to be a religion and, by others, a way of life.

One thing that becomes clear when you begin to study and compare world religions or practices is that they share some universal human values and seek to create a more just and sustainable world society. Learning more about religious practices can help to increase tolerance toward others. This is an important aspect of the spiritual-wellness dimension. Many of the world's religions also encourage health and wellness. As you read through the following descriptions, ask yourself these questions:

✔ What role does religion play in the social health of the elderly? (Social dimension)
✔ How do the doctrines of some of these religions encourage reflection and commitment to one's life work? (Occupational dimension)
✔ Do the religious doctrines encourage followers to experience love, joy, peace, and fulfillment? (Spiritual dimension)
✔ What role does diet play in the lives of the followers of these religions? Which religions emphasize physical activity? (Physical dimension)

✔ Which religions encourage lifelong learning? (Intellectual dimension)

✔ How might prayer and meditation influence stress levels and mental and emotional health? (Emotional dimension)

## Religion in Canada

Canada is a religiously diverse country. Figure 17-4 shows a graphic representation of religious service participation by geographical area of Canadians, while Table 17-1 shows Canada's 10 largest faith groups and a comparison of membership in specific denominations between 1991 and 2001.

Warren Clark, in an article titled, "Pockets of belief: Religious attendance patterns in Canada,"[63] reports that attendance rates at religious services do vary across our country. In the past, Newfoundland and Labrador, Prince Edward Island, and New Brunswick have had the highest monthly attendance rates. Alberta, British Columbia, and Quebec have had the lowest. However, as the title of his article suggests, pockets of high attendance rates can exist in provinces that appear to have overall low attendance. During the 1990s, attendance at religious services dropped the most in the province of Quebec. We have already seen that age appears to have an impact on attendance, but research also shows that the immigrants attend religious services more frequently than Canadian-born adults, too.

There are numerous books about religions of the world. If you would like to discover more about the similarities and differences between the world's religions, you might find David Levinson's book *Religion: A Cross-Cultural Dictionary* (Oxford Press, 1998) helpful. The brief descriptions here, taken from various websites and books, are a way of celebrating the different doctrines of formal religions, but they are by no means a detailed account.

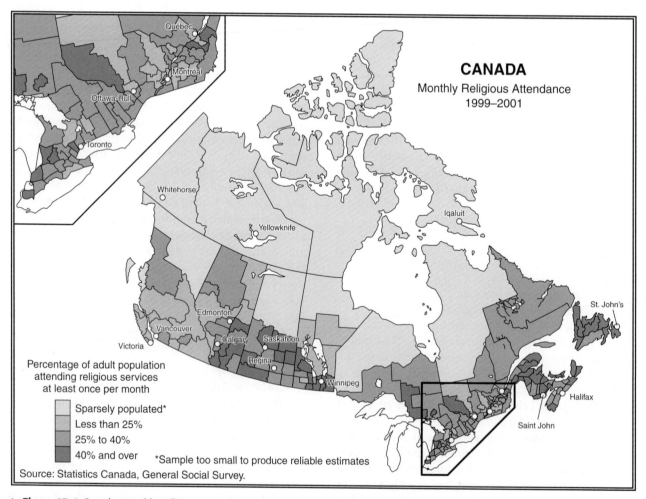

▲ **Figure 17-4** Canada. Monthly Religious Attendance 1999–2001 by Geographical Location

Source: Clark, Warren. (2003, Spring). Pockets of belief: Religious attendance patterns in Canada. *Canadian Social Trends,* 3. Available at www.statcan.ca/english/freepub/ 11-008-XIE/2002004/articles/6493.pdf.

▼ Table 17-1 Major Religious Denominations, Canada, 1991[1] and 2001

| | 2001 | | 1991 | | Percentage change 1991–2001 |
|---|---|---|---|---|---|
| | **Number** | **%** | **Number** | **%** | |
| Roman Catholic | 12 793 125 | 43.2 | 12 203 625 | 45.2 | 4.8 |
| Protestant | 8 654 845 | 29.2 | 9 427 675 | 34.9 | −8.2 |
| Christian Orthodox | 479 620 | 1.6 | 387 395 | 1.4 | 23.8 |
| Christian, not included elsewhere[2] | 780 450 | 2.6 | 353 040 | 1.3 | 121.1 |
| Muslim | 579 640 | 2.0 | 253 265 | 0.9 | 128.9 |
| Jewish | 329 995 | 1.1 | 318 185 | 1.2 | 3.7 |
| Buddhist | 300 345 | 1.0 | 163 415 | 0.6 | 83.8 |
| Hindu | 297 200 | 1.0 | 157 015 | 0.6 | 89.3 |
| Sikh | 278 415 | 0.9 | 147 440 | 0.5 | 88.8 |
| No religion | 4 796 325 | 16.2 | 3 333 245 | 12.3 | 43.9 |

Source: Statistics Canada. Analysis series. Religions in Canada. Canada. Overview: Canada still predominantly Roman Catholic and Protestant. Table. Major religious dominations, Canada, 2001 and 1991. Available at www12.statcan.ca/english/census01/Products/Analytic/companion/rel/canada.cfm; and www12.statcan.ca/english/census01/Products/Analytic/companion/rel/tables/canada/cdamajor.cfm.

[1] For comparability purposes, 1991 data are presented according to 2001 boundaries.
[2] Includes persons who report "Christian," as well as those who report "Apostolic," "Born-again Christian" and "Evangelical."

## The Baha'i World Faith

The **Baha'i** faith was founded in Iran during the mid-nineteenth century by Siyyid 'Ali-Muhammed. Baha'is believe that there is a single God who sends prophets into the world through whom the word of God is revealed. One of Siyyid 'Ali-Muhammed's followers, Mirza Husayn-'Ali-i-Nuri, was one of those prophets and assumed the title Baha'u'llah or "Glory of God" during the 1800s. He taught about world peace, democracy, civil rights, acceptance of scientific discoveries, and equal rights for women. These ideas were decades ahead of their time. Some Muslims look upon the Baha'i faith as a breakaway sect of Islam.[64]

## Buddhism

**Buddhism** is the fourth-largest religion in the world. It was founded in Northern India by the first known Buddha, Siddhartha Gautama, a prince of the Sakya clan. In 535 BCE, he attained enlightenment and became Buddha the Awakened One. Buddhism encourages a connection with both the natural world and the spiritual world. It has evolved into two main forms. Thervada Buddhism, sometimes called Southern Buddhism, is largely found in Thailand, Burma, Cambodia, and Laos. The philosophy, meditation, and ethics of Thervada is based on the Pali texts which were written by Buddhists in India and Sri Lanka. Mahayana Buddhism, sometimes called Northern

Buddhism, is largely found in China, Japan, Korea, Tibet, and Mongolia and is based on Sanskrit texts.[65]

Tibetan Buddhism, sometimes believed to be separate from Thervada and Mahayana, is led by the Dalai Lama, a Tibetan monk who promotes non-violence, compassion, religious harmony, world peace, and universal responsibility.[66]

The Buddha taught that we are responsible for our own happiness and suffering. What we experience is dependent on our previous actions. Good moral actions lead to happy states, and bad actions lead to future suffering. We cannot escape responsibility for what we do. This is the process of *Karma*—reaping what we sow, which can happen in this life or the next. There are four noble truths:

1. Dukkha: suffering exists.
2. Samudaya: there is a cause for suffering.
3. Niordha: there is an end to suffering.
4. Magga: to end suffering follow the eightfold path. The eight factors of the eightfold path are Right Understanding, Right Thought, Right Speech, Right Action, Right Livelihood, Right Effort, Right Mindfulness, and Right Concentration.[67]

## Christianity

There are multiple meanings of the term **Christianity**. It can mean any person or group who believes themselves to be Christian. It can mean someone whose life has been transformed by the grace of God, anyone who has repented their sins, or who has been "born again."[68] What is common is the belief that Yeshua of Nazareth, a Jewish preacher, commonly referred to as Jesus Christ, was the Son of God. He was born of the Virgin Mary, was crucified for his beliefs and teachings, his body was resurrected after his death, and he later ascended into Heaven.

After his death, a Jewish Christian movement was formed. Other Christian movements such as Pauline Christianity and Gnostic Christianity were directed to specific groups of people. Further splits in different versions of the Christian movement resulted in Roman Catholic, Eastern Orthodox, and Protestant Reformation. There are more than 1500 different Christian faith groups in North America, promoting different and sometimes conflicting beliefs about Christianity. About 80 percent of Canadians identify themselves as Christians; however, the percentage of Christians is declining.[69]

The Ten Commandments guide Christians as they live their lives. They are intended as a universal set of rules for all people to follow. They include believing in one God only; not taking the name of God in vain; remembering to keep the Sabbath day holy; honouring our father and mother; and not killing, committing adultery, stealing, bearing false witness against neighbours, or coveting neighbours' goods. There are Protestant, Catholic, and Hebrew variations of the Ten Commandments.[70]

Christians believe that there is life after death, but the various Christian groups do not necessarily agree on the way souls are saved. All Christians believe that those who repent their sins before God will be saved and will go to Heaven. Belief in Hell and Purgatory, a place believed by Roman Catholics to be where there is a process of cleansing before most souls go to Heaven, varies among the many Christian groups.

## Confucianism

Founded by K'ung Fu Tzu, **Confucianism** is an ethical system to which certain rituals at specific times during one's lifetime are practised. K'ung Fu Tzu was born in 551 BCE in the state of Lu, which is the modern-day Shantung province in China. His teachings deal with individual morality and ethics. In some areas in Asia, the social and moral ethics of Confucius are blended with Taoism and Buddhism.[71] There are approximately six million Confucians in the world. Most live in China and other parts of Asia. Approximately 26 000 live in North America.

Confucian ethical teachings include Li (ritual, propriety, etiquette), Hsiaso (love within the family), Yi (righteousness), Xin (honesty and trustworthiness), Jen (benevolence, humaneness toward others, the highest Confucian virtue), and Chung (loyalty).[72] Four life passages at which the Confucian rituals are performed are birth, reaching maturity, marriage, and death.

## Hinduism

**Hinduism,** the world's third-largest religion after Christianity and Islam, does not have a single founder or central religious organization. It consists of thousands of different religious groups that have evolved in India since 1500 BCE[73] and is considered the world's oldest religion. There are about 120 500 Hindus in Canada.[74] Hindus recognize a single deity while honouring other Gods and Goddesses as manifestations or aspects of that supreme God. Most Hindus follow one of two major divisions with Hinduism. They are Vaishnavaism, which regards Vishnu (Krishna, The Preserver) as the ultimate deity, and Shivaism, which regards Shiva, the Destroyer, as the deity.[75]

Hindus follow the aims of Hinduism. These are Dharma (righteousness in religious life), Artha (success in economic life), Kama (gratification of the senses), and Moksa (liberation from samsara, the continuing cycle of birth, life, death, and rebirth for many lifetimes). Karma determines how you live your next life. People who live with pure acts, thoughts, and deeds can be reborn at a higher level, eventually achieving enlightenment. Hinduism is highly tolerant of other religions.

## Islam

Religious historians credit the founding of **Islam** to Muhammad the Prophet (peace be upon him) in 622 CE. They also suggest that the angel Jibril (or Gabriel) read the first revelation to Muhammad (pbuh). However, most Muslims, followers of Islam, believe that Islam did exist before Muhammad (pbuh) was born, that the origins of Islam date back to the creation of the world, and that Muhammad (pbuh) was the last of a series of prophets.[76] Islam is the youngest of the world's largest religions, which include Christianity, Hinduism, and Buddhism. About 21 percent of all people on Earth follow Islam. If current trends continue, Islam will become the most popular world religion sometime in the mid-twenty-first century, moving past Christianity.[77]

Muhammad the Prophet (pbuh) met considerable opposition to his teachings but did become the most powerful leader in Arabia, where Islam became firmly established. The two main texts Muslims consult are the *Qur'an,* or the words of God, and the *Hadith,* collections of the sayings of Muhammad (pbuh).[78] The six fundamental beliefs of Islam are a single, indivisible God (Allah is often used to refer to God and is the Arabic word for God); the angels; the divine scriptures; the Messengers of God, which include Adam, Noah, Abraham, Moses, David, Jesus, and Muhammad the Prophet (pbuh); the Day of Judgment; and the supremacy of God's will.

Muslims have duties to perform. They must recite the shahada (the creed: There is no God but God and Muhammad is his Prophet). They must perform the salat (prayer) five times a day if possible. They must donate regularly to charity, or zakat. They must fast during the lunar month of Ramadan, the month it is believed that Muhammad (pbuh) received the first revelation of the Qur'an from God, and, if able, they must make a pilgrimage to Mecca.[79]

Other practices include Jihad—the attainment of a noble goal. Jihad is probably the most misunderstood religious word in existence. From a western perspective, it is often used to imply a holy war or a call to fight against non-Muslims in defence of Islam. Most Muslims believe it to be a personal, internal struggle with one's self. Muslims are also expected to explain Islam to followers of different faiths but do not have to recruit. This is left up to Allah. As well, suicide is forbidden. Only Allah is allowed to take a life.[80]

## Jainism or Jain Dharma

The roots of **Jainism** begin in ancient East India. Jainism contains a number of elements that are similar to Hinduism and Buddhism. Jainists believe that the universe, which has no beginning or end, exists as a series of layers. These layers consist of the Supreme Abode where Siddha, the liberated souls, live; the Upper World, or 30 heavens, where celestial beings live; the Middle World, which is the Earth and the rest of the universe; the Netherworld, the seven hells; the Nigoda, where the lowest forms of life live; the Universe Space, or layers of cloud that surround the upper world; and the Space Beyond, a place without soul, matter, time, or motion.[81]

Those following Jainism are expected to follow the five principles of living: Ahimsa—non-violence in all parts of a person (mental, verbal, and physical); Satya—speaking the truth; Asteya—not stealing from another; Brahma-charya or soul conduct—remaining sexually monogamous to one's spouse; and Aparigraha—detaching from people, places, and material things.[82]

## Judaism

**Judaism** originated with a divine covenant between the God of the ancient Israelites and the prophet Abraham. (The term G–d is used in some textbooks to respect the Jewish prohibition against spelling the name or title of the deity in full.) The next leader of the Israelites, Moses, led his people out of captivity in Egypt and received the Law from God. Another prophet, Joshua, later led the Israelites into "the promised land," where the Israelite kingdom was established with King Saul. The second king, David, established Jerusalem as the religious and political centre. The third king, Solomon, built the first Jewish temple. Divisions of the kingdom occurred after the death of Solomon. In 70 CE, the temple was destroyed, and the Jewish Christians were scattered throughout the world.[83] In the 1930s, Adolph Hitler, leader of the Germany's National Socialist Party (Nazi Party), attempted to exterminate all of the Jews in Europe. About six million Jews were killed.

The creation of the state of Israel occurred in 1948. There are currently about 18 million Jews throughout the world.

Jews believe in one creator who is to be worshipped as the absolute ruler of the universe. He monitors people's activities and rewards good deeds and punishes evil. Jews believe in the inherent goodness of the world and its inhabitants as creations of God. They follow the *Tanakh*, which is composed of three groups of books, including the *Torah*. They also follow the *Talmud*, which contains stories, laws, medical knowledge, and debates about moral choices.[84] Jewish practices include observation of the Sabbath as a day of rest; strict discipline, according to the Law; regular attendance by Jewish males at Synagogue; and celebration of annual festivals that include Passover, Rosh Hashanah, Sukkoth, Hanukkah, Purim, and Shavout.[85]

## Shinto

**Shinto** is an ancient Japanese religion, closely connected to nature. This religion recognizes the existence of Kami or nature deities. The first two, Izanagi and Izanami, gave birth to the Japanese Islands, and their children became the deities of the various Japanese clans. All Kami sustain and protect the people. Shintoists generally follow the code of Confucianism. Shinto also shares Buddhist beliefs. Within Shinto, Buddha is viewed as a Kami.[86]

The Four Affirmations in Shinto are tradition and the family, love of nature, physical cleanliness, and Matsuri—the worship and honour given to the Kami and ancestral spirits. Shinto practices include the recognition of many sacred places such as mountains and springs; respect for animals as the messengers of the Gods; shrine ceremonies, which include cleansing, prayers, and dances that are offered to the Kami; and seasonal celebrations held at spring planting, fall harvest, and special anniversaries of the history of a shrine or local patron spirit. Many followers are also involved in the "offer a meal movement," where they give up a meal once per month and then donate the money they saved to their religious organization for international relief.[87]

## Sikhism

The Sikh faith was founded by Shri Guru nanak Dev Ji in what is now known as Pakistan. **Sikhism** is sometimes believed to be a part of the Hindu religious tradition. Many Sikhs disagree and believe that their religion is a direct revelation from God. Sikh means "learner." The goal of Sikhs is to build a close, loving relationship to God. Sikhs believe in a single God with many names. They believe in samsara (the repetitive cycle of birth, life, and death), Karma (good and bad deeds), and reincarnation (the belief in a rebirth following death).[88]

They do not believe in the caste system as Hindus do. Sikhs believe that everyone has equal status. Many Sikhs follow living gurus. Their practices include prayers, which are repeated many times each day; worship; attendance in temples or shrines; and strict clothing practices.

## Taoism

The founder of Taoism, Lao-Tse, was a contemporary of Confucius in China. **Taoism** started as a combination of psychology and philosophy, but it became a religion in 440 CE. Tao, sometimes translated as "path," is a force that flows through all life. If you are a believer, your goal is to become one with the Tao.[89] Taoism currently has about 20 million followers in the world, with most living in Taiwan. Taoism has also provided an alternative to Confucian tradition in China. The two traditions coexist within the country.

Taoists do not pray to God. They seek answers to life's problems through meditation and observation. There is commitment to health and vitality. Development of virtue is important. Taoists search for compassion, moderation, and humility.[90] The Yin Yang symbol represents the balance of opposites in the universe. Many Taoists participate

▲ Practising Tai Chi balances energy flow.

in Tai Chi, an exercise and movement technique that balances energy flow.

The debate about whether or not spirituality and religion are similar or different will most likely continue for years to come. However, we can begin to move from this debate to a thoughtful reflection on how spirituality and religion can support our personal and global health and well-being.

## Meaning, Purpose, and Potential

Meaning, purpose, and potential are connected just like the body, mind, and spirit. **Meaning** can be defined as significant quality or an implication of a hidden or special significance.[91] **Purpose** is something set up as an object or end to be attained,[92] and **potential** expresses possibility.[93] Searching for meaning or special significance makes us more aware of worthy purposes in our lives. A worthy purpose might be living in a healthy and well way and helping others to do the same. It may be completing your education or educating others. The purpose may be small or grand. Having purpose helps us grow and learn about our own human potential so that we might express our own possibility.

For many people, finding meaning, discovering purpose, and realizing potential begins when they integrate the spiritual dimension of health and wellness into daily living. Spirituality, whether based on religious or secular beliefs, allows us to move back and forth from self-reflection to serving others. It moves us beyond thinking about spirituality only as an intellectual exercise to something that guides our intentions. It opens us up to possibilities—to see the world as a place that we can be engaged in, not fearful about. It can support our health and well-being. It is a dimension that connects us to each other and all things.

## An Invitation to Health and Wellness

This textbook began with an overview of health and wellness models and ended with a chapter on spirituality. In between you were presented with information on psychological and emotional health, physical activity and nutrition, and sexuality and reproductive choices. You also discovered more about major diseases and drug, alcohol, and tobacco use. There was a chapter on Canada's health-care system, an encouragement to stay safe and protect yourself from injury, and a hint that a lifetime of health prepares us for growing older. Then there was a gentle reminder that personal wellness depends on global wellness.

You are invited to learn more about health and wellness and how lifestyle choices affect your personal potential. You are invited to continue to "live well."

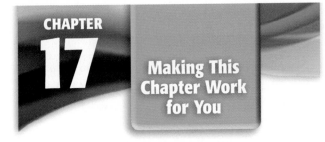

**CHAPTER 17**

**Making This Chapter Work for You**

1. Religion is
   a. a connection with the spirit only.
   b. a specific system of belief about deity, often involving rituals and a philosophy of life.
   c. something to be fearful of.
   d. the only way to salvation.

2. Spirituality is
   a. a formal religion.
   b. only available to those who attend church services.
   c. a New-Age term.
   d. a search for the sacred or divine through any life experience or route.

3. A holistic way of living includes
   a. following a strict set of religious practices.
   b. studying the major religions of the world.
   c. a connection between body, mind, and spirit.
   d. becoming physically fit.

4. Studies have found that a religious or spiritual connection is associated with
   a. less cardiovascular disease, lower blood pressure, and less hypertension.
   b. good jobs.
   c. a perception of less control over our lives.
   d. a guarantee that we will not get sick.

5. Transcendence is
   a. a major religion of the world.
   b. part of many religious services around the world.
   c. a spiritual practice in Christianity.
   d. a moment or moments of joyful experience, togetherness, and great satisfaction.

6. Native spiritual life is
   a. a short-term journey.
   b. only available to First Nations' peoples.
   c. a type of religion that honours the Kami.
   d. a connection of all natural things.

7. Followers of Islam pray to
   a. Allah.
   b. Buddha.
   c. Jesus.
   d. the Dalai Lama.

8. Shinto
   a. practices include reciting the shahada.
   b. began in ancient East India.
   c. is an ancient Japanese religion.
   d. is part of the Hindu religious tradition.

9. According to a national survey of college undergraduate students,
   a. most students reported that they did not discuss religion or spirituality.
   b. 78 percent of the students said they discussed religion or spirituality with their friends.
   c. 46 percent of the students said that they had no spiritual or religious beliefs.
   d. most students did not think spirituality or religion belonged in an academic institution.

10. Conscience is
    a. the same as ego.
    b. self-centredness.
    c. connectedness.
    d. Shivaism.

Answers to these questions can be found on page 450.

## Self Responsibility

*Every one of us has a special place in the Life Pattern. There is guidance which comes from within to all who will listen.*

**Peace Pilgrim**

A spiritual journey can take a lifetime. You can prepare for this journey by learning more about the spiritual dimension. Action might mean participating in a yoga class or attending a church service. Maintenance will demand from you the ability to face challenges that come your way. The spiritual journey is never easy. Human traits such as impatience, judgment, and irritability make their way into our daily lives.

## Social Responsibility

*Service is the rent that you pay for room on this earth.*

**Shirley Chisholm**

Yet, as we come to realize that challenges are seeds of opportunity, we become more spiritually confident and trust that things will work out.

When we gain confidence and trust in ourselves, it becomes easier to reach out to others. When you are feeling down, try doing something for another person. Make healthy lifestyle choices so you can realize your potential.

## Critical Thinking

1. How do you support the spiritual dimension of your life? What actions do you take to learn more about your personal values? How might you change your lifestyle habits to become more in tune with your spiritual self?

2. How do you serve others? What type of activities do you participate in that "make a difference" or "leave legacies"?

3. What do you know about the major religions in the world? What religious doctrines or philosophies do you find meaningful? Why? How does religion link to spirituality as you define it?

If your textbook package includes CengageNOW™, go to http://west.cengagenow.com/ilrn/ to link to CengageNOW™ for Health, your online study tool. First take the **Pre-test** for this chapter to get your personalized **Study Plan,** which will identify topics you need to review and direct you to the appropriate resources. Then take the **Post-test** to determine what concepts you have mastered and what you still need work on.

# SITES & BYTES

### Centre for Spirituality in the Workplace
www.smu.ca/institutes/csw

Established in 2004 at St. Mary's University in Halifax, the centre assists faculty, other universities, religious organizations, and the community to promote multi-faith research and programs.

### Four Worlds International Institute
www.4worlds.org

This website is a family of people and organizations who are attempting to create solutions to difficult problems faced by First Nations' communities across Canada and around the world.

### Religious Tolerance.org
www.religioustolerance.org

This Ontario-based agency encourages people to follow the religious path of their choosing. On their site, you will find information about many religions of the world. Tolerance toward various religions and spiritual beliefs is their goal.

### Roberta Bondar
www.robertabondar.ca

Roberta Bondar calls herself a passionate Earthling. Visit this site to learn more about her work as a scientist and marvel at the messages of hope and the connection of nature and the human spirit.

### Volunteer Abroad
http://volunteerabroad.ca/home.cfm

Volunteer Abroad, an organization owned by the Canadian Federation of Students, is a non-profit student organization that connects motivated students with non-profit organizations, communities, and government agencies that need help around the world.

Please note that links are subject to change. If you find a broken link, use a search engine such as www.google.ca and search for the website by typing in keywords.

### InfoTrac® College Edition Activity
Bryant, A.N., & Astin, H.S. (2008, January–February). The correlates of spiritual struggle during the college years. *Journal of Higher Education, 79*(8), 27.

1. Define "spiritual struggle" as described by the authors of this study.

2. Describe two potential consequences of spiritual struggle that the college students participating in this study faced.

3. Discuss two ways you might reflect on your own spiritual struggle as you complete your academic journey.

You can find additional readings relating to spirituality with InfoTrac® College Edition, an online library of more than 5000 journals and publications. Follow the instructions for accessing InfoTrac® that were packaged with your textbook; then search for articles using a keyword search.

For additional links and resources, visit our text-specific website at www.health.nelson.com.

## Key Terms

The terms listed here are used within the chapter on the page indicated. Definitions of terms are in the Glossary at the end of the book.

| | | | |
|---|---|---|---|
| **Baha'i** 441 | **ego** 437 | **meaning** 444 | **Sikhism** 443 |
| **Buddhism** 441 | **Hinduism** 442 | **potential** 444 | **spirituality** 432 |
| **Christianity** 441 | **Islam** 442 | **purpose** 444 | **Taoism** 444 |
| **Confucianism** 442 | **Jainism** 443 | **religion** 432 | **transcendence** 437 |
| **conscience** 435 | **Judaism** 443 | **Shinto** 443 | |

# References

1. Shahjahan, R.A. (2004). Centering spirituality in the academy: Toward a transformative way of teaching and learning. *Journal of Transformative Education, 2*(4), 294–312.

2. Estanek, S.M. (2006). Redefining spirituality: A new discourse. *College Student Journal, 40*(2), 270–82.

3. Bryant, A.N., & Astin, H.S. (2008). The correlates of spiritual struggle during the college years. *Journal of Higher Education, 79*(1), 1–27.

4. Merriam-Webster Online. (n.d.). Available at www.m-w.com.

5. Travis, J.W., & Ryan, R.S. (2004). *Wellness workbook,* 3rd ed. Berkley, CA: Celestial Arts Ten Speed Press.

6. Erriker, C., & Erriker, J. (eds.). (2001). *Contemporary spiritualities: Social and religious contexts.* London and New York: Continuum, p. xv.

7. Scherurs, A. (2002). Psychotherapy and spirituality. Integrating the spiritual dimension into therapeutic practice. London: Jessica Kingsley Publishers.

8. Tisdell, E.J. (2003). *Exploring spirituality and culture in adult and higher education.* San Francisco: Jossey Bass.

9. National Institute for Healthcare Research. (1997). *Final report. Scientific progress in spiritual research.* Rockville, MD: Author. As quoted in: Mytko, J.J., & Knight, S.J. (2004). Body, mind and spirit: Towards the integration of religiosity and spirituality in cancer quality of life research. *Psycho-Oncology, 8,* 439–50.

10. Hunglemann, J., Kenkel-Rossi, E., Klassen, L., & Stollenwork, R. (1996). Focusing on spiritual well-being: Harmonious interconnectedness of mind-body-spirit use of the JAREL spiritual well-being scale. *Geriatric Nursing, 17*(6), 262–66.

11. Kulchyski, P., McCaskill, D., & Newhouse, D. (eds.). (1999). *In the words of elders: Aboriginal cultures in transition.* Toronto: University of Toronto Press.

12. National Wellness Institute, Inc. (n.d.). Six dimensional model. Available at www.nationalwellness.org/aboutus/index.php.

13. Berry, D. (2005). Methodological pitfalls in the study of religiosity and spirituality. *Western Journal of Nursing Research, 27*(5), 626–47.

14. Estanek, S.M. (2006). Redefining spirituality: a new discourse. *College Student Journal, 40*(2), 270–82.

15. Ingersoll, R.E., & Bauer, A.L. (2004). An integral approach to spiritual wellness in school/counseling settings. *Professional School Counseling, 7*(5), 301–8.

16. Religious Tolerance.org. (2008, October 2). About specific religions, faith groups, ethical systems, etc. Available at www .religioustolerance.org/var_rel.htm.

17. Berry, D. (2005). Methodological pitfalls in the study of religiosity and spirituality. *Western Journal of Nursing Research, 27*(5), 626–47.

18. Starbuck, E.D. (1901). The psychology of religion: An empirical study of the growth of religious consciousness. New York: Scribner.

19. James, W. (1902). *The varieties of religious experience: A study of human nature.* New York: Random House.

20. Jung, C.G. (1923). *Psychological types: Or the psychology of individuation.* Translated by H. Godwin Baynes. London: Kegan Paul, Trench, Trubner.

21. Frankl, V.E. (1959). *Man's search for meaning.* New York: Pocket Books.

22. Seeman, T.E., Dubin, L.F., & Seeman, M. (2003). Religiosity/ spirituality and health: A critical review of the evidence for biological pathways. *American Psychologist, 58*(1), 53–63.

23. Cousins, N. (1979). *Anatomy of an illness.* New York: Norton.

24. Cousins, N. (1989). *Head first: The biology of hope and the healing power of the human spirit.* New York: Dutton.

25. Ingersoll, R.E., & Bauer, A.L. (2004). An integral approach to spiritual wellness in school/counseling settings. *Professional School Counseling, 7*(5), 301–8.

26. Duerr, M., Zajonc, A., & Dana, D. (2003). Survey of transformative and spiritual dimensions of higher education. *Journal of Transformative Education, 1*(3), 177–211.

27. Shahjahan, R.A. (2004). Centering spirituality in the academy: Toward a transformative way of teaching and learning. *Journal of Transformative Education, 2*(4), 294–312.

28. Nagel, E., & Sgoutas-Emch, S. (2007). The relationship between spirituality, health beliefs, and health behaviours in college students. *Journal of Religion and Health, 46*(1), 141–54.

29. Statistics Canada. (2008, October 2). Who's religious? Available at www.statcan.ca/Daily/English/060502/d060502a.htm.

30. Ibid.

31. Lindsay, Colin. (June 2008). Canadians attend weekly religious services less than 20 years ago. Component of Statistics Canada Catalogue no. 89-630-X. Matter of Fact, No. 3. Available at www.statcan.ca/english/freepub/89-630-XIE/2008001/article/ 10650-en.htm.

32. Levy, Abe. (2004, August 28). Campus religious groups offer prayer meetings, discussions for students. *The Wichita Eagle.* Knight-Ridder/Tribune Business News.

33. Adams, T.B., Bezner, J.R., Drabbs, M.E., Zambarano, R.J., & Steinhardt, M.A. (2000). Conceptualization and measurement of the spiritual and psychological dimensions of wellness in a college population. *Journal of American College Health, 48*(4), 165–73.

34. Kuh, G.D., & Gonyea, R.M. (2006). Spirituality, liberal learning and college student engagement. *Liberal Education.* Winter 2006.

35. Muller, S.M., & Dennis, D.L. (2007). Life change and spirituality among a college student cohort. *Journal of American College Health, 56*(1), 55–60.

36. McGee, M., Nagael, L., & Moore, M.K. (2003). A study of university classroom strategies aimed at increasing spiritual health. *College Student Journal, 37*(4), 583–95.

37. Mussolum, E. (2008, May 5). Trinity Western University. First of its kind—TWU creates new Religion in Canada Institute. Available at www.twu.ca/about/news/general/2008/religion-in-canada-institute .html.

38. Mueller, P.S., Plevak, D.J., & Rummans, T.A. (2001). Religious involvement, spirituality, and medicine: Implications for clinical practice. *Mayo Clinic Proceedings, 76,* 1225–35.

39. Seeman, T.E., Dubin, L.F., & Seeman, M. (2003). Religiosity, spirituality and health: A critical review of the evidence for biological pathways. *American Psychologist, 58*(1), 53–63.

40. Ibid.

41. Mytko, J.J., & Knight, S. (1999). Body, mind and spirit: Towards the integration of religiosity and spirituality in cancer quality of life research. *Psycho-Oncology, 8,* 439–50.

42. Yangarber-Hicks, N. (2004). Religious coping styles and recovery from serious mental illnesses. *Journal of Psychology and Theology, 32*(4), 305–18.

43. Wyatt Nelms, L., Hutchins, E., Hutchins, D., & Pursley, R.J. (2006). Spirituality and the health of college students. *Journal of Religion and Health, 46*(2), 249–65.

44. McGee, M., Nagel, L., & Moore, M.K. (2003). A study of university classroom strategies aimed at increasing spiritual health. *College Student Journal, 37*(4), 583–95.

45. Faver, C.A. (2004). Relational spirituality and social caregiving. *Social Work, 49*(2), 241–49.

46. Merriam-Webster Online. Available at www.m-w.com.

47. Bondar, R. (1994). *Touching the earth.* Toronto: Key Porter Books, pp. 76–77.

48. Faver, C.A. (2004). Relational spirituality and social caregiving. *Social Work, 49*(2), 241–49.

49. Montes, S. (1996). Uses of natural settings to promote, maintain and restore human health. In B.L. Driver, D. Dustin, T. Baltic, G. Elsner, & G. Peterson (eds.), *Nature and the human spirit: Toward an expanded land management ethic.* State College, PA: Venture Publishing, Inc., pp. 105–15.

50. Elsner, G., Snell, F., Lewis, D., & Spitzer, W. (1996). The role of public lands in maintaining and rejuvenating the human spirit. In B.L. Driver, D. Dustin, T. Baltic, G. Elsner, & G. Peterson (eds.), *Nature and the human spirit: Toward an expanded land management ethic.* State College, PA: Venture Publishing, Inc., pp. 10–13.

51. Suzuki, D. (2003). *The David Suzuki reader: A lifetime of ideas from a leading activist and thinker.* Vancouver: Greystone Books, p. 11.

52. Hammond, H., & Judy, S. (1996). Belief, wholeness, and experience: Sensitizing professional land managers to spiritual values. In B.L. Driver, D. Dustin, T. Baltic, G. Elsner & G. Peterson (eds.), *Nature and the human spirit: Toward an expanded land management ethic.* State College, PA: Venture Publishing, Inc., pp. 367–81.

53. Bopp, J., Bopp, M., Brown, L., & Lane, P. Jr. (1985). *The sacred tree.* Lethbridge, AB: Four Worlds International Institute for Human and Community Development. Available at www.4worlds.org.

54. Ibid., p. 7.

55. Ibid., p. 7.

56. Ibid., p. 22.

57. Ibid., p. 22.

58. Ibid., p. 23.

59. Ibid., p. 24.

60. Ibid., pp. 81–82.

61. Major religions of the world ranked by number of adherents. (n.d.). Available at www.adherents.com/Religions_By_Adherents.html.

62. Ibid.

63. Clark, W. (2003). Pockets of belief: Religious attendance patterns in Canada. *Canadian Social Trends.* Statistics Canada – Catalogue No. 11-008. Spring 2003. Available at www.statcan.ca/english/freepub/11-008-XIE/2002004/articles/6493.pdf.

64. Religious Tolerance.org. (2008, August 18). The Baha'i world faith. Ontario Consultants on Religious Tolerance. Available at www.religioustolerance.org/bahai.htm.

65. The Canadian Encyclopedia, Historica. (2008, August 18). Buddhism. Available at www.thecanadianencyclopedia.com/PrinterFriendly.cfm?Params=A1ARTA0001082.

66. The Government of Tibet in Exile. (2008, June 9). His Holiness, the Dalai Lama. Press release. Available at www.tibet.com/NewsRoom/londonphoto1.htm.

67. Religious Tolerance.org. (2008, August 12). Buddhism. Ontario Consultants on Religious Tolerance. Available at www.religioustolerance.org/buddhism.htm.

68. Religious Tolerance.org. (2008, February 3). Who is a Christian? A simple question with many answers. Ontario Consultants on Religious Tolerance. Available at www.religioustolerance.org/chr_defn2.htm.

69. The Canadian Encyclopedia, Historica. (2008, August 18). Christianity. Available at www.thecanadianencyclopedia.com/index.cfm?PgNm=TCE&Params=A1ARTA0001613.

70. Which ten commandments? (n.d.). *Positive Atheism Magazine.* Available at www.positiveatheism.org/crt/whichcom.htm.

71. The Spiritual Sanctuary.org. (2008, July 4). Confucianism. Available at www.thespiritualsanctuary.org/Confucianism/Confucianism.html.

72. Ibid.

73. Religious Tolerance.org. (2008, September 28). Hinduism. A general introduction. Ontario Consultants on Religious Tolerance. Available at www.religioustolerance.org/hinduism2.htm.

74. The Canadian Encyclopedia, Historica. (2008, August 18). Hinduism. Available at www.thecanadianencyclopedia.com/PrinterFriendly.cfm?Params=A1ARTA0003777.

75. Religious Tolerance.org. (2008, September 28). Hinduism. A general introduction. Ontario Consultants on Religious Tolerance. Available at www.religioustolerance.org/hinduism2.htm.

76. Religious Tolerance.org. (2008, August 23). Introduction to Islam. Part 1. Ontario Consultants on Religious Tolerance. Available at www.religioustolerance.org/isl_intro.htm.

77. Religious Tolerance.org. (2008, August 7). Islam. The second largest growing world religion and growing. Ontario Consultants on Religious Tolerance. Available at www.religioustolerance.org/islam.htm.

78. Religious Tolerance.org. (2008, August 23). Introduction to Islam. Part 1. Ontario Consultants on Religious Tolerance. Available at www.religioustolerance.org/isl_intro.htm.

79. Ibid.

80. Brym, R.J. (2008). Religion, politics, and suicide bombing: An interpretive essay. *Canadian Journal of Sociology, 33*(1), 89–108.

81. Religious Tolerance.org. (2008, August 15). Jain Dharma (a.k.a. Jainism). Ontario Consultants on Religious Tolerance. Available at www.religioustolerance.org/jainism.htm.

82. Ibid.

83. The Canadian Encyclopedia, Historica. (2008, August 18). Judaism. Available at www.thecanadianencyclopedia.com/PrinterFriendly.cfm?Params=A1ARTA0004186.

84. Religious Tolerance.org. (2008, August 12). Description of Judaism. Ontario Consultants on Religious Tolerance. Available at www.religioustolerance.org/jud_desc.htm.

85. Ibid.

86. Religious Tolerance.org. (2008, August 23). Shinto. Ontario Consultants on Religious Tolerance. Available at www.religioustolerance.org/shinto.htm.

87. Ibid.

88. The Canadian Encyclopedia, Historica. (2008, August 18). Sikhism. Available at www.thecanadianencyclopedia.com/PrinterFriendly.cfm?Params=A1ARTA0007391.

89. Religious Tolerance.org. (2008, August 17). Taoism (a.k.a. Daoism). Ontario Consultants on Religious Tolerance. Available at www.religioustolerance.org/taoism.htm.

90. Ibid.

91. Merriam-Webster Online. (n.d.). www.m-w.com.

92. Ibid.

93. Ibid.

## Chapter 1
1. b; 2. a; 3. d; 4. c; 5. a; 6. d; 7. b; 8. c; 9. d; 10. a

## Chapter 2
1. b; 2. d; 3. a; 4. d; 5. a; 6. b; 7. c; 8. a; 9. c; 10. d

## Chapter 3
1. b; 2. d; 3. a; 4. c; 5. c; 6. b; 7. b; 8. a; 9. d; 10. b

## Chapter 4
1. c; 2. c; 3. d; 4. b; 5. b; 6. a; 7. d; 8. c; 9. b; 10. d

## Chapter 5
1. c; 2. a; 3. d; 4. d; 5. b; 6. a; 7. c; 8. a; 9. d; 10. b

## Chapter 6
1. d; 2. b; 3. b; 4. c; 5. c; 6. a; 7. c; 8. d; 9. a; 10. c

## Chapter 7
1. d; 2. a; 3. b; 4. a; 5. c; 6. d; 7. c; 8. a; 9. d; 10. b

## Chapter 8
1. c; 2. d; 3. a; 4. c; 5. c; 6. b; 7. d; 8. a; 9. b; 10. d

## Chapter 9
1. a; 2. c; 3. d; 4. b; 5. c; 6. a; 7. a; 8. d; 9. b; 10. c

## Chapter 10
1. b; 2. a; 3. a; 4. b; 5. d; 6. a; 7. d; 8. a; 9. c; 10. b

## Chapter 11
1. a; 2. c; 3. d; 4. b; 5. c; 6. c; 7. d; 8. a; 9. b; 10. d

## Chapter 12
1. b; 2. a; 3. b; 4. c; 5. d; 6. c; 7. c; 8. b; 9. b; 10. c

## Chapter 13
1. b; 2. c; 3. c; 4. d; 5. b; 6. a; 7. d; 8. d; 9. c; 10. b

## Chapter 14
1. d; 2. b; 3. c; 4. b; 5. d; 6. c; 7. b; 8. a; 9. c; 10. b

## Chapter 15
1. b; 2. a; 3. d; 4. c; 5. b; 6. b; 7. d; 8. c; 9. c; 10. b

## Chapter 16
1. d; 2. c; 3. b; 4. a; 5. b; 6. c; 7. b; 8. a; 9. d; 10. b

## Chapter 17
1. b; 2. d; 3. c; 4. a; 5. d; 6. d; 7. a; 8. c; 9. b; 10. c.

# Glossary

**abscess** A localized accumulation of pus and disintegrating tissue.

**abstinence** Voluntary refrainment from sexual activities that include vaginal, anal, and oral intercourse.

**acquired immune deficiency syndrome (AIDS)** The final stages of human immunodeficiency virus (HIV) infection, characterized by a variety of severe illnesses and decreased levels of certain immune cells.

**action** Modifying behaviour according to a plan. A commitment of time and energy is required.

**active living** A way of life in which physical activity is valued and integrated into daily living.

**acupuncture** A Chinese medical practice of puncturing the body with needles inserted at specific points to relieve pain or cure disease.

**acute injury** Physical injury, such as a sprain, bruise, and pulled muscle, that results from sudden trauma, such as a fall or collision.

**adaptive response** The body's attempt to reestablish homeostasis or stability.

**addiction** A behavioural pattern characterized by compulsion, loss of control, and continued repetition of a behaviour or activity in spite of adverse consequences.

**additive** Substance added to food to lengthen storage time, change taste in a way the manufacturer thinks is better, alter colour, or otherwise modify it to make it more appealing.

**advance directive** Document that specifies an individual's preferences regarding treatment in a medical crisis.

**aerobic exercise** Physical activity in which sufficient or excess oxygen is continually supplied to the body.

**aging** The characteristic pattern of normal life changes that occur as humans grow older.

**alcohol abuse** Continued use of alcohol despite awareness of social, occupational, psychological, or physical problems related to its use, or use of alcohol in dangerous ways or situations, such as before driving.

**alcohol dependence** Development of a strong craving for alcohol due to the pleasurable feelings or relief of stress and anxiety produced by drinking.

**alcoholism** A chronic, progressive, potentially fatal disease characterized by an inability to control drinking, a preoccupation with alcohol, continued use of alcohol despite adverse consequences, and distorted thinking, most notably denial.

**altruism** Acts of helping or giving to others without thought of self-benefit.

**Alzheimer's disease** A progressive deterioration of intellectual powers due to physiological changes within the brain; symptoms include diminishing ability to concentrate, disorientation, depression, apathy, and paranoia.

**amenorrhea** The absence or suppression of menstruation.

**amino acid** Organic compound containing nitrogen, carbon, hydrogen, and oxygen; the essential building block of proteins.

**amnion** The innermost membrane of the sac enclosing the embryo or fetus.

**amphetamine** A stimulant that triggers the release of epinephrine, which stimulates the central nervous system; users experience a state of hyper-alertness and high energy, followed by a crash as the drug wears off.

**anabolic steroid** A synthetic artificial version of the male sex hormone testosterone.

**anaerobic exercise** Physical activity in which the body develops an oxygen deficit.

**androgynous** Refers to people who neither identify as male nor female.

**angioplasty** Surgical repair of an obstructed artery by passing a balloon catheter through the blood vessel to the area of obstruction and then inflating the catheter to compress the plaque against the vessel wall.

**anorexia nervosa** A psychological disorder in which refusal to eat and/or an extreme loss of appetite leads to malnutrition, severe weight loss, and possibly death.

**antibiotic** Substance produced by microorganisms or synthetic agents that is toxic to other types of microorganisms; in dilute solutions, used to treat infectious diseases.

**antidepressant** A drug used primarily to treat symptoms of depression.

**antioxidant** Substance that prevents the damaging effects of oxidation in cells.

**antiviral drug** A substance that decreases the severity and duration of a viral infection if taken prior to or soon after onset of the infection.

**anxiety** A feeling of apprehension and dread, with or without a known cause; may range from mild to severe and may be accompanied by physical symptoms.

**anxiety disorder** Psychological disorder involving episodes of apprehension, tension, or uneasiness, stemming from the anticipation of danger and sometimes accompanied by physical symptoms; causes significant distress and impairment to an individual.

**aorta** The main artery of the body, arising from the left ventricle of the heart.

**appetite** A desire for food, stimulated by anticipated hunger, physiological changes within the brain and body, the availability of food, and other environmental and psychological factors.

**arteriosclerosis** Any of a number of chronic diseases characterized by degeneration of the arteries and hardening and thickening of arterial walls.

**artificial insemination** The introduction of viable sperm into the vagina by artificial means for the purpose of inducing conception.

**assertive** Behaving in a non-hostile, confident manner to make your needs and desires clear to others.

**atherosclerosis** A form of arteriosclerosis in which fatty substances (plaque) are deposited on the inner walls of arteries.

**atrium** (plural, **atria**) Either of the two upper chambers of the heart, which receive blood from the veins.

**attention deficit/hyperactivity disorder (ADHD)** A spectrum of difficulties in controlling motion and sustaining attention, including hyperactivity, impulsivity, and distractibility.

**autoimmune disorder** A disease caused by an immune response against antigens in the tissues of one's own body.

**autonomy** The ability to draw on internal resources; independence from familial and societal influences.

**aversion therapy** A treatment that attempts to help a person overcome a dependence or bad habit by making the person feel disgusted or repulsed by that habit.

**avian influenza**  A contagious infection that also comes from a virus that infects many kinds of birds and other animals.

**Ayurveda**  A traditional Indian medical treatment involving meditation, exercise, herbal medication, and nutrition.

**bacterial vaginosis (BV)**  A vaginal infection caused by overgrowth and depletion of various microorganisms living in the vagina, resulting in a malodourous white or grey vaginal discharge.

**bacterium**  (plural, **bacteria**) One-celled microscopic organism; the most plentiful pathogen.

**Baha'i**  A faith founded in Iran during the mid-19th century by Siyyid 'Ali-Muhammed. Baha'is believe that there is a single God who sends prophets into the world through which the word of God is revealed.

**barbiturate**  Anti-anxiety drug that depresses the central nervous system, reduces activity, and induces relaxation, drowsiness, or sleep; often prescribed to relieve tension, treat epileptic seizures, or as a general anesthetic.

**barrier contraceptive**  Birth-control device that blocks the meeting of egg and sperm by physical barriers (such as condoms, diaphragms, or cervical caps), or by chemical barriers (such as spermicide), or both.

**basal-body temperature**  The body temperature upon waking, before any activity.

**basal metabolic rate (BMR)**  The number of calories required to sustain the body at rest.

**behaviour therapy**  Psychotherapy that emphasizes application of the principles of learning to substitute desirable responses and behaviour patterns for undesirable ones.

**benzodiazepine**  Anti-anxiety drug that depresses the central nervous system, reduces activity, and induces relaxation, drowsiness, or sleep; often prescribed to relieve tension, muscular strain, sleep problems, anxiety, or panic attacks; also used as an anesthetic and in the treatment of alcohol withdrawal.

**binge drinking**  For a man, having five or more alcoholic drinks at a single sitting; for a woman, having four drinks or more at a single sitting.

**binge eating disorder (BED)**  The rapid consumption of an abnormally large amount of food in a relatively short time.

**biofeedback**  A technique of becoming aware, with the aid of external monitoring devices, of internal physiological activities in order to develop the capability of altering them.

**bipolar disorder**  Severe depression alternating with periods of manic activity and elation.

**bisexual**  Sexually oriented toward both men and women.

**blood-alcohol concentration (BAC)**  The amount of alcohol in the blood, expressed as a percentage.

**body composition**  The relative amounts of fat and lean tissue (bone, muscle, organs, water) in the body.

**body mass index (BMI)**  A mathematical formula that correlates height and weight with body fat; a better predictor of disease than weight alone.

**botanical medicine**  An ancient form of medical treatment using substances derived from trees, flowers, ferns, seaweeds, and lichens to treat disease.

**botulism**  Possibly fatal food poisoning, caused by a type of bacterium that produces a toxin in the absence of air; found in improperly canned food.

**breech birth**  A birth in which the infant's buttocks or feet pass through the birth canal first.

**Buddhism**  The fourth largest religion in the world; founded in Northern India by the first known Buddha, Siddhartha Gautama. Buddhism encourages a connection with both the natural world and the spiritual world.

**bulimia nervosa**  Episodic binge eating, often followed by forced vomiting or laxative abuse, and accompanied by a persistent preoccupation with body shape and weight.

**caesarean delivery**  The surgical procedure in which an infant is delivered through an incision made in the abdominal wall and uterus.

**calorie**  The amount of energy required to raise the temperature of 1 gram of water by 1 degree Celsius. In everyday usage related to the energy content of foods and the energy expended in activities, a calorie is actually the equivalent of 1000 such calories, or a kilocalorie.

**candidiasis**  An infection of the yeast *Candida albicans*, commonly occurring in the vagina, vulva, penis, or mouth, and causing burning, itching, and a whitish discharge.

**capillary**  A minute blood vessel that connects an artery to a vein.

**carbohydrate**  Organic compound, such as starch, sugar, and glycogen, that is composed of carbon, hydrogen, and oxygen; source of bodily energy.

**carbon monoxide**  A colourless, odourless gas produced by the burning of gasoline or tobacco; displaces oxygen in the hemoglobin molecules of red blood cells.

**carcinogen**  A substance that produces cancerous cells or enhances their development and growth.

**cardiorespiratory fitness**  The ability of the heart and blood vessels to efficiently circulate blood through the body.

**celibacy**  Abstention from sexual activity; can be partial or complete, permanent or temporary.

**cell-mediated immunity**  The portion of the immune response that protects against parasites, fungi, cancer cells, and foreign tissue, primarily by means of T cells, or lymphocytes.

**cervical cap**  A thimble-sized rubber or plastic cap that is inserted into the vagina to fit over the cervix and prevent the passage of sperm into the uterus during sexual intercourse; used with a spermicidal foam or jelly, it serves as both a chemical and a physical barrier to sperm.

**cervix**  The narrow, lower end of the uterus that opens into the vagina.

**chanchroid**  A soft, painful sore or localized infection usually acquired through sexual contact.

**chiropractic**  A method of treating disease, primarily through manipulating the bones and joints to restore normal nerve function.

**Chlamydia**  A sexually transmitted infection caused by the bacterium *Chlamydia trachomatis*, often asymptomatic in women but sometimes characterized by urinary pain; if undetected and untreated may result in pelvic inflammatory disease (PID).

**chlorinated hydrocarbon**  Highly toxic pesticide, such as DDT and chlordane, that is extremely resistant to breakdown; may cause cancer, birth defects, neurological disorders, and cause damage to wildlife and the environment.

**cholesterol**  An organic substance found in animal fats; linked to cardiovascular disease, particularly atherosclerosis.

**Christianity**  A religion derived from Jesus Christ. Christians are individuals who believe their life has been transformed by the grace of God, or anyone who has repented their sin, or who has been born again.

**chronic obstructive pulmonary disease (COPD)**  A lung disorder that causes airways to become partially obstructed.

circumcision  The surgical removal of the foreskin of the penis.

climate change  Any long-term significant change in the "average weather" that a given region experiences; variations within the Earth's atmosphere and include such processes as variations in solar radiation, the Earth's orbit, and greenhouse gas concentrations.

clitoris  A small erectile structure on the female, corresponding to the penis on the male.

club drug  Illegally manufactured psychoactive drug (including ecstasy, Special K, and Rohypnol) that has dangerous physical and psychological effects; often used at all-night rave or trance events.

cocaine  A white crystalline powder extracted from the leaves of the coca plant that stimulates the central nervous system and produces a brief period of euphoria followed by depression.

cognitive-behavioural therapy (CBT)  A technique used to identify an individual's beliefs and attitudes, recognize negative thought patterns, and educate in alternative ways of thinking.

cohabitation  Two people living together as a couple, without official ties such as marriage.

coitus interruptus  The removal of the penis from the vagina before ejaculation.

colpotomy  Surgical sterilization by cutting or blocking the fallopian tubes through an incision made in the wall of the vagina.

complementary and alternative health care (CAHC)  All health-care approaches, practices, and treatments not widely taught in medical schools and not generally used in hospitals.

complete protein  Protein that contains all the amino acids needed by the body for growth and maintenance.

complex carbohydrate  Starches, including cereals, fruits, and vegetables. They have more than 10 units of sugar.

concentric phase  Decreasing the angle between two bones or contracting the muscle constitutes the concentric phase of an isotonic contraction.

conception  The merging of a sperm and an ovum.

conditioning  The gradual building up of the body to enhance one or more of the three main components of physical fitness: flexibility, cardiorespiratory fitness, and muscular strength and endurance.

condom  A latex sheath worn over the penis during sexual acts to prevent conception and/ or the transmission of disease; some condoms contain a spermicidal lubricant.

Confucianism  An ethical system in which certain rituals at specific times during one's lifetime are practised. Teachings deal with individual morality and ethics.

conscience  Our connectedness; our sense of moral goodness.

constant-dose combination pill  An oral contraceptive that releases synthetic estrogen and progestin at constant levels throughout the menstrual cycle.

contemplation  Awareness that there is a problem behaviour and one is considering changing it within the next six months.

contraception  The prevention of conception; birth control.

corpus luteum  A yellowish mass of tissue that is formed immediately after ovulation from the remaining cells of the follicle; it secretes estrogen and progesterone for the remainder of the menstrual cycle.

Cowper's gland  Either of two small glands that discharge into the male urethra.

crucifer  A plant, including broccoli, cabbage, and cauliflower, that contains large amounts of fibre, proteins, and indoles.

crystal meth  Also known as methamphetamine (MA). A white, odourless, bitter-tasting crystalline powder that readily dissolves in water or alcohol. It can be snorted, swallowed, or injected. Ice (or crank, crystal, glass, or tina) is a smokeable form of methamphetamine.

culture  The set of shared attitudes, values, goals, and practices of a group that are internalized by an individual within the group.

cunnilingus  Sexual stimulation of a woman's genitals by means of oral manipulation.

cystitis  Inflammation of the urinary bladder.

decibel (dB)  A unit for measuring the intensity of sounds.

deep frostbite  The freezing of skin, muscle, and bone that requires medical treatment. It usually involves the tissues of the hands and feet, which appear pale and feel frozen.

defence mechanism  A psychological process that alleviates anxiety and eliminates mental conflict; includes denial, displacement, projection, rationalization, reaction formation, and repression.

deleriant  Chemical, such as solvent, aerosol, glue, cleaning fluid, petroleum product, and

some anesthetics, that produces vapours with psychoactive effects when inhaled.

dementia  Deterioration of mental capability.

depression  In general, feelings of unhappiness and despair; as a mental illness, also characterized by an inability to function normally.

depressive disorder  A psychological disorder involving pervasive and sustained depression.

diabetes mellitus  A disease in which the inadequate production of insulin or resistance to insulin leads to failure of the body tissues to break down carbohydrates at a normal rate.

diaphragm  A bowl-like rubber cup with a flexible rim that is inserted into the vagina to cover the cervix and prevent the passage of sperm into the uterus during sexual intercourse; used with a spermicidal foam or jelly, it serves as both a chemical and a physical barrier to sperm.

diastole  The period between contractions in the cardiac cycle, during which the heart relaxes and dilates as it fills with blood.

dietary fat theory  All calories are not the same. Some studies have shown that consuming a diet high in fat calories will result in being overweight or obese.

dietary fibre  The nondigestible form of carbohydrates found in plant foods, such as leaves, stems, skins, seeds, and hulls.

dietary reference intake (DRI)  A set of values for the dietary nutrient intake of healthy people (Estimated Average Requirements, Recommended Dietary Allowances, Adequate Intakes, and Tolerable Upper Intake levels); used for planning and assessing diets.

dilation and evacuation (D&E)  A medical procedure in which the contents of the uterus are removed through the use of instruments.

distress  A negative stress that may result in illness.

do-not-resuscitate (DNR)  An advance directive expressing an individual's preference that resuscitation efforts not be made during a medical crisis.

drug  Any substance, other than food, that affects bodily functions and structures when taken into the body.

drug abuse  The excessive use of a drug in a manner inconsistent with accepted medical practice.

drug misuse  The use of a drug for a purpose (or person) other than that for which it was medically intended.

**dynamic flexibility** The ability to move a joint quickly and fluidly through its entire range of motion with little resistance.

**dysmenorrhea** Painful menstruation.

**eating disorder** A bizarre, often dangerous pattern of food consumption, including anorexia nervosa and bulimia nervosa.

**eccentric phase** Increasing the angle between two bones or lengthening the muscle constitutes the eccentric phase of an isotonic contraction.

**ecosystem** A community of organisms sharing a physical and chemical environment and interacting with each other.

**ecstasy (MDMA)** A synthetic compound, also known as methylenedioxymethamphetamine, that is similar in structure to methamphetamine and has both stimulant and hallucinogenic effects.

**ectopic pregnancy** A pregnancy in which the fertilized egg has implanted itself outside the uterine cavity, usually in the fallopian tube.

**ego** Our self and self-centredness.

**ejaculatory duct** The canal connecting the seminal vesicles and vas deferens.

**electromagnetic field (EMF)** The invisible electric and magnetic field generated by an electrically charged conductor.

**embryo** An organism in its early stage of development; in humans, the embryonic period lasts from the second to the eighth week of pregnancy.

**emergency contraception (EC)** Types of oral contraceptive pills usually taken within 72 hours after intercourse that can prevent pregnancy.

**emotional health** The ability to express and acknowledge one's feelings and moods.

**emotional intelligence** A term used by some psychologists to evaluate the capacity of people to understand themselves and relate well with others.

**endocrine disruptor** Synthetic chemical that interferes with the way hormones work in humans and wildlife.

**endometrium** The mucous membrane lining the uterus.

**endorphin** Mood-elevating, pain-killing chemical produced by the brain.

**endurance** The ability to withstand the stress of continued physical exertion.

**energy-balance equation theory** Weight will remain constant if our caloric input (energy in) and caloric output (energy out) are balanced.

**epidemiology** The study of how often diseases occur in different groups of people and why.

**epididymis** That portion of the male duct system in which sperm mature.

**epidural block** An injection of anesthetic into the membrane surrounding the spinal cord to numb the lower body during labour and childbirth.

**essential nutrient** Nutrient that the body cannot manufacture for itself and must obtain from food: water, carbohydrates, fats, vitamins, and minerals.

**estrogen** The female sex hormone that stimulates female secondary sex characteristics.

**ethyl alcohol** The intoxicating agent in alcoholic beverages; also called ethanol.

**eustress** A positive stress, which stimulates a person to function properly.

**failure rate** The number of pregnancies that occur per year for every 100 women using a particular method of birth control.

**fallopian tube** Either of two channels that transports ova from the ovaries to the uterus; the usual site of fertilization.

**fellatio** Sexual stimulation of a man's genitals by means of oral manipulation.

**fertilization** The fusion of the sperm and egg nuclei.

**fetal alcohol effect (FAE)** Milder form of fetal alcohol syndrome, including low birth weight, irritability as newborns, and permanent mental impairment; caused by the mother's alcohol consumption during pregnancy.

**fetal alcohol syndrome (FAS)** A cluster of physical and mental defects in the newborn, including low birth weight, smaller-than-normal head circumference, intrauterine growth retardation, and permanent mental impairment; caused by the mother's alcohol consumption during pregnancy.

**fetus** The human organism developing in the uterus from the ninth week until birth.

**FIT** A formula that describes the frequency, intensity, and length of time for physical activity.

**flexibility** The range of motion allowed by one's joints; determined by the length of muscles, tendons, and ligaments attached to the joints.

**food toxicologist** Specialist who detects toxins in food and treats the conditions toxins produce.

**frostbite** The freezing or partial freezing of skin and tissue just below the skin, or even muscle and bone; more severe than frostnip.

**frostnip** Sudden blanching or lightening of the skin on hands, feet, and face, resulting from exposure to high wind speeds and low temperatures.

**functional fibre** Isolated, non-digestible carbohydrates with beneficial effects in humans.

**fungus** Organism that reproduces by means of spores.

**gamma globulin** The antibody-containing portion of the blood fluid (plasma).

**gamma hydroxybutyrate (GHB)** A brain messenger chemical (also known as blue nitro or the date rape drug) that stimulates the release of the human growth hormone; commonly abused for its high and its alleged ability to trim fat and build muscles.

**gender identity** Refers to a person's self-identified sense of being male, female, neither, or both.

**general adaptation syndrome (GAS)** The sequenced physiological response to a stressful situation; consists of three stages: alarm, resistance, and exhaustion.

**generalized anxiety disorder (GAD)** An anxiety disorder characterized as chronic distress.

**genetically modified organism (GMO)** A plant, animal, or microorganism whose genetic code has been altered, subtracted, or added to (either from the same species or a different species) in order to give it characteristics that it does not have naturally.

**glycemic index (GI)** A measure of how much a carbohydrate-containing food is likely to raise your blood sugar.

**gonorrhea** A sexually transmitted infection caused by the bacterium *Neisseria gonorrhoeae*; male symptoms include discharge from the penis; women are generally asymptomatic.

**guided imagery** An approach to stress control, self-healing, or the motivation of life changes by means of visualizing oneself in the state of calmness, wellness, or change.

**hallucinogen** A drug that causes hallucinations.

**hashish** A concentrated form of cannabis containing the psychoactive ingredient TCH; causes a sense of euphoria when inhaled or eaten.

**health** A state of complete well-being, including physical, psychological, spiritual, social, intellectual, and environmental components.

**health promotion** An educational and informational process in which people are helped to change attitudes and behaviours in an effort to improve their health.

**healthy environment** The creation of conditions and surroundings conducive to health.

**heat cramp** Painful muscle spasm caused by vigorous exercise and heavy sweating in the heat.

**heat exhaustion** Faintness, rapid heart beat, low blood pressure, an ashen appearance, cold and clammy skin, and nausea, resulting from prolonged sweating with inadequate fluid replacement.

**heat stress** Physical response to prolonged exposure to high temperature; occurs simultaneously with or after heat cramps.

**heat stroke** A medical emergency consisting of a fever of at least 40.5°C (105°F), hot dry skin, rapid heartbeat, rapid and shallow breathing, and elevated or lowered blood pressure, caused by the breakdown of the body's cooling mechanism.

**helminth** A parasitic roundworm or flatworm.

**hepatitis** An inflammation and/or infection of the liver caused by a virus; often accompanied by jaundice.

**herpes simplex virus (HSV)** A condition caused by one of the herpes viruses and characterized by lesions of the skin or mucous membranes; herpes virus type 2 is sexually transmitted and causes genital blisters or sores.

**heterosexual** Primary sexual orientation toward members of the opposite sex.

**Hinduism** The world's third largest religion after Christianity and Islam. Hindus recognize a single deity while honouring other Gods and Goddesses as manifestations or aspects of that supreme God.

**holism** An emphasis on the interconnectedness between an individual and his or her mind, body, and spirit.

**holistic** An approach to medicine that takes into account body, mind, emotion, and spirit.

**holographic will** A will entirely in the handwriting of its author.

**homeopathy** A system of medical practice that treats a disease by administering dosages of substances that would produce symptoms in healthy people similar to those of the disease.

**homeostasis** The body's natural state of balance or stability.

**homosexual** Primary sexual orientation toward members of the same sex.

**hormone replacement therapy (HRT)** The use of supplemental hormones during and after menopause.

**host** A person or population that contracts one or more pathogenic agents in an environment.

**human immunodeficiency virus (HIV)** A type of virus that causes a spectrum of health problems, ranging from a symptomless infection to the development of life-threatening diseases because of impaired immunity.

**human papillomavirus (HPV)** A pathogen that causes genital warts and increases the risk of cervical cancer.

**humoral immunity** A portion of the immune response that provides lifelong protection against bacterial or viral infections, such as mumps, by means of antibodies whose production is triggered by the release of antigens upon first exposure to the infectious agent.

**hunger** The physiological drive to consume food.

**hygiene** Healthy; akin to well and to living; a science of the establishment and maintenance of health; conditions or practices conducive to health.

**hypertension** High blood pressure occurring when the blood exerts excessive pressure against the arterial walls.

**hypothermia** An abnormally low body temperature; if not treated appropriately, coma or death could result.

**hysterectomy** The surgical removal of the uterus.

**hysterotomy** A procedure in which the uterus is surgically opened and the fetus inside it removed.

**immunity** Protection from infectious diseases.

**implantation** The embedding of the fertilized ovum in the uterine lining.

**incomplete protein** Protein that lacks one or more of the amino acids essential for protein synthesis.

**incubation period** The time between a pathogen's entrance into the body and the first symptom.

**indole** Naturally occurring chemical found in foods such as winter squash, carrots, and crucifers; may help lower cancer risk.

**infertility** The inability to conceive a child.

**infiltration** A gradual penetration or invasion.

**inflammation** A localized response by the body to tissue injury, characterized by swelling and the dilation of the blood vessels.

**influenza** Illness caused by one of the highly contagious influenza viruses; symptoms include stuffy nose, headache, body aches, fever, and cough.

**informed consent** Permission (to undergo or receive a medical procedure or treatment) given voluntarily, with full knowledge and understanding of the procedure or treatment and its possible consequences.

**inhalant** Substance that produces vapours having psychoactive effects when inhaled.

**integrative medicine** An approach that combines traditional medicine with alternative and/or complementary therapies.

**intercourse** Sexual stimulation by means of entry of the penis into the vagina; coitus.

**interpersonal therapy (IPT)** A technique used to develop communication skills and relationships.

**intersexed** Refers to people who were born with both male and female anatomy, or ambiguous genitalia.

**intimacy** A state of closeness between two people, characterized by the desire and ability to share one's innermost thoughts and feelings with each other, both verbally and nonverbally.

**intoxication** Maladaptive behavioural, psychological, and physiologic changes that occur as a result of substance abuse.

**intramuscular** Into or within a muscle.

**intrauterine device (IUD)** A device inserted into the uterus through the cervix to prevent pregnancy by interfering with implantation.

**intravenous (IV)** Into a vein.

**irradiation** Exposure to or treatment by some form of radiation.

**Islam** The youngest of the world's largest religions. The two main texts that Muslims consult are the *Qur'an* and the *Hadith*. Practices include Jihad, the attainment of a noble goal.

**isokinetic** Having the same force; exercise with specialized equipment that provides resistance equal to the force applied by the user throughout the entire range of motion.

**isometric** Of the same length; exercise in which muscles increase their tension without shortening in length, such as when pushing an immovable object.

**isotonic** Having the same tension or tone; exercise requiring the repetition of an action that creates tension, such as weight lifting or calisthenics.

**Jainism** A religion that is based on the belief that the universe, which has no beginning or end, exists as a series of layers. Those following Jainism are expected to follow the five principles of living.

**Judaism** A religion developed among the ancient Hebrews and characterized by belief in one transcendent God who has revealed himself to the prophet Abraham.

**labia majora** The fleshy outer folds that border the female genital area.

**labia minora** The fleshy inner folds that border the female genital area.

**labour** The process leading up to birth: effacement and dilation of the cervix; the movement of the baby into and through the birth canal, accompanied by strong contractions; and contraction of the uterus and expulsion of the placenta after the birth.

**lacto-ovo vegetarian** Person who eats eggs, dairy products, and fruits and vegetables (but not meat, poultry, or fish).

**lacto-vegetarian** Person who eats dairy products as well as fruits and vegetables (but not meat, poultry, eggs, or fish).

**Lamaze method** A method of childbirth preparation taught to expectant parents to help the woman cope with the discomfort of labour; combines breathing and psychological techniques.

**laparoscopy** A surgical sterilization procedure in which the fallopian tubes are observed with a laparoscope inserted through a small incision and then cut or blocked.

**laparotomy** A surgical sterilization procedure in which the fallopian tubes are cut or blocked through an incision made in the abdomen.

**lipoprotein** Compound in blood that is made up of proteins and fat; a high-density lipoprotein (HDL) picks up excess cholesterol in the blood; a low-density lipoprotein (LDL) carries more cholesterol and deposits it on the walls of arteries.

**listeriosis** An illness caused by the bacterium *Listeria monocytogenes* that is acquired by eating contaminated food; the organism can spread to the bloodstream and central nervous system.

**living will** A written statement providing instructions for the use of life-sustaining procedures in the event of terminal illness or injury.

**locus of control** An individual's belief about the source of power and influence over his or her life.

**lumpectomy** The surgical removal of a breast tumour and its surrounding tissue.

**lymph node** Small tissue mass in which some immune cells are stored.

**macronutrient** Nutrient required by the human body in the greatest amount, includes water, carbohydrates, proteins, and fats.

**mainstream smoke** The smoke inhaled directly by smoking a cigarette.

**maintenance** Continued work at changing behaviour. The change may take six months to a lifetime. Some lapses may be temporary.

**major depression** Sadness that does not end.

**male pattern baldness** The loss of hair at the vertex, or top, of the head.

**mammography** A diagnostic X-ray exam used to detect breast cancer.

**marijuana** The drug derived from the cannabis plant; contains the psychoactive ingredient THC, which causes a mild sense of euphoria when inhaled or eaten.

**massage therapy** A therapeutic method of using the hands to rub, stroke, or knead the body to produce positive effects on an individual's health and well-being.

**mastectomy** The surgical removal of an entire breast.

**masturbation** Self-stimulation of the genitals, often resulting in orgasm.

**meaning** Defined as significant quality or an implication of a hidden or special significance.

**medical abortion** Method of ending a pregnancy within nine weeks of conception using hormonal medications that cause expulsion of the fertilized egg.

**meditation** The use of quiet sitting, breathing techniques, and/or chanting to relax, improve concentration, and become attuned to one's inner self.

**meningitis** An extremely serious, potentially fatal illness in which the bacterium *Neisseria meningitis* attacks the membranes around the brain and spinal cord.

**menopause** The complete cessation of ovulation and menstruation for 12 consecutive months.

**menstruation** Discharge of blood from the vagina as a result of the shedding of the uterine lining at the end of the menstrual cycle.

**mental health** The ability to perceive reality as it is, to respond to its challenges, and to develop rational strategies for living.

**mental illness** Behavioural or psychological syndrome associated with distress or a significantly increased risk of suffering pain, disability, loss of freedom, or death.

**metabolic syndrome** A cluster of symptoms that increases the risk of heart disease and diabetes.

**metastasize** To spread to other parts of the body via the bloodstream or the lymphatic system.

**micronutrient** Vitamin or mineral needed by the body in very small amounts.

**microwave** Extremely high-frequency electromagnetic wave that increases the rate at which molecules vibrate, thereby generating heat.

**mindfulness** A method of stress reduction that involves experiencing the physical and mental sensations of the present moment.

**mineral** Naturally occurring inorganic substance; small amounts of some minerals are essential in metabolism and nutrition.

**minilaparotomy** A surgical sterilization procedure in which the fallopian tubes are cut or sealed by electrical coagulation through a small incision just above the pubic hairline.

**minipill** An oral contraceptive containing a small amount of progestin and no estrogen; prevents contraception by making the mucus in the cervix so thick that sperm cannot enter the uterus.

**miscarriage** A pregnancy that terminates before the 20th week of gestation; also called spontaneous abortion.

**mononucleosis** An infectious viral disease characterized by an excess of white blood cells in the blood, fever, fatigue, bodily discomfort, a sore throat, and kidney and liver complications.

**monophasic pill** *See* constant-dose combination pill.

**mons pubis** The rounded, fleshy area over the junction of the female pubic bones.

**mood** A sustained emotional state that colours one's view of the world for hours or days.

**morbidity** The number of disease rates in one period of time or in one place.

**mortality** The number of deaths in one period of time or in one place.

**multiphasic pill** An oral contraceptive that releases different levels of estrogen and progestin to mimic the hormonal fluctuations of the natural menstrual cycle.

**multiple chemical sensitivity (MCS)** A sensitivity to low-level chemical exposure from ordinary substances, such as perfumes and tobacco smoke, that results in physiological responses such as chest pain, depression, dizziness, fatigue, and nausea; also known as environmentally triggered illness.

**muscular fitness** The amount of strength and level of endurance in the body's muscles.

**mutagen** An agent that causes alterations in the genetic material of living cells.

**mutation** A change in the genetic material of a cell or cells that is brought about by radiation, chemicals, or natural causes.

**mutual aid** The actions people take to help each other cope.

**myocardial infarction (MI)** A condition characterized by the dying of tissue areas in the myocardium, caused by interruption of the blood supply to those areas; the medical name for a heart attack.

**naturopathy** An alternative system of treatment of disease that emphasizes the use of natural remedies such as sun, water, heat, and air. Therapies may include dietary changes, steam baths, and exercise.

**neoplasm** Any tumour, whether benign or malignant.

**nicotine** The addictive substance in tobacco; one of the most toxic of all poisons.

**nongonococcal urethritis (NGU)** Inflammation of the urethra caused by organisms other than the gonococcus bacterium.

**nonopioid** Chemically synthesized drug that has sleep-inducing and pain-relieving properties similar to those of opium and its derivatives.

**norm** Unwritten rule regarding behaviour and conduct expected or accepted by a group.

**nutrition** The science devoted to the study of dietary needs for food and the effects of food on organisms.

**obesity** The excessive accumulation of fat in the body; a condition of having a body mass index (BMI) of 30 or above.

**obsessive-compulsive disorder (OCD)** An anxiety disorder characterized by obsessions and/or compulsions that impair one's ability to function and form relationships.

**opioid** Drug that has sleep-inducing and pain-relieving properties, including opium (and its derivatives) and nonopioid, synthetic drugs.

**optimistic** The tendency to seek out, remember, and expect pleasurable experiences.

**oral contraceptive** Preparation of synthetic hormones that inhibits ovulation; also referred to as birth control pills or simply the pill.

**organic** Term designating food produced with, or production based on the use of, fertilizer originating from plants or animals, without the use of pesticides or chemically formulated fertilizers.

**organic phosphate** Toxic pesticide that may cause cancer, birth defects, neurological disorders, and damage to wildlife and the environment.

**osteoporosis** A condition common in older people in which the bones become increasingly soft and porous, making them susceptible to injury.

**ovary** The paired female sex organ that produces egg cells, estrogen, and progesterone.

**overload principle** Providing a greater stress or demand on the body than it is normally accustomed to handling.

**overloading** Method of physical training in which the number of repetitions or the amount of resistance is gradually increased to work the muscle to temporary fatigue.

**over-the-counter (OTC) drug** Medication that can be obtained without a prescription from a medical professional (i.e., over the counter at a retail outlet).

**overtrain** Working muscles too intensely or too frequently, resulting in persistent muscle soreness, injuries, unintended weight loss, nervousness, and an inability to relax.

**overuse injury** Physical injury to joints or muscles, such as a strain, fracture, and tendinitis, which results from overdoing a repetitive activity.

**overweight** A condition of having a body mass index (BMI) between 25.0 and 29.9.

**ovulation** The release of a mature ovum from an ovary approximately 14 days prior to the onset of menstruation.

**ovulation method** A method of birth control based on the observation of changes in the consistency of the mucus in the vagina to predict ovulation.

**ovum** (plural, **ova**) The female egg cell.

**panacea** To heal; a remedy for all difficulties; a cure-all.

**panic attack** A short episode characterized by physical sensations of light-headedness, dizziness, hyperventilation, and numbness of extremities, accompanied by an inexplicable terror, usually of a physical disaster such as death.

**panic disorder** An anxiety disorder in which the apprehension or experience of recurring panic attacks is so intense that normal functioning is impaired.

**pathogen** A microorganism that produces disease.

**PCP (phencyclidine)** A synthetic psychoactive substance that produces effects similar to other psychoactive drugs when swallowed, smoked, sniffed, or injected, but may also trigger unpredictable behavioural changes.

**pelvic inflammatory disease (PID)** An inflammation of the internal female genital tract, characterized by abdominal pain, fever, and tenderness of the cervix.

**penis** The male organ of sex and urination.

**perimenopause** The period from a woman's first irregular cycles to her last menstruation.

**perinatology** The medical specialty concerned with the diagnosis and treatment of pregnant women with high-risk conditions and their fetuses.

**perineum** The area between the anus and vagina in the female and between the anus and scrotum in the male.

**phobia** An anxiety disorder marked by an inordinate fear of an object, a class of objects, or a situation, resulting in extreme avoidance behaviours.

**physical activity** All leisure and non-leisure body movement produced by the skeletal muscles and resulting in an increase in energy expenditure.

**physical dependence** The physiological attachment to, and need for, a drug.

**physical fitness** The ability to respond to routine physical demands, with enough reserve energy to cope with a sudden challenge.

**physiotherapy** Sometimes known as physical therapy, this health-care treatment is used to assess, restore, and maintain physical function.

**phytochemical** Chemical that exists naturally in plants and has disease-fighting properties.

**placenta** An organ that develops after implantation and to which the embryo attaches, via the umbilical cord, for nourishment and waste removal.

**plaque** Deposits of fat, fibrin, cholesterol, calcium, and other cell parts on the lining of the arteries.

**pollutant** A substance or agent in the environment, usually the by-product of human industry or activity, that is injurious to human, animal, or plant life.

**pollution** The presence of pollutants in the environment.

**polyabuse** The misuse or abuse of more than one drug.

**population health** A way of thinking about the social and economic forces that shape health. It builds upon public health and health promotion, but goes beyond our more traditional understanding of the causes of health and illness.

**post-traumatic stress disorder (PTSD)** The repeated reliving of a trauma through nightmares or recollection.

**potential** Expressing possibility.

**preconception care** Health care to prepare for pregnancy.

**precontemplation** Not even aware that you have a problem, whereas others around you might; no intention of making a change.

**prediabetes** A condition where blood glucose (blood sugar) levels are higher than normal but not high enough to be called diabetes.

**premature labour** Labour that occurs after the 20th week but before the 37th week of pregnancy.

**premenstrual dysphoric disorder (PMDD)** A disorder that causes symptoms of psychological depression during the last week of a woman's menstrual cycle.

**premenstrual syndrome (PMS)** A disorder that causes physical discomfort and psychological distress prior to a woman's menstrual period.

**preparation** Intent to change a problem behaviour within the next month.

**prevention** Information and support offered to help healthy people identify their health risks, reduce stressors, prevent potential medical problems, and enhance their well-being.

**prion** (proteinaceous infectious particle) Infectious self-reproducing protein structure.

**progesterone** The female sex hormone that stimulates the uterus, preparing it for the arrival of a fertilized egg.

**progestin-only pill** *See* minipill.

**progressive overloading** Gradually increasing physical challenges once the body adapts to the stress placed upon it to produce maximum benefits.

**progressive relaxation** A method of reducing muscle tension by contracting, then relaxing certain areas of the body.

**pro-life** A term that refers to the opposition to abortion and support for fetal rights.

**proof** The alcoholic strength of a distilled spirit, expressed as twice the percentage of alcohol present.

**prostate gland** A structure surrounding the male urethra that produces a secretion that helps liquefy the semen from the testes.

**protection** Measures that an individual can take when participating in risky behaviour to prevent injury or unwanted risks.

**protein** A substance that is basically a compound of amino acids; one of the essential nutrients.

**protozoan** Microscopic animal made up of one cell or a group of similar cells; its enzymes and toxins can harm or destroy healthy cells.

**psychiatric drug** Medication that regulates a person's mental, emotional, and physical functions to facilitate normal functioning.

**psychiatrist** Licensed medical doctor with additional training in psychotherapy, psychopharmacology, and treatment of mental disorders.

**psychoactive** Mood-altering.

**psychodynamic psychotherapy** Interpreting behaviours in terms of early experiences and unconscious influences.

**psychological dependence** The emotional or mental attachment to the use of a drug.

**psychologist** Mental health professional who has completed a doctoral or graduate program in psychology and is trained in a variety of psychotherapeutic techniques, but who is not medically trained and does not prescribe medications.

**psychoprophylaxis** *See* Lamaze method.

**psychotherapy** Treatment designed to produce a response by psychological rather than physical means, such as suggestion, persuasion, reassurance, and support.

**psychotropic** Mind-affecting.

**purpose** Something set up as an object or end to be attained.

**pyelonephritis** Inflammation of the kidney.

**quackery** Medical fakery; unproven practices claiming to cure diseases or solve health problems.

**rape** Sexual penetration of a female or a male by means of intimidation, force, or fraud.

**recover** Refurbishing old items such as computers; salvaging parts.

**recycle** The processing or reuse of manufactured materials to reduce consumption of raw materials.

**reduce** Buying products packaged in recycled materials or purchasing products that have less packaging.

**reflexology** A treatment based on the theory that massaging certain points on the foot or hand relieves stress or pain in corresponding parts of the body.

**reinforcement** Reward or punishment for a behaviour that will increase or decrease one's likelihood of repeating the behaviour.

**religion** A specific system of belief about deity, often involving rituals, a code of ethics, and a philosophy of life, usually representing a special doctrine or group of people.

**resting heart rate** The number of heartbeats per minute during inactivity.

**reuse** Repairing items instead of purchasing new ones; finding new uses for old items.

**reversibility principle** The physical benefits of exercise are lost through disuse or inactivity.

**rhythm method** A birth-control method in which sexual intercourse is avoided during those days of the menstrual cycle in which fertilization is most likely to occur.

**rubella** An infectious disease that may cause birth defects if contracted by a pregnant woman; also called German measles.

**satiety** A feeling of fullness after eating.

**saturated fat** A chemical term indicating that a fat molecule contains as many hydrogen atoms as its carbon skeleton can hold. These fats are normally solid at room temperature.

**schizophrenia** A general term for a group of mental disorders with characteristic psychotic symptoms, such as delusions, hallucinations, and disordered thought patterns during the active phase of the illness, and a duration of at least six months.

**scrotum** The external sac or pouch that holds the testes.

**seasonal affective disorder (SAD)** Extended and severe bouts of malaise, low energy, problems with sleep and appetite; people who have difficulty functioning at home and at work during the fall and winter seasons.

**secondhand cigarette smoke** The most hazardous form of indoor air pollution, ranked behind cigarette smoking and alcohol as the third-leading preventable cause of death.

**sedative-hypnotic** A drug that depresses the central nervous system, reduces activity, and induces relaxation and sleep; includes the benzodiazepines and the barbiturates.

**self-actualization** A state of wellness and fulfillment that can be achieved once certain human needs are satisfied; living to one's full potential.

**self-care** The decisions and actions individuals take in the interest of their own health.

**self-efficacy** Belief in one's ability to accomplish a goal or change a behaviour.

**self-esteem** Confidence and satisfaction in oneself.

**self-talk** Repetition of positive messages about one's self-worth to learn more optimistic patterns of thought, feeling, and behaviour.

**semen** The viscous whitish fluid that is the complete male ejaculate; a combination of sperm and secretions from the prostate gland, seminal vesicles, and other glands.

**seminal vesicle** Gland in the male reproductive system that produces the major portion of the fluid of semen.

**semi-vegetarian** A diet that consists of no red meat but includes poultry and fish with plant foods, dairy products, and eggs.

**set-point theory** The proposition that every person has an unconscious control system for keeping body fat (and therefore weight) at a predetermined level, or set point.

**severe acute respiratory syndrome (SARS)** A respiratory illness caused by a previously unknown type of coronavirus. Normally, coronaviruses cause mild to moderate upper respiratory symptoms, such as the common cold. SARS is new, and scientists are still searching for answers about this illness.

**sexual coercion** Sexual activity forced upon a person by the exertion of psychological pressure by another person.

**sexual orientation** The physiological, psychological, and social factors that attract a person to members of the same sex or members of the opposite sex.

**sexually transmitted infection (STI)** Any of a number of infections that are acquired through sexual contact.

**Shinto** An ancient Japanese religion, closely connected to nature. This religion recognizes the existence of Kami, or nature deities.

**sidestream smoke** The smoke emitted by a burning cigarette and breathed by everyone in a closed room, including the smoker; contains more tar and nicotine than mainstream smoke.

**Sikhism** A monotheistic religion of India; the goal of Sikhs is to build a close, loving relationship to God. Sikhs believe in a single God, with many names.

**simple carbohydrate** Sugar; like all carbohydrates, it provides the body with glucose; consists of one simple sugar unit.

**smog** A greyish or brownish haze caused by the presence of smoke and/or chemical pollutants in the air.

**social determinant of health (SDOH)** Income inequality, job security, working conditions, housing and food security, education and care in early life, and social exclusion of individuals and groups; each of these are all aspects that are very important to health and wellness status.

**social isolation** A feeling of unconnectedness with others caused and reinforced by infrequency of social contacts.

**social phobia** A severe form of social anxiety marked by extreme fears and avoidance of social situations.

**social responsibility** A principle or ethical theory that suggests governments, corporations, organizations, and individuals have a responsibility to contribute to the welfare of society.

**social worker** Helps individuals, families, groups, and communities resolve individual and personal problems as well as broader social issues such as poverty and domestic issues.

**specificity principle** Each part of the body adapts to a particular type and amount of stress placed upon it.

**sperm** The male reproductive cell produced by the testes and transported outside the body through ejaculation.

**spermatogenesis** The process by which sperm cells are produced.

**spinal block** An injection of anesthetic directly into the spinal cord to numb the lower body during labour and childbirth.

**spiritual health** The ability to identify one's basic purpose in life and to achieve one's full potential; the sense of connectedness to a greater power.

**spirituality** A sacred matter of things of an ecclesiastical nature or something highly valued or important.

**sport** A form of leisure-time physical activity that is planned, structured, and competitive.

**static flexibility** The ability to assume and maintain an extended position at one end point in a joint's range of motion.

**sterilization** A surgical procedure to end a person's reproductive capability.

**stimulant** An agent, such as a drug, that temporarily relieves drowsiness, helps in the performance of repetitive tasks, and improves capacity for work.

**strength** Physical power; the maximum weight one can lift, push, or press in one effort.

**stress** The non-specific response of the body to any demands made upon it; may be characterized by muscle tension and acute anxiety, or may be a positive force for action.

**stressor** Specific or non-specific agents or situations that cause the stress response in a body.

**stroke** A cerebrovascular event in which the blood supply to a portion of the brain is blocked.

**subcutaneous** Under the skin.

**suction curettage** A procedure in which the contents of the uterus are removed by means of suction and scraping.

**syphilis** A sexually transmitted infection caused by the bacterium *Treponema pallidum*; characterized by early sores, a latent period, and a final period of life-threatening symptoms including brain damage and heart failure.

**systemic disease** A pathologic condition that spreads throughout the body.

**systole** The contraction phase of the cardiac cycle.

**Taoism** Sometimes translated as "path," Taoism is a force which flows through all life. If you are a believer, your goal is to become one with the Tao.

**tar** A thick, sticky, dark fluid produced by the burning of tobacco; made up of several hundred different chemicals, many of them poisonous, some of them carcinogenic.

**target heart rate** The heart rate at which one derives maximum cardiovascular benefit from aerobic exercise; 60 to 85 percent of the maximum heart rate.

**termination** Can take two to five years for a behaviour to become so deeply ingrained that a person can't imagine abandoning it.

**teratogen** Any agent that causes spontaneous abortion or defects or malformations in a fetus.

**testis** (plural, **testes**) The paired male sex organ that produces sperm and testosterone.

**testosterone** The male sex hormone that stimulates male secondary sex characteristics.

**toxic shock syndrome (TSS)** A rare, potentially deadly bacterial infection that primarily strikes menstruating women under the age of 30 who use tampons.

**toxicity** The dosage level at which a drug becomes poisonous to the body, causing either temporary or permanent damage.

**transcendence** Extending notably beyond ordinary limits.

**trans-fatty acid** Fat formed when liquid vegetable oils are processed to make table spreads or cooking fats, and also found in dairy and beef products; considered to be an especially dangerous dietary fat.

**transgendered** Refers to people whose gender identity is different than the sex they were assigned at birth; alternately, can be used as a general term to describe individuals whose gender identity differs from traditional gender roles.

**trichomoniasis** An infection of the protozoan *Trichomonas vaginalis;* females experience vaginal burning, itching, and discharge, but male carriers may be asymptomatic.

**triglyceride** Fat that flows through the blood after meals and that is linked to increased risk of coronary artery disease.

**tubal ligation** The suturing or tying shut of the fallopian tubes to prevent pregnancy.

**tubal occlusion** The blocking of the fallopian tubes to prevent pregnancy.

**12-step program** Self-help group program based on the principles of Alcoholics Anonymous.

**unsaturated fat** A fat molecule that contains fewer hydrogen atoms than its carbon skeleton can hold. These fats are normally liquid at room temperature.

**urethra** The canal through which urine from the bladder leaves the body; in the male, also serves as the channel for seminal fluid.

**urethral opening** The outer opening of the thin tube that carries urine from the bladder.

**urethritis** Infection of the urethra.

**uterus** The female organ that houses the developing fetus until birth.

**vagina** The canal leading from the exterior opening in the female genital area to the uterus.

**vaginal spermicide** A substance that kills or neutralizes sperm, inserted into the vagina as a foam, cream, jelly, or suppository.

**value** The criteria by which one makes choices about one's thoughts, actions, goals, and ideals.

**vas deferens** Two tubes that carry sperm from the epididymis into the urethra.

**vasectomy** A surgical sterilization procedure in which each vas deferens is cut and tied shut to stop the passage of sperm to the urethra for ejaculation.

**vector** A biological or physical vehicle that carries the agent of infection to the host.

**vegan** Person who eats only plant foods.

**ventricle** Either of the two lower chambers of the heart that pump blood out of the heart and into the arteries.

**video display terminal (VDT)** A screen or monitor that emits electromagnetic fields from all sides; these fields may lead to increased reproductive problems, miscarriages, low birth weights, and cataracts.

**virus** Submicroscopic infectious agent; the most primitive form of life.

**visualization** An approach to stress control, self-healing, or motivating life changes by means of guided imagery.

**vital sign** Measurement of physiological functioning: temperature, blood pressure, pulse rate, and respiration rate.

**vitamin** Organic substance that is needed in very small amounts by the body and that carries out a variety of functions in metabolism and nutrition.

**waist circumference (WC)** Used along with body mass index as a practical indicator of risk that is associated with excess abdominal fat.

**waist-to-hip ratio (WHR)** The proportion of waist circumference to hip circumference; an indicator of cardiovascular disease risk.

**wellness** A deliberate lifestyle choice characterized by personal responsibility and optimal enhancement of physical, mental, and spiritual health.

**withdrawal** Development of symptoms that cause significant psychological and physical distress when an individual reduces or stops drug use.

**zygote** A fertilized egg.

# Index